Robert G. Kaiser

RUSSIA

The People and the Power

PUBLISHED BY POCKET BOOKS NEW YORK

POCKET BOOKS, a Simon & Schuster division of
GULF & WESTERN CORPORATION
1230 Avenue of the Americas, New York, N.Y. 10020

Copyright © 1976 by Robert G. Kaiser

Published by arrangement with Atheneum Publishers
Library of Congress Catalog Card Number: 75-34069

ISBN: 0-671-43285-0

First Pocket Books printing November, 1976

10   9   8   7

POCKET and colophon are trademarks of Simon & Schuster.

Printed in the U.S.A.

Contents

"Russia—a country in which things that just don't happen happen."

Peter the Great

Introduction

RUSSIA: MYSTERIOUS DARK continent, "a riddle wrapped in a mystery inside an enigma" in Winston Churchill's phrase, remote, inaccessible to foreigners, inexplicable even to natives. That is the myth, encouraged by the Russians themselves, who would prefer that no one discover who they really are and how they really live.

I spent three years in Russia and concluded that the myth is true in a way, but also exaggerated. True because big, complicated, isolated societies with rich but alien traditions and cultures are inevitably baffling. America is baffling too, for that matter. But exaggerated because in the end Russia is just another country, a synthesis of history, character, politics and economics, child-rearing customs, jokes and happy nights out on the town. The elements of Russian life are—with a few exceptions—now accessible to outsiders. They can be observed, felt and described. And that is the purpose of this book.

I had the extraordinary good fortune to be sent to Moscow as the correspondent of the *Washington Post* in 1971. Good fortune, because foreign correspondents are paid to learn, and I had three years to learn all I could about the Soviet Union. My wife, Hannah—a wise and energetic partner—and I arrived in Moscow with a year's intensive study of the Russian language behind us, carrying a small library of books on the Russian past and Soviet present, but without expert knowledge. In the subsequent three years we had time to master the language, to poke around Moscow and travel throughout the country, to meet hundreds of Soviet citizens, to catch up on the reading we should have done before we got there, and generally to discover what kind of country it is. In this book I want to try to share the experience of discovery.

What we discovered was surprising, because nothing we had read prepared us fully for the Russia we encountered. I have tried to write the kind of book I looked for but could never find when we were preparing to go to the Soviet Union, a plausible explanation of Soviet life and society written for a curious amateur.

I confess to a journalist's bias about the best way to understand something new or foreign. The important question, I think, is how does it work? But there is no simple answer when the subject is a huge and complex society. So I have tried to build a portrait of Soviet life by explaining the workings of hundreds of its components: the Communist Party, the ritual of marriage, the betting at Moscow's racetrack, the editorial board of a Soviet newspaper, and many more.

I could not find equally satisfying answers to all of my questions. For instance, I learned nothing startling about the Politburo of the Communist Party, and cannot claim to have uncovered the secrets of high-level Soviet politics. Those secrets are hidden from all but a few hundred people, and I did not breach that magic circle. Nor did I overcome all the barriers that Russians set up almost instinctively to frustrate foreign curiosities. The Russians are a nervously secretive people who mistrust the motives of foreigners, and mistrust their own ability to cope with them. They hide or lie about things they think might help an enemy or reflect badly on their country, an inclination that blossoms into a kind of spy mania. Maxim Litvinov, the Soviet commissar of foreign affairs during the 1930s, used to tease his countrymen about this. "I think we're afraid of spies," Litvinov would say, "not because they'll see what we have, but because they'll see what we don't have."

On the other hand, a great deal of information about how things work is readily available—probably more available in the 1970s than at any time since the 1920s. On the most basic questions of human existence a foreign resident of Moscow has a vast laboratory in which to pursue his curiosity—the city of Moscow itself. I grew fond of that gray, eclectic capital, a city unlike any other in the world, a ragged, disorganized combination of ancient, old and new built on a huge scale. Moscow is the perfect capital for the Soviet state, a clear reflection of the society's true elements. First of all it is Russian, dominated by the ancient Kremlin at its center, dotted still with Russian Orthodox churches, breathing its age and agelessness on almost every street and boulevard of the old city. Its chaotic combination of architectural styles—from log houses to glass skyscrapers, scattered across the landscape like dice carelessly tossed on a board—evokes the disorganized Russian character. Its pretentious new boulevards, built in recent years to prove that the Soviet system has brought old Russia to the forefront of the modern age, actually accentuate the fact that downtown Moscow is still a 19th-century city, dominated by ornate stucco façades with rows and rows of windows. But most of all Moscow is crowds of people, great masses surging along sidewalks with shopping bags and satchels, dressed in grays and blacks except during the short, bright summer, people coming and going with a stubborn, unsmiling purposefulness.

An outsider can study Muscovites in shops and markets, undress with them in the public baths, gamble with them at the racetrack and talk with them in all these places. In the 1970s a substantial number of Muscovites are not afraid to invite a foreigner into their small apartments, to reveal Russian family life and discuss the subjects that matter most to them.

The Russians who invited us into their homes were not politicians or journalists or people with official careers, but artists, musicians, writers, Jews who had applied to emigrate to Israel, old people living on pensions, political dissidents and others who did not fear official retribution for befriending an American journalist. My life was hardly private—agents of the political police, the KGB, watched it closely—but it was not isolated from Russian reality. There were strange aspects to Soviet life in the early 1970s. Though the country's authorities controlled the nation's life, they did not control every life in the nation. I could meet and talk with one of the country's most distinguished atomic scientists, Andrei Sakharov, who gave up his official work as a designer of thermonuclear weapons and became a leading political dissident. I could meet Alexander Solzhenitsyn, the best-known writer of Russian prose of this generation. I could discuss scholarship and science with distinguished professors, men who would not have dreamed of talking with me before they had applied to emigrate to Israel. After applying, they talked freely. Traveling on trains, eating in restaurants, visiting acquaintances in their apartments, I had chance encounters with dozens of fascinating people from unexpected places and backgrounds. Whenever I could I asked these people to tell me stories from their own lives, incidents from their jobs or other personal experiences that might help a foreigner understand how the society worked and why.

I gathered additional stories from Russians now living outside their country. More than 100,000 people have left the Soviet Union as emigrants since the late 1960s, most of them Jews. They come from all over the Soviet Union and from almost every conceivable walk of life. I recorded many hours of interviews with Soviet émigrés in Israel, Western Europe and the United States. This is a rich source of information about Soviet life, as yet unexploited by western scholars.

So, much of this book consists of the words of Russian people telling stories from their own lives. I have tried to use these stories, my own observations and excerpts from books by Russians about their own country to construct the image of Soviet society I took away after living there for three years. Three years of impressions, I discovered, cannot fit into one book, even a big one. What follows is not a diary or a re-creation of our experiences in Russia, but description and analysis in which our experiences are the principal evidence.

Writing about a foreign country invites comparisons. An American or Western European reading my description of Soviet life will inevitably compare it to his or her own country. The comparisons will often be unfavorable for the Soviet Union. It may appear to some readers that I am determined to malign the USSR in this book—that I am another cold-warrior out to prove the superiority of the western way of life.

I readily acknowledge that I would prefer to live in any of the western countries I know than in the Soviet Union. That preference reflects my own background and values. But when I criticize some aspect of Soviet life, implicitly or explicitly, I hope it is clear that I am not simultaneously trying to endorse the corresponding feature of western life. Only a blind and foolish American could claim that his country has solved the problems of human society. A wise Russian journalist I knew in Moscow said something to me which made a deep impression: "Of course there are aspects of our reality which you don't like," he said, "but I can assure you there are many things in your country which appall us." He mentioned unemployment and organized crime, two curses which we take for granted, neither of which afflicts the USSR.

So I ask readers to keep in mind that the Soviet Union does not exist in American or British or German terms. It exists in Russian terms, in a unique setting and cultural environment unlike anything we know. Comparisons are inevitable but usually irrelevant. Russians could not live like Englishmen or Americans even if they wanted to, which they do not. They must live like Russians, which means they cannot turn their society into a copy of ours.

The uniqueness of Russia is so important that the first chapter of this book is devoted to it. I begin with a series of anecdotes and stories which are meant to convey one crucial fact: the special combination of politics, economics, national character, history, fate and circumstance that defines contemporary Russia can be found only in Russia.

RUSSIA

1 · Only in Russia

"BEGIN YOUR BOOK in the baths," a friend in Moscow suggested. "Describe us with our clothes off, then dress us slowly." A beguiling idea. Many Russians still take baths in communal facilities. Some of them are splendid pre-revolutionary establishments with carved and gilded—though peeling—moldings, marble staircases and vast mirrors. The bathers buy bunches of dried branches, roast themselves in sauna-like dry heat, whack the poisons out of their skin with the leaves, then wash it all away in rushes of cold water.

Russians with their clothes off at the bath do reveal something about their country: that it is filled with sociable people who savor their pleasures; that the national diet produces bodies that bulge and droop; and that the Soviet dictatorship isn't as fierce as it sometimes seems. Signs posted in the Sundonovski Baths in an old corner of Moscow say flatly: NO SMOKING. Everyone smokes. It's against the rules to drink vodka in the baths, too. For a modest tip, one of the attendants will run out and buy half a liter.

The heart of the bath is the hot room. Natural-gas fires heat giant bricks to a fierce temperature, and the bricks radiate the heat through an iron door into the small room where the bathers gather to sweat and swat. To the uninitiated the temperature is high enough to make breathing painful, but the regulars often find it too weak, in the vernacular of the bath. One or another of them is bound to open the oven door with the handle of a broom and begin tossing water onto the glowing bricks. This creates a hot steam which eliminates the "weakness," makes everyone cry out in alleged delight, but invariably begins an argument. "Enough!" someone will cry. "No, more, more!" another will shout. Those who ask for more usually prevail, and someone continues to toss water into the fire, often until it gets so unbearably hot that everyone is forced to run out into the shower room for air.

The baths are an introduction to the people, but a country is more than people. A country is a state of mind, and a way of coping with the human condition. Russia is unusual on both counts. Take, for example, the story of the national anthem without words.

The Soviet Union has a stirring national anthem. It was introduced in 1944 as a successor to the "Internationale." The new anthem is a more specifically Russian, more patriotic hymn than that old revolutionary standard. The music, written by a man named A. V. Alexandrov, churns the blood and raises the spirits. But there are no words.

There used to be words, verses that extolled the "united and powerful Soviet Union" and the personal role of Joseph Stalin:

Stalin raised us and inspired us
To be true to the people, to work, to perform heroic deeds.

Stalin had himself written into the anthem. When Nikita Khrushchev began to discredit Stalin and disavow many of his acts, Khrushchev and his colleagues decided that these words would have to be changed. They established a commission to write new verses. Nearly 20 years later, no new words have been introduced. Schoolchildren don't even know that words ever existed.

Normally the absence of words creates no special difficulties. In 1972, however, it caused some embarrassment. That year several thousand Canadian ice-hockey fans came to Moscow to cheer on their national team. Before each match against the Soviet team, the anthems of both nations were played to the crowd at Luzhniki Stadium in Moscow. The

Canadians sang the words to "O Canada" in strong voice. The Russians in the arena had to hear their anthem out in silence—an obvious and awkward silence.

From an official guidebook to Odessa, the principal Soviet seaport on the Black Sea, in the Ukraine: "Mud is indispensable in the treatment of several diseases. ... The mud of the salt lakes near Odessa, which is considered to be unequaled in curative capacity, has long since been recognized as a world standard for mud."

Russians boast about more than mud. "You don't have a railroad this long in your country, do you?" a passenger asked on the Trans-Siberian as it neared the city of Irkutsk, the capital of Eastern Siberia. "Do you have trains in the West?" the manager of the dining car asked. "Do they have dining cars?"

We may have dining cars, but we have nothing like Siberia: as far from Europe as remotest Asia, but part of a European country and populated by familiar Slavic faces; cold, remote, barren and rich. The Trans-Siberian is 5600 miles long; from end to end, a ride of a few hours less than a week—if it's on time, which it sometimes is.

Siberia is far, far away, both on the map and in the mind. The director of a regional museum in Khabarovsk on the broad, muddy Amur River boasts of the local family whose members have captured 36 tigers with their bare hands. The director of the farmers' market in Novosibirsk, where collective farmers can sell the produce from their tiny private plots, asks an American visitor whether "you eat meat in America." Avid sports fans in Khabarovsk, the capital of the Soviet far east, must stay up all night to watch big games on television. They are victims of the time zone, seven hours later than Moscow's.

Like most of Russia, Siberia is a vast plain. Its only hills are gentle; even the Ural Mountains seem to have been depressed by some giant flattener. Out the window of the Trans-Siberian, a traveler sees only fields, woods of birch and pine, villages of wooden cottages and an occasional town or city. The scenery hardly changes from one end to the other.

The railroad crosses a relatively populated and developed strip of southern Siberia. This strip is farther to the north than the continental United States, but it represents just a fraction of Siberian territory. More than half the region is north of the 60th parallel—farther north than Juneau, Alaska. There are barely three months a year without snow and ice, and the brief summer is hot and mosquito-infested. Yet most of the vast natural riches of Siberia lie beneath the permafrost and summer swamps of those far-northern reaches.

"In Siberia," the Siberians like to say, "we have nine months of winter, and then it's summer . . . and summer . . . and summer. . . ." There are many jokes in a similar vein, the Soviet equivalent of Texas jokes, though Texans would be rash to put themselves in the same class. More than 16 states of Texas could fit into Siberia's four million square miles.

The Siberians are pioneers, though not always by choice. Thousands of them (and the parents of thousands more) arrived in Siberia in prison cars, sentenced there by czarist or communist courts, or swept to the east in some great purge or forced relocation. Exile to Siberia is still common today.

Millions chose Siberia voluntarily, though. Many were young enthusiasts like Sasha Gurevich, who left his Jewish mother and Ukrainian home in 1957 and set off for Bratsk, the hero project of those years.* A giant hydroelectric dam was being built on the Angara River, deep in the central Siberian *taiga*, or forest.

The propaganda for Bratsk was intense: only the toughest could do the job, they said. Sasha still remembers that line. Thousands of young people applied to work on the dam, to prove that they were among those toughest. There were more applicants than the project could absorb. Sasha had a college degree in engineering, but he ended up with an airhammer, crushing rocks for the foundation of the dam. "My mama wrote me letters," he recalled years later: 'Why is a boy with a college education playing with an air hammer and those devil rocks?' " A good question, perhaps, but Sasha remembers it now with a grin, even a laugh from inside his barrel chest, earned with the air hammer in his youth and sustained by weight lifting as he approached forty.

---

* There is always a hero project of some kind under construction in the Soviet Union. The latest is a railroad across northeastern Siberia which won't be finished before 1982. Branches of the Young Communist League all over the Soviet Union are recruiting young people to join in its construction.

Those early days on the Siberian frontier are as sweet and romantic to recollect as any pioneer's early triumphs. They lived first in tents, then in temporary dormitories, fighting the cold or swarms of mosquitoes, without the most basic conveniences, including electricity in the beginning. At the time it must have been rough, but 15 years later it sounds sublime. And the dam is built, an heroic monument to their heroic deed. "We are the real communists," Sasha insists. Throughout Siberia the locals speak with disdain of the bureaucrats and spoiled city people west of the Urals.

Yevgeni Yevtushenko, the popular poet, wrote a long hymn of praise to the Bratsk pioneers, Sasha and his friends. That made them famous, but it didn't keep them young. There have been half a dozen other hero projects since Bratsk's dam was finished, and all that's young about the original Bratsk generation is their children. Sasha lives with his wife and daughter in a five-story apartment house not far from the dam, a building duplicated in tens of thousands of copies throughout the Soviet Union. Sasha's building, at least, is surrounded by trees, something seldom seen in the housing developments of European Russia.

The Gureviches set a table in their 10-by-15-foot living room for guests from America, whom Sasha was entertaining in his capacity as a part-time journalist and promoter. He had also invited Mr. and Mrs. Alexei Marchuk. Marchuk is one of Bratsk's most famous pioneers. His "tartar eyes" struck Yevtushenko, and his exploits on the dam are the subject of a popular song known throughout the country, "Marchuk Plays on His Guitar." As an engineering student in Moscow, Marchuk wrote a thesis suggesting a new method for blocking a river to begin construction of a high dam. His idea was used successfully at Bratsk.

By the early 1970s Marchuk's brush cut was turning gray, though his full mustache remained a rich black. He was in charge of a factory that made prefabricated concrete sections for new apartment houses, a frustrating job for a dam-builder. Mrs. Marchuk was dark, earthy, lovely.

It was a gay evening. The Gureviches served vodka, cucumbers and tomatoes, then vodka, then smoked fish, then vodka, then canned peas, then vodka, then a cake Mrs. Gurevich had made according to her own Ukrainian recipe, then vodka and Soviet champagne. Mrs. Gurevich, a friendly woman who worked in an art gallery in Lvov before she moved to Siberia, doesn't approve of heavy drinking, and she protected the women from many of the toasts. But it was a man's duty to drink every one. Many a soul, living and dead, had the benefit of a toast that night, from V. I. Lenin to the editor of the *Washington Post*.

Soon Marchuk's famous guitar appeared, followed by all kinds of songs in all kinds of languages. This Russian engineer in the middle of Siberia knew more words to "Goodnight, Irene" than the chagrined Americans he was entertaining. "There's no justice," he complained. "We learned all the American songs at Moscow State University, and you don't know any of the Russian songs."

The party broke up after midnight. The guests shuffled out of the two-room apartment. The halls and stairwell of the apartment house—scarcely a mile from one of the biggest hydroelectric dams in the world—were pitch black.

Three years later, in a long conversation in Rome, a young student named Vova Azbel described a starkly different Siberia. Azbel and his parents were on their way to America, part of the new emigration from Russia, an unexpected phenomenon which is bringing tens of thousands of Soviet citizens, mostly Jews, to Israel and the western world. They bring with them tales from Russian reality, like Vova Azbel's story of a country village only about 100 miles north of Bratsk.

Vova had studied at the medical institute in Irkutsk in central Siberia. All the students there were obliged to donate labor to the state, either as construction workers in the summer months, or by helping with the harvest in September. September is supposed to be the first month of school, but for Azbel and many of his classmates it was a month on the farm. This is what he remembered.

"They sent us to a very poor, very remote Siberian collective farm. It was about twenty-four hours by train to the north of Irkutsk, then several hours more on a dirt road by truck. . . . They put us up in the village school—there were no other facilities. There were about thirty of us. . . . They threw some dirty blankets on the floor of a big room used for sports in the school, and we all slept there, men and women together. . . .

"They didn't turn the heat on for us because it was 'summer,' though in northern Siberia by that time of year it goes below freezing at night. For an entire month they promised to turn on the heat, but they never did. The boiler didn't work. The bath, which we could use once every ten days, was heated by an open fire. The smoke went out a window.

"They didn't feed us too badly, but we had to cook everything for ourselves. They didn't just bring us meat—they brought us a calf, and we had to slaughter it, cut it up ourselves, everything. The only butcher was sixty miles away. If they wanted a calf butchered, they had to take it that distance, wait for the butcher to do the job, then bring back the meat. The director of the collective farm decided that he couldn't spare a truck to make the trip for our meat. He decided that the students should butcher their own.

"The first thing we discovered was that nobody in the village spoke Russian. At first we thought they were Buryats [a Soviet ethnic group closely related to Mongolians], but it turned out they were Chuvashes [natives of the Chuvash Autonomous Republic on the northern Volga, in European Russia]. They all spoke the Chuvash language. We found out that they had all been deported, sent off to this place. They'd been living there for more than twenty years in extremely impoverished conditions. . . . It was an awful thing to see. . . .

"They got a road connecting them with civilization only in the last few years. Still every spring a bridge on that road gets washed out in the thaw. Until it's fixed they have no ties to the outside world. . . .

"I've never seen people that poor. They had ramshackle old houses. Nobody could afford to keep a cow. They could keep a pig, but not a cow, because they couldn't get grass to feed it. To get grass they had to cross a wide river and travel a long distance—the fields around the village all belonged to the collective farm, so they couldn't use that grass to feed their own cows . . . So of course they didn't have enough milk, or enough of many other basic food products. Every time they bought bread they had to stand in a long line at the village store.

"But regularly, every day, a truck came with more vodka. They used a lot of vodka in that village, and there was always plenty—and plenty of customers. The people didn't work. I saw only students in the fields. Every morning the men gathered at the village store and bought whatever vodka was available. By midday they were all drunk, men and women. Nobody wanted to work. Only the chairman of the collective farm stayed sober. He ran around yelling at the students to work harder. . . .

"We worked for a month, but only harvested a quarter of a huge potato field. It was funny to see—a huge field, no machinery at all, or maybe just an old, broken-down combine, and in the distance a group of three people working, and nearly a mile farther, three more, and so on. . . . The collective farmers themselves either did nothing at all, or they picked some potatoes for themselves, but not for the farm's deliveries to the state. . . . In the middle of September it starts to frost, real frost. The frost kills the produce still in the ground—potatoes, carrots. . . ."

The fate of those Chuvashes in Siberia is hardly typical. Most Soviet citizens live better than that. "You can live," Russians like to tell each other when they talk about conditions in their country in recent years. It may sound like a modest compliment, but by Russian standards it is more. When a Russian has enough to eat, his own small apartment or the reasonable expectation that he will eventually get one, and no serious reason to doubt that this situation will last indefinitely, then life in Russia is good—better than it has ever been.

It is best of all in Moscow, where stores are better stocked than anywhere else. Permission to live in the capital is a privilege; only those with a special stamp in their internal passports can do so. This stamp is a coveted possession, and one rarely meets a Russian who voluntarily moves out of Moscow.

So it was a surprise to meet a man in the ancient city of Pskov, in northwestern Russia, who had left the capital for life in what seemed a dull, small metropolis. "The stores here don't have as much for sale," he admitted. The reason he had chosen to move involved a lady, and, in the end, two of them. The first was his wife.

"One day I came home from a business trip and she announced that she was finished with me, we were getting a divorce. It happens. This wasn't the first time a marriage failed."

To the husband's misfortune, the flat they'd been living in was registered in the name of his wife's family. When she kicked him out of it, he had nowhere to go. Permission to live in Moscow is invalid without a place to live. When he heard of a job in Pskov with a factory that would give him an apartment, he decided it was time to leave the capital for the provinces.

As a bachelor, he expected the factory in Pskov to give him a one-room flat, but he received two rooms. He enjoyed them contentedly for several months, then decided to switch jobs again, this time to another enterprise in Pskov. Though he was technically entitled to keep the apartment the first factory had given him, the factory was understandably upset and wanted it back. They said a single man wasn't entitled to two rooms. "They wanted me to live in a dormitory."

"Between you and me," he recounted, "I hadn't planned to remarry, but I decided I had to keep the apartment. I had an old girlfriend in Moscow, and I asked her to come to Pskov to marry me. At first it didn't work out too well, but lately we've managed to make contact, so to speak, and it's working out better, it's all right now. She's a good girl."

Russian insecurity:
When the Nazis invaded the USSR in 1941, the NKVD— the political police, since renamed the KGB—organized special "rear security units." These were troops equipped with machine guns who were stationed just behind the front-line Red Army forces that were fighting the Germans. Their mission was to kill any Soviet soldiers who tried to break from the front and flee.

In the 1970s the Soviet Union suddenly permitted thousands of its citizens to travel to the United States, mostly on official exchanges. Many of them were scientists who spent several months working in American laboratories and universities. Most of these scientists had to travel without their families. A few could bring their wives, but never their children. Children were left in Russia to insure that the parents would return home.

From the "Memorandum for a Foreign Tourist" published in booklet form by Intourist, the Soviet State Tourist Agency:

ARTICLES WHICH MAY NOT BE TAKEN INTO THE U.S.S.R.

1. Military weapons of any kind and ammunition for them.
2. Opium, hashish and smoking utensils.

3. Pornographic literature and pictures.
4. Publications, negatives, used camera films, photographs, gramophone records, cinema films, manuscripts, drawings and other items harmful to the U.S.S.R. politically and economically.

RULES FOR CAMERAMEN AND PHOTOGRAPHERS

... It is prohibited to film, as well as to draw pictures of all kinds of military weapons and equipment and objects of a military character, sea ports, large hydroengineering structures, railway junctions, tunnels, railway and highway bridges, industrial plants, research institutes, designing bureaus, laboratories, electric power stations, radio beacons and radio stations. It is forbidden to take pictures from a plane, to photograph and draw pictures of industrial cities on a large scale, as well as to take pictures and make drawings within two kilometers of the border.

Geographers in the Soviet Union face an unusual occupational hazard. For reasons which must have something to do with national security, no published map of the USSR published in the Soviet Union can be accurate. Each river, city and town must be moved slightly from its actual location. Western geographers discovered this idiosyncrasy by comparing old and new maps of Soviet territory. It is hard to imagine the purpose of this subterfuge in the age of spy satellites.

Visiting a Soviet university, I once found myself alone for a few moments with a young geographer. I asked if the practice of altering maps made life difficult for geographers. "It might," he replied, "but not for me. I specialize in the Middle East."

Political power in the Soviet Union:

A professor of medicine from the Soviet Ukraine told the following story.

"There has been a new slogan in recent times, 'National Cadre.' That means that people from local nationalities must be represented in local jobs. [This would mean giving preference to Ukrainians in the Ukraine, or Uzbeks in Uzbekistan.] This policy creates good opportunities for scientists who can promote their careers not on the basis of their talents, but on the basis of their nationality. The requirements for a dissertation by such a scientist would be lower than for mine. . . .

"In this atmosphere falsification becomes easier. Since these 'national cadre' can get away with so much else, why not try falsification too? So this is what happened.

"A group of young physicians, including one of my students, a Russian, a wonderful doctor, discovered that someone had made 'corrections' in the records of patients in the hospital files—excisions from the records, revisions of diagnoses, amazing things. Patients' records are serious documents, they can't be altered. My student pursued the matter, and found that more than two hundred and fifty medical histories in the files had been altered. All the alterations were similar: they all made the the patients' illnesses look more serious than they really had been. Say someone suffered from a light form of rheumatism. His record was altered to look as though he had a serious case. The doctor who had been forging these records used them to show that he had cured very serious diseases. His course of treatment was made to look very effective.

"My student and his colleagues told the rector of the medical school that this man—a Ukrainian—had falsified his dissertation. However, the [Communist] Party organs defended this pseudo-scientist, and actually brought legal charges against one of the complaining doctors, accusing him of slander.

"Not a single lawyer in the city would agree to defend that doctor at his trial. This was in 1971. They said that if they agreed to defend a doctor who had been accused by the Party, they would lose their jobs in the legal-consultation office. Not one would agree to take the case. Finally the accused doctor got a lawyer from Moscow to defend him. The charge was personal slander, which meant a private suit, not a state accusation, not for slandering the state, but for slandering an individual. . . .

"And despite the fact that there were two hundred and fifty examples of altered, 'corrected,' falsified medical records lying on the table in front of him, the judge ruled that the accusation of slander was justified. He made this ruling without looking up at the accused. It must have been too embarrassing for him. He sentenced the doctor to six months in prison, for slander. The doctor was found guilty even though two hundred and fifty examples of falsification lay on the table

and thirty witnesses, all doctors in the hospital, confirmed
that the records were falsified. . . .

Book reviews are less common and less influential in the
Soviet Union than in the West, largely because the public
isn't used to a wide choice of reading matter, and usually
buys what is available. (A new edition of Dostoevski or
Tolstoi sells out in a few hours, and Soviet bookstores *never*
have the great Russian classics in stock.) Nevertheless, many
Soviet journals publish book reviews. Writers can make a few
extra rubles reviewing books, but only if they are willing to
hide their true opinions. In the Soviet Union, when an editor
assigns a book review he stipulates what it should say—praise
or damnation, in what degree, and why.

In 1972 a Leningrad musician, a Jew, applied to emigrate
to Israel. He was summoned to a meeting with a mild-man-
nered young man who identified himself as an officer of the
political police, the KGB. The KGB man asked the musician
why he wanted to emigrate, then said suddenly, "In 1963 you
befriended the French spy La Farge—why?"

The musician was shocked and scared. Spy? What spy? He
denied befriending or even knowing a Frenchman named
LaFarge. "This is a ridiculous accusation," he said.

"Come, come," the KGB man replied, "are you going to
pretend that you don't remember the Frenchman you met in
the House of Books on Nevski Prosekt in August 1963?" The
KGB man then recounted a story which slowly came to life
in the musician's memory. A Frenchman who was obviously
lost in the old bookstore, which had been the Petersburg office of the Singer Sewing Machine Company before the Revolution, bumped into him on a stairway and asked if he spoke
French or German. The musician did speak German, and
helped the foreigner find the section he was looking for—
books in foreign languages. They could not have been together for more than five minutes, but the KGB had a detailed report on the encounter.

And yet the same KGB is capable of egregious sloppiness.
One of its jobs is to keep track of foreigners traveling inside
the Soviet Union, a job it performs with the help of Intourist,
the state travel agency. I once traveled from Kiev to Odessa
on the Black Sea coast by train. I arrived in Odessa at eight

in the morning, but no one was there to meet me—neither the young man or woman from Intourist I had come to expect, nor the older men in raincoats and dark hats who often loitered in the background to watch my arrival. I found the woman who was in charge of the Odessa railroad station at that hour and explained my problem. She telephoned the local Intourist office, but no one was yet at work. She consulted colleagues, looked helplessly at my wife and me, then finally instructed a baggage porter to take us to the parking lot and find a taxi. He did so. "You've got some rubles?" he asked. Assured that we did, he went off to negotiate, returning a few minutes later. "This man will take you to the hotel for two rubles," the porter announced. He did not explain that his friend was a bus driver. No matter. The friend put us, all alone, into his big bus and drove through Odessa to the hotel.

A statue of Vladimir Ilyich Lenin, leader of the Bolshevik Revolution and founder of the Soviet state, stands in the main square of every town and city in the Soviet Union, probably without exception. Lenin's portrait hangs in every Soviet classroom. His slogans appear in every issue of every newspaper. His authority is invoked at the beginning of nearly every scholarly book and article that appears in the Soviet Union, even if the work in question covers a subject Lenin never heard of. World War II—the Great Patriotic War, as the Russians call it—began 17 years after Lenin died, but the authors of an article about the war in the latest edition of the *Great Soviet Encyclopedia* began their bibliography with five references to the *Collected Works of V.I. Lenin*.

The cult of Lenin is an unmistakable indication that Soviet politics doesn't work like ours. Yet this idea is difficult to accept. A friend in New York wrote me a letter in Moscow just after Alexander Solzhenitsyn was expelled from the USSR. "While you still can," he recommended, "you should find out all there is to know about the expulsion of Solzhenitsyn—how it was decided on, how exactly it was done, what they told him when they arrested him, everything. It would make a great story."

It would indeed have made a great story. Alas, that was not the only consideration. Who was going to explain to an American what had happened? The Politburo of the Communist Party, a committee of 16 members who keep their own counsel, had voted to expel Solzhenitsyn. The Politburo has no public-relations office, no press secretaries to brief foreign or domestic correspondents. Even senior officials of the Communist Party often don't know how or why the Politburo reaches its decisions. The activities of the KGB, which carried out the Politburo's wishes in Solzhenitsyn's case, are even more remote from public view. The Politburo, at least, is composed of politicians who gossip, spread rumors, occasionally leave a few clues. The KGB is not composed of politicians.

When Nikita Khrushchev was in power, the men who ran the country were occasionally accessible to foreigners. Khruschev liked diplomatic receptions and attended them regularly. His colleagues began to attend too, perhaps to keep an eye on Khruschev. A diplomat or journalist could take the measure of the Soviet leaders at a reception, perhaps even getting a word with one or two of them. The men who sent Khrushchev into premature retirement also retired from the diplomatic-reception circuit. They are no longer accessible.

Khrushchev, incidentally, discovered just how secretive Politburo politics can be. He apparently came to the Politburo meeting which ended his career without a clue that his fate was on the agenda.

During the early days of "the relaxation of international tensions," as the Russians call *détente*, a group of American state governors visited the Soviet Union. In Moscow the government of the Russian Federated Socialist Republic, the largest unit of the Union of Soviet Socialist Republics, gave a reception for the governors. A few American journalists were invited.

The host was Mikhail Solomentsev, who had just been appointed chairman of the Council of Ministers of the Russian Federation, and was soon to be appointed a candidate (that is, non-voting) member of the Politburo. It was a rare opportunity to see one of the country's leaders, and even to talk with him.

Solomentsev and his guests stood around a rectangle of tables that were crowded with platters of king crab, smoked sturgeon, caviar and other rare treats that are brought out on special occasions. The atmosphere was relaxed, but several of the American governors were in an argumentative mood.

They debated with Solomentsev about the war in Vietnam and other subjects. The Russian was more than a match for his ill-informed American guests, but he took it all good-naturedly.

After more than an hour the leader of the American group, Governor Warren E. Hearnes of Missouri, proposed a friendly toast of thanks to the Soviet government for its hospitality. Governor Hearnes finished his brief speech and everyone took a drink. It was obvious even to the Americans, who were still not fully at home with the Russian custom of repeated toasts, that Solomentsev should reply to Governor Hearnes. But Solomentsev himself, supposedly one of the 25 most powerful men in the Soviet Union, stood at the buffet table and grinned, suddenly devoid of the composure he had displayed earlier. Everyone looked at him, but nothing happened. The pause was painfully graceless.

Then suddenly a short, stocky man stepped briskly out of a crowd of Soviet officials who were gathered in a knot off to one side. He strode toward Solomentsev, whispered a brief phrase in his ear, then strode on, disappearing into another knot of Soviet officials at the opposite end of the room. This was obviously the authorization Solomentsev had been waiting for. He immediately began a gracious toast in reply.

According to the Five Year Plan, which is supposed to guide Soviet life, a new factory in a provincial town was to open on a certain date. In fact the factory was far from ready to open when that day arrived. Work on the exterior was almost finished, but the interior was hardly begun. The men responsible for building the factory decided to buy a large quantity of kerosene and light smoky fires at the bottom of the high chimneys that were already in place. With black smoke pouring out of them, the local secretary of the Communist Party came to the factory and cut a ceremonial ribbon on the day of the official opening.

A week later the factory reported that there had been a serious accident on the premises. The director estimated that it would take four months to repair the damages. After four months he reported that the repair work was not yet complete, and asked for an extension. After a year of extensions the factory actually began operations—at 20 percent of capacity.

The Five Year Plan sets the quantities of production of most products, the amount of raw materials that goes into each, the amount of money to be invested in research, weaponry, apartment houses and children's toys.

To make use of such an all-encompassing Plan, the authorities must devise standards by which to measure its fulfillment. In some cases this is easy. If the Plan calls for the production of 800,000 passenger cars per year, the State Planning Commission can confirm that the Plan is fulfilled simply by counting the cars.

The Plan for car parts is more complicated. The Planning Commission cannot stipulate the number of distributor caps, the number of spark plugs and universal joints to be produced each year. To do so would be wildly impractical and complicated, and probably impossible. So the planners compromise. In this case they have decided to measure the output of car parts in terms of gross weight. That means that to fulfill its Plan a factory must produce a certain gross weight of parts.

A Soviet newspaper published a letter explaining the consequences of this system, written by workers at the Gorki automobile factory. The Gorki factory makes the Volga, a four-door sedan about the size of a Volvo which serves throughout the country as taxi, government car and, for a privileged few, private automobile. "The Saransk rubber factory owes us 5.6 million parts that they have failed to supply this year," the workers wrote. "The Yaroslavl technical rubber factory owes us more than forty thousand rubber moldings. . . ." The Gorki automobile plant suffered a chronic shortage of small parts because the factories making parts concentrated on heavy items—the better to fulfill and overfulfill their Plans.

The standard of achievement for factories making plate glass is square meters of glass produced. By law, each glass factory must produce the amount of glass, measured in square meters, that the Plan requires. Overproduction will lead to bonuses for workers and management. How does a glass factory increase its output of glass? By making the product as thin as possible. But thin glass breaks easily. It is common, perhaps normal, that the windows in new prefabricated apartment houses all over the Soviet Union are broken by the time they are installed.

No significant aspect of economic life escapes the Plan. Research scientists, for example, are supposed to forsee their work five years in advance. David Azbel, a Soviet chemist now living in America, described the frustrations inherent in this system:

"You have to say, five years ahead of time, what kind of equipment you'll need, what instruments. In reality, I may be working on one idea today, but if it turns out badly, I'll have to head off in an entirely new direction. But that may not be possible, because the system is so bureaucratic. You won't get anything that isn't planned for....So what happens? People start hoarding things. For instance, they'll say to you, 'Do you need such-and-such an apparatus?' And you'll say, 'No—but go ahead, give it to me, I'll save it just in case it comes in handy.' It won't cost you anything, you won't have to answer for it. The spending of money in this way is completely irresponsible, completely."

The Plan also extends to the production of medicine. Emanuel Luboshits, who practiced medicine in the Ukrainian city of Kharkov before he emigrated to Israel, explained the significance of this:

"Soviet medicines are produced to fulfill the Plan....They can be practically devoid of effectiveness. An ampule of medicine can actually come to you filled with water, perhaps because the flagon of penicillin the factory received contained less than it was supposed to, or perhaps because the factory wanted to produce 'above-Plan production.' If a factory produces vitamins, say, or penicillin, and can make a certain amount of it above their planned targets, then the factory will receive a bonus. It follows easily from there to decide to make the pills a little weaker than they should be, and to make a larger quantity of them—to produce above-Plan production....When we saw that a medicine had no effect, we often said, "That must be above-Plan production.'"

On the other hand, planning makes possible the Russians' accomplishments in science, weaponry and heavy industry. When the planners decided to build the world's largest truck factory, they assigned 70,000 workers to the task, constructing not just the enormous plant, but an entire city to house its future workers. Scientific research in a few famous institutes is given virtually unlimited financial support. The planners allocate to the arms industry everything it needs, including the power to commandeer scarce skills or materials from the civilian economy.

The Russians have produced magnificent accomplishments by concentrating vast resources on limited goals. In Leningrad, for example, the state supports a ballet school whose principal purpose is to supply great dancers to the Kirov Ballet. Each year the school receives between 1500 and 2000 applications from eight- and nine-year-olds. Of them 90 are accepted. The students spend eight years in school, arriving each morning at 8:30, seldom departing before eight or nine at night. For literally thousands of hours they repeat the same basic five movements, progressing slowly through the fundamentals of classical ballet. There is one faculty member for each five students. At the end of the course the Kirov selects perhaps five students from the graduating class; the rest take jobs in lesser companies, mostly in the provinces.

The box-office attendant at a Moscow theater once answered her telephone: "Yes, we have two tickets for Thursday night. Who wants them? Foreigners? No, these tickets are way back in the balcony. They aren't good enough for foreigners, I'm sorry."

In 1959 Nikita Khrushchev prepared the Soviet Union for its first state visit from an American President, Dwight D. Eisenhower. Khrushchev built a golf course for Ike in Siberia, the first golf course in the country and, until now, also the last. Outside Irkutsk, the principal city of central Siberia, a large residence was constructed for the President. A woman who visited Irkutsk at the time remembers that "they turned the city upside down. . . . They scrubbed it—it was a dirty, sooty town in those days. They built a new hotel downtown. Produce began to appear in the stores. Everybody was delighted with how good things were getting in Irkutsk. Then they announced that Eisenhower wasn't coming [Khrushchev canceled his invitation after the U-2 incident], and all of that disappeared." The special residence remains, however. It's now called the Baikal Sanitorium, and is open to the public.

That wasn't Irkutsk's last brush with a world statesman. In the fall of 1973 the President of Mexico, Luís Echevarría Alvarez, visited the Siberian city. Again it was cleaned up and repainted. Señor Echevarría had told his hosts that he would like to eat in a resturant in Irkutsk, so the town fathers redecorated the Arctic Restaurant for him.

Pat Nixon accompanied her husband to Moscow in May

1972 and spent much of her time sightseeing. One stop on her tour was GUM, the main department store, which looks across Red Square to Lenin's mausoleum and the Kremlin. A Moscow housewife who was in the department store that morning described what happened:

"You know what GUM is like—always crowded, with long lines, sometimes lines that go up two flights of stairs. So there I was one morning, and suddenly they closed the doors and wouldn't let anybody in. They shooed everybody out who was already inside. When I came out onto Red Square, it was empty. A lot of policemen were keeping people away from the store. . . .Apparently, they decided to create an atmosphere for Mrs. Nixon that looked like an American store— not so many people, lots of things for sale. So after the regular shoppers were all out of the store they sent in their own people—KGB agents, I guess—to pose as shoppers. And they probably brought out 'deficit' [i.e., rare] products, and the salespeople were probably very polite, and she must have thought that's how it always is in GUM."

A British delegation visited a large Soviet factory that makes scientific instruments. Members of the delegation were impressed by the crisp efficiency, cleanliness and order of the factory, and complimented their hosts. The next day one of the Englishmen who had seen something of particular interest in the factory asked to go back while his colleagues visited another establishment. The Soviet officials guiding the group made a series of excuses as to why this was impossible, but the Englishman insisted. Finally they took him. He found a completely different scene. Two workers were asleep on tables beside the quality-control line. The efficiency of the day before had vanished.

An American journalist and his wife met the dean of a large Soviet university. The journalist's wife was interested in the personal lives of students, and asked about sex. The dean replied: "We have no pre-marital sex in the Soviet Union."

This series of anecdotes could continue almost indefinitely. Russia is a land of anecdotes. According to legend, Peter the Great, Russian czar of the 18th century, once said: "Russia is a country in which things that just don't happen happen."

The point of these stories has been to bend the mind a little in preparation for an unusual sort of mental exercise: thinking about the truly unfamiliar. Russia really is different, in the most obvious ways and also subtly, sometimes nearly imperceptibly. Most obvious, perhaps, is climate, an overbearing fact in Russian life. It isn't unusual for the last snowfall of a Russian winter to come eight months after the first. Spring and fall usually amount to a few weeks stuck between the long winter and the short, green summer. Nature is more an enemy than an ally in the Russian north, a powerful enemy which traditionally has forced people into prolonged periods of inaction, which makes their food supply problematical year after year, and which must eventually influence their most basic reactions to life and fate.

Russia's uniqueness goes well beyond its weather. Cause and effect work in strange ways there. Our notions of logic, common sense and fair play often don't apply. Which does not mean that everything about the country is strange. Russians are people; Russian bureaucrats are familiar bureaucrats; Russian mothers are as maternal as any, perhaps even more. Aspects of Soviet life recognizable to a western eye will appear repeatedly in the pages that follow. But by dwelling on the familiar, one risks missing the more important strangeness, the fundamental differentness of this vast land.

A Russian carries intellectual and emotional baggage through life which we in the West wouldn't recognize. A Russian's sense of what is normal or unusual is—by our standards—unusual. His sense of history has little in common with ours. The great movements and ideas that produced the civilization of the western world, the crucial elements of our history, are far removed from the Russian experience. Western ideas began to influence Russia only in the 18th century, and have been treated suspiciously ever since. Tyrants are more important to Russian history than ideas, so Russians have their own special idea of what a government is and how it should behave.

Russians have been conscious of their uniqueness for centuries. Their awareness of it has been the central element in a long and continuing struggle between those who want to keep Russia apart from the European world and cultivate her special qualities, and those who want to push her toward the West. A brilliant young writer in Moscow who sympathized with the latter position explained why he thought Russian society was so different.

"The first thing is that we have no history of respecting the individual person as the supreme value of society, we have simply never accepted that idea. Look at the war [World War II]—we wasted men, they didn't matter. The second thing is, we have no history of individual mobility in this country. People live the lives they were born to, in the places where they were born. This has started to change a little, but not very much. The third thing is the traditions of the Russian Orthodox Church. Russian Christians have always been taught not to expect too much on this earth—the greatest rewards are meant to come in the next life. Religion isn't as strong as it was, but this idea is deeply imbedded. A Russian tends to measure his achievements not by material, earthly standards, but by what's in here. [He thumped his chest above the heart.] By your standards, his sense of possibilities is limited."

All of that is indisputably true. There is more besides. The Russian nation transmits from generation to generation an abiding fear of invasion and anarchy, both based on sound historical precedent, and both unfamiliar to non-Russians. Russia has been repeatedly invaded, and was once ruled for centuries by invaders. It has known the worst sort of anarchy, and Russians have little faith in their own capacity to combat anarchy with self-discipline and restraint. The creation of a true dictatorship is all that preserved the Russian nation in the late Middle Ages, and Russians have been relying on dictators ever since. If a dictator failed, an interlude of anarchy was the inevitable result.

The Russian inclination to anarchy is difficult to understand from the pages of a book, but it is easily grasped in real life. I saw it at the Lenin Stadium in Moscow at half time of a big soccer game. Thousands of men headed for the men's room in the brief intermission. Approaching the end of the line, I was suddenly swept into a terrifying press of humanity and literally carried down several flights of stairs by the uncontrolled shoves from behind. Only the wall of bodies ahead prevented me from crashing down the stairs. The city authorities assign *thousands* of police and soldiers to the stadium for a big game, but their only contribution to the control of the men's-room crowd is a cordon at the bottom of the stairs, just outside the toilets. Policemen with locked arms hold back the crowd at this point, letting a new group through each time the room empties out. Never were bodily functions performed with a greater sense of relief.

Fear of invasion and anarchy may contribute to the Rus-

sians' gaping inferiority complex, which they reveal most explicitly in their relations with foreigners. Russians compensate
for their insecurities in different ways; some are terrified of
foreigners, others are determined to deceive them. Travelers
have remarked for centuries on the Russian habit of deception. "I blame the Soviet Union not for having failed to
achieve more," wrote André Gide, the French author, after a
disillusioning visit in 1936. "I see now that nothing better
could have been accomplished in that time; the country had
started from too low. What I complain of is the extent of
their bluff, that they boasted that the situation in the Soviet
Union was desirable and enviable—this from the country of
my hopes and trust was painful to me."

The leaders of the Soviet Union seem to regard the western
world as an enviable but dangerous combination of skill,
wealth and treachery. They have little confidence in the Soviet citizens whom they allow to travel to the West, as though
expecting them to like life in our world better than in their
own. The Soviet authorities spare no effort to impress—and
often to bamboozle—foreign guests, while working harder
than any nation in the world's history to steal other countries'
industrial, military and political secrets.

Insecurity and defensiveness typify Soviet politics at home,
too. The Soviet system is built on the assumption that the citizenry cannot be trusted. "We cannot sell your newspapers
and magazines in our country," a Soviet editor once assured
me, "because people believe whatever they read."

It is common management practice to set the directors of a
Soviet factory against one another, to encourage the assistant
director to report on his boss, and the finance officer to report
on both of them. Important government officials, including
ministers of the Soviet government, conduct their business on
the assumption that they are being watched by official and
amateur spies. Not surprisingly, such a mistrustful society
puts little value on individual resourcefulness and enterprise.
Individualism is suspicious.

Nearly 60 years after the Bolshevik Revolution the authorities still regard any expression of opposition to any aspect
of Soviet policy as a statement on behalf of czarist rule.
When Janos Kadar, the Hungarian communist leader, began
to try to revive his country after the Soviet invasion of 1956,
he used the slogan "If you are not against us, you are with
us." In the Soviet Union it has long been axiomatic that "if

you're not with us, you favor the return of the capitalists and restoration of the landlords." The "loyalty" demanded in Richard Nixon's White House is an everyday political value in the USSR.

Suspicious, insecure, isolated, an Asian land in Europe, or perhaps the other way around, the heir to Byzantium in an era dominated by the descendants of Athens and Rome—this preliminary description lacks one crucial element. It is useless to spend even a fleeting moment in the contemplation of Russia without a sense of the grip she has on all her peoples. "It is impossible to love your own mother," a Russian actor once said with a flat assurance, as though this impossibility were beyond dispute, "unless you love your Motherland."

Nikolai Gogol, the 19th-century writer whose descriptions of Russians are as good as any written, described the power of the homeland in his masterpiece, *Dead Souls*:

Everything in you is poor, straggling, and uncomfortable: no bold wonders of nature crowned with ever bolder wonders of art, no cities with many-windowed tall palaces built upon rocks, no picturesque trees. . . .Everything in you is open, empty, flat; your lowly towns are stuck like dots upon your plains . . . there is nothing to beguile and ravish the eye. But what is the incomprehensible, mysterious force that draws me to you? Why does your mournful song, carried along your whole length and breadth from sea to sea, echo and re-echo incessantly in my ears? What is there in it? What is there in that song? What is it that calls, and sobs, and clutches at my heart? . . . Russia! What do you want of me? What is that mysterious, hidden bond between us?

2 · From Birth to Death: "We're Living Well"

IN THE SOVIET UNION about one family in 70 owns an automobile, which means most people use public transport. Buses and trolleys are usually full, and the passengers are used to pushing and shoving. The atmosphere is seldom congenial.

So it was a surprise one afternoon in Leningrad to be standing in the aisle of a crowded, malodorous bus when one of the passengers, a young man, burst into melodious song. The singing startled everyone on the bus, and the young man attracted the challenging stares of his fellow passengers. He tried to explain: "My wife just had a baby!"

"Ahhh, a baby," a round, grandmotherly figure said with magnanimous understanding, nodding the kerchief that covered her head. The skeptical stares of the other passengers dissolved into broad grins. The young man got off at the next stop. "A new baby!" someone shouted from farther back in the bus. "Now, that's a *real* joy."

New fathers are more often encountered on city sidewalks (or on the dirt that so often substitutes for sidewalks), gesticulating toward a nearby building. The scene is baffling until one follows the young man's glance to the window above;

there a woman in a robe is smiling and waving, announcing as best she can that a healthy new Soviet citizen has arrived.

Husbands are not permitted to visit the maternity hospitals where Soviet babies are born. Russians share a national phobia about germs and babies. Even the mother is separated from her child for the first 24 hours of its life, sometimes longer. Mother and infant generally spend 10 days in the hospital. During that time, waves from windows must substitute for any closer contact with the new father. Giving birth is a lonely experience for Russian women.

Like every aspect of Russian life, childbirth is governed by a rich collection of customs. The Soviet regime has also added a measure of bureaucratic regulations. At a lecture for expectant mothers in Moscow, a doctor—a woman, like most Soviet doctors—warned her audience: "Stay calm and take long walks every day. Don't eat too many sweets or your skin will itch. Wear only wool or cotton clothes, baby doesn't like it when you wear synthetics. Come to the clinic regularly for your ultraviolet rays." (The rays are a source of Vitamin D.)

The young women in the audience were shy, and asked no substantive questions. One inquired if it was all right to cry during childbirth; the doctor said no one cried. Many in the audience were teenagers. More than half the brides in Moscow are now eighteen or nineteen.

As a rule, Russians do not practice birth control. Neither loops nor pills are generally available. It is occasionally possible to obtain a diaphragm—in just one size. Men's condoms are crude and unreliable, when available. Abortion is the most widely used means of preventing unwanted children. In Moscow, Leningrad and other large cities 80 percent of all pregnancies are deliberately aborted.

Pregnant women receive general instructions on how to give birth. Breathe deeply, the lecturer advised, oxygen is the best antidote to pain. She demonstrated how to rub the stomach during labor. But there is no equivalent to the elaborate exercises and breathing patterns now taught to women in the West who want to have babies without anesthetic. Practitioners of the Lamaze method of natural childbirth in America and Western Europe describe it as based on a Russian technique, but Russian doctors say they are unfamiliar with it. There is no choice about anesthetic in Russia; it is used only in emergencies.

Toward the end of pregnancy the neighborhood clinic gives

each expectant mother the address and telephone number of the maternity home where she is to go when labor begins. Occasionally this system breaks down. One woman called the number she'd been given, but there was no answer. While she went through the early stages of labor, she had to locate another home with space for her. Later she learned that the place she had been scheduled to use was closed for *remont*—repair and refurbishment, a ubiquitous harassment in Russian life.

Another woman had been treated at a special clinic for those who showed signs that they might give birth prematurely. Doctors there examined her regularly during the first eight months of pregnancy, then told her she was no longer likely to have a premature baby, and discontinued treatment. Her labor began before she had made arrangements to give birth at an ordinary maternity home. It was late at night, and she and her husband set out to find a place where she could have the baby.

One maternity home turned her away because there were no empty beds. But first the nurse on duty bawled her out for coming to have a baby without the proper change of clothes. They went next to the clinic for premature babies, but were turned away because the baby could not be considered premature; space had to be saved for serious cases. Finally a third establishment agreed to let her in. She produced a boy, healthy and noisy. The delivery was uneventful, though loud.

Most births probably are uneventful, but the horror stories are sufficiently common that many Russian women are afraid of childbirth. They seem put off by the long separation from one's husband, by the sure knowledge that birth will be painful and by the communal facilities in the maternity homes. (Two or three women may give birth in the same delivery room at the same time.) These factors may contribute to the low birthrate in the European part of the Soviet Union.

A young married couple is most unlikely to have its own flat, so the arrival of a baby affects more lives than the parents'. But all involved, grandparents, aunts and uncles and parents, share a typically Russian enthusiasm for the prerogatives of the newly born.

"When a baby arrives, it's as though we were all marched to the wall and told to put up our hands," a Moscow father once explained with a defeated grin. " 'Go ahead,' we say, 'take it all, take everything.' Why do we act that way? Russians are an irrational people. We are afraid of the unknown. And what could be more unknown and unknowable than this little creature who suddenly appears among us? So we devote ourselves entirely to it, in hopes this will somehow satisfy it, or at least remove the mystery."

Little is left to chance. Strict rules and traditions are passed from generation to generation, and they are respected. The new baby must be wrapped up like a sprained ankle, head to toe, often with a piece of wood as a splint to hold head and neck stiff. The baby must sleep on its back, swaddled in blankets. Sleeping on the stomach is bad for the heart, and for breathing, and much else besides, according to the conventional wisdom. Breast feeding is mandatory. If a mother cannot provide enough milk herself, she can buy human donors' milk at special shops. The Russians haven't heard of baby formula. When told of it they tend to shudder, and to doubt its efficacy. As infant can be bathed only in boiled water, and there must be enough of it to submerge the baby up to its neck. This is said to prevent chills, a common danger in the Russian climate. The recommended treatment for diaper rash is corn oil. Petroleum jelly is one of hundreds of western consumer products that don't exist in the Soviet Union. Rubber pants are another. At the maternity clinic the doctor suggests that mothers make their own diapers from old sheets.

After several months a typical child is taken off mother's milk and put on a mild diet of thin cereal and milk products sold at special baby kitchens. A mild yogurt, especially sterilized, is the most popular product. To receive it, a mother must be registered on the baby kitchen's list. If she doesn't pick up her supply every few days, the kitchen will take her name off the list. Mothers are advised not to stop nursing in the spring, when fruits and vegetables are beginning to appear after the long, barren Russian winter. Better to wait until midsummer, the theory goes. By then baby will have absorbed the stronger vitamins and minerals in those fresh foods from its mother's milk, and will be better prepared to digest them when independent feeding begins.

But "independent" isn't exactly the right word. Russian parents (including, it seems, those who have read contrary advice in Dr. Spock, whose book has been published in Russian) don't believe in letting a baby try to feed itself. The mess is offensive and the inefficiency wasteful. It is not unusual to see a Russian mother patiently spooning an entire meal into the mouth of a four- or five-year-old.

From its first day at home, the baby is subjected to extraordinary attention. No amount of fussing is considered excessive by the rest of the family. Parents, grandparents, aunts and uncles withdraw energy and resources from most other pursuits and redirect them enthusiastically to the baby. Expenditures on baby carriages, blankets and other paraphernalia can destroy the family budget. It is currently fashionable to buy a carriage (an East German one is best) and clothes all in pink for a girl, blue for a boy.

Arkadi Raikin is one of the two or three most famous entertainers in the Soviet Union. He is a comedian, a product of the same tradition of Jewish humor that gave America the Marx Brothers, Milton Berle and Jack Benny. Raikin practices his art in a society that disapproves of public displays of cynicism, so his humor is more sentimental than those American comedians'. In one of his sentimental routines Raikin mimics an old grandfather conversing with a grandchild of two or three:

"I look at you and I ask myself, 'What have I done special or unusual in my life?' I'll tell you what. Nothing. Everything has been done for the sake of the children. If we had a glass of milk—give it to the children. Two apples? For the kids. Vitamins? Likewise. When your Aunt Irina needed a violin, we hoarded our kopeks. We suffer when you are sick, we go absolutely mad when you take the college entrance exams. . . ."

In the winter parents take their small children outside on aluminum sleds.* On a winter Sunday there are thousands of sleds in the city's parks. Each transports a carefully bundled-up minicreature, usually wrapped in the same outfit: felt boots, overcoat, a long scarf around the neck on the outside of the overcoat, and an all-enveloping hat of fur or wool. This little being rides triumphantly behind mama or papa, who pulls the sled by a rope.

If there's a little hill in the park, the children will yell to be pushed down it. The parent in charge finds that idea disquiet-

---

* The sled itself is a prized possession; when the Children's World department store in Moscow receives a shipment of them, the line of would-be purchasers may wait six hours. One proud uncle got a sled by helping the store's employees unload several hundred of them from a truck.

ing, so there is a compromise. Papa pulls the sled up the tiny hill, turns it around and, still holding the rope, runs down the hill ahead of the sled. He never lets go.

That is the theme of Russian parenthood: don't let go. It means that children remain dependent on their parents until they are well past the toddling stage. Children under the age of six or seven are rarely allowed to go outside by themselves. An eight-year-old still needs help getting into his winter clothes. I once asked the eight-year-old son of a family we were visiting in Moscow to bring me a box of matches from across the room. Before the bewildered boy had a chance even to shrug his shoulders, papa was on his feet, patting his son reassuringly on the head and jumping for the matches. "Here they are," he said. Little Mishka hadn't moved an inch.

In public, at least, a Russian child's behavior is sternly regulated. The courtyards of many Moscow apartment houses contain sandboxes, which are popular with the children. But mothers don't allow them to sit in the sand. They must learn to squat on their haunches, in the manner of Asian peasants, to keep their bottoms dry and the sand out of their clothing. Anyone who slips into a more comfortable and natural posture is certain to be lifted out of the sandbox with a jolt.

Inherited wisdom also dictates the method of toilet training. The rule is that a year-old baby uses a toilet—perhaps not always, because no one is perfect, but in principle. No more diapers after the first birthday. The rule is applied by anxious parents and relatives, who learn the schedule of a baby's bodily functions and put the child on the toilet when they are due to occur. Many American child psychologists now believe that a child must be old enough to understand what is happening to be properly trained, but the Russians don't agree. If one asks a Russian mother about the possible psychological implications of her method of mandatory toilet training, the answer is likely to be a look of surprise. "But this is the way everyone does it, and always has."

Continuity—the passing of traditions from generation to generation—is enforced by grandmother, or *babushka*, a formidable Russian institution. Not every young couple has a *babushka* living nearby, of course, but a high percentage still do. Her role is often greater than mama's own, especially after mama returns to work. Virtually every Russian woman of childbearing age living in a town or city holds a full-time job.

After she has a baby, her job is held for her for a year, but no longer. If mama is back at work and her mother is home with the baby, she is unlikely to challenge the older woman's methods of child-raising.

Babushka's guiding principle is love and affection, praise and appreciation to the highest degree. This is combined with the traditional deprivation of independence and extreme protectiveness which Russians take for granted, and which would be unacceptable in a culture that valued self-reliance more highly.

*Babushka*s demonstrate total confidence in their own wisdom. They are apt to look into other people's baby carriages to check on the child's protection against Russia's unpredictable weather, and freely express an opinion if one seems called for. They may berate young parents on the street, even total strangers, for alleged violations of the parental code. One Sunday in May I took my daughter, then fifteen months old, for a walk in Moscow. She was dressed in rain gear from rubber boots and pants to sou'wester, and was running merrily back and forth through a big puddle. An elderly lady passing by came up short.

"Papa!" she said sternly. "How dare you? How can you allow it? Her mama would *never* allow it."

A Russian childhood has much in common with everyone else's. Discovery, adventure, frustration, toy guns and summer camp, nagging parents and homework—all these have a place. The seven-year-old son of a friend in Moscow disappeared from home one day. His best friend, also seven, disappeared at about the same time. Hours later police in a remote corner of Moscow telephoned the distraught parents. They had intercepted two seven-year-olds who were riding the trolley to Alaska.

The same seven-year-old discovered—perhaps by watching Canadian hockey players on television—that it was fashionable to wear one's hair over the ears. He insisted that his locks be left to grow. His teacher began to write comments in the grade book that every Soviet student carried with him at all times: "Anton needs a haircut" or "Please see that Anton has his hair cut at once." Anton's mother found it easier to disregard these instructions than to convince her son to cut his hair. "A lot of the older kids have long hair," he complained, "why shouldn't I?" The answer, his grandmother explained, was that the school authorities still thought they controlled the seven-year-olds, even if they had lost some of their influence over the teenagers.

A young child in Russia finds it difficult to be different. His own parents are usually the most anxious that he adhere to the accepted norms. Parents are constantly apologizing for rambunctious or disobedient children, as though a child's misstep implies some parental inadequacy. "No crying!" mothers repeat to children who cry in public. At kindergarten—and two-thirds of the children in the Soviet Union between four and six attend kindergarten—the curriculum demands group ("collective") behavior.

Some of the meaning of collective behavior emerged from a conversation with the director of a kindergarten in Volgograd (the name Nikita Khrushchev gave to the city once called Stalingrad). The director wanted to show off her students' art work; she held up a beautifully painted watercolor of a tree on a riverbank. "One of our six-year-olds did this," she beamed. "Look, here are some others." She held up a dozen more watercolors of a tree on a riverbank—precisely the same picture, the same colors, the same strokes. How did they turn out all alike? "That's how we do it. The teacher puts a picture up on the board and asks the children to copy it."

An inventive teacher—in Russia as elsewhere—can overcome the system. In Moscow a kindergarten music teacher taught her children the principles of high and low notes, harmony and rhythm, then encouraged them to invent dances to accompany the tunes she played on the piano. In the same kindergarten, though, another teacher brought a sprig of pine to class and asked the children to draw it. She then posted their pictures at the front of the room and asked each child to come forward and explain what he did *not* like in the other children's drawings. She set the tone for this discussion by observing that one of the children had used blue to draw the pine, which was the "wrong" color, and another had made a "mistake" by drawing the sprig in the corner of her piece of paper, not in the middle.

Parents and teachers constantly remind children of the right and wrong ways of doing things. The only right way to dress for playing outdoors, for example, is to overdress, in layers of protective covering. Children thus encumbered sweat like a cold glass of beer under their winter clothes. The right way to eat or draw is with the right hand; left-handedness is considered abnormal. Teachers use some corporal punishment in school, and a child trying to write left-handed is likely to get whacked for doing so.

The right way to learn one's lesson is by rote. "They don't care if you know how to solve a problem," a ten-year-old American in the fourth class of a Soviet school once told me—"only if you know the answers to the problems assigned for homework." The homework is memorization, and classroom participation by the students often amounts to nothing more than recitation of what was memorized. Teachers are looking for one right answer, and for one right way of finding it.

The same young American remembered that at his old school in Washington "you could get up from your desk and walk around the room if you wanted to. Here, if you get up just to get a pencil, they bawl you out. And you've got to raise your hand a special way, too." Discipline is meant to be strict, and school life is meant to be regimented. The children all wear uniforms.

A Russian child is made aware of his relative standing among his peers at an early age. Class assignments are based on grades and perceived talents. Older children supervise younger ones at recess—which is almost always indoors—and are authorized to use force to maintain order.

The rules and traditions of Russian childhood may seem foreign, but they don't deter the universal instincts of youth. On a winter's afternoon I could join twelve-year-olds in a hockey game which seemed identical to the games I played when twelve myself on frozen ponds around Albany, New York. The players shared the same contempt for sissies and bad skaters, the same interest in a new pair of skates or a fancy stick, the same zeal for victory and the same excuses for defeat as Americans of the same age.

The awkwardness of adolescence is another universal phenomenon. It was on display one Saturday night in Volgograd at the Theater for Young Spectators. Hundreds of young people had come to see a melodrama called *Return Address*, so popular—or so enthusiastically endorsed by the Ministry of Culture in Moscow—that it has been playing in theaters throughout the Soviet Union for several years.

Before the play began, dozens of bare-cheeked young men

primped in front of mirrors in the men's room. Many helped each other tie or adjust the neckties that come out of the cupboard on rare special occasions. A cigarette dangled uncertainly from almost every lip. The suits and sports jackets that Russians call "going-out" clothes clashed with scuffed, unpolished shoes and dirty fingernails.

Upstairs in the lobby, girls pressed together in front of every available square centimeter of mirror space. In the Russian fashion, they combed and primped in full view, without a hint of self-consciousness. The dresses were bright; many looked new, and a few were flattering. Like the boys, the girls wore wrist watches clipped into thick watch straps, mostly plastic ones meant to look like leather. Some of the girls' stockings had seams that ran up the backs of their unshaven legs. They teased and shaped their bouffant hairdos, many in bright shades of blond blond or red red about which not only their hairdressers knew for sure.

One girl gripped five drooping daffodils wrapped in a piece of cellophane, a valuable treasure in Volgograd in March. She talked busily with a circle of friends, moving with them into the theater. "Did you hear about the mixer Friday night?" she asked. "There'll be 150 girls and 150 soldiers—a nightmare!"

The play itself was a sentimental and barely plausible account of a teenage boy's first encounter with adult realities. In the first scene he opens a letter meant for his father, an understandable mistake since father and son have the same name. It is a note from an old girlfriend whom the father left during the war. The boy eventually meets this woman and is attracted to her. She has recently lost a foster child she'd been caring for to its real parents, so she is drawn to the boy. Other young people are brought into the plot, which ends inconclusively, but with all the adolescents wiser about the uncertainties of life ahead. The play was a huge success with the audience, perhaps because it was written from such an unswervingly adolescent point of view.

During the applause that followed the final curtain, the girl with the daffodils and her friends debated which of the actors shold be presented with the flowers. Finally, they split the five daffodils among three of the performers, and giggled nervously as they stepped forward to hand the flowers over the footlights during the curtain calls.

It would be impossible to exaggerate the gulf that separates those teenagers in Volgograd from the most sophisticated adolescents in Moscow. The students at one of the capital's special schools for bright (or well-connected) children would have little patience with the style of life on display at the Theater for Young Spectators. They are interested not in sentimental melodrama, but in a recording of *Jesus Christ Superstar*. Ideally, their wardrobes include a pair of Levi's or Wranglers (*not* the Polish imitations), a British sweater, a suede jacket.

In 1972 the authorities closed one of the schools in which this sophisticated adolescent culture thrived, a special mathematics school in Moscow. The pretext for the unpublicized decision was that some of the students had visited the main Moscow synagogue and signed a guestbook there as representatives of "Mathematics School No. 3." But according to a former student at the school, the authorities acted because they had lost control of the school. "The atmosphere there was too free. We had a Russian-literature teacher who told us that Solzhenitsyn was the best living Russian writer"—a bold violation of the official line on Solzhenitsyn. In September 1973 the former students of Mathematics School No. 3 scattered to ordinary schools throughout the city.

A girl of seventeen who attended another of these institutions, a special high school for biology, spent an evening telling me about it. Her story deserves recounting:

She and her friends don't see how it is possible to get an education in the ordinary schools that most of their contemporaries attend. ("They're lousy.") They do feel they are learning a lot of biology in their special school, for which the students are chosen in a tough competition. They work hard, hoping to win a place at Moscow State University or one of the best institutes (colleges) of biology.

Of the thirty-two students in her class, four are children of ordinary workers. The rest are products of the "intelligentsia," the sons and daughters of officials and intellectuals. All but three belong to the Young Communist League (the Komsomol), "but very few take it seriously. It's a credential you have to have to get into the university." In every Soviet school Komsomol activity is the responsibility of a paid professional Party worker. (Twenty years ago these posts were filled by students or part-time people.)

Most of the students who participate actively in Komsomol

activites are completely cynical about it, "or they are fools." They know that most fringe benefits go to the active young communists. When the director of the school chose six students for a tourist trip to Poland, an extraordinary privilege, he picked only active Komsomols. "Anyone who has been abroad has the highest status in school."

The students must attend regular political lectures. "We had one recently on the *coup d'état* in Portugal. The Komsomol secretary produced a resolution condemning the previous regime and welcoming the new government. 'Who's for this?' she asked. A few people raised their hands, a few didn't, but it was announced as a unanimous vote."

Political lessons are part of the curriculum at every level. In the 10th grade (which is the last) they're called the "Lenin Lesson"; students study Lenin's writings and achievements.

There is also a "military preparations" class conducted twice a week by "a dumb retired colonel" from the Red Army. He too is a member of the school's permanent staff. Girls and boys march together. "But the boys are anxious to avoid being drafted into the Army—that's ghastly. Their parents try to help. Lots of mothers are always looking for physical defects that might keep their sons from being drafted." No one from the school would want to make a career in the military. "There's no prestige in it."

"Steady romances aren't too common," but there is an active social life. On holidays the school organizes its own "evenings"—speechmaking, a concert of some kind and a dance afterward. On ordinary weekends the kids gather at one another's apartments for parties, if they can persuade someone's parents to allow it. "There are always some liberal parents who are willing, but most parents don't like to see vodka on the table."

Boys in this group began experimenting with vodka at 13 or 14, by which time many were already regular smokers. (There is almost no propaganda against smoking in the Soviet Union.)

The girls must wear a uniform to school, but that does not prevent sartorial competition. "Only the dress is required—we can wear different shoes, coats, stockings, pocketbooks. It's a big deal." In the evenings a girl's prestige depends a good deal on her clothes. The most prized possessions are items of clothing from abroad.

But social life is a diversion from the main business—success in school, and success in the entrance examination for the university or a good institute. Many of the 10th-graders hire private tutors to prepare them for the entrance exams. The school curriculum doesn't cover all the material that the students will need to know for the examinations; the tutor fills the gap. The students suspect that teachers in the universities and institutes created and maintain this gap so they'll get more business as tutors. An instructor at Moscow State University, whose salary might be 200 rubles a month, can earn up to 10 rubles an hour tutoring.

As members of the faculties of colleges and universities, tutors can help a student gain admission. "It's what we call *blat* in Russian—influence." The admissions committees that choose new students are known to be susceptible to various kinds of inducements; bribery is not uncommon.

What do 17 year-olds in a privileged school like this care about? "Biology. They've got biology in their blood. They all have a pretty clear idea of what kind of work they would like to do later on—research or practical work or whatever."

Not all Soviet young people are so cynical, but there is a general feeling in the country that the young are more frivolous and freer of spirit than their elders. Which isn't surprising. Their elders grew up with famine and poverty, Stalin's official terrorism and World War II, in which perhaps 20 million Soviet citizens were killed. The younger generation could hardly come from a more different environment: peaceful, relatively prosperous, without terror.

I once rode in a Moscow taxi driven by a young man whose brown locks fell over the collar of his jacket. He looked barely twenty. I asked if he got a hard time for wearing his hair so long. "Oh, they'd like to give me a hard time," he replied, "but I play on our garage's soccer team. I'm pretty good, so they don't dare say anything."

By such arrangements, the long hair that the Beatles gave the rest of us in the mid-1960s began to appear on young Russian men in the early 1970s. Long hair does not challenge the Communist Party. It is hardly counter-revolutionary. But it does depart from the strict standards of an outwardly puritan and fiercely conformist society.

One Moscow mother told me about her children's generation with a combination of satisfaction and alarm. By the age of about twelve, she said, "the kids have stopped thinking that they have to do every single assignment in school and obey every single instruction they hear. By that age most of the boys and a lot of the girls have started to smoke. Teachers who used to maintain iron discipline now find that they can't. Naturally, this makes them nervous. Some try to rush through their lessons and escape from the classroom before they lose control. The teacher no longer enjoys full authority just because she's the teacher."

Official Soviet newspapers have confirmed that juvenile delinquency is a serious national problem. Soviet sociologists—a harrassed group of intellectuals who are not always able to publish their findings, because they contradict the official image of how things ought to be—have suggested that a deprived underclass exists which breeds juvenile crime. According to published official reports, 84.4 percent of all juvenile offenders began drinking alcoholic beverages before the age of sixteen—43 percent before they were thirteen. A television documentary not long ago described a teenage gang that killed two tellers in a savings-bank holdup in a Ukrainian city. The gang's leader was sentenced to death.

The newspapers have also revealed the existence of bands of young dropouts from many different backgrounds who roam remote areas of the country, working when they need money—and earning the relatively higher salaries paid in remote regions—then quitting their jobs when they get bored, and blowing their earnings on easy or wild living.

Soviet newspapers and television don't report on isolated events or unrepresentative social phenomena. That would be "sensationalism," and therefore unacceptable. So it is reasonable to assume that these reports describe social problems which the authorities consider serious.

Milder challenges to official authority can be seen on city streets. There is no disguising the black market in phonograph records conducted daily in front of the secondhand store on Moscow's Sadovoye Koltso, for example. There a copy of that recording of *Jesus Christ Superstar* could change hands for as much as 100 rubles—the monthly salary of a young scientist.

Jesus Christ Superstar is a piece of the international youth culture which thousands, perhaps millions, of young Russians have heard about but never seen. I met many who craved an opportunity to share it. Judging by his reaction, the

biggest compliment I ever paid a Russian was a chance remark to a young man in Sochi, a beach resort on the Black
Sea. He was wearing an Ohio State University tee shirt and
Levi's. "Where are you from?" I asked in English. "Oh, oh, I
am Russian," he replied, beaming with satisfaction at the mistake. Later he asked for the latest news about Jethro Tull,
Led Zeppelin, the Jefferson Airplane and a long list of British
and American rock bands and singers.

At another chance meeting with young people in Tbilisi, the
capital of Soviet Georgia, a group of university students sat
for an hour talking about where they would travel if they had
the chance. "I know where I want to go," one announced
with finality. "Japan, France, the Scandinavian countries and
America." He had met a girl from Philadelphia on the beach
at Sochi the previous summer. She had given him a Frisbee.

Those students in Tbilisi claimed to have smoked hashish.
In Moscow it is difficult to find a young person who admits
to any use of drugs, though everyone knows that they are
fashionable in the West. In 1972, however, the police arrested
at least one scientist from the Institute of Natural Compounds in Moscow after seizing a kilogram (2.2 pounds) of
LSD that had allegedly been made in the institute's laboratories.

Some Russian young people show an interest in the outside
world that goes beyond clothes and rock music. "My son
wants to be a poet," the wife of a prominent Soviet musician
told me at a diplomatic reception. I said he had picked the
perfect ambition for his homeland, since Russians were so enthusiastic about poetry and poets. "Oh," the mother said excitedly, "I wish you'd tell my son that! He only talks about
how good things are in the West—the freedom, the lack of
censorship . . ."

He is hardly typical. Russian children are lectured from
the age of eight or nine on the need to prepare for a career,
work hard, stay in line. Nearly all of them take the advice to
heart. A Hungarian girl studying at a provincial Soviet college
of engineering found her fellow students universally bored by
world politics, the works of Alexander Solzhenitsyn and other
subjects outside their own narrow worlds. A teacher of English at a Moscow institute described her own discomfort at
the sight of career-oriented students who compromised their
way toward good jobs and other material benefits: "I asked
one of them recently, 'Aren't you ashamed of yourself?' And

he said, 'What do you mean? I'm building a career. I want to live, to *live*.' " The Russians have a saying: *"Nado Zhits"* —you have to live.

Away from Moscow and the colleges and universities that breed cynicism, simple, patriotic enthusiasm is still common. It is vividly evident at the giant Kama River truck plant which 70,000 young people, half of them teenagers, have been building 600 miles east of Moscow.

Like the dam at Bratsk, the Kama plant is a hero project, the subject of massive publicity and the beneficiary of high official priority. Kama is located in the Volga River basin, an area severely affected by food shortages in 1972. But the young people building the factory suffered no shortages. The Komsomol lured them to Kama with promises of exciting jobs, apartments and fun with thousands of their contemporaries, and the Komsomol insures that the food supply is adequate. The national concert bureau in Moscow, which organizes the tours of the country's leading performers, sent more of them to Kama in 1972 than to any other town or city in the entire country.

The government must rely on young people to work on projects like the Kama factory, because young men and women leaving school at seventeen or eighteen are the country's principal reserve of mobile labor. The young workers on the job seem enthusiastic. Anna Guzenka, for instance, read about Kama in a youth newspaper when she was twenty-one, and decided, with a girlfriend, to give it a try. "My friend's father died and she went home, but I'm staying." She was twenty-four when I met her, and was promised a one-room apartment the following year. No one that age would have her own apartment in Moscow or Leningrad.

In the spring of 1973, 80 couples were getting married each weekend at Kama's Palace of Weddings, a mock-elegant structure draped in gold sateen.

Valentin and Valentina, a play by Mikhail Roshchin, was the smash hit of the 1971-2 theater season in Moscow and throughout the Soviet Union. It was still playing in 1975, and appeared likely to run for years in the repertoires of many Soviet theaters—a gold mine for Roshchin, and a minor revelation about Russian life for the rest of us.

Valentin and Valentina is a Soviet variation on the Romeo-and-Juliet theme, but with a happy ending. It takes place in the present-day Soviet Union, a land—as Roshchin depicts it—of generation gaps, obvious class distinctions and a pervasive preoccupation with living space. All the play's characters are absorbed in their own lives. They reveal not a hint of interest in the world around them.

All this seemed to have the ring of truth for audiences in Moscow, which gave the play a rapturous reception. A critic wrote in the Ministry of Culture's official newspaper: "The merit of the play is that the author is not afraid to speak about simple and even commonplace aspects of daily life." The subject matter of *Valentin and Valentina* also explained—according to this critic—why so many theaters around the country liked the play. There is a "natural desire," the paper said, for plays about problems of everyday life. *Valentin and Valentina* is certainly that.

Valentina, a college freshman studying mathematics, is the daughter of a self-appointed member of the better classes, an earnest woman of unfailing bourgeois morality whose husband deserted the family several years before. Valentin studies history. He lives with his widowed mother, an earthy and sensible memeber of the proletariat, an attendant in a railroad car, who takes tickets and makes tea for the passengers.

As the play begins, the two young people are already hopelessly in love. Both families disapprove of the romance. Valentina's mother and grandmother dismiss it as a youthful infatuation, and hope it will end before it produces a catastrophe—a premature marriage. Her mother tries to forbid Valentina to see her Valentin, with consequences (or, rather, a lack of consequences) that any western parent would recognize. Her grandmother predicts that "when she marries the train attendant's son, she will use obscenities." Her mother obviously worries that Valentina will squander the benefits of her upbringing—her training in English and music, for instance, which are supposed to set a better girl apart from the crowd. "Love comes and goes," Grandma counsels Valentina, "but a husband sticks around."

Valentin's mother is also worried about the gap between her son's humble family and Valentina's classier surroundings. "What would you feed your young wife?" she asks him at one point. "She is not a common girl, she wouldn't eat just potatoes and noodles." He answers that he'll take her to restaurants. Later the train attendant warns her son, "She is not a proper match for you."

Oleg Yefremov, one of the most talented directors in the Russian theater, staged *Valentin and Valentina* at the Moscow Art Theater. He dressed Valentina's family in fancy western clothes and furnished their three-room apartment with pieces that hint at some wealth, and put Valentin's family in a crowded, functional room in a communal apartment, emphasizing the class distinction.

The action of the play, such as it is, turns on practical and philosophic disputes between children and parents. On the philosophic plane the dispute involves love—does it exist, and if so, what is it? Every character has a go at answering that one.

A more practical problem is where the couple can live if they do get married. Valentina's mother doesn't want them in her apartment, and Valentin's mother couldn't have them in her small room. Meanwhile the young people cannot find a private place to make love. When his mother is away on a train trip, Valentin bribes his younger sister to go to the movies and leave them alone. The sister accepts the ruble bribe, but returns in a few minutes—before anything can happen. The only movies in the neighborhood, she announces, are forbidden to children under sixteen.

Finally a neighbor goes away for the weekend and leaves Valentin the key to her room. By this time Valentin's mother (the sensible member of the working class) has accepted this love affair as a serious matter. She even lays out Valentina's nightgown on the neighbor's bed before departing on another train trip.

A scene clearly implying premarital lovemaking is bold for the Soviet stage. Oleg Yefremov tried to accentuate its boldness in his original production by taking most of the clothes off Valentin and Valentina and setting them like statues in a hazy spotlight just for an instant. The chairman of the Council of Ministers, Mr. Kosygin, was in the audience for the premiere of this spectacle. The nude scene never appeared again.

But Valentin and Valentina do manage to consummate their affair. The morning after, when Valentina realizes how her life has changed, the drab, borrowed room where they have made love appalls her. "Who am I here? I oversleep in someone else's room. They could come in at any minute. I'm even afraid to run out into the corridor for a second. Everything is strange, shameful, dangerous. . . ."

The lovers overcome this awkward moment, and as the play ends they seem determined to make their new life together a success. The audience leaves the theater convinced that Valentin and Valentina will achieve their vision of happy-ever-after, which Valentin enunciates midway through the play: "You and I have our whole lives ahead of us. Let's go somewhere and teach in the same school. You can torment the children with your mathematics [her specialty] and I'll torment them with history [his]. And then I will write a dissertation."

Valentin and Valentina disappeared into the wings before they got married. Volodya and Luba, two real young Russians, went through the entire ritual.

They were both nineteen when they decided to get married. Both are the children of working-class families in Moscow, but Volodya's parents are relatively prosperous, so they took responsibility for the wedding.

The expenses were considerable, and in the end there had to be some economies. The groom wanted a new suit, but it would have cost at least 100 rubles, two-thirds of his mother's monthly salary. The young couple thought about giving a wedding party in a Moscow Café, but at 10 rubles a guest this idea also proved too extravagant. They decided to hold the party in the two rooms of the communal apartment that Volodya, his parents and sister had shared for 15 years.

On the day of the wedding there was so much still to be done that Volodya's mother skipped the ceremony to finish preparing food for the party. While she made salads and cold hors d'oeuvres, the young people, their friends and a few representatives of the older generation set off for the Palace of Weddings on Griboyedova Street.

Volodya and Luba had first gone to the palace three months earlier to apply to marry. With other nervous, giggling young couples, they had sat at one of the small wooden tables and filled out the form. They wanted to have a wedding ceremony at the Palace of Weddings on a Saturday or Sunday. Fifty couples can be married at the palace every day, but there was a three-month wait for a weekend wedding. They could have gone to a neighborhood registry office, where marriages are made by shuffling papers, but they wanted a proper ceremony in the grand, high-ceilinged palace, which was a rich merchant's mansion before the Bolsheviks put an end to such things.

Their turn had finally come. They arrived at the palace in taxis which Volodya's father had commandeered—at a price—with the help of a friend of his, a taxi driver. Two of the cars were decorated with crepe-paper streamers and balloons. The taxi that led the procession had a doll attached to its front grill, a good-luck symbol that would have cost more than 10 rubles had Volodya's mother not found a friend who had a doll from her own daughter's wedding. A teddy bear was similarly fastened to the second taxi. Four other caravans of cars, decorated identically, were already parked on the street when Volodya and Luba's party arrived.

Inside, the palace was bustling. One newly married couple was leaving as the new arrivals gave their coats to the cloakroom attendant. They found a seat in one of the waiting rooms. Luba nervously rubbed the wrinkles and folds out of her long white gown, which, for 90 rubles, had been made to measure in a state tailor shop. They waited with four other young couples, each surrounded by a group of friends and relations.

Every 10 minutes a small, stern-faced woman in high-heeled shoes came into the waiting area and called out a name. The members of that party then lined up in two rows behind the bride and groom. Finally it was their turn. The clerk threw open double doors and led them into a brightly lit room with elaborate moldings, a red carpet and a large statue of Lenin looking down on the whole scene.

Two more female officials conducted the ceremony. They described the solemnity of marriage, and the Soviet government's interest in its success. Volodya and Luba signed a document. An official handed them their internal passports, now amended to show their new marital status. One of the women declared them man and wife and they kissed.

Their friends and relatives gathered around; many gave Luba a flower, and she accumulated a large bouquet. They went into an anteroom for a glass of Soviet champagne. Volodya and Luba had decided not to spend 21 rubles to have an eight millimeter movie made of the wedding (they knew no one who owned a projector), but a friend took snapshots. In keeping with the atmosphere of the palace, the mood of

the group was restrained. No one laughed. They all seemed
self-conscious. Strangers kept staring at them.

After several minutes, yet another woman official asked
them to move along, their time was up. They got into their
overcoats and went out to the waiting taxis. From the palace
they drove to Red Square, where Luba and Volodya laid a
bouquet near Lenin's mausoleum. Several other newlyweds
were doing the same thing. This is an officially encouraged
custom that has taken hold, particularly in the working class.
From Red Square they went home to begin two days of
celebrations.

They had invited relatives, close friends of both sets of
parents, their own friends from school and the neighborhood,
but not the neighbors who lived in their apartment. Volodya's
family had shared a communal kitchen and bath with four
other families for 15 years, living with them intimately.
Someone suggested inviting them to the wedding, but after a
discussion it was agreed that they didn't want the neighbors
at the party.

Volodya's sister agreed to spend that night with their aunt,
so the bride and groom had a room to themselves for their
wedding night. Later they planned to move in with the same
aunt. She had a two-room flat, but lived alone, so there was
room for them.

Early marriages have become increasingly common in the
Soviet Union. Both bride and groom are now under 20 in
more than half the marriages in Moscow. The reasons for
this are not clear.

Russian young people are not puritanical about sex. An
unpublished poll of twenty-two-year-old students at Leningrad University found that less then 5 percent of them were
virgins. According to numerous young people from the West
who have studied in Soviet universities, the sexual atmosphere
is relaxed. Sleeping together on the first date is not uncommon—provided one can find a place to do it. A young psychologist in Moscow told me that many educated young
women in the capital thought it was fashionable to disdain
formal marriage, though "many want to have a legal husband
briefly so they can have a legitimate child."

If this is indeed a new fashion, it hasn't reached the vast
majority of the population. On the contrary, Soviet social
scientists are worried by the haste with which the young are

rushing into marriage. The state maintains an Institute of the General Problems of Upbringing, where Alevtina Suvorova conducts research on young couples. She wrote in one article, "Accelerated sexual development does not run parallel with social development. Young people do not have sufficient psychological maturity. As a result there are early marriages—ill-considered alliances, doomed in many cases to a short existence."

"Our children . . . are not properly prepared for marriage," Mrs. Suvorova wrote, referring to the most practical matters. Young couples about to marry "haven't yet encountered questions of the family budget, housekeeping, or a husband's role in domestic duties." Subsequent surveys of the same couples early in their married lives found that "husbands who used to worry about their girlfriend's cooking abilities soon realize that those abilities may perish in oblivion if they and their wives cannot learn to balance income and expenditures. But alas, it turns out that only 17 percent of newlyweds know how to plan a family budget."

It isn't easy to leave a protective Russian home at the age of eighteen or nineteen and try to set up housekeeping. Many young couples don't try; they simply move in with one set of parents and carry on as before. Life alone is unexpectedly difficult, even for a couple fortunate enough to find a room or flat of their own.

Russians live in rooms and apartments, unless they are country folk still housed in log cabins or cottages. Detached homes in the western sense are virtually nonexistent. Even on collective farms, prefabricated buildings of flats are beginning to replace the cabins. According to the norm established by V.I. Lenin himself, a Soviet citizen is entitled to 98 square feet of living space, plus kitchen, hallway and bath. That amounts to a room 10 feet square. In fact the average citizen has a good deal less. Probably a third of the urban population of the Soviet Union still lives in communal housing—a room or two per family, several families sharing one kitchen and bath. Young workers often live in dormitories, five or six to a room, sometimes even after they are married.

Citizens of the Soviet future will live in high-rise boxes of flats clustered in vast "micro-regions" around towns and cities. These enormous communities are reminiscent of the apartments Western European and American governments built for their poor in the 1950s and 1960s—rows of repetitive towers laid out on a vast scale. The plan for the future of Moscow includes great forests of towers around the old central city.

In architects' renderings these new neighborhoods are neat, attractively landscaped and well serviced by their own shops and public facilities. They often fail to live up to that image. The official newspapers regularly report on sloppy construction, new communities without shops and schools, and the complaints of tenants who have to repaint and refinish the floors in brand-new apartments. In spring and autumn the new regions around Moscow—like the villages in the Russian countryside—are seas of mud.

The same street address often applies to four or five huge buildings, each containing hundreds of flats. A resident of one of these will direct visitors to Building X, Entry Y, Apartment Z at a given address. At dusk these communities present an eerie spectacle: countless dark figures shuffling to and fro in the half-light of dim streetlamps, carrying string bags and briefcases full of groceries or books, bustling solemnly along well-worn paths.

In town the big apartments in older, grander buildings have been divided and subdivided into communal quarters. Apartments with broad hallways and high ceilings in pre-revolutionary buildings which once provided plush accommodations for a single family may now be home for six or eight. Each family has its own doorbell tacked or screwed onto the ancient molding around the front door.

There is also newer housing in the city centers. Millions of flats have been built since the war. Apartment houses built with outsized bricks in the 1950s are now equipped with wire-mesh screens just above the ground floor; the screen sticks out from the building to catch the bricks that come loose from the facade above. Buildings higher than five stories have elevators, which are generally turned off at 11 or 12 at night, when the "lift lady" goes home. One attendant looks after the elevators in several buildings, and responds to their alarm bells when passengers are stranded or stuck. This happens so often that it is considered imprudent to use the elevator without an attendant on duty nearby.

The close quarters in which Russians live help determine the quality of their existence. The Russian language has no word for "privacy," perhaps because the concept has no real place in Russian life. The government has set a goal of one room per citizen, but officials won't hazard a prediction as to when it might be met. Meanwhile, Russians live with each other—constantly. Housing is so scarce that it is not uncommon for divorced couples to continue living together because neither can find new accommodations.

"I hope you never have to live this way," Vladimir Maximov told John Shaw of *Time* magazine and me in the summer of 1972.* As he spoke he waved an arm around his dingy one-room apartment, then out the window at rows of five-story prefabricated apartment houses identical to his. Maximov was utterly disillusioned that night; he hated the land his country had become, and wanted his guests to understand why. "This is no life, is it?"

His contempt was probably misplaced, but also instructive. It is indeed a life for most Russians, a better life than they have ever known. Dingy one-room flats, Maximov knew, were not an American journalist's idea of good living. He had decided he didn't think much of them either. But millions of ordinary Russians are delighted to have a one-room flat of their own, with a private kitchen and private toilet. Such a flat can transform the lives of a family or couple who have known only crowded, communal living.

An outsider, particularly a foreigner from a richer land who is used to a richer existence, cannot easily grasp the essential quality of life in Russia. Maximov accepted foreign standards when he judged his homeland. But it is crucial to understand that most Russians do not. An ordinary Russian's notions about the dimensions of life, the possibilities of life, are not the same as ours. Russians who live in one-room flats and eat fresh meat no more than once a week, or perhaps not at all, who wear the same outfit for months on end and never dream of the material goods we take for granted, can nevertheless be proud and satisfied. Proud because they know how much life has improved since the 1930s and 1940s. Satisfied perhaps not because they are completely comfortable and content, but because they sense that it would be foolish to hope for much more. So they cope. "We're living well," Russians say repeatedly.

---

* Maximov, a dissident writer, was permitted to leave the Soviet Union in 1974, and now lives in Paris.

Coping means different things to different kinds of Soviet citizens. The life of a cotton farmer in Asian Tadzhikistan has almost nothing in common with that of a Muscovite. Even within Russia, the standard of living varies enormously; it is best of all in the capital. The subject here is urban life in Russia because a foreigner can see enough of urban Russian life to describe it. The life of a Tadzhik peasant is still hidden from view.

"If you wanted to have potatoes every day," a young man responsible for the family shopping explained, "you would have a hard time getting them. Some parts of Moscow just don't have potatoes on some days, you might have to go way across town. And you wouldn't know which direction to set off in, because there's no telling where potatoes might be. So you don't have potatoes every day, you buy them when you can."

The same could be said of any commodity except bread. Bread shops in every neighborhood of the capital are well stocked seven days a week. (This is not true in the provinces; in many towns and cities a day's supply of bread is sold out in a few hours.) Otherwise, people buy and eat what is available. Russians carry string bags with them at all times, in purse or pocket. They're known as "just in case" bags, for use in case one happens across a desirable product for sale on the daily rounds.

As they walk along the city's crowded streets, good shoppers keep an eye on the store windows. An unusual line of shoppers inside a store, or gathered around the many kiosks that state shops set up on the sidewalks, is a signal that a desirable product may be available. The custom is to line up first and ask questions—what is for sale?—afterward. On a busy Moscow sidewalk four or five people can attract a crowd merely by lining up together at the same kiosk. "What are they giving?" passing grandmothers will shout from beneath their kerchiefs. Russians talk about "giving" and "taking" rather than selling and buying, which may be a linguistic consequence of a consumer economy that has always been a sellers' market.

Shopping seems to be the principal occupation of thousands of old women. There is no more typical Russian scene than a bulky grandmother wrapped in a black coat and wool kerchief, both arms weighted down by heavy shopping bags, moving purposefully along the street like an oversized, self-propelled pear.

In the Russian families I knew, one member was likely to do some shopping every day of the week—perhaps just a trip to the bread store, perhaps a major expedition to one of the farmers' markets where collective farmers can sell the produce of their legal private plots. Poor families won't shop in the farmers' markets because they are much more expensive than state stores. But they offer goods the state stores don't carry, and many families use them regularly. (The produce of the tiny private plots which farmers are entitled to cultivate provides a third of the food eaten by Moscow's eight million residents; the entire country depends on this private economy for food.)

Shopping is time-consuming. To buy bread means waiting in line at the cashier's desk in the bread store, paying in advance, the exact price of the loaves you want, taking a receipt for that amount to the end of a second line at the bread counter, then finally trading your receipt with a saleswoman for your bread. The same procedure is repeated in every kind of shop—for sour cream and yogurt, for cheese and salami, for cabbage and canned peas. The stores all close for an hour for lunch, but different kinds of stores close at different times.

The most striking aspect of the shopping routine, at least to a foreign eye, is the contentious atmosphere in which it is conducted. Two comedians in Arkadi Raikin's troupe captured this in a skit:

A man approaches a kiosk that is selling souvenirs and small gifts. The woman running it looks bored. "What do you have nice for a little girl?" the man asks. "How would I know, why ask me?" the saleslady snaps. The man tries again to evoke her help and sympathy, and is again treated to a nasty snap in reply. "I guess you haven't seen this article in the paper," he says, pulling out his newspaper. "It says that salespeople will receive 100 percent more pay if they treat their customers politely." "Really?" the woman says, interested. "Yes, really. Listen to this . . ." and he reads her the story. Suddenly her manner is transformed. She asks solicitously about the little girl, recommends a gift and carefully wraps it, chatting gaily all the while. Finally she says, "Could I see the newspaper?" He hands it over, and she looks for the article about her pay raise. She finds it and bristles: "Say, this article is labeled 'satire,' it's a joke! You were putting me on!

You no-good . . ." The audience chortles its appreciation for an all too credible scene.

Russians are fiercely and deliberately rude to each other in public. This is obvious to a foreigner, because foreigners are usually given kind, polite attention, often out of turn and ahead of any waiting Russians. (Foreign clothes are so distinctive that most Russians recognize them at once.) If you ask Russians why they are so rude to each other, the answer is an embarrassed shrug. Gentle, kind Russians can become ferocious combatants on the street, trading insult for insult with shop attendants, pushing and shoving with the worst bullies in lines and on crowded subways. The official newspapers periodically publish articles exhorting all citizens to mind their manners, with no consequences whatsoever.

Waiting in line is endemic to Russian life, like eating borscht or drinking vodka. To buy a glass of beer in one of Moscow's rare "beer bars," establishments with the physical characteristics of an American school cafeteria, a citizen can expect a wait of 20 to 40 minutes on the sidewalk outside. To buy a fur hat at GUM, the main department store on Red Square, one might stand in line for six hours. To buy a railroad ticket to a Black Sea resort in summer might require 10 hours or more in a queue at the station.

At the end of 1973 about 500 intellectuals in Moscow waited in line for 10 *days* to buy a copy of a newly published collection of the poems of Osip Mandelstam. Though he was one of the two or three best Russian poets of this century, Mandelstam has not been published for years. When members of the Moscow branch of the Union of Writers heard that they would have a chance to buy this new book (which was not offered for public sale), several hundred rushed to the union's book shop. All 500 did not have to stay there for 10 days. Russians know how to organize a line. They arranged the queue by registering every person waiting on a master list. Once registered, one had to return periodically to take a turn on the line. Someone remained on duty, protecting the interests of the entire group, at all times.

To see a doctor at a neighborhood clinic is often an all-day proposition. Acquiring a new set of kitchen cabinets may take a year; it did at the House of Furniture on Leninski Prospekt in Moscow. A woman suffering from high blood pressure, advised by a physician to spend a month in a special sanitorium for treatment, may wait two or three years for a place in such a sanitorium. She may never get it.

Occasionally frustration is visible. Once, in a Moscow tailoring shop that was repairing my winter overcoat, I was waiting for service with eight or nine women. The shop's only visible employee devoted all her attention to one customer. The rest of us just stood there. Finally one of the women started to shout. "What's going here? Where is everybody who is working?" Her loss of patience inspired the rest of the group; suddenly everyone was shouting for service. Two more employees emerged from the back room.

At two o'clock on a Monday afternoon in a downtown Volgograd café there was a five-minute wait to check one's coat in the cloakroom, then a 20-minute wait to get some food—in the express line. One man lost his temper just as he was about to be served:

"Listen, I've been standing here thirty minutes, I'm already late for work."

"What do you want me to do about it?" asked the woman in a white smock behind the counter. She went on ladling bouillon out of a huge caldron at a comfortable, deliberate pace.

"I know a woman," a friend in Moscow said, "who complains that when she dies, no one will know what kind of taste she had. 'All my life,' she says, 'I have bought what was available, not what I wanted.'"

When a Russian discusses his need to acquire a new overcoat, say, or a refrigerator, he seldom speaks of "buying" the item in question. Instead he will use the Russian verb *dostats*, which one Russian grammar defines as "to acquire with difficulty." When someone asks, "How can I *dostats* a refrigerator?" everyone knows that it won't be easy.

In early 1974 the word went out that a furniture store in a new section of southwest Moscow would take orders for carpets to be delivered during the year ahead. Anyone interested had to sign up on a designated weekend. "We were asleep, it was about two in the morning," a man who lived in the neighborhood recalled, "and suddenly we heard the sound of hundreds of people milling about outside. We had no idea what it was about, but I can tell you, we were scared. Why would hundreds of people be milling around our courtyard at two in the morning? Finally my son got dressed and went down to find out what was happening. It was people who had come to buy a rug! They came in the middle of the night to be first in line."

By the next afternoon, this engineer estimated, 10,000 people were in the line. Yes, he agreed, this might sound implausible, but he had taken a photograph. He brought out a blurry snapshot. It showed a three-cornered queue which did indeed contain thousands of bodies, lined up like the hungry unemployed outside American soup kitchens in the 1930s. They were in line merely to put their names on the list for subsequent delivery of a rug, probably one of the mock-oriental ones made in the Central Asian republics. The customer could say what size he wanted, but color and design were left to chance. Not surprisingly, the floors of most Russian apartments are bare.

A woman in Moscow decided to buy her husband a new bed. She went to one of the capital's barren furniture stores, and was about to buy the best bed she could find when a man walked up to her and said, "Why do you want to spend 110 rubles for that lousy bed? I can show you where to buy a good Romanian bed for 90 rubles—plus 15 for me. Interested?" She was interested, and accompanied him to a furniture store on the edge of the city. There indeed were Romanian beds, better made and more attractive than the Russian one she had been prepared to buy. The tipster showed her how the back seat of a taxi could be adjusted so the bed would fit inside, and she rode it home in a victorious mood.

Possessions and the money that buys them have a special meaning in Soviet society. Because the acquisition of goods is so difficult, the accumulation of wealth loses much of its potential significance.

A typical family budget is tight. In the cities, more than 90 percent of able-bodied Russian women hold jobs; most families need two incomes to make ends meet. A few numbers are instructive. The minimum wage, paid for lowliest manual jobs, is 70 rubles a month. The average industrial worker's wage is about 135 rubles a month. A beginning physician, just out of medical school, gets 90 or 100 a month.

The average family, according to published statistics, has an income of about 220 rubles each month. At the official rate of exchange prevailing in 1975, that is about $285. But the comparison is misleading, because the ruble has no real value in terms of the dollar, and Russian prices are so inconsistent that direct comparisons are meaningless. In terms of purchasing power, those 220 rubles are not very much. A Soviet book called *Family Needs and Income*, published in 1967, estimated that a well-balanced, nutritional diet cost about 50 rubles per person per month. So a family of three would spend 150 rubles just on food. In fact most people get by with less than that ideal diet, but it is a rule of thumb in Soviet households that 40-60 percent of the available money will be spent on groceries. Another 10-20 per cent is spent on rent, gas and electricity. Rents are heavily subsidized by the state.

So an average family may have 50 to 100 rubles a month for clothing, transportation, medicines (partially covered by the state health system) and incidentals. A good wool overcoat costs 120 rubles; a good pair of ladies' boots, 40; a flimsy nylon raincoat, 40; a man's shirt, 5 to 10. A substantial purchase—a 200-ruble television set, for example—will absorb the family's spending money for several months.*

Families with higher incomes, members of the growing Soviet middle class, may earn 350 to 600 rubles a month, and their lives are easier. A chemist and his wife with a joint income of 500 rubles told me they spend 220 or more on food for themselves and their two growing sons, and the rest disappears on ordinary expenditures. "We never have anything left at the end of the month."

Someone who acquired his sense of money in the capitalist world expects that greater income will lead to a higher standard of living, but in Russia this is not automatically the case. Money without privilege is insufficient to acquire a better apartment, a car or a summer vacation in Yugoslavia.

Those thing are allocated, not just sold. The best apartments are assigned to officials of the Communist Party and other influential citizens. The opportunity to buy a new car is similarly allocated as a privilege. (Some used cars are now sold freely.) Foreign travel is the rarest and most coveted privilege of all. No amount of money can buy the official permission needed to go abroad.

A film director in Moscow once tried to persuade me that many Russians would prefer to remain poor rather than com-

---

* Large department stores now sell a few major items—pianos, for instance—on *kredit*, but installment buying in the western sense is not normally possible.

plicate their lives with money. "Money doesn't give satisfaction—it creates difficulties. Spending money is difficult."

His argument—perhaps too condescending, but still plausible—was that a family without pretensions can maintain a simple life quite easily: a basic diet, a modest wardrobe worn until threadbare, vodka and television for entertainment. If the same family suddenly finds itself with more money to spend and decides to live a little better, life gets complicated. For example, to improve their diet, members of the family would have to devote much more time to shopping. Good foods are the hardest to find, and they attract the longest lines in the shops. The search for a half-kilo of ham took one friend three hours and stops at half a dozen shops in different parts of the city. But a basic Russian diet of salami, potatoes, bread, cabbage and dairy products is relatively easy to buy.

Good food is also intimidating. I knew a Jewish couple in Moscow who both lost their jobs when they applied to emigrate to Israel. They lived partly on gifts from Jews in the West, who could send hard currency to them as a gift. The state took about a third of the money in taxes, and my acquaintances got the rest in coupons which they could spend in the hard-currency shops. One of these, a grocery store established to serve the diplomatic colony, sold fine fillets of beef, something never sold in an ordinary Russian grocery store. "I'm afraid to buy it," Sarah confided one evening. "I've never cooked such a good piece of meat, I wouldn't know what to do with it."

Buying better clothes is complicated too. "Some people," the movie director said, "never buy a new suit. When they've got the money, there are no suits, and when there are suits, they haven't got the money." Women who want to acquire the best Yugoslav or Hungarian clothes that are sometimes sold in Moscow must spend hours visiting numerous shops and checking with friends for inside information about where and when something good might be put on sale. A tip from a salesgirl who knows about the future disposition of a shipment of Polish sweaters is more useful than a week of window-shopping.

So it may be easier to hold on to one's simple life. And the society does not pressure its members to consume and display their wealth, to keep up with the Ivanovs or the Kuznetsovs. There is no cult of youth and beauty in the Soviet

Union, no compelling need to get teeth whiter or hair darker.

There appears to be no embarrassment or sense of inadequacy in a Russian family when parents and children dress in the same shapeless clothes, when everyone slurps his soup and spills down the front of his shirt, when the two-room flat is not equipped with an upholstered sofa or colorful curtains. The overwhelming majority of Russians now living in cities are just a generation or two removed from the primitive life of the Russian peasant. There is a reminder of that on the gound floor of GUM. Next to the counter selling neckties (appalling neckties in synthetic fabrics and unlikely patterns) there is a poster on the wall showing two ways of tying a tie. I walked by it one day and saw a young man carefully copying the diagram into a notebook. The traditional and middle classes that might have provided models of behavior and a sense of style have been wiped out several times since the Bolshevik Revolution. The only class that lives well now, the privileged elite, lives well privately, usually out of public view.

If there are Russians who really don't care about acquiring more money and a more luxurious standard of living, a growing number do seem anxious to be "fashionable," to own consumer goods, to acquire symbols of prosperity and enjoy an easier life. Soviet society is in the midst of wrenching transformations—inevitable transformations in a country that is leaving behind an era of poverty and beginning to offer its people the prospect of a new kind of life. By the quite fantastic standards of the affluent West, Russians still live at a subsistence level, or just above it. But by their own standards the Russians' existence is changing fundamentally, and has already improved appreciably. In a society that long took communal living for granted, true privacy in self-contained apartments has become common. Purple plastic boots and brightly printed scarves now appear on women who long knew nothing but gray, black and brown. The possibility of owning a car—albeit still remote for most—challenges the established, stable and stolid Soviet way of life. In 1960 there was no television to speak of in the Soviet Union; now it reaches most of the population.

The Russians living through these changes can accept them or not, as they like. Everyone seems to accept television, but not everyone is interested in a Polish sweater. The embourgeoisement of Soviet society proceeds steadily, but leaves many behind.

"There are just three people in our family, me, my wife and the daughter," a Russian comedian protests to his audience. "Wouldn't you think 500 rubles a month would be enough to take care of us? Of course it would, except for one little word: fashion." There follows a long list of the absurd things the women in his life claim they need to stay in fashion, accompanied by an appreciative string of guffaws from the crowd. His 500 rubles disappear before their eyes.

The current fashions in Moscow's middle class are antique furniture (scorned and thrown away just a few years ago), old jewelry, fancy china, crystal, carpets and just about anything foreign. Money can buy such things, and they can be expensive. The government runs "commission" stores which sell unwanted belongings for members of the public, taking a percentage of the proceeds. A handsome antique grandfather clock cost 4000 rubles in the commission store on the Arbat in old Moscow. A Japanese tape recorder could change hands for 1000 rubles.

There is also an extensive black market in the Soviet Union, though the term may be misleading, since many black-market transactions are merely unofficial exchanges between acquaintances at free-market prices. A pair of American blue jeans might sell for 100 rubles on the black market maintained by sailors in the port city of Odessa. For six to eight rubles one can buy a one-ruble coupon valuable in special hard-currency shops which sell goods not available for ordinary, "soft" rubles. High fashion is particularly expensive. In the winter of 1974 the black-market price for a pair of ladies' boots on platform soles was 150 rubles.

Many Soviet officials accept bribes, as periodic exposés in the official newspapers attest. A man with a wife and a daughter who is theoretically entitled to a two-room apartment could offer the right local official 1000 rubles and find himself with three rooms. Someone building a cottage in the country might acquire his lumber with a well-placed gratuity to an official of a state construction trust.

Money is sufficiently appealing for millions of Russians to regularly risk a little in hopes of making a lot—on a lottery, in a bet at the racetrack or in an office pool. In many offices in Moscow the female employees maintain a "black cashbox" to which each contributes five or ten rubles a month, then takes her chance in a winner-take-all drawing.

Russians can earn two percent on their savings in state savings banks, and total deposits are large. In 1974 the banks held 70 billion rubles in citizens' deposits, an average of 280 rubles per man, woman and child in the Soviet Union. Most of the Russians I spoke with about money said they saved almost nothing, and they were surprised to hear how much others managed to hoard. Part of this can be explained by the fact that there are no checking accounts in the Soviet Union, and most people are paid twice a month, so many citizens probably use the savings bank to hold their disposable income. Others are undoubtedly saving for major purchases, such as a car. Soviet models cost from 4000 to 10,000 rubles, or two and a half to six years' salary for an ordinary industrial worker.

Russians buy insurance on their own lives, often so they can leave an inheritance to children and grandchildren. The state sells policies on remarkably unfavorable terms, but with some success. When the Soviet Union achieves "communism," the ideal state beyond the socialism of today, money is supposed to disappear. Meanwhile it seems to be holding its own.

Russians know countless ways to make their lives a little nicer without the help of rubles and kopeks. Playing the angles of Soviet life is an elaborate game, but many Russians find the effort worthwhile. Goods and services acquired outside normal channels—"on the left," in the Russian phrase—can make an important difference in one's standard of living and general comfort.

The best angle-players try to avoid official channels for nearly every service they need, from medical care to haircuts. This can be done, but not without a lot of work. The results are rewarding, because everyone in Russia seems more attentive to a friend than to any ordinary client or customer. Playing the angles can give a person friends in all sorts of places, and that is a powerful antidote to the impersonal bureaucracy that hovers over so much of Soviet life.

Irina, the wife of a flutist in the orchestra of the Kirov Opera and Ballet in Leningrad, can acquire tickets to the ballet and opera through her husband. Most seats are now reserved for important people or sold to foreigners, so a ticket to the

Kirov is one of the prizes of Leningrad life. Irina uses these tickets as her basic currency; she builds an entire life on them.

An old family friend (he shared the same communal apartment during the war, throughout the Leningrad blockade) is a distinguished surgeon at a big hospital. For years he has helped Irina and her family with medical care, introducing them to specialists that they needed, finding beds in the hospital if someone had to have an operation, helping find medicines that were unavailable in ordinary pharmacies. The surgeon does all this for Irina's family out of friendship, but she reciprocates with occasional tickets to the Kirov. This is a form of self-interested gratitude. Having given the tickets, she feels free to ask the surgeon for occasional assistance for her friends.

For example, her dressmaker—an extraordinarily good one who can make a blouse or skirt that looks as if it came from Helsinki or London—might suddenly need special medical attention. If the dressmaker's illness is serious, Irina might ask her friend the surgeon to help. She is genuinely fond of the dressmaker, but there is self-interest at work here, too. A talented tailor is a rarity. Irina usually doesn't tell her friends about the dressmaker, for fear the dressmaker will get too many clients and begin to do shoddy work.

But this is not an inflexible rule. The wife of one of the conductors of the Kirov orchestra once admired a blouse the dressmaker had made, and Irina quickly offered to introduce her. This woman's husband would help decide which of the Kirov's musicians would make a tour of Western Europe the following summer, and Irina's husband hoped desperately to be chosen.

The dressmaker, by the way, regularly receives a pair of tickets to the ballet.

Irina's network also includes a good hairdresser who knows how to shingle her hair around the neck, the way it was on the models in *Vogue* a couple of years ago. Irina's sister works for Intourist, guiding Finnish tourists around Leningrad; the Finns sometimes give her copies of fashion magazines and other foreign literature.

And there's an elderly woman who works in a box office that sells theater tickets. She trades with Irina—tickets to the ballet or opera for seats at a popular play in one of Leningrad's many legitimate theaters. The old lady is supposed to sell the tickets she gets on a first-come, first-serve basis, but she can arrange quite a nice life for herself by selling them more selectively.

Other Russians get special treatment without barter to trade. A workingman in Moscow who underwent two unsuccessful operations for an ear problem (in fact the operations aggravated his problem) was eventually examined by a well-known ear specialist; his wife worked in a laboratory that sometimes did analyses for the professor, and she badgered him for several months to look at her husband.

Others take advantage of their jobs more crudely. A Moscow newspaper reported a typical case involving two kitchen workers at a day nursery in the capital: "One day when they were leaving the nursery carrying heavy shopping bags, inspectors of the state financial organs stopped them. . . .In the bags they had oranges, cookies, butter, milk, potatoes, cocoa and sugar. They claimed that they had bought these foodstuffs during their lunch break at a neighboring store. The inspectors visited that store and discovered that those foodstuffs weren't on sale that day. . . ." The women had skimped on the meals for the babies in the nursery and kept the extra ingredients for themselves.

Stealing by employees—a common occurrence—got so bad at the restaurant in the House of Writers, a club for writers in Moscow, that the restaurant's director resigned in a huff. He took a similar position at the House of Journalists a mile away. "Our staff doesn't steal as much," a journalist explained.

The living room of a Soviet apartment: four women sit around a table, playing cards and throwing down small glasses of vodka. Loudly, they are telling war stories. A man wearing an apron, the husband of one of them, enters with a tray of steaming cups of fresh tea.

With nervous, jerky gestures he tries to clear empty vodka bottles off the table and serve the tea. The women complain to him about the supper he had made, the dirty table, the absence of cognac and other matters. He shrugs his shoulders helplessly. Finally the three guests decide that it's time to go. The husband fetches their coats and boots.

As he shuts the front door on the last of the company, the man's wife throws her arms around him drunkenly. He cringes and shouts, "Don't touch me!"

She is indignant. "Whatsa matter," she slurs, "doncha think I can drink? I drink on my own money, you know . . ."

Speaking of money, he says, she isn't giving him enough housekeeping money, he can't do the shopping. She brushes him aside.

An unlikely scene? A Soviet audience watching a group of comedians act it out found it hilariously implausible. The theater rocked with laughter.

Reality, as one of the performers explained in an introduction to the skit, is different. Papa comes home from work and reads the paper. Mama comes home from work and goes shopping, makes supper, does the laundry and ironing and helps the children with their homework. Sometimes Papa helps out after supper by turning on the television set.

In Russia, "A good wife does not let her husband help her keep house. She keeps it clean herself, sews and weaves for her husband and children. A good wife is always merry. She always smiles and makes her husband's life easy and pleasant. A good wife doesn't interfere in her husband's business talks, and in general is mostly silent."

Those rules were part of the *Domostroi* (roughly, "Household Regulations") that were accepted by church and state in 16th-century Russia. The Soviet Union of today bears faint outward resemblance to 16th century Russia, but the influence of the *Domostroi* is still evident. As Russian women will readily confirm, theirs is the greatest burden in the Russian family.

The fact that most women hold full-time jobs reduces the time available for housework, without reducing the volume of housework at all. Soviet sociologists report that young couples are beginning to share domestic chores more equally, but this is still atypical. I once asked a workingman how his family celebrated International Women's Day, a "red letter" holiday (that is, a day off for everybody) in the Soviet Union. "Well, I usually buy the wife a little present, maybe a bunch of flowers." Did he cook dinner for her, too? "What? Me? Cook dinner?" He chuckled, and that ended the conversation.

Labor-saving devices are difficult to obtain and poorly made. Less than half of all Soviet households have a refrigerator, and the most common size is tiny. Just more than half have a washing machine, but Soviet washers are simply tubs in which the water is gently agitated. One family in seven has a vacuum cleaner. No clothes-dryer or dishwasher is made in the USSR. Nor is there an effective dishwashing detergent. Many women do the family laundry by hand every day.

Most Russian women with university degrees apparently want to work outside the home, and 60 percent of the college graduates in the country are women. (As a result of World War II, women comprise 54 percent of the population.) In Russia a diploma is considered a practical tool for life, meant to be fully exploited. Published surveys of educated women conclude that they are eager to pursue their careers.

But educated women represent a fraction of the female population. Other surveys have found that about half of all Soviet women say they are working because they need the money, not because they enjoy it. Women sometimes do heavy physical labor, a fact that outrages some Russians. One is Alexander Solzhenitsyn, who has written: "How can one fail to feel shame and compassion at the sight of our women carrying heavy barrows of stones for paving the street . . . ? When we contemplate such scenes, what more is there to say, what doubt can there possibly be? Who would hesitate to abandon the financing of South American revolutionaries to free our women from this bondage?"

Women doing hard physical labor are an embarrassment. But the general idea that women should work is no embarrassment at all. "The state's interest presupposed only one decision," Elena Ivanova, a senior editor of *Izvestia*, the government newspaper, told me. "The country needs hands for work, including women's hands." In fact, 51 percent of the country's workers are women.

Women in the wealthy western countries who want to work, but not at the expense of their family obligations, can sometimes find compromises—part-time work, or careers they begin at thirty-five or forty. But the Soviet economy is rigid, and Soviet institutions live by a stern rulebook; either you work or you don't. Women are given two months' paid leave to have a baby, and they can take 10 months more without pay. If they fail to return to work after that year, they will lose their jobs.

The state does provide day-care facilities for working mothers, though not enough to care for the entire infant and child population. There is room in state nurseries for about a quarter of the children aged three months to three years. Children generally spend an 8-to-12-hour day in these nurseries. The state's experts take the position that children should enter a nursery when they are three months old. This releases the mother for a speedy return to the work force and brings the child into "the collective" at an age which makes its physical and psychological adjustment the easiest. Not surprisingly, many mothers resist this idea. Even the experts argue about it.

Kindergartens for four-to-six-year-olds are less controversial. They care for about two-thirds of all the children in the country in that age group. The curriculum—provided from Moscow in a handbook for teachers—calls for singing, dancing, drawing, memorizing and some reading, all in groups. The best kindergartens are happy refuges of laughter and fun, but many don't live up to the ideal.

Komsomolskaya Pravda, the national daily newspaper of the Young Communist League, reported on the grimmer realities in Semipalatinsk, a city in Asian Kazakhstan with a predominantly Russian population. Semipalatinsk had a shortage of nurseries and kindergartens, the paper reported. The nurseries in the city had places for 1030 infants, but they were caring for 1631. The kindergartens were also overcrowded.

Workers in large factories which could afford to build their own day-care centers found adequate facilities for their children, but other citizens of Semipalatinsk did not. Mrs. T. Stepanova wrote the newspaper that she had to take her daughter across town to kindergarten, riding two different trolleys, though she could see a kindergarten from the window of her apartment. It belonged to a factory, and was open only to children of the factory's employees.

A working Soviet mother is pressed for time to perform her chores, particularly the shopping, but work discipline in Soviet enterprises is generally lax. Many women are able to do errands on office time. "In our institute," a research chemist once told me, "a woman scientist is about one-third as productive as a man."

There are virtually no baby-sitters in Russia, apart from willing grandmothers. If the *babushka* isn't available, the baby either goes out with the adults or mama stays home. Soviet teenagers have neither the entrepreneurial spirit nor the confidence of their elders that makes baby-sitters of American teenagers.

Like most Soviet citizens, a working mother is entitled to a month of paid holiday each year. This vacation might be devoted entirely to the family, but it is common for Soviet parents to take separate holidays. This is officially, albeit co-incidentally, encouraged. Rooms in trade-union resorts, rest homes and sanitoria—the most popular vacation spots in the Soviet Union—are allocated at work. Unless husband and wife work in the same place, they are likely to take vacations in different places at different times of the year. Popular writers on family problems have repeatedly criticized this situation, without apparent effect.

The most obvious antidote to the difficulties of mother-hood is to avoid it, as millions of Russian women have. Despite the enthusiasm that Russian parents and grandparents put into the raising of a first child, it is increasingly likely that the first will also be the last. It is difficult to find a family in Moscow with more than one child, and three or four is all but unheard of. I asked an engineer in Moscow who often boasted about his wide circle of friends if he knew anyone who had more than two children. "Just one," he replied after thinking about it. "He's an Orthodox priest." But it was the priest's wife who took care of the three children.

Rural families are a little larger, but Russia proper is fast approaching, and may have reached, zero population growth. The major cities would now be shrinking were it not for migration from the countryside. The population of the Soviet Union continues to grow, thanks to the high birthrates in Central Asia and the Trans-Caucasian republics (Azer-baijan, Armenia and Georgia). This is a source of anxiety to Soviet demographers and state officials, though the anxiety is expressed in muted terms—it might sound racist. By 1975 ethnic Russians probably represented less than half the Soviet population, and their share of the total is shrinking. (Under the Bolsheviks as under the czars, ethnic Russians have dominated the other nationalities under Moscow's—or Peters-burg's—control.)

The declining birthrate is much discussed in the press and in professional journals, but no one has proposed a practical way to convince Russian women to have more babies.* The

---

* There has been a suggestion for increasing the "Russian" population in other ways. Lawyers working on a new Soviet constitution, I was told, have proposed allowing citizens born of other-than-Russian parents to designate themselves as ethnic Russians if Russian is their principal tongue and "culture."

rare mother with eight or ten children is assured of publicity in the national press and recognition as a "Hero Mother of the USSR," but her example seems anything but infectious. The state could withdraw the right to abortion on demand which helps Soviet women hold down the size of their families, but there is no certainty that this would increase the birthrate. Stalin made most abortions illegal in 1936 and produced a brief surge in births. But eventually the birthrate declined again, going even below 1936 levels. When abortion was legalized again in 1955, the birthrate did not fall. Women obviously had found ways to prevent unwanted pregnancies. Illegal abortion was one of them.

Unofficial abortion is still common. Many doctors will come to a private apartment to perform the operation. In Moscow the charge for this unofficial service is 30 to 50 rubles. It appeals to women who want to avoid the humiliation of an official abortion, accompanied by lectures on the need to bring children into the world.

There have been proposals to improve the economic benefits for working mothers, to encourage more children. Soviet benefits are less generous than those in some of the Eastern European countries. A cash allowance for mothers, common elsewhere in Western and Eastern Europe, is paid in Russia only after the birth of a fourth child: it is only four rubles a month. Several social scientists told me that there was no money in the state budget for a larger allowance; even if there were, no one is sure that a few rubles would convince even one mother to have another child.

It has also been suggested that more day-care facilities might induce more children, but there is contrary evidence. From 1960 to 1966 the number of spaces in Moscow's day-care centers grew by 61.5 percent; the birthrate fell 52 percent in the same period.

Ada Baskina, a journalist who writes about family life, told me, "The fairest solution to this problem may be for the state to take responsibility for housework—government agencies doing the work at home." That way, Mrs. Baskina thought, a woman could hold a job, raise two or three children and not feel she was a victim of life instead of a beneficiary. But the authorities have given no indication that they would accept such an enormous responsibility.

The family is the strongest institution in Russian life. Ideally it is a fortress of love and mutual protection whose walls shield all within from an uncertain world. Most families may not live up to that ideal, but sentimental and affectionate Russians (which means nearly all of them) tend to overlook the family's failures and romanticize its strengths.

Soviet society does not challenge traditional family relationships the way the West's hyperactive, hypermobile societies do. Children are likely to live in the same town as their parents, and the extended family sticks together. It's still common for three generations to live in the same quarters. The hedonistic life-style that lures westerners out of their homes has no counterpart in the Soviet Union. The Russians have no amusement industry, no leisure industry, no travel industry to sweep them hither and yon. Relations between parents and children in Russia seem closer than in the Anglo-Saxon world.

I once discussed this subject with a woman in Moscow, a member of the privileged intellectual elite who has traveled abroad. Her son of twenty had been ill for several months, and on his account she had turned her own life upside down. It was her strong impression that parents and children are much more intimate in Russia than in the West.

"I was invited for dinner to a fancy apartment in Paris," she recalled. "The family had a teenage son, and I sat next to him. We had a long talk. He told me that he wanted to go to Chile to see what was going on there. He told me all about his girlfriend. After dinner his mother asked me what we had been talking about so avidly, and I told her. 'Why,' she said, 'you've found out more about my son than I ever knew before.'

"You know, in Moscow a boy that age wouldn't go to the family *dacha* [a cottage in the suburbs] without discussing it thoroughly with his parents. But that French boy was planning a trip to Chile that he'd never even mentioned at home."

Russian parents and children both complain of a generation gap, but it strikes a westerner as much narrower than ours. Young people accept a parental involvement in details of their lives that western adolescents would regard as private.

The strength of family ties is especially noticeable in times of crisis—for instance, during a student's last year in secondary school. "We have examinations this year," a Russian parent announces with a combination of pride and trepidation. In other words, their eighteen-year-old is hoping to win a place in college or university, and the entire family is mobilized for the entrance exams. I once asked a journalist what his plans were for a summer holiday. "It depends on my son," he replied. "He's taking the entrance exams to Moscow University in July. If he passes, we can take a holiday in August. If he doesn't, we'll have to help him prepare for the entrance exams to the institute of physics, which are given in August."

Not all Russian parents can pay so much attention to their children. One of Arkadi Raikin's sentimental skits is about Slavik, a little boy whose grandmother used to take care of him. Grandmother died, and now Slavik's mother makes various stops around the neighborhood asking for favors on her way to work. She asks a pensioner in their apartment house to knock on the wall to be sure that Slavik is up in time for school. She asks a nurse to feel his forehead if she sees him after school. She tells the policeman to blow his whistle if Slavik gets into a fight. "But I don't think," Raikin says, "that any of those people can substitute for a mother who can sing a lullaby, answer any question, feed, pity and comfort. Mothers should probably work a little less and pay a little more attention to their children. Everybody would benefit—children, parents and the state."

The audience applauds warmly, but the state does not agree. Nor do all Russians. I once met a young mother in Moscow who thought parental interest in children's lives was excessive. "Sometimes it's silly. We sit around in our apartment—me, my husband, my parents, maybe an aunt and uncle—and everybody is looking at Kolya [age eight]. 'What's new with you, Kolya?' 'How's life, Kolya?' 'What's happening in school, Kolya?'—that's all you hear for hours on end."

Families reveal the best in themselves at times of celebration. Russians are a people with a grand sense of occasion. Families organize celebrations for the major holidays— November 7, the anniversary of the Bolshevik Revolution, New Year's and May Day—and in the days prior to those events anything remotely worth eating or drinking is likely to disappear from the shops. In late November a woman I knew bought two chickens for her New Year's dinner. "There won't be any nearer the time," she explained.

The Russians' New Year celebration is similar to our Christmas: a New Year's tree, presents and a big dinner. It is as grand a holiday as Russian life can offer. In Moscow, ladies in prosperous families think of New Years's Eve as the one occasion all year when wearing a long gown is justified, and some women have a new one made every year. Many families end their own celebration with champagne at midnight, then go out visiting friends for the rest of the night. Driving through Moscow at four o'clock New Year's morning, one sees thousands of people on the streets, both downtown and in suburban neighborhoods. Many wave at passing cars in hopes of flagging down a taxi, professional or amateur.

In my experience the best celebrations were family birthdays, when the emotions are personal. The party will be held at home, because it is expensive to go out and not worth the effort. The "table" for a family celebration is one of the things Russians love most about their country.

It is heavy with culinary riches. There could be a dozen different hors d'oeuvres (*zakuski* in Russian), from simple things like sprats in oil out of a tin to elaborate Caucasian dishes like chicken in walnut sauce. The company may spend an hour or two over these delights, washing them down with the eloquent toasts that inevitably accompany the consumption of vodka or wine.

A soup may follow the *zakuski*, then a piece of meat or perhaps a Polish duck. Mama and grandma serve and clear the dishes (none of which matches any other) and yell at the young people to eat more of everything. Three generations plus assorted friends crowd around the table, many sitting on stools because there are never enough chairs, and all squeezed tightly together because the table is always too small. The men tell jokes and make toasts, the women gossip and tease. There is no cocktail hour, no coffee in the drawing room afterward (there is no drawing room) and somehow it is usually more fun than any dinner party in Washington or London.

At one party in an overcrowded kitchen in Moscow I found myself next to an old uncle of the woman whose twenty-fifty birthday had brought us together. Between toasts and jokes we had a long conversation about life, the state of the world and especially Italy. As a boy, before the Revolution, he had been cared for by an Italian nanny. She had taught him Italian, which he had later pursued on his own. He knew and loved Italian literature, painting, architecture and opera, but to his great regret he had never been to Italy. He didn't explain why. Nor did he have anything to say about the Soviet Union. He did remark that the Georgian wine we were drinking had been Stalin's favorite.

He began to yawn and excused himself while the party was still animated. Later his niece explained that he would never go to Italy, because after World War II he had spent 10 years in a prison camp. He was a marked man, and had no hope for permission to travel abroad.

What had he done to be sent to a camp? I asked.

"Oh, nothing. He was just one of the unlucky ones."

The Russian capacity for having a good time is regularly on public display in the country's restaurants, which aren't numerous—Moscow, a city of seven million, has about 130, or one restaurant for every 55,000 inhabitants. Nor are they very good, with the exception of a handful of unique establishments specializing in the cuisine of provincial Soviet republics. The basic menu is the same from the Baltic to the Pacific, with variations depending on the availability of ingredients: basic *zakuski* such as sprats, cold chicken salad, smoked fish, cold meat, cucumbers and tomatoes, then a choice of two or three hot dishes; perhaps *shashlik* (a sort of Caucasian shishkabob), *beefshteks* (a hunk of beef), beef stroganoff, perhaps a fish dish. The main courses are invariably served with fried potatoes, a few strands of purple cabbage and a dozen or so cold canned peas. Lunch ("dinner" in Russia) may also include a choice of several soups. Restaurant service is notoriously slow, though occasionally one encounters an efficient waiter or waitress. It is possible to spend three hours trying to get lunch.

So it isn't the greatest—it can still be fun. The Russian definition of a restaurant is an eating establishment with a band to play live music, and that's what is fun. Moreover, restaurants serve vodka and wine.

The Dynamo Restaurant in Kiev, the capital of the Ukraine, is one of the handsomest in the country. It's an old wooden building atop a hill in Kiev's central park. The restaurant is on two levels—a ground floor with several nooks opening off it, and a second story overlooking the first from balconies on all four sides. On a Saturday night it is booked solid; an old sign on the front door, which is locked, announces: NO PLACES. A doorkeeper admits those with reservations. (He'll also admit a foreigner who claims to have a reservation although his name is not on the list.)

Two wedding parties have established a gay atmosphere inside. Both brides and grooms rise out of their chairs again and again to accept the toasts of their friends and relations. They also seem to dance nearly every dance. When the band takes a break, one of the wedding parties fills the silence with songs of its own, sung loudly, unabashedly, for the benefit of the entire restaurant.

Both wedding parties sit around long tables on the second floor. On the lower level, tables have been set up for a special dinner. Sixty new graduates of Kiev's naval college have come to the restaurant in full dress uniform: black jackets and trousers with gold buttons and trim, and a long sword hanging at the hip. The girls, an unusually handsome group, are dressed as if for a senior prom, most with elaborate hairdos piled on top of their heads. Though late arrivals, the young officers and their companions quickly get down to business. After a brisk series of toasts, they begin to blend into the atmosphere set by the wedding parties.

The band plays a mixture of music, fast and slow, foreign and domestic. The crowd obviously prefers the fast numbers, and rushes onto the dance floor whenever one begins. Young and old perform personal interpretations of the jerking, jumping dances that America has imposed on so much of the world. Responding to the general enthusiasm, the musicians play a series of fast numbers, and the dancing gets wild. The old wooden beams of the Dynamo begin to sway, and dancers bounce off one another's hips and bottoms. Just in time, or so it seems, the band switches to a waltz. Most of the dancers return to their tables, and to their food and drink.

The party continues until 11:30, when the waiters and waitresses begin to circulate with checks and firm announcements that it is time to leave. The young officers and their girls are the last to go, at about 11:45. They march down the hill into the center of town, singing and shouting. Many of the girls wear their boyfriends' white dress hats. The couples kiss and embrace openly, something rarely seen on the street in the Soviet Union. But why not? It's 12:30 in the morning.

The Dynamo in Kiev is an attractive, well-run establishment. More typical is a café on Rustaveli Avenue in Tbilisi. It is a modern three-story building, just a few years old, in the shape of a crescent. The first floor is an entrance hall and cloakroom, the second contains a long bar, the third small formica tables and a stage for the band. The roof leaks, and the plaster on the ceiling and walls of the top floor is blotched with damp. Large windows along the front wall are coated with greasy dirt. Along the back wall, light fixtures hold bare bulbs, also coated with grease and grime. When the band plays its electric instruments here, no conversation is possible. On the Friday night when I happened into the place, the orchestra knew four numbers. It played them in succession, took a break, then repeated the cycle.

The waitress suggested a wine cocktail. It came with pieces of apple and a cherry floating in it, and tasted of fruit juice. A second one, ordered 20 minutes later, had neither apple nor cherry, and tasted entirely different. Dinner (roast chicken) was served with a makeshift variety of utensils, including feather-light aluminum cutlery. The waitress apologized, but she couldn't serve any coffee—all the cups were in use.

The crowd here, mostly young people, looked sullen and bored. No one danced.

On a Sunday in autumn the woods of birch and pine around Moscow—or any Russian city—are filled with people hunting for mushrooms. Round women bend over their bellies to shuffle among the leaves, searching for toadstools that have sprouted underneath. A little boy screams with delight at a discovered red mushroom with white polka dots, only to be told that it is poisonous. An old man who knows his business carries a big cloth bag already full of fine specimens.

Russians are in love with nature. It seems a cruel trick of fate that a people so devoted to the outdoors has been given such a prosaic land and such a harsh climate. As Gogol wrote, "No bold wonders of nature crowned with ever bolder wonders of art. . . .Everything in you is open, empty, flat . . . there is nothing to beguile and ravish the eye. . . ." Most of Russia is flat as a pancake; most of the countryside is the same combination of old villages of log cabins and wooden cottages, flat open fields, woods and an occasional river.

But the Russians make the most of nature's spare gift. Like

mushroom-hunters scouring the floor of the forest, they leave no leaf unturned. If there's a river—well, swim in it, no matter if it's the dirty Moscow River flowing right through the capital. On one June Saturday, when the nip of a Russian spring was still in the air, eager bathers lined the banks of the Moscow River/near the university, diving happily into the water as though the weather were hot and the water fresh and clean.

The best place to observe the city's nature-lovers is on one of Moscow's many railroad stations. On a weekend morning or evening the stations are full of Muscovites rushing to and from the *elektrichkas*, electric trains serving the city's suburbs and nearby villages. Those coming home from the country often carry a souvenir of nature, a bunch of wild flowers in summer, or the yellow leaves of a birch in fall. Fishermen carry long bamboo poles, and occasionally even a fish. Families travel with a basket full of lunch and a volleyball.

In winter the baggage is skis, the long, thin skis on which Russians propel themselves through woods and fields for hours at a time. Nothing is more Russian—or more fun—than a day in the forest on cross-country skis. Once you've got the knack of it you can make them go quite fast through the parallel troughs made by earlier skiers. After half an hour clothes begin to be shed, even when the temperature is far below freezing. It is glorious exercise and, after a fresh snow, fantastically lovely. A long ski followed by a little vodka and hot soup is enough to compensate for almost any pain or frustration.

I knew a man in Moscow whose daughter was in prison camp for her political activities. He always feared he might lose his job as an editor because of her transgressions. Many of his friends were part of the dissident opposition to the regime, people constantly on the edge of personal catastrophe. His life was a continuous strain, but this seldom showed. Every weekend he set off for the countryside—alone, or with his wife if he could persuade her to come—to ski for miles and miles through fields and forests.

A Russian winter is intimidating, and a lesser race might be deterred from all this outdoor activity in such cold weather. The sun barely rises out of the horizon; even at noon it hangs low in the southern sky, casting a yellow light and long shadows. Even when the sun is out, the air may be filled with what looks like fine snow, but is actually nature's thermometer. "A real Moscow frost," the natives call it.

The sky is blotched with great clouds of steam from the chimneys of factories and power stations. In the evening rush hour Moscow's trolley cars ply their routes with golden, frosted windows. It is impossible to see in or out. The Moscow River, which flows briskly through the city in warmer weather, is frozen to a dead halt, as if stopped in its tracks by the sight of a ghost.

The Russians take care to keep the winter outside. Each fall the cracks around windows and doors are plugged with cotton and covered with tape. The people dress sensibly, wrapped in layers of wool, never without a hat, and they are quick to ask a stranger why he hasn't got one. Except in the most bitter cold, few people seem to avoid the outside. Most Russians remain true to their beloved nature.

The luckiest Russians have a little place of their own in the country, a *dacha*. The connotation of that word in English is much grander than in Russian. A *dacha* may consist of a single room 10 feet square, without running water, electricity or interior walls. No matter, it is a shelter nearer to nature than a room or apartment in the city. Its plot of ground may be no more than 10 yards square, but that is enough to grow some tomatoes and cucumbers.

There are thousands of *dachas* around Moscow, and they are popular throughout the country. Land to build a *dacha* is allocated, usually as a privilege, by state organizations, enterprises or the Communist Party. Members of the privileged elite may get a proper house in the country; ordinary citizens are happy with a small hut. Only a fraction of the population can get one. Once a *dacha* has been allocated, it is as good as private property. A legal private market in *dachas* thrives. The buyers are often the parents or grandparents of a new child. According to the folk wisdom passed from generation to generation, it is nothing short of a tragedy for a baby to spend the summer in the close, unhealthy air of the city.

A Russian's best chance to escape the city is his annual vacation. Most are entitled to a full month, and it is a month that is taken deadly seriously. The Russian word for vacation is *otpusk*, which means, literally, letting go, and that is the Russian idea of a "rest," which is the purpose of every *otpusk*. Let everything go, forget all ordinary concerns and relax.

A good rest does not depend on luxury or even comfort. Camping in the wilds or living sardine-like in someone else's apartment in a resort area is consistent with the general objective. In Volgograd the enormous Red October steel factory maintains its own "sanitarium," where many of the workers take their holidays. The sanitarium looks something like an American school, and is located right in town. Its guests live two or three to a room, eat in a big dining hall and loaf. There is a "sun room" where one can escape to a more exotic atmosphere. It is brightly lit, and two walls are covered with a large mural depicting the Black Sea coast. A tape recording of ocean surf plays continually at low volume.

Several people staying in that dreary sanitarium when I visited it assured me that there was no better place to have a rest. But most Russians prefer to get closer to nature and farther from home.

Each year two million Soviet citizens decide to take their rest in Sochi, an attractive resort town on the Black Sea. The atmosphere on the streets of Sochi evokes images of Alantic City or Blackpool; the crowds of holiday-makers are determined to enjoy themselves and—above all—to bake their skins. In Sochi in July the light but incessant drumbeat of feet marching to a place in the sun begins at 6:30 each morning. Early arrivals are assured of a good place on the narrow strip of pebbles that passes for a beach. The typical Russian figure is not well suited to the bathing suit, but that stops—or embarrasses—no one, as the vast acres of flesh on display at Sochi attest.

Perhaps half the vacationers in Sochi have beds in a proper hotel, rest home or sanitarium. Gigantic sanitaria offering special cures and baths in the local mineral waters dot the seacoast in and around Sochi. There are also many rest homes and a few hotels. But only the fortunate get places in these facilities, most of which are controlled by trade unions. An ordinary citizen hoping for a vacation by the sea must come to Sochi as a "savage," in the local vernacular, and hope for the best.

The best in Sochi means a room in a private flat. The city government runs an office that helps visitors find a place to stay. It is crowded with travelers, all looking for a quiet room "in the center, not far from the beach." Most settle for something quite different, such as a bed in the kitchen of an apartment in the suburbs. The standard rate is a ruble per person per night. A resident of Sochi who can squeeze three visitors into his apartment can earn 270 rubles in the summer season alone—the equivalent of two months' salary.

The same landlord could earn twice as much by renting his room "on the left." Landlords looking for unofficial business can be found under the shade trees outside the Sochi railroad station night and day, scrutinizing the tourists for a face that looks reliable and discreet. I happened onto this scene at nearly midnight on a hot July night. Mothers holding sleeping young children pestered several men who appeared to be offering rooms. "No, no children," one said without any apology, "no children." Occasionally a grin and a handshake signaled a successful deal.

A holiday in Sochi is not elaborate. Though the occasional water skier zips through the harbor and a few home-movie cameras are visible, the age of consumer gadgetry is only dawning in the Soviet Union. The average vacationer relies entirely on a bathing suit. Some also have sunglasses with a white plastic shield to keep sun off nose. Besides lying on the seashore, the most popular activity in town is strolling. Sochi is a handsome old town, with many parks and tree-lined boulevards, all filled with people until about 10:30 p.m., when the town closes up. There are concerts in the parks, often performed by visiting orchestras and ensembles from the north.

A night on the town might be dinner and dancing at the Cascade Restaurant, a sprawling two-story establishment with a standard menu and seats for perhaps 1000 diners. The front door is guarded sternly by a little man in a uniform. In the manner of such doormen, he keeps the door locked, and appears to get some satisfaction from snarling "No places!" to tourists who look hopefully through the glass. However, he will accept a ruble or two and let someone in. Upstairs a band plays from an eclectic repertoire, old American rock-and-roll and sentimental Russian ballads. The music attracts dozens of couples to the dance floor in the middle of the dining room; girls gladly dance with each other if the men are too busy with the vodka. It makes for a good party, but the orchestra goes home at 9:30 p.m. On the way out the doorman is still snarling, but a new message: "The restaurant is closed!"

Officious doormen are just one of the many touches of Soviet life that one cannot evade simply by going on holiday.

The buses in Sochi are crowded, the lines are often long. It took me half an hour to get into a telephone booth to call Moscow from the Sochi post office. I tried one day to take an excursion to Adler, the next town up the coast. After I had waited an hour for a boat ticket, the saleslady announced that none were left. At the bus station across town, 50 people waited in line to buy a ticket to Adler, but the lady in that ticket office refused to sell any, and refused to explain why. I never did see Adler.

Not everyone wants or needs a vacation in Sochi. One man I knew who didn't was an old writer in Moscow. As a boy peeking from behind buildings and barricades, he had watched the street fighting and marches that marked the Bolshevik Revolution in Petrograd. In his old age he was a spectator of a different kind. He took his holiday every Sunday at the Moscow Hippodrome, the capital's racetrack. It was, he always said, the best escape in town.

Russia imported horse racing; the start is *start* in Russian, the finish *finish*, the favorite *favorit* and the bookmaker *bukmaker*. But the Russians have taken the sport as their own, and there are thousands of loyal enthusiasts like the old writer in Moscow who have made the horses part of their lives. The writer used to buy the program for Sunday's races as soon as it was available on Friday evening. By the time he got to the track at about noon on Sunday, an hour before the first race, he had chosen all his bets for the day's dozen or so races.

The present Hippodrome was built after the war in what was then a new section of Moscow. From the street the grandstand looks like a bad Italian copy of ancient Greek grandeur—giant columns and porticoes topped by statues of rearing steeds. Inside, the accommodations are divided into three classes (this happens everywhere in the classless Soviet Union). The more one pays for admission (20, 40 or 80 kopeks), the closer one stands to the *finish*.

The grandstand and its facilities echo the exterior façade's attempt at grandeur. High-ceilinged rooms where ladies behind wire-mesh screens sell and cash tickets, wooden railings between the high-backed seats, portraits of horses on many of the walls—but all a little dingy now, worn down by many years of use and too little maintenance. The grandstand looks out on a classic Moscow panorama: first the infield of the half-mile track, and beyond, from one end of the horizon to the other, a jumbled collection of Soviet architecture. The mock-gothic towers that Stalin loved are interspersed among sterile new high-rise apartment houses, old hulking factories and every sort of living accommodation. It all looks like so many children's blocks scattered at random across the landscape.

A day at the races usually begins in the queue to buy a program, which is sold at a tiny window on the edge of the grandstand. The line behind the window is revealing. Perhaps half the customers take a place behind the last man and wait their turn. The other half walk to the front, adopt a jovial, good-sport sort of manner and approach someone near the head of the line: "Hey, sport, here's 15 kopeks, buy me one, will ya?" Because the "sport" in question was meek enough to join the line in the first place, he is usually meek enough to comply with this request, too. I always did.

The program provides scant information: the name of the horse, its parents, its driver (most of the races are for trotters and pacers which pull sulkies behind them) and its times in four previous outings. These times mean nothing unless one knows what the weather was like when the horse ran, and the program provides no clue about that. The program is sufficient for a serious betting man, though, because he probably saw the horses' earlier outings and can remember them in detail. There is racing at the Hippodrome on Sunday afternoons and Wednesday evenings the year around, on snow in the winter and in thick mud in spring and fall. The old writer missed a Sunday program only when he was sick or out of the city. Once he even abandoned a holiday at the Union of Writers' sanitarium on the Baltic coast to return to Moscow for a big race.

The regulars often sit or stand in the same spot week after week, some on the terrace down by the rail, others up in the stand. The old writer had a dozen friends with whom he shared big tips, anxieties and the satisfaction of a big win. Some of them had been coming to the races together for 20 years, but they knew only each other's first names. The writer had no idea where most of his comrades worked. One, I suggested, looked like a professor. "Oh, him—he makes his living helping people exchange apartments, on the black market."

In cold weather (in other words, for most of the year) the

crowd consists of a horde of men in dark overcoats, wool scarves and fur hats. Only a handful wear anything else, and there are just a few women and children. These dark figures move about like so many toy soldiers, up to the rail, back to the betting windows, to the snack bar for a beer. Sometimes the round old lady on duty behind the bar demands that the customer buy an open-faced salami sandwich with a beer—she won't sell beer separately. Why? "I've got to sell all these sandwiches, don't I?"

The horses are the property of collective farms, and are trained by one of 32 "training departments" under the direction of the Ministry of Agriculture, which is responsible for the Hippodrome. The quality of the training is mediocre. Trotters regularly break out of their gait, and are even allowed 10 paces at a gallop before they are disqualified.

It is widely assumed that the drivers fix the results of races. Several scandals of this sort have come to light over the years. The regulars realize that they may be entrusting their money to a pack of scoundrels, but it's no good complaining—this really is the only game in town. Many of the bettors prefer to risk their rubles on a particular driver rather than try to divine the relative merits of the competing horseflesh, though this seems no more fruitful than any other racetrack system. (A young woman driver named Anna Polzunova has attracted a wide following largely because she is thought to be honest.) "Damn," one may hear in the grandstand, "I bet on that sonofabitch Karamov [a driver], but he just sat there until the very end, then he started to push that nag. He should have started in the turn." Russians are natural commentators and *post facto* analysts; any number of spectators will happily explain anything that's going on at any time.

After every race, long lines form at the betting windows. Many people like to go to the front of the queue and look at the sheet of paper on which each cashier records the tickets she has sold. This is the only way to find out which horses are attracting the most bets. There is no tote board to announce the odds, though somehow the old hands sense a favorite and can sometimes even guess what the payoff will be. It will be small, with rare exceptions. The Hippodrome pretends that its system of wagering is mechanized and impersonal. It's called a "Totalisator," the American trademark of a computerized odds-making system used throughout the United States and much of Europe—but obviously not used in Moscow. The regulars say they think there is some kind of machine in the back room which takes the numbers off the cashiers' sheets and converts them into real odds and reasonably fair payouts, but this seems highly unlikely. The payouts are just too small and too consistent to be fair.

The basic bet at the Hippodrome is on two races; the object is to pick the winners of both, a double. There is no place or show option, and although it is possible to bet on one race at a time, few do because the payoff for picking a single winner is negligible. Only by picking a double can one win any money. Even then the winnings are often no better than three or four rubles on a one-ruble wager. In 10 visits to the track, the highest payout I ever saw for a ruble bet on a double was 39.60. Once it was 1.80. Anything more than 10 rubles was rare. The state is doing well at the Hippodrome, though not as well as it might.

"Betting ouside the totalisator is categorically forbidden," says a warning printed in the program. "Guilty parties will be held strictly responsible." Nevertheless, half a dozen private bookies do a thriving business in the grandstand every Sunday, operating quite openly. One bookie named Misha stood near the spot where the old writer and his companions used to gather. He was a handsome young man with dark, curly hair and a flashy, foreign-made wardrobe for every season of the year. The winter version consisted of an expensive fur hat (perhaps of Soviet origin, but if so, made for export), a long sheepskin overcoat and bell-bottom trousers. The suede of his coat was worn bare and dirty above the right-hand pocket, where Misha deposited every wager. He and his clients communicated in a private tongue, often no more than a wink and a nod. He scrawled his records in the margins of his program, which by the end of the afternoon suggested the ledger book of a meticulous Chinese accountant.

Misha accepted bets of less than a ruble, which the Totalisator would not. He also took larger wagers for anyone who preferred his service to the long lines at the cashiers' windows. His payouts were identical to the track's, a hint that they must be profitable to the house. The old writer once guessed that Misha cleared 100 rubles in an afternoon, assuming he had to pay about that much to the police for the privilege of doing business.

There is a lot of serious betting at the Hippodrome. The program warns that the cashiers are instructed not to allow anyone to wager more than 10 rubles on a single race, but this regulation is easily evaded. I once watched a man throw a wad of tickets to the ground in disgust when the result of a race was announced, and I picked up the records of his failure. He had 28 one-ruble tickets on the same double, though he looked very much like that average Soviet worker who earns 135 rubles a month. Many friends bet together, sharing the cost of tickets on a variety of combinations. The program speaks to this issue too: "Payment for a winning ticket will be made ONLY to the person holding that ticket. No claim by third parties to a share of any winnings will be recognized." Moral: know with whom you share a bet.

The racing itself is somewhat haphazard. The trotters start from behind a gate that is attached to an old Russian station wagon which speeds ahead of them at the starting line. Accidents, broken gaits and other difficulties are common. Once the car that pulled the starting gate wasn't working, so the races started without a gate, and without much regard for a fair start. The horses never go off at exactly the stated post time, and by the end of the afternoon the program may be running 25 minutes behind schedule. No matter. No one is in a hurry to leave. After the last race many of the fans linger in the grandstand, analyzing and re-analyzing the day's results. "They have nowhere to rush to," the old writer explained.

A day at the Hippodrome (or at one of the racetracks in half a dozen other Soviet cities) is a risky proposition, and it isn't especially comfortable. Millions of Russians prefer another sort of escape, a long morning or afternoon at the baths.

There is nothing imported about a Russian bath. Russians have been cleaning themselves for centuries with a combination of intense heat, birch leaves and cold water. Every village has a bath, every city has a number of them. The village version is a simple wooden hut with a stove, but in the cities the bath is an elaborate institution. The grandest of all are the 19th-century Sundonovski Baths in Moscow.

Sundonovski built his establishment at the bottom of a hill on a side street a long block from Kuznetski Most, the most fashionable street of shops in pre-revolutionary Moscow. He put up a three-story building a block long, built in the style of 19th-century Moscow—stucco-fronted neo-classical, with rows and rows of large windows. Sundonovski's name is no longer advertised, but everyone still uses it to describe the old building, which has changed very little (and not at all for the better) since 1917.

Sundonovski divided the baths into three classes, a distinction that survives, though the word "class" has been replaced by "department." The present management (the city of Moscow) demonstrates less concern for the preservation of the old building than the Sundonovski family undoubtedly did, but there is still something grand about the first-class facilities on the second floor.

One senses the grandeur on the circular marble stairway that leads to them. An imposing chandelier and multicolored, carved ceilings mark the way. The first rooms are paneled in warm, dark wood, and divided into cubicles. Naked men, some wrapped in white sheets, lounge on upholstered seats, some drinking beer, most smoking and talking. (Smoking and drinking are both forbidden by the posted regulations.) They are resting between sessions in the hot room, the shower room or the pool. This last is a Roman monument, Olympic size, surrounded by Corinthian columns and marble walls. The intricate tile floors that Sundonovski selected a century ago are still in place, though whenever a fault appears the repair work is done in a contemporary orange tile that distorts the beautiful old patterns.

According to published descriptions of the baths at the turn of the century, they were then a bastion of luxurious hedonism. A large staff of underpaid boys did the bidding of a wealthy clientele, fetching refreshment, scrubbing and massaging, pressing suits and shining boots. It isn't like that now, though elderly men in white smocks will press a suit or fetch some beer or a bottle of vodka. And the feeling one gets lounging around the baths of a Friday morning must still approximate the pleasurable sense of self-indulgence that made the establishment so popular before 1917.

The bath attracts all kinds of clients.* A group of distinguished professors from the Academy of Sciences likes to spend most of Saturday there. They come to the first-class section with a good supply of vodka and Armenian brandy, salami, smoked fish and loaves of bread, which they consume—between visits to the hot room and the pool. Their

---

* Including women, whose section of the baths I cannot describe.

neighbors may be scruffy laborers who come to the bath once a week to dislodge the grime they absorb on the job. Many of the bathers come at the same time on the same day every week, creating societies of friends who have been steaming, drowning and caressing themselves together for years.

One such group met on Friday mornings in the third-class section. Third class is the scruffiest, but that does not mean it attracts the scruffiest clientele. Until late 1974 draft beer was sold in the third-class section, an attraction that drew a better crowd of customers, as well as a lot of drunks. (Russian draft beer isn't bad; it tastes quite a lot like English bitter. The bottled beer is much less appealing.) It wasn't clear who the men in the Friday-morning group were, or why they were able to while away a weekday morning in the Sundonovski Baths. An outsider didn't ask about such things. Some of them belonged to the intelligentsia—an editor of scientific books and a film-maker from Moscow television. Others appeared to have office jobs of some kind. Once a dark little man who looked as if he came from Soviet Central Asia happened into the Friday-morning group and began teasing its members: "I think I'll have to write a letter to the People's Control Commission [a state inspection agency]," he said, "and ask them to investigate why so many able-bodied men spend weekdays in the bath."

The atmosphere in the baths is something like that of a locker room, but it isn't a place to dress and undress for some other activity—it *is* the activity. The sheet and pillowcase one gets (for 13 kopeks) to wrap around the body and put under the seat make the clients look like Romans in a B movie. The fact that no one has any clothes on seems to reduce the barriers between people. Conversation is easy.

The talk covers every conceivable subject. Jokes are a favorite pastime. The Friday-morning crowd could spend most of the morning chewing dry smoked fish, drinking beer and telling jokes. Like the one about Igor and Zhenya, both discussing their troubles:

IGOR: You know, Zhenya, I think my wife is cheating on me.

ZHENYA: Oh, with whom?

IGOR: I think with a florist.

ZHENYA: Oh, why?

IGOR: Because when I came home unexpectedly the
            other morning, there was a rose on the table.
ZHENYA: You know, Igor, I think my wife is cheating
            on me, too.

IGOR: No kidding? With whom?
ZHENYA: With a man who works on the railroad.

IGOR: Oh, why do you think that?
ZHENYA: Well, when I came home unexpectedly the
            other day, I found my wife in bed with a man
            who works on the railroad.

One Friday a middle-aged man covered with tattoos appeared in the third-class bath and took a seat in the row of
benches where the regular group was gathered. Somebody
asked him about his decorations; on one bicep "STALIN" was
inscribed, on the other "LENIN." His chest was a forest of
flourishes in dark green. "It was fashionable once, but now
. . ." He didn't have to finish the sentence. That led to a discussion about how things are in "the West." Someone said
he'd heard that in the West you could get a technicolor tattoo
without any needle work at all, they just stamp it on you.

Toward the end of the year the man from the publishing
house that specialized in scientific books told the group that
his office was going to the dogs. A new young editor who had
come to work in a supervisory position had decided to get all
his colleagues more actively involved in "social"—which
means political—work in their free time. He was always proposing lectures and study groups and whatnot, a pain in the
neck. Then the accountant had botched the books, and instead
of the usual year-end surplus, they were short of funds. They
had been accustomed to taking business trips in December
to spend the surplus money; no trips that year.

The soccer team from Yerevan, the capital of Soviet Armenia, was popular with the Friday-morning group. "They
play like Europeans," one of the regulars said. "They're indi-
vidualists. And they'll chew out the referee if they don't agree
with him." Another popular subject was the bath itself. "If I
ran this bath," somebody announced, "it wouldn't just be the
best in the Soviet Union, it would be the best in the whole
world! You could do wonders with this place if you gave it a
good going-over." On another Friday the talk was about
building one's own bath in the country. "I think it could be

done for about 600 rubles, if you knew the right people," one man said. The others weren't so sure. The subject of food filled many a morning, often beginning with a dissertation on the type of smoked fish one of the group had found to accompany the beer.

Grisha, a little Georgian who would go out for vodka for a tip, was always good for a laugh. He wore a gray smock over an old and filthy brown double-breasted suit. The lapels on his jacket were covered with the souvenir buttons and pins that Russians love to swap and save. Grisha would do a dance for half a glass of beer, manipulating the glass all around his body, between his legs and behind his back, then setting it on the floor, going down on his knees and picking it up with his teeth, emptying it in the process.

One morning was nearly ruined by an obstreperous old man—senile or drunk—who started shouting his complaints about life at the top of his lungs. "How dare they put up a sign outside telling people to finish their baths in two hours? [There is such a sign, but no one pays any attention to it.] How can they push us around like that? What's wrong with these goddam authorities?" He shouted his protests between hastily gulped infusions of air until he was red in the face. No amount of cajoling by the good-natured attendants would shut him up. Finally one of the men in white smocks lost his temper. "You're a political illiterate!" he shouted. "I'm going to kick you out of here!" That calmed the angry man, and he kept still.

Most of one's time at the baths is spent on the benches in a series of interludes separating the main business. From the benches in the third-class section the bathers pass through a heavy door into the showering and scrubbing room, a long hall, perhaps 100 feet by 30, lined with marble slabs arranged like beds in a hospital ward. The ceiling of this hall is held up by ancient girders which have been eaten away by rust for decades in the steamy atmosphere, but somehow continue to bear the weight. Men lie asleep on the marble slabs, lounge on them, massage themselves or each other, scrub from head to toe with great mountains of soapsuds. At the end of each marble platform two ancient spigots with smooth wooden handles dispense hot or cold water. Above some of them are shower heads that make it possible to lie under a stream of water for extended periods. Some men fell asleep this way.

The hot room opens off the far end of this hall. It is relatively small, perhaps 25 feet square, on two levels. Just inside the door the heat is strong but not intense. To really feel it one must walk up the tiled steps to the second level, where the old physics lesson about heat rising comes to life. Here the real zealots stand for 20 or 30 minutes, some dressed in little peaked caps and gloves. The head is most sensitive to the heat. The hands start to burn as they collide with the hot air when one whacks himself (or his neighbor) with bunches of leaves. The whacking is meant to open the pores and promote circulation. Serious bathers keep hitting themselves until the leaves come off the dried branches, so the floor is covered with slippery leaves.

The assembled company can never agree on the temperature in the hot room. The fanatics always think it is "weak," and toss small quantities of water onto the big bricks which—made red hot by a gas fire—heat the room. The water creates a fine steam which raises the temperature.

The only unpleasant moments in the bath are the inevitable arguments in the hot room about the temperature. The pretensions to expertise are quite remarkable; at any time there are at least two or three people in the hot room who confidently explain that they know exactly what is best for everyone, what the history of the Russian bath is, why the heat should be higher or lower or unchanged. These experts never agree with each other. Usually, whoever wants it hotter prevails, because he can himself continue tossing water onto the bricks when the others have stopped doing so. Finally it gets too hot for everyone, and there is a stampede of bare bodies down the stairs from the second level.

The hot room is an acquired taste. Breathing can be painful in the heat, and the hands do burn. Heart patients are advised to stay out of it, and one can feel that the circulatory system is under considerable pressure. Yet after a few minutes of heat and a long session under the cold shower, the body feels wonderfully clean and exhausted—and ready for another half-liter of beer on the benches outside. The skin continues to tingle from the beating it has taken for an hour or more.

In this fashion the morning slips by. Some of the Friday regulars liked to arrive at the baths around 8 and leave at 11:30 to be first in line at the Uzbekistan restaurant nearby, one of Moscow's best. There one could buy a few grams of vodka and a big bowl of spicy lamb soup, served (when the baker was working) with hot Central Asian bread. It is a satisfying conclusion to a morning in the Sundonovski baths.

> *It is Russia's joy to drink.*
> *We cannot do without it.*
> —St. Vladimir (965-1015)

Those few grams of vodka continue to reappear in this description of Russian life, which is not surprising. Vodka and Russia are inseparable. Vodka and, to an increasing extent, wine are the central elements of almost every Russian celebration, private or public. An evening at home with friends is unlikely to pass without a drink of something. A walk through any city or town is unlikely to end without meeting someone drunk or drinking.

The Russians have their own sociology of drinking. Vodka is sold in half-liter bottles with tops made of heavy metal foil. Once the top is torn off, there is no way to replace it; an open bottle is meant to be drunk to the end. Few Russian homes have anything like a liquor cabinet. Either there is vodka in the house, probably for some special occasion, or there is none. "I can't keep it around," the wife of a writer in Moscow explained. "If it's here, it gets drunk." The idea of a single cocktail before dinner is unheard of. So, in fact, are cocktails, except in films and a few pretentious new "bars" in big-city hotels and resort areas. Vodka is drunk straight, often in amazing quantities, and in glassfuls at a time. Only the ladies sip vodka.

There are no bars in Russia; only cafés and restaurants sell vodka in public. It is supposed to be impossible to buy spirits in one of those establishments without a meal, and there is a limit (though it is generally ignored) of 100 grams of vodka per person (about 3.5 ounces). Workingmen who want a drink on their way home gather outside a shop selling vodka, looking for comrades to go "three on a bottle" with them, an old tradition. Three on a half-liter bottle means 5.6 ounces of straight vodka per man, usually drunk in one gulp with only a piece of dark bread or perhaps a slice of cucumber as a chaser. A man with more money in his pocket (that half-liter costs at least 3.62 rubles) may buy the entire bottle for himself. I saw one man who did in Khabarovsk, a city in the Soviet far east, near Japan. He was sitting on a hillside in a downtown park with the empty bottle between his legs, looking at nothing in particular. "Tanya," he suddenly shouted, "I love you!"

Vodka marks the dividing line in Russian life between simple pleasure and escape. Per capita consumption of hard liquor in the Soviet Union is the highest of any country in the world. Stumbling drunks are a common sight on the streets of every Russian village, town and city. And consumption is rising all the time. The cost of alcoholism and drunkenness to the society is staggering in terms of work days lost, lives shortened, families broken up, crime caused, and more.

Russia's drinking problem is older than the Revolution. George Turberville, an Englishman who visited Russia in 1568, described the nation's proclivity for drink in a letter in verse to friends in London:

Folk fit to be of Bacchus trained, so quaffing is their kind.
Drink is their whole desire, the pot is all their pride,
The soberest head doth once a day stand needful of a
 guide. . . .*

There are no statistics on the consumption of alcohol in the 16th century, but figures from more recent times demonstrate that the drinking problem has grown steadily worse since 1917. Just why this is true is a difficult question. It might be tempting to conclude that the victims of a poor, totalitarian society have nowhere else to turn—that vodka performs the narcotic function of *soma* in Aldous Huxley's *Brave New World*. There is probably some truth in this, but it is far from the entire answer, as is obvious on a visit to Russia's neighbor, Finland. There—in a liberal democracy, where life is much more comfortable than in the USSR—public drunkenness on the Russian model is widespread, despite stern official policies to discourage drinking, including rationing. Finns come to Leningrad or Tallinn in Soviet Estonia for weekend holidays which consist of little more than drinking Russian vodka.

Millions of Russians regularly decide quite consciously to go on a bender. I once spent several weeks asking every Russian I met what ordinary workers did for a night out or a celebration. There were a number of answers, but the first

---

* Quoted in *Voyages and Discoveries* by Richard Hakluyt.

thing everyone mentioned was "Buy a bottle of vodka." The consequences of this are evident to the most casual observer.

One Saturday afternoon in Pskov, an ancient city in northwestern Russia, a group of four or five men who had been drinking waited restlessly for a bus. Two of them began to quarrel. The soberer of the two (a narrow distinction) threw a few quick punches, knocking his comrade to the sidewalk. The victim took a long moment to pull himself up. In no mood for a fight, he tried to sneak away.

A woman, apparently sober, tried to intervene in the brawl on behalf of the drunker fellow by forcing herself between the two of them. The man who threw the punches thanked her with a sharp kick to the shins. By this time there was a crowd of perhaps 15 people watching from the opposite side of the street. When the drunk kicked the woman, ladies in the crowd gasped. One shouted for the police. But the disputing parties made peace of a kind, and the crisis atmosphere passed.

I moved closer and could overhear an emotional conversation between the woman who had tried to intervene and a bystander. "Last week he did *that* to me," she said, pointing to a bright red bruise on her cheek. The man who had kicked her—not for the first time, apparently—was her own husband.

Suddenly a policeman appeared. "What's going on here?" he demanded, in the universal manner of policemen.

The lady with the red bruise sped 10 yards to her husband's side, slipping her arm tenderly into his. "Nothing, nothing at all," she answered with a winning smile. "He's forty-five years old today, forty-five he is," she went on, as if to say there is nothing extraordinary about a little birthday celebration, as indeed there isn't.

The policeman accepted her explanation, though he urged all the celebrants to "keep it down." The lady with the red bruise kept her smile, but said in a stage whisper to her forty-five-year-old husband, "I'll deal with you later, I will!"

Perhaps the closest thing to a personal-advice column in the Soviet Union is a radio program called "Man and Society." The announcer reads citizens' letters to the program, then offers some guidance. Drinking is a topic that is raised again and again on the show. A typical letter came from

Magadan, a remote city in the Soviet far east, not far from Alaska.

"My life has been a nightmare," a woman there wrote. "I got married in 1946, and hoped to raise a happy family." Her first son was born in 1947, and—"perhaps to celebrate this event"—her husband drank some vodka. That was his downfall; a lifetime of drinking followed. "Our family survived extreme material difficulties, since more than half our income was spent on vodka."*

After 21 years of marriage, the defeated wife and her three children agreed that they could no longer put up with papa. They fled to Magadan, leaving him in their old home in European Russia. He continued to drink. After a time he remarried, then divorced, then moved in with another woman. Several years ago he had a stroke which left him paralyzed. When they learned of this, his former wife and children decided to invite him back into their lives.

He's getting better now," the woman wrote. "He's back at work and, most important, he isn't drinking any spirits. But life has already passed us by. We can't relive our youth."

Losses due to drinking (including the enormous losses of industrial alcohol, which serious drinkers readily substitute for ordinary—and expensive—vodka) run into billions of rubles every year. A recent rise in the Soviet Union's crude death rate is partly attributable to increasingly heavy drinking. About half of all divorces in the Soviet Union are blamed on drunkenness; so are two-thirds or more of the country's crime, 60 percent of all serious accidents and 90 percent of the new cases of syphilis. And the drinking problem gets steadily worse. Teenagers drink more than previous generations, women drink more, men do too. Drink may be Russia's joy, as St. Vladimir put it, but it is also Russia's curse.

That same St. Vladimir, the Prince of Kiev, was the first Russian Christian. He took the faith to marry the sister of the Emperor of Byzantium. In the year 988 he made Eastern Christianity Russia's state religion, and the consequences of that decision are still being felt. If millions of Russians regu-

---

* According to the research of Vladimir Treml, an American economist, the average Soviet family spends two months' salary a year on drink.

larly escape their lives with alcohol, millions more find solace in church.

According to a survey published in a Soviet magazine, 60 percent of the babies born in the industrial city of Gorki in the late 1960s were baptized. Priests in Moscow say at least a third of the children in the capital have been baptized in church. A curious outsider can witness baptisms every week in several of Moscow's 45 active churches. An American once saw a woman in a Chaika, a limousine used only by important state or Party officials and their wives, bringing her baby to be baptized. On Easter and other holidays the country's churches are jammed with worshipers. There are no reliable statistics, but churchmen estimate that 30 to 50 million Russians regard themselves as believers and attend church at least occasionally. This guess is based on church income, and is probably accurate. That means there are vastly more Christians in the Soviet Union than communists. (The Party has about 14 million members.) The state may disapprove, but it does not forbid its citizens to practice their religion.

An outsider can sense the strength of Russian Orthodoxy at any working church on one of the high holy days. The large congregations are composed predominantly of older women, but not exclusively; there are always a few young people, and sometimes quite a few. The most I ever saw was in Pechori, an old town in northeastern Russia where the church maintains a monastery. The monastery consists of a lovely cluster of Hansel-and-Gretel churches, brightly painted and nestled at the bottom of a deep, wooded hollow that is surrounded by a high wall. One enters through that wall and leaves the Soviet Union for a glimpse of what old Russia must have been. Even church bells are permitted in the hollow (they are forbidden elsewhere).

On the winter Sunday I visisted the main cathedral at Pechori, it was crowded with local citizens and pilgrims. They were Russians of all shapes and descriptions, including many teenagers and young couples. Many, no doubt, were tourists there for the spectacle, but many also knew the words to the service, and knew when to sing or chant aloud with the priest, deacon or choir.

The scene in church is familiarly Russian. The congregation is another mass of barely distinguishable people, dressed in gray and black, moving together down onto their knees, up to sing, out the door to the street. There are no pews, and the ordinary Sunday service lasts for three hours, but no one wants it shortened.

The physical trappings of a Russian church are unlike anything else in an ordinary citizen's life, and this is no small part of its appeal. Yellow candlelight reflected in brass, silver and polished glass, incense in the air, old icons in gilt frames, the glorious music of the service and the imposing robes of the priests all contribute to an otherworldly atmosphere. Judging by the faces of the worshipers, the atmosphere is appreciated. Many seem to come to church determined to have an emotional experience, just as many Russians sit down to a family celebration determined to be sentimental. Church is a slice of the next world right here in this one. "A Russian does not see worship as something to *do*," an American Episcopal minister once said, "but as something to *be*."

A priest in Moscow told me about a young woman who came to him several years ago and asked to be christened.

"Why do you want that?" the priest asked. "Do you believe in God?"

"I don't know anything about God," she answered. "But please, christen me at once."

"Buy why, then?" the priest persisted.

The young woman explained that she had been to church many times. At home she was quarrelsome, a complainer, always fighting with her parents and friends. But she left church a changed person, feeling warm and benevolent.

"I can't cross myself in church when everyone else does," she said, "because I haven't been christened. I want to cross myself."

The priest happily christened her the next afternoon.

The Church's influence in modern Soviet life is more easily felt than described. It consists largely of habits of mind and speech. "God save us," Russians still say, even leaders of Party and state. An American mountain-climbing team listened helplessly with a group of Russians in a base camp in Soviet Asia as a team of Russian women climbers died literally over the radio, audible to the entire group. They were trapped on a high peak in a blizzard, unable to move up or down. "We can't hold the button down any longer on the radio to transmit," one of the women said in the last radio message. "We are going to die. Goodbye. We are very sorry." Robert Craig, an American who was there, recalled later that everyone was crying. "The Russians, for the most part, all crossed themselves in silence. That was it."

In small towns and villages the priest is still a central figure in society. A workingman fom Moscow returned to his native village for his mother's funeral, expecting to perform certain filial duties in connection with the burial. But he did nothing at all. "The priest took care of everything," he told me. "I didn't even know the customs any more."

Christianity utterly dominated the life of a toothless old woman I met in Zagorsk, the ancient monastery 44 miles north of Moscow. With surprising candor she recounted her life history, and the Church was always near the center of the tale. She lived in a small town in the Urals, and recommended a visit. "We have a young, new priest," she said, beaming proudly—nothing mattered more to her.

This ancient creature traveled to Zagorsk every few years. It is an important pilgrimage for the devout. The monastery there is rich in holy objects, lucky icons and a well that produces miraculous holy water. She had a jar of it in her black plastic bag the day she set out for home, as well as some special rolls baked by the monks. It would take five or six days to get home, she reckoned; she had no ticket, and wasn't sure how she would get one. She didn't even know how she would get from Zagorsk to Moscow when she stopped to talk to us on her way out of the monastery. She looked well past seventy, walked with stiff legs and a bent back, and it was difficult to believe that she would be able to complete her journey. But she was delighted with herself, and with the treasures she had accumulated in the magical monastery at Zagorsk.

The Orthodox Church is not the only one that is thriving in the Soviet Union. The Baptists are in some ways stronger, winning converts and actually opening new churches, something the Orthodox have not done in years (primarily because they are not allowed to). Richard Nixon worshiped with Moscow's Baptists on his first presidential visit to Moscow in May 1972. The overflowing congregation included two young men in the uniform of the Red Army. The Russian Baptists practice a hellfire-and-brimstone religion familiar to anyone who has visited a fundamentalist church in the Bible Belt of the American south.

In Soviet Lithuania the Catholic Church is still strong; in Armenia the Armenian Church is a symbol of national identity. It is one of the Armenians' most useful tools in proclaiming and maintaining some independence from Moscow and the Great Russians. The Moslem influence is still strong in Soviet Asia; traditional religious and social customs have survived, especially in small towns and villages. The religious comprise a minority of the Soviet population, but they are a substantial minority.

An outsider in Russia is repeatedly beset by the disquieting realization that every generalization about the country must be hedged and qualified. This frustrating truism is brought to life by periodic reminders, such as that toothless old pilgrim encountered in Zagorsk.

This book describes urban Russians. It does not explain the lives of country folk like her, or of a majority of the Soviet population. Though urban Russia dominates Soviet society, it includes less than a third of the citizenry. An encyclopedia of Soviet life, describing all of its forms in detail, would fill many volumes.

Urban Russians, particularly Muscovites, live better than most Soviet citizens. Moscow itself is an artificial showpiece, a world capital because the authorities will it so. Most of the cars sold to Soviet citizens are sold in Moscow, so the capital's streets are crowded, while the broad avenues of Volgograd, to name one city of many, have almost no traffic at all. Consumer goods go first to Moscow, then to half a dozen other "hero" cities, so designated for their roles in World War II, then down a hierarchical list on which every community is ranked. The state stores in Moscow are always supplied with fresh meat, but the shops in Novosibirsk, a city of a million souls, sell no meat at all for months on end. Some meat is usually available at Novosibirsk's farmers' markets, but only at high prices. There are smaller cities and towns that *never* get fresh meat in any form. After the disastrous harvest of 1972, much of the country suffered serious shortages of staples, including bread, as well as meat and other more esoteric items, but Moscow remained well supplied. Muscovites complained bitterly that autumn about the long lines to buy potatoes, but they did have potatoes. The police were instructed to inspect the baggage of travelers leaving the city to prevent them from taking the capital's spuds to the countryside.

Citizens from all over the country regularly come to Moscow to shop. City officials have said that on any day of the year there are at least a million visitors in the capital. They buy foodstuffs, clothes, toys and all kinds of consumer goods. I asked a man on a train from Moscow to Tallinn, the capital of Soviet Estonia, why he was carrying three new fishing rods. In the Baltic seaport of Tallinn, he explained, fishing rods are seldom available. But they are freely sold in land-locked Moscow.

Nikita Khrushchev told this anecdote in his reminiscences*:

> I met a man recently who asked me, "Say, Comrade Khrushchev, do you think a camel could make it all the way from Moscow to Vladivostok [a trip of more than 6000 miles]?"
>
> I could tell from the way he was smiling that there was more to the question than met the eye. I answered cautiously, "Well, the camel is a strong animal with lots of stamina, so I think he could probably walk all the way to Vladivostok."
>
> "No, Comrade Khrushchev, you're wrong. The camel would be lucky to make it as far as Sverdlovsk [about 1200 miles east of Moscow]."
>
> "Why?"
>
> "Because, assuming he gets to Sverdlovsk, the people there would eat him."

It is difficult for a foreigner to visit the poorer areas of the Soviet Union. More than half the country is closed to foreigners, some of it for strategic reasons, but a great deal, no

---

* *Khrushchev Remembers: The Last Testament* (Boston: Little, Brown & Co., 1974). The Khrushchev memoirs will be cited often in this book. There is now no doubt that the two books of memoirs published in English are translated from tape recordings made by Khrushchev himself. The recordings are on deposit in the Columbia University library, and independent voice experts have confirmed their authenticity. In Moscow I was told by people very well placed to know the truth of the matter that the memoirs were genuine, if incomplete. Incomplete, because the tapes reached the West through dubious channels, including, apparently, agents of the KGB. The tapes have probably been edited. Moreover, Khrushchev displays a chronic disregard for truth in these recollections; many of his assertions are demonstrably untrue. To me, the memoirs are most interesting not for the factual (or allegedly factual) material they include, but for their revelations about Khrushchev's personality and the workings of the system he dominated for seven years.

doubt, because the Russians are embarrassed by it. Yet ·the poverty is visible from the windows of trains traveling between open cities, and many of the areas open to foreigners suggest that rural life is far harder than life in the cities.

In Petrozavodsk, a city of 210,000 in far northwestern Russia, near Finland, many people live in log houses, some in the center of town. Carefully stacked mountains of firewood in dusty vacant lots and wisps of smoke coming from chimneys on a warm summer's day suggest the continued importance of wood-burning stoves in the city. Thousands of people live in a community of two-story wooden buildings reminiscent of American army barracks, built on a muddy plateau across the railroad tracks from the main part of town. New, prefabricated apartment houses are going up in Petrozavodsk, but the local authorities acknowledge that there won't be a new apartment for everyone for many years. According to the mayor, the city is allocated 500 automobiles a year for sale to private citizens. At that rate, each family in Petrozavodsk would get a chance to buy a new car about once in 100 years.

Despite all this, the citizens of Petrozavodsk probably have more rubles per capita than the residents of Leningrad or Moscow. They earn 45 percent more than workers in central Russia, a bonus that is meant to compensate for the harsher life in the far north. But there is nothing to spend the money on, and capital investment in Petrozavodsk, particularly in housing, has relatively low priority in the national Plan. So the city looks poor, though its people may be relatively well off.

This is not true of rural villages, which look poor, and whose residents *are* poor. Foreigners who ask for official permission to spend some time in a Russian village are usually turned down or sent to one of a few well-known showpieces. I was refused permission several times to make extended visits to the countryside, though I was taken to several relatively wealthy villages in different parts of the country. A village's wealth is almost entirely a function of nature's blessings; the villages in fertile areas can be prosperous, but those farming more barren land are poor.

Andrei Amalrik, one of the most outspoken intellectual dissidents of recent years, was exiled to a Siberian village in 1965, and later described it in detail. Amalrik's village, Guryevka, may have been poorer than many, but it is certainly representative. Parts of his *Involuntary Journey to Siberia* bear repeating here; there is no comparable glimpse of the realities of life in the Russian countryside.

Amalrik wrote about the small wooden homes in the village:

The furniture was mass-produced: round tables, dressers and iron bedsteads, tha latter being regarded as the first sign of prosperity. . . .One house had a leather divan which everyone else joked about but secretly envied. No one ever sat on it, however—it was covered with a clean white cloth and was intended only for show. As a rule, the houses are divided into four rooms. The first is where the cooking is done (and fodder is prepared for the livestock) and the family have their meals. The second is the bedroom, which in the daytime serves a purely ornamental purpose: bedspreads are put on the beds, pillows are piled one on top of the other, and on the wall, except in the poorest homes, there was always a cheap print: swans swimming on a lake in front of a white castle, or a knight in shining armor riding out of the castle gates while a lady in a white dress waved good-by. Such pictures were sold in Tomsk [the nearest city] at 10 rubles apiece. Icons hung in almost every house, but the attitude towards religion was one of utter indifference, and the old men would ask: 'Who can tell if God exists or not?' . . . The houses had outbuildings for livestock, but newly born calves and pigs were kept in the house itself. Many houses had radio sets, but half of them didn't work because the strength of the electric current kept changing. Electricity had been brought to the village three years earlier; two generators in Novokrivosheino [a nearby town] supplied the current, chiefly at milking times—early in the morning, at midday and at night and until 11 o'clock.

Amalrik was constantly surprised at the collective farmers' attitude toward work:

Several years previously they had started building a garage for tractors in Guryevka; it was still standing unfinished, and the timber was gradually pilfered for fire-

wood. The summer I arrived the foundations were laid
for a day nursery, but it was still unfinished a year later
and looked as if it would suffer the same fate as the garage. Leaving the nursery unfinished, the *kolkhoz** next
started building a new barn. By the following summer
this too was unfinished, yet next door to it a space was already being cleared for a drying shed. I imagine these
things happen mainly because labor is paid so little that
nobody thinks it worth economizing. There is also perhaps the mentality of the *kolkhoznik*:** he has ceased
to be a peasant but has not become a laborer, and hence
cares nothing about what happens to the results of his
work. Finally, though the *kolkhoz* is a big unit, the
methods of running it are more appropriate to a small
family farm: things needing attention are done in the
same spirit as that in which a fence is mended on a small
holding.

Amalrik found that most members of Guryevka society
would periodically drink themselves into a stupor. Scenes of
drunken misbehavior recur throughout his description of village life:

The peasants' life was remarkably dull; all their free
time was spent working on their private plots. Their
main distraction was drink, especially in winter, when
they drank nearly every day. Ordinary vodka bought in
the village store was kept for special occasions; they usually drank the home-distilled variety. Made from rye,
this is singularly unpleasant to the taste, muddy green in
color and about 70 proof. Not every villager had his
own still. In preparation for a holiday or to repay a
neighbor for some good turn people borrowed a still
from someone and made an extra supply. Homemade
beer ... was brewed by everybody, and all year round.
Boiled water is poured into a bucket, six—or, if the
brewer is mean, four or five—pounds of sugar are
added; yeast is put in when the water has cooled, and
sometimes tea for coloring and hops for taste. Hops are
always added if the beer is going to be offered to guests,

---

* Collective farm.
** Collective farmer.

so they should get drunk quickly and drink less. . . . Illicit brewing is an offense punishable at the very least by a fine of 100 rubles, but it can also lead to forced labor for several years. Many of the villagers had paid fines, and one had spent a year in camp, but this deterred no one.

The residents of Guryevka were constantly on the lookout for ways to make their private lives easier. Women without men did whatever they could to trap a mate, not necessarily a formal husband, but at least a man to share the bed and help cut firewood. The villagers were intrigued with one another's private affairs. Amalrik found that "curtains for the window [of the small hut he shared with his wife, who came from Moscow] were absolutely essential because in the villages people are very curious: in the mornings I sometimes found footprints under our windows, and even the woman in charge of the village store warned me that several people came to eavesdrop under our windows, trying to peer in."

That village shop, Amalrik thought, was something in Guryevka's favor:

> To the credit of Siberia, it must be said that every village there had its own store—presumably because of the great distance between places. Ours was open in the morning and evening when the villagers were not working. It sold vodka, wine, sugar, grain, biscuits, candy, vegetable oil, canned food, household utensils, and a small selection of men's and women's clothes; occasionally bicycles and pieces of furniture could be got on order. Thanks to the efficiency of our storekeeper, we were well supplied by village standards.

Nevertheless, the shop had run out of flour by mid-November. The villagers' diet depended on their own produce; most were able to keep a cow and a pig and grow their own potatoes.

"The children," Amalrak wrote,

> were brought up very strangely, as though they were midget adults and, from early childhood on, they were initiated into all the most intimate problems of the grown-ups. Everybody used filthy language—neither men nor

women could say a sentence without it—and nearly all of them swore in front of their children, whether they were three or sixteen years old. You would hear a boy of four who had only just learned to speak using the same choice expressions as an elderly drunk. No one stopped him. Teenage girls also used the same remarkably coarse language.

While Amalrik was living in Guryevka the system of payments to the villagers was changed, much to their advantage. He was in the village when they each received a windfall of 150 to 200 rubles:

For people who were used to getting only 15 or 20 rubles in cash a month, this was a great deal of money indeed, and they all immediately started drinking. For three days the village store was open from early in the morning till late at night; the woman in charge of it was run off her feet, but she exceeded her sales plan for January four times over. The kolkhozniks bought not only vodka but lengths of cloth to make dresses and curtains, good trousers to wear on weekends, jars of preserved fruit, gingerbread by the pound, and in general all the stuff that had been lying around unwanted in the store all year. There were also one or two accidents: the drunken Kritsky, for instance, set out to visit us, but on the way he fell into the snow and went to sleep. When he woke up both his hands were frozen and he was in the hospital [in a nearby town] for more than a month; they amptuated two fingers on one hand and three on the other. From all over the village we could hear drunken shouting and the shrieking of women.

It would be a mistake to conclude that the entire Soviet countryside is nothing but a succession of Guryevkas. Amalrik was sent to that village not least because of its remoteness. Many villages are now within the reach of both normal electric power and television. Guryevka has no doctor of its own, but many villages do—more than in America, no doubt. The standard of living in the rich agricultural areas of southern Russia and the Ukraine is much higher then Siberia's.

But even in those fortunate villages, life is surprisingly primitive. The same wooden cottages Amalrik saw in Gu-

ryevka house farmers all over the USSR. Roads are still a
rarity in the Soviet countryside, and mud is overwhelming for
several months each year. Farmers don't have their own cars
or trucks which they could drive into town for a lively Saturday night. In fact, for years it has taken special permission
from a senior official of the collective farm to leave its con-
fines. Soviet villagers have not had their own internal passports, and thus have not had the right to travel freely around
the country on their own. The government announced late in
1974 that this would change, but it remains to be seen how.
Education in the countryside is far inferior to education in
the towns and cities, as the government itself has acknowledged. Wages, pensions and all the benefits of the welfare state are less generous in the villages than in urban areas.

Amalrik's account of life in Guryevka has circulated
among intellectuals in Moscow in typescript, and is well
known among a slice of the capital's intellectual society. It
startled many of those Muscovites in the same way it startles
us. A Russian living a relatively comfortable life in the capital finds Guryevka difficult to imagine. The gulf which separates the urban intelligentsia from the peasantry is one of
the enduring facts of Russian life, long predating the
Bolsheviks.

If there is a portrait of the Moscow intelligentsia's life
comparable to Amalrik's description of Guryevka, perhaps it
is the 25,000-word story by Yuri Trifonov called "The Exchange." Trifonov was a prodigy at twenty-four, when he
won the Stalin Prize for literature in 1951. In middle age Trifonov is one of the Soviet Union's few really accomplished
writers, though he is virtually unknown abroad. In this story
he explains and illuminates an entire way of life.

The exchange of the title is an exchange of flats in Moscow, one woman's idea of how to improve living conditions
for herself, her husband and daughter. But this is Russia, so it
is complicated. The idea is that Viktor Dmitriev and his wife,
who live in one room of a communal flat, and Dimitriev's
elderly mother, who has her own room in another communal
apartment, should pool their resources, trading their separate
rooms for one two-room flat in which all four could live together.

Dmitriev has been suggesting this idea for years. They

would just have to find someone with a two-room flat who wanted to trade it for two separate rooms—perhaps a couple getting a divorce. But until recently his wife, Lena, was not interested. She didn't like Dmitriev's mother, and didn't want to live with her. Now, suddenly, Lena herself has revived the idea, and the reason for this pains Dmitriev. His mother is dying of cancer, and Lena realizes that they can make the exchange in her last days—while she is still alive, and therefore still entitled to "living space," as the Russians call it—confident that they won't have to live with her for long. It is a cruel idea, but also eminently practical. Dmitriev knows that he, his wife and daughter are not comfortable in their single room. He ought to go through with it for their sake.

But going through with it would mean persuading his mother to agree. Like most cancer patients in Russia, she hasn't been told that she has the disease; she thinks she is recovering from an operation for ulcers. Dmitriev is afraid to raise the idea of an exchange with her. In his struggle with himself to find the courage to do so, he reviews the most important facts of life, and they are depressing.

Dmitriev is thirty-seven. Though "sometimes it seemed to him that everything was still ahead," in fact he knows that it isn't. He had wanted to be an artist, but failed the entrance exam for the art institute. He has ended up as an engineer specializing in some sort of pumps. (Trifonov gives no further explanation of Dmitriev's work, one of the literary devices he uses to convey his characters' total preoccupation with their private lives.) Dmitriev's job bores him. His marriage, which began as a torrid love affair, has soured. His wife is fat and tactless. Her inability to get along with his family has alienated Dmitriev from his mother and sister. Dmitriev no longer likes her, though this is too much to admit outright. He tried another woman for a summer; it was an exciting infatuation, but fleeting. The other woman is still available and would like to revive the liaison. Dmitriev is tempted—but not really tempted.

As Dmitriev's life is revealed, so is the flavor of human existence among the people best described as Moscow's middle class, the college-educated and white-collared who call themselves the intelligentsia. The elements of that existence come to life in Trifonov's story like the shiny bits in a piece of quartz rock that happen to catch the sun.

These are several scenes from the story.
Dmitriev and his wife going to bed in their room:

... Their daughter, Natasha, was sleeping behind a
screen in the corner. ... Dmitriev and Lena slept on a
wide Turkish mattress of Czechoslovak manufacture,
luckily purchased about three years before, which was
the envy of their friends. ... It turned out to be not very
durable, quickly getting rickety and squeaking with every move. ... Dmitriev and Lena always listened for a
long time for sounds from the cell [the family's name
for Natasha's space behind the screen], trying to figure
out whether their daughter had gone to sleep. Dmitriev
would call, checking, in an undertone: "Natash! Hey,
Natash!" Lena would go on tiptoe and look through the
crack in the screen. ...

Dmitriev arriving at the Moscow crematorium for the funeral of his grandfather:

He came to the crematorium straight from work, and
looked foolish with his thick yellow briefcase, in which
he carried several cans of Saira, a popular but rarely ob-
tainable fish, bought by chance on the street. Lena loved
Saira. When they entered the crematorium from the
street, Dmitriev quickly went to the right and put his
briefcase on the floor in a corner, behind a column, so
that no one would see it. "Don't forget the briefcase," he
repeated to himself, "don't forget the briefcase." During
the funeral ceremony he remembered about the briefcase
several times and looked back at the column. ...

In a painfully vivid scene Dmitriev goes to the office of a
colleague whom he doesn't really know to ask for a favor.
Dmitriev has heard that this man once made the same sort of
exchange for a flat that Dmitriev's wife wants to make—a
hurried exchange before a dying relative died. "He had connections in the local housing commission," Dmitriev has
heard, so he forces himself to ask for help:

Dmitriev began clumsily to put forward his request,
or, more precisely, to hint at his request. Neviadomsky
had to guess at it ... but he didn't guess.

Dmitriev tries to explain that he needs help to initiate a speedy exchange, but Neviadomsky insists that he only knows the normal, bureaucratic method:

"Start with the exchange bureau, I don't know any other channels." Neviadomsky stuck a thumb into his nostril and began with concentration to extricate something from it. Obviously he was tensely trying to figure out whether or not to let Dmitriev in on his connections. He decided it wasn't worth it. "I didn't have any other channels. . . ."

Dmitriev's father-in-law had been successfully playing the angles since the 1920s. His success didn't help him later, when fears and suspicions gripped the land. There were "slanders and libels from various rats who wanted to ruin him," but he escaped because he had once served in the Cheka, the original political police. He had learned to keep an eye out for his own interests:

The habit of constant distrust and unremitting vigilance had insinuated itself so much into his nature that Ivan Vasilievich [the father-in-law] displayed it constantly. . . . For example, he'd ask Dmitriev before going to bed at night [when they were living together], "Viktor, did you put the latch on the door?" "Yes," Viktor replied, then he listened as his father-in-law slipped down the hall to check the door. It was amusing that the same mistrust for absolutely everyone—beginning with the people with whom they lived—infected Vera Lazarevna [Dmitriev's mother-in-law] too. She would call from somewhere and ask for Lena [her daughter], and Dmitriev would say Lena was out. In a little while there would be another call, and Vera Lazarevna, disguising her voice, would ask again for Lena. . . .

In the end Dmitriev finds the courage to suggest the exchange to his mother. Her first reaction is to say no, but two days later she telephones to say she will do it. Two months later her health takes a drastic turn for the worse, but she survives long enough for Dmitriev and his wife to find someone with whom to make the exchange and get it approved by all the relevant offices. They get a two-room flat. After his mother's death "Dmitriev had a high-blood-pressure crisis, and he stayed in the hospital for three weeks, confined strictly to his bed."

That short story doesn't support the image of the Russian family that Russians like to believe in, but it is a realistic story nevertheless. The Russians have not found a secret way to make all families happy and loving; they only have a fierce desire to make them so.

The fact is that one in three Soviet marriages ends in divorce, nearly one in two in Moscow and Leningrad. This is nearly as many divorces as occur in the divorce-happy United States. Among the class described in Trifonov's short story it is unusual to find on adult couple of whom neither was previously married to someone else. Thirty percent of all divorces involve "young" couples—presumably under thirty or thirty-five—more than half of whom have one or more children.

Russian marriages collapse for the most obvious human reasons, but the special characteristics of the society also contribute. According to one sociologist's study of 1000 divorced couples in Leningrad, drunkenness causes more divorces than any other factor. Of the 500 women in this sample, 210 said they had left their husbands because they were drunks. Twenty-two percent of this sample blamed arguments with parents for their divorces, a hint of the consequences when generations are forced to live together in close quarters. Eleven and a half percent said a shortage of living space caused the breakdown of their marriages.

Under Soviet law every citizen has a right to divorce. Marriages can be dissolved almost as easily as they are formalized. When there are no children, a couple need only make joint application for divorce at their neighborhood records office, wait three months and pay 50 rubles each. In return they receive a piece of paper solemnizing the dissolution of their union. It is simply a matter of paperwork. The procedure is slightly more complicated when there are children. The parents must appear before a counselor, who makes an attempt, usually a *pro forma* attempt, to persuade them not to divorce. If they insist, the paperwork proceeds.

If one of the spouses is reluctant to divorce, or if there is a dispute over custody or the distribution of joint property, a court fight is possible. This is rare. A reluctant partner can only postpone, not prevent, the divorce. Except in extraordinary circumstances, mothers get custody of the offspring.

Russians are used to red tape, and I met several who were surprised at how easy a divorce was. One woman fairly beamed with satisfaction while recounting her experience. "I went to the records office on Tuesday—it was noon, I looked at the clock. I had a letter from Yuri [her ex-husband] agreeing to everything. I gave the man the papers. He said, "Do you have any questions for me?" I shrugged—no. He said, 'You can pick up your document in the clerk's office.' That's all there was to it. I walked out a free woman. It was four minutes past twelve, I looked at the clock."

The Little Hall of the Moscow Conservatory looks like the auditorium of an American high school built in the 1930s— once nearly grand now dilapidated. Concerts are given in the Little Hall several times a week, usually by soloists or small ensembles. At other times it is used by students of the conservatory, who give free concerts for practice.

Many elderly Muscovites regularly attend the free concerts. The seats are comfortable, the music can be soothing and it doesn't cost anything. A nice outing. I went one night to a concert given by violin students. Several of the white-haired spectators looked like regulars. One round woman carefully arranged herself in a corner seat, tucking her shopping bags in all around her, and opened a scarf on her lap that was decorated with an embroidered design. As the aspiring violinists played their pieces, she busily folded the scarf into a square, unfolded it, held it up to look at the design, turned it around to look at it from the back, refolded it into a square, and so on, over and over again. She didn't even notice the musicians.

On the other side of the auditorium three women who appeared to be old friends sat together. One of them held forth on one subject after another. She didn't let the music interrupt her commentary, nor did she heed the pleas of other spectators to keep still.

About half the people in the audience that night were old. Some came late, others left early. They seemed to treat the Little Hall as a sort of hangout.

There aren't many proper gathering spots for the elderly in the Soviet Union. The only special service the state provides for most old people is a modest pension. Instead of clubs, the old are drawn to the Little Hall at the conservatory, or to the park in Tverskoi Boulevard, where they sit over chess sets and gossip away the afternoons. Boredom takes its toll. An editor of *Izvestia*, the government newspaper, told me that pensioners write half of the thousands of letters to the editor that the paper receives each week.

The strains of ordinary life are most difficult for the old. Three sisters, all in their late sixties, who live together in Moscow try to share the most burdensome chores. The youngest and healthiest does the shopping. Instead of going out every day, as most people do, she tries to make a single shopping trip every two days, burying as much as she can carry home in two shopping bags. "If you're old and don't have a family to help you," a friend once remarked, "it's terrible." Another friend told me about an old woman who lived alone in one room of a communal apartment on a pension of 40 rubles a month. She was so poor that she had to think twice before taking a five-kopek bus ride. She ate meat only two or three times a month.

The Soviet government has not recognized old age as a social problem deserving special services and attention. A scientist in Moscow whose specialty is old age once talked about this with me. He complained that geriatrics, the branch of medical science that deals with old age and its problems, is not recognized as a separate specialty in Soviet medicine. There are almost no special hospitals or clinics for the elderly. (A famous exception, sometimes shown to foreigners, is the home and hospital for Old Bolsheviks in Moscow.) There are no popular or professional journals dealing with old people and their problems. Existing homes for the aged meet less than 10 percent of the country's needs, and many of them are inadequate. In the town of Kaluga, for instance, residents of the home for the elderly live in dormitory conditions, several in each room, in an uncomfortable building.

The state forbids the gathering of accurate statistics on mortality, so it is impossible to know what diseases are the most common or what regions the least healthy. Apparently the authorities want to hide this information from the citizenry, and to exaggerate the longevity of Soviet citizens. In 1966 the Institute of Gerontology (old age and its diseases) opened a statistical unit, but it was closed soon afterward for want of statistics to work with.

The state pays about 20 billion rubles a year in pensions to its old and disabled citizens. This sounds like a good deal, but it is distributed among 43 million recipients, so the average pension is less than 40 rubles a month. A retirement pension depends on one's income when he worked, but no one receives more than 120 rubles a month. Women are generally eligible for a pension at 55, men at 60.

Many old people supplement their pensions by continuing to work. The state encourages this to reduce the general labor shortage. Members of undermanned professions who reach retirement age can go right on working as before, collecting both salary and pension. Many doctors do this. The classic pensioners' profession is cloakroom attendant. Every Soviet office, theater, restaurant, museum, school and factory has a cloakroom manned by one or more old people.

The best insurance against the tribulations of old age is the extended family, which is still a healthy institution in the Soviet Union. Although statistics are not available—they seldom are for social phenomena in the USSR—I'm confident that in Russia many more old people live with their children then in the United States or Britain, for example. Even if they live separately in the same town, relations between the older generation and its heirs seem close and mutually protective. In our world we try to make the old disappear. Russians don't seem so eager to do that.

The universal scourge of old age is bad health, and it is no more fun to be sick in Russia than anywhere else. A 61-year-old woman with high blood pressure, for example, has trouble every fall and spring when the seasons change. Each time she goes to her neighborhood clinic, which refers her to a hospital, which puts her through a series of tests that take two or three days to complete. Each time the tests show that she has high blood pressure. A brief rest is prescribed, and some pills. No Soviet doctor has ever suggested that her diet—which includes large quantities of eggs and fatty milk products—might contribute to her illness.

Valentin Alexandrovich was seventy-nine. He had liver trouble, and some years ago had a heart attack. One evening at home in Moscow he developed a pain in his chest and became nauseous; his wife thought it was another heart attack and called an ambulance. It took two hours to get to their apartment, but the old man was still alive and the ambulance took him to a hospital.

No one in the family was consulted about which hospital, and they had bad luck. It was an old one, overcrowded and shabby. The wards were full, so Valentin Alexandrovich had to sleep on a bed in the hallway. Some of the doctors were sympathetic, others were not. Soviet hospitals are reluctant to admit patients who are likely to die. Giving them beds is seen as a waste of space. People should die at home.

Valentin Alexandrovich was not interested in dying. He had survived 10 years in one of Stalin's prison camps and numerous other hardships; he wanted to keep going. His wife, his fifty-nine-year-old son by an earlier marriage and the son's wife and daughter took turns at the hospital looking after him. They kept watch around the clock.

Soviet hospitals do not provide much nursing care. The nurses on duty perform functional tasks—cleaning up, keeping order, serving the one basic menu that is offered all patients. They seldom provide individual care to the patients. Relatives make up for this by attending the sick themselves and bringing food from home. It is also common for the family to find whatever medicines are needed—often the medicines that the hsopital's doctors prescribe, but cannot provide themselves. Soviet hospitals are irregularly supplied with medicines, especially modern drugs. The newest antibiotics and miracle drugs are generally not available, except in the special hospitals for high officials.

Valentin Alexandrovich spent more than a month on the bed in the hospital hallway, but he didn't die. He went home with his son, regained his appetite and started to go out for walks.

Most old people do die at home. Even a victim of lung cancer will stay in his own bed at the end, attended by a doctor who comes every day to give him an injection. (Soviet doctors still believe in house calls.) For the rest of the family it is a difficult experience, but the patient must be grateful for these last days at home.

When Ivan Mikhailovich finally died of cancer, his daughter called the hospital and asked what to do. She was told that a doctor must certify the death; the hospital gave her another number to call. Two hours later the inspector arrived to record the details of Ivan Mikhailovich's passing. (These inspectors sometimes ask whoever is living with the deceased to present their documents, part of the authorities' continuing campaign to uncover people who are living in Moscow without proper registration. That didn't happen in this case, however.) When the inspector left, the daughter called the morgue, which promised to send someone for the body before the end of the day. The children were afraid to stay home with the corpse, so they were sent to an uncle's.

A friend had given the daughter the telephone number of the state agency that helps arrange funerals. She called and asked what services it provided. "Come and see us in person, we don't do business on the telephone," a woman on the other end replied sharply.

The daughter then called the new municipal crematorium, which she hoped would cremate her father's remains. It is located in a small village just beyond the circular highway that marks Moscow's outer limit, and its telephone is on a village switchboard. She couldn't get through all morning. Finally she asked the village switchboard operator how to get from the city to the crematorium. "How do _I_ know? Is that my job, to give directions?" The operator hung up.

Toward evening two men from the morgue came to take Ivan Mikhailovich's body away. The next day his daughter was able to make arrangements for a funeral by traveling from one office to another. She had to get a certificate of death from the neighborhood registry office. For a 10-ruble tip the men at the morgue agreed to make the body presentable for display in an open coffin. (Some people do this themselves at the morgue, to save money.)

Through a friend, and with the help of several more tips, she arranged for a bus to take the coffin and the mourners to the crematorium the following Saturday. They would have 30 minutes in one of the crematorium's chapels for a farewell ceremony. The family would have to organize this themselves.

The new crematorium, the only one serving the capital, sits in a field on the outskirts of the city, a serene box of white marble. In the parking lot outside, groups of mourners huddle around the buses that brought them and the corpses of their deceased friends or relations. They are waiting for their turn in one of the three chapels, talking quietly among themselves, sometimes comforting a crying wife or daughter. The parking lot and the sidewalk in front of the crematorium are lined with wreaths from earlier funerals, some as big as a man, some made of plastic flowers, many of them wilting and falling apart.

Finally a man in a work smock comes up to the bus and says, "It's your turn now." The pallbearers lift the coffin out of the bus and carry it 20 yards to a door in the marble façade. There they set it on a kind of pushcart which is rolled into the chapel. This is a high-ceilinged room about 40 feet square, carpeted and furnished in a modern style rarely seen in Russia. The far wall is all glass, and looks out onto an open field. The coffin is rolled up to an altar-like platform near the big window, then slid onto it. Then it is common to remove the top of the coffin for a last look.

There is no lectern and no leader of the "service." Several people may stand on a chair to deliver brief orations. Mournful music is piped into the room. It seems to be a custom for the womenfolk to weep and wail loudly. The atmosphere in this strange setting, reminiscent of the ballroom of a big American motel, seems to intimidate the average Muscovite, who isn't used to such things. Many of the people look self-conscious and eager to leave.

After 30 minutes an employee of the crematorium, a young woman, enters the chapel and makes a short speech. She announces that "Ivanov, Igor Valentinovich" has ended his life, and that "the Motherland is burying its son." Another woman, dressed in a black smock, nails the top back onto the coffin. Somewhere a button is pushed, and the true function of the altar on which the coffin sits is revealed. It is a trap door, which opens, and the coffin gently disappears from view. Several days later the widow or a child can return to pick up an urn full of ashes

On the way out of the chapel the eye is caught by a brightly painted sign: FOR BURIAL OF URNS WITH ASHES, THE MANAGEMENT SUGGESTS A NICHE OR A PLOT IN THE CEMETERY.

A niche is a recess, about 18 inches square, in a specially built wall which accommodates row upon row of urns with ashes. The urn goes into the recess and is covered with a stone plaque that can be suitably inscribed. These walls, about 20 yards long, are going up one after another in the fields around the crematorium. They look like miniature versions of the new housing developments in which more and more Soviet citizens live.

Fewer families choose burial, which is more expensive and more complicated. But religious families do. At the Nikolo-Archangelskoe cemetery next to the crematorium, grave after grave is marked with the distinctive cross of the Russian Orthodox Church.

The cemetery is in dilapidated condition. The asphalt walkways are cracked and crumbling. Maintenance of the graves and the shrubs that grow around them is left entirely to the families of the dead. Many of the graves are marked with crudely painted wooden signs.

I was walking around the cemetery one April afternoon when a middle-aged man approached and asked if I had a relative buried there. "I'd happily take care of the grave for you, only a few rubles a month," he said. "Look there, that nice grave, that's one of mine . . ." He pointed to one of the small plots, about six feet square, surrounded by a metal fence, like most of them. This one was neat and trim, however; it stood out from its neighbors. "Would you like me to do that for you, just a few rubles a month?"

3 . The System: USSR, Inc.

DURING THE EARLY negotiations between the Soviet Union and the United States on control of strategic weapons, the American negotiators made a curious discovery. When they initiated a discussion of the Soviet Union's missiles and weapons, the Americans found that they knew more about them than some of the Russians. The civilians in the Soviet delegation, including a Deputy Foreign Minister, did not know details of their own country's strategic weaponry. The military men, however, were well informed. One day the senior military officer on the Soviet delegation, Colonel General Nikolai V. Ogarkov, took an American delegate aside and reproached him: there was no reason, the General said, for the Americans to reveal their knowledge of Soviet military matters to the civilian members of his delegation. That sort of information, the General said, was strictly the military's business.*

I know of no better introduction to the Soviet system than that anecdote. Like the rest of us, the Russians have govern-

---

* This story is taken from *Cold Dawn*, by John Newhouse (New York, 1973).

ment, politics and bureaucracy, but their system is hardly familiar.

The Soviet system is "totalitarian"—in the words of the *Oxford Dictionary*, it permits "no rival loyalties or parties." The Communist Party has a monopoly on political power and political wisdom. The entire society is dominated by the capital, Moscow, the center of a vast bureaucratic apparatus, all of whose elements are subordinate to the Politburo of the Party. All ideas in the USSR must be tested against an official ideology; any idea thought to contradict the ideology is unacceptable. An enormous police force, much of it operating secretly, enforces the decisions made in Moscow.

All that is indisputably true, but it is not enough. In Russia things are often not what they seem. Soon after I moved to Moscow I attended a performance of Gogol's comedy *The Inspector General* at the old Moscow Art Theater. The audience was composed almost entirely of schoolchildren of twelve or thirteen who had been brought by their Russian Literature teachers. When the curtain rose the young spectators began to whisper excitedly to each other. In the first five minutes of the play I could hear teachers in various parts of the theater ordering their charges to keep still, but the effect of these warnings was fleeting; the buzz quickly resumed. Within about 10 minutes the teachers had given up, and the rest of the performance was accompanied by a steady hum from the auditorium. The children of this totalitarian society seemed unintimidated by the authority that was meant to control them. (Some of the actors were so annoyed by the competition that they made faces at the audience while taking their curtain calls.)

Russian totalitarianism is often less than total. Neither state nor Party really tries to impose complete control on the entire country, or to impose the official ideology universally. The state permits the existence of organized religion, though the ideology ridicules it. Despite official adherence to "socialism," legal private enterprise flourishes; without it the Soviet public would not have enough to eat. In recent years citizens have even been able to organize protest demonstrations. A group of Jews conducted a sit-in in the offices of the Central Committee of the Communist Party, the most powerful institution in the country.

Many westerners have accepted George Orwell's image of totalitarian power, the bleak, remorseless, all-powerful state of 1984. In Orwell's vision the state and party allow no compromises. They control not only behavior, but even thoughts. Orwell invented "Thought Police" to enforce the official orthodoxy. His Big Brother sees everything; no infraction goes unpunished.

The Soviet Union hasn't turned out that way. There is more bumbling confusion, improvisation and luck involved in running the USSR than the traditional totalitarian image would allow. The country's rulers do not insist on limitless power in all things.

Their attitude toward the Orthodox Church suggests the limits of their ambitions. There is a huge and active Church in the atheist Soviet state. It maintains 12 monasteries and three seminaries for the training of priests, where about 750 young men pursue the four-year course leading to ordination. The state even helps restore many fine old churches, on the grounds that they are "architectural monuments." Churches are open throughout the country, about 45 of them in Moscow. In the past decade the Church has enjoyed a mild revival, particularly noticeable in Moscow and other large cities. Many young members of the intelligentsia have turned to the Church to find a spiritual haven or a link to the Russian past. Orthodoxy has become fashionable in some circles. Icons and other religious artifacts are in great demand.

All the same, as the Russians like to say, the Church is not really free. The state strictly forbids any form of organized religious instruction for children. It effectively prevents most of the brightest boys who apply for the priesthood from pursuing that vocation. (Probably a majority of the priests in training in the mid-1970s were farmers from rural villages.) The state restricts enrollment in the seminaries, insuring a national shortage of priests. In new industrial cities, some with populations of a million or more, no churches are permitted.

The Church is subject to the guidance of the State Council for Religious Affairs, which can overrule the Patriarch (the ruling bishop) or any Church authority on any issue, religious or secular. The council exacts huge "contributions" from the Church treasury for various worthy—and government-supported—causes,* and compels Church elders to lend

---

* These donations run into tens of millions of rubles, but the Church has enough left over to pay its priests relatively handsome salaries of several hundred rubles a month. The Church raises money by soliciting donations from the faithful.

their presence to state occasions, particularly large receptions in the Kremlin to which foreigners are invited. According to believers in Moscow, the hierarchy is riddled with agents and informers, especially the international section, which deals with foreigners. This so infuriated Alexander Solzhenitsyn (himself a believer) that he wrote an open letter to the Patriarch accusing the Church of betraying its own values. He called it "a church dictatorially ruled by atheists."

There was a hint of the true nature of Church-state relations one morning in May 1974 when a propaganda agency of the allegedly atheistic and revolutionary Soviet state arranged a press conference for American journalists to tell them that the Russian Orthodox Church was alive and prospering. The American department of the Novosti "press agency" (in fact a propaganda organization responsible for dealing with foreign news media) arranged the press conference with Metropolitan Yuvenalyi, a youngish priest with a pepper-and-salt beard who wears a cylindrical white hat decorated with a small cross of diamonds.

Metropolitan Yuvenalyi is the director of the Church's foreign department, thought to be controlled by the Committee for State Security, the KGB. His performance that day consisted of a ready grin and numerous reassurances. "The state does not interfere with the Church," he insisted. Another bishop with him told the journalists, "It is logical and normal that the demand for priests is greater than the supply available." The Metropolitan said the Church was publishing many new Bibles—80,000 of them in the last 20 years, or 4000 a year for 30 to 50 million believers. The man from Novosti nodded approvingly. One of the journalists lost a fraction of his temper and asked the Metropolitan how he could possibly say that there was no state interference in the Church when glaring examples of such interference were obvious to all. He replied with a lesson in the Russian character, a display of an old Russian technique for dealing with a difficult situation; he smiled, and asked the two bishops with him to answer the journalist's question. Both spoke at length without addressing the question at all.

But the Metropolitan did not duck the issue entirely. He spoke confidently of one fact: "The Church is not losing its flock." The number of believers is growing, he said, and he asked his visitors to "keep this in mind when you reach your own opinion about the Church."

At the end of the press conference the Metropolitan offered a special gift to each of his guests. It was a set of four long-playing records containing most of the liturgy of the Church, sung by a marvelous choir. The state record monopoly made the album, but it has never been sold to the public. It is a special edition, made for the Church to hand out on occasions like this one. Metropolitan Yuvenalyi had a set for everybody at the press conference, including the propagandist from Novosti, who seemed particularly pleased to receive the records.

As that strange press conference suggested, the Church still seems to hold some power over the Soviet authorites. This was true even in Stalin's time. In the 1930s he closed all the monasteries and seminaries, arrested many rural priests and otherwise harassed the Church, but in the terrifying days after the Nazi invasion in 1941 Stalin abruptly changed his attitude. Suddenly he needed the Church to support his desperate war for survival. He offered the Orthodox bishops an unprecedented peace offering, reopened eight seminaries and allowed a great revival of religion. The Church responded in kind and became Stalin's stanch ally on the home front.

Secure again in the late 1940s, Stalin turned on the Church once more in a bitter anti-religious campaign. Khrushchev also campaigned against religion. But neither of them could undo the effects of that brief wartime revival. A majority of the working clergy in the 1970s was trained during the war years.

Now the relationshiop between Church and state seems stable. The Church endures the state's interference, and the state endures the Church. This is hardly a solution to the basic challenge that the Church poses to the official ideology and the ultimate authority of the Communist Party, but it is a satisfactory arrangement nevertheless, because both sides can live with it. Party zealots argue that the Church is slowly withering away, that the clergy is getting old and cannot replace itself, that in a generation or so Orthodoxy will quietly die out. Though there is some concrete evidence to support such a theory, especially the aging of the clergy, it is also apparently true that more people are going to church now than 10 years ago. Baptisms continue, and young people continue to find something they need in the Church.

The authorities realize that religion still gets in the way of communism. Every Easter the Party mobilizes members of the Young Communist League to taunt and harass Christians going to church. It is an ugly scene, sometimes violent, but also apparently futile—an indication of the authorities' unwillingness to take the fierce coercive steps that would be necessary to really eliminate religion. The man who run the country are even older than the aging Orthodox clergy, and they do not plan to solve the religious question while they are in power. The status quo is quiet and apparently stable, which must be good enough for them.

The Soviet authorities reveal a similarly limited ambition in the new policy they have hit upon for coping with the non-Russian ethnic groups in their society—"nationalities policy," as they call it. Half the country's population is non-Russian, 25 percent non-Slav—that is, neither Russian, Ukrainians or Belorussians, the traditional ethnic components of the Russian population. Many of the non-Russian peoples are indifferent to Moscow's domination of their lives; many more are probably hostile to it, though quietly hostile.

The Russians who rule the country* have made practical compromises with the ethnic minorities to achieve broad control without abject subservience. The results of these compromises are inconsistencies—sometimes striking inconsistencies—in Soviet policies. The rules that apply in Russia itself are often bent or ignored in the other Soviet republics.

The Georgians have traditionally been allowed more private enterprise than others; the Baltic republics, Estonia, Latvia and Lithuania, have a higher standard of living; traditional customs of the Soviet Union's Asian peoples (Uzbeks, Kazaks, Azerbaijanis and others) have been indulged. Cultural and ideological controls are substantially weaker in many of the small republics. The Union of Artists in Estonia, for instance, openly recognizes abstract art, which is scorned in Russia. The Estonian theater in Tallinn, the republic's capital, has produced Edward Albee's *Who's Afraid of Virginia Woolf?*—a daring slice of the avante-garde by Moscow's standards, and one that has not appeared in the capital, or anywhere in the Russian republic. The Armenian Christian

---

* Stalin was a Georgian, but since his death the Russians have dominated the Party leadership. Even Stalin was a fierce Russian nationalist who showed no sympathy for the national ambitions of ethnic minorities.

Church prospers under a Patriarch who isn't even a Soviet citizen (he was born in Romania).

The flavor of life in these non-Russian republics is distinct. In Estonia, for instance, the atmosphere is German or Scandinavian; it strikes a westerner as part of *his* world, not Moscow's. In Tallinn, high television antennas rise above the roofs of the neatly arranged homes and apartment houses. They are aimed at Helsinki, 50 miles to the north across the Gulf of Finland. The Finnish and Estonian languages are so nearly identical that every Estonian understands Finnish. Thousands of Estonians in Tallinn spend their evenings watching Finnish television, which broadcasts western entertainment, including the most popular American television series, and news broadcasts with a western orientation. Moscow's official line has serious competition in Estonia.

Estonia (like Latvia and Lithuania) was forcibly absorbed into the Soviet Union in the summer of 1940, when Stalin secured his Baltic flank. Before that the Estonians had 21 years of genuine independence, a consequence of the Versailles Treaty and the only period of independence in Estonia's long history. Stalin sought to bring the country abruptly into his domain, and to that end forcibly relocated perhaps 100,000 Estonians to Siberia. Many died there; the rest have now returned. Estonia is still very Estonian.

Its special character is visible. Unlike the look-alike towns and cities of Russia, Tallinn has a real personality. It suggests the atmosphere that interior decorators have in mind when they design restaurants called "The Hofbrau House." Tallinn is one of the old Hanseatic trading towns, dominated for generations by German merchants, and still looking much as it did in the 15th century. The old town, now carefully preserved, rises on a steep hill. Its narrow, winding streets are still paved with rough cobblestones. Thin church spires slice the sky. Romantic courtyards snuggle behind stone arches.

Newer sections of the city have not escaped the stamp of Soviet architecture. The traditional prefabricated apartments appear in Tallinn, too. But they are laid out in a more orderly pattern, and the yards are attractively landscaped with grass and shrubbery, something rarely seen in Russia.

The Estonians' independent spirit is also something a visitor can sense. It appears in simple encounters. Speaking Russian, I ordered a pastry in a café. An Estonian girl behind the counter refused to respond to my request, and said in heavily accented Russian, "You ought to know the language of the place you live in." She apparently took me for a Russian, and she wasn't friendly. A young actor from Moscow who spoke English found he was received more cordially in Tallinn when using that language rather than his native Russian.

Disregarding the standards of their Russian neighbors, Estonia's farmers are efficient—as efficient as Scandinavians, according to comparative statistics. A Russian engineer working in Estonia said the Estonians have a respect for "quality" in their work that was new to him. The Estonians are rewarded with a higher standard of living. Their shops are better stocked than those in comparable Russian cities, and the food supply is said to be better even than Moscow's.

Estonian intellectuals have found numerous ways to protect their culture and language. More books are being published in Estonian now than when the country was briefly independent. The local intelligentsia seems disinclined to master Russian, and most speak it ungrammatically, with a heavy accent. With official blessing, the Estonians are introducing their children to traditional cultural values through huge festivals of folk songs and literature.

This sort of cultural autonomy should not be confused with real political power, which the Estonians do not have. They are used to foreign domination: they've been controlled at various times by Danes, Swedes, Germans and Russians. Their latest master is perhaps the most demanding they have ever known, but they have made a kind of peace with him. At least they know where they stand. "We used to have many enemies," one Estonian told a friend from Hungary, with whom he had shared theories on how to cope with the Russians. "Now we have only one."

The authorities are unable to control the populations of other outlying republics with anything resembling the discipline that prevails in the Russian republic. This is publicly admitted, which probably means the problem is far worse than it appears. In the Soviet Union, dirty linen is exhibited in public only in the most extreme circumstances.

In recent years the First Secretaries of the Communist Parties in the republics of Azerbaijan, Georgia and Armenia have all been remarkably candid about their failure to impose Party or state authority. These are southern republics, all bordering on Turkey, and life there has always been more relaxed than in the Russian north. Georgians are known throughout the Soviet Union as a high-living breed. Their mountainous little land must be the only place in the world where, if one orders wine with dinner in a restaurant, the waiter first asks what kind, and then "How many bottles?" Socialism seems never to have taken firm root in Georgia, where money talks too loudly to suit proper communists.

Azerbaijan adjoins Georgia, but is separated by an entire culture. It is a Moslem land, once united with a province of Iran, but long under Russian control. The corruption typical of the Moslem world thrives in Azerbaijan still, despite numerous campaigns against it. In Baku, the hilly and attractive capital on the Caspian Sea, I asked the conductor on a trolley bus for four tickets—a 16-kopek purchase. Thanks to my accent and my clothes, the conductor quickly realized that I was a foreigner. He accepted the 16 kopeks and moved down the aisle without handing over the tickets he is supposed to give to every paying passenger. Thus the conductor pocketed 16 kopeks, and the state lost a little of its just revenues.

Since 1969 the campaign against corruption in Azerbaijan has been the responsibility of G. A. Aliyev, once the chairman of the republic KGB and then First Secretary of the republic Communist Party. Mr. Aliyev's rhetoric is startling:

"Some Party members misuse their official positions and take advantage of Party membership for mercenary purposes, plunder socialist property, accept bribes and carry on in other ways incompatible with membership in Lenin's Party. . . . We are talking about acts that occur before the very eyes of our people. . . . One reason for bribery is the striving for private property, the basis of which is individualism, selfishness, worrying only about one's own benefit and the wish to get as much as possible for oneself and less for society."

In public speeches Mr. Aliyev has lambasted citizens who acquired scientific degrees by buying their dissertations and school administrators who gave gold medals for scholarship to their own children. He has acknowledged that among "some communists, including leading workers and representatives of the intelligentsia, the struggle for atheism has weakened." He named Dr. Zulfugarli, a member of the Azerbaijani Academy of Sciences, and Moussa Mirzoyev, a composer, who "visited [Moslem] mosques in order to give them financial gifts."

I met a taxi driver in Baku in the usual way that travelers meet taxi drivers, but when he discovered that he was carrying American passengers he immediately invited the four of us to his home. It was a one-story box of stone and stucco that he and his cousin had built several years earlier in an unkempt suburb of the city. They had both married since and divided the house in half. Ahkmet, the driver, and his young bride, who hid herself in the background in the manner of Moslem women, had two rooms, four chairs, a brass-plated bedstead, a short-wave radio and a record player which emitted the wavering wail of Middle Eastern music that is so popular in Azerbaijan. It took a bribe of 500 rubles to get permission to build this bungalow, Ahkmet explained. It would have taken as much again to get his job—desirable because it allowed for a high degree of independence and provided a good income—had it not been for a well-placed friend at the taxi park who got him hired. Ahkmet thought the high-rise apartment houses going up all around Baku were "beautiful," but he had no hope of living in one. That would also require a big payoff, he explained. Why not just put his name on the official waiting list? He grinned: Yes, and then wait 20 or 30 years.

Apparently, the Georgians have been living even further outside the norms of Soviet society. Their new leader, a police official before he was named First Secretary of the Party, is more outspoken than Mr. Aliyev, and the transgressions he has exposed seem a good deal more serious.

The juiciest case was that of Otari Lazeishvili, sentenced in 1973 to 15 years in prison for a fantastic combination of transgressions. Formally he was accused of embezzling about a million rubles in state funds, but wise Georgians said an accurate figure would have been many times greater. Lazeishvili and nearly 100 collaborators had established a large network of underground factories and retail outlets, producing and selling consumer goods such as turtleneck sweaters and "wet-look" raincoats that were unavailable in the state stores. The profits from Lazeishvili's enterprises must have been stupendous. I was told by several trustworthy people that he was able to operate on such a large scale because he was in partnership with Mrs. Vasily Mzhavanadže, the wife of the previous First Secretary of Georgia's Communist Party, a man who sat in the highest body in the land, the Politburo of the Communist Party of the entire Soviet Union.

The Mzhavanadze affair was perhaps the biggest political scandal of modern times. He was dropped from the Politburo in 1972. Mzhavanadze was seventy at the time, and his departure was advertised as a routine passing of leadership from one generation to another. But his successor, Eduard Shevardnadze, quickly began arresting high officials (including a Deputy Minister of the Interior and perhaps others whose arrests were not publicized), lambasting Party functionaries and imposing new discipline, apparently to convince his fellow Georgians that things really would have to change. For example, he closed the borders of the republic to farmers who traditionally took the produce of their private plots to markets in large Russian cities, where prices were high. What was grown in Georgia, he said, should be eaten in Georgia.

Shevardnadze's techniques were radical, and a mythology quickly grew up around him. One night, it was said, he filled the trunk of a small car with tomatoes, dressed in the clothes of a peasant and drove himself toward Georgia's northern border with Russia. He bribed the border guards himself, the story goes, to let him pass with his load of tomatoes, in violation of the new First Secretary's explicit order. That episode supposedly led to a purge of the border patrol.

According to another anecdote, Shevardnadze was holding a meeting with leaders of the Georgian government and Party and asked for a vote. "But this time, comrades," he said, "let us vote with our left hands." When all the left hands were raised, Shevardnadze remarked that foreign wrist watches seemed to be popular among his colleagues. "Let's give up these expensive watches, take them off right now, and from now on let's wear reliable Soviet-made watches."

This story reached Moscow, where I heard it. Later I traveled to Georgia by plane and happened to sit next to a Georgian government official (he told me that's what he was, but declined to be more specific). He was gregarious, quick to laugh and delightful company, like so many Georgians. After we had talked for some time I noticed that his watch, a flashy new calendar model, was a Pilot, one of the best known Soviet brands. I told him the joke that was going around Moscow about Mr. Shevardnadze and foreign wrist watches. He grinned and nodded in what I took to be affirmation, then checked the time on his new Russian watch.

For all of his heroics, Shevardnadze failed to transform Georgia at a stroke. His failure has been publicly acknowledged. Nearly a year and a half after he became First Secretary, the Georgian Party issued a report which said:

> There are still cases of bribery, cheating, abuses of power and so forth. . . .Many Party organizations have tried to pretend that nothing extraordinary has happened [since Shevardnadze began his crackdown]. . . .One hundred enterprises have not fulfilled their plans. . . .Remnants of capitalism and tendencies toward private ownership have been restored in the Republic. . . .The Central Committee of the Communist Party of Georgia categorically demands the establishment of a Bolshevik order in every region and every city of the Republic. No mercy will be shown to anyone who dares ignore the instructions, demands and proclamations of the Party. No one will be indulged, regardless of age, rank or former merits.

Language of this kind is extraordinarily rare in public political dialogue in the Soviet Union. It can only mean that after three years in power Shevardnadze is still struggling unsucessfully with the stubornly lackadaisical Georgians.

The men who rule the USSR cannot rule with the ferocious efficiency of Orwell's Big Brother. They are forced to tolerate numerous deviations from the formal norms. This doesn't mean they are happy with local nationalism or deviant behavior, nor that they ignore such things. They are capable of ruthless repressions to try to reimpose discipline—these have occurred most recently in Lithuania and the Ukraine. But in other cases the authorities have been more tolerant. The important point is that the central authorities do not now have the power to impose consistent, reliable discipline throughout the country.

The Soviet system of administration and control is based on two bureaucratic structures, the government bureaucracy and the Communist Party apparatus. The first, recognizable to a westerner, is an organization of ministries, departments, committees and commissions that provide government services and oversee the state-owned economy. The Party apparatus is less familiar. It consists of a central bureaucracy in Moscow, miniature copies of that bureaucracy at every administrative level from village to province to autonomous republic, and an organized unit in virtually every insitution and enterprise in the country. There is a Party secretary and a Party organization in every school, every trolleycar garage, every factory, department store and hotel in the Soviet Union. Though the Party is not directly responsible for administering government, industry or agriculture, it is ultimately responsible for all of them, and the Party bureaucracy is usually more influential than the government's at every level. Officially the Party plays a "leading role" in virtually every aspect of Soviet life. The First Secretary of the Estonian Party runs Estonia; the chairman of the Estonian Council of Ministers helps him. The same is true in each province or *oblast*. The *oblast* Party committee (*obkom*) is the dominant political institution, and its First Secretary has the powers of a satrap.

The satrap is Moscow's agent in his territory, rather like a prefect in a province of Napoleon's France. His principal duty is to see that the inhabitants of his domain fulfill the obligations Moscow has established for them, and he enjoys wide discretion to accomplish this mission. Subject always to a last word from Moscow, the satrap enjoys a significant degree of independence. Local units are sufficiently autonomous that different *oblasts* and cities have distinct reputations for harder or softer Party lines. In Leningrad, for instance, intellectuals regard their Party as especially harsh and unforgiving of any individualistic expression. The university in Vladivostok in the Soviet far east can invite someone from Moscow to lecture who is not allowed to make public appearances in the capital because of his ideological unreliability.

The most influential body in Moscow is the *apparat* of the Party Central Committee's Secretariat. It is unlikely that any important policy can be changed without the acquiescence of the Secretariat, and most changes are probably initiated within its *apparat*, a staff of powerful officials working in 23 different departments, from culture and ideology to the chemical industry. The *apparat*, which reports to the elected secretaries of the Party (all of whom are full or candidate members of the Politburo), is probably more influential in the day-to-day governing of the country than the Central Committee itself.*

Relations between the state and Party bureaucracies are generally harmonious. During their careers, officials often move back and forth between Party and government posts. In recent years the men promoted to the highest posts in the Party have come from practical administrative backgrounds.

The supremacy of the Party is most explicit at the top. There is no question that the Politburo—the party's executive board—rules both bureaucracies. The point is made with unmistakable clarity each November 7 and May 1, the principal national holidays, when the portraits of Politburo members are posted in prominent places all over the country.

The pre-eminence of the Politburo means that in the Soviet Union state authority is subservient to the leaders of a political party. As a practical matter, state authority is *not* sovereign in the USSR. The sovereign state authority is a formal structure whose officials would never dream of taking any action not formally sanctioned by the Party. Nor would any other institution in the country.**

A group of young American politicians who toured the Soviet Union in 1973 was overwhelmed by the consequences of Party rule of every aspect of Soviet society. "This is like one big corporation," one of the Americans concluded, "USSR, Incorporated." It is a nice image.*** The Soviet System is more like a corporation than a government in our sense of the word, because it is responsible for *everything* within its domain. Laws, constitutions and—probably most important—cultural traditions constrain the powers of western governments. Only practical considerations limit the powers of the Soviet regime.

Practical considerations guide Moscow's nationalities policies and its attitude toward the Church. The country's leaders

---

* Officially the Central Committee is the governing body of the Party between national congresses, held every five years. In fact it usually meets only twice a year to ratify decisions already taken by the Secretariat and the Politburo. Nevertheless, the Central Committee's members are the country's most powerful individuals, and they can make their will known informally, and within the Party bureaucracy. The Committee has about 190 full members and 160 alternates.

** The KGB may be an exception to this generalization. The armed forces are probably not an exception to it.

*** Alfred Meyer, an American scholar, used the "USSR, Inc." phrase in 1961.

evidently prefer the status quo to the disruption and difficulty that would be caused by a serious attempt to change it. But one reason the status quo is acceptable, surely, is that Moscow does control the outlying republics and the Church, too. The methods used to maintain this control are indirect and may appear ambivalent, but they work.

Moscow's most useful tool for controlling the republics is its economic system. Because the economy is centrally planned, the center can impose a division of labor on the republics which insures tight interdependence with other parts of the country. Thus, for example, Uzbekistan in Central Asia is compelled to produce an enormous cotton crop each year; the Uzbek Republic provides more than half the country's cotton. The Plan demands this level of production. The Plan has the force of law, and is drawn up in Moscow. Uzbek officials know that their republic would be wealthier if they could grow more fruits and vegetables and less cotton, and the population might be healthier if they raised more livestock for local meat consumption, but Moscow requires the cotton. (Moscow also determines the price that will be paid for it.) On the other hand, Uzbekistan depends on Russia and the other republics for numerous manufactured goods and raw materials for its own industries. This pattern is repeated throughout the country.

A second technique at Moscow's disposal is the imposition of ethnic Russian domination of the republics, which has been largely successful. Nearly a third of Estonia's 1.2 million people are Russians or Ukrainians. Every republic has a significant Russian population, and it is probably growing in all of them (though perhaps not proportionately, since the birthrates of ethnic minorities are usually higher than the Russians'). Armenia is one exception: its population is just three percent Russian.

The central authorities use economic development as a means of drawing Russians into the republics. In Estonia, for example, surplus labor was long ago exhausted. If Moscow orders the construction of a new factory in Estonia, it must also supply workers from Russia or the Ukraine to man it. The Estonians realize this, and now oppose further industrialization, but they do not have the last word.

Qualitative Russification is more easily imposed than the mass movement of population. Though it has been traditional for the First Secretary of a Communist Party to be of the local nationality, the Second Secretary is almost always a Russian. The Second republic's Secretary is responsible for "cadre," which means he decides who gets what jobs in the Party apparatus throughout the republic, an extremely powerful role. Often the Second Secretary doesn't even speak the language of the republic in which he serves. Judging by my conversations with numerous present and former residents of the ethnic republics, the locals assume that the Second Secretary has an independent relationship with Party authorities in Moscow, and that in a pinch he may prove to be more influential than the First Secretary.

The Second Secretaries are not the only Russians imposed on local bureaucracies. The chairman of each republic's branch of the KGB is appointed directly from Moscow, and is often a Russian. In Central Asia it is common for Russians to serve as deputies to the local directors of all kinds of enterprises.

It is an official point of pride in the USSR that Soviet power protects and encourages local culture, particularly language. The authorities publish books and newspapers in local tongues, make movies in them, broadcast on television and radio in them. But there is a catch. Official policy often discourages *traditional* culture at the same time that it encourages *local* culture. For example, the Tadzhik language was traditionally written in the Persian alphabet, but in the 1920s it was transcribed into the Russians' Cyrillic. Young Tadzhiks cannot read the classics of their national literature unless they've been "translated" into the Cyrillic alphabet, and some have not been. The same young Tadzhiks are taught in school that their own history was meager indeed, and that it was only because of the brotherly help of the great Russian people that their country amounted to anything.

Moscow's representatives in the republics follow a hard line on the basic issue of local independence versus central (i.e., Russian) control. Local scholars, writers, movie directors and the like are cautioned repeatedly, by explicit warning and threatening example, never to question the legitimacy or justice of Moscow's rule.

By chance I met a young writer from Tadzhikistan who told the following story: In 1967 a Tadzhik literary critic wrote a letter to the local newspaper suggesting that it wasn't necessary to paint the signs on stores and public buildings in both the Tadzhik and Russian languages. Since Tadzhik is written in Cyrillic, why not just leave the local name, he wondered, and save some effort?

The Second Secretary of the Tadzhik Party—the Russian secretary, "who of course has his network of agents reporting to him," according to the writer I met—interpreted this letter as an anti-Russian declaration by the newspaper (printed in the Tadzhik language) which published it. The Party fired the editor of the paper and deprived him of his official posts, including his seat in the republican parliament and on the Party's Central Committee. He lost access to the government clinic for high officials, and the special store for important people. His car was taken away. Some Party officials even wanted to move him out of his apartment, but that idea was dropped because he had a big family of six or seven people.

Not everyone on the Tadzhik Central Committee endorsed this punishment, according to the writer, who seemed to be in a position to know such things. Several Party officials privately supported the editor, but they could not do so openly. After a brief interval the editor's supporters got him a job in the local publishing house, simply to give him an income. But the Russian Second Secretary heard about this, and ordered that he be fired again. Books are a branch of the press, he said, and the editor might try another of his anti-Russian tricks at the publishing house. Finally his friends got him a job on the editorial board of the Tadzhik encyclopedia, which the Russian apparently accepted.

The Politburo manages Soviet society through immense bureaucracies. Bureaucracy in the Soviet Union shares the characteristics of bureaucracy everywhere: it is conservative, ponderous, self-interested and inefficient. But it is also Russian, which means that it has a number of special characteristics.

Like Russian life for centuries past, Soviet bureaucracy is pervaded by mistrust and suspicion. Mistrust is part of the national character now, an intutitive reflex, conditioned over centuries by rapacious rulers and a social order which has never discouraged scheming and exploitation oy some at the expense of others. Russians have learned to look over their shoulders, to protect their own interests first.

Leo Tolstoi was driven to distraction by his serfs when he tried to free them voluntarily in 1856. When Tolstoi announced his plans to give them land, the serfs decided it was a trick and refused to accept. Later he tired to organize a school for peasant children in his home at Yasnaya Polyana; the rumor spread through the village that the master wanted to educate the young men so he could sell them to the czar as foot soldiers. Andrei Amalrik found irrational suspiciousness in Guryevka, his village in Siberia. When he proposed a new method of doing some job on the collective farm, the peasants rejected it out of hand, despite its compelling good sense.

These ancient reflexes operate at the highest level of the Soviet regime. Leonid Brezhnev once described the petty selfishness of state officials as "the bureaucratic style," which he defined as "the disregard of state and nationwide interests for the sake of departmental and parochial interests."

A Soviet bureaucrat—I know this from extensive personal experience—thinks nothing of making a commitment to do something for someone outside his organization when in fact he has no intention of ever keeping his word. Arkadi Raikin's comedy troupe does a routine about this: the officials of a factory in a provincial city receive an order from Moscow for a product they cannot make. Rather than admit this, they reply that the order will be filled, then forget all about it. When the agency issuing the order asks for it repeatedly, the factory's officials begin to dissemble in their answers, in obvious hope that the whole bothersome matter will disappear.

An American doctor who visited several medical institutes in Moscow expressed surprise at the way they hid information from each other that might have been mutually helpful. He learned that at the only institute in Moscow which performs organ transplants the kidney-transplant program was hampered by a chronic shortage of kidneys. (These are best removed from bodies immediately after death and transplanted within a few hours.) In another part of Moscow the American visited an institute which daily disposed of numerous fresh corpses, kidneys and all. Did this institute know about the kidney shortage at the other one? When the American asked, he got a shrug in reply.

Mistrust is now built into the system. In industry, for example, the director of a large enterprise cannot appoint his own chief engineer, assistant director, chief accountant, chief of staff or secretary of the factory's Party committee. Higher authorities appoint these officials independently, and often encourage them to compete with one another and report on each other's shortcomings. A similar motive is at work in the Party apparatus. For instance, in the republic's Party organizations the Russian Second Secretary is meant to keep an eye on his colleagues.

A second distinctive feature of Soviet bureaucracy is its instinctive distrust of individual initiative. Marxism-Leninism and Russian traditions both value collective behavior above individual accomplishment. Olga Korbut, the young Soviet gymnast, became a heroine in America, but at home she was publicly reprimanded for taking an individualistic approach to her sport. Emphasis on the collective approach to all problems reinforces the normal bureaucratic tendencies toward caution. There is no incentive to risk-taking in Soviet life. The big gamble for a big payoff is unheard of.

The best way to get ahead is to plod ahead—no surprises, no initiatives that might make a superior nervous. A frustrated Soviet biologist once told me that the system itself weeds out the best people—and also the worst. Promotion goes to the steady, the reliable, the undistinctive. After many years during which this rule has prevailed, it is the reliable, steady and undistinctive people who are running the country and most of its institutions. The influential members of Soviet society now have a stake in maintaining the inertia.

Among much else, this means reducing the rules for success and promotion to clear and unmistakable formulas. A chemist from Kiev, the capital of the Soviet Ukraine, explained what this means in terms of the Ukrainian Academy of Sciences:

"In Kiev, members of the [Ukrainian] academy are chosen because they hold certain posts. It is virtually impossible for an ordinary scientist to be voted into the academy. Members must be the directors of institutes, or perhaps assistant directors, something of that kind. And they don't make you director of an institute because you're a brilliant scientist. To receive one of these top jobs you have to be in the good graces of somebody important. And once you get the job, then you become a member of the academy. . . . So the academy consists of a lot of people whose scientific credentials are low, and, not surprisingly, they bring in more people like themselves."

Rather than do something outstanding and be rewarded for it, Soviet bureaucrats, it seems, prefer to avoid doing something unusual for which they might be punished or remembered. An engineer I met described his experience in Angarsk, in Siberia, where he worked in a large factory:

"They had a monster crane that could lift enormous weights, but they couldn't find the right kind of steel to build the tracks on which this crane was supposed to move. There were all kinds of high officials on the scene, but no one would take responsibility for deciding to substitute some other kind of steel for the one that was recommended—which they didn't have. Finally I said the hell with it, *I* would sign the order—not that I had any authority to do it. But they were all delighted to have somebody take the responsibility. I signed it and we went ahead and built the rails with the substitute steel. That's the system—everybody's afraid. And the higher they go, the more they have to fear."

By now this must sound like a foolish way to run a railroad—which leads to a final distinctive feature of the Soviet bureaucracy. Our standard of how to run a railroad, or anything else, is relatively clear: does it work efficiently, make a profit, please its customers? In the Soviet Union these three questions are seldom asked.

Efficiency is a relative notion. In a western economy, where the prices of most things are determined by a relatively free market, we measure efficiency in terms of cost, but the Russians can't do that. Thir prices are set arbitrarily; the value of products, labor and time is literally immeasurable, except in the vaguest, most general sense. The goal in Soviet society is to fulfill the objective. If the railroad completes its daily runs, that's enough. If the Ministry of Education keeps the schools open, and the schools produce the specialists that are needed, and the specialists keep the railroads running, then everyone is happy.

Except, perhaps, the ordinary citizen. But his preferences are seldom directly influential. As a general rule, the Soviet bureaucracy answers to *itself*, not to its public. This is an inevitable consequence of a political system in which wisdom is assumed to come from above, not from below. It is an unshakable assumption in Soviet life that the leadership knows best, so it is important only to please the leadership. On a practical level, a bureaucrat knows he can probably insult the people he deals with, provided he is pleasing his own boss. Sometimes the bosses are displeased by employees' rudeness, but this seems rare. If it were more common, Soviet bureaucrats would be a great deal more polite than they are.

Lenin recognized the dangers of an unresponsive centralized bureaucracy, and he insisted on "openness" to counteract them. He hoped the officials of the new Soviet state would take their revolutionary responsibilities seriously. When cases of arbitrary behavior by state or Party officials came to his attention, Lenin sometimes ordered that they be fired or even imprisoned.

Lenin believed in strong leadership, but the current leaders of the country do not. Their overriding interest in stability has persuaded them to diffuse leadership, and thus responsibility, so widely that it virtually disappears. I knew a wise old man in Moscow who looked on his country's history with a bemused skepticism. "In the beginning," he used to say, "we had democratic centralism," Lenin's strong leadership based on a tightly knit group of Party leaders. "Then we had bureaucratic centralism," a metaphor for the system that Stalin created in the 1930s, when a burgeoning bureaucracy administered a true revolution in the life of the country. "And now we have bureaucratic decentralism," he would say, grinning at the ungrammatical accuracy of his own observation.

"Bureaucratic decentralism" is a nice description of a political system whose leaders are happy to limit progress and efficiency for the sake of stability. Under stronger, more dynamic leaders, bureaucratic decentralism could quickly turn back into the strong, centralized rule of the Stalin era, but these leaders are content to rule by *managing*, accepting the status quo in most areas of society. The status quo is stable, so why change it?

The Soviet bureaucracy is not as foreign as it may sound—or so it seemed to me after I had spent several months in the USSR. The more I saw, the more I felt I had seen it already, in the United States Army. They are not identical, naturally, but the Army and the Soviet system have a surprising number of similar traits. Both demonstrate that behavior which an outsider considers silly if not irrational is perfectly acceptable to the participants in a closed bureaucratic system. Once one has enlisted in such a system, its rules of behavior are no longer open to question. Any challenge would be self-defeating for whoever posed it. The Russians call this Party loyalty; American Army officers call it staying on the team.*

---

* I use the Army, not the Navy or Air Force, as my example here only because I got to know it well during 18 months as a correspondent

By American standards, the Army is an unusual institution. We try to apply objective, or at least independent, criteria in judging most of our bureaucracies. The bureaucracy at General Motors, for instance, is judged not only by the cars and profits it produces, but also by the achievements of the bureaucracy at Ford. The bureaucracy at the Commerce Department must satisfy elected and appointed politicians, not merely officials from its own ranks. The Army is ultimately subject to civilian control, but this is felt only at the highest level. Generally it runs itself. And it cannot be judged by the customary criteria, because the Army's usual task is not to perform a function, but to be ready to perform a function. Readiness is intangible and unmeasurable.

The Army is an extremely conservative organization. Its officers know that staying out of trouble is more important than looking for ways to impress their superiors with originality or initiative. Soviet bureaucrats repeat endlessly, "That is not my responsibility." The equivalent expression in the Army is "Cover your ass"—make certain you can't be blamed if something goes wrong. The Army prizes loyalty and self-discipline, and encourages intellectual conformity. Promotion is based solely on the recommendations of superiors, and the criteria for advancement are clearly understood by all participants. Obsequiousness is common in the Army and endemic in the Soviet Union.

Reform alarms the Army establishment, which resists it successfully. It is now a cliché that the Army is always ready to refight the last war, but never prepared for the next one.

In the Army as in the USSR, performing "the mission," as our soldiers call it, is all-important. Goals are set with scant regard for how they may be achieved, and the institutions are left to achieve them as best they can. (In the Army's case, to be fair, the goals are usually set by civilian politicians.) The officer's duty is to perform the mission, not challenge it. If the mission has priority, draw resources from other missions to accomplish it. This is how the entire Soviet economy works. In the Soviet Union and in the U.S. Army this mentality produces a great many graphs, statistical tables, briefings and pieces of paper, all sharing a common self-congratulatory tone.

---

in Vietnam in 1969–70. No doubt the other services would serve equally well to illustrate this point.

Perhaps the most striking similarity is the way both institutions diffuse responsibility for the sake of individual protection and institutional survival. The Joint Chiefs of Staff, the senior officers of the three military services and a fourth senior officer who is their chairman, claim to reach decisions only by unanimous vote; so does the Politburo. The Army handled the embarrassment of the My Lai massacre in much the same way that the Russians coped with Stalin's crimes—a "thorough investigation," mild punishment for a few senior officers, severe punishment for some junior men, hints that the guiltiest parties had already died, and a speedy conclusion to the whole affair. The Soviet Communist Party tried to deal with its past by blaming a few dead comrades, making some adjustments to the official history of the country and rehabilitating the victims, a large percentage of them dead people. There are anti-Stalinists in the Soviet Union who still hope the Party will disown the dictator and punish his accomplices more systematically, but this is now unlikely. Similarly, General William R. Peers, who conducted the Army's internal investigation into My Lai, later expressed dismay that his colleagues failed to thoroughly face up to the My Lai aberration, which is how he thinks of it.

Several examples of how things work in the USSR may convey a flavor of the system that simple analysis and description cannot. Analysis always seems to distort Russian reality by reducing it to declarative sentences; anyone who has lived in Russia senses that declarative sentences simply don't take it all in.

Soviet hotels are required to keep extensive books and ledgers, financial figures for the planning and financial organs, records of who stayed where and when for the police and security organs. Within moments of checking into any hotel, a traveler's name is inscribed in at least one large ledger.

And yet if someone calls a hotel on the telephone and asks if a Mr. Ivanov is staying in the establishment, and if so, in what room, the answer will be (if it isn't an insult and a severed connection), "What day did he check in?" If the caller doesn't know, he won't get an answer. A Soviet hotel doesn't keep a daily list of its residents; it has only the ledger book which shows when someone checked in and, eventually, when he left. It occurred to me when I first discovered this in

Moscow that the switchboard operators in large hotels must have a difficult time handling calls for visitors. Then I learned that there are no switchboards in Soviet hotels, or almost anywhere else, for that matter. If a hotel room has its own telephone, that phone has its own outside line. The number is usually (though not always) unrelated to the room number—and there is no way to get a guest's number unless you know what day he checked in.

In Sochi the director of a large hotel told me about the great demand for rooms which could never be fully satisfied. I asked if a citizen anxious to stay in his hotel during the summer season could reserve a room in, say, January or February for the following July. "I don't know," the director replied, "but I wouldn't try it."

A crisis at the Institute of Natural Compounds in Moscow, described for me by a senior biologist, reveals what happens in a decentralized bureaucratic system when someone breaks the rules. Somehow the police learned that scientists in the institute, a branch of the Soviet Academy of Sciences, were making narcotics, apparently LSD (which was almost unheard of in Moscow). Perhaps an unhappy user had gone to the police. The director of the institute, a distinguished member of the academy, was away from Moscow when the police found one kilogram of LSD at his laboratories. One young scientist was arrested.

"It's a big scandal," my informant told me. "A report has been circulated to all chemical and biological institutes, where it has been read to scientific workers and discussed. Every institute has been instructed to take measures to prevent such events from recurring."

The scandal blossomed only because the institute's director was out of Moscow at the time—or so his friends and colleagues thought. They were distressed at his bad fortune. Had he been there, my informant said, he would have persuaded the police to stay out of the institute and let him handle the investigation as an internal matter. The police would have agreed because a member of the Academy of Sciences is a formidable figure. But not when he is out of town.

A Jew from Central Asia who once served as a minor functionary in the Party's Central Committee in his republic told me this story in America, where he is now living:

"There was one Secretary of an *oblast* Party Committee in our republic who was a true patriot. He knew that Marxism-

Leninism allows for criticism of anyone who does his job poorly, even the First Secretary of the Party. And he made some criticisms of the apparatus of the Central Committee in our republic. And what did they do? They proposed liquidating his *oblast* in order to get rid of him. 'We don't need that *oblast* any longer,' they said. Everyone knew what they were doing. For a long time after they did it, the old Secretary complained, and tried to get the decision reversed. But it never was."

It is time to muddy the waters. The preceding impressions of the Soviet bureaucracy are incomplete—true, I think, but misleading, because they leave out too much.

For example, if the bureaucracy often ignores the wishes of the people, a large section of the bureaucracy exists only to serve them. The Soviet Union is a welfare state. It provides cheap housing (though not yet enough to go around,) guaranteed employment, free education at all levels, free medical care, subsidized day care for infants and preschool children and pensions for the old and disabled. The system surrounds each Soviet citizen with a reassuring security blanket. It doesn't dispel all anxieties, obviously, but Russians need not fear the financial consequences of a serious illness, the cost of putting a child through school or the possibility of unemployment. The state tires to remove uncertainty from life, to insure stability of the basic elements of everyday existence.

When first encountered, the benefits of the welfare state are impressive. I first arrived in the Soviet Union by way of Siberia, and took the train across the country to Moscow, stopping at the rare "open" cities (that is, cities which foreigners may visit) along the way. My Intourist guides took me to see or visit a succession of kindergartens, clinics, schools and colleges, all of which made a favorable impression. I particularly remember a clinic in Khabarovsk, an industrial city near the Chinese border. The clinic was a two-story building serving a scruffy neighborhood in a generally unkempt city. Its exterior was the gloomy gray brick of the neighborhood, but inside the clinic was bright white, as clean as a compulsive housewife's kitchen counters. It was Saturday afternoon, and the clinic was closed, but my guide was able to show me around. The facilities were functional, neat and attractive.

What I missed then, and only realized slowly during the three years I spent in Russia, was that the welfare state is not outside the rest of the Soviet system; it is perhaps the most admirable part, but still very much a part of the whole.

Medical service is at the heart of the Soviet welfare state, and a description of the way it works may explain what I mean. The state has committed itself to provide free medical care, so it provides free medical care. The task is fulfilled. The government builds hospitals and clinics, even in rural communities. It trains more doctors than any other country in the world, and assigns them to work where they are needed, not where they might like to practice. The Soviet system has brought medical care to the masses, but on its own terms.

I met a doctor from Moscow whose reputation among his friends was almost idyllic. He was, they said, one of those rare doctors who care for everyone, who really try to help whomever they can. He had given up on his life in Russia and emigrated with his Jewish wife to Rome, where I met him. I asked him what work in a Moscow clinic was like.

"Say 50 people show up for office hours at a neighborhood clinic. One doctor will handle them all. He or she will have five hours to see them. That's about six minutes per patient. And the patient must undress and dress, he has to tell the doctor what's bothering him, the doctor has to prescribe something and fill out the patient's 'hospital list' [a document certifying his illness, which excuses the patient from work]. In other words, the time available is simply insufficient.

"And if there is such a thing as a good, serious doctor who thinks about the patients and cares about them, . . . who gives a patient 20 or 30 minutes of undivided attention, then there will be long lines. People will start complaining to the head doctor, and the head doctor will bawl out this physician who is holding everyone up. In other words, in a typical clinic a good doctor is simply unwanted.

"And a patient can't choose his doctor. In a neighborhood clinic one physician is assigned to treat all the residents of one apartment house—you can't get out of this arrangement. . . ."

And yet I knew people in Moscow who received fine care through the state system. Inconsistency seems common, even typical. One day I visited an elderly friend in Moscow, a woman with heart trouble, who announced that during the previous night she had survived the worst and the best of Soviet medical care, all within a few hours. After going to bed she had felt a sudden sharp pain in her chest and feared a heart attack. She telephoned the ambulance service, which claims it has special "trauma" teams on duty around the clock to treat cardiac emergencies in the home. The voice on the phone promised that someone would come at once, but nothing happened. A second call elicited a second promise, but produced no doctor. Finally she called a friend with a car, who drove her to the Bodkin Hospital nearby. The Bodkin is one of the capital's finest hospitals, and my acquaintance found the emergency room there nearly empty at midnight. "A brilliant young surgeon," in her words, gave her a thorough examination, some pills and a reassurance that she hadn't had a heart attack. Despite the hour, he was kind and thoughtful. "But not everybody has a friend with a car," she added. "And the ambulance never showed up."

The Soviet authorities put more emphasis on the extent of medical care than its quality. They train doctors in six years, without sending them first to an ordinary college, and put them to work right out of school. Some medical institutes have 10,000 students, which means the students cannot get the personalized instruction and experience that, for example, British and American schools provide. The result is doctors with less formal training, but, as the Russians like to point out, a doctor's real training comes on the job.

When it is time for the workers at a factory to receive a "physical examination," hundreds of them line up at once. A doctor will pass down the line, glancing at each, and ask if anyone has a complaint. More serious preventive medicine, except for children, is almost unheard of. There has never been a serious campaign against smoking in the Soviet Union (a nation of heavy smokers).

Dentistry is simple and relies heavily on extraction; stainless-steel teeth shine in a large percentage of the nation's smiles. Only later did I realize the significance of the dental facility I saw at my first clinic in Khabarovsk. It consisted of a small office "for repair work" and a second room several times larger "for extractions." A handsome set of white, healthy teeth is a rare sight in Russia.

Medical service is run on an austere budget. Doctors are poorly paid—90 to 100 rubles a month for a physician just out of a medical institute. Nurses and lower grades of medical workers earn less, and much less than workers in other sectors of the economy. "We are expected to work for the love of the profession and mankind," one woman doctor told me. Most doctors are women, no doubt in part because men look for better-paying careers. This also creates problems, as the doctor I met in Rome explained: "What is a doctor thinking about while examining patients: Often about what she has to buy on the way home, and where she might find that product. You know, many doctors think the best kind of patient is a sales clerk from a shop, someone who can help the doctor buy something useful."

There is an enormous black market in medicine, though it isn't readily visible to an outsider. Of the intellectuals I knew in Moscow, none relied on the state health system. All had friends, relatives, connections of some kind through whom they got personalized care. Some of these relationships are based on friendship, others on the outright payment of money or gifts. The doctor I met in Rome said the hypocritical attitude toward money and bribes in medicine helped convince him to emigrate:

"Because doctors are so poorly paid, they try to find alternative sources of income. This leads to a whole series of ugly and unpleasant complications in their relations with patients. The doctor wants to get some extra money, but since this is illegal, the whole business takes on the character of some kind of black-marketeering.

"For instance, you have to have an operation, and you know that ordinarily it would be a three-week business—first tests, then the operation, then recuperation. But you want to get it over with quickly, so you make a deal with the doctor, and both of you get what you want. But this is offensive to both parties. It's dishonest, unpleasant. And it complicates relations among doctors. You hear complaints—'So-and-so took too much, So-and-so didn't take enough,' and so on. . ."

The amount of hospital space available does not satisfy the demand, and overcrowding is not unusual. I realized this after seeing a movie made in Soviet Georgia which included scenes of a hospital whose patients had to sleep in the hallways—an unusual acknowledgment of inadequacy in a movie passed by the state's censors. Later I asked a young surgeon what an overcrowded hospital was like.

"That's really something to see. Beds are jammed into corridors, sometimes so tightly that there is no room to pass through. Beds are put next to the elevators, next to the dining rooms. I remember one case when a nurse couldn't find a place for a patient anywhere, and ended up putting him on two tables in the dining room that she pulled together. The next morning other patients came in for breakfast, saw this makeshift arrangement and refused to eat. It was a big scandal. A commission came to investigate it."

A foreigner living in Russia soon learns that medicines are in short supply. Russians in need of a drug turn to foreign acquaintances for help. I was asked for a dozen or more drugs, from the latest antibiotics to basic preparations, including antacid for an ulcer patient. Russians turn to foreigners because foreign medicines have an exotic reputation in their world: if it is Hungarian or—the best one can hope for—French, it *must* be more effective. The Russians don't produce many of the new "miracle" drugs, and make only small quantities of many others. I heard of several cases in which doctors told relatives that a patient could be saved only with a type of medication that the doctor could not obtain. One doctor told a worried daughter how to look on the black market for a medicine her father needed.

The welfare state inevitably assumes the character of the entire system. The story that demonstrated this to me most clearly was the history of an official campaign against rheumatism, recounted by the same professor of pediatrics:

"About eight years ago it was suddenly discovered that rheumatism was five or six times more common in Russia than in England. How was this possible? England, with its fog, damp weather and poorly heated buildings, *had* to have a higher rate of rheumatism, and always did. At one point rheumatism was known·as 'the English disease.' What had happened?

"What had happened was that they had created so-called rheumatism centers in the big cities of the Soviet Union. The doctors working in these centers were told that the number of service personnel they would have—nurses and so on—would depend on the number of patients that came to see them. If they had, say, 100 patients, they'd get one nurse; 200 patients, two nurses; and so on. So the statistics began to rise.

"If every doctor invented only two or three phony patients, on a nationwide scale, that becomes thousands of cases. And suddenly it became known that rheumatism in Russia was becoming very common. . . . There was an order from the Ministry of Health to recheck all the lists of patients and remove those which weren't confirmed cases of rheumatism. Commissions were sent out, they studied medical records and so on. . . ."

When Lenin died in 1924, his new revolutionary state was in disarray. The Bolsheviks had prevailed in a messy, difficult civil war and secured their power, but could not decide what to do with it. Lenin's last important idea had been the "New Economic Policy" or NEP (the acronym is the same in Russian), a limited revival of free enterprise intended to invigorate the devastated Russian economy. The Five Year Plans, the huge and centralized bureaucracy, the Communist Party's rigid monopoly on all ideas—the Russia that still survives—did not exist when Lenin died, and he never dreamed of them.

A joke about this is still being told in Moscow. It concerns the recent invention of an elixir that can restore the dead. The elixir is given to Felix Dzerzhinski, a Polish communist who was one of Lenin's stanchest allies and the first head of the political police Lenin formed after the Revolution. When Dzerzhinski comes to life and realizes what has happened, he says to himself, "If they've revived me, they must have revived Vladimir Ilyich [Lenin] as well. I must find him." He rushes to Lenin's tomb in Red Square, and finds that the glass-enclosed case in which the founder has lain for nearly 50 years is empty. A note in Lenin's unmistakable hand is stuck to the outside of the coffin: "To whom it may concern. I have looked around, and am leaving at once for Zurich [the place of his last exile prior to the Revolution in 1917]. We must begin all over again. Lenin."

For vaguely disaffected Russian intellectuals, that is a fine joke. It is also a telling commentary. There is no knowing what Lenin would make of the contemporary Soviet Union, but there is no doubt that he would be amazed by it. This isn't what his Revolution produced. It is the product of the dictatorship of Joseph Stalin, which lasted for 24 years.

Many scholars argue that Stalinism was a logical extension of Leninism, and perhaps it was. Had he lived, Lenin himself might eventually have adopted Stalin's harshest policies. But the fact is that Lenin died in 1924, when the Bolsheviks were still looking for ways to turn the backward country they inherited into an industrialized socialist state. When Stalin died in 1953, that process was well under way, and Soviet society had been transformed.

Life in Russia has changed radically since Stalin's death. The country is vastly wealthier, its people are far more comfortable and immeasurably more secure. Citizens don't disappear in the night to be shot in unmarked prisons or shipped off to Siberian camps. Children don't betray their parents to the political police. High officials no longer need fear the sudden loss of their jobs and privileges without cause or warning.

But none of that alters the fact that the Soviet system Stalin built is virtually intact. Stalin brutally reorganized rural life, forcibly eliminating the "peasant question" which so baffled Lenin. He regimented the population behind his massive development schemes, and finally completed the process of industrializing Russia which had been interrupted in 1917. Stalin destroyed the animated—if one-sided—intellectual life that enlivened Moscow in the 1920s, organizing the "creative intelligentsia" into the unions of writers, artists, composers and so forth which still dominate the cultural world. Stalin inspired the modern version of Soviet bureaucracy and made the bureaucrats the country's managers. If he could drink a life-renewing elixir, Stalin would probably be horrified by his successors' "softness" and "liberalism." But if he held his famous temper for a moment and looked carefully at contemporary Soviet society, he would find that most of his works remain much as he left them.

They have survived because they were effective. Lenin left no successful model for running the country. Stalin did. His successors have dismantled the apparatus of terror and tinkered with the rest of the machine. They have changed its character substantially through the evolution of bureaucratic decentralization, a process which has allowed a limited redistribution of authority and responsibility. Stalin allowed virtually no decentralization.

Because of his political strength and the terror he instilled in those beneath him, almost any order from Comrade Stalin would be swiftly implemented, no matter what its consequences. At the time of his death, for instance, loyal underlings were apparently preparing for the mass deportation of all Soviet Jews to the far east because Stalin had expressed interest in a scheme of this sort.

Now the various elements of the machine are more independent, and they can find ways to evade instructions from the center. The government tried to conduct a significant economic reform in the mid-1960s, but the bureaucrats sabotaged it—probably not deliberately, but simply by giving inertia a free reign. Stalin's dictatorship, in sum, fitted George Orwell's totalitarian model in ways the present regime does not.

In place of terror the current system relies on the shared realization—shared by a large and growing ruling class—that cooperation is more useful than any kind of protest. This system works more slowly than Stalin's, and the absence of fear breeds a lackadaisical attitude, but it works.

The present leaders must be grateful for Stalin's accomplishments. Although they have abandoned some of his tactics, they still rely on the structure he built.

Soviet ideology is a bewildering phenomenon. It cannot be defined or neatly explained, because ideology serves many masters and different purposes. One man's Marxism-Leninism may be another's good joke, and both may think of themselves as good communists. But what is a good communist, or a communist of any kind? The general confusion is nicely summarized in an old Russian joke: A student asks an instructor of Marxism-Leninism to explain the difference between communism and capitalism. "That's easy," replies the instructor. "Under capitalism, man exploits man. Under communism, it's just the opposite."

The ideology is called Marxism-Leninism, but it excludes much of what Karl Marx believed, particularly on questions of individual dignity, democracy and the proper role of state authority. Leninism is not a clear body of ideas; it amounts to the life's work of a prolific thinker and politician who, during the course of a long career, often came down on several sides of the same question.

Marxism-Leninism is important in a way the ideologists rarely mention—it sets the style for Soviet politics and the framework for Soviet political analysis. The enduring contribution of Lenin was to teach his comrades the arts of manipulation and control, the conspiratorial tools so crucial to his victory in 1917, and to Bolshevik successes since. Marxist-Leninist analytical categories color the views of virtually every Soviet citizen, I decided. These are the categories of dialectical materialism, the intellectual formulas which persuade so many Russians that they can see how history is moving, and that it is moving in their direction. Once absorbed, a Marxist-Leninist view of the world is not easily shaken off, as Alexander Solzhenitsyn testifies eloquently in the first volume of *The Gulag Archipelago.*

The advertised Soviet ideology can be reduced to a few basic formulations. These are the ones that seem to come up most frequently:

The Communist Party knows best. The Party's monopoly on political power and ideas is normal and correct, because the Party is the repository of all wisdom. Moreover, people and Party are united.

The Soviet Union is a workers' state and a socialist state, organized on the "scientific" principles of Marxism-Leninism for the maximum possible benefit to the working class. As a result, it progresses from triumph to triumph along the road to perfect communism, the ideal state in which men will live in total harmony with each other, without private property, government or class distinctions of any kind. Under perfect communism, society will operate according to Marx's maxim: "From each according to his abilities, to each according to his needs."

Soviet society is molding a "new Soviet man," unselfish, honest, hard-working and utterly devoted to building communism.

The Party and thus all the Soviet people are engaged in a perpetual "ideological struggle" with the "imperialists" of the western world. Peaceful coexistence in the ideological sphere is impossible. Because they are run by representatives of a hostile "class," the bourgeoisie, the capitalist states must inevitably be hostile to socialism, communism and the Soviet State.

The curious thing about these formulas, and others in the same vein, is that almost no one takes them literally, yet no one within the system would dream of challenging any of them. Orthodoxy reigns in the absence of faith.

The Party has indirectly acknowledged its own grave errors, particularly in its denunciations of Stalin's murderous excesses, which were themselves, of course, conducted in the name of the Party. The Soviet attempt to build communism is obviously not scientific, and it is obviously not progressing toward the communist ideal at anything like the speed that should be possible and must be desired. In fact, the Soviet economy can't even grow as fast as capitalist Japan's. The classic Marxist distinctions between the proletariat and the bourgeoisie have been hopelessly blurred and confused in both the socialist and the capitalist worlds. The dream of a new communist man is contradicted daily in the government's own official newspapers, which report on greed and corruption, crime and alcoholism. The "imperialists" long ago relinquished whatever dreams they had of toppling the Soviet state, and there is no indication that the Russians expect a socialist revolution in the capitalist world in the foreseeable future.

The Russians did not invent this kind of ludicrous contradiction between ideology and obvious fact. The United States began its life as a nation with a declaration that all men were created equal, and an understanding that some of those men could be bought and sold as slaves. Politicians everywhere are capable of perceiving just what they want to, and believing whatever slogans may suit their fancies.

The reason for this is that ideologies provide the justification for those in power to hold power. The Soviet Communist party's monopoly of power is an ideological matter, explained not by the desires of a relatively small group to protect their powers and privileges, but by a great historic mission. Or so it is made to appear.

Stalin understood that the Bolsheviks' original claim to rule Russia and its possessions was neither legally justified nor clearly supported by the population. The Bolsheviks were not czars who could claim legitimacy through a long line of succession; on the contrary, they were usurpers. Nor were they democrats who could point to a clear popular mandate; they never sought a mandate. Their best claim to legitimacy was Lenin himself, a leader extraordinarily popular in many segments of the population. Stalin understood this and promoted the speedy deification of Lenin after his death in 1924. Once in power, Stalin rewrote the early history of the Party, putting himself at Lenin's side in pre-revolutionary years when in fact they barely knew each other.

Simultaneously, Stalin abandoned Lenin's ideas about how to run the Party and the country. No more hand-wringing or intellectual disputes about the problem of the peasants, or about how backward Russia could be transformed into a socialist state. Instead he took action—drastic, revolutionary action, without regard for the disruptions his tactics caused. It wasn't too much for Stalin to abolish the days of the week—he did, and replaced them with numbers.

Hitler nearly destroyed everything in 1941. When the Germans attacked, Stalin himself apparently believed that they would overwhelm the Soviet Union. "Everything is lost," Stalin allegedly said. "I give up. Lenin left us a proletarian state, and now we've been caught with our pants down and let the whole thing go to shit."* For two weeks Stalin was immobile, perhaps the victim of a nervous breakdown. But he revived, and the people responded to his remarkable personality and to their own patriotism. Soldiers rushed into battle shouting, "For the Motherland! For Stalin!" The Germans were defeated.

This was Stalin's greatest accomplishment. Not only had he saved Russia, he had saved Lenin's "revolutionary state" as well. The experience of the war fused the causes of Russian nationalism and the Communist Party. The Bolsheviks could legitimately claim to rule the land.

But by that time the Communist Party bore little resemblance to Lenin's original Bolsheviks. Stalin had destroyed the Party, perhaps destroyed it twice—first in the purges of the 1930s, then in the war, when hundreds of thousands of devoted Party members were killed, many in the first disastrous weeks when the most eager volunteers rushed to the front to be devoured by the Nazis. The early Bolshevik spirit, the desire to build a true workers' state on a genuinely popular foundation, had disappeared. Stalin's Party had no time for logic or persuasive argument. The dictator's approach to power reflected a profound distrust of ordinary Russians, even a contempt for them. People would do what he wanted them to because they worshiped him, or because they were terrified of him. Traditional ideology mattered less to Stalin than Russia's status as a world power.

So Stalin achieved the final legitimization of Bolshevik rule at a time when he was losing interest—he may have lost it entirely—in the original content of Bolshevism. After the war the cult of Stalin all but displaced the cult of Lenin. Stalin paid little heed to ideological or Party issues. He didn't call a single Congress of the Communist Party between 1940 and 1953.

After Stalin's death his successors quickly revived Lenin. The highest honor in the land had been called the Stalin

---

* The quotation comes from Khrushchev, who says he heard it from Lavrenti Beria, Stalin's most intimate associate.

Prize; it became the Lenin Prize. The statues and pictures of Stalin that covered the land like a fungus were removed and replaced by portraits of Lenin. Eventually Stalin was condemned, but not the Party. Stalin erred, the Party triumphed. Schoolchildren are now taught that the Party industrialized the country, and that the Party led the nation against the Germans. Stalin is gone and "ideology" is back.

And yet Stalin's attitude toward ideology survives. His successors share his view that ideology is most useful as a tool. They take from it what is helpful, reject what is not, all the while invoking Marxism-Leninism as the source and justification of their power. Marxism-Leninism is the mythology of Soviet society. (As the anthropologists have demonstrated, no society can exist without a mythology of some kind.) Nor is it wholly disingenuous. If they are cynical about its application, the ideology remains a source of comfort for those who invoke it. The rulers of the land find in their Marxism-Leninism reassurance that they are doing what is best in the long run. Granted, it has proven impossible to relax the dictatorship or permit the freedoms Marx dreamed of and Lenin seemed to endorse. True, state ownership of the means of production has not brought economic miracles, or even as much progress as private ownership has achieved elsewhere. Nevertheless, the Soviet Union is pursuing its historic goals. It has destroyed the class of wealthy exploiters and eliminated the worst poverty, improved the lives of workers and peasants, industrialized the land and created a formidable military machine to defend socialism. This may be a rosy view of what has been happening in Russia, but it is plausible, all the more so if one wants to believe it.

I puzzled over the significance of ideology for three years. I spent too much time looking for a logical explanation of it. Lenin thought of ideology as a science, but the science has gone out of it. Now ideology provides a kind of mystical adhesive which is important to the stability of Soviet life. This isn't the sort of explanation that comforts pragmatists, but Russians are not pragmatists.

The rituals of Marxism-Leninism are rather like the rituals of an American college fraternity; secret handshakes and mottoes in fraternity life signify nothing but a common *belonging*. If you know the handshake, you are one of us; if not, you are one of them. In Russia, if one performs the expected ideological rituals, one demonstrates loyalty to the cause—an important demonstration, since the cause depends on loyalty, or so most of the adherents believe. This is a conspiratorial notion; Russians are conspiratorial by nature. Lenin was perhaps the most successful conspirator in all history.

Soviet citizens are called upon to show their loyalty in countless ways. Every bureaucrat is well advised to hang a portrait of Lenin in his office. Ambitious university students know it is best to take an active part in the Young Communist League. An engineer who finds himself moving up through the hierarchy of his factory knows he should join the Party if he wants to reach the very top. A sociologist writing a scholarly article realizes he must begin with a reference to the works of Lenin.

These ritualistic displays reminded me of an old Jew entering his synagogue, touching the holy *mezuzah* beside the front door and kissing his fingers. The gesture is habitual, an act of reverence (the *mezuzah* contains a piece of holy scripture), but it is also a source of reassurance, tangible proof that this is indeed a Jewish house, the House of the Lord, a safe refuge.

For Soviet communists the safe refuge is ideological orthodoxy. Those who demonstrate it prove that they are with us, not against us. In societies whose leaders rule with self-confidence, this kind of ostentatious display of loyalty is superfluous, but not in the Soviet Union.

The most basic proof of loyalty is membership in the Communist Party; not incidentally, membership is also a virtual prerequisite for admission to the highest level of Soviet society. The Party has about 15 million members, only seven percent of the entire population, but in certain important groups the percentage is much higher. For example, more than half of the men over 30 with a college education are Party members. More than 99 percent of all members of government executive bodies, heads of departments in city, *oblast* and republican governments, and directors of state enterprises are members of the Party.

Party membership is meant to be the privilege of the best members of society, the most serious, dedicated and hardworking, but in practice this not always the case. An engineer in Moscow who had worked in various branches of Soviet industry told me he thought it was common for the best workers to try to stay out of the Party, since Party membership gave them formal responsibilities which made it more difficult to jump from factory to factory, selling their skills to the highest bidder. Poor workers, on the other hand, seek out Party membership as a means of self-protection. A Party member, my acquaintance thought, was less likely to be punished for poor work.

The official newspapers regularly report that Party members are prey to the same temptations as everyone else—bribery, drunkenness and sloth. The Party recently asked every member to exchange his card for a new one, a ceremonial means of purging undesirables, but the overwhelming majority seemed to receive their new cards without any trouble. I knew several intellectuals in Moscow who joined the Party years ago and, despite growing disillusionment and even hostility to the regime, maintained their membership. Somehow they passed muster whenever Party officials examined the purity of the ranks. Those examinations must not be too thorough.

The heart of the Party is the large group of Soviet citizens who work directly for it or in closely associated, essentially political jobs, full- or part-time. Several *million* citizens fall into this category if one counts part-time Party agitators, most officers of the KGB, Party and Komsomol workers, political lecturers and teachers. There is probably no society in the western world with as large a percentage of politically active citizens. Its size is a good indicator of its significance as a stabilizing influence.

These activists see to it that ordinary citizens feel the presence of the Party in their daily lives. Each fall, for example, Party organizations put millions of city dwellers to work as temporary potato-pickers. The fields around Moscow are filled with these "volunteers." A friend who taught French at a scientific institute recounted her experience "on potatoes," as the Russians describe this duty:

"We were picked up at the institute in a bus before dawn, about five in the morning. We rode for four hours on the bus, picked potatoes for four hours in the rain, got back in the bus and rode home. A crazy, inefficient use of time, the bus, its gas and everything else, but that didn't matter—the Party secretary had done his job, he'd taken us on potatoes."*

A former resident of Irkutsk in Central Siberia told me that in September, "If you toured the streets in early morning, you'd see people from all kinds of different enterprises—accounting offices, stores, research institutes—standing around in work clothes outside the places where they worked. They were waiting for city buses to pick them up and take them to the fields for the day."

Political meetings organized by Party functionaries are even more common interruptions in a citizen's routine. Schools, factories and offices regularly assemble for a report on the international situation, a recitation of the goals of the Five Year Plan or a warning against ideological laxity. One of the most popular Soviet movies in recent years included a brief parody of this phenomenon: the Party agitator on the staff of a small restaurant in northern Russia gathered his colleagues around a long table and read them an impassioned editorial from an official newspaper. His colleagues pretended to listen, but their faces could not hide the signs of unmitigated boredom.

Svetlana Alliluyeva, Stalin's daughter, who now lives in America wrote in her remarkable book *Only One Year* about a young woman doctor in a Moscow hospital who told her, "If you only knew how much of a doctor's time is wasted on Party meetings. How much unnecessary chatter, papers, lists, reports! We are supposed to treat the sick; it would be better to spend an extra hour at a patient's side."

The Party, naturally, sees all this differently. Its intrusions on daily life are part of the system of governing the country; they remind the governed who is in charge, and they convey what the governors want known, even if it is boring. The Party has a "leading role" in every facet of Soviet life, a role that must be actively performed if the citizenry is to take it seriously.

The Party's most practical duty is to get the Plan fulfilled. Agitation, stimulation and entreaty are all part of the Party officials' daily repertoire. Some of this has been reduced to

---

* Potato-picking had more ceremonial than practical value in this case, but the labor of millions of urban workers in the fields is needed every fall to bring in the harvest—even though a third of the Soviet population still lives on the farms.

routine—a routine so familiar that almost no one notices it. For instance, every Soviet factory or enterprise is decorated with red banners covered with slogans. From 1971 to 1976, in the period between the 24th and 25th Congress of the Party, the most common slogan has been "Fulfill the Decisions of the 24th Party Congress!" Another popular one was "Fulfill the Plan Ahead of Schedule!"

But there is more to Party agitation than sloganeering. Local Party officials share responsibility for the success or failure of every enterprise in their domain. They must explain why a factory failed to meet the targets of the Plan, because they share responsibility with the director of the factory concerned. So the Party's agents constantly prod the workers to work harder, drink less, produce more of better quality.

The Party protects the regime and system. It provides stability, brings millions of people into the political life of the country, helps make things happen. And it is a symbol of uniqueness, too, a special source of strength that Russia's rivals in the western world cannot match.

Foreigners—the word itself resonates in a Russian's ear, a promise of exotica, or treachery, or boundless cunning. Foreigners, curiously, are an important element of Soviet politics. A hunger for foreign admiration, fear of foreign enemies and foreign ideas—both powerfully influence affairs of state.

Russians live with the outside world in a state of tense ambivalence as old as Russia itself. The first Russian monarch, Rurik, was a Scandinavian whom the tribes of ancient Russia invited to rule and protect them in the ninth century. Russia was brought into the European world by Peter the Great, a ruthless westernizer who even made French the language of his new court in Petersburg, the European capital he built in a Baltic swamp to give his people a "window on the West." Peter's transformation of Russian life was preserved by Catherine the Great, a fierce Russian patriot, although she began life as Princess Sophia of Anhalt-Zerbst, a tiny German principality. The Bolshevik Revolution grew out of foreign ideas, was partly financed by Germans and succeeded because Russia was engaged in a foreign war.

Russian misgivings about foreigners are also ancient. The first Russian word used to describe them, *nemtsi,* appeared in the tenth century and meant, roughly, "the dumb ones." (The word is still in use, but now means Germans. Most of the first foreigners in Russia were from Germany.) In 1568 an Englishman named Thomas Randolfe visited Moscow as an ambassador of the English crown, and recorded this description of his arrival:

We were brought to a house built of purpose by the [Russian] Emperor for ambassadors, fair and large. Two gentlemen were appointed to attend upon me, the one to see us furnished of victuals, the other to see that we should not go out of the house, nor suffer any man to come unto us. He that looked to our persons so straitly handled us that we had no small cause to doubt that some evil had been intended unto us. No supplication, suit or request could take place for our liberty. . . .*

Randolfe spent 17 weeks under that special kind of house arrest before the czar finally agreed to meet him.

The Marquis de Custine, a French nobleman who visited Russia in 1839, recorded this exchange with a Russian policeman during the prolonged series of searches and interrogations which consumed most of a day before he was permitted to come ashore in Petersburg:

"What are you going to do in Russia?" [the policeman asked.]
"See the country." [Custine replied.]
"That is not a motive for traveling." . . .
"I have no other."
"Whom do you intend to see in Petersburg?"
"Any persons who will allow me to make their acquaintance."
"How long do you expect to stay in Russia?"
"I do not know."
"Say approximately."
"Several months."
"Do you have a public diplomatic mission?"
"No."
"Some scientific purpose?"
"No."
"Have you been sent by your government to observe social and political conditions in this country?"

---

* Quoted in *Voyages and Discoveries* by Richard Hakluyt.

"No."

"By a commercial company?"

"No."

"You are then traveling freely and entirely through curiosity?"

"Yes."

"Why did you head toward Russia?"*

And so on. My own experience 132 years later, after arriving on a Soviet ship in Nakhodka, on the Sea of Japan, was comparable, if less quotable. My wife and I were informed 75 minutes after the ship docked (at a point approximately 4200 miles from Moscow, as the crow flies) that the visas the Soviet Embassy in Washington had given us were valid only at the airport in Moscow. All our fellow passengers disembarked. The ship's ventilation system was turned off. We waited alone and wondered what could possibly happen next. Back to Japan on the next boat? A plane direct to Moscow? The ship had landed at 4:30 in the afternoon. At 7:20 I saw a military truck stop beside the ship's gangplank on the dock. An officer got out and walked up the gangplank. Several minutes later he walked down the passageway, past our cabin, whose door was open, to the next door. He knocked; no one answered. Then he came back to us. I announced who I was, and he nodded, mumbling something about customs. There was a strong smell of alcohol on his breath. He left. Ten minutes later a young man came with our passports and said the visas had been accepted. We were driven hurriedly to our train, and just caught it.

Our experience was not typical. The Soviet government now welcomes foreign tourists, not least for the hard currency they bring. The authorities even permit about 5000 foreigners (not including foreign students) to live in Moscow. But the old suspicions persist.

Like almost all foreign residents of the capital, I lived in a ghetto of apartment houses reserved for foreigners and surrounded by a concrete wall nine feet high. A policeman checked me in and out each time I left by car or on foot.

The KGB's microphones are imbedded in the walls of every foreigner's apartment, and every telephone is bugged. My wife and I once left Moscow for five weeks; when we re-

---

* Quoted in *Journey for Our Time* by Phyllis Penn Kohler.

turned we found a fresh patch of plaster in the ceiling of the dining room, just above the table. One usually didn't know where the microphones were, but an American businessman in Moscow decided to find out. John Connor, Jr., the resident director of the Soviet-American Trade and Economic Council, asked security men from the American Embassy to check the five-room apartment that the Soviet agency which cares for foreigners had allocated to him. Their devices located 23 microphones in the walls. Foreigners can hire domestic help through that same agency. A young diplomat in the British Embassy told me that his unusually well-educated maid read through his mail when no one was home.

Hella Pick, a correspondent for the *Manchester Guardian*, came to Moscow in July 1974 with President Nixon. She stayed in the Intourist Hotel in downtown Moscow with the other journalists on the trip, but did not leave on the President's plane with the rest of them. She returned to the Intourist after the others had departed. On the way to get her suitcase she passed the open doors of a dozen or more rooms, all of them occupied by American journalists until a few hours before. In each one Miss Pick saw a microphone hanging from a vent in the ceiling, apparently waiting to be cleaned or serviced.

KGB agents sporadically follow foreigners around Moscow. Sometimes their surveillance is blatant, suggesting that they want the person being followed to know it. The security police in provincial cities follow foreigners more assiduously. In Tbilisi once with another American I was followed by a team of five agents. Half a dozen or more followed three of us around the ancient town of Pskov one Saturday.

Much of the USSR is closed to foreigners. A trip to one of the open areas requires official permission in advance. It is impossible for a foreigner to simply buy a ticket on the train to Leningrad, or reserve a room in a hotel in Kiev. All tickets and reservations must be ordered through the agency that looks after diplomats and other foreigners, or through Intourist, the state travel agency.

As a result of all this, most foreigners who live in the Soviet Union don't really live in the Soviet Union. Foreigners inhabit a special world of their own, rather like the foreigners' quarter in Peking before the Boxer Rebellion. There are even special hard-currency shops for foreigners, so they are spared the long lines and erratic supplies in the local stores.

Mistrust of foreigners extends to business dealings. Western businessmen who have repeatedly demonstrated a willingness to deal fairly and honestly with the Soviet Union are still treated like pickpockets trying to rob the national treasury. "Every negotiation is based on suspicion, mistrust," one such trader from America told me. "They're always implying that you're trying to trick them, fool them, when in fact you're trying to make a buck for yourself and for them, too."

Negotiations between westerners and Soviet bureaucrats sound like the haggling in an Oriental bazaar. When the Russians want something that the foreigner will not or cannot provide, they refuse to accept a simple no, but return to the matter again and again.

Mistrust is not only an official policy; for most Russians it seems to be an intuitive response to foreigners. I saw this countless times myself in Russians whose whole demeanor changed abruptly when they realized they were in my presence. On a train from Murmansk, a port city in the extreme northwest of Russia, to Mosocw, I rode in the same car as a group of Soviet sailors, and tried to strike up conversations with several of them. All brushed me away, and one slammed the door of his compartment in my face. An American student at Moscow University asked a Russian acquaintance why the government refused to allow unhappy Soviet Jews living in Israel to come back to Russia. "That would be impossible," the Russian student answered. "They'd all be spies."

Spies—they are as common in Russia as miracles in Alice's Wonderland. Stalin encouraged spy mania with a vengeance. His successors discuss the presence of foreign agents less often, but they still promote the old fears. Lectures on "vigilance" make up a large part of every Soviet citizen's political education. Books and movies on the evil intentions of visiting foreigners are common and popular.

Out of fear of saying the wrong thing to a foreigner, many Russians will fabricate fantastic tales. When the wife of an American official visiting Moscow asked to meet a Russian psychologist who specialized in family problems, particularly the tensions between parents and children, her Russian guide replied, "We have no tensions between parents and children in this country."

Obviously, that Russian lady was not only worried that the American official's wife was a spy. She had something else in mind besides—something Russians seem to have constantly in mind in their dealings with foreigners. That is: How will it look: What will they think?

The Marquis de Custine discovered this frustrating trait in Russians on the boat he took from Germany to Petersburg in 1839: "I am struck by the excessive uneasiness of the Russians concerning the opinion that a foreigner might form of them; it would not be possible to show less independence. The impression that their country must make on the mind of a traveler disturbs them endlessly."

Russians are plagued by the fear that foreigners will judge them inferior to other peoples. This fear infects even those Russians who think their country and their countrymen *are* inferior. Russians permit self-criticism, but not in front of foreigners. A precise if inelegant line on this subject is attributed to Ivan Pavlov, the Russian psychologist. "This is our own Russian shit," Pavlov reportedly said of a scientific scandal at the turn of the century, "and we will sort it out ourselves without any help from abroad."

A foreigner in Russia is overwhelmed by countless references to international prestige, "world standards," reputations abroad and the like. Purely Russian criteria are rarely invoked when a Russian wants to find lavish praise for some piece of art or work of science. In Yalta, on the Crimean coast, at the former imperial residence where Stalin met with Franklin D. Roosevelt and Winston Churchill at the end of World War II, a man showed me his collection of souvenir pins and buttons. One was issued by a local winery—"a famous winery," he assured me. "Its wine is sold all over the world, in America, Asia, everywhere." No better compliment could be paid, though it was utter nonsense.

I met numerous Soviet Jews in Israel who used the same vocabulary of praise to describe institutions in their former, Soviet lives. One couple had worked in a large steel mill in the Ukraine—"the steel mill named for Lenin, famous throughout the world, of course you've heard of it," the man said to me, his face betraying a hint of uncertainty despite his confident tone. No, I said, I never heard of it. This friendly young man with huge blue eyes, sitting in a refugee center in the mountains outside Jerusalem, was crushed.

The Russians face an unresolvable dilemma: they want to

please and impress foreigners, but can't bring themselves to *trust* foreigners. Not surprisingly, once the foreigner realizes how profoundly he is mistrusted, he is no longer in a mood to be pleased or impressed. The Russians offered their most lavish hospitality to the American official's wife who was interested in family tensions, but she remembers and retells the story of the guide who claimed that parents and children live in perfect harmony in the USSR.

A young Russian who won the extraordinary privilege of a trip to Brazil in the late 1950s (when travel abroad was still extremely rare) was briefed and rebriefed before his departure. The relevant authorities told him how to behave in public, how to eat with fork and knife, how to spot a western intelligence agent or *provocateur*. He departed by train for Rome, thence by Italian steamship to Brazil. On board ship he was offered an artichoke. No one sitting near him had one, and he didn't have the first idea what to do with it. After some hesitation he cut the artichoke into large pieces and ate them, whole. The waiter looked on in amazement.

At the port of Rio de Janeiro a Brazilian official asked for his health card. "You need one more shot," the official said. "We'll give it to you?"

"Shot? What kind of shot? Not me, you aren't going to trick me." The Russian smelled a classic entrapment.

The exasperated Brazilian police finally found a diplomat from the Soviet Embassy, who came on the scene just as the student was declaring that he would rather go back to Russia than take this so-called shot. The diplomat told him to keep still and do as he was told; he got the shot and saw Brazil.

I heard that story from a friend in Moscow, a well-traveled member of the official elite. He giggled appreciatively as he recalled it. But surely, I said, Russians are more sophisticated now, nearly 20 years later? Well, perhaps, my friend allowed. That reminded him of a joke: Do you know how to cook a behemoth? Easy, he answered himself—put it into a behemoth pot, bring it to a boil and add asparagus. He laughed again. I asked if he knew what asparagus was. He didn't. Had he ever heard of broccoli? Never. Would he know what to do with an artichoke? As a matter of fact, no.

The working of their Communist Party and its ideology and the Russians' relationship with foreigners have been considered consecutively here because together they lead to the

Soviet system's vast police apparatus. The Committee for State Security (KGB) and other agencies in the same line of work are police forces in a familiar sense, but they are *Russian* police forces. Their functions have a distinctly local aspect. The KGB and the others are meant to preserve the orthodoxy from internal rot and foreign influences. Their success means the preservation of the leading role of the party, and thus the leading roles of the Party's leaders.

The mentality of the Soviet police—the political police of the KGB as well as the more ordinary police of the Ministry of Internal Affairs—is the familiar mentality of policemen everywhere. A policeman prefers to find out whatever he can about life on his beat, simply because he feels better if he knows. All policemen rely on informers, eavesdropping and other informal devices to get the information they think they need. Most policemen seem to agree that the public underestimates the seriousness of crime and the rapacity of the criminal classes. Policemen tend to be conformists, even hyperconformists, to the conventions of the community they are meant to serve.

If the Soviet police are unique, it is because of their exalted status, not their attitudes. The Soviet police, particularly the "security organs," are lavishly financed and, by all appearances, enthusiastically supported by the politicians who run the country. Intelligence agencies in the West estimate that the KGB has 90,000* officers at home and abroad; these are men and women whose only responsibility is "state security." All ordinary crimes are taken care of by the militia of the Ministry of Internal Affairs, a force several times larger.

Like the Party, the KGB is virtually ubiquitous. Each college, factory and enterprise in the country has its "First Department," a secretive office in charge of personnel and security, manned by representatives of the KGB. (Apparently, the employees of some First Departments are not full-time officers of the Committee, but Russians all assume that the

---

* This is a guess, made by competitors who are themselves bureaucrats competing for highest budget allocations to counter the KGB, so perhaps it should be taken with a grain of salt. But there is no doubt that the KGB is enormous. In addition to its agents, it has several hundred thousand uniformed troops, most of whom guard Soviet frontiers.

First Department's business is the KGB's business.) Every town and city has its own branch office.

But the real sweep of the agency depends on its official staff, an army of paid and self-appointed informers, snoops and gossips. Intellectuals whom I knew in Moscow assumed that their lift ladies—the women who look after elevators in apartment houses—reported on anything unusual in their domain, such as the visit of a foreigner. Russians develop a sixth sense about stool pigeons. Acquaintances assured me they could find them at work, in the courtyard, at holiday camps and in all sorts of unlikely places.

Though they must have tens, perhaps hundreds of thousands already, the KGB is constantly searching out new collaborators. A professor from Leningrad told me about a teenager who was caught in illegal dealings with Finnish tourists, trading vodka for western clothes. This young man was about to take college entrance exams, and the KGB told him he had a choice: go to college and work as an informer, or spend five years in a labor camp. The choice was not difficult.

I never met a Russian who had a friend in the KGB, though virtually everyone I knew had at one time dealt with its agents. Those who serve the Committee live in a separate world. The KGB provides apartments, access to special shops, its own holiday resorts and more. I once asked a Soviet journalist, a man with an important job on an official newspaper, how people like him felt about those who worked for the KGB. "It depends," he replied, "on whether they are open about what they are doing. If they're working for it secretly, that isn't especially appreciated." I rarely heard such candor from a Soviet official.

Like so many Soviet institutions, the KGB appears to operate on the principle that too much is enough. No effort is spared, even efforts that seem superfluous. A young man who worked in the port of Tallinn, the Estonian city on the Baltic, told me how the KGB supervised that institution (which, like all port and border facilities, is under its control):

"The security is something. It takes two months to get checked out to receive the pass you need to enter the port area—the KGB issues it. At work you never know who might be following you, keeping an eye on you—including your colleagues. A lot of them seem to be full-time informers. They have to make reports all the time—who they talked to, what they talked about, etc. And they'll report on anything—a smile someone gave a foreigner, or the fact that one of the girls changed her blouse before she went home, anything. A report like that provides a reason for the KGB to call you in for a talk. They tell you how they are just standing behind you, that all they want is good security and a happy work force, that they need your help to keep track of foreign spies. But they think that every foreigner is a spy. If you get called in like that, they'll give you a warning. God forbid that after such a warning somebody should accept a pack of cigarettes from the captain of a foreign ship or something like that. Then they'll really put the pressure on and say, 'All right, now you have to agree to work for us.' They might say, 'You've got until five p.m. today to state officially that you agree to work for us.' And if you refuse, they'll get you fired, or have your pass lifted, which amounts to the same thing.

"When you go on board a foreign ship, you have to get a special pass and register what time you go on board and what time you come off. If they think you stayed on too long, they'll ask, 'What held you up?' They'll look through your briefcase to see if you have anything suspicious. They did this to a friend of mine, a girl who had worked in the port for a long time. They found a copy of some Solzhenitsyn book in her bag. Later they went to her apartment and searched it; she knew she was finished. . . . They can fire you for lack of trustworthiness. That's a legal basis for firing somebody."

A French teacher in Leningrad recounted this experience: "I was once called to the KGB, but not directly. I got a call from Intourist. They said they had a group of French educators visiting the city and asked me to come and talk to them. I said sure, and set off for the Astoria Hotel. As I was walking in, a little man stopped me and identified himself as a KGB officer. [The Committee's agents have military ranks.] He said he wanted to talk with me. 'Wait here 15 minutes,' he said, 'then come upstairs to room 348.' I did as he said. He conducted the standard sort of interview. 'We talk to everyone who speaks a foreign language,' he explained. Then he asked about foreigners I had met—'Oh yes,' he'd say, 'we know about that one,' and so on. He asked me who my friends were. Finally he said, 'Remember my phone number. If you ever see anything unusual, call me.' I asked if I could write the number down. He said, 'Just the last two digits, no more.' And he ordered me not to tell anyone about our meeting."

I met a young woman in Israel who had been called to the KGB in Kiev for an interview when she first applied for a visa to emigrate. One officer asked: "You spent the night in a Moscow hotel in 1963 next door to some Italians. What did you talk about with them?" She started to protest that this was nonsense, then suddenly remembered that she had indeed been in a hotel with Italian tourists many years before.

If the KGB is effective, it is not always intelligent. A young American journalist named Paul Browne discovered this at the United Nations. Browne, a graduate student at the Columbia University School of Journalism, was taking a course at the UN from two American journalists when he met Alexander Yakovlev, a Russian who worked as a radio announcer. Yakovlev began courting Browne. He invited him to lunch and offered to pay him $30 each for any articles he might like to write. Yakovlev said he would try to sell the articles in Russia. Browne didn't take this offer seriously, but Yakovlev repeated it, and repeatedly invited Browne to lunch or dinner. Finally he made specific suggestions:

"Perhaps you could take notes in class about what your foreign students there say, and about what your professors think and say about different issues—about the Mideast, for example. . . . Tell me, so I can analyze how students think, what the professors say, whether they are Democrats or Republicans, if they are Jewish. . . ."

Browne went to the FBI, which encouraged him to maintain the contact and even provided "articles" for him to sell to Yakovlev. The Russian happily paid $30 for an analysis of suburbanites' reactions to Watergate which the FBI had rewritten from upstate New York newspapers. He asked if Browne might write something about the Jewish Defense League. Yakovlev kept calling Browne, who finally stopped answering a year after their first meeting. Browne then wrote an article for the *Washington Post* about his experience. Shortly after it appeared, Yakovlev was called home to Moscow on "extended consultations."

Reading Browne's story and recalling my own experiences with hypercurious Russians in Moscow who sought my opinion on all sorts of irrelevant subjects, I realized that the KGB's offices must be overwhelmed by memoranda, documents and reports. An elderly woman in Moscow who had lived through many years of trouble with the KGB and its predecessors warned me about this with a question I didn't fully understand when she posed it. "Why should we believe," she asked, "that the KGB is so much different from the Ministry of Agriculture?" Of course, it isn't.

But with its huge budget and staff the KGB can perform Herculean tasks. Zhores Medvedev, a Soviet biologist once incarcerated in a mental hospital for his political beliefs and now living in England in involuntary exile, has demonstrated that the KGB must examine most of the letters sent by Soviet citizens abroad, or sent to them from foreign countries. Medvedev reached his conclusion after conducting elaborate experiments with various correspondents abroad, and although the magnitude of such a job is staggering, his evidence leaves little doubt that this is indeed what the KGB does.

Medvedev also looked into the use of sailboats along the Soviet coast. He found that "there are many yacht clubs" in the Soviet Union, "but only on lakes and reservoirs. There are none on the sea, except on gulfs which penetrate deep into dry land." Along the Baltic coast,

> Dozens of kilometers of shoreline ... are wound around with coils of barbed wire, and there is no access to the sea. Every day a roller goes along the shore trampling down the sand and earth so that all traces of fugitives can be seen. ... only rare small boats appear on the sea, each one by permission of the [KGB's] frontier posts. ...
>
> Only a few local people manage to get permission for a boat; these are generally harbor employees, scientists, employees of the militia, the most active members of the Party and Soviet organizations and those employed in sanatoria and rest homes. ... [One] has to notify the frontier post of the surnames and given names of everyone who is going out in the boat [on an excursion]. After going for a sail, it is not enough to draw the boat up to a safe place on shore, or to leave it at anchor...; it has to be taken to a special "pound" sealed off by barbed wire, with padlocked gates and an armed guard. The boat, too, has to be padlocked.*

---

* *The Medvedev Papers.*

Perhaps nothing makes the KGB more nervous than foreign travel by Soviet citizens. Soviet delegations traveling to other countries routinely include a KGB officer or reliable representative of the Party. Most ordinary citizens will never travel overseas, and the lucky exceptions are likely to go somewhere in Eastern Europe.

Medvedev described the questionnaire that anyone trying to go abroad—a scientist invited to an international conference, for instance—must fill out. It includes "the usual questions" about close relatives and any terms of imprisonment, a list of every job the applicant has ever held, a detailed autobiography, copies of birth certificates of the applicant's children, a copy of the applicant's marriage certificate, a medical report, the itinerary of his or her proposed journey and a character reference. All these papers must be provided in duplicate, with 12 photographs affixed to them. The character reference must include a statement on the applicant's political maturity and moral stability. His immediate supervisors must endorse it in triplicate, then the Party committee at his place of work must confirm the endorsement. Finally, the local regional committee of the Party must give its approval, put its formal stamp on the file and send it on to Moscow.

I met a young man from Leningrad who had been screened as a possible "volunteer" to teach foreign languages in Cairo. He was interviewed by six commissions, including two at the regional committee of the Party, by Party workers and by KGB officers. "I had given them a huge amount of written material, but they asked questions, too, about politics, about Marxism-Leninism, the standard formulas." The sixth commission deemed him politically unreliable and he didn't make the trip.

And yet the KGB is human, and Russian, too. I knew a musician in Moscow who went abroad with the symphony orchestra she played in. She filled out all the forms, but many of the answers she gave were wrong or incomplete; she forgot the address of her husband's new job, so put down the old one, and she failed to mention some trouble she'd once had in the Young Communist League. She was never questioned, and received her passport without delay.

Andrei Amalrik, who was the subject of KGB investigations for many years and who never disguised his contempt for the political police, once asked a KGB man to help his father get the pension he was entitled to but hadn't received because of a bureaucratic mix-up. "When I next went to the Welfare Department," Amalrik wrote, "I was received with great solicitude and the following day the pension came through. For this reason I cannot speak only ill of the KGB."

Galya Gabai, the wife of a dissident (he later committed suicide), was about to be fired from her job as a teacher when her husband was put in prison. The KGB intervened and saved her job, apparently on the grounds that her husband's imprisonment was punishment enough.

An old joke:

"Why did the soldier get five years at hard labor for calling the general an idiot? Wasn't that a little harsh?"

"Not at all. He got six months for insulting his commanding officer, and the rest for revealing a state secret."

Joseph Stalin created the governmental and legal structures of Soviet society, but while he ruled, both were regularly ignored. Laws meant little, the high-minded constitution of 1936 meant even less. The political authorities, led by Stalin himself, regularly disregarded laws and regulations to mete out justice to suit their own whims. This is one prerogative of absolute rulers, and Stalin's successors are regularly tempted to exploit it. Periodically they do succumb, but when they do they try to disguise the fact. Stalin's successors, particularly the latest batch, would like to be thought of as law-abiding citizens.

For the dissident intellectuals in Moscow, this is probably the single most heartening change in their society since Stalin's death. The ostensible respect for the law and for orderly legal procedures has given Soviet citizens a means of contesting the state's (which is really the Party's) authority. This means that a chance exists for a contest between citizens and state—a new idea in the Soviet Union, even if the contest is seldom fair and sometimes profoundly corrupt.

An independent legal system has no logical place in the Soviet system. Traditionally, every individual and institution in the country has been subject to orders from Moscow; everything is subject to a fix. Khrushchev let his cat out of its bag in the second volume of his memoirs in an aside about the architecture of the Palace of Congresses, a hideous glass box which he ordered built within the walls of the Kremlin. It was designed by a team of architects led by M. V. Posokhin, chief architect of Moscow. "I liked [it] very much," Khrushchev said of the palace. "I couldn't understand why the Lenin Prize committee failed to recognize its merits. I remember the government had to intervene in favor of Comrade Posokhin." Posokhin won the Lenin Prize for the design of the palace in 1962.

Failings like these are a matter of personal weakness. Khrushchev didn't have to intervene on Posokhin's behalf, he just wanted to. Similarly, Soviet leaders are tempted to intervene in the legal process to insure that it produces the results they want. Soviet lawyers are beginning to feel that their society could accept stricter legal procedures without threatening the leading role of the Party or any vital element of the system. They are becoming something of an interest group, lobbying as best they can on behalf of the law.

They wage their struggle in a hostile, or at best indifferent, environment. Respect for the law is one of those western notions—like fair play or rationalism—which don't find a natural refuge in the Russian character. Several foreigners who have spent time with Soviet lawyers found them more "like us" than other Russians, no doubt because they tend to share the value we place on the law, which only means they take it seriously. Ordinary Russians take it seriously as a threat—the punishments handed down in Soviet courts are harsh by our standards—but seldom as a force to protect their civil rights. Russians rarely think of civil rights. Moreover, legal formalities don't sit well with Russians. To an American eye a Soviet courtroom is remarkably cavalier and undisciplined.

Russians at all levels tend to see the law as a means to an end—punishing criminals, preventing undesirable behavior, allocating the blame in a dispute. This is evident at the most basic level—for instance, in a traffic policeman's handling of an accident. A bus once eased into the front fender of my car while we were both making the same turn in parallel lanes. As is customary, the bus driver stopped dead when he realized what had happened. I did the same and we waited for a policeman, trying to ignore the enormous traffic jam we were causing by blocking a busy intersection. Passers-by stopped to study the scene; many passed judgment, usually in the bus driver's favor—that is, against the foreigner. The policeman, however, recognized that the bus had been at fault, and wrote out a formal charge on the spot. "I'll make him sign this," he said to me, displaying a handwritten confession of guilt.

Unhappily but resignedly, the driver signed. The decisions of traffic policemen, in accidents or even cases of missed red lights, are virtually unappealable. For minor offenses they collect a fine on the spot.

The country's leaders take a similar view of the law. They generally issue decrees to make things happen, not to broaden the rights of the governed or make the society more "fair." In 1966 the authorities were upset by the popularity of jokes directed against the regime, so they issued a decree outlawing "anti-Soviet jokes." When they get upset by the extent of drunkenness as they periodically do, the leaders promulgate new orders governing the sale of vodka, in hopes of discouraging it.*

Soviet law is not immune from the bureaucratic inertia that dominates so much of the society. Andrei Amalrik recorded an example of this inertia in his recollection of a fellow prisoner in a Moscow jail:

A geologist from the Carpathians, he had arrived in Moscow as a tourist. Soon after he got there all his money was stolen from him. He reported this to the police and settled down for the night at the railroad station in the naïve hope that he would be sent back home at official expense—there was no other way he could get home. The police warned him several times that he could not live in Moscow without registration. [That is, without the stamp in his official passport that entitled him to reside in the capital.] He paid no attention, as it did not occur to him that in the eyes of the law he was no longer a victim but an offender. Three days later he was arrested and sent here to the Butyrki prison. The inquiry had been going on for over half a year. I could not understand why the investigation was taking all this time. He explained that part of the delay had been due to his examination by psychiatrists, who, however, had found him completely sane. His investigator thought him out of his mind not to have got out of Moscow in time. [He was entitled to stay for three days.] When he was

---

* But not too much: the government makes a lot of money selling vodka. According to one western expert, the tax on alcoholic beverages is the single most important source of revenue in the Soviet budget, producing 10 to 12 percent of all the state's income.

finally taken to court he hoped he would be sentenced to seven or eight months in prison, and, since he had already been there for longer than this, that he would then be allowed to go home. Whether his hopes came true or not I don't know—I was removed from the cell before he came back from court.

After the publication of Aelxander Solzhenitsyn's *Gulag Archipelago* and Solzhenitsyn's expulsion from the country, the Novosti press agency asked if I would like to interview a prominent Soviet lawyer who would refute Solzhenitsyn's accusations against the USSR's legal system. I accepted the offer and was taken to meet Professor Vladimir Kudryavtsev, director of the country's leading law institute.

Kudryavtsev was a tall, angular man whose vacant expression belied his scholarly status. He was not particularly eloquent, but he did seem genuinely indignant about the accusation—which he thought Solzhenitsyn had made—that Soviet law was no better now than it had been under Stalin. I asked if, under Stalin, people had been punished who had done nothing wrong. "Of course," he said, but went on to list the many changes—and there have been many—in legal regulations and procedures since 1953. I said western scholars who have followed Soviet legal developments agreed with him that the situation had changed substantially, but it still seemed that the authorities could disregard the law when it suited them. I asked about several cases in which dissidents got something less than the legal treatment they deserved; the professor said he wasn't familiar with the cases. My last question was about Solzhenitsyn: under what law had he been expelled from the Soviet Union? (He was deposited in Frankfurt, West Germany, by plainclothesmen who flew him there on an Aeroflot jet.) The professor replied that he had been forcibly exiled by a decision of the government. He could cite no law which provided for this punishment. In fact, there was none on the books.

"Socialist democracy" is the term the Soviets use to describe their methods of protecting and expanding the rights of the citizenry. Periodically the propaganda organs publish eloquent defenses of socialist democracy as far purer and more significant than the West's "bourgeois democracy."

The heart of socialist democracy is its protection of economic and social rights. Soviet citizens have the right to work, the right to inexpensive living quarters, the right to free education and free medical care. The constitution Stalin promulgated in 1936 also guarantees the political and personal rights which the bourgeois democracies claim to cherish, but these are seldom given equal treatment in the official propaganda—or in the value system of the average Russian, no doubt. And yet the country's leaders would never admit that they disregard the population's political rights, even if in fact they do. The leaders obviously want to appear fair and democratic.

While I was in Moscow the government ratified several United Nations conventions on human rights, promising the free right of emigration, the free movement of books and newspapers across international borders, and a number of other rights and guarantees which the Soviet government routinely ignores. The newspapers made much of this event, which occurred—not by accident, as the Russians like to say—at a time when the Soviet Union was receiving a lot of unfavorable publicity in the West about Solzhenitsyn and Andrei Sakharov. Professor Kudryavtsev, the lawyer I interviewed, boasted about the ratification of these UN conventions as further proof of the growth of socialist democracy. I noted that the government hadn't changed any of its policies, even those forbidden by the newly ratified conventions. He replied that the UN documents explicitly stated that nothing in them should contradict local laws or endanger a country's national security.

Only a transparent attempt is made to suggest that the leaders of Soviet society are chosen by the people. The country does vote for members of the Supreme Soviet, which is described as a legislature, but which in fact has only ceremonial functions. There is one candidate for each seat, chosen by the central authorities in Moscow, and voting is compulsory for all. It has become a test of the vitality of Soviet democracy—at least in official eyes—to get out the vote; in each election the percentage of eligible voters casting ballots must rise. This has created a palpably absurd situation; in the last elections 99.98 percent of the adult population allegedly voted. In a country of 250 million this is a statistical impossibility, even allowing for extensive efforts to collect the votes of travelers on trains, the sick in hospitals and so forth. More than one percent of the population is surely drunk, lost, dead since the last census, camping in the mountains or otherwise beyond the reach of the energetic vote-collectors. I met a man in Moscow who once worked in a polling station in the capital. He said the real number of non-voting adults in his region was about 11 percent; the Party had ordered in advance what figures should be reported.

· The real rulers of the country, the officials of the Communist Party, are promoted by pleasing their superiors, not by winning the votes of the public or their peers. This is a sensitive point among Party officials, particularly younger ones, and particularly in conversations with foreigners. They have to admit that no one ever voted to give them their power and privileges; both came down to them from above.

The most interesting political activity in Soviet society goes on out of sight. Debates, disputes and power struggles are deliberately hidden from public view. Occasionally the camouflage is insufficient and an observant Kremlinologist can discover something significant, but this is rare.

On the other hand, much ceremonial political activity is conducted in public. Soviet life is filled with formal, rehearsed events which create the impression of political activity. Foreign journalists stationed in Moscow are invited to most of the ceremonies, so I saw many.

One sort of ceremony, which the Soviets have adapted from western practice, is the press conference. For example, one was called in the Kremlin in March 1972 to announce plans for the celebration of the 50th anniversary of the formation of the USSR, scheduled for the following year. The press department of the Foreign Ministry sent an elaborate invitation, including a pass enabling me to drive into the Kremlin grounds. The large, ornate room where the conference took place was jammed. An official stood up and read a long speech full of statistics, dates and other facts from the Soviet Union's history. Movie cameras made in Eastern Europe whirred noisily while Soviet and Eastern European journalists scribbled prolific notes. After the speech, which contained not a sliver of new information, an intermission was announced. Soft drinks were served, and a text of the speech just read was handed out. Then the speaker announced that he would answer questions, and began reading queries from unnamed journalists. There had been no announcement that

questions should be handed in. (Written questions were almost always required at Soviet press conferences. Officials
would not answer oral questions spontaneously.)

"A representative of the United States has asked, what
about the people in the north of the country?" the official
read. This reporter, who received a detailed answer, must
have been the Moscow correspondent of the *New York Daily
World*, a communist paper. A Soviet journalist asked, "Will
there be a monument built in Moscow in honor of the 50th
anniversary of the USSR?" "That question," the spokesman
answered, "is still being considered. Maybe there will be a
monument, maybe not." The question period ended without a
hint of news passing the speaker's lips.

Grander occasions take place in the Kremlin's Palace of
Congresses, the giant hall whose architecture Khrushchev admired, which seats 7000 souls. In 1974 it was the site of an
"election meeting" at which Brezhnev met the voters from
the region of Moscow which elected him to the Supreme Soviet. The meeting began with a series of short speeches by citizens of the region. Each spoke in lavish terms of Brezhnev's
personal contribution to his or her area of concern: Brezhnev
the benefactor of science, the model for young people, the
workers' hero, and so forth. Though the wording was never
precisely identical, the message of each speech was the same,
suggesting that one editor was responsible for all of them. At
each compliment the entire audience, including all of
Brezhnev's colleagues in the leadership, applauded. This
meant clapping one's hands after every one or two sentences.

Brezhnev listened for an hour and 15 minutes with a dead-
pan expression. Finally it was his turn. He got up, adjusted
his spectacles and began reading a speech. Like those that
preceded it, his address contained not a single new idea—just
slogans. He read at his familiar slow pace, slurring the words,
apparently because of a speech defect, though many citizens
think it's a sign he's been drinking. When he finished, the hall
exploded in applause. The crowd stood on its feet to cheer.
Many shouted "Glory! Glory!" in unison.

The next day I happened to hear the three-o'clock news on
the radio. The announcer said all of Moscow was talking
about Brezhnev's speech, and then switched to a correspondent in one of the city's factories "for the reaction of the
workers." The reporter put his microphone in front of a

woman who read a prepared morsel of enthusiasm in a monotone voice.

Twice a year the delegates of the Supreme Soviet assemble to pass legislation. Its members meet in the Kremlin, a long hall under an arched roof. The deputies sit in rows behind desks reminiscent of Victorian schoolrooms. When a proposition is put to the group, the chairman announces the question and then calls for affirmative votes, demonstrating as she does so how to raise the right hand. Everyone in the hall, more than 1000 deputies, follows her lead, each forearm making a right angle at the elbow. Once when I was in the gallery the chairman watched the hands go up, said "Good" into the microphone, then brought her hand down; the others followed. Then she asked for votes against the proposition or abstentions, but there were none.

On this occasion the voting was followed by a long speech by Vladimir Kirillin, a deputy premier, on the problems of pollution. With lists of statistics and a series of promises he outlined what should and would be done to preserve natural resources. The speech was too much for many in the audience; some slept, some read newspapers or magazines. Members of the leadership sitting in a tribune behind Kirillin were no more attentive. Many chatted among themselves without paying him any heed.

The biggest ceremonies of the year are parades on November 7, the anniversary of the Revolution, and May 1, the May Day workers' holiday. After watching half a dozen of these spectacles, I decided that they deserve careful attention. They reveal both what the leaders of the society hope it looks like, and also something about its true nature.

There are two principal themes in these parades: the country's strength and the people's enthusiasm for their lives, their work and their leaders. The parades take place in Red Square, a beautiful architectural space surrounded by the walls of the Kremlin, the storybook cupolas of St. Basil's Cathedral and the neo-classical façade of GUM, Moscow's principal department store. The country's leaders watch from atop the red marble mausoleum in which Lenin* lies in a

---

* Or a reasonable facsimile. The Russians claim to have found a process which has preserved Lenin's body for more than 50 years after his death. No western embalmers claim a similar ability to preserve dead skin and flesh. Lenin in the mausoleum has a waxy look.

glass coffin—atop the corpse that symbolizes the Soviet state and its claim to power. The mausoleum stands midway down the square, just in front of the red-brick Kremlin wall. On each side of it, relatively small reviewing stands are filled with foreign diplomats and journalists and several thousand Soviet citizens.

On the day of the parade, central Moscow is closed to traffic. Those fortunate enough to have an invitation are instructed to come well before the spectacle begins, and to bring full identification. I showed my invitation and press card at least half a dozen times, and once to 10 or more inquiring policemen on my way into Red Square. At the entrance one must pass through three different lines of uniformed KGB men, each time presenting one's documents for careful inspection. A KGB man is stationed in every nearby hotel room which overlooks the square.

On November 7 the parade begins with an awesome display of military might. First the Minister of Defense reviews an honor guard of troops from an open car while loudspeakers blare with pre-recorded "Hurrahs!" as though they were coming from the soldiers. Then the parade begins. Military units march by in the goose-step that the Russians borrowed from the Prussians, an intimidating evocation of Hitler's loyal forces. The men are followed by machines, tanks, personnel carriers, amphibious vehicles, mobile rocket-launchers, then enormous intercontinental ballistic missiles pulled on long trailers by trucks, their warheads painted a bright red.

For several weeks the parade has been carefully rehearsed (in Red Square itself, in the middle of the night), and it is executed with awesome precision. The military weapons roar through the square, always in perfect formation.* The noise echoes off the Kremlin's walls as the vehicles race past, adding to the impression of power.

In May the military display is replaced by an exhibition of coordinated gymnastics and dancing by young people dressed in colorful outfits. Hundreds of bright-eyed young men and women execute maneuvers reminiscent of a Big Ten college band at the half-time of a football game, accompanied by

---

* I saw only one accident. On November 7, 1973, a tank broke down just as it entered the square, and it was abandoned next to the Kremlin wall. It still sat there forlornly hours later as the crowd began to leave.

pre-recorded cheers and salutes to the leaders looking on from Lenin's tomb.

Both parades end with mass "demonstrations" by thousands of Muscovites who have been marching from all corners of the city to converge on Red Square. They come from schools and factories, where they are selected to take part in the parade. An ordinary citizen who wants to march along with them is likely to be sent home. The marchers carry artificial flowers, Party slogans and photographs of the members of the Politburo (who thus look at pictures of themselves from the mausoleum). The marchers pull floats decorated with upward-thrusting graphs depicting economic achievements and other symbols of the country's strength and energy. These demonstrations last for several hours, but they continually repeat themselves: the same posters and floats, the same artificial flowers, and all the time, in the background, the same recorded hurrahs and slogans. ("Glory to the Central Committee of the Communist Party—glory!") The demonstrators march between long rows of plainclothes policemen. There must be several thousand soliders and police in the square during the parades to provide security. Stalin's daughter Svetlana has written that there are stacks of rifles behind Lenin's mausoleum—"just in case . . ."

Superficially these great parades convey precisely the message they are meant to. One leaves Red Square on November 7 awed by the Soviet military machine, impressed above all by its rockets, tanks and machines, all so shiny, so loud and so swift. On May 1 it is the healthy young people, all smiles and salutes, who leave the strongest impression. And on both occasions the throngs of loyal citizens, apparently so willing to walk for miles, usually in unpleasant weather, to salute their leaders suggest the popular enthusiasm that the leaders cultivate.

But the real message, I decided, was very different; it was more the message I took away from the other Soviet political ceremonies mentioned earlier. This is a society whose leaders mistrust the citizens, and therefore forbid any sort of spontaneous behavior. It is a society whose leaders aren't confident of their mandate to rule, and therefore contrive elaborate demonstrations of loyalty and enthusiasm. Nothing in the visible political ceremonies of the Soviet state is *real;* literally every event, every meeting of the Supreme Soviet, every May Day parade, is contrived. Each of these displays exudes unanimity, solidity and strength; never is there a hint of doubt or confusion. When votes are taken publicly, the results are unanimous. Every speech or resolution on a public occasion praises the leaders and the society's accomplishments. The real substance of Soviet politics is hidden, treated as a state secret.

In every society, leaders have ceremonies through which they demonstrate the legitimacy of their power to their followers.* It is common for the leader to travel around his domain and among his people, to show his face and the trappings of his power. The parades of November 7 and May 1 seem to be the Soviet version of this universal phenomenon, but in these parades the leaders barely move from their Kremlin fortress. The people are brought to them to pay homage; the leaders do no more than wave from a platform above the corpse of the man in whose name they rule.

Soviet leaders occasionally travel around the country, but by law—the censorship law—the news media cannot report in advance on their itineraries. Generally, the leaders meet ordinary people only in formal surroundings. A spontaneous crowd to cheer a leader is almost unheard of. (I heard of one in the city of Magadan in farthest Siberia. The day before Premier Kosygin visited Magadan, the shops received a supply of oranges, a treat rarely seen in that remote city. The next day people turned out on the sidewalk to welcome Mr. Kosygin.)

Soviet ceremonies are one manifestation of a national urge to make things look different than they really are. This is an ancient Russian inclination, one foreign travelers have remarked on for centuries, often bitterly, as though Russian deceptions were meant as personal insults. In fact the Russians practice the same deceit with each other.

In modern times they have even coined a new word for the phenomenon, an onomatopoetic gem, *pokazuka*. Only after living in Russia for more than two years did I discover *pokazuka*, but it was worth waiting for. Just as the Russians have no word for privacy, we have none to cover *pokazuka*. It comes from the Russian verb which means to show or show off. The slang noun means, roughly, something one does

---

* I am indebted to Clifford Geertz, an American anthropologist who has done striking, original work on the role of ceremonies.

for the sake of doing it, for show, so one can say it's been done. By definition, the act involved is of no material conse-quence, but it looks good. *Pokazuka* is a central element of Soviet life, part of the social landscape. Perhaps it is unnecessary to add that it also defies rational explanation, it is so perfectly Russian.

Political ceremonies are a form of *pokazuka*; so are the rules that govern them. It wouldn't do for the First Secretary of the Community Party of Georgia to make a speech on the anniversary of the Bolshevik Revolution describing how bad things are in Georgia. So on November 7 the First Secretary makes a speech about how wonderful life is in Georgia, how glorious are the accomplishments of Georgian communists, and so forth. Several weeks later the same official, speaking in a less ceremonial forum, may tell his colleagues (as he has on many occasions) that conditions in Georgia are terrible, that the Party is in disarray, that drastic reforms are required at once. No one will challenge him on the contradiction of his rosy holiday speech, because everyone knows the rules about holiday speeches: they are filled with good news, whether the real news is good or not.

Pokazuka goes far beyond political ceremonies. A false display for a foreign delegation is a form of *pokazuka*. The Party official who organizes white-collar workers to pick potatoes is performing another variety. A schoolteacher who gives passing grades to inadequate students because her school director wants to report a higher rate of "successfulness" in his annual statistics is also engaged in *pokazuka*. Another piece of *pokazuka* flies constantly above the Kremlin—red flags which billow perpetually in an artificial wind that blows out of their flagpoles. *Pokazuka* is everywhere. A Soviet engineer now living in America tried to explain it:

"For instance, say some big cheese is going to visit some enterprise. Now, any enterprise, no matter how insignificant, has a friend who will warn it when somebody important is going to drop in for a visit. That's the way the bigshots themselves want it, so that whoever they are going to visit will have time to fix things up in advance. I remember once I was teaching a course in a big Moscow factory, a pretty good factory, but one that sometimes got dirty. I was walking through the plant one night on the way to my class. One of the factory's managers was with me. We ran into a janitor who didn't know me, and I complimented him on how clean everything was—they were expecting some kind of delegation. 'Is this factory always so clean?' I asked the janitor. 'Oh yes,' he said, 'we have a great factory, a wonderful director,' etc., etc. And the guy I was with lit into him. 'What kind of nonsense are you talking?' he said. 'You know the place gets dirty all the time.'

"That janitor was interested in playing the game, because he knew that his own well-being depended on the factory director's standing with his bosses. If the janitor could help the director out, he would. Bonuses, rates of pay, benefits— everything depends on how well the factory director is doing. It's all interconnected—everybody's involved. Take another example, a quality-control worker in a factory. By law, he is supposed to reject any faulty product that comes off the production line. Just let him try! If he did what he was supposed to, they'd get rid of him in an instant. Everybody wants to create a false impression. Or another kind of example. A commission comes to see the new shops that a factory has built. They ask, 'How many of these new shops are already working?' 'Ten,' the factory director will reply, though he knows it's really three or four. But not one worker will speak up with the truth. I even saw this happen in a factory where they had prisoners working, forced labor, but none of them said to the visiting commission, 'Just a minute, comrades, you're being lied to.' Hell, no. Everybody wants the deception to succeed."

They are all in it together.

Soon after my arrival in Moscow I paid a call on the journalists who run the American Department at *Pravda*. It was late 1971, and the Russians questioned me for 90 minutes about the 1972 presidential election. It was a friendly chat, but unproductive for me. Finally I said I had talked enough about my country, could they tell me what was going on in the Soviet Union?

There was a long pause. Eventually, Georgi Ratiani, chief of the American Department, thought of an answer. "Cattle-breeding," he said, then paused again, apparently to muster an explanation. "There have been some interesting developments in cattle-breeding, you probably read about them in *Pravda* . . ." He said it with a straight face.

The issues of Soviet politics are not considered the proper concern of a foreigner. Many of them, in fact, aren't considered the proper concern of a Soviet citizen. Numerous topics that the Politburo must discuss are never mentioned in public—Soviet aid to foreign countries, for example, or the level of military spending.

Nevertheless, there isn't much doubt about what the issues are. Politicians everywhere have the same basic concerns: their own careers first of all, then budgetary issues, stability and prosperity at home, tranquility and invulnerability in relations with other countries. These are the substance of Soviet politics, too.

On the other hand, the Soviet political system has certain unique features. The most obvious of these, at least to a western eye, is the significance of formalistic mumbo-jumbo associated with the official ideology.

In the Soviet Union the politicians must decide what the people should be told. How should *Pravda* explain President Sadat's expulsion of Soviet advisors from Egypt? Should a book by Pasternak or Solzhenitsyn be published? Is a new play consistent with the standards of "socialist realism"? The Party organization has ideological workers at every level who consider such questions. The trickiest ones go all the way up to the Politburo for final resolution.

An outsider is tempted to ridicule the posturing involved in ideological disputes, but the fact is that they absorb the energies of countless Party functionaries, and therefore, one must conclude, of Party leaders too. Christian Duevel, a Kremlinologist who works for Radio Liberty in Munich, West Germany, found a remarkable example in 1974.

When a collection of speeches by Leonid Brezhnev was published in 1974, Duevel compared the texts with the original texts of the same speeches as they had appeared in Soviet newspapers during the preceding 20 years. He found that the new versions had been extensively altered so that Brezhnev's words of 20 years ago would appear consistent with the Party line of 1974. (Winston Smith, the hero of Orwell's *1984*, did this kind of editing for a living.)

For example, in 1955 Brezhnev said: "Fulfillment of the Party's directives will make it possible in the next few years to have an abundance of all agricultural products."

In the 1974 version of that speech the same sentence shrank: "The growth of all agricultural production will make it possible to raise the welfare of the toilers."

Presumably, the editors feared that if they published the

original version, readers in 1974 would ask what had happened to that promised "abundance of all agricultural products."

Information is a crucial factor in all politics, but in the USSR it has a special status. In western societies politicians absorb vast quantities of unofficial political information from newspapers, magazines and books, candid meetings with citizens and reports from political allies. The last of these may be a source of information in the Soviet system, too, but important officials are denied those other sources. They must depend almost entirely on official information—that which their superiors allow them to know, or which their subordinates believe deserves reporting. It is difficult to judge the consequences of this arrangement, but it must produce relatively narrow-minded officials, and it certainly helps the men at the very top control those below.

Just how the men who rule the country reach their decisions remains a genuine mystery. Presumably, Soviet politics involves argument, compromise, trades and bargains, but none of this is visible. Some western scholars have suggested that interest groups on the western model are beginning to operate in the Soviet Union, competing for the spoils of power among themselves, but I doubt the accuracy of this image. Interest groups in our sense are not possible in Soviet society, because no group except the senior leaders is permitted to pursue a narrow interest which does not fit into the leaders' grand design. The farmers of Uzbekistan and Tadzhikistan, were they able to pursue their own true interests, would grow fruits and vegetables instead of cotton, but in fact this is unthinkable. Soviet citizens—including Uzbek farmers—do what they are told. Every potential interest group must conform to the prevailing line, even when it contradicts the group's own immediate interests. Our interest groups are possible because we believe in the autonomy of individuals and groups. In the Soviet Union no one is granted the rights of autonomy.

The intense machinations of the Stalin and Khrushchev years encouraged the theory that Soviet politics consists of a permanent struggle for power among competing factions and individuals, but times have changed, and that theory may be out of date. Western experts doubted that the collective leadership of Brezhnev and Alexei Kosygin could long survive after it deposed Khrushchev. History suggested that this was a temporary arrangement. A similar group which ruled the country after Stalin died dissolved within four years, when Krushchev emerged as the dominant figure. But Krushchev's successors did survive as a real group, and their survival may mean that bitter struggles for personal power are not an inevitable aspect of the Soviet system.

This doesn't mean the members of the Politburo are a band of brothers all working together for nothing more than the good of the cause. According to the unconfirmable stories that circulate among well-informed citizens in Moscow, these are suspicious men. There appear to be only a few real friendships among members of the ruling group. In public, almost all call each other the formal "you" instead of the intimate "thou," which ordinary Russians use freely.*

Competition for power is part of any political process, and it is a rare politician who wouldn't like to be more important than he is. Soviet leaders obviously do maneuver for position, try to edge one another out of important posts, build networks of allies and supporters and otherwise promote and protect their own careers.

Cronyism is common in Soviet politics, and cannot be hidden. A number of Brezhnev's protégés from earlier stages of his career showed up in important positions in Moscow after he became the Party's general secretary in 1964. Roy Medvedev, the dissident historian and former Party member, who has many acquaintances in the ruling elite, has written bitterly about cronyism in *Our Socialist Democracy*:

> The alarming thing is that advancement is largely dependent on personal patronage, on friendships or family connections—political and professional qualifications are secondary. How else can one explain the fact that a man who invariably is the subject of scorn and ridicule in scientific circles has for seven years been head of the science section of the Central Committee? ... A senior Party official who has been working in Minsk [the capital of Belorussia] finds jobs in Moscow for those who assisted him in Belorussia, while a different leader, who was in Moldavia, assiduously pushes his colleagues

---

* An exception is the warm relationship between Brezhnev and Marshall A. A. Greshko, his Minister of Defense and an old comrade from the war.

[from there] up the administrative ladder. In this way extraordinary "spheres of influence" and "private domains" are formed within the apparatus of government—with "one of our boys" in charge. Individuals are often referred to as "so-and-so's man."

No doubt various alliances compete with each other, looking for ways to advance their power and prestige. But the Soviet Union is maturing, and in the process is probably finding ways to regulate the struggle for power and make it orderly. Such controls are part of every advanced civilization. Internecine political warfare never helped the Soviet system or the men who ran it, so the men who run it now have brought the warfare under control.

There are many hints of this in the public record of the Politburo's behavior. Most obvious has been its reluctance to alter its own membership or change the composition of the senior organs of state and Party. The 11 years from Krushchev's removal through 1975 were a period of unprecedented stability in the USSR's political leadership. Only the inevitable consequences of old age seem capable of disrupting it significantly.

The few senior leaders who were demoted during those years, without exception, were demoted honorably. Even Mr. Mzhavanadze, the Georgian leader whose wife was fleecing the people of Georgia, was allowed the appearance of a normal retirement due to old age. Stalin often shot the losers of political struggles; now the losers qualify for a comfortable if lonely retirement. Khrushchev had a *dacha*, a car, people to look after him and keep an eye on him. This is probably a typical pattern now.

Events in Czechoslovakia in 1968 created the severest crisis the post-Khrushchev leadership has faced, and its behavior then was revealing. At one crucial meeting of Soviet and Czechoslovak comrades, the entire Soviet Politburo turned out. Perhaps this was a demonstration that they all mistrusted one another, or could not trust any small group of their colleagues to do the talking. But I suspect that extraordinary meeting at Cierna Nad Tisou, on the Soviet-Czechoslovak border, was more a demonstration of the group mentality of the Soviet leaders. Because all were present, no one could claim to have misunderstood the situation; all would share equally the responsibility for whatever course of action was ultimately agreed upon.

This sort of politics-by-committee suits the personalities of the Soviet leaders. Roy Medvedev has observed that "the Party has no leaders who are genuinely popular and close to the masses, nor has it any theoreticians capable of giving a new impulse to Marxism-Leninism." A harsh judgment, but apparently true. These are not inspiring leaders, but good committee men.

None of this means that the members of the ruling elite share identical opinions. On the contrary, there is evidence of significant disagreements within the ruling circle.

I am in no position to explain how the leaders of Soviet society think, or how they argue among themselves about sensitive political subjects. I never had a candid conversation with a member of the Party's Central Committee or a provincial Party official. The closest I ever came to the Politburo was in the Great Hall of the Kremlin, an extraordinary room the size of a 19th-century railroad station, decorated in white with mammoth chandeliers. I was invited there in July 1974 for a reception in honor of President Nixon. With several thousand others I was swept into the room, which was lined with two tables nearly 100 yards long laden with drink and food on the most elaborate platters I have ever seen. I stopped to look around and realized suddenly that the entire Politburo was beside me. Andrei Gromyko, the Foreign Minister, was holding forth to several colleagues, apparently describing some aspect of the just-concluded talks between Mr. Nixon and Mr. Brezhnev. I moved within range of his voice just in time to hear him say, "But we weren't interested, we said no." Alas, Gromyko did not repeat what it was they said no to.

I was with Joseph Kraft, the syndicated columnist. We saw Boris Ponomarev, then a candidate member of the Politburo, and struck up a conversation. Kraft had met Ponomarev in Washington. Standing just two feet away was Mikhail Suslov, the fourth-ranking member of the Politburo, the Party's senior ideologist and probably the leader of the group that removed Mr. Khrushchev in 1964. Kraft told Ponomarev (I was acting as an interpreter) that he would love to meet Suslov. As I translated this, Suslov shuffled away; apparently he overheard the request.

So firsthand experience cannot help me describe the politics of the Politburo or the private views of the country's most powerful citizens. The only members of the elite whom I got to know belonged to an international-affairs establishment in Moscow—journalists, diplomats and academics who specialize in international relations. They are a fascinating group, but not representative, because they have traveled widely, studied the outside world and overcome the narrowness of their own backgrounds.

Nevertheless, concrete evidence and the testimony of well-informed Russians are both available. Because the subject here is political struggle, it cannot be kept entirely secret; where there is a fire, there must also be a little smoke. The most unmistakable wisps suggest the existence of right-wing opposition to the relatively moderate line of the present leadership. Much of this opposition grows out of extreme Russian nationalism; some of it can be called neo-Stalinism.

The best evidence of these tendencies is to be found in recent literature. Reactionary elements have sufficient influence to sponsor the publication of literature which reflects their views. The most successful have been writers associated loosely with the *Russiti,* Slavophile Russian nationalists who argue that traditional Russian society must be preserved against both western influences and—implicitly—the homogenizing effect of the multi-national Soviet state.

Influential members of the Soviet elite sympathize with the view that Russia is more important than the Soviet Union, and that things uniquely Russian—the Orthodox Church, for example, or the ancient Russian village—need to be protected.

Literary Gazette, the weekly organ of the Union of Writers and the most serious Soviet newspaper, confirmed the existence of a serious dispute over Russian nationalism in November 1972. The paper published a 10,000-word article by an important Party official, Alexander Yakovlev, acting director of the Central Committee's propaganda department, which sharply criticized the Russian nationalists, naming more than a dozen of them. Like the material he attacked—largely short stories and novels which only hinted at Russian nationalist arguments—Yakovlev's article was indirect and at some points indecipherable. The first of these points was its title, "Against Anti-Historicism," as ambiguous in Russian as it sounds in English. Yakovlev's arguments seemed mild enough: writers had to recognize the continuing pre-eminence of the working class; they had to stop romanticizing the "stagnant daily life" of the Russian village; they should show less concern for old churches and monuments and more respect for the anti-nationalistic "internationalism" of Marxist-Leninist ideology.

Yakovlev's article, I was told by credible informants, caused prolonged controversy. *Literary Gazette* held it up for months until powerful figures in the Central Committee, perhaps even in the Politburo, pushed it into print. If publication of the article represented a victory for Yakovlev and those who agreed with him, the victory was shortlived. Several months later Yakovlev suffered one of the classic demotions of Soviet politics: he was named the Soviet Union's ambassador to Canada.

Roy Medvedev writes in *On Socialist Democracy*:

> The Russian nationalists have up to now been openly supported in such influential bodies as the political department of the army and the central committee of the Young Communist League, where their ideas are used for the purpose of "patriotic education." One may assume that in the face of growing political apathy among young people and soldiers, their loss of interest in the vulgar and oversimplified Marxism so inadequate for the needs of our time, many of the officials responsible for political education in the Young Communist League and the army are falling back on an appeal to deepseated nationalist sentiments and ideas. Internationalism goes by the boards as they attempt to rouse feelings of national exclusiveness. In this way our youth is being taught a kind of patriotism most inappropriate for citizens of the first socialist country of the world.

> The crudest forms of nationalist preaching by the *Russiti* have been condemned in the Party press, and even in a special resolution of the Politburo [never publicized]. However, in other more veiled forms, the *Russiti* movement continues to develop and to receive highly influential support.

Medvedev's book contains a remarkable revelation about an extreme nationalist group in Moscow whose "racist program speaks of the 'Russian race,' 'the voice of the blood,' 'the cosmic mission of the people,' the 'duty to our ancestors,' and calls for the 'sterilization of women who give themselves to foreigners.' "

According to Medvedev, whose information has proven accurate in the past, "This program was summed up in 1965 by a leading official of the Moscow Young Communist League, Valery Skurlatov, in his 'Rules of Morality,' duplicated and distributed among the activists of the Moscow City Committee [of the Komsomol, or Young Communist League] and the Komsomol central committee."

This sort of extreme nationalism is traditionally associated with anti-Semitism and intense anti-foreign feeling, both of which are still widespread. Medvedev learned of a lecture by a senior officer of the Red Army's political department "in which he urged that the number of international industrial exhibitions in the USSR be reduced" as a means, apparently, of minimizing foreign influences.

Reactionary neo-Stalinism also has strong supporters in important places. Since Khrushchev's demise in 1964 Stalin's official standing has improved. He is still rarely mentioned and almost never praised, but occasionally he is portrayed sympathetically in a movie or book. In recent years the most striking of these was a novel called *War* by Ivan Stadnyuk, published in the magazine *Young Guards*, an organ sympathetic to the neo-Stalinists. Stadnyuk wrote an apologia for the dictator, absolving him of all wrongdoing in the early days of the war, forgiving his cult of personality and even offering an indirect justification for his purges, which killed millions. The novel is the work of a sycophant, as one small excerpt may demonstrate. This is a description of Stalin sitting at his desk, drafting his first wartime speech to the people while staring at a portrait of himself:

> Yes, in the picture he breathed with immortality. Stalin himself thought that was just how he looked when he sat at his desk with a pen in his hand, writing, looking into the recesses of his own knowledge, freely and generously guiding obedient thoughts, giving them energy, determining new basic principles and connections between comprehensive scientific ideas and practical realities.

Medvedev, a proponent of democratic socialism, abhors neo-Stalinism, which he says is powerful and perhaps gaining strength. The neo-Stalinists, he writes, want to restore " 'firm' leadership and a 'strong' regime—essentially to bring back Stalin's administrative and terrorist methods, excluding only some of the extreme forms". They favor more censorship, tighter control of all spheres of life, an end to economic reforms and a hard-line foreign policy, particularly toward other communist countries. Medvedev blames neo-Stalinists for promoting the invasion of Czechoslovakia in 1968, and writes that extreme neo-Stalinists also proposed intervening in Romania and Yugoslavia. "Neo-Stalinism springs essentially from a conviction that socialism is so weak that it cannot defend itself except by totally suppressing all forces supposedly antagonistic to it."

The existence of neo-Stalinists is not surprising. In America we still have McKinley Republicans, Roosevelt Democrats and Kennedy New Frontiersmen. Politicians are usually molded by the age in which they come to power or maturity; for several generations of Russians, that was the age of Stalin. It must be especially painful for older communists to watch the current leadership pursue *détente* with the West, to end the jamming of BBC and Voice of America broadcasts in Russian, to allow Soviet scientists to travel abroad. These are signs of softness, the sort of softness Stalin would never tolerate.

More surprising, I think, is the fact that there is also opposition from another extreme, from relatively liberal and progressive people who want to push the country further away from Stalinism. I met some of these people myself, mostly academics, some of them with access to powerful figures in the Party hierarchy. Traveling through Eastern Europe, I met Poles, Hungarians and Yugoslavs who knew of progressives in various branches of the Soviet elite. Economists who favor reform, sociologists who propose honest research into the nature of Soviet society, Party officials who want to break out of the confinement of traditional ideology—all exist in the Soviet Union today.

Like oppositionists on the right, these "Party democrats," as Medvedev calls them, come in many different shades. Some are only vaguely progressive; others favor radical changes in the system. All of them together, however, comprise "the weakest trend . . . inside the Party," in Medvedev's words—a painful admission for him, because he so fervently wishes them well. But all the available evidence does suggest that this is the weakest single faction.

The strongest, of course, is the great conservative middle which runs the country, and to which the majority of the ruling elite remains loyal. Medvedev calls them the "moderate conservatives":

> What chiefly distinguishes them is simply a desire to preserve the present regime and to prevent any kind of appreciable shift either to the left or to the right. Turning a blind eye to the many acute political and economic problems facing the country, they oppose the modernization of our social system, deny the need for a comprehensive review of all our past and present policies, and obstruct the application of new and more progressive principles to domestic and foreign affairs. . . . [They want] to avoid any kind of crisis or open conflict, and as far as possible to maintain or in any case to prolong the none-too-stable equilibrium which now exists in the top ranks of the Party. . . .

So there are differences at the top. At the same time there is a remarkably broad consensus about a subject the ruling elites of western countries can never agree on: the basic goals of the society. Soviet officials may argue about Russian nationalism, about economic reform and tolerance for non-conformity, but they seem to agree on the goals they are trying to achieve. They want a prosperous and strong Soviet Union (though some might call it Russia instead—a potentially serious disagreement); they want more status and influence abroad; they want more health, welfare and prosperity at home; they want stability in their country and throughout the communist world. There are no serious arguments about the objectives of domestic or foreign policy, no serious disputes about the proper role of the government or Party in the lives of the citizenry, very little uncertainty about the shape of the ideal future.

An American professor went to Moscow several years ago to try to find out how the Soviet system worked. He was an official guest, and had interviews with many Soviet citizens, mostly academics like himself. One assured the American that the Soviet system really wasn't much different from any other, and then he drew a rough diagram. Here on the left, he said, we have the national goals. In the middle we have the interests of various groups in our society. The goals are filtered through these interests, he explained, producing government policy over here on the right. Isn't it the same in America? the Russian asked.

No, the professor answered, it isn't. In America no two people can agree on what the national goals are.

The urge to interpret Soviet politics as a constant conflict among contestants for power has probably distorted our view of what really goes on. For example, many western experts have claimed to perceive a debate about how much the Soviet Union should spend on armaments. The temptation to see a conflict, and also to see Soviet politics in familiar, western terms, has led to the view that a group of hawks associated with the Ministry of Defense presses for more spending, while doves anxious to improve the standard of living favor less.

There probably hasn't been any such dispute. No doubt—as Khrushchev indicates in his memoirs—military men are always ready to spend more money: no doubt, too, some Soviet officials think more should be spent on the civilian economy. Yet there has never been any evidence that real doves can be found in the Politburo. The Bolsheviks have always put great emphasis on military strength, which secured their Revolution in the civil war and legitimized their rule in World War II. The Soviet defense establishment has grown steadily since the 1930s. Brezhnev, to cite one example, is a past soldier and a constant supporter of the Ministry of Defense. He may be remembered as an architect of *détente*, but the period of his leadership is more notable for its military accomplishments. I suspect that the entire Politburo agrees on both the desirability of *détente* and the necessity for continued expansion of the country's military forces.

The Politburo makes all important decisions, but an outsider is repeatedly surprised by the Soviet definition of "important." I knew an old communist in Moscow who once attended a Politburo meeting chaired by Khrushchev. The topic of the day was errors in book-publishing. Each member of the Politburo worked from a thick dossier containing samples from several books to be discussed. The first was a book on China, written three years earlier and obviously far off the increasingly anti-Chinese Party line by the time it appeared. The director of the publishing house responsible was fired. A second book under consideration was about the care of pets. It recommended that dogs be fed meat, eggs and other good foods at a time when people couldn't find enough of these commodities for themselves. The head of that publishing enterprise was fired, too.

Khrushchev described a discussion among the "collective leadership" about Svyatoslav Richter, the brilliant pianist: "Comrade Richter . . . appealed for permission to go abroad as part of a cultural exchange. . . . Right away the people around me started shaking their heads and saying it would be risky to send Comrade Richter abroad because of his German background. He had a mother living in West Germany and people warned me that he probably wanted to be reunited with her."

Khrushchev recalled with evident pride that he had told his colleagues, "We simply can't mistrust everybody and suspect everybody of being a traitor." He allowed Richter to travel to the West, and noted happily that "he came back."

What does it signify about a huge and powerful country that its senior leaders must decide on the foreign travels of concert pianists? That is one formulation of the basic question about the Soviet system which hounded me for three years: What's going on here? I pursued an answer to that question in countless conversations over tea and cold supper in the apartments of Moscow's intellectuals, forcing my unanswerable questions into otherwise relaxed conversations, demanding explanations of things that Russians seldom question.

One night, in a stark new neighborhood of high-rise apartments in a remote corner of Moscow, two changes on the subway and three bus stops from my apartment downtown, I heard a satisfying answer. It came from an unusual man named Mikhail Agurski, an engineer whose father was an American citizen and an early Communist Party emissary to the United States after the Bolshevik Revolution, a Jew later purged by Stalin. Agurski said he thought he could explain Soviet society to an American with the help of two diagrams, and he drew them.

American society, Agurski said, might be graphically described in this fashion:

This arrangement doesn't guarantee absolute stability. The ball can move back and forth, but only within the limits of the diagram—limits generated by the society itself. The turbulent 1960s and 1970s demonstrated that the ball can move back and forth dramatically; the survival of America despite the turmoil proved that the barriers were effective.

Soviet society, by contrast, might be pictured like this:

Here, obviously, the immobility of the ball is crucial. In place, it is stable. But a good jolt could throw it out of its protective groove, and the society provides no additional barriers to control it. The men who rule the country realize this, and therefore apply restraints, pictured as lines in the diagram. These internal controls are the anchors that hold the ball in its niche.

Why are the barriers in the Soviet diagram so low? This is a graphic device to depict the precariousness of stability in Soviet society, Agurski said, a precariousness explained by two factors. First, centrifugal forces within the Soviet Union, especially local nationalism in the outlying republics, tend to pull its components apart. Americans accept their common nationality without question, but some Soviet citizens do not—a potential source of grave troubles. Second, Russian governments have always been authoritarian, so Russians have no experience with democratic practices, self-discipline and self-restraint. Any experiment with those untasted fruits might produce the anarchy that Russians have feared for centuries.

That is Agurski's theory, not mine. It raises several questions, some about its optimistic view of America, which is not the subject here. I also questioned the idea that Soviet society is on the brink of instability. An outsider doesn't sense this. On the contrary, Soviet society looks stable; in Russia it looks almost serene. The people seem proud and loyal, devoted to the slogans of communism and fully willing to accept the legitimacy of the regime. My reaction to most of the regime's arbitrary controls was that they weren't necessary. The system would survive without them.

But what did I know? Perhaps the appearance of stability was deceiving. Or, more realistically, perhaps the country's leaders share my impression of stability, but worry constantly that the impression is wrong, or that the stability is artificial. The leaders realize that their power was never granted by popular mandate, nor endorsed even tacitly by the people of many outlying republics. They understand the potential strength of local nationalism among their non-Russian subjects. Today's stability, they must reckon, depends on today's controls. They have discomfiting memories of 1956, when Khrushchev jolted the ball by denouncing Stalin; uprisings followed in Hungary and Poland which shook the entire empire. So the diagram, with its implied precariousness, just might be correct. If it is, any change in the status quo, any jolt to the ball, would be extraordinarily dangerous. The fear that the diagram *might* be accurate would be enough to make the leadership act as though it *is* accurate. After all, these are cautious men who don't take chances.

I once had a long talk with a prominent Russian journalist about the painfully slow pace at which his country seems to change, which he explained with a proverb, "Every vegetable ripens at its own speed."

4 · *The Rulers*

"... maybe gaiety is a national characteristic of the English."

—*Nikita S. Khrushchev*

THE MEN AND women who make the Soviet system work lead different lives than do the ordinary Russians described in Chapter 2. In many ways they are different people. In Russian they are called the *nachalstvo*, an untranslatable word, often used ironically, whose literal meaning is "the authorities," but whose true sense is more "the big cheeses." They live in a world apart.

My apartment in Moscow was on Kutuzovski Prospekt, a boulevard seven lanes wide which begins at the Moscow River. It carries traffic out of the city toward Minsk to the southeast, and toward the villages outside the capital where important citizens have country *dachas*. Many of the country's leaders also live along Kutuzovski Prospekt, so official limousines are a regular part of the traffic. One day I stood on the sidewalk with a Russian workingman and watched one of the long, handmade Zil limousines used by Politburo members (copied from an American Lincoln) roar down the center lane of Kutuzovski Prospekt, preceded by a yellow police car. (The center lane is reserved for cars of the *nachalstvo*.)

"The *nachalstvo* never see how the rest of us live," my companion said, nodding toward the passing limousines. "They go from home to office and home again, escorted all the way. They never go shopping—stuff is brought to them. They don't even go to the barber, the barber comes to them and gives them all kinds of special services. Their wives don't do the cooking, their maids do. They are always under control—I mean surrounded by police, escorted here and there. No, they don't see what you and I see. They never wait in line. What kind of life is that?"

A good life, by Soviet standards, but still a very Soviet life by ours.

The society works because the Soviet people recognize its sanctions, its ladders of success and its standards of achievement. The people who run the society are those who accepted, climbed, achieved more than the others. They have that in common, but they differ among themselves. Some are cruel and corrupt, others kind and upstanding; some are fools, some are shrewd. All are privileged.

It is illegal to turn left from Kalinin Prospekt onto Granovskovo Street, just opposite the Lenin Library in central Moscow. But if a car whose license plate begins with the letters MOC appraoches that intersection with its left-turn signal blinking, the policeman on duty will stop oncoming traffic and wave it through.

License plates beginning with MOC belong to members and staff of the Party's Central Committee, and illegal left turns are one of the privileges that accrue to such citizens. They come to Granovskovo Street to collect more privileges—food and clothing sold in a special store open only to them. The store is hidden behind a door marked BUREAU OF SPECIAL PASSES in a building where—according to a plaque on the wall—Lenin spoke to Red Guards on their way to the civil-war front in 1919. Granovskovo Street is usually lined with chauffeur-driven cars waiting for their official proprietors to come out of the store. Most of the customers emerge carrying nondescript packages wrapped in brown paper.

There are more limousines around the corner on Kalinin Prospekt in front of the Kremlin Polyclinic, a special medical facility for a privileged few. The clinic belongs to the

"Fourth Department" of the Ministry of Health, an entire division of the Soviet Union's health service which serves only the elite. Every major city has a Fourth Department clinic, and perhaps also a hospital, for the privileged.

The Fourth Department of the Ministry of Health publishes a book which tells its employees exactly what sort of treatment officials at each level of the bureaucracy are entitled to, what kind of room, with what furnishings, and so forth.

The entire system of privileges is rigidly hierarchical. An ambitious young man working his way up through the ranks can see ahead to the privileges he will receive at each level. Even inside the same enterprise there may be several dining rooms, each with a different quality of food, each open to a different rank of official.

Privileges insulate those at the very top, a tiny group of perhaps only two or three dozen men, from all the harassments and discomforts of an ordinary citizen's life. Attended by servants and chauffeurs, housed grandly in country *dachas*, hunting lodges and beach houses, provided with an abundance of fine food and drink, they must live about as well as the ruling classes of any capitalist society. There is a joke about this involving Mr. Brezhnev and his late mother, who (in the joke) still lives in a country village. Mr. Brezhnev had invited her to his hunting lodge in Zavidovo on the Volga, and shows her around the paneled dining room, the sunken bath, the swimming pool, the forest stocked with deer and bear. "Well, Mama," he finally says, "how do you like it?" "Oh," she replies, "it's marvelous! But aren't you afraid the Bolsheviks might come back?"

It *is* marvelous, at least that part of it an outsider can glimpse. The nicest spot around Moscow is the section east of the city where the *nachalstvo* have their *dachas*, a serene area of regal old pines, birch groves, winding rivers and open fields. On the day after a snowstorm the woods around the village of Uspenskoye are something out of a fairy tale. Snow clings to the trunks and boughs of pine trees like too much sticky frosting to a cake. Thin streams of smoke rise out of the chimneys of the big *dachas*—two- and three-story houses, many made of brick, most surrounded by several acres of land and high walls. The *dachas* of the leaders of state and Party are in this area, but out of view, at the ends of long driveways whose entrances are marked with DO NOT ENTER signs. But even a foreigner can walk and ski nearby, around the *dachas* of prominent scientists, important officials of bygone days and other privileged citizens.

The loveliest section of the Crimean coast, near Yalta, is similarly reserved for the *nachalstvo*. From a boat traveling along the coast one can see that large sections of the beach have been walled off for the exclusive use of important people. A man who worked in the Nitikski Botanical Gardens in Yalta told me that an ordinary citizen who made the mistake of going too close to these closed beaches would be shooed away gruffly by a guard.

When Dmitri Polyanski, a member of the Politburo, built a new hunting lodge near Kaluga, southeast of Moscow, the woods in the area were closed off. They were stocked with game and deer, and residents of the region could hear the shooting of guns on the weekends.

Only in Moscow do the leaders live anywhere near the common folk. Khrushchev* decided that they should move out of the Kremlin, where many had lived during the Stalin years, and now the senior men all have apartments in the city. Several, including Premier Kosygin, live in a specially built modern apartment house on the Vorobyevskoye Way atop the Lenin Hills, overlooking all Moscow. But others, including Brezhnev, have apartments—no doubt large apartments—in buildings along Kutuzovski Prospekt that are occupied by much lesser mortals, too. Judging by the traffic of limousines, the leaders prefer their suburban *dachas* to these city apartments.

The senior leaders never encounter the usual difficulties of shopping. Their food, it is said, comes from a special shop to which they pay a nominal fee of 50 to 70 rubles a month. For this amount, which is less than most workers' families spend for food, they are entitled to order whatever they want, including rare products, such as fine beef and caviar, which

---

* Khrushchev had the reputation, especially among intellectuals in Moscow, of being a relatively austere man, less interested in the privileges of power than many of his colleagues. One rumor which spread through the capital a few years ago was that Brezhnev, Kosygin and the others moved against Khrushchev in 1964 when they learned that he planned to do away with many of their privileges. I never learned where this story originated, and it may be baseless, but it does indicate the sort of thing many Muscovites are prepared to believe about their leaders.

are not sold to the public. Special tailors make their clothes. They can acquire foreign cars and gadgets otherwise never seen in the Soviet Union. In sum, they live in a contrived environment. Even their vodka is better than the ordinary man's.

Svetlana Alliluyeva has explained how Anastas Mikoyan, the only important Soviet leader of modern times to enjoy an honorable retirement, was affected by the false environment in which he lived when he was responsible for the Soviet food industry:

> At Mikoyan's dacha, even in winter, fresh green vegetables from his own hothouses were always served. Helping me to some, he once said, "In the USSR people haven't got the habit of eating green vegetables." To which I told him that everyone loved green vegetables but couldn't buy them anywhere.
>
> "What are you saying!" exclaimed Mikoyan. "This year we sold twice as many green vegetables to the people as in any previous year!"

Immunity to the difficulties of ordinary life ends abruptly just below the highest level. (So, one might add, does responsibility for running the country.) But privileges pervade the system, and reach far down into the bureaucracy of state and Party to induce participants upward.

The inducements amount to lesser versions of the privileges available at the very top. In Central Asia I met a man with access to privileges who explained the system in the capital city of an outlying republic:

"There are privileges for the *nachalstvo*. There are government *dachas* and other kinds of special *dachas*. . . . There are special polyclinics. There are special stores. And there are privileges in the form of free trips to resorts. There are special closed dining rooms. The best one is the Council of Ministers dining room. They cook very well there, the selection is good and the prices are lower than in ordinary cafeterias. There are closed stores for staff of the Central Committee [of the republican Communist Party] and the Council of Ministers. Those stores sell fresh meat, and at a good price. Say in the farmers' market meat costs four rubles a kilo; in the closed store it is 1.80. And it is always available. So are a lot of other products—for instance, Armenian cognac. That's very popular in Moscow, but it's almost impossible to get in our ordinary stores. They also have good canned foods, good salami, vegetables and fruit. . . ."

An Armenian scientist told me about the "closed distributor" in Yerevan, a shop which provides rare goods on the basis of written allocations. Before a big holiday those entitled to use the store receive written notification of what they can buy. A senior Party official, for example, might be permitted to buy as much caviar as he likes, while someone of a lower rank can buy only 300 grams.

The distribution of private cars works similarly. An official is given a piece of paper entitling him to buy a car without waiting in line—a line that may last a year in Moscow, five years in a provincial city. Senior officials get good apartments while others wait. They get a piece of land in the country to build a *dacha*, or, above a certain level, they are allocated the *dacha* itself. Special box offices sell tickets to the privileged for popular concerts and theaters that ordinary citizens can virtually never attend—the Bolshoi in Moscow, for instance.

Privileges begin at an early age. During a national congress of the Young Communist League in Moscow, selected delegates and guests were invited to shop in a makeshift store, set up just for the congress, which sold stylish western clothes.

Officers in the armed forces have a system of privileges all their own, and represent one of the largest groups of pampered citizens. I met a young man in Moscow whose father was a dentist in the Army, a colonel stationed near the Chinese border. He earned 550 rubles a month—three times the earnings of an ordinary dentist, and an extraordinary salary by Soviet standards.

Of all the regime's inducements, none is stronger than the rarely granted privilege of travel abroad. A westerner whose foreign travel is limited only by financial considerations cannot begin to understand the exotic significance of a trip abroad for a Soviet citizen. Not least because it is so unusual, a week in Paris is something utterly fantastic, exciting, exhilarating. Not everyone feels this way: it is a point of pride among some patriots that they don't need to see the western world. Judging by my experience, though, such patriots are few. For most of the Russians whom I got to know, nothing could compare with a trip to another country, particularly a western country.

Officials of the Young Communist League now have a

chance to go to America on exchanges of young political
leaders. According to the Americans who take part in this exchange, the Russians flaunt their eagerness for an invitation.
Journalists on the major newspapers seem to be constantly
maneuvering for a trip overseas. Trading officials obviously
relish their excursions abroad. The lucky few who see the
world return home with foreign clothes, romantic tales and
the latest rock records for their children—who thus become
the envy of every other kid on the block.

Some privileges that accompany rank in Soviet society are
allocated less formally. For instance, the First Secretary of an
oblast Party committee receives foreign films from Moscow
that are deemed unsuitable for general distribution. He can
invite whomever he likes to his private screening room, as a
means of rewarding those who have pleased him in his own
little fiefdom.

Privileges are also available to those bold enough to ask
for them, a function of Russians' reflexive response to official
titles. I knew a man in Moscow who telephoned one of the
capital's most popular restaurants and said he was calling
from the Central Committee. He wanted a table for twelve,
with a special menu which he enumerated, and the best possible service. The restaurant made no attempt to verify the
identity of the caller, and filled his order with alacrity. The
manager of a theater or concert hall knows from experience
that he should save a few of the best seats until the very last
moment, a hedge against the unexpected appearance of someone important (or someone who claims to be important).

The privileged few usually understand the advantages of
helping one another. An editor whose son was a journalism
student at Moscow State University once complained to me
bitterly that a colleague had let him down. His son needed to
publish a few articles to demonstrate professional competence. The father had approached the editor of a small magazine who could easily have cooperated, but the editor never
published the son's work. "Why, I'd never behave that way,"
my acquaintance said, visibly angered. "I hope he doesn't
have any children who need favors from *me*."

The children of successful people tend to inherit a part of
their parents' status. It generally isn't possible to pass on great
wealth or political power, but the privileged life is shared by
the younger generation. According to a graduate of the Mos-

cow State Institute for International Relations, a special college that trains diplomats and other officials for foreign assignments, a high percentage of the students were "children of the privileged class."

"You can see whose children are admitted even before the entrance exams," he said, "when, for instance, generals come into the school wearing all their decorations and go right to the rector's office. They come out after a while, confident that their sons will be admitted."

I heard of numerous cases in which the children of famous people received unsolicited special treatment. Whoever was responsible simply thought it would be wise to favor the young person with a famous name.

It is difficult to form an opinion about people who hold positions of responsibility without doing some kind of business with them, and an American journalist living in the Soviet Union seldom has an opportunity to do business with anyone. I met numerous officials and often heard them boast, but rarely saw them perform. Officials who do their jobs poorly may make a good impression on visitors, an impression not easy to test.

I had brief encounters with hundreds of officials all over the Soviet Union. Those who made a striking impression were few and far between. The vast majority seemed colorless, unimaginative, uncritical and contented. What was lacking—it is lacking in most Soviet citizens—was a sense of personal sovereignty, a feeling that individual action was possible and could be effective.* The few officials I met who seemed to be unusually competent all defied this general rule. They conveyed a conviction that by themselves they might do something significant and useful.

A good example is Lev Vasilyev, a deputy minister of the Ministry of the Automobile Industry, who is in charge of building the world's largest truck plant on the banks of the Kama River, 600 miles east of Moscow. In a meeting with half a dozen American correspondents, Mr. Vasilyev fairly brandished his self-confidence. By adopting an open and engaging personal manner, by admitting some problems, by demonstrating a mastery of detail and a winning way with his

---

* We sometimes speak of a person's "sense of self." This concept does not exist in the Russian language.

own subordinates, Vasilyev convinced those present that the Soviet government had made a good choice when it put him in charge of the single most important industrial project of the Five Year Plan.

Arguably, Mr. Vasilyev had to be an impressive fellow: if the Soviet Union didn't have a good man to run its most important industrial enterprise, the country would be in dire straits. But there are also good people in far lesser jobs—Kadzhibaba Abassov, for example, the director of the Southern Caspian Fishing and Water Resources Administration. I met Mr. Abassov in Baku, the capital of Soviet Azerbaijan.

His job was to try to protect the fish in the Caspian Sea and its tributaries. This put him at odds with a great many other bureaucrats who were supposed to exploit the sea and the rivers for industrial purposes—the most important purposes there can be in the Soviet Union. Mr. Abassov spoke frankly about the strength of his competition, and their success in making the Caspian's tributaries so dirty that fish could no longer survive in most of them.

The biggest polluter in the Caspian is oil. The sea (actually a saltwater lake) sits on a giant oil field which produces seven to eight percent of the Soviet Union's petroleum. A lot of it is spilled. "If you asked me," Mr. Abassov said, "I would say stop drilling oil. Of course that's only my opinion." He acknowledged that it stands no chance of being accepted by higher authorities, so Mr. Abassov and his colleagues are trying to persuade the enterprises that extract, transport and handle the oil to do so carefully.

To this end Mr. Abassov's organization can fine transgressors as much as 100 rubles. This wasn't a great deal, he agreed, but it could come from the pocket of an individual, which made it more significant. He had tried to impose much stiffer fines on flagrant violators of the pollution regulations, but he didn't want to discuss these cases in detail. "Moscow will decide on them," he said. He acknowledged that some executives (presumably the most influential ones) didn't pay their fines. The director of a chemical factory, for example, said he was "confused" by the first notice that he had been fined, which he ignored. The second time, Mr. Abassov said, he paid.

This enthusiastic little man talked at length about ways of saving the precious caviar that the Caspian's sturgeon produce less of every year. (Because of pollution, the Russians now import huge quantities of caviar from Iran, across the Caspian Sea. Iran's tributaries are still relatively clean.) Mr. Abassov spoke as though the sturgeon were his relatives. There were plenty of sturgeon, he said, but they were stuck in the Caspian—they couldn't swim up the tributaries to spawn. Many would never lay their eggs. I left a long discussion with Mr. Abassov with the good feeling that comes from an encounter with a public official who knows his business and cares about it.

More typical Soviet officials make no impression at all. Looking back at my notes of meetings with dozens of officials, I find it impossible to conjure up a clear image of most of them. I recall a stream of mostly smallish, heavy-set men, dressed in formless suits of gray or dark brown, with hair flowing back from their foreheads in the classic Russian manner, solemnly reciting statistics or a memorized briefing about their factory, store, school, whatever.

These briefings are so common that they are given without thought. Soviet officials are not used to questions of the kind western journalists ask, and rigorous questioning can catch them unprepared. There was an example of this when Alexei P. Shitikov, chairman of one house of the Supreme Soviet, the national parliament, met with a group of American journalists. Earlier in his career Shitikov was Party Secretary in the tiny Jewish Autonomous Oblast in the Soviet far east, to which Stalin apparently considered relocating the entire Jewish population of the Soviet Union.

Shitikov answered several questions about Jewish emigration, and said at one point that no Jews living in the autonomous *oblast* had asked to emigrate. Why was that? he was asked. "Because conditions there are good," he answered, "there is no discrimination." Did that mean that conditions in Kiev (where thousands had applied to emigrate) were bad? There was an awkward moment. "Oh, I don't know about Kiev," Shitikov replied. He smiled self-consciously. You caught me, he seemed to be saying but he didn't say it. He changed the subject.

The gray sameness of Soviet officialdom inspired a movie director I knew in Moscow to concoct the following idea for a film: The bigshots in a Russian river town get together one night for a celebration in a local restaurant. The restaurant is on a riverboat tied to a dock downtown. Unbeknownst to those on board, the riverboat breaks away from its mooring;

while the party gets drunker and drunker, the boat sails to the next town downstream, where by chance it bumps into a dock and stays put. The next morning the celebrants emerge from the boat and go off to work, not noticing that they are in the wrong town. (Like bureaucrats, towns in the USSR tend to look alike.) The locals are surprised by the strange faces that appear in the offices of important officials, but no one has the courage to ask what has happened, because they aren't sure that anything has happened.

Privately, the men and women who hold power in Soviet society make sharp distinctions among their colleagues; they wouldn't accept the idea that all are interchangeable. A Russian diplomat once startled me by dismissing Jacob Malik, the Soviet ambassador to the United Nations, as "an extremist." Another official told me there was a world of difference between two academics who have advised Mr. Brezhnev about the western world. One of them, Georgi Arbatov of the USA Institute, was a strong man who said what he believed, no matter who asked him. The other, Nikolai Inozemtsev, "says whatever he thinks Brezhnev wants to hear."

The people I got to know best in Russia were journalists, who are important figures in Soviet society. Propaganda—a word with positive connotations in Russian—is one of the Party's principal preoccupations, and journalists produce the most important propaganda. They are officials of the regime, not independent reporters or critics.

The journalists I knew were not all alike. Some were timid. I asked one young man who gave me a tour of his newspaper where the censor sat.

"What censor?" he said.

"The censor from Glavlit," I replied, using the Russian acronym for the censorship agency whose representatives work in every newspaper office in the country.

"We have no censor here," my host replied. "There is no censor on this newspaper."

Others were bolder. When I asked an editor of *Pravda* about Glavlit, he replied without hesitation that the censors had a small room in the building where they read the proofs of every article.

In other ways, too, the journalists I met or heard about from colleagues tended to fall into two general categories. One group might be called patriotic cynics. They are skeptical men who make clear their private distaste for the posturing and ideological rhetoric of the regime, who confide personal displeasure with some official policies, who try in small ways to be honest and honorable, but who are not ashamed to work for their country. A few examples of their behavior may be more revealing than further description.

A British correspondent in Moscow once complimented a Soviet colleague on an article he had written about the situation in the Middle East. "Don't pay me false compliments," the Russian replied brusquely. "You know I have to write that stuff."

The editor of an important Soviet magazine laughed when an American economist visiting Moscow suggested that the western world might at last be entering the series of ever-worsening economics crises that Karl Marx predicted. "Somehow those predictions of Marx have never come true, have they?" No, I'm not expecting that to happen any time soon."

I once asked a Soviet colleague over a long and vodka-sodden lunch why his country was so aggressively isolated, so hostile to foreign ideas. "A lot that you don't like will change," he answered, "when our economy is stronger and our leaders are no longer afraid to let the people compare Soviet life to life in the West."*

Another Russian journalist over another liquid lunch talked at length with a French correspondent about Solzhenitsyn, Sakharov and the dissident intellectuals. "Of course our intellectuals want more freedom," he said, "but let's face it, how much experience has Russia ever had with freedom? Seven months in 1917, that's how much. What do they expect?"**

After I had experienced or heard about several dozen cases in which Soviet journalists violated the rule that they adhere to the Party line in conversations with foreigners, I concluded that these morsels of candor were important to those who proffered them. They were claims advanced on behalf of the

---

* According to Roy Medvedev (*On Socialist Democracy* [New York, 1975]), "A member of the Central Committee [of the Party] told Academician [Andrei] Sakharov: 'Given the present state of the economy and the workers' inadequate standard of living, it is too soon to put through various measures to democratize society.' "

** He referred to the brief period of parliamentary democracy between the February Revolution, which overthrew the czar, and the Bolshevik Revolution, which brought Lenin to power.

speakers' essential humanity, testimony that they were still whole men. The testimony was serious precisely because it was offered to a colleague from the enemy camp, an imperialist journalist.

Another important fact about these Soviet journalists is that they believe in serious journalism. A Soviet correspondent in Washington once told an American colleague there that he wrote honest, straightforward dispatches "just like you do," but, alas, they were not intended to appear in the open press. These journalists would like to print more news and less propaganda, to break down some of the conventions of Party-line journalism. That is a dream for an imprecise future; meanwhile they think of themselves as realists making the best of an imperfect situation.

The second broad category of journalists are the super-loyalists—careerists who simply don't care what others think of them, and who cannot be budged from the official line, except by mistake. They are generally less bright than members of the first group, less curious, less willing to enter serious discussion of any kind. The man at *Pravda* who recommended that I look into cattle-breeding was typical.

The archetype, however, is another *Pravda* man, Yuri Zhukov. Zhukov is big and overweight, with an oversized round face. He is *Pravda*'s "senior commentator," but that is not all. The large red button on his jacket lapel announces that he is a member of the Supreme Soviet. He has been chairman of committees on peace in Indochina and European security, and often speaks for the regime at foreign meetings and conferences. Zhukov has survived Stalin, Khrushchev and Brezhnev with constant demonstrations of loyalty to all of them, and to each succeeding version of the Party line.

I paid a call on Zhukov soon after I arrived in Moscow. My Russian then was hesitant at best, but I knew Zhukov spoke English. He greeted me with a brisk shake of his big hand and a cold eye. What did I want to discuss? he asked in Russian. I replied in English, but he cut me off—he spoke poor English, he said, so I should speak Russian. I gulped and tried to go on. The meeting was short, and I remember only one thing he said. When I commented that the recent settlement of the Berlin problem demonstrated that both his government and the Americans seemed ready to make compromises, he replied that the Soviet side had made no compromise. Its position on Berlin—which Stalin blockaded,

Khrushchev surrounded with a wall and Brezhnev had just signed over to West Germany, with a few reservations—had never changed.

Later I heard Zhukov speaking English often. However, he forgot who I was. Our paths crossed half a dozen times in the subsequent two years, but he never seemed to recognize me.

The Zhukoz personality might have been invented by central casting. He seems the ideal *apparatchik*—utterly loyal and, beneath a studied exterior, cold and ruthless. During the period of *détente* he has repeated the new Party line, praising relations with the western powers and trying personally to be more friendly with westerners. But I always had the feeling that this posture discomfited Zhukov. His true colors seemed on display one evening in 1973, on his television show. From his office in *Pravda*, Zhukov regularly answers viewers' questions on world affairs. On this evening his message was an attack on foreign radio stations which broadcast to the USSR in Russian. Only a few weeks before, the Soviet government had stopped jamming most foreign broadcasts, an obvious gesture to the West. But Zhukov warned his viewers not to listen:

"Those who touch this mud which is pouring through the airwaves on alien radio beams pollute themselves and besmirch the dignity of a Soviet citizen. And others do more than just listen. Either wishing to boast before their friends of how well they are informed, or simply because they misunderstand the alien voices conveyed to us on the radio, these people, by all kinds of gossip, pollute others as well. But we, comrades, come out for cleanliness!"

In June 1973, Zhukov and I were among the journalists who traveled from Moscow to Washington to cover Mr. Brezhnev's first trip to America. My newspaper, the *Washington Post*, invited a number of Soviet journalists to lunch during the summit conference. Zhukov was among them. When he appeared, he recognized me warmly, and in English.

There were a number of other journalists at that same lunch. Zhukov was late, and before he arrived the others bantered among themselves with their American hosts. They all referred to each other with the intimate "thou." When Zhukov came, the mood changed. The others called Zhukov by the formal "you," and quickly yielded to him as the spokesman for the Soviet side. What had begun as a friendly gathering turned into a pompous ceremony. Zhukov gave a

long speech (in Russian, so it had to be translated) on the
Soviet view of the summit conference, which he might have
been reading from *Pravda*.

Zhukov is not popular among his colleagues, but they defer
to him instinctively. He may not be one of the guys, but he is
the most influential journalist in the Soviet Union.

A young Soviet diplomat I met in Paris suggested that this
kind of distinction appears in other areas of Soviet life. He
was thirty-five, a graduate of the Moscow State Institute for
International Relations, the school that trains diplomats, journalists and others who will serve overseas. It is a prestigious
institution whose graduates have important jobs throughout
the government and, to an increasing extent, inside the Party
apparatus. The diplomat thought of himself as a progressive.
He felt that the war in Vietnam and the invasion of
Czechoslovakia were both "terrible" events from which it
would take my country and his many years to recover. At the
present time, he said, the people who shared his views were
overwhelmed by the traditional Party officials, the conservatives who still held sway. "That might change," he said. "Our
approach might someday be accepted."

Young scientists convey similar messages to the westerners
they meet at international congresses. Every Soviet writer
knows the difference between the careerists and the honest
men. It is tempting to conclude that all the important people
in Soviet society can be classified as good or bad, honest or
careerist, progressive or reactionary.

Alas, it is never so simple. The most common type of Soviet official combines contradictory human qualities within
himself. He may be a careerist with flashes of honesty, a progressive who constantly yields to the conservatives, a good
man who occasionally must do something dishonest or cruel
to retain his job or his influence. The most common compromise, it seemed to me, was one that many made between
their private and official lives. Officially one does what is required, because there is no real choice. Privately one can
redeem his self-respect by behaving according to high personal standards.

There is nothing uniquely Russian about this sort of life.
Hypocrisy and deceit are the common property of all mankind. The human urge is to compromise. I heard more private philosophizing on these subjects in Russia than I had

heard in a previous lifetime—which leads to what *is* uniquely Russian about the situation there.

In the Soviet Union there is seldom a satisfactory way out of a confrontation with unpleasant choices. One submits or voluntarily chooses martyrdom; the authorities rarely offer a third alternative. A Soviet lawyer asked to participate in a corrupt trial—in a political prosecution, for example, whose result is rigged in advance—must agree or voluntarily imperil his entire career. The people who asked for his participation control his employer, and every potential employer he might find in the entire country. A factory director ordered to alter the statistics in his annual report cannot resign in moral indignation and look for a job at another factory, because every factory is run by the same directors. He agrees to dissemble or accepts dire consequences.

Theoretically, all but an unlucky few should be able to avoid these ugly situations. There aren't enough political trials to involve every lawyer: a factory director who fulfills his Plan—as most do—would never be asked to distort his statistics. But in practice the system defies this logic. It does so by degrading the truth and denying common sense, then demanding that its adherents do the same. A Soviet official may see sloth and drunkenness all around him, but he must speak about the emergence of a new communist man. A politician whose entire style of life depends on special privileges must pretend to be a leader of the first classless society in history. An industrial minister whose factories have fallen behind schedule must—for public consumption—transform failure into triumph. *Pokazuka* over all; the truth is not a defense.

This does not mean that Soviet life is utterly corrupt and venal. On the contrary, most people go about their business in an honorable and business-like fashion *most of the time*. Ordinary citizens may never have to make choices that they perceive as moral compromises. Officials can avoid these difficult confrontations for months, even years at a time. It is occasionally even possible to defy authority on moral grounds and get away with it.*

---

* The best example I know of a man who refused for ethical reasons to do the regime's bidding is Pyotr L. Kapitsa, a physicist and one of the greatest scientific minds in the USSR. Lavrenti Beria, chief of Stalin's secret police and, in 1945, the man responsible for organizing the Soviet effort to build an atomic bomb, asked Kapitsa to work on the project. He refused on humanitarian grounds. Beria wanted to

However, the crucial fact is that the authorities will usually succeed in imposing moral corruption when they choose to do so. Most people will give in at once. The tiny number that do hold out will eventually accept the suggested compromise or pay an extraordinary price for their defiance.

Like all of us, Russians cope with life by constructing comforting rationalizations. Among Soviet officials I found a rich variety of rationalizations, ranging from high-minded idealism to the crassest sort of cynical selfishness.

The high-minded position can be eloquent, and a great many Soviet officials believe in it. One version might go something like this:

We have transformed Russia, eliminated exploitation of the poor by the rich, immeasurably improved the lives of working people and built the foundations for a new kind of human society. We have made our Motherland the world's second strongest nation, secured her against all enemies, extended her influence into every corner of the world and into outer space, too. We are working on the side of history; decadent, self-indulgent, self-destructive capitalism cannot survive. Of course we have made mistakes, particularly in Stalin's time, but also in the years since. There is much left to be done. We are still bureaucratic, narrow-minded, inefficient, lazy and too afraid of foreigners. We still cannot trust the people to withstand the temptations of bourgeois life, because we have not yet made our socialist life good enough. But someday we will show the world. We'll build the best society men have ever known, right here in Russia. Not in our lifetime, but someday it will happen.

The driving force behind this vision is Russian patriotism, as strong an emotion as any known to man. I am an American, I have lived in Britain and Asia and traveled throughout the world, but I have never seen anything to compare with Russian patriotism. Russians weep with happiness when they cross the Polish border on the train returning home. A man I

---

arrest him, but Stalin refused, apparently realizing that Kapitsa's arrest would cause a furor abroad and demoralization among scientists at home. Kapitsa was fired from the Institute of Physics, which he himself had founded before the war, and for nearly a year and a half could get no new job. Eventually he was hired by the Institute of Crystallography. After Stalin's death he returned to the Institute of Physics. He has continued to speak his mind on all subjects and do what he can for friends and colleagues who get into trouble for speaking theirs.

met in Siberia told me he wasn't interested in sports "unless one of our national teams is playing some foreigners. Then I watch on television." A Russian diplomat in Washington looked into my face when I came home from three years in Russia and said, "Well, there is something there, don't you think, something special?" Who could deny it?

A fervent patriot is an effective rationalizer. Yes, one of the journalists I knew agreed, more could be said and written about Stalin's crimes, which were indeed abominable. But Stalin was like a brutal father: "After his death, do you expect all the children to reject him completely? A country cannot spit on its own history." For the good of the Motherland much can be excused.

General Eisenhower discovered this mentality in a conversation with Marshal Georgi Zhukov, the Soviet commander in the last years of World War II. Reminiscing after the war, Zhukov told Eisenhower how the Red Army had cleared minefields. In his memoirs Eisenhower paraphrased Zhukov's comments, "When we come to a minefield our infantry attacks exactly as if it were not there. The losses we get from personnel mines we consider only equal to those we would have gotten from machine guns and artillery if the Germans had chosen to defend that particular area with strong bodies of troops instead of with minefields."

The biography of Rostislav Ulyanovski is revealing. Ulyanovski was arrested during one of Stalin's purges and spent 21 years in prisons and camps. An expert on India, he became deputy editor of a magazine called *People of Asia and Africa* after Stalin's death. Then he was appointed deputy director of the Institute of Eastern Studies of the Academy of Sciences, and is now deputy head of the Central Committee's international department in charge of relations with Asia and Africa.

I never met Ulyanovski, but heard about him from a former colleague who described him as a man with an independent mind, an effective political operator utterly dedicated to his work. I asked what motivated such a man.

"He is a patriot, no doubt about that," my acquaintance replied. "He loves Russia the way only a Russian can. Communist ideology is his second nature. He takes it seriously— he grew up in the late 1920s and early '30s, and that generation does take it seriously. He is really thinking about a communist revolution throughout the world, but he isn't dogmatic about how to pursue it."

And yet, my acquaintance continued, "there is an element of cynicism in him." Thanks to his 21 years in prison, Ulyanovski is a bitter anti-Stalinist, but his ambition overcame even this emotion. In the late 1960s, when Stalin was regaining favor at the highest level of the Party, Ulyanovski made a speech to a meeting in his institute trying to suggest that there had never been a period of the "cult of personality" in Soviet history.

"It's impossible to judge these officials straightforwardly," my acquaintance said. "You can't just call them good or bad. They are much more complicated than that. A lot of them have complexes. Ulyanovski, for example, feels he has lost a lot of time; he's had to wait a long time to show his talents—21 years—although I understand he did a lot of serious work for the government while he was in prison, in a *sharashka*."

Sharashka is slang for a special scientific institute staffed by prisoners. Stalin created dozens of them after the war. Solzhenitsyn described one in *The First Circle*. Thousands of Soviet intellectuals, including Rostislav Ulyanovski, worked in *sharashkas* for the good of the state that had imprisoned them—imprisoned them in most cases for no reason.

Patriotism and idealism can be invoked by anyone, but I left Russia with the feeling that simple self-interest was usually the best explanation for the way Soviet officials behave. Men may he induced to work hard for the sake of a glorious if uncertain future, but it is more likely that they will work hard for a more comfortable present. The system of privileges in Soviet society insures that relative comfort is available.

"Relative" is an important word in that last sentence. The regime's inducements do not equal the emoluments of western capitalists, but they represent a dramatic improvement over the lot of ordinary Russians. They are more than adequate to persuade millions of people to compete for them. "We are attracting good young people," a senior official and Party member told me, "not for idealistic reasons, but for practical reasons."

A Soviet citizen motivated by material self-interest quickly perceives the benefits of good behavior. Once he has them, a Soviet citizen is likely to value the privileges of official status, and to do what is necessary to keep them. And there is no other way to get those privileges—no private sector. Only *official* status gives one a better standard of living.

Many of those who play the game as they feel they must are troubled by their own lack of independence. I say that confidently because numerous Russian officials tried to signal to me private reservations about their public poses, as I have mentioned. At the same time, I sensed, they tell themselves they must stay inside the system to improve it: the good people must not abandon it to the bad. Of course that may be true. In any case, this rationalization allows for continued participation in the system.

Participation requires an extraordinary degree of self-discipline. A Russian journalist posted in Washington in the early 1960s, before the blossoming of *détente*, persistently refused invitations to the homes of American acquaintances and neighbors, because in those days he was not supposed to fraternize with the enemy. Returning to Washington in 1973, after the drastic improvement in at least the mood of Soviet-American relations, the same journalist evidently had new instructions. He went back to those old acquaintances and all but solicited renewed invitations, all of which he accepted. One former neighbor was astounded to hear him invent a series of anecdotes for her dinner company intimating that he had often dined in her home during his previous tour in Washington.

I heard about a high-ranking official who travels abroad regularly and who leads what amounts to a double life. Riding with friends in his chauffeur-driven car, he is likely to discuss a recent trip to London or Paris in aggressive, ideological terms, emphasizing the poverty he saw, the crass materialism and the cruelty of the ruling classes. "That's for the benefit of his chauffeur," a friend of this official told me. "He knows the chauffeur reports on him. But alone with us later, walking in the woods near his *dacha*, he tells a very different story—how nice life seems to be in England, how glamorous Paris is. He assumes his phone is bugged, too. The higher up you go, the more they spy on you."

Cynicism is an obvious reaction to the values that prevail in the higher reaches of the society. The journalists I knew realized that Yuri Zhukov is neither a good journalist nor a nice man, but they put up with him. Others equally patiently put up with domination by mediocre men.

There are code words and phrases which cover awkward situations at the highest levels. "Yes," one might say, "he is a knowledgeable fellow, but he wouldn't be good for [Party] apparatus work." Thus a talented but independent-minded man might be ruled out of consideration for a senior Party job. "He's a hard man to cooperate with" is another stock phrase, used to write off strong-willed people who won't yield to the views of others. I learned these phrases from an engineer who worked in Soviet industry. He also told me about a factory director who once said, "If the Party ordered me to make my factory unprofitable, then of course I would make it unprofitable."

The same engineer told me the advice he received from his first supervisor in a Soviet industrial establishment: "Think one thing, say something else and do a third thing."

"That's where the cynicism comes from," my acquaintance said. "Everyone is taught not to say what he thinks."

After living this way for years, inevitably some people stop thinking independently. Svetlana Alliluyeva was in Sochi on the Black Sea coast when President Kennedy was assassinated. She was staying in a rest home for Party officials. "The Party members in the rest home did not know how to react," she has written, "until the Moscow newspapers published the telegram of condolence sent by the Soviet government to the United States."

Another important ingredient of life at the top is obsequiousness. Western visitors to China in recent years have noted the ease with which low-ranking officials challenge the statements of senior leaders, even in their company, as though they really were just comrades. No visitor to Russia could take away a similar impression.

The Bolsheviks are not responsible for this obsequiousness; it is a Russian reflex. Gogol captured it superbly in *Dead Souls*. The anti-hero of the book, Pavel Ivanovich Chichikov, visits the country estate of Sobakevich, a landlord, and the two of them discuss the czar's local officials:

> ". . . Of course [said Chichikov] every man has his weaknesses, but you must admit that the governor is a most delightful person."
> "The governor a delightful person?" [replied Sobakevich.]
> "Yes, don't you think so?"

"He's the biggest brigand on earth!"

"The governor a brigand?" said Chichikov, who was entirely at a loss to understand how a governor could be a brigand.

For those Russians like Sobakevich who can see how a governor could be a brigand, the governors take special precautions. Andrei Amalrik noticed this phenomenon in his village in Siberia: "The police jealously guarded the authority of the *kolkhoz* chairman and the other local bosses, for insulting them you could get at least two weeks in jail, while they could yell at you in the foulest language with impunity."

I saw countless examples of the obsequiousness reflex at work. A typical one occurred at a Moscow theater. The deputy director of Tass, the Soviet news agency, was already sitting in an orchestra seat when he noticed Georgi Arbatov, Brezhnev's advisor on American affairs. The Tass man, Alexander A. Vishnyevski, is well over six feet tall, and he had wedged himself down into his seat with his knees pulled up in front of him, Nevertheless, he decided he should rise to greet Arbatov, and executed some quick contortions to bring his large frame upright. Then he bowed slightly. Arbatov returned the greeting with a wave.

In Armenia I was taken to a collective farm by the local correspondent of the Novosti press agency, a round and bald little man of about fifty with a red nose. Also with us was a local KGB agent, a young man with the unlikely name of Spartacus who had been detailed to look after two visiting American journalists in the guise of an Intourist guide.* Spartacus was no older than thirty-five. The director of the farm gave a dinner in our honor, for which he brought out some homemade vodka (an illegal product, but no one seemed to mind). Midway through the dinner the little man from Novosti offered a long, saccharine and ingratiating toast

---

* We suspected Spartacus was not really an Intourist guide from the time we first met him. Then one afternoon he failed to appear for a scheduled appointment, and I went to the Intourist office in our hotel to look for him. "Where's Spartacus?" I asked. "Who?" a young man on duty replied. "Spartacus." He insisted that no one by that name worked for Intourist. Then I explained that I was an American journalist, he was my guide—and the young man interrupted with a knowing "Ahhh, just a minute." He disappeared. A few minutes later Spartacus materialized.

to the KGB man, praising him as the finest sort of young Soviet citizen upon whom the future of the country depended. It was a pathetic scene, but it prompted two other men at the table, both functionaries of the collective farm, to chime in with toasts in a similar vein to their director—"whose leadership we depend on here at the farm," as one of them put it.

At its extreme, self-interest produces the least attractive Soviet officials, the unqualified careerists. Some of them, I decided, were simply too stupid to be condemned: dull-witted, automatically selfish people to whom moral or even intellectual considerations were alien. Because merit alone is often insufficient to earn advancement, the best people often do not rise to the top. Many of the worst people get there.

The narrow-minded, self-absorbed bureaucrat appears in Soviet anecdotes, movies and plays: he is the object of official ridicule and popular indignation. Despite all that, he and his brethren thrive. I met dozens of examples of the breed myself in a variety of situations. "Oh," an acquaintance in Moscow said when I told him how frustrating these people could be, "you mean Ivan Ivanov? All he cares about is feathering his own nest." The nickname is common.

Perhaps the most frustrating characteristic of this class of Soviet officials is their insistence on exaggerating their own importance. This happens at every level of Soviet society. The woman who scrubs the floor of a restaurant in Moscow takes enormous pleasure in shouting "Closed!" at hungry citizens who have the temerity to knock on the door after closing time. An Intourist guide took me for a ride on a riverboat in Khabarovsk. When we got to the ticket window, the woman working there looked me up and down and said, "No, I won't sell you any tickets, foreigners aren't allowed on this boat." The Intourist guide—whose job it was to know just what foreigners were allowed to do—told the woman she was wrong, but she adamantly refused. The guide asked us to wait 50 yards away, then went back to shout and argue. After several minutes the guide returned with a flushed face—and the tickets.

"They all pretend to be working in the name of the Party, in the name of patriotism," a former Party official in an outlying Soviet republic told me in Israel, where he now lives. He was describing his former colleagues in the republican Central Committee. "But of course some of them are just doing what is best for their careers. If somebody has to be criticized at a meeting, they'll each stand up and make their critical speech, no matter what they know about the situation. . . .

"And if you argue with them when they criticize you, they get all the angrier. You're supposed to say, 'Yes, comrades, you're right, I was wrong, I'm sorry, I'll do better in the future.' It's inadmissible to say that you're not guilty.

"In theory they're supposed to stay close to the people, to know what people are saying, to help them. In fact they are cut off. If somebody tries to come in to the Central Committee to make a complaint or ask a question, he'll be asked for his pass. If he asks to see someone, they'll ask 'Why?' and give him a hard time. Eventually he may meet some minor official who will listen but won't do anything."

A harsh portrait, not meant to apply to every Party official, but it fits a good many of them.

Even more common, not surprisingly, are men and women in official positions who just do what they are told. Bureaucrats and officials in every society find comfort in the thought that they are only following orders. This notion probably provides particular comfort in Russia, because following orders is, from earliest childhood, a fundamental part of Russian life.

A Soviet official with an embarrassing or difficult order to carry out is capable of the most astounding doubletalk. The director of Intourist in Sochi, the Black Sea resort, had obviously been ordered not to help me in any way when I visited that city. She told me that no car was available to be rented; no driver could take me; no foreigner could visit such-and-such, though I knew that foreigners constantly did. All of Intourist's regular services simply evaporated as soon as I asked for them.

The psychiatrists who had to answer for the forced incarceration of Zhores Medvedev in a mental hospital put on a more vivid performance. Medvedev, a biologist and dissident intellectual who was later exiled involuntarily to England, was arrested in May 1970 and confined to a mental hospital in Kaluga, not far from Moscow. His twin brother, Roy, and numerous friends, including several Old Bolsheviks (elderly communists of many year's standing) and prominent intellectuals, exerted pressure to get him released. They repeatedly visited the hospital and pressed their arguments on the doctors there, but the doctors were not moved.

"In this kind of situation," Dr. Galina Bondareva told two

of Medvedev's friends, "it is very difficult for psychiatrists to find a common language with relatives or other people who know nothing of the subject. It sometimes happens that a patient shows no external signs of illness and behaves like an absolutey healthy person."

In the same conversation, however, Dr. Bondareva revealed the true source of her intransigence. Political officials, not doctors, she hinted, were responsibile for Medvedev's incarceration. In other words, she was only following orders and was not personally responsible for what had happened to Medvedev.

Soviet officials rarely need to take personal responsibility for their decisions—which are rarely made without the collaboration of others. Occasionally the head of an important enterprise is fired for symbolic reasons; Ministers of Agriculture have been prone to this fate over the years. But in general men and women who achieve high status in Soviet society retain it regardless of how badly they do their jobs. They are not held personally responsible.

The case of S. A. Radzhabov is instructive. For many years Radzhabov was the rector of the university in Dushambe, the capital of Soviet Tadzhikistan. Corruption in the university was rampant; Radzhabov was accepting bribes to admit students, giving jobs to his relatives and publishing under his own name books that others had written for him. Finally he was fired—but not disgraced. First a new department of the Tadzhik Academy of Sciences was created for him to direct. Later he was made chief editor of the Soviet-Tadzhik encyclopedia, though he didn't even speak the local language fluently. The *nachalstvo* looks after its own.

In cases like Medvedev's, bureaucratic inertia carries Soviet officials to abnormal extremes. Merely by following orders, qualified professionals end up doing appalling things. The use of mental hospitals forcibly to treat political dissidents is an established part of the Soviet "penal" system.* This means that trained psychiatrists, medical men and women who belong to one of the world's most honorable professions, pervert

---

* This has now been documented so thoroughly that there is no longer any doubt about it. Interested readers can pursue this subject in numerous books, including the Medvedev brothers' *A Question of Madness* (New York, 1972) and Valery Chalidze's *To Defend These Rights* (New York, 1975).

their values to do the regime's bidding. This may involve the forced use of drugs that can permanently damage the mind of the patient taking them.

A brief digression. The Russian officials I knew always told me what good fellows they and their countrymen were, yet I had indisputable evidence that some of them were perpetrating horrors. How can perversity be explained?

This is no place for a treatise on man's capacity for evil, nor for an accusation which implies that only Russians are capable of evil on this scale. This is more a personal aside. Exposure to official Soviet evil pricked my curiosity, and I tried to satisfy it. That led me to a number of studies by American social scientists which may help explain why Soviet (and American) officials defy the norms of civilized behavior to please a superior.

A number of persuasive studies demonstrate that even Americans—brought up in a society that encourages self-reliance and independence—are prone to abandon their personal judgment and even their moral code to conform to a group or carry out an order.

In one classic experiment an individual was brought into a group whose other members—unbeknownst to the subject—were briefed in advance on how to behave. The group was asked to decide which of three lines drawn for them was the same length as a fourth line, also put before them. The briefed members of the group all answered identically, one at a time, but the answer they gave was obviously wrong. The subject was then asked for his or her answer. One third of the subjects tested defied the evidence provided by their own senses in order to agree with the rest of the group. Such is the power of the urge to conform.

Another study demonstrated that conformity is habit-forming. Experimenters asked California housewives for two kinds of assistance. The first request was for something simple—for instance, a statement over the telephone about what kind of soap product the woman used. The second request was much more substantial—for example, that the woman construct a sign on her front lawn which said DRIVE CAREFULLY. Both requests were made by people who identified themselves as representatives of the "California Consumers' Group." The experiment showed that of those who agreed to the small request, 55 percent also agreed to put up the sign. Another group of housewives who had not been approached with the original, small request were asked to put up the same sign; only 20 percent agreed. This experiment was called "Compliance without Pressure: The Foot-in-the-Door Technique." Its authors concluded that people who acquiesce to a small request may develop a new, more pliant attitude toward "compliance in general."

The most interesting study I found in this field provides vivid, disheartening evidence of man's capacity for inhumanity. It is a study of obedience conducted by Professor Stanley Milgram, a social psychologist, who invited subjects to participate in what he called a learning experiment. The subject was told that he would be the teacher; his job would be to teach another subject to memorize certain pairs of words with the help of electric shocks.

In fact the other subject was an actor, and the electric shocks were faked, though they were applied by a most realistic-looking piece of machinery whose dial was marked with increments of LIGHT SHOCKS (15 volts) to DANGER: SEVERE SHOCK (450 VOLTS). To heighten the sense of authenticity, each teacher was given a 45-volt shock before the experiment began.

Once the experiment had started, the learner (that is, the actor) began making mistakes, and the figure of authority conducting the experiment, Professor Milgram or an associate, would order the teacher to begin inflicting shocks. Each mistake called for a severer shock.

As the voltage increased, the actor began to protest. At 150 volts he insisted on being released from the experiment, at 200 he complained of heart trouble, at 285 he screamed in agony. Some of the subjects defied the order to administer shock, forcing an end to the experiment. But 60 percent of those tested, people from a wide variety of backgrounds, obeyed every instruction, which meant inflicting what they thought was a 450-volt shock on a "student" who by that time wasn't saying anything or showing any sign of life. The person conducting the experiment volunteered to take responsibility for its outcome, and repeatedly insisted that there was no way to abandon the experiment midway—it had to be completed. Most subjects went along.

Milgram's report on the experiment is hair-raising. Some subjects perspired profusely as they inflicted fiercer and fiercer shocks; others laughed uncontrollably; others showed no signs of tension at all. The actors spared no histrionics. "Ohhhh," one shouted after 270 volts, "I absolutely refuse to answer any more! Let me out of here! You can't hold me here! Get me out. Get—me—out—of—here!" The experimentor ignored these screams and ordered the subject to continue. He did.

Milgram concludes that most people are too intimidated by authority to refuse to carry out even inhumane orders. "The subjects do not derive satisfaction from inflicting pain, but they often like the feeling they get from pleasing the experimenter. They are proud of doing a good job, obeying the experimenter under difficult circumstances."

He also found that "Many of the people were in some sense against what they did while they obeyed. Some were totally convinced of the wrongness of their actions but could not bring themselves to make an open break with authority. They often derived satisfaction from their thoughts and felt that—within themselves, at least—they had been on the side of the angels."

"The most fundamental lesson of our study," Milgram believes, is that "ordinary people, simply doing their jobs, and without any particular hostility on their part, can become agents in a terrible destructive process. . . . Relatively few people have the resources needed to resist authority."

Morality survives in this situation, Milgram believes, but "it acquires a radically different focus: the subordinate person feels shame or pride depending on how adequately he has performed the actions called for by authority," without regard for the consequences of the actions themselves.

As Milgram notes, his findings lend support to Hannah Arendt's analysis of Adolph Eichmann as little more than a loyal official carrying out the orders of his superiors. "Even Eichmann," Milgram writes, "was sickened when he toured the concentration camps, but he had only to sit at a desk and shuffle papers. At the same time the man in the camp who actually dropped the Cyclon-b into the gas chambers was able to justify *his* behavior on the ground that he was only following orders from above. Thus there is a fragmentation of the total human act; no one is confronted with the consequences of his decision to carry out the evil act. The person who assumes responsibility has evaporated. Perhaps this is the most common characteristic of socially organized evil in modern society."

Milgram's study seems to prove something ugly about human beings, not about Americans, Russians or any other particular group. But his findings were incomplete. Moral behavior often—I suspect usually—grows out of a social context. Moral courage for most people probably derives from their ties to others, from a desire to do something which a person knows his peers would approve or applaud. Milgram isolated his subjects, depriving them of their peers.

Before conducting his experiments, Milgram asked a variety of Americans how they thought such an inquiry would turn out. The overwhelming majority predicted that nearly everyone tested would refuse to obey the order to inflict ever stronger electric shocks. Those optimists probably didn't realize the significance of isolating the subject. And Americans do tend to assume that their ethical and political traditions insure more moral behavior than in fact they do—hence the public outrage when optimistic assumptions are proven unwarranted, as in the Watergate affair. Americans may also underestimate the strength of authority because authority is so diffuse in their society.

I suspect that if one asked a variety of Russians to predict how an experiment like Milgram's might turn out, they would be much more pessimistic. Soviet society is not imbued with the Judeo-Christian ethic. Russians expect the worst from human nature. Russian governments, czarist and communist, have long been organized to limit the damage men can do if they follow their worst instincts. Their leaders have always assumed that Russians left to their own devices will get into trouble.

Another point deserving note here is that few Soviet officials occupy themselves by inflicting high-voltage electric shocks, or the equivalent, on the populace. Most Soviet officials undoubtedly maintain good opinions of themselves as men and women who are trying to do what is best for their country. Like all people compelled occasionally to make uncomfortable compromises, they tend to forget those compromises as soon as they can, and to keep in mind what pleases them most about their work and their lives.

At the same time, Russian communists come from a tough tradition. Lenin readily accepted the idea that the end justified the means. In his view, moral considerations were often symbols of weakness. Stalin was vastly harsher. Political ethics don't seem to concern many Soviet leaders.

Until the appearance of Nikita Khrushchev's reminiscences, outsiders had only smidgeons of unreliable evidence about the character, personality and private attitudes of Soviet rulers. The Khrushchev volumes, particularly the second, therefore fill a void. Often inadvertently, Khrushchev draws a revealing self-portrait of the kind of man who rises to the top in the Soviet Union.

Not that he is typical of them all; on the contrary, his personal idiosyncrasies contributed significantly to his downfall. Numerous Russians told me that Khrushchev should have been the director of a collective farm, not the ruler of the country. He is faulted for his unpredictable behavior, his inconsistent policies, his blustering and his attempts to be an expert on every subject. And yet it is probably safe to assume that many of Khrushchev's political attitudes and habits of mind are similar to those of his colleagues and successors. The laws of probability suggest as much: how likely is it that an utterly untypical man would be chosen by the others as their leader?

Khrushchev's attitudes toward the Soviet system are fascinating. His memoirs describe not a fanatic adherent to the Party line, but a pragmatic politician: "It's time for us to realize that the teachings of Marx, Engels, and Lenin cannot be hammered into people's heads only in the classroom and newspapers and at political rallies; agitation and propaganda on behalf of Soviet power must also be carried on in our restaurants and cafeterias. Our people must be able to use their wages to buy high-quality products manufactured under socialism if they are ultimately to accept our system and reject capitalism."

Khrushchev did not belittle capitalism: ". . . we still have a lot to learn from the capitalists. There are many things we still don't do as well as they do . . . those 'rotten' capitalists keep coming up with things which make our jaws drop in surprise."

Nor was he confident of the leadership's ability to control the Soviet Union, as he revealed in an observation on the "thaw" in Soviet life which followed his denunciations of Stalin: "We were scared—really scared. We were afraid the thaw might unleash a flood, which we wouldn't be able to control and which could drown us. How could it drown us? It could have overflowed the banks of the Soviet riverbed and formed a tidal wave which would have washed away all the barriers and retaining walls of our society."*

Khrushchev revealed a gaping sense of inferiority, partly about himself but more about Soviet society and its accomplishments. Evidence of this recurs throughout his recollections. For example, Khrushchev described a middle-aged American woman who sat next to him at a banquet in Hollywood during his tour of the United States: "I could imagine her thinking to herself: 'How exciting! Here's a real Russian bear! In Russia, bears actually roam the streets. This one has come to our country and is sitting right here beside me. How interesting! And the bear isn't even growling!' "

In all the foreign countries Khrushchev visited he seemed haunted by the fear that he would be snubbed. When President Eisenhower proposed that he come to Camp David, Khrushchev sensed an affront. His own diplomats didn't know what Camp David was. Finally they learned that "far from being an insult or an act of discrimination . . . it was a great honor for me to spend a few days at Camp David. . . ."

He feared the comparison that foreigners would make between their airplanes and the Soviet models in which he traveled. In the mid-1950s, he acknowledged, "we were embarrassed to land in a two-engine plane [for a Four Power meeting in Geneva] while all the other leaders arrived in four-engine ones." Later he convinced himself that a Soviet turbojet, driven by propellers, was really just as good an airplane as a Boeing 707 propelled by purely jet engines.

Khrushchev seemed especially concerned about how important western capitalists would receive him. He described this encounter in Paris:

> Our ambassador whispered to me that I would now meet the biggest capitalist in all of France, Rothschild. Of course it's a terribly famous name. I'd known about the Rothschilds from the newspapers back in the days when I was a worker because their own workers were always going on strike.**

---

* Don't those sound like the words of a man who would accept the precarious diagram of Soviet society that appears in Chapter 3?

** This appears to be a figment of the Khrushchev imagination, since the Rothschilds have always been bankers and—only in the years since Khrushchev was a worker—winegrowers, but not industrialists.

When he was introduced to me, I said, "I'm very pleased to meet you, Mr. Rothschild. I've heard a lot about you. I'm glad to have the honor of shaking hands with you. I welcome you as a guest of our embassy.". . .

The reason I'm relating this incident is that we attached some significance to Rothschild's attendance at our reception. . . . As Comrade Vinogradov [the Soviet ambassador] said, "If Rothschild does come, it means he isn't boycotting our invitation, and therefore he's expressing his recognition of us."

Nelson Rockefeller and the King of Denmark made similarly intimidating impressions on Khrushchev.

Khrushchev's recollections reveal the effects of Marxist-Leninist ideology and years of isolation on the intellectual processes of a Soviet leader. His intuitive shrewdness was remarkable, but his grasp of complicated issues, particularly those involving foreigners, was often weak. His ability to distort foreign reality and project his own prejudices and experiences onto foreign situations matched that of the most parochial American politicians.

In America Khrushchev met Walter Reuther, the late president of the United Auto Workers, and didn't like him. "He made as much money as the directors of the biggest corporations, like Ford," Khrushchev remembered. "In other words, the capitalists had bought him off. . . . I have always favored peaceful coexistence among countries, but Reuther favored peaceful coexistence among classes, which is in fundamental contradiction to our Marxist-Leninist teaching. Worse, it is treason to the cause of his fellow workers. I'm afraid such treason is all too common among American trade-union leaders."

Khrushchev was equally contemptuous of the opinions of ordinary Americans: "the average American had long since been conditioned to think whatever he was told to think."

My favorite line from all of Khrushchev's recollections is the one that begins this chapter. It was prompted by the wife of the French official who was his host in Marseilles in 1960. She "turned out to be a very nice Englishwoman," Khrushchev recalled. She drank Russian vodka and surprised him with her charm and gaiety. "I don't know," Khrushchev began, with a rare acknowledgment of ignorance, "maybe gaiety is a national characteristic of the English."

Khrushchev's readiness to attribute gaiety to the reserved English—the masters of what Tennyson called "a stony British stare"—suggests the ignorance of the outside world which still afflicts many Soviet leaders. Mr. Brezhnev's only exposure to the western world came on his official visits of the early 1970s, which provided no opportunity to see even as much as Khrushchev did on his cross-country tour of America. A few of his colleagues have seen more of our world, but most have seen even less.

On a visit to Canada several years ago, Dmitri Polyanski, a member of the Politburo and the Minister of Agriculture, visited a large factory. A parking lot outside was filled with the workers' cars. Polyanski asked his hosts why they had gone to so much trouble to fill the lot with cars to impress him.

Mikhail Zimyanin, the chief editor of *Pravda* and an important member of the Party's Central Committee, met a group of American congressmen in Moscow. The congressmen asked him why the Soviet authorities had treated Alexander Solzhenitsyn so harshly. Because, Zimyanin replied, Solzhenitsyn had slandered his homeland and even its founder, Lenin. What would happen, he asked, if a writer in America wrote a book slandering Lincoln or Jefferson?

A thoughtful, well-trained man who moves in the highest circles of Soviet society once assured me that the members of the Warren Commission, which investigated the assassination of John F. Kennedy, knew that he was killed by a conspiratorial group of right-wing politicians. If that were true, I asked, why would members of the commission hide what they knew? "For patriotic reasons," my Russian acquaintance replied without hesitation. "They didn't want to show America in that dirty way."

Today's Soviet politicians grew up in an environment where words did not always mean what they seemed to, in which conspiratorial explanations were often correct. They have developed an Asian sensibility which they now project with dismaying ease. They also tend to overestimate the Soviet Union's importance in the calculations of other countries' leaders.

All these inclinations were evident in the most popular Soviet interpretation of the Watergate affair. To avoid insulting Mr. Nixon, Soviet newspapers printed almost nothing about Watergate, but political lecturers told their audiences that enemies of *détente* with the Soviet Union were out to get

President Nixon. Important citizens also believed this. I asked one of the country's best-known political commentators, a man who had lived in the West himself, if it wasn't possible that Nixon was in trouble simply because he had misused his power and lied about it. Possible, he acknowledged, but unlikely. "Isn't it more likely that there is some kind of conspiracy at work?" he asked. He meant a conspiracy against the Soviet Union, at least by implication.

There are intelligent men in the USSR who study the western world closely and know a great deal about it. One, a man who had personally advised Brezhnev on foreign policy, admitted that the experts have trouble sharing their knowledge with the politicians who run the country. We were talking about the fact that the American President could not impose his will on Congress. "People [in the Soviet Union] who are not familiar with the situation," he said, "often think that all of this"—the alleged independent power of the Congress—"is arranged to deceive *us*."

Russian ethnocentrism is peculiarly ferocious. Living apart in their own vast land, formed by their own history and only peripherally influenced by outsiders for many centuries, Russians tend to believe that they live in the center of the world, and that their lives and customs are the only normal ones. Nothing hurts a Soviet patriot more than the discovery that Lenin is not idolized or even highly respected in the West, that most Soviet writers are unknown abroad, that Russia is not universally admired.

As Khrushchev's recollections suggest, however, ethnocentrism coexists with a confused awe of the outside world. Some Soviet officials who have visited the West are overwhelmed by it. "I know you have serious problems here," one told an American acquaintance, "but I *love* America. And now I have to go home and invite my American hosts to the Soviet Union. What can I show them there? We have nothing that could impress them."

Officials of Soviet foreign-trade organizations seem to love the luxurious entertainment that American and European businessmen provide. An official in Moscow told me excitedly about the reception a friend of his was given by a large American corporation. "Why, they sent their company jet to pick him up in New York, can you imagine?" Many important Soviet citizens are fascinated with the wealth of the West, and obviously wonder what life would be like for them had they been born under another flag. On a flight from Washington to Moscow with Henry Kissinger, the Soviet ambassador in Washington, Anatoli Dobrynin, repeatedly asked Marvin Kalb of CBS News how much he had earned from the biography of Kissinger that he had written with his brother Bernard. "It was something," according to another American journalist who rode on the same airplane. "Dobrynin just couldn't drop the subject, even when it was obvious that Marvin wasn't going to answer his question."

The best-educated Russians rise above the narrowness I have been trying to describe, but there are few intellectuals among the country's leaders. Intellectuals serve the leadership, but seldom join it. Members of the Politburo with higher educations—which is not all of them—generally studied technical subjects. Brezhnev graduated from an institute of metallurgical engineering. President Nikolai Podgorny studied at the Kiev Polytechnic Institute of the Food Industry. They are true products of the Soviet system's early years, Russians far removed from the intelligentsia of Moscow or Leningrad, Russians whose language has no word for "sophisticated."

As a practical matter, it is probably impossible for a leader of the Soviet Union to learn about the world in a way we would regard as normal. The educational system which trains Soviet citizens directs them away from our intellectual world at an early age. It subtly imposes an ideological cast of mind whose residue is difficult to expunge. It minimizes the value of what we call the liberal arts, so that most university graduates have barely a passing acquaintance with them.

Stalin, his daughter wrote, "never acquired any knowledge about modern history, philosophy, contemporary social thought, and remained therefore to the very end of his days a dogmatic and, in essence, an uneducated man."

Stalin restricted the flow of information in ways that assured the ignorance not only of the masses, but even of his senior colleagues. Khrushchev has written that Stalin never consulted the Politburo on questions of military policy, and rarely on foreign affairs. With one or two advisors he handled these matters independently, so his successors had to begin their education afresh when he died.

Even at high levels of the government and Party, individuals are deprived of sensitive information unless they crucially need it. As a result, important officials remain ignorant of significant facts only because those lie outside the officials' immediate area of responsibility. Khrushchev recounted an extreme example of the effects of this restrictive policy. In the mid-1950s he and several other members of the Politburo observed naval maneuvers in the Black Sea:

> . . . One of our commanders gave a report on how "our" fleet had met and routed "the enemy" in the [maneuvers]. . . . He started rattling off how "our" fleet was sinking "enemy" ships right and left. . . . He was terribly cocky. It made me sad to listen to him. Finally I couldn't restrain myself any longer. I interrupted him and said: "Stop! Wait! You keep talking with such certainty about how you've made short work of the enemy, and now you're telling me there's nothing left to do but polish off the enemy. Have you really assessed the situation correctly? If this were a real war and not just a map exercise, your ships would all be lying on the bottom of the sea by now."
>
> He looked at me with complete surprise.
>
> I went on: "You haven't taken into account the missiles which the enemy would certainly be using against you from his shore defenses and from missile-launching planes. We have such a system ourselves, so surely the other side has it, too. It's terribly dangerous to underestimate your enemy's capabilities."
>
> The commander was obviously perplexed. "Comrade Khrushchev," he said, "I've never heard of missile-launching planes before. You're telling me something entirely new."
>
> "Then it's our own fault," I told him. "All this information must be classified." I turned to the other members of the Presidium [the old name for the Politburo] and suggested, "Comrades, let's interrupt our conference and take our naval officers ashore so they can familiarize themselves with our missile system."

In the twenty years since that incident occurred, officers of the Soviet Navy have undoubtedly learned a great deal. The ignorance Khrushchev described would no longer be found among its senior officers. But I'm sure there are similar contemporary examples of the debilitating consequences of trusting almost no one with a full range of sensitive information.

"You are going to a country where the hard-hats are in charge," a colleague in Washington told me before I set out for Russia. He was right. A sort of hard-hat mentality dominates the Soviet system and Russian society. Hostility toward non-conformists, intolerance of the frivolous or the avant-garde, fierce public puritanism (often accompanied by private licentiousness) and rigid patriotism all seem typical of the USSR. These attitudes infect even the intellectual dissidents, some of whom—Solzhenitsyn is an obvious example—are nearly as intolerant of liberal democracy as are the country's leaders.

One of the first Russians I met, a journalist in Khabarovsk, asked me why American authorities allow demonstrators in New York to shout obscenities at Soviet diplomats. I explained that we took freedom of speech seriously, and that crowds also occasionally shouted obscenities at the President of the United States. That appalled him. Right to his face, to the President? Yes, I said, it had just happened to Mr. Nixon in Kansas City. That was a strength of our system, I suggested. Quite the contrary, he replied.

Svetlana Alliluyeva, Stalin's daughter, described a meeting with Mikhail Suslov, the Politburo's ideological guardian and probably the man most responsible for Khrushchev's removal from power. Suslov was trying to dissuade Svetlana from going to India with the ashes of Brajesh Singh, her lover, who had died in Moscow. " 'Why are you so anxious to go abroad? [Suslov asked her] . . . Take my family and my children—they never go abroad, don't even want to. Not interested!' he concluded, proud of his family's 'patriotism.' "

Svetlana also wrote of Andrei Zhdanov, one of her father's colleagues and the man who imposed "socialist realism" on Soviet culture: "Zhdanov viewed art from the bigoted and puritanical points of view prevalent in the Party. Zhdanov's wife once expressed them admirably in one of her unforgettable aphorisms: "Ilya Ehrenburg [the Russian poet of Jewish origin, who lived in Paris before and after the Revolution, then in Moscow] loves Paris so because there are naked women there."

A description of the people who run the Soviet Union should end on a contradictory note. Though their power is enormous, their privileges extensive and their lives rich and comfortable compared to the mass of Soviet humanity, the *nachalstvo* also have their problems. They work harder than most people (though the parking lot at the Party Central Committee rarely has more than half a dozen cars in it on a Saturday or Sunday). They have to put up with an inordinate amount of ceremony. To the extent that anyone is, they are held responsible for failures in the system. They get the ulcers.

Moreover, life at the top isn't quite as good as it is supposed to be. One would think that Party officials whose connections were good enough to get a new, oversized apartment would also be able to get a telephone, but sometimes this isn't the case. I knew one such man who went without a telephone for many months. His wife was furious. Another man, given the rare privilege of a plot of land in Uspenskoye, may, despite his windfall, have to go without a *dacha* for many years—or until he can raise the 10,000 to 20,000 rubles he'll need to build a good one.

It turns out that the medical care provided by the Fourth Department of the Ministry of Health—the department which serves only the *nachalstvo*—isn't very good. The doctors who work in the Fourth Department are not the most talented physicians, but those with the best personal connections and the most reliable personal records.

"There's an old joke," one physician told me, "that in the Fourth Department they have parquet floors and doctors with good questionnaires." By questionnaires he meant the documents on which a citizen records his Party affiliation, his "social activities" and other indications of political reliability. In Russian the words for "parquet" and "questionnaire" rhyme, so the doctor's old joke is a couplet.

"A self-respecting doctor won't work in the Fourth Department," a surgeon told me. "The people who work there must be ready to wait on their patients like servants. A bigshot demands that an experienced surgeon give him an enema, even though a midwife could do it."

Doctors in the Fourth Department get less experience than those working in the ordinary health-care system, so have less occasion to improve their skills. "If a serious problem arises," the doctor said, "they immediately call in a famous professor to deal with it." The surgeon confirmed that this was true. "All the professors at our medical institute were used as consultants to the Fourth Department. . . . The *nachalstvo* know that in a difficult situation they'll get a good doctor."

A final note on the hazards of life at the very top. Of the men who have held supreme power in Russia since 1917, only Lenin and Brezhnev still enjoy a good reputation. In 1967, when the country celebrated the 50th anniversary of Soviet power with an outpouring of self-congratulation, the authors of all the books and articles on the jubilee worked under one bizarre constraint: in writing about 50 years of Bolshevik rule, they could not mention the men who led Party and country for 40 of those 50 years. In 1967 Stalin, Georgi Malenkov and Khrushchev were all non-persons.

Khrushchev died in 1971. Although even astronauts are buried in the wall of the Kremlin, he was not. Instead his successors decided he should be buried in the Novodyevichi ("Young Maidens") Cemetery beside one of Moscow's loveliest architectural monuments, a 17th-century monastery. It is an honorable resting place, though it hardly befits the country's former leader. Many distinguished Russians are buried there—Chekhov, Prokofiev, Stalin's wife Nadezhda. Russians flock to the cemetery on a sunny day to walk among the headstones, searching for famous names.

I attended Khrushchev's funeral. The KGB insured that no ordinary citizens got near Novodyevichi on that gray and drizzly autumn day. Only plainclothesmen, foreign journalists, members of the Khrushchev family and a few close friends were admitted. No member of the country's new leadership attended, but the Central Committee and the Council of Ministers jointly sent a large wreath. So did Anastas Mikoyan, then living in honorable retirement. Khrushchev's successors obviously wanted him to pass finally from this world as inconspicuously as possible.

Nevertheless, Khrushchev's son Sergei, an engineer who was then thirty-six years old, brought some drama to the ceremony. Shortly after the open coffin was placed on a platform beside the grave, Sergei stepped up on the pile of freshly dug earth beside the empty hole and addressed the crowd. We all stood in the narrow spaces between other graves nearby.

"We simply want to say a few words about the man whom we are burying now, and for whom we are crying," he began. He paused to regain composure, and his lips quivered. "The sky is crying with us, too," he said as rain fell lightly.

"I won't talk about the great statesman," Sergei continued. "In recent days the newspapers of the whole world, with rare exceptions, talked about this. I will not evaluate the contributions which Nikita Sergeyevich, my father, made. I don't have the right to do that. History will do that. . . .

"The only thing I can say is that he left no one indifferent. There are people who love him and people who hate him, but no one can pass him by without turning to look. . . . A man has gone from us who had the right to be called a man. Unfortunately, there are very few such real people. . . ."

His reference to "the newspapers of the whole world, with rare exceptions" was an oblique commentary on the official Soviet reaction to Khrushchev's death. No obituaries were published, no commentaries on Khrushchev's role in Soviet and world history. The death of "pensioner Khrushchev" was noted in a six-line newspaper announcement on the day of the funeral, two days after he died.

Guests were given the opportunity to walk past the coffin as a small band played a mournful funeral march. Khrushchev's body lay on red satin, dressed in a white shirt, black tie and black suit. His lips were pursed in an unnatural expression and the face was waxen, but the famous profile was unmistakable. Because of the rain, someone held an umbrella over the head of the corpse.

After all who wanted to had walked past, Mrs. Khrushchev tearfully put her hand on the forehead of her dead husband. Others in the family did the same. Workmen then put the top of the coffin in place and nailed it down. A man stood at the head of the grave holding a red pillow on which all Khrushchev's 27 state medals, including the very highest awards, were pinned. The coffin was lowered into the hole.

Later Khrushchev's son had the bold idea of commissioning a memorial to his father from Ernst Neizvestni, a modernist sculptor whose work Khrushchev himself had once lambasted as "shit." That was a famous moment in Khrushchev's ambivalent relationship with the country's creative artists. Responding to the thaw that Khrushchev's program of de-Stalinization had initiated, artists began experimenting with new and more abstract forms. Neizvestni helped arrange an exhibit of this work, which Khrushchev visited, then vilified. For some years Neizvestni received no official commissions.

After Khrushchev's death the sculptor was pleased to be asked to do the memorial for his grave. By then Khrushchev's successors had established a much harsher cultural climate, and Neizvestni looked back on his confrontation with Khrushchev nostalgically.

He created a realistic head of Khrushchev on a platform in front of two intertwined forms of black and white stone, suggesting the struggle between good and evil that dominated Khrushchev's life. Three years after Khrushchev died the relevant officials gave permission to erect the sculpture over the grave.

5 · *Propaganda*

VIKTOR PERELMAN WORKED for many years on the magazine *Soviet Trade Unions,* edited by Konstantin Amelchenko, a prominent Party ideologist who once directed the state censorship agency. Amelchenko assigned Perelman to write an article about "trade-union collective control of inventors and rationalizers" at a large factory. Perelman, who now lives in Israel, has related what happened:

"When he assigned me this subject Amelchenko was quite uninterested in whether such a thing existed at the factory or not. He only knew that such a conception was required for the pages of his magazine.

"I went to the chairman of the factory [trade-union] committee and told him what I wanted to write. I said my job consisted not so much in writing my own article, but in helping him write, or, in practical terms, writing for him, if he would tell me something about his experience and about the organization of this trade-union collective control.

"He gave me rather a strange look, as if I had come to force him to indulge in some hocus-pocus. I realized from his look that there was no trade-union collective control at this factory. But he was no fool, and he understood what was required. He said he gave me carte blanche and I could do whatever I liked. All the workshops were at my disposal and I could go and look for any kind of collective control I wished.

"I went off to search the workshops for forms of collective control, but could find nothing. All I could find were a few workers who actually had introduced some quite interesting suggestions for improving the efficiency of production, but when I mentioned collective control to them, they just gave a strange smile. I realized that further exploration of this problem would have to cease, and that now everything depended on me. I locked myself up in my hotel. I could not go back without an article; the chief editor did not understand how one could fail to find what one was looking for.

"I . . . wrote the article according to a quite simple principle. I already knew what collective control was, and I knew about inspection brigades and other forms of public control—checking and controlling of one another's work, things like that. So I introduced all these formulas into my account of life at the factory, and I also used some touches from real life—for instance, the people I had actually met who had done something for efficiency, but who had nothing to do with collective control and had no idea what it was.

"Then, when I had read my article through, I took it along with bated breath to the chairman of the factory committee. How could he possibly put his signature to all of this when in fact there was no real collective control at the factory?

"He put on his glasses and wore a very serious expression as he read. He finished reading and signed it. His face lit up with a smile, and he said: 'An excellent article! Here we are, working away, but we simply don't know how to write about it!' "

Thanks to émigrés like Viktor Perelman and to numerous Soviet journalists in Moscow who told me about their work, I know more about Soviet journalism than about any other Soviet institution. I can provide no better example of the regime's mentality and how it works in a practical way.

Soviet journalism is propaganda, avowedly and unabashedly. The word has a positive connotation in Russian; one popular Soviet dictionary defines it as "the spreading and profound explanation of some ideas, theory or knowledge." Lenin said a newspaper's job was to propagandize, agitate and organize on behalf of the Party. He vigorously opposed freedom of the press. Two days after the Bolsheviks seized power in 1917 they began closing down newspapers which opposed them.

The Party's Central Committee recently described the role of the country's newspapers in these terms:

> The major tasks of the press are to popularize, in a prompt and easy-to-understand manner, with a deep knowledge of the matter under discussion and using lively, concrete examples, advanced methods of labor, management and administration, to work persistently for their introduction everywhere, and to educate tirelessly in all Soviet people a conscientious, creative attitude to work, a feeling of being master of the country and a high sense of responsibility to society.

The New York Times publishes "All the News That's Fit to Print." At *Pravda*—not surprisingly, in light of this official set of objectives—news in our sense is barely mentioned.

Pravda, organ of the Party's Central Committee, is the most influential national daily newspaper. Its name in Russian means "Truth." *Izvestia*, which means "News," is the organ of the Soviet government, and it is almost as important. (According to an old joke, *"The Truth* isn't news, and *The News* isn't true.") Eight other national dailies are published around the country. (Local printing plants receive matrixes by airplane or facsimiles by wire.) They include *Trud* ("Labor"), organ of the trade unions; *Selskaya Zhizn* ("Rural Life") for the farmers; *Sovietski Sport* for sports fans; and so on. There are variations in subject matter, but not in style or theme. All papers are controlled by the propaganda department of the Central Committee.

Pravda's staff is divided into departments—information department, foreign news, industrial news, military news, letters to the editor, and so on. The biggest and most important department is called Party Life. Sergei Selyuk, the editor of Party Life who agreed to meet me in 1972, said I was the first "capitalist journalist" he had ever spoken with.

What, I asked, was a big story for the biggest department of the world's biggest newspaper (its circulation is nearly 11 million)? The letter from Pavel Abashkin which the Party

Life Department received a few years ago was a big story, Selyuk replied. Worker Abashkin, a member of the Party and a Hero of Socialist Labor (the most distinguished title a Soviet civilian can carry), wrote *Pravda* that he was dismayed: he had noticed that not all communists were active, many were indifferent to their Party work, and in general there was too much laxity in the Party.

Selyuk seemed to get excited telling the story of Worker Abashkin's letter. With his wrinkled skin and twinkling eyes, he reminded me of a good old boy from North Carolina. When Abashkin's letter reached the Party Life Department, *Pravda* sent a correspondent to his hometown to investigate. The correspondent interviewed numerous local communists, solicited opinions of Abashkin's letter and came back to *Pravda* with full notebooks but no clean idea what to write. A meeting was convened in the Party Life Department. It was decided to help Abashkin himself write an article—something that is done, Selyuk explained, for people who have a good idea but don't know how to put it into writing. The *Pravda* men prepared the article, worked it over, but finally realized that it no longer sounded like the ideas of a worker. So they went back to Abashkin's original letter, which they finally published with some of the interviews the reporter had recorded on his first trip. Thus began a long discussion in the pages of the world's largest newspaper about the work of members of the Communist Party of the Soviet Union.

That was a big story. Decidedly *not* a big story was the most dramatic airplane crash of recent years, the mid-air explosion of the Soviet Union's super-sonic jet transport in front of television cameras and thousands of spectators at the Paris Air Show. That disaster in June 1973 was the major news of the day in most of the world's newspapers, but *Pravda* dealt with it in a 27-word item tucked away at the bottom of page six, its back page.

In late 1972 what was then the biggest accident in aviation history occurred outside Moscow. An Aeroflot jet flying from Leningrad crashed in a muddy swamp, killing 176 people. That one got 42 words on *Pravda*'s back page, and probably would have been ignored entirely had there not been 39 foreigners on board. Because of the foreign casualties, Soviet officials knew the story would get out. Ordinarily the censor's regulations forbid any mention of domestic airplane accidents.

Plane crashes come within the purview of the Information

Department. Its values were explained to me by its editor, Irina Kirilova, a smily woman with a gravelly voice who smokes cigarettes one after another. "The reader," she said, "must know something new and *good*."

An airplane crash can be good news, she added—well, almost an airplane crash. She recalled the story of a plane that was flying to Moscow from Khabarovsk, a 10-hour flight by jet. After takeoff the plane's front landing gear jammed. The pilot warned Moscow that he would probably crash on the runway. Someone at the airport called *Pravda* while the plane was still in the air, and a reporter hurried to the scene, arriving just in time to record the heroic combination of piloting skill and ground-crew precautions which resulted in a safe landing.

"If there is some connection with heroism, courage or overcoming a great risk," Mrs. Kirilova said, "then we write about it." What about unluckier occasions, when planes crash? "What's the point of writing about every one? It happens that accidents occur for technical reasons—that doesn't interest us very much."

A Russian scientist told me about a girl from Central Asia who went to Moscow to take university entrance examinations. She did not come home as scheduled, and failed also to notify her parents, who began to worry. After waiting for several days they decided to go to Moscow to look for her. There they learned that she had never taken the examinations. They finally found a police official who told them that the plane she took to Moscow crashed. All on board perished, but Aeroflot, the state airline, had no idea how to contact next of kin. The airline had only the passengers' names, not their addresses. No news of the accident was published.

Soviet papers are only four to six pages long, but they have much more space for editorial matter than comparable western papers because they carry no advertising. This small size is dictated by a general paper shortage,* though I suspect that even with more paper Soviet newspapers would remain small. Smallness makes them easier to control.

To a western eye, the most striking aspect of Soviet news-

---

* The Soviet Union has the world's largest timber reserves, but inadequate industrial capacity to convert trees into paper.

papers is their indifference to news. Reports on events that occurred the day before, at home or abroad, take up only a small fraction of a Soviet paper, perhaps 15 percent.

When the editors of *Pravda* come to work each morning, the next day's *Pravda* is waiting for them in proofs—tomorrow's paper today. It is ready for the printers except for a few small spaces left blank for late-breaking official announcements or perhaps a story from overseas. All the papers work in this way, putting the final touches to Tuesday's paper on Monday, but devoting most of the day to Wednesday's edition.

In *Pravda*, this is how the space is allocated:

The front page is usually dominated by one or two photographs of Soviet citizens at work, accompanied by an article on a farm or factory. A typical story began: "Carrying into life the decisions of the 24th Congress of the Party, the workers of the Severodonetsk chemical factory are successfully fulfilling the tasks of the ninth Five Year Plan. . . ." These pieces appear in the most prominent positions on page one under large black headlines—for instance, "Introduce and Assimilate Capacity More Quickly."

Each day *Pravda* carries an editorial down the two left-hand columns of the front page. It is printed in boldface type, and usually consists of an elaboration of the Party line, a celebration of some accomplishment or an exhortation to work better and harder. "The birthday of Vladimir Ilyich Lenin," began the editorial on that day, "has become a festive day for the Soviet people, and for the working people of all countries. . . ."

Important official news appears on page one. If one of the leaders has made a speech, its text will begin on *Pravda*'s front page. So will the texts of a friendly exchange of telegrams with a fraternal party, or a resolution from the Central Committee. On the day of that plane crash in Moscow which killed 176 people, *Pravda*'s front page was filled with the 61 slogans the Central Committee had approved to mark the November 7 holiday. All were printed in large, bold type, and conveyed such messages as "Long Live the Great, Unbreakable Unity of the Party and the People!" or "Workers of the Soviet Union! In all possible ways, increase the role of workers' collectives in communist education, and in further developing the work and social activity of every person!"

Pravda also occasionally prints poems on the front page,

particularly in conjunction with holidays. This verse appeared soon after my arrival in Moscow:

> Exciting statistics of the five-year plan
> Are filled with glittering light;
> They are like branches becoming green
> On the white tree trunk of a dream. . . .

Each day there are a dozen or more short news items from around the country and the world on page one. The domestic stories report economic developments—the opening of a new factory in Omsk, or the exploitation of a new chemical process in Leningrad. The foreign news is brief and flat—small earthquake in Peru, Soviet trade mission in Algeria.

The page has a cluttered look. Stories are piled on top of one another under a bewildering variety of headline typefaces.

Page two is for Party news, and the country's several million Party workers and agitators are expected to read it carefully. Articles by Party officials and members of *Pravda*'s staff and letters from readers inform the faithful about new methods of Party work, new (or old) lessons about the Party line.

Perhaps the most common sort of story on page two describes the work of a party committee which has increased efficiency or production in its enterprise. Others are meant to take heart, or learn something concrete, from this example. Worker Abashkin's concerns about laxity appeared on page two. Other items suggest the attitudes communists should adopt toward problems of the day. For instance, a Party member in Pskov named V. Davidov wrote a letter about the exchange of Party membership cards:

> The exchange of Party cards is . . . a kind of examination for each Party member. . . . One has to justify the high honor of Party membership by one's attitude to work and one's behavior. When a communist makes a mistake (for instance, communist I. Sherbina came to work drunk) he or she should be strictly reproached. . . . If mistakes are repeatedly made, one must be expelled from the Party, as happened to the same I. Sherbina. . . ."

Page three is for domestic reports on many topics, from nuclear science to ballet and painting. The stories are often written by experts not on *Pravda*'s regular staff. Page three also carries investigative reporting on official malfeasance, about which more presently.

Page four often carries material continued from page one, the texts of long speeches or official announcements. Foreign communists write long articles for page four. So do *Pravda*'s commentators on international affairs.

The principal foreign news appears on page five, the newsiest and the most popular in the paper. About a fourth of the space is devoted to routine reports from the "socialist camp," and another fourth may go to tendentious articles about the struggles between "progressives" and "imperialists." Coverage of the Angolan civil war, the new government in Portugal or the left-wing states in Latin America falls into this category. Page five also carries objective factual information from the world's major capitals. There is a *Pravda* correspondent in almost every one of them except Peking.

The bottom of page five is often the most interesting spot in the paper. Authoritative commentaries appear there. So does the most readable correspondence from abroad, and short essays by *Pravda* writers on new developments or old customs in foreign lands.

Page six is also well read. It contains articles on sports, humorous pieces, practical advice for family life ("Beware: Flu") and reportage from around the country. Radio and television listings appear on the back page. So do the letter and numbers, printed in the bottom righthand corner, with which the censor announces that he has read and approved the paper.

The censor at *Pravda* is little more than a technician. His job is to make certain that nothing which appears on his voluminous list of forbidden items slips into the paper. In fact the journalists on *Pravda* are careful craftsmen and rarely if ever produce a faulty item. They know the rules as well as the censor, and seldom try to challenge or bend one. They are agents of the Central Committee and know their place. "We are never embarrassed to admit that we express the will of the Party," the editor of Party Life told me.

The will of the Party is that the newspapers, radio, television, movies and the arts all help convey the Party line. The newspapers have by far the biggest role in this process. The Party line is more important than the facts about any situation described. When the facts don't conform to the line, the line prevails.

The Party line consists of a few basic propositions: The *USSR is a rich, strong nation whose citizens are happily and energetically building communism, the envy of the world's toiling masses and history's ally in the march toward tomorrow. The USSR is ruled in the name and tradition of Lenin, a prince among men. It is ruled by the Communist Party, the vanguard of the working class, for the benefit of the workers and the common good. The Party embodies the popular will on all subjects; anyone who opposes the Party must favor the restoration of capitalism and the return of the landlords. The spirit of capitalism lives on in the imperialist camp (the western world); imperialists are a natural enemy, progressive forces a natural friend. The struggle for freedom and democracy—the contest between progressive forces and imperialists—is naturally the great event of our time.*

The line is a combination of slogans, invoked to suit the people who control official propaganda, without regard to the facts of any concrete situation. Vietnam was a good example of the way Soviet propagandists use their slogans as they see fit. Until 1972 the Soviet Union supported North Vietnam staunchly in word and deed. But in May 1972, several weeks before President Nixon first visited Moscow, the line on Vietnam changed. *Pravda* and the other papers reduced their coverage of the war and took much of the usual invective out of it. When President Nixon mined North Vietnam's harbors, thus isolating the country from the sea and, according to French diplomatic reports, even killing several Russians on board a Soviet ship in Haiphong harbor, the leaders of the Soviet Union turned the other cheek. The papers only mentioned the mining as an aside, in a story from Washington on another subject. The message to the Vietnamese was clear: Soviet-American relations took precedence over their war.

When *détente* blossomed in the early 1970s, the Soviet press began to treat the western powers with new sympathy. But not—until 1974—Britain. The British did not participate in the first rushes of *détente*, and they paid a price for that in Soviet propaganda. Nothing they said or did could change the hostile tone of news stories about them. When Sir Alec

Douglas Home, then the Foreign Secretary, tried to bury the hatchet with a most conciliatory speech, *Pravda* reported that the speech was hostile to the Soviet Union. The press dwelt on Ulster, blaming the troubles there on Britain's "occupation" of a country that sought its independence. In 1974 and 1975, when a new British government finally improved the diplomatic climate, press coverage changed accordingly. The acid pens were retired, and Ulster became a small story.

Pravda eschews ambiguity. In its descriptions of Ulster, for example, there is no historic struggle between Catholics and Protestants, no sense that perhaps the Ulster problem is too complicated to solve. Instead it is a simple matter of cruel imperialism. The same kind of categorical interpretation recurs in the Soviet treatment of virtually every issue, at home or abroad. The Arabs are designated friends, so they can do nothing wrong. After they started the Yom Kippur War in 1973, *Pravda* reported the precise minute at which, it said, Israeli forces began the fighting. In the next few days, according to *Pravda*, the Israelis "fell back" into defensive positions—an unprecedented maneuver for an army supposedly attacking with the advantage of surprise, but that is what happened on the pages of Soviet newspapers.

When a truly ambiguous event occurs, the Soviet press often chooses to present it as the consequence of conspiracy. The assassination of King Faisal of Saudi Arabia, Soviet newspapers implied, was the work of the CIA. A report on the defeat of Senator J. William Fulbright in a primary election in 1974 began with this paragraph:

> On May 30 American press organs under the control of Zionist capital or sympathetic to Zionists, including the *New York Times* and the *Washington Post,* took malicious pleasure in informing their readers that the distinguished politician and chairman of the Senate Foreign Relations Committee, William Fulbright, did not get enough votes in the Democratic primary election.

Thus wrote the weekly magazine *Abroad,* which blamed Fulbright's defeat on the machinations of Zionists, particularly Robert Strauss, a Jew and the chairman of the Democratic National Committee.

The Soviet press conveys a sense of serene domestic tranquility in the USSR. The citizens are happy, the Party wise and just, the country prospering. But there is a certain amount of muckraking in the Soviet papers; the tranquility can be stirred by an occasional revelation of corruption or stupidity.

Critical material is meant to be functional. Its publication is supposed to clear up the problem it reveals, if that is possible, or simply to demonstrate official concern for essentially insoluble problems. A typical insoluble problem—this one involving a newly purchased glasscutter—prompted a school technician named N. Fedchenko to write to *Pravda*:

> ... At home ... I tried to read the instructions, but I needed the help of a magnifying glass. They said: "Place the tool perpendicularly to the surface of the glass. . . ." I did so. It didn't work. I tried to adjust the tool to make it work—in vain. Does every person who buys a tool like this at a store have to fix it before using it?

The answer to that question may well be yes. No amount of publicity seems to improve the quality of Soviet consumer goods. But the subject is written about prolifically, and this at least conveys the idea that the authorities care about the problem, even if they can't solve it.

Letters like Mr. Fedchenko's appear regularly in most of the nation's papers, including *Pravda*. Soviet citizens love to write to their newspapers; 30,000 write to *Pravda* each month. Only a few of these letters are printed, but a staff of 26 letter-readers carefully screens the mail, referring complaints to relevant Party or government offices and collating trends in public opinion for the Central Committee.

Certain kinds of complaints don't get into the paper, as Ludmilla Yemelyanova, the deputy editor of *Pravda*'s Letter Department, acknowledged. She told me about a rash of letters from Kazakhstan complaining about the behavior of local policemen. "It's not convenient to publish such letters in *Pravda*," Mrs. Yemelyanova said, so the letters were forwarded to the Kazakhstan Party organization, which, she said, rectified the problem.

It *is* convenient to publish letters in which citizens complain of the noise their neighbors make, or suggest that a new stadium be built in their town, or praise the Politburo for the wisdom of its foreign policy. A senior editor of the paper once admitted to me that some letters in this last vein are contrived by *Pravda*'s correspondents. This was evident after Alexander Solzhenitsyn was expelled from the country. The next day Soviet papers printed letters applauding the expulsion that were allegedly written by citizens living in remote cities—cities from which letters to Moscow take at least a week to arrive.

Soviet papers periodically publish articles exposing misbehavior by Party and (more commonly) government officials. The nature of these exposés reveals the authorities' practical concerns. The most common topics are petty corruption and bribe-taking, laziness and irresponsibility, drunkenness and narrow-minded stupidity. Occasionally—rarely—the journalists' targets are important officials.

The best example of this during the three years I spent in the USSR involved the scandals in Soviet Georgia. Shortly after the "retirement" of the Georgian First Secretary whose wife was a thief, *Pravda* published a humorous "fantasy" about senior Georgian officials who built summer houses for themselves with state-owned materials. Several weeks later an item appeared under the oft-used heading "After a Criticism." *Pravda* had received a letter from the new First Secretary in Georgia, who wrote that the "fantasy" described in the original article "conformed to reality." *Pravda* then listed a dozen Georgian officials who had lost their jobs—and their summer *dachas*—for participating in this intrigue.

When I visited the Letter Department of *Pravda*, its editor, Viktor Grishin, told me excitedly about Deputy Minister Buikov of the Ministry of Civil Aviation, whom *Pravda* had accused, almost directly, of lying to its reporter when he claimed that a problem involving the sale of airplane tickets had been cleared up. Grishin said that it was "just nonsense" to claim that Soviet papers won't take on the bigshots.

It would be equally nonsensical to claim that this happens very often. The limits of investigative journalism are neatly summarized by the following story, which *Pravda* itself reported a decade ago: A journalist who had written critically about a local Party official was summoned to the Party office. So was his editor. The journalist was told: "You think you're smarter than everyone else! We'll fire you now, and no one will give you work. I mean it! And you [to his editor], remember this: Communists, especially the [Party's] officials, are not to be criticized without the knowledge of [this] committee. Is that clear?"

The list of subjects ignored by Soviet newspapers reveals as much as the material printed. The official Soviet image of reality depends heavily on omissions.

In Moscow I obtained a partial list of the censor's forbidden topics from an unofficial but reliable source. The list speaks very well for itself. Here are some of the items that the censor in each newspaper office must keep out of his paper:

* The itineraries of trips and locations of stopovers or speeches of members and candidate members of the Politburo.
* Information about the organs of Soviet censorship which discloses the character, organization and method of their work.
* Activities of the organs of state security and Soviet intelligence organs. . . .
* . . . The amount of crime, the number of people engaged in criminal behavior, the number arrested, the number convicted. . . .
* Information about the existence of correctional labor camps. . . .
* Facts about the physical condition, illnesses and death rates of all prisoners in all localities.
* The number of illiterate people.
* Reports about the human victims of accidents, wrecks and fires. . . .
* Information about the consequences of catastrophic earthquakes, tidal waves, floods and other natural calamities. . . .
* Calculations of the relative purchasing power of the ruble and the hard currency of foreign states.
* The size of the total wage fund [that is, wages paid to the population], or the amount of money which comprises the population's purchasing power, or the balance of income and expenditure of the population. . . .
* Information about hostile actions by the population or responsible officials of foreign states against representatives or citizens of the USSR.
* The correlation between the cost of services for foreign tourists in the USSR and the selling price of tourist trips in the USSR.
* Information about export to foreign countries of

arms, ammunition, military technology, military equipment. . . .

* Information suggesting a low moral-political condition of the armed forces, unsatisfactory military discipline, abnormal relations among soldiers or between them and the population. . . .

* The number of drug addicts. . . .

* Information about occupational injuries.

* Information about the audibility of the radio stations of foreign states in the USSR.

* Information about the duration of all-union [i.e., nationwide] training sessions for athletes; information about the rates of pay for athletes; information about the money prizes for good results in sports competitions; information about the financing, maintenance and staff of athletic teams. . . .

The list I obtained was not complete. Any regular reader of Soviet newspapers knows other subjects which they never mention. For example, there is no coverage of domestic political disputes or disagreements among the country's leaders. The papers never report that Communist Parties in Eastern Europe and elsewhere often disagree with, and sometimes even criticize, the Soviet Party. *Pravda*'s readers have never read about the electoral platforms of the French and Italian communists, both of which promise the full range of human rights and reject the Soviet model for their own societies. The fact that the standard of living in Poland, Hungary, Czechoslovakia and East Germany is substantially higher than in the USSR is not reported in Soviet newspapers. Similarly, the social services provided by "capitalist" states—for instance, the welfare program in Sweden, which is far superior to the Soviets' own—are never mentioned.

As the list hints, embarrassments are never mentioned. When President Sadat of Egypt expelled 10,000 or more Soviet advisors in 1972, *Pravda*'s first reaction was silence.* After a delay of more than 24 hours, the Soviet papers pub-

---

* The length of time it takes *Pravda* to react to an event can be an indication of its importance—or the confusion it causes inside the Soviet leadership. There was a similar long silence, for instance, when Mr. Nixon mined the harbors of North Vietnam. *Pravda* finally reported that development as an aside in the third paragraph of a dispatch from Washington.

lished an official announcement that the Soviet troops stationed in Egypt were coming home by mutual Soviet-Egyptian agreement because they had completed their mission.

Another kind of material shunned by *Pravda* and the other Soviet papers is admission of error. Like the Party that rules it, the Soviet press projects an image of infallibility.

Rather than acknowledge an error when—for example—a reporter incorrectly describes the work of some factory, *Pravda* prefers to wait a few weeks then print another article on the same factory with the correct facts. Individuals aggrieved by the treatment they receive in a Soviet paper theoretically have a right to sue, but this has happened only a few times in Soviet history. To my knowledge, no newspaper has ever lost a libel suit.

In the 1930s *Pravda*'s hypersensitivity to errors had comical consequences. As part of a new propaganda campaign, officials in Moscow were looking for "shock workers" whom they could lionize as models for the nation—men or women with heroic reputations for overfulfilling their norms. Someone found a suitable coal-miner in the Ukraine, and *Pravda* rushed his life story into print. The paper put his name in the big black headline: "Nikita Izotov."

Soon "Nikita Izotov" was a household word. (People still remember the name.) But it wasn't quite the name of the coal-miner in question, whose mother had called him Nikifar, not Nikita. The name was garbled in transmission to Moscow.

What to do? The question was hotly debated. The final decision avoided the need for any admission of error. Mr. Izotov was taken to a local court in the Ukraine, where his name was legally changed to Nikita so *Pravda*'s headline and real life would coincide.

Inconsistencies sometimes do appear in the press, and they sustain the western world's Kremlinologists. My favorite involved Khrushchev, who, at various stages of his reign as First Secretary of the Communist Party, was referred to in *Pravda* as First Secretary, First secretary and first secretary.

Shortly after I left the USSR, I met a man in London who had worked as a journalist in Tashkent, the capital of Soviet Uzbekistan in Central Asia. Unlike many émigrés from the Soviet Union, this man was not bitter about his previous life, and he retained some pride in the work he had done. He gave me a vivid description of Soviet journalism:

"A newspaper is not only a collective propagandist and agitator, but also a collective organizer—that's what Lenin said. And that's the goal before every [Soviet] newspaper—to be a good organizer and propagandist, a propagandist in support of the Party's ideas.

"Every newspaper works on a Plan. The Plan sets out the basic needs for the coming months—what has to be done, what subjects have to be written about. In Uzbekistan, for instance, one of the most important things was cotton. Every summer our paper's Plan called for lots of articles about the cotton crop—how to bring it in more effectively, how to avoid the mistakes made in past years, etc. In the area of ideology the Plan always emphasized 'Friendship Among the Peoples' [that is, among Russians and other minority groups] and atheist propaganda against religion. Political education of party cadre was important; we had to give material about Marxism-Leninism to every communist, because every communist is supposed to sharpen and improve his political education.

"The newspaper's plan is coordinated with appropriate departments of the Central Committee [i.e., the Central Committee of the Uzbek Communist Party, a miniature copy of the Central Committee in Moscow]. The paper never took a step without the Central Committee. Once a week there was a meeting in the Central Committee at which important questions were decided. We did everything the way they do in Moscow, but on a smaller scale. The meeting was attended by all the members of the bureau of the Committee [the local equivalent of Moscow's Politburo], and by all the nomenclatured staff of the Central Committee. [In Soviet terminology, key officials of Party organs are called "nomenclatured." It means their job is listed in the nomenclature of the *apparat*. The chief editor and "responsible secretary," or managing editor, of a provincial Party newspaper would be nomenclatured officials.]

"The bureau considers the paper's plan. If comments are required, they are made at the meeting. The chief editor is the only person from the paper who attends.

"When a big issue came up we always had to consult the Central Committee. For example, a professor in Tashkent complained that we didn't really need a new steel combine which the Planning Commission in Moscow had decided we needed. The professor wanted to write about this. So we had to discuss it with the Central Committee. They'd have to decide, because if we published such an article, there would have to be some official decision about it afterward. If they didn't want to make a decision, they'd tell us not to publish it. . . .

"You see, if a newspaper writes about something that isn't right, something has to be done to correct it. After a while the paper must publish an article reporting what happened after it made the original criticism. There was a man on the staff whose job it was to cut out copies of the critical articles we ran and send them to the appropriate offices. For instance, if we published a criticism of a hospital, he'd send the article to the local Ministry of Health, to the city government and to the hospital itself, and he'd expect answers, including measures that were taken to correct the problem that was criticized.

"Sometimes we had to resort to Aesopian language in critical articles. I remember one of our journalists wrote about a group of people who were stealing clothes from a clothing factory where they worked and selling them. When the journalist looked into it he found that even the secretary of the local Party Committee was involved in this black-market deal. So was the head of the Party Committee's industrial department. These local princes—local czars, so to speak—were stealing. But we couldn't say in the paper that such important officials were involved in criminal behavior. We had to hint at it by writing that this Party Committee was badly managed—things like that. But they did remove that Party Secretary from his job.

"Once I wanted to write about an old man who died because a doctor gave him the wrong medicine. My idea was to write about it as a warning to doctors to be careful, but the Central Committee said, 'You don't have to write about such things.' . . .

"If we made a mistake, our Central Committee had to answer for it to Moscow. . . . The authorities in Moscow were especially concerned about things that tended to exacerbate nationalist feelings. In Uzbekistan there is a local intelligentsia. They have a national feeling—they express it subtly, but they feel it. They want recognition for the ancient Uzbek culture, they're proud of it. But from the center, from Moscow, they demanded that we recognize that the outlying republics didn't amount to anything before the Revolution, before they were helped by the great Russian people—they had no culture, no education. If you wrote that way, it pleased Moscow but not the local intelligentsia. . . .

From Moscow, Tass [the government's news agency] sometimes sent word on its wire that we had to publish some official item on the front page. Tass would also send messages saying, 'Wait for an important dispatch' that was to come along soon afterward. Sometimes they would say what it was about, sometimes not. Sometimes these messages would come in after we had closed the paper, put it to bed, and we had to stop everything and remake it. If we didn't, the Central Committee would be after us. . . .

"The most important department on the paper was Party Life, just as it is on *Pravda*. It had a rule: never publish two heavy articles on propagandistic or ideological themes in one issue.

"Soviet papers aren't interested in sensations, in accidents or murders. Many years ago there was an airplane crash in Uzbekistan. A lot of people were killed but nothing was printed. Rumors flew like leaves in autumn, but nothing was printed. That wasn't what the journalists wanted. We wanted to print something. . . . A group of us were always trying to print things that people wanted to read, and we proposed new ways of handling news, but nothing ever happened. . . . As I said, everything depends on the Central Committee."

I asked if the Central Committee realized that people would doubt the reliability of the newspapers if they failed to report on events that were widely known, like that airplane crash.

"You know, fear is what is operating. Some of those officials in the Central Committee really aren't very smart. What they worry about is the reaction—not the reaction of the people, but the reaction of their bosses. There's fear for oneself. Say an editor on the paper gives permission for an article about an accident. Then somebody up the line will say, 'Who gave permission for such a sensational item?' And the editor could get fired for that, or at least punished. So it's easiest not to write anything. Of course the journalists know this discredits their work, but their hands are tied, they aren't free. . . ."

I asked who bought the paper, and how subscriptions were sold.

"Armies of people—thousands of them—from the Central Committee, from the ministries and other offices, all joined in the campaign to get new subscribers for the papers. . . . People received norms—numbers of new subscribers that they personally were supposed to sign up. Formally it was forbidden to make someone subscribe but the fact is you *have* to subscribe. Somebody comes to you and says, 'What, you haven't subscribed to the most important magazine in the republic?' And you subscribe. Or someone says, 'Is it possible you haven't subscribed to *Pravda*, the central organ of our Party?' And you sign up."

A staff of 150 journalists works in *Pravda*'s dark gray, once-modern building designed by students of Le Corbusier. (A new building is going up next to the old one on Pravda Street, but construction is far behind schedule because much of the frame of the building collapsed, killing an undisclosed number of workmen. The accident wasn't reported in *Pravda*.) The journalists sit at blond wooden desks in small rooms which open off wide corridors, all lined with mock-oriental carpet runners trimmed in red. There is no big newsroom in the American style, no men in eyeshades and shirtsleeves shouting for a copyboy, no excitement in the air.

Pravda is not just a newspaper, it is an official institution. When a journalist there needs a car, he calls the Central Committee's garage—a good measure of *Pravda*'s status. The editors work in oversized offices. Each has a long conference table, half a dozen telephones on a table beside his big desk and a bottle of Scotch or vodka in a closet behind. The ambience is executive, not editorial.

The boss is a politician. Chief Editor Mikhail Zimyanin was the Soviet ambassador in Prague and Hanoi and a Deputy Foreign Minister before the Central Committee named him the Soviet Union's most important journalist in 1965. Zimyanin has the last word at *Pravda* (though he is in turn fully responsible to the Central Committee). He chooses his principal deputies, most of whom are professional journalists, and the Central Committee ratifies his choices.

It is impossible to say with certainty how the journalists at *Pravda* or any other Soviet newspaper see their own roles, or how they feel about the journalism they produce. Judging by those I met, journalists' attitudes toward journalism parallel the views they take toward life in general. The "patriotic cynics" I mentioned in Chapter 4 are, as a rule, interested in seeing more professional journalism and less propaganda than the politicians now permit. The "careerists" tend to be the people who don't really care what they have to write.

The first group can rationalize about the unpleasant things they have to do. For example, there is the concept of the "literate reader." I heard about it from a Russian journalist who was based in America. I asked him about the fairness of the picture of American life that emerges from Soviet newspapers. He acknowledged that, for example, Soviet papers wrote little about the modest improvements in the status of blacks in American life in recent years. A Soviet reader, he agreed, might conclude that America's blacks were little better off than South Africa's. "But we have literate readers who know better," he went on. "For instance, they know that Negroes go to college in America, because we have referred in our stories to the fact that Paul Robeson and Angela Davis graduated from college."

Some—a few—Soviet journalists like to sneak things into print for the sake of the literate reader. One common technique is to report on and respond polemically to some foreign commentary on Soviet life or policy; if cleverly done, a piece of this kind can tell Soviet readers what foreigners are saying about their country, information usually forbidden by the censor.

Another rationalization I met often was the idea that the Soviet public has to be dealt with carefully. One writer who lived for several years in America told me that Walter Cronkite could safely announce the discovery of a possible new cure for cancer, because Americans are used to sensational stories which often turn out to be untrue. "But a tiny article in *Pravda* about a possible cancer cure would cause a furor here, because papers are read differently," he went on. People assume that if *Pravda* mentions something, it must be important. So cancer victims would flood the paper with requests for the new treatment.

I heard this story before I obtained the copy of the censor's regulations. One of those regulations forbids publication of "information about new methods for treating or diagnosing malignant tumors in humans without permission of the Ministry of Health of the USSR."

Many Soviet journalists do what is expected of them automatically, without trying to improve on the standard formulas, and without protesting against them. In 1967 Lev Tolkunov, then the chief editor of *Izvestia*, commented on this phenomenon with unusual candor. He wrote about the great outpouring of propaganda to celebrate the 50th anniversary of the Revolution: "In a number of instances, this work is purposeless, inconsequential, superficial and, finally, simply dull. Page through newspapers and you see a large headline on the [50th] jubilee, and under this a hope-filled, ringing sub-headline. And under the headline, ordinary, gray, incidental items."

Viktor Perelman, who told the story about "collective control" that began this chapter, has recalled that many of his colleagues on the magazine *Soviet Trade Unions* smiled at the fact that they had to "create and build mythical 'castles,' indulge in hocus-pocus and propagate myths which had no foundation in real life. That was how things were, and that was really how we worked. It was not the most pernicious sort of work, one gathered, and *Soviet Trade Unions* was not the most unscrupulous journal. So what if people didn't read it and didn't particularly like it? What if it wasn't very popular? What did that have to do with us? Our business was to do what was demanded, otherwise we would be dismissed. This was the general philosophy."

Perelman did not mention another relevant fact: the journalist's life is a pretty good one. Journalists enjoy a vaguely romantic status in Soviet society. They can travel, sometimes even abroad. They meet interesting people. They are better paid than most Soviet intellectuals. In Moscow they belong to the House of Journalists, a pleasant club in an old, ornate building that was once a wealthy merchant's mansion. The club has one of the best restaurants in the country and a bar in the basement which sells draft beer and peanuts.

If Soviet journalists rationalize (and who does not?), some of them also speak with wit and subtlety about their work. One of *Pravda*'s deputy chief editors, Vadim Nekrasov, admitted in an interview that "even in our news [coverage], we try to persuade the reader in the way we understand things." Doesn't *Pravda* distort reality? Nekrasov, a charming man who likes to grin, grinned. He recalled a photograph he'd once seen in a British paper when he was *Pravda*'s correspondent in London. The photograph showed an artist at his easel. In an outstretched left hand the artist held his model, an egg. On the canvas he was painting a hen. "In essence, that gives our point of view on the world," Nekrasov said, still grinning.

Several months after I arrived in Moscow I realized that almost every time I visited a Soviet journalist in his office there was a thick stack of mimeographed sheets on the desk. The stack looked the same at *Pravda*, at *Izvestia* and at other papers and magazines. Once a man with whom I was talking had to leave his office for a moment, and I had a chance to look at the stack. It was from Tass, the news agency, and contained translations of foreign newspapers and radio broadcasts, including an article of mine published two days earlier in the *Washington Post*.

This, I learned later, was one of the special news services the authorities provide to journalists and Party and government officials to keep them informed of events not covered in the open press. The editors of *Pravda* don't count on *Pravda* to tell them what they need to know, nor do the men who run the country.

In the Soviet Union, information is a privilege; the amount one gets depends on rank, influence and connections. The chief editor of a newspaper in a provincial city receives *Atlas*, a weekly round-up of world affairs which quotes the foreign press. That provincial editor is told to restrict the use of *Atlas* to a few senior people on his staff, and to burn every copy at the end of each year. In Moscow, according to the dissident historian Roy Medvedev, *Atlas* is available in the reading rooms of most Party organizations. But there are many subjects that *Atlas* ignores—the award of a Nobel Prize for literature to Alexander Solzhenitsyn, for instance.

"Much essential information can only be found in special Tass reports, which are subdivided into three classifications and distributed only to restricted categories of recipients," according to Medvedev, who has many contacts inside the Party and was once a member himself. "The 'green' or 'blue' Tass reports are more accessible, while the most complete 'white' Tass reports cannot be obtained even by most of the 'instructors' [a bureaucratic title] and consultants of the Central Committee *apparat*. Yet not less than 90 percent of the information contained in these 'white' reports is readily available to the ordinary person in the West who reads several newspapers of different political complexions."

Even Party officials are allowed to know only as much as some higher authority feels they can be trusted to know. Even Party officials are told that the egg is really a chicken. I found it difficult to comprehend the degree of mistrust which must motivate this kind of allocation of information.

The authorities also provide the general public with alternative sources of information, most commonly in the form of lectures. Every factory, school, neighborhood club, university and Party organization offers regular lectures at which professional propagandists supplement the open news media.

Lectures are needed because foreigners can read the newspapers. Sometimes the image the Soviet leaders try to project abroad does not coincide with the image it wants to convey to its own people. And the authorities are willing to admit more to their own citizens than they want to acknowledge to outsiders.* One of *Pravda*'s senior editors told me there was a "certain reluctance" to allow his paper to be quoted abroad "on some issues."

The most interesting lecturers are probably those given to the staffs of academic institutes or Party organizations, and they are effectively closed to outsiders. But a foreigner can attend lectures at the central lecture hall in downtown Moscow, and occasionally at local "Agitation Points" in the capital's residential neighborhoods. I attended numerous lectures myself.

Much of every lecture comes right out of the newspapers. It is slightly eerie to hear a man reciting the stilted rhetoric of a *Pravda* editorial in a conversational tone of voice. One evening a pudgy little lecturer looked out into his audience and said: "The recent meeting of the heads of the socialist states in the Crimea represents not just a great step forward in the area of technical and economic development of the socialist countries, and of their cooperation, but also in the area of foreign policy!" He delivered the line almost breathlessly, as though it were a news bulletin.

---

* In provincial Soviet cities the local evening papers often publish more revealing information than the morning papers. Foreigners living in Moscow or abroad are allowed to subscribe to the morning papers, but not to the evening ones.

At the opposite extreme, a lecturer occasionally provides revealing factual information of a kind not seen in the open press. In early 1973, for example, after the disastrous harvest of 1972, rumors spread in Moscow that rationing had been imposed in the provinces. One lecturer was asked about these reports.

Yes, he said, he had seen it himself in Gorki, an industrial city of 1.2 million, where certain "controls" had been imposed. In Gorki, he explained, workers who did their shopping at the end of the working day found that potatoes* and butter were already sold out. To make sure that everyone got his share, the lecturer said, measures were taken to restrict the amount of these commodities each family could buy.

In other words, the food situation was serious; rationing had been imposed. The lecturer tried to make the decision look sensible and fair, and also to suggest that there was enough butter and potatoes for everyone, even if the supply had to be rationed. I sensed, however, that the audience understood the import of his admission.

In May 1972, when the Soviet Union and the United States signed the first strategic arms limitation agreements, the Soviet papers printed the texts without any explanation, and with one striking omission. The Russians did not print the protocol accompanying the temporary agreement on offensive weapons which listed the numbers of missiles and submarines each country was allowed.

I never knew why these numbers were omitted. They showed that the Soviet Union was permitted a marginal advantage in both categories, so they could not have embarrassed the authorities. Perhaps the government was reluctant to set a precedent for publishing what would ordinarily be considered a state secret in the hypersecretive Soviet Union. The biologist who suggested this theory to me said that if they published those numbers, many scientists and intellectuals would ask why they couldn't publish a lot of other things, too.

In any case, lecturers were authorized to give the numbers of missiles and submarines to their audiences, and did so frequently. They also gave some explanation of the agreement,

---

* Russians eat potatoes at every meal; with bread they form the basis of the national diet. The average Russian consumes five to ten times as many potatoes as the average American.

always implying that the Soviet Union got the best of the bargain.

The papers neglected to print anything about the Soviet Union's enormous purchases of grain from America in 1973. The censor has a rule against revealing details of such agreements. But lecturers used news of the purchases—without ever saying just how huge they were—to assure the public that there would be no famine, despite the bad harvest of 1972.

After sitting through a number of these lectures, I decided that their real purpose was to lend a little human plausibility to the Party line. *You understand, comrades,* a good lecturer seemed to be saying, *we can't print everything in the papers, you and I realize that, but let me give you the straight poop* ... As it turns out, the lecturer's confidences never contradict the published material. Occasionally they may come to the same conclusion by a different path, and the way they are presented is often more interesting and more believable.

The lecturer's credibility depends on the implicit suggestion that he isn't just another propagandist, but a friendly fellow who is going to let his audience in on a few secrets. Selective candor helps to convey this impression.

For instance, I attended a lecture by a Soviet journalist who had just completed an assignment of several years in West Germany. He wore a German tweed jacket, German shoes and German eyeglasses. Someone asked him if people lived well in West Germany.

"Yes," he said, "it's a good life. But the working class is under great stress. There's no time for fun; it's work, work, work. The pay is high, but they get no joy from it. A German once said to me, 'Our stores sell more goods than your [Soviet] stores, but when we go to visit relatives here there's never anything on the table! But in Moscow, when one is received as a guest, the table is always piled high with food and drink!'"

At that, the audience gave an audible sigh of understanding.

The lecturer continued: "Once I had two teeth filled; it cost 145 marks. For the same amount of money I could have bought a good Phillips tape recorder." He mentioned the brand name, and some members of the audience appeared to recognize it.

At the lectures I attended, the western press was, curiously, the most frequently cited source for authoritative information. Once I even heard a lecturer cite an article of mine on the Soviet Union's stature in international diplomacy. Another lecturer began a discussion of public opinion in Western Europe by saying: "I was recently in Europe, where I was able not only to read the newspapers and listen to the radio, but also to meet real people."

One lecturer was asked—before President Sadat expelled his military advisors from Egypt—to evaluate Soviet-Egyptian relations. "They're good," he answered. "Even the western press says so."

There is an ugly side to the system of lectures. Because lecturers are not speaking for the record and no record is kept, these occasions provide an excellent opportunity to spread misinformation. The opportunity is regularly exploited. The more confidential the setting, it seems, the stronger the temptation to spread some lie.

Lies and blatant errors of fact were common at the lectures I heard. "American bread now costs more than a dollar a loaf," a lecturer said in Moscow in 1973. "Seventy-five percent of the means of mass communication in America are under the control, directly or indirectly, of Zionists and Jews," said another. Lyndon Johnson's visit to the Soviet Union—which he canceled after the Soviet invasion of Czechoslovakia in August 1968—did not take place because "we could not agree to have President Johnson in the Soviet Union after he began the Vietnam War," according to another lecturer.

In recent years lectures have been used to spread anti-Semitism. At the Institute of Adolescence of the Academy of Pedagogical Sciences, for example, a lecturer said that on secret Israeli maps the "northern border" of "Greater Israel" is just south of Kiev in the Soviet Ukraine. At another academic institute a lecturer said "the Israelis" had killed a large number of Soviet citizens traveling abroad. Someone asked why this fact had never been mentioned in the newspapers. Because "we'd be accused of anti-Semitism," the lecturer replied.

In March 1972 another American correspondent and I were the first journalists ever to interview Alexander Solzhenitsyn. The main information he wanted to convey was that a "campaign against me"—a campaign of innuendo and accusations—had been going on for several years in lecture halls throughout the country. Acquaintances and well-wishers had told him what the lecturers were saying: that his books were "criminal"; that he had been incorrectly rehabilitated during Khrushchev's de-Stalinization, implying that he had done something serious in 1945, when in fact he was arrested for writing letters to a friend which were critical of Stalin; that he had cooperated with the Nazis and even worked for the Gestapo; that his middle name, the Russian patronymic Isayevich—"son of Isaiah"—indicated that Solzhenitsyn was really Jewish.

Lecturers have told similar stories about Andrei Sakharov, the dissident physicist. One lecturer said the real Sakharov was dead and the man speaking in his name was an imposter. Another said his mind had been affected by nuclear radiation when he was inventing the Soviet Union's hydrogen bomb and he was a little crazy.

If the Soviet Union had evolved according to the Orwellian image of *1984*, propaganda—"thought control"—would by now be sophisticated, elaborate and effective. In fact it is elaborate, but it is also crude and only partially successful. Soviet propaganda is boring and crude because—like so much else in Soviet life—it is distorted by the insecurity of the country's rulers. They are so anxious that the propaganda organs treat them and their works in a princely fashion that they lose sight of the impression the propaganda makes on ordinary people.

"Fear is what is operating," the journalist from Uzbekistan told me when I asked if the Party officials there worried about the credibility of their official newspapers. Better to publish an unbelievable newspaper than to risk the wrath of senior Party officials who dislike a more complete account of the news. So the journalists distort their work to please their bosses, without regard for the readers. This same fear is at work at *Pravda,* on Soviet television and throughout the propaganda organs.

The main evening news program on Soviet television usually appears from 9:00 to 9:10 p.m. After watching it several times one begins to understand the weaknesses of Soviet propaganda. If one of the country's leaders has done something in public that day, it is invariably the lead item. In the era of collective leadership it is rare for one leader to do something alone, so other members of the leadership are usually mentioned. Each time any of the leaders is named, the announcer—one of a stable of monotonous men and women—reads his first, middle and last names, and usually his full title. If the leader is Brezhnev, he will be named and titled in full at every mention. If the Politburo is meeting Brezhnev at the airport on his return from a trip abroad (as it always does), the announcer will read the name of every high-ranking comrade who showed up at the airport. These lists of names often take up three or four minutes of a ten-minute broadcast.

When President Nixon made his first visit to the Soviet Union in 1972, hundreds of journalists from all over the world covered the event. The Russians set up a press room with a bar, where I met a number of Eastern European radio and television broadcasters. I watched the evening news with several of them; we heard how Leonid Ilyich Brezhnev, General Secretary of the Communist Party of the Soviet Union, and Richard Nixon, President of the United States of America, did this, that and the other during the day, their names and titles repeated in full for each event. I looked around at the bar and saw that the Eastern Europeans—a Pole, an East German and a Hungarian—were smiling. "Do you know what would happen if we did that kind of stuff in East Germany?" one asked. "People would laugh at us—and switch the channel to West German television." But there is no West German television in the Soviet Union.

The leaders' prejudices also dictate that television and the press describe a happy nation, prospering citizens and a powerful economy. In every case the image is more important than the reality. The propaganda is so overdone that even ordinary people can recognize its exaggerations. No matter, it makes the country look the way the leaders would like it to. Propaganda is a basic form of *pokazuka.*

Fears and prejudices compel Soviet propagandists to do things that detract from the effectiveness of their own work. At the most basic level, no one has the courage to change the old, essentially Stalinist traditions of the Soviet press—to throw out the old-fashioned make-up, the turgid political and ideological articles, the crude censorship and slanted news.*

Soviet sociologists have discovered that the old formula is not particularly successful. In 1969 a survey of *Izvestia* readers based on 8000 interviews and 18,000 questionnaires found that only 18 percent of them regularly read articles classified as "propagandistic," meaning ideological and political. Twenty-three percent regularly read articles on economic subjects; thirty percent read *Izvestia*'s editorials. The most popular subjects—to which two-thirds or more of the readers paid close attention—were "morals" (human relations, crime, etc.), satire, family life, exposés of official malfeasance, international news and commentary. Many readers indicated skepticism about the news they read. More than a third expressed less than full satisfaction with "the completeness and objectivity of the international news" in *Izvestia*.

Less formal propaganda can also be ludicrously ineffective. Andrei Amalrik described the haphazard approach to political propaganda in his Siberian village, where it was the responsibility of his friend Vera:

Her job was to write slogans on posters, such as "Tractor Drivers! Bring the harvest in on time and without waste!" These texts were provided by the district Party Committee and she wrote them in chalk on strips of red material that she hung up in various places in the village. . . . It was also her duty to issue bulletins written on special sheets of paper with a letterhead design which showed a peasant boy and girl in profile with a flying Sputnik in the background. If the foreman told her that X and Y had worked well during the haymaking, she wrote: "Honor and glory to collective farmers X and Y, who have worked well at bringing in the hay." Or if he said that such and such a herdsman had worked badly and should be criticized, she wrote: "So-and-so is bad at his job and is too fond of vodka." All the names and facts were invariably mixed up, and there were many grammatical errors.

---

* Khrushchev's son-in-law, Alexei Adzhubei, substantially altered the appearance—and slightly changed the content—of *Izvestia* when he was its editor. These were the only real changes in the Soviet press in several generations.

Marxist-Leninist ideology is itself a barrier to effective propaganda. The mass media, particularly television, are not recognized as powerful forces capable of molding human attitudes. In the Marxist view, economic factors and social class determine human behavior. Soviet ideologists stick by the old formulas even on subjects like this one, which has been transformed by purely technological factors since Marx and Lenin died.

A sociology student in Soviet Azerbaijan was sent to a remote mountain village to find out why the people there had suddenly begun to abandon their traditional culture in the mid-1960s, throwing off customs that were thousands of years old to mimic urban fashions and mores. The young scholar spent some weeks in the village. He learned that its customs had begun to change just after the first television sets had appeared in the region. Television had brought the outer world into those mountains, and had transformed the residents' attitudes. The student put his conclusions into writing and took them back to his professor, who rejected them angrily. "This is not a Marxist analysis!" he said, and told the student to re-do it.

Insensitivity to its power must be one explanation for the mediocrity of Soviet television programing. When the Russians care deeply about something—bombs and missiles, for example, or good athletes—they find ways to develop them. If they cared about television, they could certainly use it much more effectively.

As it is, the Russians use television as though it were a newspaper, allocating "space" (in this case, time on the air) to various official spokesmen and different kinds of entertainment without regard for the way the flow of programs affects the viewer. The viewer obviously doesn't matter. What matters is pleasing the boss.

Not surprisingly, the bosses are themselves permanent fixtures on television. Every week a variety of military, Party and government officials appears on the main channel, which reaches about two-thirds of the Soviet population. These officials read long-winded, dull speeches, usually in a monotone voice, usually without looking up from the text. One Saturday afternoon in May I sat through 45 minutes of Marshal A. M. Vasilevski of the Soviet Army reading a dissertation called "Exposure of False Stories about the Great Patriotic War" (the Soviet name for World War II). Occasionally the Marshal looked up from the text, though his eyes rarely found the lens of the camera. Mostly he just read, a monotonous recitation of the Army's great victories in the war. Such programs are regularly inserted between sports events and more popular entertainment shows.

The latter, too, are primitive by western standards, but they seem to satisfy their audience, which knows nothing else. There are game shows, movies, variety entertainment shows and documentaries. World War II is a favorite subject. Adventures and movies are, with few exceptions, low-budget affairs with mediocre acting and sloppy sound tracks and film editing.

The priorities of Soviet television were on display one spring day in Moscow at a press conference given by John V. Lindsay, then the mayor of New York. Lindsay made an eloquent statement on the need for greater trust between Russians and Americans, and he answered questions about Soviet Jews and other delicate subjects. The camera crew from Soviet television ignored all of this. When Lindsay had finished answering the questions of western correspondents, the Soviet television reporter rose to his feet. The lights went on, the camera began to whir and the reporter asked the mayor of New York City his question:

"How did you like Moscow?"

Lindsay answered that he was impressed by Moscow, an ideal answer from the Soviet reporter's point of view—one immortalized for rebroadcast to millions of citizens at some later date.

There was one stunning exception to all of this during the years I spent in the Soviet Union, a 12-part film called *Seventeen Flashes of Spring*. It lasted for 14 hours, which was much too long, but the acting was superb, the story exciting and the photography excellent. It was also brilliant and powerful propaganda—proof that Orwell's vision can still be realized.

The movie, made in mock-documentary style with periodic snippets of actual wartime newsreels, was about a man named Stirlitz—at least, that was one of his names. Stirlitz was a Soviet spy who became a senior official in the political-intelligence section of Hitler's SS. Using personal relationships with most of the famous Nazi leaders, Stirlitz managed to sabotage an attempt by Heinrich Himmler and Allen Dulles to make a "separate peace" between Germany and the United States in February and March 1945—a peace which would have allowed the Nazis to concentrate their last forces on the eastern front, against the Soviet Union. (Dulles was the senior American intelligence official in Europe at the time.)

Stirlitz was played by an actor named Vyacheslav Tikhonov, whose aristocratic bearing and dark, distinguished features were "almost not Russian at all," as a friend of mine in Moscow put it. Other parts were played by some of the Soviet Union's most talented actors. The film portrayed senior Germans with intelligence and some sympathy, avoiding the standard Soviet cliché of barbaric Nazi monsters. Nevertheless, Stirlitz was smarter than all of them. So were the other Soviet spies, diplomats and officials who appeared in the film. One of them was Joseph Stalin, who was portrayed as a shrewd leader heading off the Americans' wily plan.

Nothing else that appeared on television when I was in the Soviet Union, except perhaps international hockey matches, attracted as much attention as *Seventeen Flashes of Spring*. It was shown first in August 1973, when much of the country was on vacation. Nevertheless it was an enormous sensation; I overheard strangers talking about it in buses and while waiting in line to buy bread. For 12 days millions of people organized their schedule around the day's episode. Apparently by popular demand, all 12 episodes were repeated in December, again attracting an enormous audience. Virtually every Russian I knew or met in that period saw at least several episodes. The movie was strikingly realistic, and many took it as historically accurate. One paper printed a letter from a much-decorated war hero who praised its authenticity and the great achievement of Soviet intelligence in sabotaging "the talks about a separate peace between the leaders of Hitler's Germany and the western nations."

In fact, however, the whole story was fiction, only loosely connected to events that actually took place. The Russians had no spy remotely as influential as Stirlitz. According to American diplomatic documents, a group of Nazis made a vague approach to Dulles in March 1945, but it never led to anything like talks about a separate peace agreement.

Perhaps because of these inaccuracies, the authorities withheld *Seventeen Flashes of Spring* for 18 months after its completion. I could never find out why they finally permitted it to be shown—or why exactly they suppressed it for so long, though presumably they feared embarrassing the United

States in the early days of *détente*. In any event, the movie made a stunning impression on the Soviet public, and demonstrated that the Russians could use television brilliantly if they set their minds to it.

Seventeen Flashes of Spring was sophisticated propaganda, good enough to appeal to a western eye jaded by a generation of slick films and television. The Soviet Union does not produce very much good propaganda, I decided, because the people who rule the country are not very sophisticated. Their concerns are more basic.

The editor of *Pravda*'s Information Department, Mrs. Kirilova, repeatedly described her journalistic mission with the Russian word *vospitanie,* the word Russians use when they discuss the *upbringing* of their children. At first I was startled by her use of the word, but as I thought about it, upbringing began to make sense.

Soviet children begin to hear propaganda slogans before they can feed themselves. The teachers' manual for Soviet nurseries and kindergartens stipulates that instructors of two- and three-year-olds (called "upbringers" in Russian) should teach their charges "to recognize V. I. Lenin in portraits and illustrations." The teacher is told to "arouse feelings of love and respect for him." From that modest beginning, the education in Lenin gets more complicated every year. The children learn poems and songs about him, which are invariably recited for visitors to their kindergarten. On the founder's birthday, teachers of six-year-olds are instructed to take children to the Lenin monument in town to lay a wreath.

A Lithuanian woman told me something about the impact of this sort of early indoctrination. Many Lithuanians are struggling against Russification and communist ideology, among them the woman I talked with. She told me about a friend who came to work one day in a bad mood. " 'What's the matter?' I asked her. 'Oh, it's my son, he's full of all that Lenin stuff they feed him in kindergarten—Grandpa Lenin, everybody's protector, all that stuff. He came home yesterday and said, "Grandpa Lenin gives us everything," and I got angry with him. "Stupidity!" I said. "No Lenin gives you anything. Your father and I are the ones who give you everything. I stood in line for two hours yesterday to get you those boots, and don't you forget it!" ' "

My Lithuanian acquaintance, who had no children herself,

was intrigued by this story, and began asking other mothers what their children learned about Lenin. All of them could recount similar experiences. Women who lived alone, without husbands, said their children were told in school that they *did* have a papa of their own—Lenin.

One story in a reading book for second-graders is about a little boy who wanted to go hunting in the forest with the grownups. The older man dismissed him as too little. The boy was crestfallen until a man named "Ilyich" appeared and took his side. Let the boy join the hunt, Ilyich said, he can take care of himself. Ilyich, of course, is Lenin—Vladimir Ilyich Lenin.

By age ten a student's reading book provides drawings of children living "under capitalism"—in slums, surrounded by turmoil. Adolescents read about the fate of capitalist society: "History long ago passed sentence on imperialism [the "last stage" of capitalism]. It is doomed, because the objective realities of social development have put the revolutionary transition to socialism on the agenda of this century." War, they read, "is a means of quickly enriching capitalists." The workers of the western world are mercilessly exploited, one of the textbooks reports: "The system of hired labor is a system of hired slavery.... The exploitation of the proletariat in the capitalist world is growing."*

"Upbringing" for adults consists of repetition of the basic themes and a variety of practical lessons. Thus Mrs. Kirilova was fond of the story about the airplane that didn't crash—an inspiring example of heroism and skill. Thus the papers and television provide numerous accounts of lives ruined by vodka, crime or sloth. Thus the Central Committee could describe the goals of the press without mentioning information or ideas—except those concerning "advanced methods of labor, management and administration." Soviet propaganda deals with facts and ideas because they are unavoidable, not because the men who rule the country want to encourage them.

---

* *Détente* has not altered this rhetoric. The quotations in this paragraph are taken from two high-school texts that were revised during 1973, the year after President Nixon's first and most successful visit to Moscow, when Soviet relations with the western powers were ostensibly cordial.

6 · *True and False*

Q. Is Comrade Nyetyev the greatest and most important
inventor of all time?

A. In principle, yes. Comrade Nyetyev invented toilet
paper, the electric razor, the registry office, the automatic fleatrap, the ultra-short wave and the beer
glass. But Comrade Potalov was an even greater inventor.

Q. Why? Did he invent more things?

A. No. He invented Comrade Nyetyev.

"Describing something that exists is much easier than
describing something that doesn't exist, even though you
know it's going to exist. What we see today with the unaided
human eye is not necessarily the truth. The truth is what
must be, what is going to happen tomorrow. Our wonderful
tomorrow is what writers ought to be describing today"
(from Alexander Solzhenitsyn's *Cancer Ward*).

Q. The chart on the wall of our factory shows a sharply
falling production curve. What can we do to change
this?

A. Grasp the chart and rotate it 90 degrees. Then the curve will rise.

In 1972 I wrote an article for the *Washington Post* about the translation of American literature into Russian. (Thanks to a group of determined Soviet scholars, American literature has become well known in the USSR.) One of the people I interviewed was Tanya Kudryavtseva, a senior editor of *Foreign Literature* magazine, a monthly journal which publishes prose and poetry translated from other languages. Mrs. Kudryavtseva, a stocky, middle-aged woman, spent more than an hour discussing American literature with me. Toward the end of the conversation she volunteered the information that her magazine was paying some American authors in dollars for the rights to translate their works. This was interesting news, since the Soviet Union was not then a signatory to any international copyright convention (it is now), and was not obliged to pay such royalties.

"Yes," Mrs. Kudryavtseva said, "I paid Mary Hemingway to publish *Islands in the Stream* [Ernest Hemingway's posthumously published novel]. I think we paid her about two thousand dollars." She went on to say that Mrs. Hemingway, the author's widow, was a personal friend. "I just received a Christmas card from her—here it is," Mrs. Kudryavtseva said. She held it up and began reading the message inside. I sat across the desk and could easily read Mrs. Hemingway's closing sentence on the back of the greeting card. It said she had never received any money for the publication of *Islands in the Stream;* she asked if something had gone wrong.

I left that meeting thinking I had never before been lied to quite so boldly, but Mrs. Kudryavtseva had done it with such a pleasant smile that I was never sure—until I got back to America and wrote Mrs. Hemingway myself. She replied that she had never received $2000—or any amount at all—for *Islands in the Stream*, and had never received an answer from Mrs. Kudryavtseva to the question on her Christmas card.

In 1905, 12 years before the czar was deposed in the revolution of February 1917, the first Russian revolution nearly plunged the country into chaos. The first workers' "Soviets," or revolutionary councils, appeared in 1905, the most important of them in Petersburg. Leon Trotski, a brilliant twenty-six-year-old orator, became its chairman. This was Trotski's first great contribution to the revolutionary cause.

Today tourists can visit a grand old building on Gorki Street in central Moscow that was the English Club before 1917, and is now the Museum of the History of the Revolution. The museum has a "1905 Room" dedicated to the events of that year, but one can search its exhibits in vain for any hint that Trotski was involved in the first revolution.

"Where is Trotski?" I asked the old woman who watched over the 1905 Room.

"Enemy of the people," she replied. That is what Stalin called Trotski when he banished him.

"Yes, later," I said, "but in 1905 he was a leader of the Petersburg Soviet and an important revolutionary."

The old lady shook her head and repeated: "Enemy of the people."

In retirement, Nikita Khrushchev said:

Frankly, I hardly ever read any of these memoirs that are now coming out about World War II. I find them too upsetting. I'm getting along in years, and my nervous system simply can't stand all the self-serving distortions and outright lies. Maybe it's just my subjective viewpoint . . . what makes me furious is that while these other people who are writing memoirs should be pinning the blame on Stalin, they're more worried about vindicating themselves. They're all too willing to be yes-men and to present events the way someone else would like to have them presented rather than the way they happened. . . .

[Marshal] Zhukov's memoirs are a special case. Even though they bear his name, I don't think they contain many of his thoughts. Who the real authors are, God only knows. . . .

I firmly believe that the truth will come out in the end. Someday, we'll have another Leo Tolstoy to write a *War and Peace* for our own era. That's in the area of fiction.

"Although the Russians are the most incorrigible liars in the whole world," wrote Ivan Turgenev, the 19th-century author, "there is nothing they respect so much as the truth—to nothing do they respond so readily."

The relationship between Soviet society and the truth must be as tense and complicated as the emotional relationships in a sheik's harem. Turgenev captured the essence of the Russians' ambivalence: they lie like troopers, yet long for "a true word," as they call it. An outsider, particularly one raised on the Judeo-Christian moral absolutes, is baffled. I was.

There is a cultural trait at work here which I cannot explain but can describe. Russians find it easy to fib. In Moscow I lived closely with three Russians—a woman who took care of our apartment, a secretary/translator and a driver, all of them provided by the agency which cares for diplomats. All three reacted identically when caught shirking, loafing or otherwise misbehaving. They quickly invented some improbable story, or simply denied the obvious, to avoid acknowledging guilt. I decided these must be tricks that children learn from their parents, because they are endemic to Russian life. "No Russian," wrote Gogol, "likes to admit before others that he is to blame."

But the lie is more than a means of coping with life's embarrassments. In the contemporary Soviet Union, in Solzhenitsyn's bitter but indisputably accurate phrase, "the lie has become not simply a moral category, but a pillar of the state." It is a harsh judgment, but there is no way around it. In the land of *pokazuka* the truth often does not matter.

There is no moral authority in Soviet life which can call a lie by its rightful name. Though allowed to exist, the Church is denied the right to speak out, especially on secular matters. Philosophers, writers and other thinkers who might be expected to fill this role are denied access to the means of communication. When the issue is faced at all, it is faced indirectly.

An unusual musical play staged in Moscow in late 1974 included an example of the indirect approach. The play, *Rock and Roll at Dawn*, written by two *Pravda* editors, incorporated rock music into a wild story about America involving Chinese agents, heroin, student demonstrations and police brutality. At one point a character in the play, an honorable young narcotics agent, flung his badge at his boss and said, "I want to tell the truth at least once in my life, Chief."

He turned toward the audience and continued: "We lie, level by level. I lie to you. You lie to your chief. And he lies to the very top. A pyramid of lies. What holds it up? I don't know. Perhaps it is built on fear that someone will get out of the pyramid and it will collapse. But sometime all this must end. I personally am quitting the game."

His monologue ended to loud applause; the actor turned away from the audience and left the stage.

The cheap lie is an everyday occurrence in Soviet life. When a spy scandal drove Willy Brandt from office in West Germany, the Soviet Union seemed to be embarrassed; its ally, East Germany, had helped bring down the Russians' best friend in the West. So the Soviet papers simply reported that Brandt had resigned. They never mentioned the spy scandal.

In Baku in Soviet Azerbaijan I passed a large building under construction. It was a weekday morning, but there wasn't a worker in sight. "Where are the workmen?" I asked the Intourist guide. "Oh," the guide replied, "this project is entirely automated."

In Armenia a dean at the University of Yerevan boasted confidently that Armenia had more university students per capita than any western country—222 per 10,000 was the statistic. Later I calculated the corresponding figure for the United States; it was more than 350 per 10,000.

For years Intourist ran an advertisement in the American magazine *Foreign Affairs*. "Meet me at ten near the fountain in GUM," it began. "You know, the Macy's of Moscow. Caviar for a song. High fashion fur pieces at reasonable prices. Those famous Orenburg wool shawls. Try to be punctual. We have such a full day ahead. Lunch at the University . . ." An appealing ad. However, GUM almost never sells caviar, and on the rare occasions when it does the prices are steep. "High fashion" furs do not exist in the Soviet Union. Those wool shawls haven't been seen in Moscow's scruffy department store for years. Foreign tourists are not permitted to "lunch at the University."

After three years in the Soviet Union, my list of personally experienced lies could easily fill the rest of this chapter. Longer still would be a list of the daily lies in the newspapers and on television—the eggs described as chickens that Soviet citizens now take for granted, and sometimes also take for chickens. A journalist stationed in London or Washington for three years would also accumulate a long list of personally experienced lies, but the Soviet lie seems to me different because it is unassailable. No one blows a whistle. There is no whistle to blow. When lies are accepted as readily as the truth—and that is just what happens in the Soviet Union—

then the distinction between them inevitably begins to disappear.

Joseph Brodsky, an exile who lives in America and probably the most talented poet now writing in Russian, considered this phenomenon in an article on the 20th anniversary of Stalin's death. Soviet life under Stalin and afterward, Brodsky wrote, has led to a kind of doublethink:

> By doublethink I do not mean simply "I-say-one-thing-I-do-another" and vice versa. Nor do I mean what Orwell described in 1984. I mean the rejection of a moral hierarchy, not for the sake of another hierarchy but for the sake of nothing. I mean that state of mind characterized by the formula "it's-bad-but-in-general-it's-good" (and, more rarely, vice versa). I mean the loss of not only an absolute but even a relative moral criterion. I mean not the mutual destruction of the two basic human categories—good and evil—as a result of the struggle between them, but their mutual decomposition as a result of coexistence. Putting it more precisely, I mean their convergence. . . .

Like Solzhenitsyn's, Brodsky's words sound harsh, particularly in a western world lately more conscious of its own mendacity. But it is impossible to deny their essential accuracy. Let me try to illustrate with an example. The editor of a Soviet journal in Moscow explained to my colleague Peter Osnos why Soviet newspapers never told the whole story of the Watergate affair: "To tell the whole story would have required that the seamy side of Nixon be exposed. For us to say that he was bad would put a shadow on all the agreements and achievements of Soviet-US relations in the past few years. We are not prepared to do that."

Was Nixon bad or wasn't he? Is there a shadow over the agreements he reached with Mr. Brezhnev or not? In the Soviet context these are irrelevant questions. The editor seemed to be saying that a good agreement made with a bad man will look worse if that man's badness is revealed. Only someone who has lost sight of what is truly good or bad could make such a remark.

The lie begins with history, particularly the history of the Soviet Union since 1917.

"We have constructed three great myths," according to a sagacious old man I once met in Moscow. "They are the basis of our new society: the myth of Lenin, the myth of the October Revolution and the myth of the Great Patriotic War [World War II]." It was a wise remark; each of the myths bears examining.

On January 30, 1924, nine days after Lenin succumbed to the series of strokes that had begun to disable him in May 1922, *Pravda* published this appeal from his wife, Nadezhda Krupskaya:

> I have a great request to you: do not allow your mourning for Ilyich [Lenin] to take the form of external reverence for his person. Do not raise memorials to him, name palaces after him, hold solemn festivals to commemorate his life, etc. To all this he attached so little importance in his life; all this was so burdensome to him . . .

A widow's desires could not have been more flagrantly ignored. All that Krupskaya pleaded against happened, plus a lot more in the same vein, including things she could never have dreamed of, like the mummification of Lenin in the mausoleum in Red Square.

Lenin's successors understood his popularity and the service he could perform for them even in death. Construction of the mausoleum and subsequent speedy deification of Lenin gave the young Bolshevik movement a martyred prince and a holy monument. Stalin was especially astute about Lenin's symbolic significance. Once he was in complete control, as I mentioned earlier, Stalin ordered that official Party history be rewritten to put him at Lenin's side in early struggles when in fact they barely knew each other. The Lenin deity was eclipsed only by the cult of Stalin's own personality; as that became wilder and wilder, Stalin began to insist on his own ascendancy over the founder.

After Stalin's death his successors hastily revived Lenin. In the years since, Lenin's figure has become the symbol of the regime. A head of Lenin perhaps 50 feet high is the backdrop to the podium at the Palace of Congresses in Moscow, where important Party meetings are held. The Party does not have just a foreign policy, but a *Leninist* foreign policy. A bust of

Lenin overlooks every wedding palace in the country, so the founder is a silent guest at every marriage.

There is a Lenin Museum in virtually every city in the country, and the places where he actually lived and worked are maintained as shrines. At Leninski Gorki, for example, a small village outside Moscow, the house in which he died is now a tourist attraction. Lenin spent his last months in this splendid house, once the property of a wealthy member of the exploiting classes. Its elegance belies the image of Lenin—cultivated elsewhere in the official hagiography—as a humble, simple man, but no one seems to mind. Tour guides lead citizens around the house, their shoes wrapped in canvas slippers to keep down the dust and protect the floors. The rehearsed spiel is melodramatic, ending in the room where Lenin died: "Here, at 6:50 in the evening of January 21, 1924, the life of Vladimir Ilyich Lenin, friend of the people, great leader, founder of the Soviet State, ended."

After taking this tour my wife, Hannah, and I sat down in the park outside to eat our picnic lunch. We sat on a bench facing a huge and appalling statue of the dead Lenin being borne on the shoulders of half a dozen young men. All the figures were dressed in togas, as though this were a scene from antiquity. While we ate we watched a group of about 30 Young Pioneers walk in formation toward the statue. They planned to put flowers beside it. We noticed two girls of about fourteen talking to each other and looking over at us. Finally they walked up to us and said this was an inappropriate place for a picnic, it was a sacred memorial. They had obviously decided to make this announcement to us entirely on their own. Bluffing, Hannah said we didn't understand Russian, and the girls grinned in embarrassment and shuffled off. We, too, decided it was time to move on.

That statue's image of Lenin as a dead Roman emperor suggests the dimensions of the Lenin myth. In fact it has almost no boundaries. The Lenin that children now read about was the wisest, kindest, strongest and most competent of men. The myth is powerful, and Russians seem to take it literally.

The truth about Lenin—like the truth about every leader who captures first the admiration and then the adulation of his people—is much more complicated than posthumous myth would allow. His life, or at least the version of it recorded in brilliant western books such as Bertram Wolfe's and Adam Ulam's,* was an engaging combination of brilliance, single-mindedness and fluke. His real gift was that of a brilliant political opportunist and tactician. He was inconsistent and sometimes self-contradictory, and he made numerous mistakes. For instance, in February 1917, when the first revolution of that year overthrew the czar, Lenin wrote from his exile in Zurich that these events were obviously the work of the British and French embassies in Petersburg. These countries, with some elements of the Russian army and bourgeoisie, wanted to prevent the czar from making a separate peace with Germany, Lenin reasoned. He did not believe that the ordinary people—in whose name he would claim to lead the country just eight months later—were capable of rising up to overthrow the House of Romanov.

In power Lenin was suspicious, sometimes vain, often confused about how to run the Russia his revolution had bequeathed him. With enormous, perhaps crucial, assistance from Trotski, he led the Bolsheviks to victory in the civil war, which lasted until 1922, but he had no real plan for transforming backward Russia into a socialist state.

Precisely none of this emerges from today's official portrait of Lenin. The myth is all-enveloping. It has made of Lenin a superman who not only understood every aspect of life, politics, revolution and Marxism in his own time, but foresaw the future as well. Today's policies are correct, the regime declares, because they are *Lenin's* policies.

The myth of the October Revolution is intertwined with the myth of Lenin. October's was the second revolution of 1917, in which the Bolsheviks forcibly displaced the provisional government then led by Alexander Kerenski, seizing power in their own name and installing Lenin as the country's leader. The Bolsheviks' success followed a wild spring and summer in which Lenin led his party to the brink of utter disaster (in July), then haltingly back to the verge of success. Unpredictable twists of fate repeatedly played into the Bolsheviks' hands, and in October Kerenski's foolish, helpless regime collapsed. By then the Bolsheviks were a real

---

* *Three Who Made a Revolution* by Bertram Wolfe (New York, 1964), and *The Bolsheviks* by Adam Ulam (New York, 1968).

political force, in that they had won over numerous army units and the Soviets of workers and peasants in Petersburg, Moscow and other principal cities. But they still had no mass following; the public was essentially indifferent to their seizure of power. The great majority of Russians, those living in the countryside, had demonstrated no sympathy for the Bolsheviks. Their ascendance was so tentative, so improbable, that even some Bolshevik leaders doubted it would last.

Today's official version of the October Revolution is altogether different, and much simpler. It is essentially the same in the heaviest historical tomes and in schoolbooks for children. The breathless account of the period between February and October in the textbook used by Soviet students in the ninth class (seventeen-year-olds) describes an inexorable growth in Bolshevik strength and popularity under Lenin's brilliant leadership. The final seizure of power appears as the culmination of a great wave of popular sentiment. The chaos of the time, Lenin's almost disastrous attempt to promote a premature armed uprising in July, Trotski's crucial role and the fragility of the first days of Bolshevik rule have all disappeared.

The myth of the Revolution is an important element in the Soviet regime's claim to legitimacy. The myth says Lenin was swept into power by the enthusiasm of the populace, and that Lenin's victory brought the workers and peasants to power. In fact Lenin's Bolshevik Party was a tightly disciplined, elitist band of revolutionaries, almost none of whose early leaders were workers or peasants.

The Bolsheviks conspired to seize power, then imposed a dictatorship on the country—a relatively relaxed dictatorship by the standards Stalin would later establish, but still a dictatorship. Like Stalin and Soviet leaders in modern times, the first revolutionaries *said* they were ruling in the name of the workers and peasants, but in fact neither group has ever had direct influence over the Soviet authorities.

This is no place for an analysis of the true nature of Lenin's Revolution, and my abbreviated account hardly does it justice. None of what really happened is surprising. Revolutions have to be conspiratorial. Revolutionary leaders are inevitably confused and uncertain, and most of them are much less successful than Lenin was. The true story of Lenin and the Revolution would be, by our standards, a triumphant account of ingenuity and daring. The fact that he had to use harsh, sometimes cruel methods might be explained by the exigencies of the chaotic revolutionary situation. But a true account would be subtle; it would paint the revolutionary actors in shades of gray, and leave many questions about what happened and what might have happened. That sort of portrait would not interest the leaders of this Soviet regime, so they have invented another one.

The myth of the Great Patriotic War—World War II—struck me as the most interesting of all. A few old people can remember Lenin and the Revolution, but the war is still a vivid memory to anyone born before about 1938—for example, this artist in Moscow:

"I was evacuated to Tataria during the war, but in 1944 the shoe factory in Moscow where my mother worked called her back. This was the only way you could get back to Moscow in those days, with an invitation from a factory. We had to ride two days on a horse-drawn sled to get to the nearest railroad station. During the trip all our belongings were stolen—that was common in those days. But we got to the station. Then we had to wait for a place in a freight car to take us west, toward Moscow.

"I was seven at the time. My mother tried to keep me next to her, but I always wanted to explore around. In the station I stuck my head behind a door that was propped open. There, in the corner, was a tiny baby with a terrified look on its face, all wrapped up in a blanket. It must have been abandoned—just sitting there, looking terrified and alone. I can't remember now whether I told Mama about it or not, but I can still see that baby. . . ."

He can still see that baby, just as millions of Russians can still see that appalling war. Thirty years after its conclusion the war remains a haunting presence in Soviet life—like a retarded child or a dying parent in the back room, a permanent piece of the emotional furniture.

The regime selectively encourages the survival of war memories. The war must still be the single most popular subject for official propaganda, movies and television programs. The younger generation, which missed the war itself, is bombarded with recollections of the wonderful days when the Soviet people suffered and survived together.

My first reaction to this was that it resembled the nostalgia so popular in the West in recent years. There is an element of that, but Russia's war memory goes much further. It is a prolongation of pain—partly inevitable, partly deliberate and even orchestrated—by a nation that has discovered the joys of masochism, or at least the difficulty of separating pain from pleasure. Russia is cursed with a collective memory of a war in which 20 million died and babies were abandoned in the recesses of railroad stations—and which was an exciting, exhilarating experience, especially toward the end, for those who survived.

Exhilarating but also horrible, horrible in a way few other people can understand, horrible the way war can be only when it is fought at home, in backyards and native villages and big cities. "We know what war is like," Russians tell a foreigner in their midst time and again, and there is no denying it. They do know, and most of us do not.

The participants in World War II all remember their own wars. British schoolchildren now learn about Dunkirk, the Battle of Britain, North Africa and Normandy. American recollections are similarly ethnocentric: Pearl Harbor, the Pacific campaign, D-Day and the Bulge. This is understandable, but it is also slightly perverse. The Russians deserve more credit in everyone's recollections, for reasons well stated by the current edition of the *Great Soviet Encyclopedia:*

> The Soviet Union played the decisive role in the victory over Fascist Germany. The basic military forces of the Fascist coalition were destroyed on the Soviet-German front—in all, 607 divisions. Anglo-American forces destroyed or took prisoner 176 divisions. On the Eastern [Soviet] front the German forces lost about 10 million men (approximately 77 percent of total German losses in World War II), about 62,000 airplanes (62 percent of all German losses in the war), about 56,000 tanks and assault weapons (about 75 percent) and approximately 180,000 guns and mortars (about 74 percent)....

The figures are essentially accurate. Perhaps as a result, the Russian recollection of the war is at least as ethnocentric as anyone else's. The Russians tend to regard World War II as their own, going so far as to rename it. Today's Soviet schoolchildren are barely told that any other countries fought against Hitler, let alone that assistance from other countries, particularly America, made victory possible. (Stalin acknowledged this last fact openly during the war.)

Accounts of the war written at various times since 1940 contradict one another, though a conceivably "final" account has now been agreed on. It is a tale of glory virtually without reservation. Embarrassments have been deleted.

For example, it is embarrassing to acknowledge that Stalin made an arrangement with Hitler in 1939 which allowed the Soviet Union to seize large sections of pre-war Poland and the Baltic states. These were the provisions of the secret protocol to the Nazi-Soviet pact, but they contradict the image of Soviet power that the regime tries to cultivate. So the protocol disappeared from Soviet history—it has never been mentioned.

At the same time Stalin justified the annexation of Polish lands as Poland's just deserts. The 1940 edition of the *Great Soviet Encyclopedia* explained what happened:

> The internal rottenness and weakness of Poland, the aggressive policies of its ruling classes, its political dependence on the imperialists of England and France, which drew it into war with Germany—all these caused Poland's disintegration at the very first blow of Germany's forces in [September 1939].

> As a result of the disintegration of the Polish state, *oblasts* of the western Ukraine and western Belorussia [i.e., Polish lands] were reunited with the brotherly Ukrainian and Belorussian people [i.e., the Soviet Union], and the remaining part of the former Poland passed into the sphere of the state interests of Germany.

The 1971 edition of the same encyclopedia tells a different story. According to the new version, Poland was overwhelmed by massive German forces. "The courageous defense by the Polish army [of many Polish cities and towns] . . . wrote brilliant pages in the history of the Polish-German war, but could not prevent the defeat of Poland."

As for the Soviet absorption of Polish territory, it is now explained as the result of "an order by the Soviet Government" to the Red Army to undertake a "liberation campaign" in these areas, to help their populations realize their desire for "reunification" with the Soviet Union.

The entire Nazi-Soviet pact is ignored in history books for schoolchildren, though it is mentioned in more specialized literature. There it is explained as the inevitable consequence of the western powers' failure to build a united front against Hitler.

Many other embarrassments have disappeared from Soviet historiograhpy. Soviet historians do not discuss the consequences of Stalin's purge of the Red Army in 1937–8, which decimated the officer corps and contributed to Germany's stunning early victories in the war. Stalin's failure to prepare for the German attack in 1941 is now hinted at but not fully described. His personal collapse after the German invasion is ignored. Soviet histories berate Britain and America for postponing the opening of a second front in Europe, but there is no hint that extensive Soviet trade with Nazi Germany helped Hitler wage war against Britain during 1940–1. (The word "Nazism" does not appear in Soviet accounts, apparently to avoid legitimizing Hitler's description of his system as "national socialism," a blasphemous misuse of socialism's good name.)

The official war was all heroism and valor. Children learn about an entire galaxy of war heroes, many of them children, who gave their lives to save the Motherland. A classic example is the Panfilov Regiment, which, according to legend, fought to the last man in defense of Moscow.

In 1966 a writer named E. V. Kardin published an article called "Legends and Facts" in a literary magazine. He noted that some members of the Panfilov Regiment survived the entire war. Kardin could not get any of his work published for several years after the appearance of that bit of irreverence.

The official version of the war cannot correspond closely with reality, because it is meant to legitimize Soviet power. The Russians almost lost the war in its first months, when Nazi forces raced deep into their homeland, but there is no hint of that today. For four years the Red Army and Soviet nation lived on foreign aid, but that fact, too, is gone from the official histories. Instead there is this sort of paragraph, taken from the *History of the Communist Party*, 1973 edition: "The Soviet Union's victory over the aggressors was perfectly logical. The sources of the strength and might of the Soviet people and their armed forces lay in the very nature of the country's socialist social and political system, in its great advantages over the outdated and decayed capitalist system. . . ."

The Party waged the war, assured the victory, proved its strength and wisdom. Stalin, who truly was a brilliant war leader after his initial collapse, though he continued to make expensive errors throughout the war, now gets almost no credit for the war effort. The Party—which he nearly destroyed three years before the war began—gets the credit.

Sudden changes in the Party line on the war have bewildered some propagandists, as Khrushchev's recollection of war memoirs, quoted above, suggests. Marshal Zhukov's memoirs, which Khrushchev mentioned, have appeared in different versions with varying degrees of praise for Stalin and other wartime leaders, depending on the political climate when each was published.

Missing from the official version of the war is any sense of the way it debased the Russians themselves. An engineer in Moscow talked about that:

"When the war began, my father was in exile in Kazakhstan. [He was an old Bolshevik purged by Stalin.] We had to go and join him in August 1941. . . . We had no means of support. My father had no right to work. My mother got a job in a kindergarten—an orphanage, really. We never had enough to eat. The daily ration was 300 grams [10.5 ounces] of bread and a glass of sour skimmed milk. My two sisters and I lived on that for three years—with some lucky intervals. There were potatoes and melons in the fall, for instance. Not only food was short. We had no water, no coal, no wood. . . .

"In 1941 I was eight. The Chichentsi were exiled in that part of Kazakhstan. [The Chichentsi were a small ethnic group from the Caucasus, one of the minorities which Stalin forcibly transported out of European Russia.] I used to see their dead bodies in the streets of the town, just lying there. Once a little Chichen boy was brought to my mother's kindergarten. His stomach was bloated from hunger. As soon as he recovered a little bit, he made an attempt to escape. He tried several times, but always was caught. Then finally he got away. But it was 15 miles to the next dwelling in any direction, and he didn't make it. The next morning they found only his bones on the road. He had been eaten by wolves.

"Once I saw a hungry Chichentsi try to take a watermelon out of someone's garden. He was shot dead right in front of me. . . ."

In the 1950s and 1960s, when the war was a fresher memory, a few writers did describe this side of the war years in published works. One can find accounts of the looting of dead Germans, the collaboration of some Soviet citizens with occupying Nazis, the panic in the first days of the war and a variety of official stupidities and cruelties. But such material is no longer published, and such memories have been eased out of the official version of the Great Patriotic War.

There is no place in the official history of the war for a description of the "rear security units" established in 1941 by the political police, the NKVD. Armed with machine guns, they took up positions behind Soviet troops that were fighting the Germans. These were the troops who had orders to kill any Red Army soldier who tried to flee from battle.

The authorities now exploit the war for several contemporary purposes. For example, it provides a good excuse for those occasions when comparisons must be made with the West. On my first trip through Siberia I met a young architect in the city of Irkutsk. I was new in the Soviet Union then, and surprised by the low quality of construction work. I asked this young man, an official of the city government, why the new apartment houses looked so shoddy. "Well," he answered, "perhaps if we hadn't lost 20 million people in the war, we could pay more attention to things like quality."

I heard similar explanations for all sorts of deficiencies in Soviet life. You may be richer, countless Russians told me, but our country was destroyed in the war, we lost 20 million people.

It's true. The Russians rebuilt Leningrad, Kiev, Stalingrad, Minsk and dozens of other partially or totally destroyed cities, all without benefit of the Marshall Plan. The country's population still shows signs of the grotesque disfiguration inflicted by the war. Women outnumber men by 20 million in the total population of 250 million. It is often said, probably correctly, that every family in the country lost someone in the war.

But this does not excuse every Russian failing. East Germany was more thoroughly devastated by the war than was the Soviet Union. The remnants of its former wealth that did survive were taken away by the Russians as reparations. But today East Germany has a higher standard of living than the Soviet Union. Its construction work is not shoddy.

The war serves a more important purpose as a justification for the Soviet Union's huge military expenditures—which are necessary, according to the official pronouncements, to prevent another conflagration. The horrors of the Great Patriotic War are vividly re-created for new generations of Soviet citizens. This, for example, is an excerpt from a fourth-grade reading book:

> Here's a letter from a little girl: "The Germans were cooking their dinner in Petya's log house [in occupied Russia during the early years of the war]. Petya ate a slice of their meat and one potato. For that, the Germans burned Petya to ashes. Zina Petushkova was walking along the street and saw that the Germans had an open box of candy. She was five years old and she didn't even know what Fascists were. She ate one piece of the candy. For that the Germans killed her."

The ten-year-olds who read that may well have nightmares afterward; perhaps that's the idea. Stories like these instill the official image of war: a cruel invading army, foot soldiers, tanks, the last war all over again. The scenarios of nuclear warfare familiar in the West—surgical strikes, massive retaliations, second strikes and so on—are unknown to most Russians. Even relatively sophisticated journalists of my acquaintance who should have known about such things understood them only vaguely. Instead the authorities encourage an outdated image of war because it supports their "Fortress Russia" posture. It justifies defense spending, tightly sealed borders, the militarization of the population through military training in school and the draft, and constant "vigilance" against external evil.

I read a good deal about Soviet history and talked to many Russians about the way it is officially presented. I concluded that the Soviet authorities have managed to destroy the history of their own country. Because history has been rewritten so often, people cannot keep up with the latest version. So instead of official history there is just a muddle of historical explanations which don't hold together. The numerous and often contradictory changes in the official version have numbed the national mind.

The old man who suggested the idea of the three great myths proposed tracing the history of the Bolshevik Revolution as reported on its anniversary each year in *Pravda* and other official organs. "First it was Lenin and Trotski" he noted, "then just Lenin, then Lenin and Stalin, then mostly Stalin, then just Lenin again"—depending on when one read about it.

Many other subjects have undergone blatant revision. Tour guides are a good source of these revisions. In Odessa my Intourist guide talked at length about the German Fascist occupiers of that seaport during the war. She seemed genuinely not to know that Odessa was occupied by Romanians fighting with Hitler, not by Germans. (Romania is now part of the fraternal socialist camp.) In Petrozavodsk on the Finnish border a stocky woman led me around the local museum which supposedly depicted the history of the area of the past 50 years. At the end of the tour I asked why there was no mention of the Soviet Union's war with Finland in 1940, which must have been an important event in the life of Petrozavodsk and the surrounding area. "That material is not on display," she answered, immediately flustered. Will it be? I asked. "Probably," she said, and turned away. In Soviet Estonia the guides report that Estonia *asked* to join the USSR in 1940—when in fact Stalin seized the country as one of the fruits of his secret protocol with Hitler.

The great rewriter of history was Stalin. During his reign massive revisions of the historical record resulted in the wholesale destruction of the careers of numerous important Bolsheviks, as if they had never lived. Stalin muddied the historical waters, and the country has never filtered them clean again. Though Khrushchev denounced his crimes, many of them have survived in official history as praiseworthy acts. For instance, Stalin's forced collectivization of the peasantry in which millions died is still described as an heroic accomplishment. His show trials of the late 1930s have never been flatly disowned, and many of the victims have never been rehabilitated. The most celebrated victim of the trials was Nikolai Bukharin, "the darling of the Party," as Lenin once called him, one of the most interesting of the original Bolsheviks. Stalin had him executed, and he has never been rehabilitated. He has disappeared from most history books. There is no entry for Bukharin in the new edition of the *Great Soviet Encyclopedia*, though he was one of the half-dozen most important men in the Revolution.

Collectively the official myths create what struck me as the fundamental distortion of Soviet propaganda: the idea that the Soviet Union is just a normal young revolutionary country with an unexceptional, though admirable and exciting, history. In fact Soviet history is filled with horrors: Soviet leaders have murdered millions of Soviet citizens and cruelly mistreated tens of millions more. Khrushchev's partial denunciation of Stalin, partially retracted in recent years, has been the country's only attempt to face up to its horrific past, and now even that is a taboo, never discussed.

I asked numerous Soviet officials, mostly journalists, why it was not now possible to begin dealing more honestly with the past. A few, who made no excuse for the disappearance of such important figures as Bukharin and Trotski, said it was time to do so. But most seemed to agree—at least in conversation with me—with one senior editor, a sensible man on most subjects, who offered this proposition:

"We can't reopen those old questions of history now. If we did, the whole country would be consumed in 'discussion groups.' ... Talking about Trotski would just distract attention from the problem at hand."

What was that? I asked.

"Catching up with the West in industrial production."

Was there no room for ambiguity in history? I asked him.

His answer was no. "History is not just for the historians," he said. "It is for the public, too." And the public, he thought, was not interested in ambiguity. "As Napoleon said, men are judged by results," he added, as though that settled the matter. And one more point: you discuss your history freely in America, but that didn't help you stay out of Vietnam, did it?

My Soviet colleague did not mention another point, but he might have: restoring an honest version of the Soviet past now would be extraordinarily difficult, probably impossible. What could the leaders do? Suddenly announce that all previous accounts were wrong, and produce a new one described as correct? And who would believe the new version? Restoring honesty to Soviet historiography now would be rather like announcing that Ptolemy was right after all—the sun does revolve around the Earth.

So in the end a Soviet citizen is left to cope as best he can with a bewildering collection of historical and mock-historical material. My experience suggested that many don't cope very effectively, particularly the younger generation. They seem tempted to ignore history altogether.

I once saw a group of several men and women in their fifties listen with rapt amazement to another member of their generation tell the following story:

So-and-so, a famous writer, was being treated for a heart attack in the Kremlin Hospital outside Moscow. His sixteen-year-old niece came to visit him on a summer afternoon in 1973. Suddenly he broke off their conversation and said, "Look! Look! There goes Molotov down the hall!" It was Vyacheslav Molotov, whose political career lasted from 1906 to 1957, and who was Stalin's principal lieutenant for 30 years.

"Who?" the sixteen-year-old niece replied.

"Molotov," said her uncle, "Stalin's henchman. Haven't you ever heard of him?"

"No," she replied, "should I have?"

At that, the circle of middle-aged people listening to the story gasped in amazement. Was it possible? It was.

Yevgeni Yevtushenko described the disappearance of the past in the open letter he wrote in February 1974, explaining his protest against the exile of Solzhenitsyn. This was a bold act for Yevtushenko, who in recent years has disowned his earlier image as a youthful rebel and cooperated repeatedly with the authorities. Yet he did protest, and then explained himself, in part, with this story:

Last year [i.e., 1973] around a campfire in Siberia, one good young girl, a student about eighteen years old, raised a toast to Stalin. I was shaken. "Why?" I asked.

"Because then all people believed in Stalin, and with this belief they were victorious," she answered.

"And do you know how many people were arrested during the years of Stalin's rule?" I asked.

"Well, say 20 or 30 people," she replied.

Other students were sitting around the fire, and they

were about her age. I started asking them the same question.

"About 200," said one lad.

"Maybe 2000," said another girl.

Only one student out of 15 or 20 said, "It seems to me about 10,000."

When I told them that the figure is reckoned not in thousands but in millions, they did not believe me.

"Did you read my poem *Stalin's Heirs*?"* I asked.

"And did you really write such a poem?" asked the first girl. "Where was it published?"

"In *Pravda*, in 1963," I answered.

"But at that time I was only eight years old," she replied, somewhat at a loss.

This exchange shook Yevtushenko: "I suddenly understood, as never before, that the young generation really does not have sources nowadays for learning the tragic truth about that period, because they cannot read about it either in books or in school texts. . . . The truth is replaced by silence, and silence is a lie."

And yet Turgenev was right. At least some Russians do seem to respect the truth, when they can find it. Yevtushenko quoted an old Russian proverb: "A lie is like a bow. You hide the ends in water, but the middle protrudes. You hide the middle, and the ends stick out."

Wherever I went in the Soviet Union I was cross-examined about American life, world affairs, even hockey and soccer football. People everywhere understood that they did not know the truth, and they often suspected that I did. Sometimes I could not convince them otherwise.

Priests in the Russian Orthodox Church attribute the recent revival of religion to the younger generation's curiosity about where it came from. One priest told me young Russians realized that only the Church provided a link to a true past.

When the first volume of Solzhenitsyn's new work on the origins of the Bolshevik Revolution, *August 1914*, circulated in Moscow in typescript, it caused a stir. The general reaction was negative. Many intellectuals were offended by Solzhenit-

---

* A famous poem critical of Stalinism which appeared at the height of Khrushchev's de-Stalinization campaign.

syn's experiments with the Russian language, and bored by the slow-moving novel. But even the harshest critics could praise Solzhenitsyn for trying to discover the truth about Russian history. Half a dozen reviews of the book by anonymous critics circulated in typescript among Moscow intellectuals. An introduction to these reviews noted that some were critical of the book, but "all [the criticisms] recede into the background ... and are transformed into a sign of general satisfaction: the book answers what is most important. What is most important is the need for a truthful word, a truthful word about history, about man, about the Motherland. ..."

Every so often I met a Russian who wanted to put a little truth on the record. I remember particularly a visit to a Soviet school in a provincial city. We were walking through a courtyard behind the director of the school, a businesslike woman of sturdy build with white hair in a bun. Suddenly a teacher who was tagging along whispered in the ear of one of the visiting Americans: "You know, this school was built on the site of a beautiful old Orthodox church. They tore the church down to make way for the school. A shame."

Rewriting history is an old Russian habit. It pre-dates the Bolsheviks. The earliest Russian history was recorded by priests who often distorted what happened to make their favorites look better, or to improve the image of their Church. In the 16th century Ivan the Terrible personally oversaw the rewriting of the chronicles of his reign. In the 19th century the reactionary Count Benckendorff, chief of Czar Nicholas I's secret police, was quoted as saying: "Russia's past was wonderful, her present magnificent, and as to her future—it is beyond the grasp of the most daring imagination. This is the point of view from which Russian history must be written."

7 · Chicken or Egg?

"In general our people are not very demanding."
—*Nikita Khrushchev*

SEVERAL YEARS AGO a Russian woman who worked as a cook for a western diplomat in Moscow asked her mistress what had really happened to Vladimir Komarov, a Soviet cosmonaut. That very day Komarov had received a hero's burial in the wall of the Kremlin after dying in a space accident—as the diplomat's wife told the Russian woman.

"Oh, it's really true, then?" the cook asked. "We'd heard that he brought his spaceship down in America and defected."

After years of experience Russians realize that part of the official propaganda is untrue, but they are never quite certain which part.

Under the best possible conditions, coping with the information glut of modern times is virtually impossible. In the Soviet Union it *is impossible*. Because of distortions and omissions, because of the absence of independent sources, because of the inability to go and see for oneself, Russians are forced to live in an artificial intellectual environment, a fairyland that does not exist.

As a practical matter, this isn't terribly important for most people. Birth, death and all in between do not depend on honest, informative newspapers or true historical accounts. Russians seem as happy exchanging rumors as facts—perhaps even happier. Like people everywhere, they are more interested in personal gossip than in political news.

No one can spend a prolonged period in Russia without beginning to wonder what this enormous mass of people really thinks. It is an ancient puzzle. The great Russian *narod*—the masses who have followed a succession of princes and tyrants through a painful history with unbelievable stoicism and loyalty—has puzzled both Russians and foreigners for centuries.

I did not solve the puzzle, and can offer here only the results of a long but unscientific inquiry. There are few published opinion polls of Russians' preferences, no elections, no systematic evaluation of popular feelings. Instead of a Gallup Poll, I have the recollections of conversations between Russian cooks and diplomats' wives; instead of systematic sociology, the opinions of Russian writers and intellectuals, fruits of personal information and tidbits from conversations of my own with ordinary* Russians.

The most important fact is that the Soviet regime succeeds. Nearly all Russians accept its leadership and organize their lives around the norms, customs and criteria of success which it sanctions. Russians complain, but seldom challenge the status quo. They accept the government and the Party. Only a tiny fraction of the population ever dreams of living in a different kind of society, under a different kind of regime.

The young compete fiercely for places in universities, for offices in the Young Communist League and for government jobs. Tens of thousands agree to work under difficult conditions on the vast hero projects such as the Siberian railway now under construction. The Army has no shortage of officers, the KGB no deficiency of gumshoes. People do as they are told—not just reluctantly, but often enthusiastically.

Russians generally think the way they are told to think. The propaganda works. Most people allow it to fix the broad outlines of their view of the world.

The proof of this is best seen in extreme examples. I heard of one from a Russian woman who married an American and moved to New York (a difficult feat in itself). After several years in the United States she returned for a visit to the industrial city in eastern Russia where she grew up. Her parents

---

* By ordinary, I mean those who are not intellectuals.

asked how she liked life in New York. It was fun, she said, very exciting. What about the criminals roaming the streets? her parents asked. The daughter replied that she had never seen a criminal on the streets. And the rioting Negroes? Never seen rioting Negroes either, she replied. Come now, her father said, don't fib to us, we've seen it on television. But, Daddy, she protested, you know that's all propaganda on television. Ah, he said, but where there's smoke, there's fire.

Many others share his suspicions. Even when they realize that the propaganda isn't entirely true (and they often do), most Russians cannot believe that it is entirely false or entirely misleading. As a matter of fact, it rarely is entirely false. There are criminals on the streets of New York; blacks sometimes do riot. Soviet propaganda about foreign countries exaggerates or simply ignores the truth, but seldom invents fantasies out of whole cloth.

At home the relationship between smoke and fire is somewhat more tentative. The politicians declare that the USSR is a workers' state, a rich and powerful state, a state dedicated to every man's welfare. All that rings a little false to ordinary Russians, I sensed, but politicians' rhetoric in any country tends to exaggerate. Perhaps life isn't as good as it sounds in the holiday speeches; still, it is vastly better than a generation or two ago. We are trying hard. We are building communism. *Someday* we will learn to be less selfish, to work harder, to care more about our fellow men—all that will come when we achieve real communism. Meanwhile we're doing fine, better all the time. New apartments are going up like mushrooms after a rain. Our athletes won the Olympics. Our cosmonauts went into space with the Americans.

The common man's patriotism is crucially important here. A patriot in Armenia, Lithuania or the Ukraine may not think of the Soviet national hockey team as his team, but a Russian certainly does. A Russian patriot in these times is a Soviet patriot. He is proud of "Our Soviet hockey team," "Our Soviet cosmonauts," "Our Soviet tanks."

A Polish intellectual who has traveled widely in Russia told me a story about an old man in a Siberian town who took his grandson to the railroad station to look at the trains. A new diesel locomotive, the first ever seen in those parts,* pulled

---

* Steam engines still run on a large section of the Trans-Siberian Railroad.

into the station. It caused a sensation. "Grandpa! Grandpa!" the little boy shouted. "What kind of locomotive is that?"

The old man didn't know, and there was a moment of silence. Finally he volunteered an answer: "Son, that's Our Soviet locomotive!"

Patriotic feelings are not all alike, I realized while living in Russia. Hungarians, for instance, are fierce patriots, but in a limited sense: they are proud of their poetry, their survival as a tiny land in the shadows of giants, their special appreciation for life. Russians, however, are patriotic on what might be called an American scale. They see no reason not to be proud of *everything* about their country. They compare it favorably with every other country on virtually every basis. This is a function of size, and of isolation from the outside—factors at work in America, too. Russians have a long history of suffering together through difficult times, which has produced a sense of uniqueness in the population. We Russians have been through a lot together, they say repeatedly in different ways; nobody else knows what we've seen and survived.

The regime's propagandists exploit this patriotism avidly. Not surprisingly, their propaganda often smacks of chauvinism. During my first weeks in the Soviet Union, in August 1971, one of America's Apollo flights went to the moon, an event the Soviet papers noted each day in tiny stories barely 100 words long. Then the Russians themselves sent up an unmanned space vehicle during the American moon mission, and the front pages of every Soviet paper bloomed with pictures and long articles on the event.

Patriotic boasting can exceed the bounds of accuracy. Tass once reported that Soviet geneticists had—for the first time in the history of biology—synthesized an animal cell. Curious American correspondents in Moscow found a responsible biologist who said that, as a matter of fact, scientists in the West had done this some years before.

This last case demonstrates an important reason for the essential success of official propaganda. When Tass reports that Soviet biologists have done something for the first time in the world, who is to know otherwise? A Russian is trapped; he has limited sources of information and no means of checking them. Someone who has seen on television films of poverty in Liverpool or rioting in Detroit, but who cannot himself dream of visiting Liverpool or Detroit, is the victim of a vivid but incomplete image that is not easily dislodged. Even people who suspect the accuracy of what they see and read are influenced by it, particularly in the absence of any competing information. "I know a guy," one young social scientist told me, "who says, 'Everything you read in the papers is crap.' Then he drinks a little too much vodka and gets into an argument, and he starts defending his position by quoting *Pravda* and *Izvestia*. You can't help it. There's nothing else."

Isolation also reinforces a natural Russian inclination to believe that other countries are really quite like their own. I discovered this habit of mind in two conversations with Russians on the unlikely subject of *valuta*, or hard currency. One was a young engineer who, with his wife, dreamed of taking a holiday in Yugoslavia. His wife had already been abroad, on a trade-union cruise around the Mediterranean. It was fun, but there wasn't much time in port, and they gave each person very little *valuta* to buy things—only about five dollars.* After telling me all this, the engineer asked: "How much hard currency do they give you when you go abroad from America?"

On the Trans-Siberian Railroad a mother and her two young children spent 24 hours sharing our compartment. She was intrigued by this opportunity to talk to foreigners. She had heard that in Moscow we could shop in hard-currency stores which sold many products not generally available. Was that true?

Yes, I said. I asked if she thought it was fair that such stores should exist for foreigners.

"Sure, why not? I imagine that if I went to New York, there would be special stores there that would accept my rubles."

The official propaganda is deeply instilled. Russians born after 1920 have been hearing propaganda all their lives. It is part of their intellectual baggage now.

In Leningrad I met a precocious six-year-old named Misha, a kindergarten student. As soon as he heard I was an American, Misha asked me for a picture of Angela Davis. This was several months before Miss Davis' trial. "I'd like to get to know her," Misha said. "I've written her three letters."

---

* The Soviet ruble, a "soft" currency, has no legal value outside the country, though a ruble can be sold on western black markets for about 25 cents. At the official exchange rate, western tourists in Moscow buy a ruble for about $1.40.

What about?

"Two on politics," he answered, fondling a plastic revolver, "and one to wish her a Happy New Year."

Miss Davis was the subject of intense publicity in the Soviet Union, though it ended soon after she was acquitted. Misha's grandmother said he had learned about her from television.

Anton also was six when he drew a picture for his grandmother of life in a fairy kingdom. He has a real gift for drawing, and it was a marvelous picture of a parade going past a grand castle. The king watched the parade from the castle's battlements. Below, his citizens marched past carrying giant portraits of the king—just as the paraders do on November 7 and May 1 in Red Square.

I left Russia convinced that, even with the advantages the propagandists enjoy—the isolation of the population, the opportunity to introduce propaganda at infancy—they succeed because Russians are the kind of people they are. I recognize the risk in advancing this proposition, but there really *is* a Russian character. It doesn't describe everyone, naturally, but it does describe basic, shared characteristics of the Russian personality which give Russian society its special quality.

Russian history, especially the sustained insecurity of Russian life over many centuries, has done much to shape the national character. The most plausible theory for the original creation of a Russian state in the ninth century is that tribes occupying Russian lands banded together in search of mutual protection. The early centuries of Russian history were dominated by civil wars and strife, and then the Mongol invasion. Strong, autocratic government became the Russian norm, perhaps in response to insecurity; later it became a habit, a habit which survived the Renaissance and liberal enlightenment because those great upheavals hardly touched Russia.

"The Russian peasant's idea of government," Sir Bernard Pares wrote at the beginning of this century, "was always that it was there because man is sinful. He did not wish himself to have the burden of the responsibility of governing, but he strongly desired that order should be maintained."

Erik H. Erikson, the psychologist, has written in his standard work, *Childhood and Society*: "Early in Russian history, the stage was set for the interplay of the people who needed guidance and protection against enemies; the oligarchic protectors who became petty tyrants; and the central super-tyrant who was a captive of the oligarchy and a secret re-deemer." This was the pattern of Russian society for cen-turies. The organization of contemporary Soviet society echoes it still.

The Russian Orthodox Church, too, has helped shape the Russian character. The ethical and philosophical tenets of the Church are the Russians' answer to our Judeo-Christian tradi-tion. Lenin's communism has not yet supplanted them. The morality of the Ten Commandments provides Russians with a basic standard against which behavior can be measured.

Philosophically, though, the evolution of Christianity in East and West has been very different. In the West, Christian-ity evolved in a way that encouraged—or at least permit-ted—the growth of liberal optimism about man's ability to build a heaven on earth in this life, without waiting for the next.

Russian Orthodoxy is Eastern Christianity, which stopped evolving centuries ago. It emphasizes the next life, not this one. The difference can be seen in the Orthodox attitude toward Christmas and Easter. Christmas—a celebration of Christ's birth as a human being—is the major holiday in western churches, but the Russian Orthodox Church mini-mizes it. The biggest Orthodox celebration is at Easter, which marks Christ's transfiguration. Christ's godliness is more im-portant to the Orthodox than His life among men.

This has left a mark on the Russian's sense of his own worldly status. Russians don't expect to make constant progress toward heaven on earth; nor do they expect to be judged as men in terms of their worldly accomplishments. Wealth and fame mean less to a Russian than to us. Their standards of accomplishment are more modest, and in a way more Christian. Is he a good man or bad? Kind or cruel? That often means more than the cut of his suit or the influ-ence of his friends. A Russian expects less from life than we do, so he is satisfied with less.*

---

* Soviet communism is out of step with the Orthodox tradition. The Bolsheviks brought Russia optimism about man's ability to improve radically his lot on earth—this is now official doctrine. Yet the old habits of mind are still prevalent in the population. Indeed, the regime seems to count on the old expectations, which allow it to proceed very slowly toward its version of heaven on earth.

The Orthodox Church also symbolizes a trait of Russian character described 70 years ago by Sir Bernard Pares:

> No matter in what field, the Russian is essentially a believer; when he adopts a foreign philosophy [which Christianity originally was] or a foreign political formula he applies to it his own native sense of reverence, and he is able to draw from it something spiritual and inspiring. This tendency may be half unconscious; but the real corporate force which underlies it can claim, as no isolated individual can, the right to live and to succeed; and history has given abundant proofs that it is not in vain that Russia has lived and still lives by that most primitive and fundamental instinct which we call faith.

The way Russians have lived—struggling against a hostile climate to work food out of a vast plain—has left a deep imprint on the national character. It is a special kind of life, idle through long winters, intensely active in brief summers, always problematical. Until 1861 the Russian peasant was a slave, a serf without rights. His life has traditionally been a matter of scraping by, a condition which does not instill great energy or high ideals. Maxim Gorki has written about the different experiences of western Europeans and Russians:

> In the West the individual is used to seeing around him . . . the monumental outcome of his ancestors' labor. From the canals of Holland to the tunnels of the Italian Riviera and the vineyards of Vesuvius, from the great works of England to the mighty Silesian factories, the entire soil of Europe is covered with grandiose manifestations of human will—the will which has set itself the proud aim of conquering the forces of Nature and harnessing them to human reason. In the West, a person imbibes this impression with his childhood and this develops in him a consciousness of human worth, of respect for human labor, and an awareness of his own significance. . . . Such thoughts and such feelings and values can never arise in the soul of the Russian peasant. . . . Around him not a tangible trace of labor and artistry [is] to be found [as in] the West.*

---

* Quoted in *Soviet and American Society, A Comparison* by Paul Hollander.

It would be difficult to overstate the importance of the peasant tradition. The vast majority of Soviet citizens are one or two generations removed from village life. Though there were sophisticated urban populations in pre-revolutionary Russia, the Bolsheviks and Stalin wiped them out. Many left right after the Revolution; most of those who stayed were killed in the purges or in the war. Even the more enterprising and successful peasants, the *kulaks*, were wiped out during Stalin's collectivization of agriculture. Soviet society was inherited by a crude, uneducated lower class of peasants and first-generation urban workers who had no models of refined behavior.

Let me put the same point in the words of Nikita Khrushchev:

I remember in 1920, when our Ninth Kuban Army defeated Denikin [in the Civil War]. . . . In May of that year, my friend Pyotr Kabinet and I were sent to Krasnodar to attend a course run by the political department of our [Red] army. We were billeted in a house that had been a school for the daughters of the nobility. We were soldiers full of fighting spirit, but we weren't gentlemen in the old-fashioned sense.

We hadn't been in the dormitory two days before it became impossible even to enter the bathroom. Why? Because the people in our group didn't know how to use it properly. Instead of sitting on the toilet seat so that people could use it after them, they perched like eagles on top of the toilet and mucked the place up terribly. And after we'd put the bathroom out of commission, we set to work on the park nearby. After a week or so, the park was so disgusting it was impossible for anyone to walk there.

At the mine where I worked after the Civil War, there was a latrine, but the miners misused it so badly that you had to enter the latrine on stilts if you didn't want to track filth home to your own apartment at the end of the workday. I remember I was once sent somewhere to install some mining equipment and found the miners living in a barracks with double-deck bunks. It wasn't unusual for the men in the upper bunks simply to urinate over the side.

Some people might ask, "Why is Khrushchev telling

us about such unpleasant incidents? Those things happened long ago, and they resulted from the low cultural level of the people." Well, my answer is that such conditions persisted for a long time. It took decades for the people to advance from their primitive habits.

Even now the average Russian knows little of the genteel social customs. Evidence of this is available in every café and restaurant in the Soviet Union, where one can see the populace wolf down its soup and *kutlet* with an extravagant disregard for the niceties of bourgeois table manners.

The way Russians raise their children is one manifestation of their character; it is also a means of transmitting national traits from one generation to the next.

Russian parents deprive their children of freedom from infancy onward. They discourage individual initiative throughout childhood. Children grow up dependent on their parents, and eventually, dependent in general.

A hyperprotective parental attitude was probably logical in old Russia. Nature made life a rigorous contest; the climate insured that many would not survive. Children had to be watched and tended carefully so they would live through childhood. Obedience insures order and loyalty to one's elders, something the elders would need to survive old age if they reached it.

These considerations have lost their validity, but the customs of child-raising that they encouraged live on and help make Russians the kind of people they are.

Erik Erikson has suggested that the swaddling of infants—a practice still prevalent in Russia—has specific psychological repercussions. The child is swaddled to "protect him against himself," but the confinement of the swaddling clothes produces a violent urge in the infant to move his limbs and head. This creates an additional need for swaddling—"he must remain emotionally swaddled in order not to fall victim to wild emotion." This sequence contributes to "a basic, preverbal indoctrination" which teaches the child that he must be rigidly restrained for his own good.

It is very tempting to conclude that dependent, swaddled children naturally grow up to be the pliant subjects of an authoritarian state. Psychologists react nervously to such sweeping generalizations, though many would endorse them. There must be some connection between a Russian childhood and the passivity of the great mass of Russian adults.

Russian submissiveness to arbitrary authority frustrates an American inclined to be optimistic about humanity. We have convinced ourselves that it is in man's nature to strive for the kind of freedom we cherish, to honor the fruits of pure reason and the benefits of justice. The Russian people defy that theory; they probably even disprove it.

Anyone who has lived in Russia has seen examples of the national impulse to subservience. Pushkin, the father of Russian literature, wrote about it early in the last century:

> Graze on, ye peaceful sheep and cattle.
> The call of honor cannot grip
> Or charm you into freedom's battle.
> For you—the knife, the shearer's clip!
> Your heritage—the herdsman's rattle,
> The yoke, the chain, the drover's whip!

Eugene Lyons, an American journalist who lived in the Soviet Union during the first years of Stalin's reign, encountered a trainload of *kulaks* in a small station in eastern Russia. Victims of the collectivization of the countryside, they were packed into freight cars for deportation to Central Asia. Lyons asked them why they were being deported.

" 'Because we're *kulaks*,' an emaciated-looking woman replied.

> No one among her fellow-prisoners contradicted her [Lyons wrote]. These creatures did not even dispute the right of the government to deprive them of everything, pack them into [railroad] cars, and haul them into Central Asia to dig canals. Government was something too far away, too omnipotent to be questioned; its decrees were like the decrees of nature, part of a harsh destiny. This acceptance of their fate in a sort of bovine stupor seemed more horrible than liquidation itself; it explained why the Kremlin could carry out policies which elsewhere would have stirred irrepressible mutiny.

Andrei Amalrik was overwhelmed by the passivity of the peasants in the Siberian village where he was exiled in the 1960s:

I think that these are people with whom you can do anything. If tomorrow the authorities decided, out of some mysterious political or economic consideration, to go back to individual farming, each man would meekly accept his share of land and start to sow wheat or flax on it; but if the government decided to abolish private plots and private houses, herding the peasants into barracks and feeding them in mess halls, this too could be done without the slightest difficulty. In other words, the authorities are free to experiment as they wish; wages can be raised or lowered, private livestock can be allowed or forbidden.

Amalrik decided that the peasants were crippled by a lack of self-respect and motivated largely by a fear of losing what little they had. I think that can be said of Russians in general. Rather than dream of how much better life could be, they worry about how it might get suddenly worse. This is the heart of Russian insecurity. Russians are not reaching for the stars; they are looking over their shoulders.

I sensed this in the reactions of Russians to the uncertainty—in their eyes it was madness—of life in the West. Is there really so much unemployment and inflation? Does the Mafia actually exist? Can citizens really call the President a fool? Do people truly go from rags to riches to rags again? It all smacks of anarchy to a Russian, as though something was terribly wrong—as though the baby had broken out of its swaddling blanket.

Alexander Galich is a sophisticated actor who had a successful career in Moscow before he became disenchanted with his country and decided to emigrate. I knew him in Moscow, and saw him again in Washington six months after he had taken up residence in the West. "At last," he said, "I understand the meaning of that old cliché, 'the wild west.'"

After I left the Soviet Union I went to Israel to interview émigrés from Russia and find out how they were doing in their new lives. Israelis, including social workers assigned to help newly arrived Soviet Jews, despaired at their inability to cope with Israeli life. The Israelis invented a joke to describe the problem: A Soviet Jew from Kiev arrives in Jerusalem and opens a tailor shop. Three weeks later he writes an indignant letter to the mayor of Jerusalem: "Much Respected Mister Mayor. I have been in business for three weeks. Why don't you send me any clients?"

According to a social worker I met, Russian Jews were uncomfortable if he gave them a list of establishments where they might find a job. Instead, they wanted to be told when and where to report for work. In general, he said, it was extremely difficult to get the Soviet Jews to take any initiative. "What is it about these people?" the young social worker asked me, as though I knew the answer. "We've had immigrants from Romania, from Poland, they're not like this. Only the Russians."*

Russians crave fundamental security—which is not surprising for a people who have been deprived of it so often, and for so long. I met a young chemist in Sochi on the Black Sea, where he was vacationing with his wife and daughter. "What the Russian people want," he told me, "is a calm, peaceful world—no upsets, no struggles, no wars. This isn't something new. It's very old." In recent years that is the sort of world Russians have been living in—an important reason, I think, why Soviet society seems so stable at the moment.

Insecurity may explain the pettiness and resentment that Russians display so frequently. Resentment seems particularly strong toward people who are better off than oneself. Amalrik saw this in the village:

> The peasants disliked the [school] teacher—not because he was a bad teacher or a bad man, but because he was outside the system of compulsion within which they themselves were confined. They resented the fact that his work was lighter than theirs, that he was paid more for it and yet also, like them, had his private plot as well. For the same reason they disliked his wife, who managed the village store, and Vera, who ran the recreation room. In general, the attitude toward "city people" was unconsciously resentful, the peasants feeling that in the cities people just had a good time, while the *kolhozniks* waded around in muck all day long—it was a kind of inferiority complex.

---

* By Soviet standards, a Jew cannot be a Russian. Jewishness is a nationality in the Soviet Union, stamped as such into a citizen's internal passport. This distinction seems absurd from the vantage point of the Israeli melting pot, where Jewishness loses all significance as a descriptive generalization about one group of people.

Nearly all the villagers were related, but they quarreled ceaselessly among themselves, keeping a close eye on each other's earnings and resenting another's good fortune more than their own setbacks.

The villagers' attitude toward "city people," I think, corresponds to the city dweller's view of foreigners. A young woman from Leningrad, the wife of a professor, told me, "The working class hates foreigners—they simply hate them." She exaggerated, but there certainly is a resentment which can turn to hate for people who seem to dress better, who travel to foreign countries, who make the machinery the Russians are so anxious to buy. The wealth and power of foreigners makes Russians nervous and defensive.

Traveling by train with another American journalist to Baku, the capital of Azerbaijan, I met two young pilots, both in uniform and both drunk. They were amazed to find themselves talking with American correspondents and had numerous questions. Both were anxious to compare Soviet and American life. One was good-natured, the other alternately friendly and hostile. He put his arm around me in one of his friendly moods, then began to brag about how efficiently the Soviet Army had occupied Czechoslovakia in 1968. Hadn't that been something terrific? No, I said, I didn't think so. Suddenly the friendly arm around my shoulders became a hammerlock around my head and he was talking about how tough the Soviet armed forces were. For a minute or two he wouldn't let go of me.

American military attachés in Moscow have had similar experiences with sober Soviet officers, though without the hammerlock. "Sometimes you can see them seething with anger at you," one American officer told me, describing his Soviet counterparts at official receptions.

The Russian capacity for denial is great. "If it isn't ours," a workingman's saying goes, "it must be worse." He doesn't believe it, but he says it.

"If you tell an ordinary worker that people in the West live better than he does," an engineer in Moscow told me, "he'll get angry with you. He doesn't want to hear that."

Several Soviet workers once spent a few months in West Germany learning how to use and maintain some machinery their government had purchased. The German company gave them a small party on the eve of their return to the USSR. A

German asked the Russian workers how they liked the shops in Germany. "They're fine," the Russians said, "we have the same stores in Moscow." The German looked puzzled. "Oh yes," the Russians said, "we have hard-currency stores which sell these western products." "But they are only open to foreigners and a few special people," the German responded—"our stores are open to everyone." "Don't kid us," the Russians replied, "these stores aren't open to the public; if they were, there would be long lines of people waiting outside them."

Thinking about what Russians are like can be made easier by considering what they are *not* like—us. In Moscow one afternoon I made a list of influences that define the nature of American life, none of which exists in the Soviet Union. The most obvious and important are our ethical and legal traditions, which are so closely tied to our notions about the worth and dignity of the individual. But most of the items on my list were more practical: the opportunity to buy whatever book or newspaper one might fancy; the opportunity to buy land and a home and create a truly private environment; the accessibility of private cars and thus freedom of movement; the opportunity to travel abroad; the possibility of acquiring wealth to pass on to one's heirs; the star system in sports, politics, literature and the arts which glorifies the accomplishments of individuals; the opportunity to let other people take care of you—laundries, restaurants, maids; the opportunity to indulge personal whim; the puritan work ethic; the cult of technology; the cult of youth and beauty; the opportunity to change jobs, change careers, change political affiliations, drop out or move on.

These are not part of every American life, obviously, and a lot of them look slightly crazy when written out on a list. But they do shape our lives and our attitudes.

Russians have none of them,* and, not surprisingly, they don't care about the same things we do. Andrei Amalrik wrote about this in his essay *Will the Soviet Union Survive Until 1984?*:

The ideas of self-government, or equality under the law for all and of personal freedom—and the responsi-

---

*Though some are coming—private cars, for example.

bility that goes with these—are almost incomprehensible to the Russian people. The average Russian will discern ... not the possibility of securing a good life for himself but the danger that some clever chap or other will make good at his expense. The very word "freedom" is understood by most people as a synonym of the word "disorders," as an opportunity of executing with impunity some kind of anti-social or dangerous actions. As for respecting the rights of the individual as such, such an idea simply evokes bewilderment. One can feel respect for force, authority, or even ultimately for education, but that human personality of itself should represent any kind of value—this is a preposterous idea in the popular mind.

A bitter dissident intellectual I knew in Moscow decided that for most Russians "it is easier to live in slavery. There are fewer decisions to make." I think "slavery" is the wrong word; it is too emotional, and suggests too much. But there is no question that Russians rely on and appreciate their dependence on authority.

When President Nixon went to Yalta on the Black Sea in June 1974, I stayed in a new hotel outside of town. It had been under construction for several years, and was rushed to completion in time for the President's visit. A middle-aged woman working in the hotel was fascinated by all the foreign correspondents who had descended on Yalta. She visibly screwed up her courage to ask me a question: "Tell me," she said, "do you have newspapers like ours in America, which print articles and pictures and so on?"

This is an extreme example of a phenomenon I encountered repeatedly. Russians are so absorbed in their own lives that they have little time or inclination to reflect on others'.

They are also so fatalistic that they seldom wonder how to make things in their own world better. "Yes," an Intourist guide once said to me as we waited and waited for an airplane, "we could ask why the plane is late, but if we did they'd only say 'weather conditions.'"

This isn't to say that Russians have no curiosity. Present them with an opportunity to find out something and they will exploit it. A chance encounter with a foreigner will prompt questions. The arrival in town of a foreign country's exhibit will attract throngs of curious people. But in the absence of these special opportunities, most Russians seem to remain apathetic.

The United States Information Agency took an exhibit on outdoor recreation in America to the new industrial city of Ufa, 720 miles east of Moscow in the Ural Mountains, a place rarely visited by foreigners and never before by an American exhibition. Young, Russian-speaking Americans served as guides in the exhibit. They had already been in Moscow, and knew that Russians had misconceptions about American life, but they were not prepared for the level of ignorance they found in Ufa.*

In Moscow the guides found it easy enough to talk with the Russians who came to the exhibit; the Russians argued the merits of Soviet society, challenged the Americans and also asked relatively sophisticated questions about politics and religion. In Ufa there were almost no interesting questions, the guides said afterward. If the people of Ufa asked questions—for example, could workers in America afford to buy automobiles?—the answers could visibly stun them. They had no image of what life in America might be like. They knew the propaganda about poverty and unemployment, but they also had the idea that Americans were very rich, an impression the exhibit was intended to reinforce. The contradiction baffled them.** "I felt," one of the guides said later, "as though I was talking to elementary-school children, preparing them for material that was over their heads."

One of the American guides, a linguist studying at Harvard, was a Negro. The people of Ufa were astounded by his presence. Some rubbed his arm or asked to feel his hair. Another guide was the daughter of Tatars, and spoke the language herself. Many of the people of Ufa are Tatars. As she related later, they asked her countless questions. "They do

---

* Russians who travel in the United States are appalled by Americans' ignorance about life in their country, no doubt justly. The misconceptions seem to be reciprocal.

** Russians all over the country are confused by the apparent contradiction. I knew several who resolved it by attributing the unattractive aspects of American life to blacks—unemployment, crime, poverty and so on thus became problems for Negroes, not for Americans in general. Racism in the Soviet Union is fierce, even among intellectuals. I heard it expressed, sometimes naïvely, sometimes deliberately, wherever I went. African students have a hard time in the USSR; several Africans have been killed by Russians for socializing with Russian women.

not believe that it is not written in my passport or identity papers that I am a Tatar," she said, "or that we can practice the [Moslem] religion freely, or that my parents [who live in New York] can even take time off for the holy days. When I tell them I go to school, they ask whether Tatars are allowed to go to college in America. They want to know whether we can speak Tatar openly and whether the authorities did not try to force my parents to speak English at home."

If the ignorance was great, interest in the exhibit was even greater. In Moscow 270,000 people saw it during the month it was open. In Ufa, for the same period of time, the attendance was 340,000. One day the crowds were so eager to get inside that they broke through police lines. I don't know how much of this was curiosity and how much it was just the thing to do that month in Ufa. There were similar wild crowd scenes in Moscow when the Mona Lisa and the treasures of King Tut's tomb were put briefly on display. Everyone felt he had to see what everyone else was talking about.

Virtually all of the ordinary citizens I met in the Soviet Union were ignorant about the politics of their own country. I don't think I met any non-official Russian who knew the names of even half the members of the Politburo. Several Russians told me that Premier Kosygin outranked Mr. Brezhnev, a basic error of fact. Even intellectuals who might be expected to know better believed and repeated the most improbable rumors. "They say there is going to be a military coup," one friend told me in 1973. "The Army thinks Brezhnev has gone too far with the Americans." He believed this was possible, too, though there has never been any hint that the Soviet Army has a Latin American approach to politics. Another friend, a Jewish writer, said he had heard from a reliable source that massive construction of apartments was under way in the Jewish Autonomous Region in the far east. "It's a prelude to moving all the Jews out there," he said solemnly. I laughed and said this had to be fanciful, but my friend was not amused. "In this country anything can happen," he said.

The widespread belief in—and repetition of—rumors indicates the failures of official propaganda. Like the official versions of history, the propaganda doesn't really satisfy. People know that they don't know. Rumors rush into the vacuum.

Occasionally the official propagandists are compelled to react to rumors that gain wide circulation. This happened in

1974, when rumors of a mad killer stalking Moscow's streets swept through the city. Citizens feared to go outside at night; soon the streets were virtually empty after dark. Finally the authorities revealed that there had indeed been a murderer loose, but said they had arrested him. Slowly the city returned to normal.

Pravda once printed a "humorous" item which must have been prompted by a popular rumor. The story concerned "an excited woman" who came to *Pravda*'s offices:

"How long should I collect metal [as opposed to paper] rubles?" she asked impatiently. "I have collected 84, and my neighbor Klavka has done her best—she's got 240."

"Are you playing some kind of game?" [*Pravda* asked.]

"What game? It's been announced on the radio that imported umbrellas, handbags and jersey dresses will be sold only for metal rubles."

"When did you hear that?"

"I didn't hear it myself, but Klavka's niece's friend was at home when it came over the radio."

"What would be the point of that?"

"Well, the state needs hard currency. Paper money is one thing, but metal is quite different. Can't you guess yourself which of them is harder? ... You probably don't even know that paper money will be printed in two colors, red and blue. Red money will buy anything but alcohol, and it's been decided to pay drunkards their salaries with red money...."

Evidently, many citizens invent their own news to supplement the official news media. At least as many ignore the official product. An obscure sociological study in Moscow's Lenin Library reported that people in the remote city of Taganrog weren't absorbing local news. Despite a concentrated propaganda campaign, for instance, only about 9 percent of the "young workers" of the community knew what the city's economic plan called for. Other figures in the same survey suggested that young people paid little attention to political news on television and in newspapers. Another survey reported on 500 divorced couples in Leningrad. Its main purpose was to determine why marriages broke up, but there was one fascinating tidbit tucked away in the tables. The sociologist running the survey asked these people what they had talked about with their spouses when they were still married. Less than 5 percent said they ever discussed politics. I suspect that the same figure would apply to couples that stay married.

In his Siberian village, Andrei Amalrik wrote, "hardly anybody listened" to the regular propaganda lectures, and "if they did listen, it made no sense because they didn't even know what [the initials] CPSU meant. One schoolboy asked her [the lecturer] what it meant, but she wasn't able to tell him. Only Filimon, the mechanic in charge of the milking machinery, who had once attended a course in the city, was able to say what it was."

CPSU stands for Communist Party of the Soviet Union— the most-often-repeated initials in the propagandists' entire repertoire, repeated day after day on radio and television and in the papers.

Ignorance and apathy are widespread but not universal. Many Russians do have political opinions, naturally. Most of the Soviet citizens I met had hard-line opinions, reminiscent of tough-talking New York taxi drivers. There are taxi drivers in Moscow who have photographs of Stalin on their dashboards. A writer I knew once got into such a cab, saw the photograph and lost his temper.

"Why do you display that hangman's picture?" he asked the driver.

"Hangman? Hah! Then you're riding with another hangman."

"He killed ten million people."

"It would have been better if he'd got twenty million. Maybe it would have been better if he got you."

Lydia Chukovskaya, a novelist and the daughter of the late Kornei Chukovski, a popular writer of children's books, has written about an encounter with another taxi driver soon after Boris Pasternak was expelled from the Union of Writers in 1958. She sat down in the front seat of a cab (sitting in front is common), ". . . and suddenly, like in a tasteless melodrama—or, to be precise, as happens in real life—the driver turned his narrow face toward me: 'Have you read, citizen?' and he squinted toward the newspaper on his seat, 'a writer, I think his name is Paster, sold himself to foreign enemies and wrote a book full of hate for the Soviet people. He got a million dollars for it. He eats our bread, then plays dirty . . . the bastard. . . .' " Miss Chukovskaya told him the writer was named Pasternak; "he is a great Russian writer, he loves you." But she realized that "There was a wall between us." The driver believed his newspaper. He refused the tip Miss Chukovskaya proffered at the end of the ride.

Most Russians evidently responded with similar indignation to propaganda attacking Solzhenitsyn and Sakharov in late 1973. Soviet journalists told me that Soviet newspapers received thousands of letters denouncing them both. Yuri Zhukov, *Pravda*'s resident hard-hat, invited several American journalists to his office to read the mail he had received.

"What is most insulting," one of Zhukov's correspondents wrote, "is that the people who make these slanders [against the Soviet Union] take advantage of our humaneness and go unpunished. . . ."

Another note: "It was said long ago and correctly: He who isn't with us is against us."

Virtually every letter he had received, Zhukov said, proposed harsh punishment for the famous dissidents. I had no reason to doubt this contention; there were no signs of popular support for Solzhenitsyn and Sakharov at the time. "Unfortunately," Andrei Amalrik has written, "the idea that nothing can be achieved except by force and coercion is deeply rooted in the Soviet people."

I think Amalrik was probably right—that if an election were held, the majority of Soviet citizens would align themselves with the hard-hats. The official line is a hard line, so it isn't surprising that people go along with it. People do tend to go along.

But I also sensed that there is a rich variety of opinions on most issues in the Soviet Union. If there are a lot of hardhats, there are a lot of tolerant and sensitive people who disagree with them, too. Soviet citizens are anything but singleminded.

There have even been cases of open protest against the regime, though they are rare. An acquaintance of mine met a man in Siberia who had once been a Party functionary in a large factory in Rostovon-Don, an industrial city. In 1961 he and several comrades organized a strike to protest against currency reforms instituted by Khrushchev which had the effect of reducing the average worker's income. The KGB eventually tracked down the organizers of the strike. This man was sentenced to 10 years in jail and five more years in Siberian exile. In recent years there have been unofficial but credible reports of other protests and riots in several cities. Some of the most violent occurred in Lithuania, where local nationalists protested against Soviet rule and Russian domination.

Grumblings of dissatisfaction with the standard of living, the bureaucracy and the official propaganda are all common; one can even hear them on the street.

I heard about a meeting of workers at the site of a huge hydro-electric dam in Tadzhikistan, in Central Asia. A secretary of the republic's Party was there, along with other important officials. The audience consisted of Party members, all thought to be reliable people. The subject under discussion was workers' living conditions. A man in the crowd stood and asked the Party Secretary, "Do you buy your meat in the same stores we do?"

"Yes," the Secretary replied, "my wife goes to the same stores you do."

"It isn't true, you have your own special stores," the worker said angrily.

I heard about another surprising example of outspoken curiosity from an artist in Moscow who was a friend of Alexander Solzhenitsyn. One afternoon in early 1974, when the Soviet papers were filled with attacks on Solzhenitsyn and Andrei Sakharov, a young man knocked on the artist's door. He said he was a schoolteacher in Central Asia and had come to Moscow to learn the truth about Solzhenitsyn and Sakharov. He had visited many apartments in Moscow; someone he met had recommended he visit the artist.

"I want to know if I can believe the radio [i.e., the broadcasts in Russian of western stations like the BBC]. After all, they are capitalists. Are they telling the truth?"

The artist spent several hours with him, trying to explain what he knew about the famous dissidents. He advised the teacher to be careful.

"What is there to be afraid of?" the teacher replied. "I'm only trying to find out the truth." Later he called the artist several times from Central Asia. In the last call he reported that he had gotten into trouble with the Party authorities there.

A skeptical attitude toward the authorities is common. I was told about a sociological experiment whose purpose was to encourage young couples to have more children. A social scientist spent millions of the government's rubles to conduct the experiment in a provincial city over a six-year period. It involved building new apartments and extensive child-care facilities, providing financial incentives and otherwise trying to induce a higher birthrate. Instead of cooperating, however, the young couples who participated in the experiment actually produced fewer offspring than the national average. The social scientist eventually found out why; the people involved realized that they were part of an experiment and feared it would end as soon as they produced the second or third child its organizers wanted. Russians are familiar with official promises that never quite get kept.

Ideological heresy is easy to find. On a train I met the chairman of a collective farm which raised sheep. He gave a 15-minute lecture on the need for more financial incentives to persuade people to work harder. As though enunciating an entirely new theory, he said: "If we are both making shoes, and I am making 500 pairs a month and you make 400 pairs, I should get proportionately more pay than you do. . . . People should be paid more for producing more."

I asked dozens of Russians if they thought private ownership would improve the country's restaurants; everyone I asked thought this would be a great boon—including a number of officials.

The most interesting demonstration of popular dissent I saw in the Soviet Union was the "question and answer" sessions held in a small Moscow church by an Orthodox priest, Father Dmitri Dudko. On nine Saturday evenings during the winter and spring of 1974, Father Dmitri stayed in church after the regular service to read answers he had prepared to questions from parishioners.

Each successive meeting was more crowded than the last. By the ninth session the old Nikolski Church, located in the middle of a cemetery in what is now a region of new apartment houses, was filled with old and young, intellectuals and humble folk. That last night there wasn't an empty space in the church. Sweating bodies were jammed against one another and against the walls, all lined with icons in gilt frames. One large icon was decorated with the name of Christ written out in electric lights.

Father Dmitri is a small, bald man with a flowing gray beard. He was imprisoned during the Stalin years. At the Nikolski Church he became popular with a wide variety of churchgoers, from prominent intellectuals to the humble old women who comprise the majority of every church congregation.

Father Dmitri understood that his Saturday-night meetings were risky. "I am afraid that I will be misunderstood," he said at one of them. "I love my people and my country. But the time has come to speak out. I have begun to do what I am doing very consciously. I cannot stop now or turn back. And I hope more of my brothers in the Church will join me. . . . Perhaps I'll be jailed again."

At that members of the congregation said, "No! No! God save you!"

Two themes recurred in his talks. The first was that a loss of belief in life after death had contributed to a breakdown of spiritual values in Soviet society: "Our state has taken away belief in resurrection from the dead, and we have seen a consequent growth in crime and immorality, because people have been taught to live only for today." On another occasion he said that officially inspired militant atheism "has destroyed human relations, turned friends into enemies and led us into a morass. Only the Church can restore us to normal life."

His second theme was more hopeful—that religion was strong in Russia, and growing stronger. "People are tired of atheistic propaganda. Books on atheism lie unsold in the bookshops in piles, but I think we all know what scenes there would be if they ever put Bibles on sale. Young people keep asking me, Where can I get a Bible? There just aren't any. . . .

"In old Russia you could get all the books you wanted on religion, and all the churches were open, but faith was not so deep. In the West they have all these things, too, all they want, but religion is still only a superficial thing there. Here we have nothing, but religion is growing stronger and stronger. . . . Religion is strong only when it must bear a cross."

That cross—official harassment—finally silenced Father Dmitri. At the ninth session he held, he did not give his usual talk. He could not, he explained, because the Patriarchate of Moscow, the governing body of the Church, had forbidden him to speak again.

When he made that announcement the crowd gasped.

"God save you!" many of the old women said. That may in fact be what happened: though he was removed from the pulpit, no sterner punishment was given to this remarkable priest.*

Religious feeling is one of the many simple emotions that thrive in Russia despite official propaganda. Russians are getting by, using the crutches available, cooperating when they want to or when they must, but also retaining private lives and private feelings. Political propaganda is a constant presence in everyday life, but Russians learn to step around it.

According to the propaganda, a Soviet citizen is meant to be coolly rational and scientific; in practice the Russians believe in a rich variety of superstitions and old wives' tales. I discovered this the first time I entered a Russian apartment in Moscow and offered to shake my host's hand through the open door. He jumped back. Shaking hands across the threshold tempts the evil spirits.

Spirits populated the world of the traditional Russian peasant, and they have not yet been thoroughly dispelled. The *leshy,* a spirit with bluish skin and bulging eyes, lives in the forest, where it protects thieves and leads good men astray. Every body of water has a spirit in it which, according to its own whim, can prompt the fish into the fisherman's net or shoo them away. According to inherited tradition, every peasant's *izba,* or house, was inhabited by its own spirits who protected those within. Dozens of other spirits live in the Russian imagination, some requiring special attention so they will remain charitably disposed. I once visited two intellectuals in Moscow as they were preparing to leave on a trip to the South. The commotion of packing and farewells subsided unexpectedly and everyone there—at least a dozen people— sat down in a circle. They kept completely still for about a minute. Then the chatter and activity resumed. I must have looked baffled, because one of the Russians explained the moment of silence: "It's for luck, for the road."

Folk medicines based on curative herbs and plants are popular in Russia. I happened into a pharmacy in Leningrad

---

* The case of Father Dmitri persuaded me that people sympathetic to the Church and to his views held powerful positions in the regime. There is no other logical explanation for the fact that he could hold nine of these public meetings in a society which does not tolerate any public dissent.

which had posters on the wall describing the curative powers
of various plants. In a Moscow subway station one day I saw
dozens of people excitedly crowding around a man selling
copies of a book with a brightly colored cover. Joining the
crowd, I discovered that the book was called *Medicinal
Plants of the Ukraine.*

There is a state-supported Institute of Curative Plants,
which claims to be in correspondence with hundreds of citizens around the country who have experimented with various cures. In a long article about the institute, *Izvestia* took it
to task for ignoring the work of a man named Korchan who
had lived in a small Ukrainian town. Korchan had written
numerous letters to the institute describing successful herbal
cures, *Izvestia* reported, but the institute had ignored them.
When Korchan died at the age of 90, his secrets died with
him.

There is a modern substitute for religion, spirits and folk
wisdom which may attract more of the Soviet public's intellectual energies than all of these and politics, too—sports.
Komsomolskaya Pravda, the popular daily newspaper of the
Young Communist League, described the situation accurately
early in 1975:

> The sports fan is a sign of the times. Everybody is a
> fan—from first-graders to grandmothers. There are
> hockey, soccer and figure-skating fans. There are also
> chess fans, motor-racing-on-ice fans, gymnastics fans
> and weight-lifting fans. Sports broadcasts are the most
> popular shows on television. The hottest arguments dur-
> ing lunch breaks are about sports. The tickets in shortest
> supplies are those to hockey games. Newspapers an-
> nounce contests for sports fans and receive hundreds of
> thousands of postcard replies.

Sport is the new opiate of the masses, in the Soviet Union
as in the West. There are millions of Russians who think of
little else outside their private lives.

Though all sports in the Soviet Union are theoretically
non-professional, there is no significant difference between
big-time soccer and hockey in the USSR and professional
sports in the West. The players devote the entire year to practice or competition and receive remuneration far above the

average, particularly for victories. The same Soviet soccer players represent their country in the Olympics, against amateurs from other countries, and in the World Cup, against the world's best professionals.

Both fans and athletes are virtually indistinguishable from their western counterparts. The crowds lose their hearts to star performers, wait for hours to buy tickets for big games, deal with scalpers when they must, argue vehemently on behalf of their favorites and regularly drink too much in the stadium or arena. *Komsomolskaya Pravda* disapproved of these carryings-on and published a sharp rebuke to unruly fans, mentioning a few bad examples by name.

Alexander Solovyev, for example, scalped a two-ruble ticket to a big hockey game for 60 rubles. A. V. Zinovyev drank so much he passed out and had to be taken from the stadium to a sobering-up station. M. V. Voznesenski, a junior research associate at the Institute of Inorganic Materials in Moscow, stole a city bus after a big game. He explained: "I looked around and there were these empty buses standing around. . . . No drivers. Who knows where they were loafing? I didn't have time to wait. I got behind the wheel and drove away." Small boys, the paper reported, can make 10 or 15 rubles by collecting empty beer and vodka bottles in the stands after a big game and turning them in for a few kopeks each.

Moreover, the paper said, a lot of fans go to games only in order to wave banners "bearing such dubious inscriptions as: 'Spartak, smash Dynamo!' They don't even know the rules or the finer points of the game."

Law and order in the Soviet Union are the responsibility of a national police force under the Ministry of Internal Affairs. When Stalin ruled, the ministry—known by its Russian initials, MVD—was deeply involved in political matters and developed a ferocious reputation. The MVD is much less ferocious now, but the reputation lingers.

In the fall of 1971 Duke Ellington and his orchestra toured the Soviet Union. In every city where they played, tickets were hoarded by officials, and the few put on sale quickly disappeared. In Kiev, members of the local police band tried and failed to buy tickets, but that did not stop them from hearing the Duke. They put on their intimidating MVD uniforms and walked unmolested into the hall an hour before the concert was to begin. They heard it all.

I like the story about the Kiev MVD band because it reveals something important about Soviet citizens who appear to be active collaborators with the regime. The fact is that Russians do what they have to do to make a living, just like everyone else. They are fully capable of the cynicism about their work and their country which we so often take for granted in the western world.

No one has captured this cynicism better than Alexander Galich, the former actor and playwright who became famous in the Soviet Union during the past 10 years as the author and performer of underground songs.

Several of his songs involve a man called Klim Petrovich Kolomiitsev, whom Galich introduces as "a shop foreman, a winner of many awards and medals, and a deputy to his city Soviet." (The Soviet is the symbolic equivalent of a city council; it has no real power.) Klim Petrovich has made a life and a career pleasing the powers that be.

For his efforts the local Party Committee invited Klim to give a speech "at a meeting in defense of peace." The unexpected invitation arrived when Klim was waiting at home for his Sunday dinner, drinking a little vodka. An official car drove up and the driver called him out. "Let's go," he said, "we're off!"

In the car he gave Klim the text of the speech he was to deliver. The driver told him to read it over—this was an important meeting, the First Secretary of the local Party organization would be in the audience.

"I'm a past master at reading," Klim thought to himself, and didn't bother to look at the speech. At the meeting hall he was called to the podium and began to read:

> The Israeli militarists, I say,
> Are notorious, I say,
> Of ambition they've a large amount.
> As a mother, I say, and as a woman
> I demand they be called to account!

Suddenly Klim realized that he was speaking "as a mother and as a woman," and his jaw "nearly dropped out from under me." He didn't know whether to go on or stop:

In the hall there was no howling or laughter
And the First Secretary, I see, was nodding at me
And waiting to hear what comes after.

Just a routine embarrassment, Galich seems to be saying, in
the lives of those who try to do as they're told.

One last point before I leave the common man—a point
tourists in Russia often miss because of the gray sameness of
Russian crowds and the blank expressions on Russian faces.
These are extraordinarily warm and sentimental people. Russians place enormous value on personal relationships and
family connections. They invest psychic energies in private
worlds which we in the West often apply to careers or hobbies.

I first sensed the dimensions of Russian sentimentality
when I heard about Agniya Barto's radio program. Mrs.
Barto is a children's writer, the author of nursery verses
known by heart to millions of Soviet citizens. In 1949 she attended the reunion of a family whose members had lost track
of one another in the chaos of World War II. This reunion
was well publicized, and in the years that followed, Mrs.
Barto occasionally received letters from other people who had
been separated from relatives during the war. On New Year's
Eve in 1965 she was invited to read some of her verses on
the radio. She did, and decided to read also some of the letters she had received.

One was written by a young woman who had lost track of
her parents during the war. She remembered very little, but
did recall the day her brother Tolik's sore tooth was pulled
out with a piece of string.

Miraculously, the woman's mother was listening to the radio that night. She had a son Tolik and a daughter lost in the
war, and she remembered the string and the tooth. Using
Mrs. Barto as an intermediary, mother and daughter were
soon reunited.

That was the origin of a Soviet institution. Soon afterward
Mrs. Barto began a series of monthly programs, always
broadcast on the 13th, in which she read letters from parents,
children, brothers and sisters who were still searching for
loved ones lost in the war. Letters flooded Moscow Radio—
180,000 of them during nine years. At one time there was a
two-year wait before a letter could get on the air. And Mrs.

Barto did not broadcast every one. She looked for those with vivid clues that she thought might really produce results. Disappointments heavily outnumbered successes, not surprisingly, but Mrs. Barto did reunite 900 families before her program went off the air in August 1973.

Mrs. Barto's broadcast became one of the most popular radio programs in the country. Tens of millions of people who were not looking for lost relatives listened each month anyhow. I learned about it from a woman who listened to the program because the clues interested her and she loved the happy stories of family reunions.

This story was told to me by a young man who emigrated from the Soviet Union in 1974:

"There was once a tiger in the circus, I think her name was Alma, she was very intelligent, very well trained. But every time her trainer turned his back to her she wanted to eat him. So the trainer's wife stood outside the cage, and whenever her husband did turn his back, the wife would say, 'All right, Alma, quiet, Alma,' and the tiger knew she was being watched, so she didn't jump. But the trainer wanted to find a better solution to the problem. For a long time he thought about how to convince the tiger that she didn't want to eat him.

"He thought of a brilliant idea. He realized that Alma was very comfortable sitting on her round platform in the cage. So he gave her a new platform that was much smaller—so small that she could only put three feet on it at one time. There wasn't room for all four paws, so she had to concentrate on keeping her balance. All her thoughts were directed toward staying on the platform. She no longer had time to think about eating the trainer.

"It seems to me that Soviet man is exactly the same. Like the tiger, he has to balance himself on a small platform. He's always standing in lines, always trying to buy something, always worrying about idiotic little problems. He has no time to worry about the big things—about freedom, or happiness, or changing the government. The government doesn't give you a chance to think—there's no time to think. If you get a chance to do a little thinking, you have to realize that life isn't too good.

"But nobody has time to think about eating the trainer."

8 · Science and Technology: The Flea That Couldn't Jump

NEXT I WANT to consider science, technology and the Soviet economy, subjects which have often confused the western world—understandably. The Soviet Union has been first in space, first in tanks, far behind in computers and last in ladies' lingerie. It is a bewildering situation.

The place to start, I think, is the Central Music School in Moscow. Now, this is also confusing, but justified. The Central Music School exemplifies Soviet methods for fulfilling high-priority objectives.

In this case the objective is the training of superior musicians. The Russians are proud of their orchestras, ballet and opera. These are cultural assets, exported abroad as testimony of Soviet accomplishments, enjoyed at home as today's contribution to a long musical tradition. The proponents of good music in the USSR are a powerful lobby. They have persuaded the authorities to devote resources to music on a scale that is reserved for the society's most important projects.

Five thousand schools in the Soviet Union offer special music instruction (though ordinary schools pay less attention to music than they do in America*). Thirty special schools,

---

* A typical Soviet school in an urban area has 10 classes. A student stays in the same school from age 7 to 17.

all attached to conservatories for music students at the university level, provide the most intensive training. The Central Music School in Moscow is the best of the lot.

It has students like Andrei Gavrilov. When Andrei was two-and-a-half, his older brother, then eight, took piano lessons. One day Andrei heard his brother play Tchaikovsky's "French Song." "Then," he told me in 1972, "I went to the piano and played the piece by ear, without a mistake." His mother, who wanted a pianist in the family, decided that perhaps the wrong brother was taking lessons. When he was three, Andrei got his own teacher. When he was six, his mother applied for a place in the Central Music School. Andrei was one of about 40 admitted. Most of them had decided at age seven what instrument they wanted to study. More than half chose the piano.

For 350 students the school has 100 teachers, an astounding ratio. Many of them are professors from the Moscow Conservatory next door who give lessons to the gifted children. Every student has a private lesson at least twice a week, and lessons in small groups every other day. Half of every day is devoted to music, half to other schoolwork. When he was a student Andrei Gavrilov practiced the piano six hours a day. In 1974 he won the Tchaikovsky competition for young pianists, the same prize that made Van Cliburn famous in 1958.

The Russians use similar techniques to build great ice-hockey teams. They began playing the game only after World War II. Now 800,000 young men play hockey for 40,000 teams throughout the country. The giant sports clubs which sponsor the Soviet equivalent of professional teams in hockey and soccer football maintain summer camps, special schools and large staffs of scouts and coaches whose principal objective is to locate young talent and develop it intensively.

What is true of music and sports is true also of rocket technology, high-energy physics and steel production. The Soviet response to any challenge to produce or develop something new or important is overkill—pour in the resources until the desired result is achieved. This solution often works, but it has obvious limitations: there are not enough resources to solve every problem in the same extravagant fashion.

When Soviet science is good, it is as good as any science in the world, and sometimes better. The best theoretical physicists and mathematicians, nuclear physicists, high-energy physicists, laser experts and a few others are superb by any standard. The same is true of Soviet specialists in a few areas of advanced technology. The Russians have methods of making steel that western firms pay to use. They have a factory in Leningrad which makes splendid electric generators for huge hydroelectric projects. They have done important work in magnetohydrodynamics, using rocket engines and powerful magnets as a means of producing cheap energy.

Soviet science has developed erratically. A few areas have received lavish attention, either because they were militarily useful or because talented scientists made the Soviet Union's contribution especially striking, and thus prestigious. Nuclear physics falls into the first category, for example; high-energy physics into the second. The great accomplishments of Soviet science represent the work of a few famous institutes. Brilliant research is done at the Lebedev Institute of Physics, for instance, but its scientists represent just a thin layer at the summit of the Soviet physics establishment. The physics departments of the country's universities and institutes of physics outside of Moscow are not—with one or two exceptions—in the same category. Perhaps more important, there are many fields in which the Russians do no distinguished work at all—organic chemistry, for one. Russians have done little interesting work in the new fields of biology, notably genetic engineering, which are expected to be the most exciting in all science during the next generation.

Soviet scientists and the scientific bureaucrats who guide their work in the Academy of Sciences are prestige-conscious. They want to compete with scientists of other nations, and to convey the impression that they are among the world's best. This striving leads to a certain amount of improvisation.

Take, for example, the Institute of Nuclear Physics at Academgorodok, a scientific community on the edge of Novosibirsk, the largest city in Siberia. The institute is run by Gersh Budker, a brilliant and resourceful scientist with a gift for original ideas. Budker established his institute in 1958. He was able to avoid the rules of seniority which frustrate many scientific institutions, and to hire a group of extraordinarily talented physicists, including many young men. I met one of them in 1974, after he had left Novosibirsk.

Budker, he told me, earned an international reputation and the support of his superiors by consistently pursuing novel lines of research which led his laboratory to the frontiers of international physics. This wasn't easy. The laboratory often lacked the equipment necessary to pursue complicated experiments, and soon it began to build its own. (Today Budker has a small industry within his establishment; half his institute's funds come from the sale of instruments and equipment which it makes.)

Budker and his colleagues knew, according to my acquaintance, that once they published their first findings in a new area, foreigners would soon overtake them, because foreigners had better facilities to conduct experiments. "You have to move quickly and skim off the cream," my acquaintance said. "Soon the western scientists will catch up with you. And this doesn't depend on how smart you are. It's because of the low level of our technology."

Budker's solution to this problem was to jump from subject to subject, trying to break new ground in each, then moving on quickly to a new area, leaving to foreigners the work of exploiting his original discoveries. This worked for years, though since the late 1960s his laboratory has apparently done less original work than it once did.

An American scientist involved in exchange programs with the USSR told me that westerners now realize what the Russians are doing. "When the Soviets make a very important discovery," he said, "it is extremely likely that we will get more benefit out of it than they do."

The best example of Soviet strengths and weaknesses, I think, is the space program. The Soviet reputation for scientific and technological prowess comes almost entirely from the success of its rockets and satellites in the late 1950s and early 1960s. For many years it was widely assumed in the West that the United States was substantially behind the Russians. This assumption prodded the Americans into an expensive race to the moon.

From the knowledge they acquired while preparing for the joint space flight with the Russians, American space officials now know that the Russians abandoned the race to the moon years ago, soon after it began. The Soviet Union never developed the rockets, capsules and other equipment needed to even attempt a moon landing. By all indications, they are still many years away from achieving that capability.

The National Aeronautics and Space Administration would

rather not talk about the Russians in this vein. It was a presumed Russian threat which gave NASA the huge appropriations it needed to complete the Apollo program. From NASA's point of view, Apollo's success has had unfortunate consequences: the American Congress will no longer appropriate billions for space exploration.

Nevertheless, both NASA's officials and American intelligence analysts now realize that the excitement caused by the first Sputnik and subsequent Soviet accomplishments was misleading. Though the Russians succeeded in putting up the first satellite, the first satellite carrying a live dog, the first man in space, the first capsules carrying two and three men in space and the first cosmonaut to "walk" in space, they never had the capacity to fly to the moon or even to conduct very extensive experiments outside the earth's atmosphere.

The differences between the American and Soviet space programs are instructive. From the Gemini flights onward, the Americans had a consistent plan of experiments and construction which culminated in the first Apollo moon landing. Each successive stage grew out of the previous one. Increasingly sophisticated rockets and capsules came into service one after another. Rocket fuels, radios, energy cells, computers and other components evolved as the program progressed. The private firms building components for the space program continually developed new skills and production capacities. Only the fire in January 1967 which killed three American astronauts testing the Apollo capsule at Cape Kennedy set the Americans back.

The Soviet program followed no coherent pattern. Its early sensations led nowhere, and to this day the evolution of Soviet rockets and other equipment has been limited. American analysts doubt that the Russians have developed anything comparable to the skills and capabilities of NASA's private contractors. In basic rocketry they have made little progress. The rocket which carried the Soviet cosmonauts into space to meet the Americans in July 1975 had not been significantly modified for 12 years. It is based on the design of the V-2 rocket built by the Nazis in World War II. The Russians have never mastered high-energy rocket fuels, and still use kerosene.

Leonid Vladimirov, a Soviet journalist who wrote extensively about the space program, defected to the West in 1966. In 1971 he published a little-noticed book called *The Russian*

Space Bluff, in which he describes the early Soviet accomplishments in some detail, and attributes all of them to a politically motivated desire to beat the Americans at each early stage of the space "race."

Vladimirov believes that political and prestige considerations were uniquely responsible for the development of the Soviet space program, at least until he left Russia in 1966. That sort of accusation is too broad to test, or to be useful, and it must be considered suspect coming from a defector. But the American space officials best informed about the Russian program accept the essential accuracy of Vladimirov's account. They now believe that the Russians improvised their spectacular early flights by stretching the same basic equipment in several directions, without a coherent plan of research and development which could have produced more substantial achievements later.

This history deserves a brief recounting. The first Sputnik was launched on October 4, 1957. It went into space on a rocket invented by a brilliant scientist, Sergei Pavlovich Korolyov, without whom there probably could not have been a Soviet space program. Soviet engineers could not build large rocket engines, according to Vladimirov, because they did not have metals that could withstand the heat large engines would generate.* Korolyov overcame this problem by clustering four engines together at the base of one rocket. This made the rocket very heavy, but it also gave it enough thrust to propel a satellite out of the atmosphere, or to deliver an atomic warhead on a distant target—the original purpose of Korolyov's Number Seven rocket.

In 1969 a Soviet magazine published an article about Korolyov in which the rocket designer explained how the decision was reached to launch the first Sputnik:

> We followed closely the reports of preparations going in the United States of America to launch a Sputnik called, significantly, Vanguard. [American plans to launch a satellite at the end of 1957 had been publicized long in advance.] It seemed to some people at the time

---

* This is still a problem for the Russians. They have repeatedly demonstrated to American scientists an interest in the metallurgy of jet engines made in the United States. The Soviets have never been able to develop reliable rocket engines as powerful as America's.

that it would be the first satellite in space. So we then reckoned up what we were in a position to do, and we came to the conclusion that we could lift a good 100 kilograms [220 pounds] into orbit. We then put the idea to the Central Committee of the Party, where the reaction was: "It's a very tempting idea. But we shall have to think it over...." In the summer of 1957 I was summoned to the Central Committee offices. The "OK" had been given. That was how the first Sputnik was born.

This passage strongly suggests that the whole idea of a Sputnik was an improvisation invented to beat the Americans. Moreover, Korolyov indicates that the satellite went into orbit only a few months after the Central Committee gave its approval. The Sputnik itself was designed to be "as simple as possible," according to this article. In fact, it consisted of nothing but a radio beeper inside a metal sphere. But it got into space before the Americans' Explorer. (The Vanguard turned out to be America's second satellite.)

A month later the Russians put up a second Sputnik with a dog on board. The first had weighted 83.6 kilograms (184 pounds), and the second weighed 508.3 (1120 pounds). This seemed to be an impressive demonstration of rocket strength. The *New York Times* speculated that "the Soviet Union might be using some new form of rocket propellant unknown in the West." Only much later did it become apparent that the two rockets were identical; in the first instance only the small sphere of the Sputnik was weighed, but in the second the entire second stage of the two-stage rocket was described as the satellite, and thus was weighed in the calculation.

To put a man in space Korolyov again had to solve the problem of inadequate thrust. (Russian scientists still could not develop large engines.) In what must have been a brilliant bit of improvisation, Korolyov put together a new, giant rocket using only the same engines that had flown the Sputnik. Instead of a cluster of four engines, the new model had *five* clusters of four engines—and enough power to put Yuri Gagarin's capsule into space.

By chance I saw Gagarin's ship in 1970, at the World's Fair in Kyoto, Japan. (I was a tourist at the time, and had no idea that in 18 months I'd be living in the Soviet Union myself.) The Russians displayed space hardware in their pavillion, including Gagarin's small spaceship with its bare, spartan cabin. The only dials or controls in it were a panel of perhaps two dozen toggle switches. It was difficult to believe that the first man in space had flown in this simple contraption.

Gagarin did nothing but sit through his entire flight—until the last few minutes, when he was ejected from the capsule and parachuted to earth. The first cosmonauts landed in this fashion because Korolyov and his colleagues could not invent a workable soft-landing system. To this day Soviet cosmonauts have much less to do in flight than American astronauts. Their ships are controlled from the ground.

Later the Russians sent up two, then three men in the same spacecraft. Again the accomplishment looked impressive from afar; again, apparently, it was improvised. The spacecraft never grew; only its interior was rearranged. To get three men into it the Russians chose cosmonauts who were small of frame, and had them fly without space suits.

Vladimirov argues that the Soviet Union dropped out of the race to the moon in early 1965. Science writers like himself, he says, received secret instructions at the same time to stop predicting that the Soviet flag would soon fly on the moon. The Soviet press commonly printed such predictions through 1964, but never thereafter.

"Going to the moon is like passing through an infinite number of keyholes," in the words of an American space official. "In theory, at least, the Soviets could have done it the way the United States did, but a lot has to go right. Very possibly things started to go wrong for them, so they gave it up."

Things have regularly gone wrong for the Russians. For example, their Salyut space station has been an almost complete failure. Each Salyut is thought by Americans to cost the equivalent of half a billion dollars, and the Russians have lost (as of late 1975) two of them, made only partial use of a third and had substantial success with just one. Instead of demonstrating a Soviet capacity for extended work in space, Salyut has demonstrated the uncertain reliability of Soviet space hardware. One of the space stations tumbled out of control and threw off its solar panels, leaving it without a source of power. A second fell back into the atmosphere after 10 days in space and disintegrated, having never responded to radio messages from earth. A flight by two cosmonauts to the fourth Salyut in the winter of 1975 had to be aborted immediately after launching. The cosmonauts landed in Siberia and spent the night buried in snow before they were rescued.

The Soviets have acknowledged that four cosmonauts have been killed in two space accidents. Other technicians and engineers have perished in launching-pad accidents. Several manned flights were concluded safely only with difficulty. The Russians have never solved satisfactorily the problem of rocket thrust.* They seldom put control of a space capsule in the hands of its pilots. They have not produced a real computer for use on board a spaceship.

The Russians have a joke about their prestige-conscious space program. It concerns an official of the Party's Central Committee who is sent to the cosmonauts' training center. "Comrade Cosmonauts," he tells them, "the party has decided to send you on a flight to the sun. We have to catch up with the Americans!"

"But we'd be burned to a crisp," one of the men protests timidly. "Don't you know that it's damn hot up there?"

"Comrades," says the man from the Central Committee, "the Party has provided for everything. You will fly by night."

None of this means that the Russians are incompetent. They have put men and sophisticated machines into space. Their Luna moon-explorer, though of limited scientific value, was a substantial technological achievement; it landed on the moon, took on four ounces of dust and flew back to earth, all automatically. The Russians performed their end of the joint space flight competently. The one piece of hardware they had to produce to American specifications—the docking mechanism which joined the two spaceships together—was well made, according to American officials.

But Russian competence must be understood for what it is—limited. Every Soviet spaceship has been designed to perform a narrow mission as simply as possible. Even with restricted ambitions the Russians have not always succeeded.

What the Americans have learned about the Russian space effort is revealing. Like the American program, it is the re-

---

* They do have huge rockets with enormous thrust, but apparently consider them insufficiently reliable to carry men into space. These big rockets would launch bombs against the United States in a nuclear war; it may be fair to wonder how reliably they would perform that function.

sponsibility of young men. "We're working with people our age," one American official told me, "people in their thirties and forties." The Americans admired the senior Soviet technicians with whom they worked, but none of the Russians overwhelmed them. There was "one man in particular who we would be happy to have working with us," a senior American official told me, but he put only one Russian in that exalted company. (Allowance must be made here for the pride of America's space scientists, which is appreciable.) The Americans also concluded that the Russians lacked "depth"; as one of them put it, "We have several people as good as each other in every field, but the Russians usually relied on one top man." Those top men had lots of assistance. The Americans decided that there were many more Russians than Americans working on each aspect of the joint flight.

Perhaps most revealing was the initial contrast in approach on both sides. The Americans approached the joint flight with lots of ideas; they laid them all out, tried to bring to bear the maximum number of considerations and work through them all to a final plan for the flight. The Russians began by proposing a narrow path to the final objective, as though they wanted to avoid dealing with any more problems or ideas than they had to. The Americans insisted on their approach, at the price of ruffled Russian sensibilities. The Russians hoped that American prying into their space affairs could be restricted to a minimum, but the Americans insisted on much more. They had to shout and threaten more than once to get access to one or another facility in the Soviet Union or to some piece of information, to see what the Russians were doing and how. In that manner Brigadier General Thomas Stafford, commander of the American crew for the joint flight, visited the Soviet installation in Central Asia to see the rocket that would carry his Soviet colleagues into orbit. In the end, the Americans realized, they learned a lot more about the Russian program than the Russians had expected when they first agreed to the joint flight.

As a consequence, the United States now knows beyond doubt that the Soviet Union is far behind in space technology. But the Americans also came to respect the Russians' capabilities. Some NASA officials see real merit in the Soviet approach to space hardware. "We always want to build something snazzy," one of them told me. "They want to build something that works. We could learn something from that. Our way is very expensive."

My object here is not to ridicule the Russians, but to try to understand their strengths correctly. The facts are clear enough on the Soviet Union's relative accomplishments in science and technology. The Russians were not first to the moon, and are not yet second. They are trying to buy technology of all kinds from Japan, Western Europe and America because they have failed to master it themselves. From 1920 through 1974, 244 Nobel Prizes for science were awarded; Soviet scientists received seven of them, although the Soviet Union has more scientists than any other country. (American scientists won 102; British, 47.)

Largely under the influence of Sputnik, we made something of the Russians that they never were—a scientific and technological superpower. The mistake was understandable, if not entirely excusable. Sputnik was a shock. In 1957 we knew very little about what had been going on inside the Soviet Union for 12 years, and it was easy to believe the worst.

Nearly 20 years later we know vastly more about the Soviet Union. We should now realize how wrong the reaction to Sputnik was. The Soviet Union was not then and is not now a great scientific power; it is a country rich in scientists and laboratories, but burdened by bureaucratic inefficiency, political considerations and isolation which hold it back.

I began to understand this by talking with American scientists who came to the Soviet Union for international meetings while I was living there. Contacts between Soviet and western scientists have increased markedly in recent years, allowing outsiders to get a much clearer idea of how Soviet science works. I talked with an American professor who has toured the USSR as an official guest and visited many of the country's most famous scientific establishments. He asked that I not identify him, but agreed to tell me what he had found. This is what he said:

Basic science in the Soviet Union is excellent, comparable to that in America or anywhere else. The Russians do fine theoretical work, particularly in physics and mathematics. But their productivity is low. American visitors were recently impressed by the accomplishments of Soviet scientists working on precise measurements with laser beams; they had matched the accuracy and stability achieved by a famous

American researcher. Then the Americans learned that 75 or 80 people had been working on this project in Russia. The American got the same results by himself, with the assistance of two graduate students.

The USSR has no reliable instrument industry. When a western scientist buys a fine instrument, he in effect buys the skill of the highly skilled people who made it. That kind of time- and energy-saving purchase is rarely possible in the Soviet Union. Distinguished researchers must take time away from their basic work to build the instruments needed to conduct it. Sometimes the necessary instruments cannot be acquired. The same is true of some chemical compounds and rare materials.

Soviet science is rigidly hierarchical. Senior men in every field dominate it, control the money allocated within it and generally hold sway, to the frustration of younger men. In the West it is widely felt that young scientists are the most creative, but young Russians—regardless of their creativity—must usually wait their turns on the ladders of seniority. The exceptions to this rule seem to occur in the fields at which the Russians have been most successful—in space and high-energy physics, for instance.

Rigidity limits the possibilities for exploiting the unexpected discovery. In general, the Russians are ineffective exploiters. For example, they published the first research paper on the separation of isotopes by lasers some years ago, but by the mid-1970s physicists in America had gone far beyond the Russians working in this field.

Rigidity also restricts Soviet scientists' contacts with the outside world. It is still a major accomplishment for a Russian scientist to get to an international meeting, let alone make a prolonged visit to a laboratory in another country. The Soviet newspaper *Economic Gazette* has acknowledged that thousands of Soviet scientists regularly duplicate experiments already completed abroad.

"I used to get worried," this American professor told me. "They were training more people, spending more money, their scientists have more prestige [than scientists in the United States]—but I said that 10 years ago. Somehow that potential never seems to flower."

Each of the points this scientist mentioned deserves some elaboration.

The productivity of Soviet scientists is extraordinarily low, both in pure research and in applied areas. At the time of Sputnik we were awed to discover how many engineers the Soviet Union was training; it has gone on training them at a furious pace in the 20 years since, yet Soviet society still seems under-engineered in virtually every sphere. Basic products such as elevators and record-players are poorly engineered. The Russians have spent millions of dollars importing engineering skills from the West for projects like the Fiat automobile plant built in Togliattigrad east of Moscow, whose design and components they bought from the Italian company.*

The Soviet definition of an engineer is different from ours. Tens of thousands of engineers work in Soviet factories in jobs held by skilled blue-collar workers in the West. Engineering training in the Soviet Union is narrow; a young man or woman graduates with a particular specialty and expects to spend a lifetime working in it. The Israelis have found that immigrants from the Soviet Union with engineering degrees are often unemployable in the Israeli economy, which does not require many narrow specialists.

In every town and city there are research institutes attached to industrial ministries and factories. According to a number of Soviet scientists, many of these establishments do almost no useful work.

"The Soviet Union tries to substitute quantity for quality," one Russian chemist told me. "For example, they create big scientific institutes. There are institutes with 8000, 10,000, even 15,000 workers. But I know many institutes whose 'coefficient of useful activity' is precisely zero.

"Just as you can't make an ocean-going liner out of thousands of little sailboats, you can't bring together 10,000 mediocre people without ideas and put them into an institute and call it science. It *isn't* science. Especially if you put a

---

* In 1972, according to the Soviet statistical office, there were 2,820,000 engineers in the Soviet economy, 990,000 in the American. In 1972 the USSR graduated 293,000 new engineers, the US 53,000.

An engineer from Moscow told me this story: "During the war I worked on the construction of an oil refinery bought from the Americans under Lend Lease. According to the American manning plan, there were to be only three engineers on the entire staff, but this wouldn't do for us. They began reorganizing the management structure, finding new jobs for numerous engineers. In the end the staff grew to three and a half times what the American plans called for."

mediocre fellow at the head of such an institute ... and there are many of them."

I knew an engineer in Moscow who had worked in many different branches of Soviet industry, including military production. Military industries maintained research institutes, he told me, in part so they would have someone to blame for delays. If a product wasn't ready on time, the factory blamed it on the institute. In other cases, he said, factories maintained relations with research institutes for purely cere- monial reasons, and didn't care if they ever did any useful work. "I knew of one institute that had a permanent arrange- ment with a big enterprise. It was supposed to do big research projects every year—the financial health of the insti- tute depended on these projects. Yet those projects were never completed, as far as I know. It didn't matter. The en- terprise paid anyhow."

Since Lenin, Soviet leaders have repeatedly claimed that theirs is a scientific society based on scientific principles. The repetition has had an effect: Soviet society honors science, though the country has not yet learned how to exploit it.

Which leads to the problem of instruments and materials. "It is a vicious circle," one physicist told me. "Science cannot give industry what it needs because industry can't give science what it needs." He oversimplified a complicated prob- lem, but the relationship between science and industry does exist—or rather, does not exist—as he described it.

The scientists' response has been either to make their own equipment, buy it abroad or do without. The first alternative is most time-consuming, but often most satisfactory. Labora- tories doing high-priority research can buy foreign equipment relatively easily, but they are a tiny fraction of the science es- tablishment. Others have to go through elaborate bureaucratic processes to acquire a foreign item, often relying on an igno- rant trade official to make the final choice among several models of the same product. Soviet scientists who befriend foreign colleagues often appeal to them directly for help. "I get a letter asking for some special chemicals, some small glass containers," an American biochemist visiting Moscow in 1972 told me, "and I spend $15 and send it to them." The same American said that in the entire scientific center at Academgorodok, with more than 20 scientific-research insti- tutes, there was one electromicroscope. At the Davis campus of the University of California, he said, there were four.

No amount of improvisation can compensate for some deficiencies. "It can happen," as the physicist just quoted once said, "that one crucial area holds back others. For example, it is well known that the Soviet Union is far behind in computers. And without computer technology, realistically, there can't be significant progress in chemistry, physics, physical chemistry. You can't just develop computers by yourself, it takes a long time, so you turn to foreigners. . . . On the other hand, you may be able to buy one, two, three computers for the leading institutes, but to create a broadly based computer science you have to begin producing computers at home."

It will take the Soviet Union a long time to recover from its failure to participate in the computer revolution of the last 30 years. This is very likely the country's most serious technological shortcoming. Though Soviet mathematicians have done brilliant theoretical work for computers, the computer industry has not been able to mass-produce sophisticated machines or software. By the mid-1970s the Russians were—slowly—making a third-generation computer modeled on an IBM machine, but apparently not by mass-production methods, and not in great quantity.

The Russians have a problem that goes far beyond the production of computers, however. They are not absorbing the computer into their national life. The space program, a few military programs and a few branches of science are now computerized, but most of society is untouched. There are no computerized bank accounts in the Soviet Union (in fact, there are no checking accounts of any kind except for a privileged few), no computerized telephone system, no computerized airline reservations. In the United States a whole new academic discipline, computer sciences, has grown up in the last few years. Most large American universities have established departments of computer sciences. There is nothing remotely comparable in the USSR, where only a few research institutes are working on computers.

This has profound implications for science. In the West virtually every branch of scientific inquiry is being computerized. The Russians may be missing an historic transition in man's intellectual evolution.

The next point in that American professor's summary concerned the stratification and bureaucratization of Soviet science. Science is something like the medical-care system I described in Chapter 3. It, too, is not immune from the short-comings of the society.

Lenin realized that science should have special status. He suggested an amendment to the post-revolutionary bylaws of the Soviet Academy of Science stipulating that no work published by the Academy should be subject to censorship. That provision is still in the bylaws, though it has long been ignored.

Since Stalin's day, science has been centralized and politicized like every other branch of Soviet life. The Academy of Sciences dominates research the way the Union of Writers dominates literature (though some kinds of military research may be the responsibility of the Ministry of Defense). The Academy favors its own institutes, most of them located in Moscow. Institutes of applied science, university faculties and the independent academies of the outlying republics all receive substantially less resources. The Academy also favors its own members, the pampered elders of Soviet science. A full member of the Academy is a prestigious figure in society, entitled to a monthly stipend of 400 rubles (in addition to a handsome salary from his place of work), use of a chauffeur-driven car from the Academy garage and other privileges. Members of the Academy need not retire for reasons of age, and few ever do. Old men rule both the Academy itself and its institutes.*

Each discipline is governed by a powerful professional society. The society of genetics, for example, decides which of its members will go to international meetings, whose books will be published, who will give important lectures and so on. The president of each society must be a full or corresponding (in effect, associate) member of the Academy.

In sum, scientists—like virtually all Soviet citizens—are deprived of autonomy. They are subject to guidance and control from above in most matters. The need to get clearance or approval for almost anything creates bottlenecks.

For example, there is an elaborate procedure to get a scientific paper approved for publication. Each paper must be accompanied by an affidavit that it contains no state secrets.

---

* Khrushchev established the Siberian Department of the Academy in 1957 partly to overcome the seniority system. Many of the new institutes established at Academgorodok succeeded in bringing together young men, unfettered by their elders, who did brilliant work. Twenty years later, however, those young men are no longer so young.

The scientific journals are inefficient, and it may take months, a year or more for a researcher to get his work into print. By that time, what had been a new discovery could be old-hat. Similar delays hinder the distribution of scientific literature from abroad, so that researchers around the Soviet Union often cannot find out whether they are pursuing ideas already dealt with in another country.*

Bureaucratic controls may be most damaging to Soviet science in their effect on travel abroad by scientists. In Chapter 3 I mentioned the elaborate procedure that precedes any trip overseas. There are many Soviet scientists for whom even that tortuous route abroad is closed. They are the people deemed unreliable, perhaps because they once signed a protest against a political trial, or because they refused to take part in Party activities, or because someone important doesn't like them. "There are a lot of young guys who could bloom if they could just get out," an American biologist visiting Moscow told me. "One young man I met told me flatly they wouldn't let him out—he's got a Jewish wife, he's half Jewish himself. There just isn't any hope, he said."

Russian scientists would benefit from travel and work abroad because even in the best institutes the Soviet Union cannot re-create either the facilities or the intellectual stimulation available in the West, particularly in the great scientific centers in America. Shortages of material and equipment insure that many Russians can never test the outer limits of their skills. The absence of invigorating discussion may also tend to limit a scientist's creative energies.

Soviet and western scientists agree that the benefits of informal contact with foreign scientists are appreciable. But most Russian researchers are not members of the increasingly interconnected international community of scholars. They have few if any informal ties with foreign colleagues, and therefore they don't pick up the latest gossip, the newest ideas

---

* Soviet readers of foreign scientific journals face another hazard, one described in some detail by Zhores Medvedev. Soviet censors cut out articles of which they disapprove. Sometimes these are articles critical of the Soviet Union, but often they are not. For example, Medvedev has written, the censor has cut out of the American magazine *Science* letters to the editor on the need for birth control and the harmful effects of smoking. Medvedev concluded that censors in charge of this work don't do their work seriously. They probably don't know much about science either.

that haven't yet appeared in scientific journals. This subject was raised in a book published in Moscow in 1970; its authors estimated that informal contacts among western researchers insured that the Soviet scientific community would remain a full year behind—the year it takes a new idea to get into print. The fact that this book was published suggests high-level recognition of the price the Soviet Union pays for isolating its scientists.

Official secrecy also takes a toll. The national preoccupation with state secrets and spies constrains Soviet science unnaturally. The political authorities forbid the publication of any ideas that might help foreign powers, particularly in scientific or military fields. To some extent this paranoia—and that word is not extreme—is part of the traditional Russian mistrust of foreigners, but I think there is another influence at work, too: the Soviets are afraid that others will steal their secrets because they work so hard to steal the secrets of others. I met several Soviet engineers who told me they had worked with blueprints of foreign equipment that were obviously stolen. One of these men had seen the plans of an American washing-machine motor. Another had worked with stolen specifications of a sophisticated West German chemical process. In some cases the Russians have made no effort to hide the source of their designs. The external characteristics of their supersonic passenger plane, the Tu-144, are identical to the Anglo-French Concorde. Their four-engine jet transport, the IL-62, is a copy of the British VC-10. I found in an acquaintance's apartment in Moscow that his new and prized cassette tape recorder was identical in every detail to my Phillips. This does not mean the Soviets depend on foreign ideas for their industrial accomplishments. None of these products, I'm sure, is beyond the imagination of Russian scientists. But it is simpler to skip the research and development and adapt a proven design. Adapting others' technology isn't so easy, either—it is difficult to imagine the Indians or the Brazilians copying a VC-10. But copying insures that the Soviet Union remains behind its competitors, because the copier must always be some years behind the original innovator.

In the United States, discoveries made by scientists working on military or space projects have had far-reaching repercussions. A spillover effect has swept military or space-related inventions—microcircuitry, for example—into the civilian economy. I remember discussing this with an amateur Kremlinologist before I left for the Soviet Union. Surely, he said, there must be a similar effect in Russia.

In fact it appears that a contradictory force is at work in the Soviet Union. A Russian scientist explained to me what happens. If a new process or piece of equipment is developed for military purposes, it is treated as a super-sensitive secret. It *cannot* be shared with the civilian economy because in the official view that is the first step toward handing it over to the West. As a result, the sophisticated technology the Soviet Union does have is concentrated in the military field.

Political interference in science can take more direct forms. Scientists, for example, are not immune from the "ideological struggle" with the West. When the authorities decided late in 1973 to put pressure on Andrei Sakharov, himself a member of the Academy of Sciences, they signaled this decision by publishing a letter signed by other Academicians attacking him. More scientists then joined the campaign in letters to *Pravda* and the other newspapers. One struck me as particularly revealing. It was from Academician I. Petryanov, who wrote that a Soviet scientist "must be more knowledgeable in the field of social affairs than even in his own specialty." "Social affairs" is a clumsy translation of a Russian phrase used to describe the correct understanding of ideological issues—that is, the Party line. It didn't matter to Academician Petryanov that Sakharov was a brilliant theoretical physicist, because his politics had gone awry.

Political considerations often determine who gets ahead in the scientific establishment. I met a physicist from Kiev who said the men in charge of science in the Ukraine were mediocre:

"What kind of man is the current president of the Ukrainian Academy of Sciences, Dr. Boris Paton? You know his profession? He is a welder. An academy of sciences shouldn't be interested in such subjects—that's technology, not science. . . . But a welder is president of the Ukrainian Academy of Sciences. He is very close to Party circles, he's a deputy to the Supreme Soviet and a member of the Central Committee of the Party, etc., etc. How did he get the job? He is the son of a famous scientist, also a metallurgist, and this family was very close to Khrushchev. Khrushchev made him president. . . . The Ukrainian Academy of Sciences is *quantitatively* a very big and powerful organization—measured by the quantity of its institutes, the number of people working for it, it is very powerful. But the level of scientific work, its significance, has become ordinary, average. Science is creativity, after all. It's more creativity than production. But now it has become a form of production in which thousands of people are working—very ordinary people. . . . The number of people is colossal, but their leadership is ungifted."

I was suspicious that this physicist was exaggerating, so I looked up Dr. Paton's biography. He is indeed a welder, albeit a doctor of welding. He is director of the Institute of Electrowelding in Kiev. He has written books with titles like *Selecting the Production System for Large-Gauge Straight-Seamed Welded Tubes*.

I heard of many other men and women whose qualifications did not seem to suit their jobs. An American economist who met many of the country's economic planners told me that the head of the computer department of the State Planning Commission—where computers could be put to excellent use—did not know how to write a program for a computer.

Party officials, particularly in outlying areas but in Moscow and Leningrad too, keep a close eye on scientific workers. "Say a director of an institute doesn't have a portrait of Lenin in his office," a provincial scientist once said. "He just forgot about it. A secretary of the regional Party Committee drops by and notices there is no portrait of Lenin, and comments on it. The director knows that if he doesn't then hang up a portrait, it will be remembered." That Party official probably cannot judge the scientific work in the institute, but he knows what is expected in the way of portraits of Lenin.

Dr. Emanuel Luboshits, a former professor of pediatrics in the Ukrainian city of Kharkov who now lives in Israel, told me what happened when he tried to publish an article in the American journal *Pediatrics*:

"To send an article to a western journal from Russia you must have the approval of the director of your institution. Even though there was . . . nothing secret about it, nevertheless the procedure is very strict. When I asked for permission to send my article to *Pediatrics*, they told me, 'We have enough journals here in the Soviet Union, there's no reason to send anything to any other country.' I argued that my work would be of interest to many American doctors who were working in the same area, and that only a few people were working in the field in the Soviet Union. And I tried to play on their patriotic feelings, saying that any article in an international journal would be an honor for our provincial institute.

"In a private meeting [with me] the rector said, 'That's dangerous, we don't need it. . . . Maybe it would be all right to send the article now, but maybe in two years or so they'll be reproaching both of us: why did you send that article? Sure, today relations with America are better, but in two years they may be bad again. . . .'

"In a public meeting of the institute's scientific council, the rector said: 'We are traveling by our own path, the Americans are traveling by theirs. We don't have to pay any attention to them. We'll pass America, we'll outstrip them. . . .' "

At its crudest, political interference has contradicted scientific finding. The most famous instance was the "biology" of Trofim Lysenko, a charlatan who argued that environment could alter hereditary characteristics. Lysenko said his genetics was "Marxist genetics," and convinced first Stalin, then Khrushchev that this was so. He ruled over Soviet biology for years at the expense of true science and numerous personal careers. Under Stalin, cybernetics was dismissed as "bourgeois idealistic pseudo-science," one reason why the Russians fell behind in computers. In recent years there have been no such extreme cases, but it is still true that a scientist with strong political influence can prevail over better scientists in bureaucratic struggles and in advancing his own career.

Under all of these pressures, science ends up resembling the other elements of Soviet society. Scientists learn to cover their flanks rather than march briskly ahead. Research institutes learn the value of non-cooperation and try to feather their own nests. Zhores Medvedev has recorded a good example of this mentality in The Medvedev Papers:

When plans were being made for our Institute of Medical Radiology [an institute under the Ministry of Health in which Medvedev once worked], it was decided to build a nuclear reactor on its site to carry out irradiations. The plans had already been drawn up, with an additional allocation of several million rubles. In another, chemical, institute being founded across the road from us . . . a nuclear reactor, an even more powerful one, was also being built. By chance one of the rank-and-file workers of the State Committee on Science and Technology noticed how close the institutes were together, and managed to get the construction of a reactor in our institute canceled. This worker did not receive any decoration, though he saved the budget many millions of rubles. And in the Ministry of Health they were very unhappy about this; they wanted to have their own reactor, which would have been more convenient than having to take samples over to the neighbors for irradiation.

If science shares some of the characteristics of other Soviet institutions, it is also unique in one respect. Science is the one important field in which independent-minded people can occasionally defy the regime and get away with it. Scientists, at least some of them, demonstrate an independent spirit that is rarely seen in the Soviet Union—which may explain the many brilliant accomplishments of Soviet scientists despite all the difficulties already mentioned.

Zhores Medvedev, quoted above, was a beneficiary of the scientific community's independence. Medvedev is a biologist and specialist in gerontology, the science of aging. As a young man he encountered the consequences of Lysenkoism in genetics, and eventually wrote a book about how Lysenko had taken power in the field. The book was never published in the Soviet Union, but it circulated widely in typescript among scientists and intellectuals. (It has appeared in many foreign languages.) Subsequently he wrote other monographs about official restrictions on travel abroad and the opening of private mail which made him a well-known member of the community of dissident intellectuals in Moscow. In the mid-1960s he befriended Alexander Solzhenitsyn.

In 1970 Medvedev was arrested and confined in a mental hospital outside Moscow. His twin brother, Roy, a historian, quickly organized their friends to protest against Zhores' arrest. More than half a dozen* members of the Academy of Sciences and numerous other scientists joined friends, dissident intellectuals and several Old Bolsheviks in protests to Soviet officials. Medvedev was released from the mental hospital. By expressing themselves boldly, his fellow scientists probably saved him from prolonged incarceration.

The case of Sakharov is another example of the partial au-

---

* The exact number isn't clear from a subsequent account written by the two brothers.

tonomy of Soviet scientists. No other man living in the Soviet Union (since Solzhenitsyn's involuntary departure) has been so vilified by the authorities, but through it all Sakharov has remained a full member of the Academy of Sciences. Apparently the political authorities have declined to tell the Academicians to kick him out for fear they might refuse.

There is precedent for such a fear. In 1972 the Academy refused to elect several candidates backed by the Party, including the Minister of Education, Vyacheslav Yelutin. The head of the national meteorological service and two hard-line ideologists were also rejected, the latter for the second time. Election to the Academy is by genuinely secret ballot, and the members evidently know how to exploit this procedure. According to one of my informants, when the name of Viktor Chkhivadze, a Georgian legal scholar who allegedly had ties to Stalin, was proposed for election in 1972, an Academician rose to his feet and asked, "Is this the same Chkhivadze on whom we voted in the past?" Yes, he was told. "I have no further questions," the member said—but he had apparently said enough to kill Chkhivadze's chances. The Academy is dominated by natural scientists who take their science seriously and apparently resent attempts by politicians to meddle in it. They are often helpless to prevent such meddling, but they have succeeded more than once.

The successes of Soviet science are hard-won, but not entirely surprising. Brilliant people do go into science in Russia. They are nourished in a distinguished scientific tradition that is far older than Bolshevism. The government spends huge sums to support their work even as it frustrates scientific inquiry.

Scientific research breeds enthusiasm in every society; the great achievements of Soviet science have usually been the work of the great enthusiasts. Sergei Korolyov, the father of the space program, is a good example. Korolyov began working on rockets in his early twenties, and his enthusiasm was evident even then. In 1937 and 1938 Stalin arrested and executed most of the scientists working on rocketry. Korolyov, still a young man, was arrested but not killed, and was able to pursue his passion in prison. He worked in one prison with Andrei Tupolev, one of the fathers of Soviet aviation, who was also arrested by Stalin. Later Korolyov was transferred to a special prison in Moscow, where he designed rockets.

The fact that he was working for a regime that held him in prison apparently did not diminish Korolyov's excitement. He won his first award from the state—the Badge of Honor, "for participation in the development and testing of rocket motors for military aircraft"—in 1945, the year he got out of jail.

For the next 10 years Korolyov worked away at mastering rocket technology. His idea for a cluster of several engines made possible the first long-range Soviet missiles, and his improvised Sputnik confirmed his ascendancy in the space program. Nevertheless, Korolyov never became a public hero. Khrushchev gives him full credit in his memoirs, but at the time the leadership chose not to lionize the space scientists. Perhaps they were afraid to give the scientists independent status, and thus political strength. In his heyday as the father of the Soviet Union's dramatic Sputniks, Korolyov was known to the public only as "the Chief Designer."

Scientific projects with the highest priority are driven to success, propelled by lavish financial support and official enthusiasm. Stalin appointed his most intimate henchman, Lavrenti Beria, chief of his secret police, to organize Soviet scientists to develop an atomic and then a hydrogen bomb. Beria's group—whose most brilliant member, probably, was Andrei Sakharov—worked in magnificent isolation for years. No effort was spared. Early experiments resulted in tragic accidents, some of them contaminating large areas of the Urals east of Moscow and causing hundreds of deaths, but nothing slowed the Soviet push for atomic weapons. We know now that the Soviet scientists had the advantage of British and American atomic secrets stolen by Soviet spies, but Sakharov has denied that these secrets gave Russia the bomb. They may have helped cut a few corners, but the Beria group succeeded on its own—at appalling cost, but it succeeded. Again the scientists responsible were denied personal fame. Sakharov and others received the state's highest prizes, but in secret. Stalin rewarded each of them with a large summer *dacha* in the village of Zhukovka outside Moscow. The *dachas* were built by German war prisoners. I saw them myself, rambling, weathered two-story houses along both sides of a lovely tree-lined lane. In the early 1970s, ironically, this country lane was no longer just the home of atomic scientists; Sakharov still lived there, but he had become a famous dissident; Mstislav Rostropovich, the cellist now living in the West, had bought one of the *dachas* from the family of its deceased owner; Alexander Solzhenitsyn wrote for several years in a small cottage on Rostropovich's property.

The most important point about the Soviet Union's great scientific achievements, I think, is that they represent exceptions to the norm. They are the consequence of special circumstances, and not the natural outgrowth of a well-balanced program of scientific research. They are the great leaps of an essentially backward society.

Backward is not too strong a word. A substantial minority of the 75 million Soviet citizens in rural areas still lives without electricity. Policemen directing the traffic on Moscow's wide boulevards don't know how to drive an automobile, and occasionally call on drivers to perform impossible tricks with their cars. The telephone is still treated as an alien instrument by ordinary Russians—most of whom don't have one in their homes. A cashier in Moscow's biggest department store tallies up customers' purchases on the beads of an abacus. An engineer in a factory may make his calculations on the same instrument.

This is not the sort of environment that breeds scientific and technological progress on the scale now taken for granted in the most developed western countries. The Russians are still at a much earlier stage. And though they want desperately to catch up, the chances of their doing so are not good. They may worship science and enshrine technology, but for the moment they live with an economy which actually resists new technology instead of absorbing it.

Nikolai Leskov, a 19th-century Russian writer, wrote a parable about his countrymen's gift for technology. It was a story about an English scientist who had made a perfect, life-size and life-like metal flea. His work was universally acclaimed as brilliant. Russian scientists wanted to match the accomplishment, but didn't know how. Finally a Russian devised tiny metal shoes for the feet of the Englishman's metal flea. This was also a great achievement, but unfortunately, wearing the metal shoes, the Englishman's flea could no longer jump.

9 · *The Economy:*
Inefficiency According to
Plan

"We could do it well, and we could do it quickly,
but we can't do it well and quickly."
—*A Soviet editor, explaining why his magazine is
printed in Finland.*

THE NATIONAL ECONOMY of the Soviet Union must be the
most paradoxical in the world. On one hand, it has given the
USSR the second largest industrial capacity in the history of
nation-states. It has imposed this industry on a backward land
at an impressive and consistent rate of growth. It has created
millions of jobs and homes, fed and clothed a huge population, built railroads and electric power plants across a vast
land.

On the other hand, the Soviet economy is utterly uncom-
petitive by western standards. The productivity of Russian industrial workers is half that of American workers. One American farmer does the work of 10 Soviet farmhands. With only
a few exceptions, Soviet industrial goods are so poorly made
that they cannot be sold in western markets. Soviet industrial
technology is second-rate or worse.

A paradox it may be, but there is nothing contradictory

about this bizarre situation. The paradox, in fact, explains the true nature of the Soviet economy.

The impressive results the Russians have achieved are the consequence of their single-minded determination and their ability to allocate the entire society's resources from one spot, the offices of the State Planning Commission. The Soviet Union is the world's leading producer of steel because it concentrates on steel. There is no Soviet pet-food industry; Soviet factories don't produce dishwashers or clothes-dryers; Russian women buy and wear out their shoes one pair at a time. The Soviet Union prefers tanks to automobiles.

In the West we are familiar with economies whose individual units are efficient. Our factories produce dog food, dishwashers and cars competitively, efficiently. So we think of ourselves as efficient, though our societies allocate their wealth so strangely that almost every prosperous western nation takes poverty and unemployment for granted. We are efficient in particular and profligate in general.

The Russians are inefficient in every specific thing they do, from training pianists to producing tanks. For example, it took two people to deliver my mail in Moscow: a mailwoman to bring it to the box in our entryway, a young man to drive the mailwoman (who didn't know how) from the post office to our apartment house. This kind of productivity is the rule, not the exception. The Russians also squander their enormous natural wealth. A soviet newspaper once admitted that of all the timber cut down in the forests, only 30 percent was actually converted into useful products. Nevertheless the Soviet Union achieves its principal economic goals—high rates of heavy industrial and military production and full employment—just as it continues to produce great pianists, by lavishing resources on a limited number of objectives. In the broadest sense the Russians are efficient; they use what they have to get what they want.

Fulfilling the objective is all that matters. Prices, profits, competitiveness, efficiency are all alien ideas to the Russians. Though some Soviet economists attach importance to all these concepts, the politicians who run the country and the workers who make it run don't really care about any of them. Instead they care about the Plan.

I have been capitalizing the P in Plan as a device to indicate that it isn't just a plan that I'm talking about. The Plan is law, and it is the only standard that workers and administrators worry about. If they fulfill the Plan, any other short-coming is usually excused, and if they fail to fulfill it, any other accomplishment is usually forgotten. "We live under a tyranny," a Soviet intellectual once said to me, "the tyranny of the Plan."

The tyrant is all-powerful. Not only factories work by the Plan. Every enterprise in the country seems to have a Plan of its own. At a restaurant the Plan stipulates how many meals will be served. A lending library's Plan calls for a certain number of loans in each category of literature; at the end of the month a reader in search of Tolstoi may have to take Engels home, too, to help the librarian fulfill her Plan. Newspapers publish articles according to a Plan. The Moscow Film Studio makes a certain number of movies every year about Lenin and the Revolution, to meet its Plan.

The Plan that matters most is the annual industrial and economic Plan drawn up by the State Planning Commission (Gosplan in Russian). Each annual Plan is part of a Five Year Plan, though the latter is more ceremonial than precise. In modern times the overall goals of Five Year Plans have never been met, usually because the goals have been revised downward from year to year. The yearly overall Plans usually are met, though they, too, are subject to frequent revision.

This is no place for a dissertation on central planning, but I do want to convey a sense of the enormity of the task. Apart from food sold in the legal farmers' markets, there is no free market for any product in the Soviet Union—at least not for any product made legally, in the official economy. Goods are allocated at prices fixed by the government. A factory making generators is allocated fixed amounts of steel, copper wire, paint and so forth in accordance with its own Plan for the year. A factory making men's suits is allocated a fixed quantity of buttons, lining, material, etc. The allocation is no guarantee that a factory will actually get the materials it needs—that depends on the efficacy with which the producers of the materials fulfill *their* Plans, among other things—but there is little hope of getting anything outside one's allocation, except by swapping with another enterprise.

Who gets how much of what is a question that only the Planning Commission can answer. It must compute how much of every raw material, semi-finished product and manufactured goods will be available during the year; then it must compute what every factory will need to make a certain amount of its product; then it must balance availabilities and needs. The planners must do this for hundreds of thousands of economic enterprises. The central authorities decide how much of what every factory will produce; they decide on plant expansions; they set prices. One small error can have far-reaching repercussions. For example, the Planning Commission might overestimate the amount of steel that will be available during the coming year by 5 percent. If it makes allocations of steel on that basis, thousands of enterprises throughout the country will eventually get less steel than they need, and will be unable to meet their targets. Thousands more factories dependent on the goods produced in that first group of enterprises will then also be deprived of needed products, and in turn will fall below planned output. In other words, any shortfall in a basic commodity will reverberate through the entire economy.

There are advantages to this system which suit the leaders of the Soviet Union nicely. Most obviously, it gives them complete control over the entire economy. It insures that the economic development of various parts of the country will serve their needs. For example, the Plan dictates that Uzbekistan and Tadzhikistan will produce cotton, although the people of those Central Asian republics might prefer to grow food and livestock on their land. The country needs cotton.

This is a "command" economy, run dictatorially from Moscow. It may be socialism in some literal sense, since private ownership is not allowed, but there is no hint of democratic worker control in the Soviet economy. Ironically, the present Soviet economy resembles nothing so much as the model of "state monopoly capitalism" which Soviet propagandists invoke as a description of the West. Only in this case there are no capitalists, just Communist Party officials.

The Plan eliminates consumer demand as an influence on the economy. If they were free to use their rubles as they wished, Soviet consumers could compel manufacturers to produce more cars and washing machines, but they cannot. When the washing machines run out, that's it for washing machines; those who didn't get one wait until next year, or the year after. There is no more steel available for washing machines, because it is needed to build tanks. Factories are not tempted to please the public by making more washing machines, because they would get no credit for doing so.

Credit—and bonuses—come for Plan fulfillment, not for increased sales. A manager who meets his Plan regularly may increase his salary by 30 percent or more with bonuses. Workers in shops which meet or overfulfill their Plans earn premiums amounting to a thirteenth month's pay or more. In other words, the benefits are substantial.

The Plan minimizes fluctuations in the economic cycle. Western governments watch growth rates rise and fall, inflation come and go, unemployment increase and decrease for reasons largely beyond their control. These variations are caused by market forces and the arbitrary decisions of businessmen and bankers. Because the Soviet planning system is so complicated, Soviet leaders cannot maintain complete control over growth rates either, but they do better than their western counterparts. The Soviet Union does not suffer from recessions.

The advantages of planning are bought at a high price. Planning as it now works insures inefficiency, waste and irrational behavior, and discourages technological innovation. Planned exploitation of the Soviet Union's huge labor force and incomparable natural wealth has made the country the world's second economic power, but Soviet planning also assures that the USSR will never match western efficiency or technological competence.

The biggest weakness of the Plan is the criteria by which its fulfillment is measured. The Planning Commission can tell a factory producing ladies' dresses that it must produce 500,-000 dresses, but what can it say about the style, the material to be used or the quality of workmanship? Almost nothing, as it turns out; these crucial decisions are generally left to the individual enterprise. Because the greatest emphasis is put on meeting the production target in the Plan, a dress factory is constantly tempted to cut corners to reach that magic 500,-000.

Izvestia published two long articles several years ago about the Bolshevichka men's-clothing factory which described many of the bizarre consequences of Soviet planning. "On the one hand," *Izvestia* wrote, "the stores plead with the factory: 'Don't send us any more suits. We have many too many.' On the other hand, the main board of the Moscow sewing-industry department raised the factory's production target at the beginning of the year...." Bolshevichka was working harder and harder to produce more and more suits that no one would buy. But marketability is not a consideration that affects the factory; it can fulfill its Plan and win its bonuses even if no one ever buys the product it makes.

One of Bolshevichka's problems was that its suits shrank. Why didn't they use pre-shrunk fabric? *Izvestia*'s reporter asked. "We can't pre-shrink," a factory official replied. "I will be given one million meters of fabric, and after pre-shrinking it will be 900,000 meters. They'll ask me what happened to the rest of the fabric." For similar reasons the textile mill that made the fabric also isn't interested in pre-shrinking; it would only shrink its chances of overfulfilling the plan.

Gross output is not the only index in the Plan. At Bolshevichka, in fact, there were 10 targets that the factory was supposed to meet: total value of sales, quantity of deliveries to stores, "normative costs of sewing," gross output in 1967 prices, etc. Apparently, every time the factory failed to do something higher authorities thought it should be doing, they applied a new target. But every one of them was meant to induce more production; none of them bore on quality.

In Chapter 1, I mentioned the consequences of the Plan for the production of auto parts and plate glass. Similar aberrations occur throughout the economy. A group of regular passengers on Train 76, which runs from Novorossisk to Novokuznetsk, once wrote *Izvestia* to ask why the train no longer had a dining car. This journey took four days and four nights, the citizens complained, and they had to bring their own food.

Izvestia sent a correspondent to investigate. He discovered that the workshop responsible for maintenance of railroad cars had a Plan which required it to clean and refurbish a certain number of cars each month. It was much easier to redo a passenger car than a dining car with all its stoves and equipment, so the shop skipped the dining cars and concentrated on the coaches. While passengers on Train 76 went hungry, the workshop that was the cause of their difficulties was reaping the rewards of Plan fulfillment (monthly bonuses for the management, annual premiums for the workers).

The Ministry of Railroads, interestingly, had realized what the workshop was doing, and had ordered that the shop alternate between passenger cars and more complicated jobs—a new index in the shop's Plan. *Izvestia*'s reporter discovered that the shop was ignoring this instruction. Ministries inevitably fail to enforce many of their own instructions, because the system generates too many instructions. Finer points are forgotten; the planners concentrate on gross Plan fulfillment.

A disregard for the ultimate consequences of one's work—except as they bear on Plan fulfillment—is endemic to the system. An acquaintance in Moscow told me about a building he frequented that was under *remont*—extensive repair and rehabilitation. "The crazy thing is that the building is scheduled to be torn down in three months, yet they're spending a fortune fixing it up right now." Why? I asked. "Different enterprises—the people who do *remont* don't talk to the people who tear down buildings, and they don't care."

Construction brigades building new apartments know that quantity is the only important criterion in their work, and they also know that citizens are so anxious for new apartments that they won't complain about shoddy construction. So it is routine for a family moving into a new apartment to begin by repainting it, connecting the plumbing, repairing faulty wiring and otherwise finishing the construction brigade's job.

Russians of my acquaintance said it was best to buy a new product as soon after it appeared as possible. "When it's new they still pay some attention to how well they make it," one friend explained. "Later they stop caring." The salesgirls in stores selling consumer goods routinely take a product out of its box and make sure it is working before giving it to a customer. Often it isn't working, but even when it is, there is good reason to wonder how long it will continue to work. The public is skeptical of Soviet-made goods, and there are long lines when a foreign item is put on sale.

The behavior of western businesses and industries is guided by a desire to make a profit, an impulse so obvious that we take it for granted. But it is an impulse that has no place in the Soviet Union. The officials who run Soviet industry and retail trade hear their own song playing.

An engineer who worked in a factory that made electrical equipment for ocean-going ships described his factory for me, and I think he explains how the Soviet substitute for the profit motive works:

"I've been working in the technical [i.e., quality] control department of the factory.... All the factory's production goes through our section. We check that it's working all right, and adjust it when it isn't—in other words, we do more than just look at it.

"Our month goes like this: for the first twenty days of the month we do absolutely nothing. We wait for various parts to reach us from the different shops. But they all work on the same kind of schedule.

"In the whole factory, on the first, second, third, maybe fourth of the month, everybody is resting up from the rush to fulfill the previous month's Plan. On the fifth or sixth, people start cranking up to do a little something ... but the production lines aren't working yet. On the tenth, maybe the twelfth, they start looking for the parts and materials that will go into the month's production. ...

"During the first part of the month they'll also be correcting the mistakes made in the previous month's production. ... Somewhere around the fifteenth or sixteenth the various shops actually start producing something. But nothing reaches our department that soon.

"Maybe about the twentieth we begin to receive the first finished production for checking. We start working on it at a relaxed pace. But then, somewhere between the twenty-second and the twenty-fifth or so, the storm begins. And then do we work! Checking, fixing, adjusting—like crazy! It gets more and more intense on the twenty-ninth, thirtieth, thirty-first if there is one. It's a good month when there's a thirty-first. Most workers work a shift and a half or two shifts during those last days of the month. Our department works as much as we're needed, sometimes around the clock.

"It's dangerous, of course, but nobody says anything about that. At the beginning of the month there are always people around talking about safety, talking about maintenance and all that stuff. But at the end of the month we never see any of those people. ... They all disappear. ...

"So we receive the production right at the end of the month, often on the very last day, and often it doesn't work, something is wrong with it. It often takes us into the first few days of the next month to get it working properly.

"Meanwhile, of course, somebody is waiting for our products. There's a shipyard next to our factory that makes ships using our electrical equipment. Several other shipyards around the country depend on our stuff. But we don't ship it out until the very end of the month, maybe even in the first few days of the next month. And a lot of it is crap, because we simply can't check out an entire month's production in a few days. . . . Our mistakes screw up those other factories—they can't do their work without our products. . . ."

The system of "storming" at the end of the month is endemic. The brother-in-law of a friend of mine in Moscow was an executive in a factory, and his wife knew he would never come home during the last four or five days of the month. He would sleep at the plant. The First Secretary of the Party in Azerbaijan said in 1971 that the average factory in his republic produced 10 to 15 percent of its monthly production during the first 10 days of the month and 50 percent during the last 10 days. A prominent Soviet economist, Leonid Kantorovich, winner of the Nobel prize in 1975, has estimated that the total national income could be increased by *30 to 50 percent* if "storming" could be replaced by efficient* use of resources.

I met a man who worked in a factory that made prefabricated sections of reinforced concrete for the construction industry. This is his description of that establishment:

"In our shop we made the metal frames around which the concrete was poured. . . . The shop was all cluttered and confused—there was no production line at all, it seemed. The organization of labor was terrible.

"There was no ventilation. In the winter it was cold and the windows had to be kept closed. When it started to get warmer the management had to remove the windows or the workers would break them out themselves. . . .

"A majority of the workers in our shop were women. They did really heavy work, much heavier than they are supposed to do according to the regulations. I was a safety engineer, but there was very little I could do in the way of making things safer. . . .

"They had two Plans to fulfill—a production Plan, simply square meters of reinforced concrete, and then a 'realization' Plan, which stipulated a certain level of sales to construction organizations or to other factories. I worked there for most of 1972, and from month to month they usually fell short in actual production. But they just added the needed amount in their reports, and always fulfilled the Plan. On paper . . .

"We were supposed to work forty-one hours a week, but in

---

* Kantorovich did not use the word "efficiency," however. It does not exist in Russian.

fact we worked a lot more. They kept people after work, especially in our shop, and if they were falling behind the Plan, they'd make people work on Saturdays, too. This happened a lot. Instead of having four free Saturdays a month, the way we were supposed to, we had one or two. During the first ten days of the month we always fell way behind the Plan. Then began the big catch-up—meetings, exhortations and so forth. . . .

"But the important thing is that they were putting out defective stuff on purpose. A lot of it wouldn't have qualified for any category of quality. It was junk. . . . The director and other officials always talked openly about the fact that we were producing junk. . . . But the construction organizations had to build their targeted number of apartment houses, so they had to make do with what we gave them. And it would hold up the required weight, it didn't collapse on them.

"Nevertheless, junk worth eighty thousand to one hundred thousand rubles was returned to the factory every year by users who refused to accept it. But we had a very clever lawyer at the factory who could juggle this and bring the figure of reported returns down to about thirty-thousand rubles' worth. He did this in various ways. For example, the people who got the stuff had only a certain amount of time in which to complain about it. If they missed the deadline, they were stuck with it. Or the lawyer could make various kinds of deals and adjustments to keep the users happy. . . ."

To fulfill his Plan, the director of a Soviet factory rarely wants to maximize anything. In other words, he does not try to get the most work that he can out of his labor force, or the most efficient use of his machinery and raw materials. Instead he wants to maximize his chances of fulfilling his Plan targets by keeping them as low as possible. An engineer in Moscow told me about a trial in the early 1960s of a factory director who tried to bribe officials of the Planning Commission to reduce the targets in his factory's Plan.

The director's interests are best served when he can build up reserves—of labor, raw materials and productive capacity—which he can hide from the planning authorities. Such hidden reserves enable the director to compensate for unexpected difficulties. If he is working at full capacity when some accident or unforeseen shortage of supplies curtails production, he is out of luck—there is no way he can meet his

Plan targets. But hidden reserves help him make up for unexpected losses and enable him to cope with higher Plan targets for next year (an inevitable feature of the Soviet economy). Instead of trying to devise more efficient production methods to increase production, he can bring into service some of his reserve capacity. The economy as a whole suffers greatly from hidden reserves—they represent waste on a huge scale—but factory directors benefit from them. The country's leaders exhort the industrial sector to exploit reserves to the fullest, but many directors ignore their exhortations.

A resourceful director looks for opportunities to accumulate reserves. When the planning authorities ask him how many workers and how much raw material he will need in the coming year, he exaggerates on both counts. The planners are aware of this, so they will cut back on the director's requests. The director tries to disguise the surplus in his request so the planners cannot eliminate all of it. In the same way, if a factory finds it has more workers than it needs, it is unlikely to make any attempt to reduce its staff. Better to hold the idle labor for a rainy day.

According to a poll of industrial executives published in *Pravda,* their biggest problems involve raw materials. Russians who worked in industry told me the same thing. Allocations from the central authorities do not insure actual delivery of the raw materials or semi-finished goods a factory requires. For example, the customers of the factory described above which makes electrical fittings for ships had received allocations for the equipment they needed, but they didn't always get the equipment itself, and seldom got it on time.

To overcome bottlenecks in the supply network, enterprises have developed—and the central authorities have indulged—an informal system of personal friendships and bribery. A good factory usually has a good *tolkach* or "pusher." A successful *tolkach* appears to have many of the personal qualities of a good door-to-door salesman, plus a large capacity for vodka and friendly relations with the chefs and managers of the best restaurants in his area. He devotes these assets to the cultivation of officials in various supply organizations. If a *tolkach* tells his factory director he needs some money for a banquet, a gift or even a payoff, the director is likely to pay up. In return, the *tolkach* finds the materials the factory needs to meet its targets.

Some supply shortages are too serious even for a good *tol-*

kach to overcome. It happens, as the Russians like to say, that a factory just cannot get what it needs to fulfill its Plan. Sometimes higher authority is understanding, and excuses the factory concerned. Sometimes the director chooses not to ask for official indulgence, and reports false results instead. It is impossible to know the exact extent of outright lying in the system, but it is common. The temptation to misreport production statistics is strong; a director knows a small lie probably won't be discovered, yet it may mean the difference between a large bonus and none. There is so much laxity in the economy—so many lost items, so much waste—that 5 percent here, 10 percent there is most unlikely to be missed. After all, this is an economy which loses 70 percent of its timber somewhere between the forest and the final product.

This laxity is part of the system now. The authorities seem to recognize that the system cannot work without it, so they are indulgent. A good *tolkach* is more effective than a new set of instructions from the Planning Commission, so the planners allow the *tolkach* to stay in business, though they periodically criticize him.

Among western businessmen who have been exposed to Soviet enterprises, it has become a cliché that the Russians are poor managers. If only a few of them could go to the Harvard Business School, westerners seem to be saying, they could do much better. The Russians have decided this may be right, and have established a new institute of management in Moscow to train executives.*

I suspect this is a misreading of the problem. Western executives may be better educated than their Soviet colleagues, who tend to be engineers by training, but this is not the principal distinction between them. The guiding principle at the Harvard Business School is maximization—of profits, productivity, efficiency, etc. That is the ethos of the western business community. But Soviet managers don't share it. They use their "management skills" to achieve the peculiar goals of the Soviet economic system, which often have nothing to do with maximization. Their problem is not a lack of skill so much as a lack of sensible goals.

---

* My colleague Axel Krause, a correspondent for *Business Week* magazine, tried to visit this institute and get the textbooks it used. A visit could not be arranged, he was told, and the texts were regarded as secret.

The preoccupation with Plan fulfillment is one of the strongest forces in Soviet life. In Uzbekistan and Tadzhikistan, the two cotton-growing republics, the need to meet the targets of the cotton harvest supersedes the state's commitment to education; schoolchildren in both republics spend much of every fall in the fields. According to a book published in Moscow in 1969, some students missed a fourth of every school year because they had to pick cotton. Andrei Sakharov has said that many of these children get sick from inhaling herbicides. I met a woman from Tadzhikistan who told me it was routine for every school, college and university in the republic to close from October 7 to November 7 so the students could help out in the cotton fields.

The desire to fulfill their Plan induces construction organizations to begin work on many more buildings than they can efficiently finish. At the beginning of a Plan period they lay foundations for buildings that will then sit unattended for months or years before anyone can return to complete them. The newspapers write about this problem repeatedly, with little apparent effect. In any big city in the Soviet Union one can see unfinished construction projects on which no one is working. I visited Tbilisi, the capital of Soviet Georgia, twice, in late 1971 and in early 1974. During the two and a half years between visits, it appeared, no progress had been made on the post office half-completed on Rustaveli Avenue. Labor shortages, irregular delivery of prefabricated reinforced-concrete panels (the principal building material in the USSR) and bad weather also frustrate the building trades.

Not surprisingly, in light of their complicated job, the planners periodically make mistakes. They build factories in places which have no labor force, or huge hydroelectric dams in regions without a significant demand for new energy, or aluminum refineries thousands of miles from the nearest source of bauxite. A classic catastrophe was reported in *Literary Gazette*, the weekly newspaper of the Union of Writers. It concerned the KSK textile combine in eastern Siberia, near the city of Chita, built to be the "flagship" of the Soviet textile industry, but in fact an almost total disaster.

According to Plan, the factory was to be built in five years, but it took eleven. Midway in the construction process the planning authorities decided that instead of making finished clothes, this enterprise should make raw textiles—so it was redesigned as it was being built. Machinery ordered soon after construction began was outdated by the time the factory was completed. "Dying machines from the Tcheboksary chemical machine-building factory didn't work. . . . They had to pack them up and send them back." When the factory finally started to operate, the first workers (all women and girls) came to work in their overcoats; there was no heat, water or sewage disposal. Many of the workers slept in the factory offices because there was no other accommodation.

The planners underestimated by more than 1000 the number of workers the factory would need, so the dormitories built were inadequate. As the factory's need for labor grew, so did its director's frustrations. He couldn't recruit workers among the women in the Chita region, many of whom believed rumors that work in the plant was unhealthy, and he couldn't attract workers from other parts of the country to this cold and remote area, which was traditionally a preserve for political exiles. When *Literary Gazette* wrote about the factory in late 1973 it had been open for five years. During that period 11,000 people had gone to work for the enterprise, and half of them had left. Housing was still a problem; 800 married couples were living apart in men's and women's dormitories, waiting for apartments. The factory was producing only a fraction of its planned output, and the director saw no hope that he could soon improve performance.

(This is not the only huge textile plant manned primarily by women. I heard of another from a man who made a documentary film about it. The textile center in the town of Furmanova employed 12,000 women and 2000 men. The women lived in dormitories, and some kept dolls on their beds, according to my acquaintance. He filmed a scene of one of them taking her doll to the store and buying it a new dress. He also filmed one of the town's rare weddings, at which he interviewed the local Party Secretary, also a woman. "I'd give all this up," she said, "title, status, everything, for a husband and a child." This film, made for Soviet television, was never shown.)

In other cases planning succeeds. I visited two good examples—the giant auto factory at Togliattigrad, bought from Fiat of Italy, and the new truck factory on the Kama River, which is being equipped by a variety of western firms. These establishments fall into the most-favored category of heavy industry. Both were top priority projects for the entire country. (Even so, neither was completed on schedule, but the schedule was probably unrealistic.) For them dormitories and apartments were built, supplies found as needed, workers recruited in adequate quantity (mostly by the Young Communist League). During the winter of 1972–3 people living in the area where these factories are located, about 600 miles east of Moscow, suffered from severe food shortages, but the workers on these two projects received special supplies.

Showcase enterprises like the Fiat factory are the ones foreign visitors are most likely to see, but they are hardly typical of Soviet industry. They represent the national impulse to make a few things worthy of showing off: pianists, space satellites, gymnasts, even the city of Moscow fall into the same category. They impress both foreigners and Soviet citizens, though in different ways. Foreigners often take them as typical; the citizenry sees them as rewards for their work and compensation for their own more ordinary lives—examples of what their country at its best can produce.

In the Soviet Union, planning has not resulted in predictability. The state has the authority to organize all aspects of economic life in the most sensible manner, but authority isn't the same as capability. Despite all the Plans and planners, things don't happen the way they should. A good example of the failures of planning is the story of the automobile.

I began to realize this one Friday at the baths. There was great excitement that morning. One of the regulars had learned that his wife was going to have a chance to buy a car. She was an engineer for the city of Moscow. Ordinarily her job would not have given her high priority to acquire a car, but there had been a mix-up. It was mid-December, and the mayor's office had just discovered that it had not disposed of its allocation of cars for the year. If they weren't sold by January 1, those cars would be lost irretrievably, so someone gave the order to get rid of them. The office of the city engineer was one of the beneficiaries.*

The man at the baths was excited but also worried. He and his wife didn't have the 5500 rubles that the car—a Soviet-made Fiat that the Russians call a Zhiguli—would cost. (This represented what the two of them could earn in 18 months.)

---

* Some cars are sold to ordinary members of the public on a first-come-first-served basis—which involves a wait of two to five years. Most are allocated as privileges to members of the elite.

They had to raise the money from friends within the week, though they wouldn't get their car for at least six months.

Only two members of the Friday-morning group at the baths owned a car. "Your life is going to change, you know," one of them warned, as though speaking to the husband of a pregnant woman. "Yes, I guess it will, I haven't thought much about it," the prospective car-owner replied.

That seems to be about the way the Soviet Union decided to enter the automobile age—without thinking too much about it. Khrushchev proposed that the USSR could avoid the social and personal costs of private car-ownership by establishing a national car-rental system, from which any citizen could take a car when he needed one. The idea got nowhere, and Khrushchev's successors abandoned it. Instead they bought the huge Fiat factory, whose output began to appear on the streets of Moscow in 1971, when I arrived there. In the subsequent three years, thanks largely to the influx of tens of thousands of Zhigulis, Moscow developed a real traffic problem.

Like Moscow's traffic jams, most of the other repercussions of the automobile were not anticipated. By all indications, the government decided to buy the factory (with a capacity of 660,000 cars a year, which it achieved in 1974) before figuring out what else would have to be built to accommodate so many private automobiles. The cars began to appear long before any service stations had been built to care for them. Only in 1972 did the factory itself begin to think that it would have to take responsibility for maintenance at 30 points around the country. (In the Soviet Union there is no equivalent to the neighborhood service station with a mechanic. State-owned gasoline stations, where self-service is the rule, are rare.) The planners miscalculated or ignored the true needs for spare parts, which have been in short supply since the first Zhigulis appeared. In 1975 an American who took his Zhiguli to the Moscow service station was told to remove any movable parts (windshield wipers, hubcaps, etc.) before he left the car so they would not be stolen.

The automobile age will also require roads, of which the Soviet Union has very few, considering its size. In the United States there are nearly four million miles of paved roads; the Soviet Union, with an area twice as large, has less than 250,-000 miles. This raw statistic says nothing of the quality of Russian roads; not one compares with an American interstate highway or a British motorway. No two Soviet cities are connected by a divided highway, and it is impossible to cross the country on a continuously paved road.

Soviet cars—Zhigulis and other models designed, wholly or in part, at home—are made without pollution controls of any kind, and with little concern for safety devices. The first seat belts began to appear in 1975. Most Soviet cars are made without shatterproof safety glass; their windshields break into small pieces on impact. Fiat insisted—over Soviet objections—that safety glass be installed in the Zhiguli.

Though no complete statistics are published, the Russians apparently have a staggering number of traffic accidents. Partial figures for individual republics have slipped into print, and they suggest that on a per-vehicle basis the accident and casualty rates may be five to ten times what they are in the United States, for example. Many of the victims are pedestrians, who still are not used to sharing the streets with fast-moving cars.

The Russians raced into the automotive age without a single traffic engineer, a discipline that has no Soviet equivalent as far as I could discover. Traffic patterns in Moscow are chaotic; almost no left turns are permitted, and trips within the city must often follow roundabout routes to compensate for illogical restrictions and one-way streets. There is not a single parking lot in downtown Moscow, and the police don't give parking tickets—there is no such thing.

In sum, though the development of the Soviet automobile industry has always proceeded according to Plan, the "automobilization" (as the Russians call it) of Soviet society has been chaotic, almost anarchic. Planning has provided the cars, but not the facilities the country needs to absorb and exploit them.

I ended the last chapter with the observation that the Soviet economy discourages technological innovations and progress. Now I want to explain why.

The factory director wants stable relations with the Planning Commission, his suppliers of raw materials and his customers. When he has stable relations with all of them, his life will proceed relatively calmly; he will meet his Plan, collect his bonuses, stay out of trouble. Logically, the longer the director can continue to use the same raw materials to make the same product for the same customers, the better chance he has of achieving stable relationships.

If a scientist or an official of his ministry proposes that the director make a new product or adopt a more efficient process to make his old product, the director's first reaction is likely to be "No, thank you." A new product means new raw materials, thus new sources of supply and the uncertainty that inevitably accompanies the search for them. It means new, unpredictable customers. A new process may also require new raw materials, and it will mean reorganizing the factory's labor force, perhaps adding new—and hard-to-find—skilled workers. If the Planning Commission thinks the new process is more efficient than the old, it will raise the factory's targets.

In short, sticking by the old products and production methods is the safe, easy way to get along. Innovation invites problems. If a factory director who is presently fulfilling his Plan agrees to try an innovation, he risks all his bonuses and his peace of mind. Yet even if the innovation succeeds completely, his rewards will be only what they were to begin with—the standard rewards for Plan fulfillment. A new product may serve the country's needs, and a new process may conserve its resources, but neither will do anything for the factory director. Often, therefore, the director isn't interested.

A Soviet engineer told me this story:

"I knew a guy who was the head of a shop in the construction-plastics combine in Moscow. He thought up a way to save a great deal of very expensive epoxy in the construction process—a colossal saving. But he never said anything about it.

"For one thing, to get a new method like that approved [by higher authorities in the factory, and perhaps in the ministry too] would take, at the very least, six months. Moreover, no one would want to take responsibility for approving a change in the production method. What if it didn't work out? So he just started doing it his new way, quietly, without telling anybody.

"Of course he started to accumulate a great reserve of epoxy, because he was still receiving the amount of it he needed for the old process. He used to give it away to people who needed it, or trade some for a bottle of vodka. But then he began to worry about the possibility of a spot inventory check by the authorities. They might say, 'How come you've got all this extra epoxy?' It made him nervous."

The same chemical engineer once visited a factory in Moscow that had just received new machines from Krupp, the West German firm, to perform a chemical process he was familiar with. "I looked at what they were doing, and I told the foreman of the shop that I could increase his productivity twenty times—and I could have, it would have been relatively simple. Very interesting, he said, very interesting. But nothing happened. Later I met the head of the laboratory in the factory and explained the situation to him. And he said, 'What's the matter with you, are you crazy? What does the foreman need with your ideas? As it is he can raise the productivity of his shop by one or two percent every month. For that he is assured of receiving a special bonus every month. And what will he get if he does what you suggest? Not as much. They'll give him credit for the improvement just once, and that will be it.' "

When a scientist invents a new machine, process or product, he can have an awful time trying to convince anyone to use it. The research institutes generally have no production facilities of their own, so the inventor must sell his idea to an industrial ministry or directly to an enterprise. In either case he will be frustrated by cautious bureaucrats. Several scientists told me that industrial managers are inclined to doubt the efficacy of an invention devised entirely by Russians. "Do they do this in America?" one was asked when he suggested a new idea. If they didn't, the official implied, it must not be worthwhile.

It is too easy to jump to the conclusion that the Soviet Union never adopts new techniques and never produces an original idea. This is far from true. In 1975 I learned of an American firm which is hoping to sell Soviet patents to western companies. This firm expects to make money selling Russian technology, particularly advanced steel-making methods, some of which have already been licensed in Japan. But despite its accomplishments, the Soviet system works against innovation, as the Russians themselves recognize. The press is full of exhortations to put new ideas into practice. For two years while I was in Moscow I heard recurrent reports that the Party's Central Committee would hold a special Plenum on the subject of "the scientific-technological revolution" and ways to exploit it, but the meeting never took place. A senior journalist told me the subject was too complicated, too sensitive, to bring out in a Plenum, although, he said, the Central Committee staff had long ago prepared for this meeting.

In some fields the country's political leadership has tried to impose technological progress from above. The best example is computers. Every factory director in the Soviet Union knows it is fashionable to use computers, and thousands of directors have tried to do so. I met a communications engineer who had worked for a large enterprise in Minsk, the capital of Belorussia, on its "automated systems management" program, a popular name for recent attempts to exploit the computer in Soviet industry. He told me this story about his firm, which made and distributed building materials:

"We knew that in the West, companies—especially progressive, intelligent companies—had discovered enormous advantages in the use of computers to control production. In the West, presumably, this developed naturally, out of the conditions that existed. But in the Soviet Union this had to be decreed from above. . . .

"The system I worked on was based on a Minsk-32 computer [a second-generation machine] which cost about half a million rubles. But all the preparation of information to go into the computer was done in old-fashioned ways—on an abacus, or with a pencil. And when the computer produced results, they too were dealt with on abacuses and with pencils. And the results were often irrelevant to the job at hand. When they got a result, they had to check it. How? On the abacus, naturally.

"This system apparently came from the Ministry of Defense. That is our richest institution—maybe they can do something with it. We used it in the area of construction materials. The administration [of the enterprise] wanted to have it. I mean, if some people came to our factory—foreigners, say, from the West—it would be 'inconvenient' to have them see everyone still working on abacuses. Just for reasons of prestige they wanted the computer. Of course, by itself the machine wasn't anything. To be effective it had to have good information fed into it. But we never managed to connect all the elements of our work with the computer. . . .

"Of course none of this means anything if the inputs aren't carefully prepared. And they have to be utterly reliable and accurate, obviously, or the computer's work is meaningless. But in the construction industry there are no honest, reliable statistics. Lying about statistics is built into the system.

"I worked on this thing for three years. I'm a communications engineer and my responsibility was to work on the transmission of information into and out of the computer—all the services, you might say. But, for example, just building the kinds of telephone connections that the system required was extremely difficult. In Minsk—the capital of a republic, a major city—the telephone system was in terrible condition, extremely backward and messed up. The lines and channels were in terrible shape. To make a long story short, it was technically impossible to provide the kind of telephone connections that the automated system of management needed. So information for the computer from our various depots around the city was sometimes brought by trolley bus—somebody got on the bus and brought the figures to the computer center."

Conversations with other Russians who worked in industry suggested that this was a rather typical experience. Computerization has been effectively incorporated at a few large enterprises, but below the highest level it has made little headway, except as a form of *pokazuka*. This probably should be expected.

In the West, computers were sucked into service like strands of spaghetti, compelled by the forces of competition. The advantages they provided were so great that if one firm in an important sector was computerized, its competitors had little choice but to follow suit. Automation also appealed to western managers because it helped reduce their dependence on their most demanding, troublesome and expensive cost item, human labor. Soviet managers are not in competition with anyone, and they can rarely dismiss unneeded labor even if they would like to. (Every Soviet citizen is guaranteed a job by law, and dismissals are almost unheard of.) A factory director may use a computer because he knows it is expected of him, but in fact he must hope it doesn't have much real effect on his operations.

The first Soviet factory I visited was one that made clothes in Khabarovsk. The director, a round, jovial man, took me to see his new "computer center." He was supposed to receive a Minsk-32 in a few months, he told me. How, I asked, would this affect his work? Well, he said, first he would have to hire some specialists to work out the system. After that he didn't know what might happen.

The authorities have similar difficulties imposing new foreign technology on the economy. Experts from the State Committee on Science and Technology and the industrial ministries usually decide what foreign equipment to buy, and officials of the state's trading organizations actually buy it. But the directors of factories must put the equipment to use. The story above about the chemical process supplied by Krupp suggests what must often happen.

In early 1974 *Krokodil*, the official weekly humor magazine, published a cartoon on its cover commenting on this problem. It showed a field behind a factory in which pieces of foreign equipment were buried in graves under their own markers. Workers were bringing the latest item, still in its original crate, from a railroad car to the field for burial. If *Krokodil* ridicules such behavior on its cover, we can fairly assume that it is widespread.

According to Roy Medvedev, figures on the introduction of new machinery—that is, crudely, technological innovation—show a slower rate throughout the 1960s than in 1956-60.

Technical innovation is a form of initiative, and the Soviet economic system discourages initiative—a cliché, perhaps, but true.

Literary Gazette reported on the case of Ivan S., deputy director of a construction brigade that built bridges in Siberia. He agreed to talk frankly with the newspaper provided he remained anonymous—an American journalistic trick seldom used in the Soviet press.

Ivan was a man who took initiative. Once he built a storehouse on a construction site to preserve some perishable building materials. But the storehouse wasn't in the Plan. He was sharply rebuked for this bit of unauthorized construction. Later he built an unauthorized nursery and kindergarten for his workers, to free more women's hands for the construction of bridges, the brigade's job. His ministry disapproved of this and punished Ivan by forcing his brigade to build an extra bridge, above its Plan. When he managed to do that, the planners responded by raising Ivan's production target for the next year by two bridges, on the theory that if he built an extra one so easily, he could surely do two more. That was the last straw for Ivan. He decided, according to the newspaper, that he would build his next bridge "the way everybody else does," without using his personal contacts to get construction materials, transport and so forth. "The main thing," Ivan said, "is to put an end to any initiative. Then life will be simpler. Why did I bother to take all those risks? For what?"

As if to head off the assumption that this was an isolated case, *Literary Gazette* took Ivan's story to three officials in the construction industry. All of them endorsed it as accurate. One said, "The situation is often even more serious and discouraging" than Ivan implied.

Overkill, the music-school system of development, has produced good results for the Soviet Union in many fields, but it does not induce technological innovation. By applying extensive resources the Russians can build a factory, buy the latest equipment for it, even train the people who will run it, but none of that guarantees its efficient operation. And no amount of resources can overcome bureaucratic opposition to new ideas and inventions. In the USSR, technological progress depends on the enthusiasm and initiative of the men and women who are in positions to bring it about. For many—no doubt most—Soviet managers, material self-interest is stronger than enthusiasm and initiative.

A truly comprehensive and enlightened national Plan would require a fantastic number of resources: detailed information from every sector of the country's life; completely accurate economic statistics and a perfect understanding of the relationships between inputs and outputs; wisdom about the best way for a society to grow and develop; and many more, none of them presently available to the planners of the USSR.

Soviet planners cannot cope with the figures, reports and data of all kinds which swamp their offices (Effective computerization would be helpful.) Political considerations dictate action which wise development policy would not—enormous expenditures on armaments, for example. An undisciplined population subverts the planning process by indulging in extensive illegal economic activity (more on this shortly). I could not here recite all the shortcomings of Soviet planning, but I think the general point is clear.

As practiced in the Soviet Union, planning is really a means of carrying out the music-school method of economic development. The Plan enables the authorities to enforce their priorities on the entire country, which is what they want and need. But it does not yet enable them to literally plan the beneficial evolution of the national economy.

Planned accomplishments are not always accomplished. The classic proof of this is Soviet agriculture. According to one of Mr. Khrushchev's ambitious plans, agricultural output during the 1960s was to grow by 250 percent; in fact it grew 35 percent in that decade.

To some extent the failures of Soviet agriculture can be explained by the low priority the government gave it for many years. Stalin concentrated on heavy industry and minimized investments in agriculture. Only in recent years has agriculture begun to receive a reasonable share of the country's investment capital. Mechanization of Soviet farms is still decades behind the most advanced western countries.* But inadequate investment alone cannot explain the low productivity, sloppiness and inefficiency of Soviet farming.

Cultural factors are significant. After Stalin's ruthless collectivization, the rural populations consisted of the poorest and least-successful peasants. (Any farmer who had prospered under the old system was branded a *kulak*, disowned and probably deported to Siberia, if he survived collectivization at all.) Rural folk had—and still have—a decidedly second-class status in Soviet society, deprived of internal passports and thus tied permanently to their villages.** Rural education has long been neglected, and is markedly inferior. As Andrei Amalrik discovered, Russian peasants are still a backward people.

The state and collective farms have never been properly organized. Fertilizer and seeds have never been efficiently distributed. Machinery is neglected, and much of it never works. The newspapers regularly print articles on foolish orders to farms from higher authorities and wild experiments which result in losses of production. For example, the chairman of a collective farm wrote in *Literary Gazette* about an official directive to farms growing sugar beets which had been in force since the 1930s. The directive instructs farms to harvest sugar beets before they are fully ripe because sugar refineries

---

* William Colby, director of the Central Intelligence Agency, told a congressional committee in 1974 that the Soviet Union has 1/20th as many trucks per 1000 farm workers as the United States.

** The authorities announced in 1974 that this system of indentured labor would be changed, but at this writing they have not explained how.

need raw materials to avoid working below capacity early in
the harvest season. The result, he said, was great losses of potential sources of sugar.

Agricultural "planning" works best when it can adopt the
overkill approach, which it does every fall. To bring in the
harvest, thousands of trucks normally used in big cities are
transported to the countryside. Millions of city workers and
students do temporary duty in the fields. Without this general
mobilization the Russians could not bring in their harvest—
although a third of their labor force still works on the farms
year-round.

That enormous farm labor force simply doesn't work very
hard, and the planners seem helpless to change its bad habits.
The collective farmers perceive—accurately—that their lives
won't change much if they work harder for the state. Work
for themselves, however, on their private plots, can be lu-
crative. So those tiny plots are exploited with impressive efficiency. They represent less than 5 percent of the cultivated
land in the USSR, but provide about 30 percent of the country's food.

Soviet planning has great blind spots—for example, distribution. The Plan concentrates on production. It provides
for railroads, an airline and some trucks, but delivery is
somehow shortchanged. What is most important is making
the product, not getting it to a customer. The maker is satisfied to see the goods leave his establishment; after that they
are someone else's problem. One newspaper reported on the
arrival of 60 11.5-ton trucks in a remote area of Kazakhstan.
A driver got into the first truck after it was lifted off the railroad car by a crane, but it wouldn't start. Nor would the second, third, fourth—or any of the 60 trucks. Vital parts had
been stolen from all of them during the journey from the
truck factory in Soviet Georgia. Vasily Pastukh, the official
who was supposed to accept delivery of these trucks, told a
journalist on the scene that spare parts for this model were
unavailable in Kazakhstan and he didn't know how they
would ever get the trucks working.

The episode of the 60 trucks points up a basic weakness in
the Soviet economy that planning cannot overcome. In the
USSR the different elements of the economy—factories,
stores, consumers like Mr. Pastukh—don't trust each other.
Distrust is pervasive. Citizens expect to be sold faulty or
shoddy goods; enterprises expect late deliveries, raw materials

different from those they ordered, last-minute instructions from above to alter their Plans. Ministries and the Planning Commission expect to be lied to. The distrust is hardly hidden. Journalists write about it and officials discuss it openly.

In a western economy implicit trust is crucial to efficient operations. A consumer makes an airplane reservation on the telephone and counts on it; a builder subcontracts the plumbing in a new apartment house with confidence that the job will be done; NASA orders a space capsule from a private firm and presumes it will be completed. Sometimes trust is misplaced; sometimes contracts—formal or understood—are broken. In such cases the legal system can be used to exact sanctions. But, in general, trust is rewarded, because few firms could survive with a reputation for unreliability.

The Russians have no comparable mechanism. A Russian wouldn't think of trusting Aeroflot to hold a reservation made by telephone—he would insist (rightly, in my experience) on holding a validated ticket before he set off on a trip. Enterprises cannot trust one another to make promised deliveries—hence the *tolkachi*, part of whose job it is to insure that formally promised deliveries are actually made. The Planning Commission routinely reduces the requests for labor and raw materials made by individual enterprises on the (correct) assumption that the enterprise has exaggerated its needs.

For the Soviet factory—or a Soviet research institute—the best response to unreliable business partners is self-sufficiency. When the planners decided to build the giant Fiat factory, they decided to make it almost entirely self-sufficient. Except for electrical equipment, window glass and tires, every part used in Zhiguli—every nut, bolt, seat cover and piston ring—is made in the factory itself. Gersh Budker's Institute of Nuclear Physics in Novosibirsk couldn't buy the instruments it needed, so the scientists there began to make their own. This kind of self-reliance is expensive and inefficient. Yet no amount of planning can provide the trust and reliability that could substitute for it.

The Plan makes little room for a consumer-service industry, a fact which helps define the Soviet standard of living. Less than 10 percent of the Soviet labor force works in consumer services. Hence, few restaurants, few repairmen, almost no leisure industry.

There might be more workers providing services if the productive sectors were more efficient—another problem that planning cannot resolve. Soviet workers don't work very hard.

Foreign travelers have remarked on the lackadaisical Russian approach to work for hundreds of years; it is another of the facts of Soviet life with ancient Russian antecedents. There are good sociological and historical reasons why Russian workers don't strain themselves. Russian society has never been infected by a puritan work ethic. Russia is a peasant country, a nation of slaves until a century ago. Russians never saw the point in breaking their backs. Except perhaps during the 20 years before World War I, great diligence has never earned great rewards; Russians have always gotten by.

An American who spoke Russian went to the Intourist office of a Leningrad hotel to ask for help with an airplane ticket. His problem was complicated, and the woman on duty had to make numerous phone calls to help him. In the midst of her calls a colleague appeared who didn't realize that this American spoke Russian. "Why are you helping this man?" the colleague asked. "Why should we bother to work today?"

For anyone who has suffered what my colleague Stanley Karnow has called "The Dictatorship of Intourist," that story is a poem. It is also a nice glimpse of the Russian worker's attitude. Everyone I met in the USSR who worked in industry agreed that the workers did just what they had to do and little more. Which means just what it says: if called upon to work heroically, Russians have demonstrated they can do that, too. But they would rather not.

Pride in workmanship is rarely encountered in the Soviet Union. I saw only one unmistakable case—the chief taster at a champagne factory in Soviet Georgia, a man who was proud of his palate. Sloppiness is endemic—in fact, it is the national standard, and I don't see how that can now be changed. The average Soviet worker wants to get the job done, little more. The parking lot in front of our apartment house was repaved by a work crew that couldn't be bothered to take up the old layer of asphalt. The new layer raised the level of the lot so high that the curbs which formerly channeled rain and melted snow became useless. The workers paved right over the manholes and drains. Another crew had to come later to dig up the asphalt around those openings. Andrei Amalrik reported his surprise at the careless attitude of the villagers in Siberia when they were installing wooden posts to carry a power line: "It amazed me that the blocks of wood which served as supports had not been treated to prevent them from rotting. I soon realized that this was the usual style of work on collective farms: who cared if the poles fell down in a couple of years as long as they stood up today!"

Official propaganda organs harp on work discipline so regularly that it must be an enormous national problem. In the spring of 1974 state bookstores received new stocks of propaganda posters exhorting workers not to steal "socialist property" from their places of employment. Other posters inveigh against drinking on the job, loafing and deliberate sloppiness. Of course, employers the world over complain about their workers; the Soviet state is not unique in this regard. But the testimony of western businessmen who have worked in Soviet enterprises suggests that the Russian worker really is less diligent than his western counterpart. The statistics on labor productivity confirm that this is so.

The Russian worker's attitude can be partly explained by his personal sense of security. Almost certainly he won't be fired, because almost no one ever is; but if by some miracle he lost this job, he could always get another. A skilled worker told me: "There is a popular saying among Soviet workers that is very revealing: 'What are they going to do, shoot us?' That's what they say when the paint is a little sloppy or something isn't just as it should be." So if the foreman or the Party Secretary or the man from the trade-union committee starts yelling—so what? Let them yell. This story appealed to me enormously; it gave Soviet workers a certain dignity.

Dignity is an imperfect substitute for material rewards, however, and on that count the Soviet worker has been consistently mistreated. According to calculations by western economists, the real income of Soviet workers reached *1928* levels only in the late 1950s. The situation has improved since, but Soviet workers still receive low wages and a disproportionately low share of the national income.

A good worker faces special difficulties in the USSR. *Pravda* explained them in an article about Georgi Ivanovich Sergeyev, a plumber from Kaluga. Georgi Ivanovich was a Hero of Socialist Labor, an inventor who had devised several new processes for the electrical-equipment factory in which he worked. But, said *Pravda*, "every passing day leaves Georgi Ivanovich less and less time for his work. Every organization thinks it is its duty to elect him to its leading organs, provisional and permanent commissions, and to invite him to meetings and conferences." He never had time to work. He'd spend two hours in the factory, then be off to some meeting—at the city trade-union committee, of which he was a secretary; at the regional peace committee; at the local electoral commission (in charge of voting in various elections); at the city's Party Committee, of which he was a member; at the city Soviet, to which he also belonged; or to make one of his many speeches; or to spend the day at the Palace of Weddings, congratulating newlyweds. He was able to do real work on only one day out of five, Georgi Ivanovich told *Pravda*'s reporter. The reporter concluded that this was a serious problem—"all the more so since this is not an isolated example."

One reason why Soviet planning is less than entirely successful deserves further elaboration—the fact that a huge unofficial economy thrives in the USSR beyond the reach of the planning mechanism.

There are no official statistics on this phenomenon, naturally, but the unofficial economy may amount to 20 percent or more of the official one. It consists of private repairmen, private manufacturers, doctors who practice "on the left," in the Russian phrase, and salespeople, public officials, professors and countless others who accept bribes of cash, vodka or other gifts to do special favors. I doubt there is a single Soviet citizen who doesn't conduct part of his life "on the left."

Large parts of the unofficial economy are taken for granted. For example, the government owns thousands of cars, used for official errands and as the personal cars of important officials. Each has a driver, who uses his car as an informal taxi whenever he can—between errands, for an hour at the end of his shift, etc. The standard rate for a ride in one of these cars in central Moscow is a ruble; the driver might ask for two or three rubles to go to one of the new regions on the outskirts of town. This money is clear profit for the driver, who never buys gasoline. It is supplied by the state.

Some drivers even sell the fuel from their tanks. One Muscovite who owned a car told me he never bought gas from a gasoline station. He had a regular deal with the driver of a government car, who siphoned gas into his tank once a week.

Trud, the newspaper of the Soviet trade unions, once described the unofficial economy in Odessa, famous for its entrepreneurs. "On the streets of Odessa," the paper revealed, "it is possible to buy a pair of pretty, handmade patent-leather shoes, although shoes of such quality and style are not made at the Odessa shoe factory. They are made by private shoemakers using raw materials stolen from the Odessa shoe factory." A private shop makes funeral wreaths in the city, *Trud* wrote, which would be legal if it were run by invalids, but "two healthy women" are in charge. To get a broken window repaired, the paper said, one has to visit Odessa's farmers' market, where handymen hire themselves out. There is supposed to be a state enterprise to do such jobs, the paper said, but "it doesn't fulfill its duties," so citizens pay three times its rates for private work. Not a single shoe repairman in the city wants to work for the state cobbler, *Trud* reported, "because there he has to work in a small, cold doghouse, whereas at home he can create good working conditions for himself and make a lot of money."

Odessa is an extreme example, so extreme that the First Secretary of the city's Party Committee was sentenced to death in the early 1970s for participating in corruption, according to a reliable informant in Moscow. (His case was never publicized.) Nevertheless, all the private enterprises *Trud* described exist in Moscow also, and probably in most big cities.

The authorities indulge a large part of this, particularly the private service industries. But when economic crime becomes official corruption they take a harsher view. During early 1975 two businessmen were sentenced to death for lining their pockets at the state's expense. One of them was a foreign-trade official who accepted bribes from a Swiss businessman, who himself was sentenced to 10 years in prison. Such harsh punishments, publicly announced, are extraordinary, and indicate that the authorities are deeply worried about economic crime.

This is not surprising. Economic crime is obviously pervasive. Russians don't really believe that "socialist" property belongs to anyone, so many don't feel it is criminal to take same for themselves. Clerks in shops assume it is a fringe benefit that goes with their jobs to be able to hide the best products and sell them to friends or customers willing to pay a little extra. A British scholar living in Armenia discovered that it was never worthwhile to look at the stock on display in a store; better to go right to a salesperson and ask, with a knowing wink, if they had whatever he was looking for.

The official newspapers report numerous cases of economic crime, most similar to an account in *Pravda* about a woman named L. Nigmatova, who managed the clothing department of a department store in Tashkent. Mrs. Nigmatova removed the price tags from garments and replaced them with tags of her own making, showing higher prices. When she sold one of these garments she pocketed the difference between the real and advertised prices.

What all this amounts to is the fact that Russians are human, too, which is surprising only if one takes seriously the propaganda about the "New Communist Man." Few Soviet citizens do. Selfishness and the acquisitive impulse are publicly condemned in the Soviet Union—and privately practiced with a typical human vengeance. The most telling indication of this that I found involved the country's big-time soccer-football players.

Successful athletes in the Soviet Union enjoy a comparatively high standard of living, but this is not usually discussed. ("The salaries of athletes," remember, is one of the censor's forbidden topics.) In two instances that I noticed, however, papers wrote frankly about how "amateur" football in the Soviet Union really works.

One article described the team at Bratsk, the new city in Siberia cut out of the forest beside a huge new hydroelectric dam. Bratsk's soccer team was of no national import. It played in a provincial league in farthest Siberia. Good players had no natural inclination to play there, so they had to be bribed. According to a story in *Trud*, two players, Terekhov and Dyomkin, were registered as highly qualified plumbers in a Bratsk factory and received good plumber's wages, though the only place they ever worked was on the football field. One of the coaches was paid as a senior engineer in an enterprise he never visited. Ten players were given apartments ahead of a waiting line of ordinary citizens.

In Odessa, according to *Komsomolskaya Pravda*, the system was similar but grander. Odessa's team was in the country's principal league until it was dropped to the second division for poor play. One factory in Odessa gave the players "50,000 rubles for nothing," apparently to be shared among the team. Star players received big cash payments, cars and apartments.

The authorities feign—perhaps truly feel—horror and indignation when confronted by corruption. I found the corruption reassuring, in the way conscientiously lazy Soviet workers are reassuring. In any case, corruption can only harm the Plan, which leaves no room for payments under tables and the like. The state is constantly losing resources—workers' time, raw materials, finished goods, cold cash—to the unofficial economy, but the losses cannot be rationally calculated or accounted for.

One aspect of the Soviet economy is difficult for an outsider, particularly a layman untrained in statistical economics, to grasp. Yet it is more important, I think, than laymen or politicians have recognized. I have in mind the statistical comparisons routinely made between the Soviet Union and the United States—which show, for example, that in 1974 the Soviet Gross National Product was about half of America's, or equal to American GNP in 1964.

This is an economists' statistic, derived after much complicated computation. American experts try to measure true (as opposed to reported) Soviet output; they try to give it true (as opposed to arbitrary) value and then to express it in terms of our dollars. They are proud of their ability to make these calculations, perhaps justly. I cannot fairly judge them. But I can fairly observe that the impression these figures create is wildly misleading.

Anyone who traveled in the Soviet Union of the early 1970s and who knew America in 1964 knows beyond the glimmer of a doubt that the economies of those two countries were not equal or comparable at those two times. The gross value of Soviet output must still be far, far behind what the United States had achieved in 1964.

This doesn't mean the economists' figures are all wrong. I don't know if they are wrong or right. The problem is that economists must work in *statistics*, and statistics never describe the fullness of reality. The statistics about me—height, weight, age, Social Security number—may be accurate and complete, but I hope no one ever takes them for the real me. Similarly, the statistics about the Soviet economy assembled by western experts may be correct, but that doesn't make them *revealing*.

For example, according to official statistics, in the early 1970s the Soviet Union surpassed the United States in steel production. A statistical fact, but a misleading one. In the United States plastics and other synthetic products are now widely used in place of steel—in plumbing, for example. Moreover, American industries make use of 95 percent of the metals they purchase as raw materials; only 5 percent is wasted or lost. In the Soviet Union the comparable figure is 75 percent—one fourth is wasted. The average Soviet machine is about one-third heavier than its American counterpart. To make it takes one-third more metal. To compound the problem, the Soviet machine would also require more energy to run, because of its weight, thus detracting something from the significance of comparative statistics on energy consumption.

Perhaps more serious, comparative statistics cannot satisfactorily weigh differences in quality. The statistician may try to make adjustments in his valuations of products because of known variations in quality, but these can only be guesses. For example, how could a statistician cope with the Soviet building industry? Construction is one of the biggest single items in the Soviet budget. The Russians are constantly building apartment houses, hotels, schools, factories, etc. With the exception of showpiece structures which get extraordinary attention, buildings put up in the Soviet Union today do not meet the standards of quality taken for granted in most other parts of the world. The ceiling in the living room of my apartment was four or five inches higher at one side of the room than at the other. The tiles on almost every bathroom wall I saw in Russia were coming loose. Soviet elevators are primitive, unreliable contraptions. Quite rightly, in their own terms, the Russians put high ruble values on these buildings. But if offered for sale in Paris, Rio or Chicago, a typical Soviet apartment house would fetch a small fraction of the price of a comparable (in size) local building. By western standards a Soviet apartment house is junk.*

---

* Khrushchev observed: "I don't think there's any secret about why everything is always so neat in the West: it's a matter of good production discipline, strict standards, and well-designed processes, especially when it comes to manufacturing and laying concrete. It's just a higher level of culture in the West."

To describe Soviet GNP as a percentage of America's or Japan's is to suggest that the Soviet economy produces products comparable to America's and Japan's, which it does not—with a few notable exceptions. The Soviet Union is still a developing country. It lacks many of the most basic elements of an advanced economy—a good network of roads, for example, and a relatively efficient nationwide telephone system. It has no consumer-service industry to speak of; almost no high-quality consumer goods; persistent shortages of basic foods like meat, fruits and vegetables; and a chronic housing shortage which leaves perhaps a fourth of the population without a self-contained apartment or cottage.

The Russians themselves cannot accurately measure their economy, even by their own standards. There are two basic difficulties: some Soviet statistics are simply dishonest, and the honest ones are based on arbitrary, not real, values.

Khrushchev provides the best testimony about dishonest statistics:

> I remember how Stalin used to treat Comrade Saveliev, who was head of the committee which determined average yield [of Soviet farmland]. If Stalin was unhappy with Comrade Saveliev's report, he'd glower at him like a boa constrictor about to devour a rabbit. Stalin would pat himself on the belly and say, "The rich, black soil of the Ukraine comes up to here; are you trying to tell me you can't get a better yield than such-and-such? You're going too soft on the collective farms! I'm sure the average yield must be at least half again what you say."
>
> In other words, Stalin arbitrarily dictated the average yield. Nowadays it isn't that bad, but I still don't trust our bureau of statistics. I think there remains a tendency among our statisticians to conceal setbacks and tell the leadership what it wants to hear. I know some of the statistical experts. They're the sort who can melt shit into bullets.* They're clever at hiding the truth. Sometimes they bury the truth so deep in a report that you can't possibly dig it out.

---

* This is a variation of the Russian colloquialism "to make shit into candy," meaning to tell lies [footnote from *Khrushchev Remembers*].

At another point Khrushchev observed that "our statisticians sometimes deliberately distort reality; the rosy figures they publish in the newspapers can't be sold in the stores and made into soup." The Russians tell a joke in a similar spirit. A citizen complains that, according to the radio, the country is producing abundant supplies of fruit, meat and vegetables, but when he looks into his new refrigerator it is empty. What should he do? Plug the refrigerator into the radio, he is advised.

Misreporting statistics is endemic to the Soviet system, and western economists know it. When measuring the Soviet grain harvest, American intelligence analysts discount the official figure by as much as 25 percent, though they admit this is only a guess. But in other fields, particularly industrial production, they usually have no basis for making such discounts, so they tend to accept the figures available. Fair enough, if one must have figures, but obviously the conclusions reached using those figures should be qualified appropriately.

More serious than deliberate deception is the relative meaninglessness of all Soviet economic figures. This is a complicated notion to explain; it is based on the fact that there is no free market in the USSR, so prices of all products must be set arbitrarily.

In a relatively free market there is a correlation between the price of a loaf of bread, the price of a car and the price of a ton of steel. The prices reflect the supply of and demand for those items, and the cost of the materials that go into them. Economists call this "scarcity pricing"; things are priced in terms of how scarce or abundant they are, and how much consumers are willing to pay for them. Competition tends to make prices roughly consistent. This is an oversimplified explanation, since there are many un-free elements in our "free market" economies, and many distortions in the market mechanism. But things have, roughly, a real value which reflects the forces at work in the marketplace.

In the Soviet economy there is no comparable mechanism. Prices are simply fixed by the central authorities in Moscow. For example, the Fiat factory in Togliattigrad began producing a new model in 1973. It had a slightly bigger engine than the old model, more chrome trim and a plusher interior. The original model was priced at 5500 rubles; the new one at 7500. Anatoli Zhitkov, technical director of the factory, told a group of American journalists who visited Togliattigrad in June 1973 that the factory was upset about this price, which was substantially higher than the value of the improvements actually made in the new model. "But we don't control the price," he said.

The prices of food products are heavily subsidized. The total cost of growing food in the Soviet Union is greater than the revenue raised by its sale—the government is losing money on every loaf of bread and quart of milk consumed. Nevertheless, food takes about half of the average family's budget, so the authorities don't want to raise the prices too much. For political reasons, food remains cheap, though the prices creep up every year.

The government maintains strict control over retail prices, but not over the prices of industrial products. A factory which makes a new machine tool, for example, charges another enterprise a price based on the alleged cost of the resources in the tool plus a fixed percentage of profit. But the director of the machine-tool factory cannot accurately calculate his own costs. For example, the value of the factory building and the land it stands on is ignored by a Soviet enterprise. The director of a champagne factory in Georgia told me his per-bottle price included nothing for real estate and buildings, because they were given to him by the state. Moreover, only the factory director knows how much labor really went into the new machine tool, and he can easily exaggerate the figure to increase its price and thus his income.

The relationships between the prices of various items are irrational. The price of a small house on the outskirts of Moscow—a summer *dacha* with plumbing, insulation, heat and electricity—might be 20,000 to 30,000 rubles. The price of a Volga to drive to and from the *dacha* is half as much, about 12,000 rubles. A paperback children's book costs the equivalent of two small packets of tissue paper.

The important point here is that the prices of things are not necessarily related in any way to the cost of producing them. I visited a fish cannery in Estonia shortly after officials in Moscow had decided to raise the retail prices of its products. I asked if its costs had gone up. On the contrary, they were declining, to the extent that they could be measured. Planners set prices to balance their accounts, or to tax the public indirectly, or perhaps to help an unsuccessful enterprise look more successful.

Yet prices are the basis of all the statistics on the value of industrial production published by the Soviet Union. Soviet national income—the statistic the Russians compile that is closest to our GNP—is calculated in terms of these arbitrary prices. Western experts must start with these figures when they try to compute the *real* Soviet GNP. They tinker with them, adjust them, push them up and down, but I fear that the original flaw cannot be completely disguised. The experts probably can produce consistent figures, so we know quite accurately the comparison between the Soviet economy this year and last year. But beyond that their conclusions must be subject to numerous qualifications.

The CIA allowed a rare glimpse of its assessments of the Soviet economy before a congressional committee in 1974. Senator William Proxmire, chairman of the committee, asked Mr. Douglas Diamond of the CIA's economic research staff whether Soviet prices indicated the true relative costs of different products in the Soviet economy. "We are not confident" that they do, Diamond replied. *"We have to assume* that the relative prices . . . do reflect relative scarcities of resources [emphasis added]." Why does he "have to assume"? Because as an economist he wants to come up with hard statistics. But the assumption may not be justified, as I hope I have shown.

There is one important exception to many of the generalizations in this chapter: the Soviet military economy. It appears to be the one sector which produces excellent products, fully competitive with the military hardware made in the industrial West. Its accomplishments seem to contradict what I have written about Soviet technology.

The easiest way out of this apparent dilemma is to conclude that the Soviet Union maintains a vast, secret military economy, manned by the best scientists and workers, equipped with the best technology produced at home or bought abroad, which manufactures superb weapons while the civilian economy flounders along all around it. For a long time I could come up with no other explanation, and I offered this one to the readers of the *Washington Post* more than once during my first year or two in the USSR. But it is wrong.

The military economy is not apart from the rest; it is the cream on top of the rest. Its accomplishments are the ultimate tribute to the music-school approach to the allocation of resources. The military economy gets the most resources and makes the best products.

To a great extent, military equipment is made by the same factories that produce goods for the civilian economy, and yet the military equipment is usually much better. The difference is quality control. When a factory is filling a military order, an officer is on the premises. If it's a big order, there may be a number of officers. They are empowered to reject any item if they think it is substandard, and the factory must either make it right or produce another one. I learned about this from an engineer with extensive experience in military industry. He had once been in a transistor factory, he told me, which was trying to fill a military order. The Army's inspector would accept only 2 or 3 of every 100 transistors the factory was making.

The man who worked in the factory that makes electrical equipment for ships, described earlier, told me what happened when his enterprise had a contract from the Soviet Navy:

"The Navy people don't mess around. An ordinary customer is different. You can tell him, 'Take it easy, we'll have it ready for you tomorrow,' things like that. But the Navy man won't listen to that kind of talk. When he comes, everybody bows down to him and listens to him as though he were a god. What he says goes.

"I remember a case where the factory had made something according to specifications the Navy had provided, and the Navy man was there to check it out. He looked it over and found that a certain transistor was marked 'V' when it should have been 'B.' We told him V was much better quality than B, that he shouldn't worry about it, but he shook his head and said no go—no exceptions to the specifications. . . .

"Curiously, the standards for ordinary production and the standards for military production are identical—what changes is how strictly they're adhered to. In our factory it would have been simply impossible to maintain the high level of quality control on all our production that we achieved on military orders. In fact, 50 percent of our ordinary [civilian] production left the factory unchecked. It was technically impossible to check it. . . .

"I imagine that in the US a truck produced for the private market and a truck produced for the Army are essentially the same, and the same amount of work goes into both. A fuse for a military rocket probably comes off the same production line as a fuse for a television set. But in the Soviet Union it's different. . . .

"The stuff we made for the military was much better than the ordinary production simply because we checked every single part, every detail as it was put together. Of course it took much longer to make it that way—twice as long, maybe three times, because we checked it all out so carefully. . . ."

This is not the entire explanation. Civilian plants produce a significant portion of the USSR's military hardware, but most of it is made in the huge and secret military economy which is run by Dmitri Ustinov, a candidate member of the Politburo and Secretary of the Central Committee. Hundreds of thousands of people work under Ustinov's direction, including the Minister and staff of the euphemistically named Ministry of Medium Machine Building, which is actually responsible for a large part of the arms industry.

The system of production, however, is apparently the same in the secret military plants as in the civilian factories which do military work. "The workers aren't any different, probably, than ordinary workers," according to an engineer I met who was familiar with military industry. "But their production is subjected to extremely careful controls. I think there must be more controllers in a military factory than there are workers. They throw out the crap, or give it to the civilian economy. For example, a lot of watch factories were built for military purposes, to provide mechanisms for mines and bombs.* The military factories may produce 98 percent junk, it doesn't matter. They can afford it."

In other words, the Russians have not found any secret formula for making high-quality military equipment. They make it the way they make everything else, and ruthlessly reject all but the very best production. In effect, the civilian economy subsidizes military production by devoting an extraordinary portion of its energy and resources to military needs.

Workers in military plants do receive extra pay, according to the engineer just quoted. In one military factory he visited,

---

* According to American specialists, virtually the entire photographic industry is also in the military sector, and military factories make most of the Soviet Union's modest output of vacuum cleaners.

he said, "spirits played a big role. They gave the workers as much to drink as they wanted—not vodka, but industrial spirits. And they fed them well, three times a day. The workers could save their money because there was nothing to spend it on."

That sort of fringe benefit goes with secret work in remote places. Many military factories which produce sensitive products are far removed from open towns and cities, some in large communities that don't appear on any map and are known only by a number—Semipalatinsk 4, or Post Office Box 4004, or Chelyabinsk 40. I heard of those three from two men who had worked in such establishments, one of them as an actor in the 1950s.

His closed city had a population of tens of thousands, the actor guessed. It was located in the Gorki *oblast* northeast of Moscow, and it provided well for its citizens—a well-stocked bookstore, beer to drink when that was almost unheard of, and a theater in which he acted.

It was a strange life, he said. You never saw the fence that surrounded the entire community unless you went cross-country skiing in the woods and happened on it. But you still felt the isolation, he said. It was an atomic city, and "there were always explosions, very feelable explosions. They were testing weapons. The houses shook. The explosions were far away, apparently, but you could feel them. Once there were rumors that the entire city would be searched. There was a big factory in the city that made those things, and, according to the rumors, a bomb had been stolen from the factory."

With the help of satellites, presumably, the Americans know where these secret communities are, and how many of them exist. Brigadier General Stafford discovered one when he was taken to the Russians' space center in Central Asia. To his surprise, he saw a city of 30,000 named Leninsk, a city not mentioned on any map of the Soviet Union. Apparently it is home for the people who launch the USSR's rockets.

Judging by the descriptions I heard, these secret arms-producing centers operate on the overkill principle, with highly paid workers, well-supplied stores and the best of everything in the arms factories themselves. Military enterprises apparently have first call on any resource in the country. One engineer told me about a civilian factory which lost its entire inventory of high-grade sheet metal because a military enterprise needed it.

In at least two ways the military economy differs qualitatively from the civilian one. First, competition plays a role in the development of new weapons. When the leadership decides it needs a new type of weapon, two or three design groups may be assigned to develop a prototype. The participants all know, one engineer told me, that they are in competition, though they don't know who the competitors are, or what the others are doing. They know, too, that it will be materially worthwhile to produce the winning design.

I heard about this system from two sources independently. Both were well-informed engineers; one had worked in military industry. Their description is supported by circumstantial evidence. Western intelligence agencies have often identified two or three models of a new Soviet weapon in testing, most recently the latest generation of intercontinental ballistic missiles, of which four new versions were tested in the early 1970s. According to Vladimirov's account of the early years of Soviet rocketry, two groups were in competition then. If indeed this is the way the Russians operate, they are relying on an ideologically alien concept in the most important sector of their economy.

The second special feature of the Soviet military economy is the relationship between producer and customer. The civilian economy could be described as a sellers' market: the producers make what the planners request, and the customers must take what they get. The military economy is a buyers' market: consumer demand is not just influential, it is dictatorial.

The descriptions above of the factory producing electrical equipment for ships indicate the importance of this distinction. When the factory was making equipment for the civilian market, the customer was an anonymous enterprise, far removed from daily concerns, and the principal object was to fulfill the monthly Plan. When the customer was the Soviet Navy, the Plan was irrelevant. The man from the Navy stood in the factory to insist on the precise product he needed, and the factory's managers did everything they could to satisfy him.

Because the needs of the military are specific and limited, enterprises can focus their energies and resources to meet them. The CIA believes that the Russians can exploit new technology more effectively in the military sector than in the civilian economy, and this is a plausible theory. For example, there is no easy way to introduce computers into an enormous civilian economy—it is much easier to use them to help design and guide ballistic missiles. For this purpose, a small number of custom-built computer systems would suffice. More generally, if the entire Soviet labor force cannot yet learn to work with sophisticated machinery and to make high-quality goods, a relatively small work force with a specific and important mission surely could learn to do both. And only a small work force would be needed to make the most highly sophisticated Soviet weapons. (As a general proposition, Soviet weaponry is simpler and more functional than America's.)

The CIA calculates that Soviet and American military expenditures are about equal. In this computation they recognize the irrelevance of Soviet statistics; the agency's analysts calculate how much it would cost the United States, at current American prices, to acquire the weapons and manpower of the USSR. So the conclusion of rough equality means it would cost the United States about the same amount to acquire its own military force or a copy of the Russians'.

That seems to be a sensible way to try to compare the two countries' military spending, but it does not tell us how much the Russians must spend in their own terms to acquire their weapons. I don't think they know themselves. For instance, how could they calculate the cost of the military production in that factory making electrical apparatus for ships? To meet military requirements, that enterprise exploits its civilian customers, minimizing or even ignoring their needs to satisfy the Navy. In effect, the Navy gets much more than it pays for, and that is probably a typical pattern in every factory that takes on military contracts.

The country's leaders obviously *want* the military to get more than it pays for. They run a system which is based on a hierarchy of priorities, and military power is the priority that dominates all others. It is no mean accomplishment for the Soviet economy—weak and inefficient in so many ways—to produce a military force roughly equal to America's.

The Soviet economy has grown modestly but steadily through the first half of the 1970s—it has not suffered a recession, so its graphs look better than those of the major western economies, except West Germany's. But the boom days are past; the growth is now 2, 3 or 4 percent a year, far less than it was in the 1950s and 1960s. The economy is sluggish, and the indicators suggest more trouble in the future. According to the Russians' own statistics, additional increments of labor, capital and resources are less productive than they used to be.

The country could not meet the targets of the 1971–5 Five Year Plan; they were steadily revised downward, largely because projected improvements in productivity never materialized. For years the Russians counted on a steadily growing labor force, but the birthrate is falling in European Russia and the agricultural economy cannot sustain further losses of rural labor to the cities and towns. The Soviet Union's natural wealth is still vast—the only natural resource it need import is tin—but this wealth can last only if ways are found to exploit Siberia's harsh northern reaches. For now, the Russians admit, they cannot persuade enough people to work in Siberia; transport is bad; costs are two to three times higher than in European Russia. Exploitation of Siberia's oil and gas resources will require a level of technology that the Russians don't yet possess.

The Russians have been able to modernize their economy continually, if slowly. They do so by imposing new technology—for example, by buying the Fiat factory, which is filled with machine tools from every advanced western country. They do so with the enthusiasm of their best government officials and industrial managers, who can overcome the inertia of the system in specific instances and introduce new machinery or techniques. I don't think the system is stagnant, but it does resist any change, usually successfully.

In the last few years this generation of Soviet leaders has reverted to an ancient Russian tactic to compensate for its weaknesses: it has turned to the West. Peter the Great first tried this nearly 300 years ago. Russian autocrats have followed his example sporadically ever since. The idea has always been the same—to preserve the existing autocracy with the help of foreign techniques, machinery and capital. But never foreign ideas, not if they could be avoided. Russian autocrats have never been comfortable with foreign ideas.

Trade with the West will help the Russians in the 1970s, but not as much as they probably hope. Trade cannot overcome the weaknesses of the Soviet economic system. Foreign products and technology may fill some of the gaps left by uneven development at home; they may enable the Russians to produce consumer goods that would otherwise be unavailable; but they cannot give the Soviet Union an efficient, productive and competitive economy.

This assessment suggests that it may be time for fundamental reforms, but the status quo has deep roots and a great many supporters. There was an attempt at significant reform in 1965, when the planners tried to introduce profitability as an index of each enterprise's success, decentralize management decisions and generally put the economy on a more rational footing. As a practical matter, the reform had almost no effect. By the early 1970s one could find little trace of it, though the economic bureaucracy had grown by half a million people. Roy Medvedev, one of those who hoped the reform would have sweeping consequences, complained that it had no effect on many officials. "Relapses into administrative methods and 'subjectivism' have been all too evident in the behavior of many factory managers, as well as ministers and highly placed Party officials," Medvedev has written. In 1973 *Pravda* reported on a poll of factory managers, 80 percent of whom said higher authorities were dictating compulsory indices for their enterprises in violation of the 1965 reform.

The 1965 reform failed for lack of will—the people who could have made it work did not want to. New ways of doing things mean uncertainty, disruption. Decentralized decision-making means the factory director has to take responsibility for his decisions, something he can often avoid now. Decentralization means loss of authority for hundreds of thousands of bureaucrats—a breed reluctant to give up its power in any society, not least the Soviet Union.

How do huge, complex societies reform themselves? It's clear that the mere need for reform does not guarantee it. Britain has needed reform desperately since the 1950s, but both of Britain's principal political parties have failed to institute reforms. Instead the British have become steadily weaker and poorer compared to other western societies. Reform of a bureaucratic society such as the Soviet Union's challenges the patterns of work, career advancement and remuneration which participants have long taken for granted. So they would be tempted by reform only if they felt that the existing system exploited them unfairly. But in the Soviet Union the managerial class has grown increasingly comfortable and pleased with itself. That class may see the need for change, but it doesn't *feel* the need.

The contemporary Soviet system is Stalin's system. It has been relaxed since Stalin died, but not reformed. Changes have occurred willy-nilly, in response to new forces in society and the outside world, and because Stalin's successors could not or would not rule with his iron hand.

Stalin reformed Soviet society, but only at the cost of millions of dead and years of deprivation. Mao Tse-tung reformed China by revolutionizing it. These aren't useful models for societies trying to institute structural reforms without great disruptions. Smaller countries have had more success with moderate but significant reforms—Yugoslavia and Hungary, for example. But political power is more efficiently exercised in small societies; the Soviet Union is huge and complex. Reform there would require great political will and an effective use of power. The Party would have to demonstrate unprecedented unanimity and determination. As it stands, the Party lacks confidence. It lacks a strong and popular leader.

Today's leaders seem incapable of innovating. Or perhaps they don't want to innovate, despite periodic talk of reform. The present system assures their personal comfort and the essential power of the state, particularly its military power. It provides steady if undramatic economic progress. Perhaps that is enough.

The Soviet leaders may feel that fundamental economic reform would have unwelcome political consequences. The heart of any reform would have to be decentralization—Soviet, Eastern European and foreign economists all seem to agree on that much. In his memoirs Khrushchev predicted that decentralization was inevitable: "Life itself will force us to tear down the bureaucratic obstacles which are impeding our economy." But that same bureaucratic structure enables the Party to maintain control over the country. It would be difficult, probably impossible, to separate decentralization of economic power from decentralization of political power; in Soviet society the two are intertwined. Economic power is a vital lever which helps the Party maintain its "leading role." Decentralization could therefore create competing centers of power, and eventually political diversity. It could stimulate local nationalism in the non-Russian republics. I met many Russians who despaired of significant reform on this basis alone.

Even if the necessary leadership and determination existed, one must wonder where reform could begin. There is no simple way to make irrational prices rational, misleading statistics accurate or inefficient workers efficient. Clumsy as their system is, the Russians are used to it. Most of them have lived with it all their lives. From afar one can speculate rather easily on possible techniques of reform, but living among them I came to doubt that the Russians could be convinced to try something fundamentally different. In the Soviet Union it was a major event when one factory tried experimentally to lay off workers it no longer needed; the experiment failed. The national impulse to conservatism, the elaborate bureaucratic underpinning of the status quo, the overbearing force of habit all work against change.

Which doesn't mean it won't happen. Russia, to repeat Peter the Great's phrase, is a country in which things that just don't happen happen. Stalin's transformation of Russian life was a fantastic event, unforeseeable before it occurred, beyond the imagination, probably, of every Soviet citizen but one. The Party may again produce a man of such strength and vision—and ruthlessness. A new generation of leaders, less insecure than these, more confident of their own technical abilities, might chance a reform without reverting to Stalin's methods.

But if Soviet society changes to the extent that meaningful reform becomes possible, that change will have to be visible to the outside world. It will involve so many Soviet personalities and institutions that no amount of discretion will hide it from outsiders. Reform cannot be secret, or it is not reform. Which means that the outside world will have ample warning of any change in the Soviet Union which could make it a more formidable economic force. Meanwhile it seems reasonable to assume that the Russians will continue to manage their economy as they have—by exploiting inefficient components to meet limited, specific priorities.

10 · The Intelligentsia: A Happy, Unhappy Few

"I KNEW ONE very old man who spent his entire professional life lecturing on electrical engineering in an institute and all the time ran a seminar at his home on 'Plato, Hegel, Christianity and Our Life.' And it wasn't just idle chatter—after his death it was discovered that the archives of the seminar amounted to something like 30,000 typewritten sheets. Another of the 'leading metaphysicians' in the USSR is a teacher of Marxist philosophy in one of the industrial institutes. He gives his umpteenth lecture on, say, 'The Primacy of Matter,' and then goes off to his *dacha* and discusses with his scientist friend the illusory nature of the material world and the reality of conscious being. . . ."

These are the recollections of Alexander Pyatigorski, an Orientalist who emigrated from the Soviet Union in 1974. I use them here to change the mood after all that economics, and because they make a nice introduction to the topic I like best in this book, the Soviet intelligentsia.

I can imagine those men Pyatigorski described: smallish men with salt-and-pepper hair that sweeps back from their high Slavic foreheads, wearing crumpled, shapeless suits of dark gray wool, their shoulders probably sprinkled with dandruff. One might wear eyeglasses, but crooked ones which don't fit over his ears. Both carry cracked and torn leather satchels filled with books, notes, ballpoint pens that don't work and an accumulation of newspapers and magazines. Seen on the street, or performing their official jobs, both men probably lack distinguishing facial expressions—just two more heads in the great Russian crowd. When they are at home, drinking tea around a small table and discussing the world's problems with friends, their faces come alive and shine with the intensity of personal ideas strongly felt.

The Russian intellectual—surely one of the great human types of our world. The Russians call him a member of the intelligentsia, and a gifted group it has long been. From Pushkin, Turgenev and Gogol to Dostoevski and Tolstoi, to Pasternak and Solzhenitsyn, the Russian intelligentsia has produced men of words and ideas that have swept through the civilized world as have few others. Russians have brought glory to music, ballet and, at one time, painting and architecture. They have established themselves as one of the great creative nationalities of the modern epoch.

Their lives have never been easy, which may help explain their brilliant accomplishments. (It is like a sieve, Yehudi Menuhin, the violinist, once said: the Russian autocracy presses down upon the intellectuals, but occasionally a talent of great brilliance shoots out of the sieve, forced out by the pressure.) In our day Russian intellectuals often lead double lives, like the men Pyatigorski described. The true intellectuals must coexist with a pseudo-intelligentsia which enjoys the advantages of Party patronage. The rich Russian intellectual tradition still survives, but it competes with a corrupt new tradition of no redeeming value. Those who maintain the old tradition in this uncongenial new era must be as appealing a group of people as could be found anywhere. The worst of the pseudo-intellectuals could not be much worse.

There is no sure way to distinguish the best from the worst. Both can be found working in the same publishing house, or teaching the same subject at the same university. Those who uphold the old traditions belong to a silent alliance whose objective is to frustrate the cultural bureaucrats enshrined by the Party. Their values and convictions are not taught in any school or university; instead they come from self-education, from reading and rereading the great Russian classics and many foreign writers. Most of the members of this brotherhood live in Moscow, Leningrad and a few other large cities. They are far removed from the Soviet masses, and they know it.

Their most attractive quality is the ability to lead private lives of the mind, lives whose rewards are primarily spiritual. Jobs and careers are often irrelevant, as they were for the men Pyatigorski described. They think of a good friend as the most valuable personal possession. A good conversation is one of life's richest opportunities. In a truly private world, pretense is superfluous, as it is among the best of these people. They can speak openly, frankly, with a new acquaintance in a matter of minutes.

In my experience it takes only one boring evening in London or Washington, one long dinner dominated by talk of shopping or restaurants or tennis and skiing, to realize why Moscow's intellectuals are so appealing. Deprived of the diversions of the western middle class, these Russians concentrate on ideas, books, intense political discussion. Not exclusively—they, too, can talk about buying a new suit or finding a refrigerator. But mundane or silly talk never seems to last very long. Someone always has a more important subject that *needs* to be discussed.

Life is difficult for these people because the men who rule the Soviet Union instinctively distrust them. The rulers are, with few exceptions, anti-intellectuals, hard-nosed Party bureaucrats and engineers from working-class families who may be embarrassed by their own modest intellectual attainments, and who are surely frightened by the values that the Russian intellectual tradition has preserved.

Yuri Andropov is one of the most intelligent of today's leaders, but he has no sympathy for intellectuals. Andropov is the chairman of the KGB and a member of the Politburo. It is said that he likes to remind his colleagues about events in Hungary in 1956, events he saw at first hand as the Soviet ambassador to Budapest. He organized the Soviet response to the uprising of 1956. "Who led the Hungarian revolt?" Andropov is said to ask rhetorically. "The intelligentsia, the writers, that's who." Such a dangerous element must be closely watched. Andropov's KGB watches it.

Today's leaders have kept intact the vast control apparatus which Stalin built—the huge national unions of writers, artists, composers, actors, film-makers and journalists. They have relaxed the utter rigidity of Stalin's "socialist realism,"

and abandoned the terror he used to insure absolute orthodoxy, but they continue to rule through the administrative
monster that Stalin constructed. It suits their needs and their
temperament.

They have nurtured the pseudo-intellectuals and encouraged them to dominate the • others. This encouragement
sustains the band of corrupt hacks who exploit fraudulent intellectual credentials to make careers for themselves in the cultural bureaucracy. They bend with the Party line, report on
their less loyal colleagues, write and perform and think precisely what is expected of them, and get along very nicely,
thank you.

The authorities try to manage the country's intellectual life
with a combination of sticks and carrots. The sticks are official restrictions and controls; the carrots are the privileges
and benefits which go to those who cooperate.

The most basic stick is the bureaucracy that Stalin created.
I have already described the Academy of Sciences, which—
with the Ministry of Higher Education and several lesser
bodies—dominates the country's academic life. The cultural
bureaucracy is comparable.

The creative unions are virtually omnipotent in their fields.
Writers or artists who are not members of their union usually
cannot publish books or participate in sanctioned exhibitions.
Expulsion from the union—a punishment invoked periodically—amounts to the termination of a professional career.

The officers of the unions are often hacks or worse. A
secretary of the Moscow branch of the Union of Writers is a
former KGB general—a fact known to every writer in the
capital. Those with talent usually aren't interested in doing
administrative work in the unions, so those jobs are left to the
mediocre people who will take them, or to ambitious people
who want them. In either case they are willing, even eager to
do the bidding of higher political authorities, who exercise
their control through the union bureaucracies.

The administrators support what might be called official
culture—the literature, movies, music and art most appreciated in the cultural department of the Central Committee, the
final aribter in these as in all fields. Official culture is nicely
described in this blurb for a novel published by a Soviet magazine:

In Issue No. 15 of the
"Novel Newspaper"

Read

"You Can't Look for Happiness Alone"
by Andrei Blinov

The life of the working class has become a leading theme
in the work of Andrei Blinov. His new novel, "You Can't
Look for Happiness Alone," is dedicated to members of
the oldest and most needed profession on earth—builders. The fate of a civil engineer, Fyodor Kidin, is at the
center of the book's action. Fyodor is distinguished by a
profound devotion to his work and an ability to work
with an eye on the future. Supported by his comrades, he
overcomes the resistance of those mired in routine. Fyodor Kidin finds happiness in the general struggle; he also
finds the inner personal happiness which he has missed so
much in his life.

One of the heroes of the book is the secretary of the
oblast Party Committee, Baskalov, a professor of
chemistry who came into Party work from the world of
science. With warmth and understanding the novel
describes its characters—Kuzma Shegolkov, an old
bricklayer; his daughters, Masha and Rita; Maya Zolotkova, a [female] plasterer; the engineer Zamchevsky
and other workers who comprise a militant collective capable of great achievements.

A far cry from Tolstoi, but this is the level of nearly all
contemporary literature in the USSR. It is churned out by
hundreds of writers like Blinov, the Soviet equivalent of
writers for the English-speaking world's true-romance magazines. Movies are similar—simple-minded adventure stories,
tales of wartime heroics, epics of construction brigades and
oil refineries.

The dominant styles in painting and sculpture are comparable. The annual spring show of the Moscow branch of the
Union of Artists in 1973 was a typical display: lifeless realistic panoramas, clumsy portraits, numerous blatantly amateurish canvases, only rarely relieved by a picture or sculpture
produced by someone with palpable talent. In music the offi-

cial taste is for classical forms, so most of what is composed today sounds a great deal like music from the past. One of the best-known contemporary composers, Rodion Shchedrin, has made a name—and a fortune—for himself with a series of pieces openly derived from great classics. In sum, it would be impossible to exaggerate the banality and artistic insignificance of most contemporary culture in the Soviet Union.

The same could be said of any western society, I think, but there is one crucial distinction: in the West, banality is a response to popular taste, inspired by greed; in the Soviet Union, it is the result of *official* preference. Any French or British writer who wants to rise above the popular taste is free to try to do so. The public's taste may determine which writers get rich, but it cannot dictate which get published. In the Soviet Union, defiance of the norms is much more difficult, because the norms are set by the people who run the country.

In the giant unions, bureaucratic values prevail over artistic ones. I happened on a copy of a confidential publication of the Union of Writers, a report on the union's activities which the document referred to as its "organizational-creative work." Labeled "For internal use only," it recounts the activities of the Moscow branch of the union from 1971 to 1973. During those three years, members of the Moscow Union gave 50,692 speeches to various groups in the capital. The union itself held hundreds of meetings, discussions, memorial celebrations and the like, each of them recorded in this 82-page booklet. For example, the "Creative Collective of Poets" met jointly with the "Commission on Military-Artistic Literature" to discuss the subject "The Battle for Moscow in Poetry." The meeting provided an opportunity for "appropriate preparations for participation in the plenum of the Moscow writers' organization. . . ."

The dictatorship of mediocrity in Soviet culture is officially encouraged. Those who rise to the top in the artistic bureaucracy naturally want to protect themselves. They sometimes do so by discouraging truly talented people under their control. One of the country's most accomplished sculptors told me about a young student of his who had been denied entrance to an official institute of sculpture apparently because "he has more talent than the professors there." The officers of the graphics section of the Leningrad Union of Artists, I was told, make sure they themselves get the best commissions to design posters and catalogues. The union's officers can easily make large incomes, 1500 to 2000 rubles a month. This is a society of old men, according to my informant. "They don't elect people to the council who are under fifty." The old men fear talented young people, and often try to frustrate their careers.

The union bureaucracies control the personnel; the state's network of publishers, museums, film studios and theaters, all answerable to the Ministry of Culture or other state organs in Moscow, control the product. A film studio in Kiev, described by a man I met who worked there for many years, is a typical example:

"The Plan of the studio consists, say, of five films on the theme of the working class; two films on historical, revolutionary themes; four films on the peasantry. It doesn't matter to anybody what kind of films they are, or who makes them, or who writes them. What matters is the thematic scheme of the Plan. . . .

"There is an editor for each screenplay. One editor is usually working on five or six screenplays at various stages of production. Your editor is the first person you deal with at the studio, or at the editorial council of the scenario department. . . . When your editor decides that a screenplay is finished, she has to take it to the editorial council of the scenario department, four or five other people, and they must all approve it. And then it goes to the editorial council of the entire studio. Already ten different people have read your scenario, and you have to please all of them. If they suggest some change, you have to make it—there's no choice. . . .

"Once they suggested to me that I write a movie about the Ulyanovs, Lenin's family. . . . It was known that the Ulyanovs had come to Kiev in 1905 and lived there briefly, but very little was known about that period. When they suggested this subject to me, I agreed to do it, because I knew that if I didn't agree, they wouldn't offer me anything else for 18 to 24 months afterward. . . . My first conversation about the film was with the editor who suggested that I do it. He said, 'Between us, this idea is shit, but if you want to keep working here, you have to do it.' . . . [Officially] a theme like that was considered an honor. . . ."

Censorship is the most formidable impediment to intellectual life in the Soviet Union, and it is pervasive. Official censorship goes far beyond the banning of books which defy the Party line; it has also been used to forbid various kinds of scientific inquiry, to obliterate the reputations of historical figures and to frustrate individual writers who get into trouble. Formal controls imposed by Glavlit, the state censorship agency, are not the only controls that exist. Soviet intellectuals censor themselves constantly before offering a book, film, play or painting for the censor's approval.

Political censorship makes certain research work risky. Sociology is a good example. Though there is not a single professor of sociology in the Soviet Union intellectuals trained in other disciplines have begun to practice sociology. There is a large Soviet sociological association which participates in international meetings. But sociology—the study of men in groups—often intrudes into sensitive areas covered by the official ideology, which holds that the "scientific" laws of Marxism-Leninism are sufficient to explain all social behavior. For example, one of those laws stipulates that the abolition of private property causes social class distinctions to disappear. Nevertheless, Soviet sociologists have demonstrated—though they avoid using the forbidden word—that their society is clearly divided into various classes, and the white-collar class has a higher standard of living and a better chance of sending its children to a university than do blue-collar workers in "the workers' state."

Because of the ideological sensitivity of their work, sociologists have repeatedly clashed with the authorities. While I was in Moscow the country's first sociological institute was virtually disbanded. Many of its best people took jobs elsewhere; others were simply fired. Then the institute was renamed and reconstituted under orthodox new leadership.

The authorities permit some research on sensitive topics—the citizenry's political attitudes, for instance—but the results are classified secret. Most published sociology is devoted to proving the obvious, or avoiding it. For example, an ambitious study of how Soviet citizens use their leisure time failed to mention drinking, which must be the country's most popular leisure-time activity.

Sigmund Freud is unacceptable because he suggests that human personalities are shaped by factors which Marxism-Leninism discounts or ignores. Soviet psychologists, however, have been able to introduce large parts of Freudian theory under new names.*

Literary censorship is elaborate. Some forbidden fruits are obvious: no challenges to the Party line or the official version of history are permitted; no works about disgraced personalities; no books, films or plays which might make czarist times or life under capitalism look too good.** Other taboos are less predictable. I heard of a book that was banned because it contained a favorable reference to the writing of James Joyce, whose work is officially disparaged. A book on the medieval history of the Russian Orthodox Church could be published only after its title was changed so it gave no hint of the religious subject. A film director who worked for years on a script about Pushkin's troubles with the censors of his era was finally told the film could not be made. No reason was given, but apparently the studio feared the all-too-obvious comparison to the present day.

Censorship without explanation is common. One author finished a book and gave it to a publishing house, then heard nothing about it for more than a year. He finally made inquiries, and was told that his book could not be published. He asked to have the manuscript back. Your manuscript has been destroyed, the publishing house told him, "in accordance with normal publishing-house procedures." That word "normal" drove the author to distraction.

The censor's inconsistencies are legion, and inexplicable. Since the mid-1960s, for example, the cultural authorities have forbidden all literary works about Stalinism. Then suddenly, in early 1973, they permitted the production of a play called *The Ascent of Mount Fuji* by Chingiz Aitmatov, a Central Asian and one of the country's best contemporary writers. Aitmatov's play, which he wrote with a Central Asian

---

* During my first fortnight in Russia I met an intelligent young journalist who had never heard of Freud. I insisted he must be joking, but he was quite serious. It was a good introduction to the officially imposed blind spots in Soviet education.

** In 1972 this last rule reportedly caused a delay of many months in the Bolshoi Ballet's production of *Anna Karenina*, a new work based on Tolstoi's novel and choreographed by Maya Plisetskaya, for many years the Bolshoi's prima ballerina. According to rumors which circulated in Moscow, the Ministry of Culture thought Anna's life looked too glamorous in the original version of the production. The fact that her life *was* glamorous beyond comparison with any life in the contemporary Soviet Union was of no consequence to the Ministry.

dramatist, posed the uncomfortable question of who was guilty of Stalin's crimes. It did so in the context of a reunion of old friends, all of whom had known a man who was arrested after World War II (at the same time Alexander Solzhenitsyn was arrested) for writing a poem the authorities thought was pacifist (a "crime" about as serious as Solzhenitsyn's, who was arrested for writing private letters critical of Stalin). One of the people at this reunion, Aitmatov reveals, must have turned in their old friend, but the play never discloses who it was. Instead it leaves the unavoidable impression that everyone shared the guilt—the actors on the stage, and the audience too.

Why this play was allowed is still a mystery to me. The most persuasive theory is that Aitmatov's name was responsible—a winner of the Lenin Prize for literature, a Central Asian at a time when the Party line encourages the culture of non-Russian republics can get away with things a Russian writer from Moscow could not. So goes the theory, anyhow.

Whatever the reason, *The Ascent of Mount Fuji* demonstrated the frustrating truism that censorship today does not enforce a consistent view of man and his world. Under Stalin it came much closer to that ideal, banning most foreign literature and even the Russian classics which contradicted the optimistic, uplifting and propagandistic tenets of socialist realism. Today "socialist realism" is little more than a hollow slogan, applied as needed by the authorities to achieve essentially political—as opposed to intellectual—ends.

The authorities ban ideas with blatantly political implications—attacks on the Soviet system, its leaders, its history and antecedents. Beyond these the censorship is erratic and ineffective. A Marxist-Leninist is supposed to be an optimist about man's capacities for self-improvement, so what is he to make of the pessimism of Bertolt Brecht? Yet Brecht is regularly performed in Soviet theaters, on the ground that he was a communist himself, so his work must be acceptable. Dostoevski's concern for human freedom has no logical place in the Soviet Union, but he is published and officially indulged as a Russian hero and a 19th-century "radical." (Stalin banned him.) William Faulkner's alien world is now accessible to Russians in brilliant translations; he is seen as an important representative of American literature and a friend of the downtrodden. (Not too many years ago he was banned and lambasted as a racist.) The list could go on indefinitely.

A Russian intellectual has no trouble reading ideas about man and society which contradict the practices and official tenets of state and Party.

The censor's principal concern is which ideas—and whose work—should *not* be published, not what or who should be. It is censorship by taboo. The principal object is to demonstrate the Party's power to dominate the lives of the citizenry. Writers understand that they must toe the line or lose the opportunity to publish their work. If they fall afoul of the authorities, they become a new taboo.

In recent times the work of Solzhenitsyn has been the archetypal taboo. Not only are his books banned; so are the books of writers who have supported him. Several were expelled from the Union of Writers for coming to Solzhenitsyn's defense or criticizing the decision to exile him. A novel by Robert Penn Warren was scheduled for publication in *Foreign Literature* magazine when a letter Warren wrote supporting Solzhenitsyn appeared in the *New York Times. Foreign Literature* quickly dropped his book from its publication plan. (But Warren's great book *All the King's Men* had already been lovingly translated into Russian, and is widely admired in the Soviet Union.)

Yet even a writer who stays out of trouble, and whose work *may* be published, can never be sure that his next book or story will appear. Arbitrariness is a vital part of the censor's power; it denies to virtually everyone the self-confidence on which writers' egos thrive. Each time a writer (or a painter, or a film-maker) offers a new work to the censor, he is making a form of supplication. The censor has the power of a confessional priest listening, week after week, to the same adolescent boy admit his masturbation. He may forgive, but he may not—at least not before he exacts suitable penitence.

Those who pass judgment do not necessarily share the same standards, and any work or individual must be approved at more than one level. Admission to the Union of Artists, for example, is decided by three commissions. The first two are composed of artists and union officials, who study the candidate's work and pass judgment on it. The third commission is interested not in the artist's work, which it ignores, but in his political and personal reputation. Composed of Party officials and perhaps KGB agents, it grants or denies the candidate what amounts to a security clearance.

While I was in Moscow a group of young artists assembled a small exhibit of photographs. The necessary permission to open the exhibit was granted, but officials from the Moscow Party Committee saw the photographs and closed the exhibition down. They said it was "anti-Soviet Zionist propaganda," apparently because several of the photographers whose work was shown were Jewish. The censors from the Party looked at a photograph of a man's head being held in the jaws of a dog, and one said: "We know what you're trying to show—the relations between Soviet power and the intelligentsia." Examining a photograph of an old wooden door with a tiny X carved in it, one said: "We understand, you're trying to say there are Jews living behind that door." Portraits of Moscow artists made up a large part of the exhibit. One of the Party officials looked at them and complained, "Not one Russian face in the group," intimating that they all looked Jewish.

Party authorities responsible for maintaining discipline within the intelligentsia have invented a verb from the noun "prophylactic" which means, in effect, to apply limited measures against someone to prevent him from getting into serious trouble. A former Party member told me about this, and gave a few examples. For instance, the author of a book or article which displeased the authorities could find that no publishing house or magazine would print his work for two or three years—a reminder of who is in charge.

Sometimes punishment can occur long after the transgression. I met a woman who had signed a petition in the late 1960s on behalf of two intellectuals put on trial for their political statements. She was a teacher at a Moscow institute. In 1973 she was informed that she would have to give up her teaching duties, though she could stay on as a researcher. She was told that her "political immaturity," as demonstrated by her decision to sign that petition more than five years earlier, disqualified her as a teacher of Soviet youth.

Nor is there refuge in simply keeping one's nose clean. The politicians periodically—unpredictably—insist on a token of loyalty or subservience, no matter how well one has behaved. For example, in late 1973 the political authorities (probably the KGB) decided that Andrei Sakharov should be condemned by his peers. Scientists, writers, and artists all over the country were pressured to sign letters attacking him. People who had no personal dispute with Sakharov found they had to repudiate him publicly or face unpleasant repercussions.

Even Dmitri Shostakovich, the best-known contemporary Soviet composer and himself a victim of Stalin's cruelty, signed one of the letters.

A single decision taken in Moscow can result in tighter controls on intellectual life throughout the country. In 1972 the word went out to remove some literature of a marginally controversial nature from the open shelves of the country's libraries to the "special reserve," or closed section. Every important library has a closed section for books which can be read by those with an authorized reason for reading them, but not by the general public. The same decision called for tighter controls on printed material entering or leaving the country. (Though Soviet customs officers search carefully when they decide to examine someone's baggage, they ordinarily do not search every person who enters or leaves the country. I left Moscow for foreign destinations a dozen times during the years I lived there, and was never once searched on the way out. On my way back to the Soviet Union my things were examined several times.)

In the spring of 1973 a scientific-research institute in Leningrad imposed new controls on communications between its staff and foreign scientists. Henceforth, the staff was told, anyone who received a letter from abroad would have to open and read it in front of a committee of his colleagues. Any letter written to a foreigner had to be copied for the institute's files.

Orders like these for heightened "vigilance," I was told by a reliable informant, are often passed down orally and not committed to writing. "It would embarrass them if a written instruction got out," my informant said.

So much for the sticks. The carrots in this system—the privileges and rewards for loyal comrades—are equally significant. Next to the political elite, the official intelligentsia is the most privileged group in Soviet society.

Members of the Academy of Sciences—that is, those at the pinnacle of the academic establishment—are not as far removed from everyday life as the country's leading politicans, but it would still be difficult to compare their existence to an ordinary citizen's. The Academician has material privileges: an automatic 400-ruble-a-month stipend, use of an Academy car, a country *dacha* and a comfortable apartment. He also has the privilege of travel abroad, which itself seems sufficient to assure the loyalty and cooperation of some.

Andrei Sakharov told me about Professor Alexander Imshyenetsky, whom Sakharov once asked for help in finding a job for a young scientist who had been in some trouble with the authorities. Imshyenetsky refused. "I am not going to make any trouble for Soviet power," he told Sakharov. "It has allowed me to go abroad thirty-six times."

"The greatest privilege of all is travel abroad," a professor of chemistry told me. "Westerners find this hard to believe, because in the West anyone who wants to can go abroad. Here it is a fantastic privilege." The privilege has two aspects, he said. The first is professional—the obvious benefits that come with exposure to distinguished foreigners working in one's field, the opportunity to become known—and thus to publish or lecture—overseas.

"Moreover, anyone who goes abroad acquires great prestige—automatically—in Soviet society. It makes him a big man. Abroad he can acquire material goods that simply aren't available at home. All this adds up to an irresistible lure to many people. Even those who have gone abroad twenty or thirty times miss no chance to go again. A few days or weeks abroad give a man a chance to feel like a real man, to do things he could never do at home, to rule his own life, for however brief a time. The merest threat of the loss of this privilege will successfully intimidate most men. . . ."

Another scientist recounted a voyage to England with a young colleague who had never been permitted such a trip before. They arrived at their London hotel and went to their rooms. As my acquaintance was unpacking, his colleague walked through the door.

"The provocations had already begun," he announced. "The water in my bathroom doesn't work, and the television is broken."

"Well," said the older man, "let's call downstairs and have them fixed."

"No, don't! That's just what they want you to do, just what they warned us against in Moscow—don't give them any basis for taking special notice of us."

Nevertheless, he called. It turned out that the water worked fine, and the television was quickly repaired. This did not allay the young man's suspicions, which effectively ruined the entire trip for my acquaintance.

On the airplane back to Moscow he asked the young man what he thought of Britain. "A terrible country, a terrible country to live in," he replied. "If I lived there, I would be constantly worrying about whether I was about to be thrown out of work."

What?

"Yes, unemployment is terrible."

What unemployment? They hadn't seen any sign of unemployment.

"Of course they don't show it to us—on purpose."

"And this," my acquaintance added, recounting the story, "this was a *scientist,* you understand."

A successful writer, a prima ballerina, a popular composer or songwriter can literally become a millionaire, and even live like one. Maya Plisetskaya, the Bolshoi dancer, and her husband, Rodion Shchedrin, the composer I mentioned earlier who borrows themes from classical music, have a large Moscow apartment, a maid, a Citroën car and a driver, a large *dacha,* foreign clothes and many other possessions that ordinary citizens do not dream of.

The few artists who rise to this pinnacle have a special relationship to life. Many of them have private alliances with influential politicans. (In the Soviet Union, too, everyone loves a star, even members of the Politburo.) The patronage of important people makes possible special privileges—extended trips abroad, a foreign car.

Wealth breeds a concern for material things; I met several successful performing artists who were consumed by gadgetry. One asked if I knew the price of a 40-horsepower Johnson or Evinrude outboard motor—he wanted to go water-skiing. Another asked me if he could buy a device in the West which would indicate whether he was in a room equipped with listening devices. Two ballet dancers spent 10 minutes studying my Volvo in detail, admiring it and asking questions. "Richter [Svyatoslav Richter, the pianist] has one like this," one of them said. "Boris Spassky [the chess player] has the smaller model, the 144. Rostropovich [Mstislav Rostropovich, the cellist now living in the West] has a Mercedes."

The privileged are encouraged to *feel* privileged, starting—in the case of the creative intelligentsia—with admission to one of the unions. In Moscow each union has its own club—the House of Writers, the House of Movies, the House of Composers—where members can gather of an evening, eat unusually good food in a comfortable restaurant and enjoy an ambience not found in any public establishment. At the House of Writers the waitresses all know the regulars by name, and vice versa. "Veruchka, another bottle of vodka, that's a girl," someone shouts, and little Vera trots off to the kitchen. The tables are usually full, but the maître d' can always make room for somebody important. When a big star comes into the paneled dining room, there is a stir and a turning of heads. One evening I saw Yevtushenko, the poet, arrive with a pretty girl and take a seat at a corner table. Soon people were just happening to walk nearby to say hello.*

One night I attended a showing of a new movie at the House of Writers. Dozens of people came in their own cars, something I had never seen at a public gathering of this kind in Moscow. Rumor had spread that this film might not be passed by the censor, so a large crowd turned out. The people looked prosperous—many wore items of foreign clothing—and purposefully intellectual, with lots of beards and even a few pipe-smokers, a rare sight in Russia.

Special showings of movies are themselves a privilege. The official intelligentsia can see—at closed performances—foreign films that will never be shown in public theaters. I was startled to find that a number of my acquaintances had seen *The Godfather,* a prototype of the kind of western film—a violent glorification of criminals—regularly attacked by official propagandists (who see such movies at the House of Journalists). Later I met a young man who was employed as a translator by the State Committee on Cinematography. His job was to provide Russian subtitles for foreign films to be

---

* Another Yevtushenko story deserves a place here. I happened to be arriving at Moscow's Sheremyetovo Airport when Yevtushenko was returning from a triumphant tour of America, during which he even met President Nixon. He had 14 suitcases—by my own count—most of them expensive Italian luggage, but he obviously hoped to breeze through customs with a wave and a smile. He approached the customs inspector with that in mind, but this official would have none of it. After much animated talk, Yevtushenko and his 14 bags were led to a little room at the rear of the customs hall. The door was closed behind him, and I never found out what happened, but it appeared that on that day, at least, his smile and fame were not enough to exempt him from import duties.

shown to government officials and other privileged citizens. Even for this narrow audience the committee provided subtitles.

There are extraordinary benefits for intellectual work with political significance—for example, anything associated with Lenin. The film director quoted earlier, who was asked to make a film about Lenin's family in Kiev, was to be paid 3500 or 4000 rubles for the screenplay; the rate for an ordinary film was 1000. Actors who play Lenin in the many movies and plays about his life receive special remuneration. I met a man who translated Lenin's works into one of the Central Asian languages—for three times the normal translating fee. The workers in Moscow's Lenin Museum are privileged associates of the Party Central Committee, entitled to eat and shop in its own cafeteria. On Fridays they can order meals to take home for the weekend (at least they could in 1970, when my informant last worked there).

The combination of carrots and sticks, not surprisingly, is effective. It has created the pseudo-intelligentsia, a class of careerists who choose to make their careers in the "intellectual" professions. Most of the people who control the system care more about loyalty than ability or talent. Movie directors are regularly told to give a part to someone because of his political connections, not his acting skill. Editors publish certain writers for the same reason.

The carrots and sticks also corrupt people of real talent, as they do in every society. The company has its reliable men.

Yet many withhold their cooperation, some just occasionally to redeem their own self-respect, some regularly and some systematically. The last group are now known as the dissidents, and I will consider them in the next chapter.

The others I will describe here—first a few of the most notorious compromisers, then some of the intellectuals who try to hold onto their integrity even while they work within the system.

Isaac Mintz "has a gift for divining the desires of our leaders," according to a professor in Moscow who has known him for many years. Mintz received the Lenin Prize while I was in Moscow, one of many state prizes he has accumulated over the years. He originally won fame by discerning that Stalin had been personally responsible for the Reds' victory in the Russian civil war. That is to say, Mintz edited the Stalinist version of the civil war which was published in 1943. Leon Trotsky, who actually organized the Red Army had helped lead it to victory over various White forces and the interventionist armies of the western powers, became a traitor and a fool in the Stalin-Mintz version. For that Mintz won the Stalin Prize in 1943. He received it again in 1946. In the same year he was elected to the Academy of Sciences as a master of historical science.

None of this protected Mintz, a Jew, from the campaign against "cosmopolites," Stalin's last anti-Semitic fling before his death. Mintz lost all his posts, but he bounced back quickly after Stalin died. By the late 1960s he was passing petitions among prominent Jews condemning Israel. "It would be good for you to sign this," he told one Jewish physicist.

I never met Mintz myself. He is an old man now, sometimes seen on Leninski Prospekt in Moscow walking his dog. I did meet several people who knew him, and asked them what kind of a man this was. No one seemed really sure. An opportunist, they all agreed, with no personal sense of right and wrong.

Even more baffling—to his acquaintances and even to his own relatives—is Alexander Chakovski, editor of the *Literary Gazette*. Chakovski also is Jewish,* the product of a family "from the Jewish intelligentsia," according to a cousin of his whom I met in Moscow. "I first heard about him when he was a teenager," the cousin told me. "They already talked about him as a complete careerist. In those days he wanted to make a career in the Komsomol [the Young Communist League]. He had no time for family and friends."

Chakovski worked briefly in the Moscow Lamp Factory—a useful credential in the workers' state—then graduated from the Gorki Institute of Literature in Moscow, a famous school which has trained many members of the literary intelligentsia. He went to work as an editor and, when war broke out, became a correspondent at the front. After the war he worked as an officer of the Union of Writers, then resumed his career as an editor. In 1962 he persuaded the appropriate officials of

---

* The fact that Mintz and Chakovski are both Jewish is of no broader significance; they are the only two Jews I heard of in Moscow who were careerists of this sort. Most are non-Jewish Great Russians.

the Central Committee to make him editor of *Literary Gazette*, then a paper of no particular merit or personality. He transformed it into a lively weekly, the best newspaper published in the Soviet Union. Though it contains a full dose of propaganda, the paper also publishes enlightening, readable reports on economic and social problems. Literature is its weakest subject; the paper is an organ of the Union of Writers and sticks closely to the most orthodox line. "In *Literary Gazette*," a writer said to me, "you can read all about Israel, all about automobiles—whatever you want, but not literature." Nevertheless, the non-literary material is sufficiently interesting that this writer, and most others I knew, subscribed to the paper, as did people who would buy no other official organ.

Chakovski's triumph has been to put out a paper which is read by people who despise him personally. This is possible because they despise him for his character, not for his talent, which obviously is considerable. Viktor Perelman, the journalist quoted at the beginning of Chapter 5, once worked for Chakovski. He has described a discussion at the paper about an article recommending an increase in the salaries paid to engineers. One editor said the article should not be printed, because the state did not have the money to increase salaries and the article would only raise expectations that could not be fulfilled. Chakovski disagreed:

"Yes, we understand the state has no money to pay engineers. . . . But you must realize that the task of our paper is not quite so primitive and elementary as you seem to think. . . . As one executive once said to me, 'You at *Literary Gazette* are like Hyde Park [Corner] under socialism.' Hyde Park—you all know what that is. An awful lot goes on there. . . . You must realize that not everything that is said in Hyde Park necessarily has to be carried out immediately, although of course that's what they say in Hyde Park. . . . We cannot raise engineers' pay today, but our readers should know that the state and the Party are concerned about this problem. . . ."

Chakovski's cleverness as a journalist is matched by his single-minded political ambition. He is one of the two or three highest-ranking journalists in the Party, and is said to have established personal ties with Brezhnev. His paper is usually chosen to inflict unseemly public punishments on prominent intellectuals, most notably Solzhenitsyn. When the authorities decided to attack his novel *August 1914, Literary Gazette* undertook an elaborate fraud to convince its readers that foreign critics had condemned the book. In fact, as Zhores Medvedev has demonstrated, the paper commissioned these "foreign" comments. One of the critics, a Finn, admitted later that he had never read Solzhenitsyn's novel.

Chakovski, I was told by credible informants, is capable of great charm and great personal cruelty. He collects pipes, and his young son once broke a favorite. Chakovski didn't speak to him for six months. According to a man who worked on his staff, Chakovski once reported a neighbor to Party authorities because the neighbor made a casual remark which he regarded as a slander on the state. Chakovski has always been able to ingratiate himself with others. As a young man, it is said, he carried four brands of cigarettes in his pockets at all times, ranging from the best grade to the cheapest. He offered a cigarette to everyone he met—the type a person was offered depended on his rank or importance. Chakovski has survived Stalin, Khrushchev and Brezhnev, rising higher under each of them. Those who know him predict he will continue to rise under Brezhnev's successor, whoever that turns out to be.

Sergei Mikhalkov, an author of verse and children's stories, is one of the most powerful men in the Soviet intelligentsia. His praise is enough to insure the publication of a children's book; his damnation can ruin a career. David Bonavia, a correspondent for the London *Times* who was expelled from Moscow in 1972, blames his difficulties in part on an article he wrote in which he described a Mikhalkov short story as "nauseating."

Mikhalkov's career has resembled Chakovski's. He, too, studied at the Gorki Institute, though he failed to graduate.* He, too, was a correspondent at the front during the war, and later an officer of the Union of Writers. But he has done more writing than Chakovski, and he made himself famous with one children's book about the police.

"That was Mikhalkov's stroke of genius," another writer observed, "to write a book glorifying the police!" Ever since, he has maintained close relations with the Ministry of Inter-

---

* He is a corresponding or candidate member of the Academy of Pedagogical Sciences, the governing body of the Soviet teaching profession. According to one story I heard, he was about to be promoted to full membership when someone discovered that he did not have a college degree. The promotion was dropped.

nal Affairs (which oversees the police) and, it is widely believed in Moscow, with the KGB as well. Mikhalkov presided at a meeting of the Union of Writers after the trial of Andrei Sinyavsky and Yuli Daniel, who were sentenced to prison in 1966 for writing books published abroad under pseudonyms. Their trial was the beginning of a prolonged campaign of repression which continues to the present day. At that original meeting a writer rose and asked how the authorities could be sure that Sinyavsky and Daniel really wrote the books attributed to them that were published in the West. "That is a naïve question, comrade," Mikhalkov replied. "Thank God, we still have the KGB!"

Mikhalkov is a big man with a "golden tongue," according to one acquaintance, but he also stutters, and is self-conscious about this disability. He is said to be mean and vindictive to enemies, but capable of great kindness to friends. He helped the children of a deceased friend to acquire a car, and has intervened at various publishing houses on behalf of others. I heard of a young children's writer who could get nothing published until Mikhalkov wrote a note saying how much he liked the writer's work. He has a weaknesss for the ladies, and was involved in a Writers' Union scandal in the 1960s provoked by the discovery of a small bordello in Moscow. Mikhalkov and other union officials had apparently set up this establishment, and he was reportedly one of its regular customers. The scandal was hushed up at the time, perhaps because it coincided with the trial of Sinyavsky and Daniel.

Many Russians told me that vanity was the key to Mikhalkov's character. The Party and state have assuaged him with a series of awards and honors, including three Stalin Prizes. He has also been handsomely rewarded financially; he is believed to be a ruble millionaire. A man of his influence can persuade the publishing houses to issue and reissue his books, a sure path to wealth in a book-happy country which seems to buy almost anything that isn't the collected speeches of some Party leader.

Mikhalkov lives like a prince, and evidently likes his comforts. In 1969 he defended them in a poem published in *Krokodil*, the humor magazine. The verse caused a scandal in some circles, but it was probably an honest statement of Mikhalkov's beliefs (which are shared by many members of the privileged class). This is Max Hayward's translation of the poem, reprinted here with his kind permission:

At a certain stud farm a worthy dobbin
trudged in harness before his wagon,
bringing stacks of oats to the stables
and carting loads of dung away.
He knew what thoroughbreds got to eat
according to their rightful due
and envied them their stalls and shoes,
their well-groomed tails and manes.
But he'd never been to the racetrack
and seen how a pedigreed three-year-old
runs the last lap bathed in lather,
gasping: "Shall I make it?"
Exactly so some citizens see fit
to stand in judgment on those above them,
carping at the way they live.

One of Mikhalkov's friends, a composer named Nikita Bogoslovski, has made himself famous among Moscow's intellectuals by playing practical jokes at the expense of Mikhalkov's vanity. Two of his tricks deserve recounting here for what they reveal about the two men, and about Soviet life more generally.*

The first was prompted by the fact that Mikhalkov was co-author of the lyrics to the Stalinist version of the Soviet national anthem mentioned at the beginning of this book. These were the words which praised Stalin by name, and which Khrushchev dropped. One day Mikhalkov received a telephone call from an official of the Mosocw Patriarchate of the Russian Orthodox Church. The caller asked if Mikhalkov, known as a gifted writer of hymns, would agree to write a new hymn for the Church.

No, Mikhalkov said, he was a communist, he couldn't do that.

Not to worry, the caller said, this proposal had been approved at a high level. The State Council for Religious Affairs had authorized it. And there would be a good fee—200 rubles per line, and the hymn would have to be at least 40 lines long. Mikhalkov said he would think it over.

A week later he agreed to write the hymn. In a month Mikhalkov reported that the hymn was finished. On such an

---

* I cannot affirm with certainty that either of these stories is true. Even if apocryphal, they are widely believed.

important occasion, the caller said, we would like you to meet the Patriarch himself. Can we send a car around for you?

A car came and took Mikhalkov to a big house tucked behind a high wall in one of Moscow's tree-lined old neighborhoods. He sat in a waiting room for half an hour, then was ushered into a large room that was dominated by a long table. Around it sat a group of his friends, including Bogoslovski who shouted: "Well then, comrade, let's hear your little hymn!"

On another occasion Mikhalkov received a phone call from a shipyard. "Comrade Mikhalkov," the caller said, "we are about to complete a large ocean-going liner which we would like to name for you. Do you mind?"

Of course he did not, and was profusely thankful. The caller said he would be invited to the launching. A month later he called again:

"Comrade Mikhalkov, you know, we had to name that ship for Lenin. I'm sorry, but we didn't have any choice. The Ministry made the decision." Mikhalkov said he understood perfectly. The caller said they would look for another ship to name for him. A month later another call; they had found a ship, somewhat smaller than the first, and again he would be invited to the launching. Then another month passed. Finally:

"Comrade Mikhalkov, you know, we had to name that boat for Gorki. We're terribly sorry, but they called us from the Council of Ministers and told us to do it." Mikhalkov was understanding. The caller said they would look for another boat. This process went on for many months, the size of the ship shrinking all the while. Mikhalkov was finally invited to help launch the ship named for him, a small craft barely larger than a rowboat. He arrived at the appointed spot to find Bogoslovsky and other friends waiting to laugh at him.

Mintz, Chakovski and Mikhalkov are famous careerists; in Moscow their corruption is taken for granted. But the corruption goes well beyond such infamous characters.

I heard a story about a prominent scientist who was asked, some years ago, to prepare a report for the Politburo on the pollution of Lake Baikal. Baikal, north of Irkutsk in Central Siberia, is the world's largest body of fresh water, a natural rarity of great beauty. As factories were built along its banks

and tributaries, the ecological balance of the lake and its surroundings was altered. Some scientists feared that the lake
was in danger, and began agitating for corrective measures.
So the Politburo asked for a report.

The man chosen for this assignment (according to a
woman who once worked with him) knew in advance what
the Politburo wanted to hear—that Baikal was in no danger
and industrialization of the region could proceed. Yet the evidence available suggested otherwise. "You understand hydro-
dynamics," his female colleague told him. "You know the
pollution will spread through the lake." Friends and even the
scientist's wife pleaded with him; he had no right to jeopard-
ize this great wonder of nature simply to placate a group of
politicans. But this was the Politburo. The scientist did what
was expected of him, and even came home beaming with
pride. "They liked my report," he said. "It was well
received."*

I also heard of corruption on a lesser scale, though it
seemed no less painful. One man who writes popular books
on science has always been compelled to accept co-authors
for his projects in order to get them published—co-authors
with good official reputations. Their contribution is to alter
what he has already written, sometimes substantially. But not
always. "Sometimes they are decent people who tell me to do
what I want, and they give me most of the money, too. When
I run into someone like this I begin to feel like a free person—I don't mind so much when it turns out that way. I can
live with it. Of course there is still a lot of nonsense in the
book. . . ."

Hypocrisy is another form of corruption—another means
of coping with the pressures created by carrot and stick. The
authorities want everyone to agree always about everything, a
grandiose request impossible to satisfy. So people pretend.

A former Soviet film director, now living in Los Angeles,
recounted a particularly vivid encounter with hypocrisy. It involved a film called *Jews in the USSR*, made to be shown to
foreign audiences to counteract the impression that anti-Semitism exists in the Soviet Union. The film was made entirely
by Jews, under the direction of a man who apparently

---

* Since then the authorities have recognized the dangers to Baikal,
and some steps have been taken to diminish them.

worked for the KGB. The former director who told this story
saw the movie at a special screening in Moscow.

First it showed successful Jews in the Soviet Union: "Ois-
trakh played the violin. General Dragunski [a Jewish gen-
eral] bravely smiled at us. All these were Jews, all were
kings—that was the message." Then the movie showed scenes
of people who had emigrated from Russia to Israel, disliked
it and, now miserable, wanted to return home.

"It was a simplistic film directed at unsophisticated audiences—primarily foreigners," the director said. "All of us
in the auditorium knew very well how many kings there really are in a deck of cards.

"The lights went on. We tried not to look at each other as
we left. It wasn't just the film; we had seen many similar ones
in our time. We just felt embarrassed for those who made the
film—our colleagues who were there with us.

"I was unfortunate, for I ended up next to one of the film's
creators while queuing at the cloakroom. Overcoats, scarves,
boots, hats—the line was long, and we couldn't go on not noticing each other, especially since we had been colleagues for
fifteen years and were friendly at one time. He started the
conversation:

" 'Do you get letters from Israel?' (He was referring to
mutual friends who had migrated there recently.)

" 'Yes,' I said.

" 'How is it over there?'

" 'Everything seems OK. They're happy.'

" 'My cousin writes that she is managing quite well, too,'
the film-maker told me. 'Just imagine, she's only a kid, a
nurse, and already has her own car and a flat with a
bathroom with blue tiles.'

"I could not believe what I was hearing. He looked straight
at me—a challenging stare. I had to look away."

This film director thought the impulse to hypocrisy among
contemporary Soviet intellectuals was something that "has not
been defined yet—that may be studied in time by psychiatrists and historians." I don't think it is so exotic. People
learn to get along—they often see no alternative.

I heard about a professor at a scientific institute in Moscow, a Jew who worked hard to stay out of trouble. One day
the entire staff of the institute was informed that one of their
colleagues—also a Jew—had applied to emigrate to Israel. A
staff meeting was called to condemn the errant comrade and

remind the others of the disgrace that follows such a treasonous act. (These meetings occur wherever a Jew who is applying to emigrate works.)

The Jewish professor, who had no intention of ever emigrating himself, was asked to give a speech denouncing the
colleague who had asked for an exit visa. "No," the professor
said, "I won't do that, I have nothing to say." A representative
of the Party committee came to him and repeated the request, but again he refused. Finally the director of the institute called the professor in and reminded him that his post
was subject to periodic competitive examinations—he could
be replaced. And by the way, the director said, it would be a
good idea if the professor spoke at the meeting.

So he did. According to a friend who was there, the professor came to the meeting hall "looking like a girl who had just
been raped. He didn't say anything directly against——, he
walked a narrow path, doing what he had to do without compromising himself completely. But the fact is he did it. Afterward he said he hoped his friends would understand."

Not everyone is corrupted by the system, nor is corrupt behavior the only norm. Some Russian intellectuals have found
other tactics for coping with Societ life which allow them
more self-respect, and in some cases satisfaction, too.

It is possible to do good, honest and creative intellectual
work in the Soviet Union—not easy, but possible. The political authorities are not universally fools and cretins; some of
them can recognize and reward genius as well as loyalty. This
takes courage; the cultural bureaucrat's easiest response is to
say no, because a no will rarely cause him trouble. Yes, on
the other hand, will lead to something concrete—a book, a
play, whatever—which could offend one of his many bosses.
So no is more likely, but it is not inevitable.

Moscow's Yuri Lyubimov is one of the best-known theater
directors in Europe; his staging of a new opera in Milan in
1975 received rave reviews throughout Europe and in the
New York Times. At the Taganka Theater in Moscow,
Lyubimov regularly stages exciting new productions—not
necessarily controversial, but theatrically adventurous and rewarding. Several other theater directors do the same. Writers
who agree to avoid obviously touchy subjects can also do
serious work. A novelist or poet would be ill-advised to begin
a new interpretation of the Bolshevik Revolution, but a story

or poem about rural life in the far north, a fantasy, an historical novel are all possible. Fine works in each of these categories have been written in recent years.

Every year while I was in Moscow there were one or two movies, two or three plays, a book or two which were really good or really interesting. The two are not always the same; I don't think *The Ascent of Mount Fuji*, the play about Stalinism I mentioned earlier, is great theater, but in the Soviet context it was provocative and significant. Even routine productions allow actors and stagehands to stretch their talents. In a movie about a team of architects the main plot line was a predictable story of workers' heroics, but the director managed to work into it a series of marvelous comic scenes which seemed inspired by Fellini.

There are many areas of inquiry which the authorities either encourage or tend to ignore. Pure scientific research of many kinds falls into the first category, and, as I wrote in Chapter 8, there are Soviet scientists doing research work comparable to any in the world. Medieval history is an example of a subject that Soviet officials don't worry much about; several Soviet medieval historians are said to be superb.

Certain institutions go about their business without constant interference from the authorities. I met a young man who worked in one of them, a large library attached to the Academy of Sciences, where numerous intellectuals worked hard and enjoyed themselves. The crucial factor there was a relaxed group of administrators. The director even gave work to people who had been in trouble for signing protest petitions.

After the invasion of Czechoslovakia in 1968, the library was instructed to assemble its employees so they could demonstrate their support for the invasion. Rather than force this embarrassment on the staff, the Party secretary and the director agreed simply to pretend they had held the meeting. Later the people running the library were replaced, apparently because they were too liberal, but their replacements did not radically change the atmosphere. (They did stop hiring Jews, however.)

What pleased this young man most was the opportunity to maintain a truly fine library, drawing on the best books published throughout the world, without undue political interference. "We did have our informers," he said. "Sometimes warnings spread among the staff—don't talk in such-and-such a spot, there may be a microphone there; beware of So-and-so; don't bring any printed material to work which might be compromising." Yet life went on calmly; the people working there liked one another and their jobs.

For those intellectuals willing to endure the strain of a political career there are numerous opportunities for serious work. The Party needs men and women who can master foreign cultures, for example; I met many officials who were extremely well informed on specific foreign-policy problems. I suspect many of them believe they have challenging, rewarding careers. One of those is Rostislav Ulyanovsky, the expert on India whom I described in Chapter 4, who went to the Central Committee staff from the Institute of Eastern Studies.

Officials such as Ulyanovsky assemble expert opinions from the academic institutes on policy questions. The Institute for Eastern Studies, for example, has a "Department of Actual Problems" which prepares reports on the Middle East and Asia for the Central Committee and the Ministry of Foreign Affairs. It can draw on an enormous staff of experts. In 1965, on the eve of the Indonesian Communist Party's attempted coup d'état, the Central Committee asked for assessments of the Indonesian situation. This one institute had 20 qualified experts who contributed to a response.

Curiously, official work of this kind is often more honest—and less influenced by the Party line—than ordinary research. The authorities do expect honest opinions, especially on foreign policy issues. Just prior to the Six Day War in 1967, I was told, an expert on Israel named Nikitin wrote an analysis of the Middle Eastern balance of power. He concluded that the Arabs would be defeated if they began another war. "Apparently," said my informant, a former member of the institute's staff, "the Central Committee disagreed with his analysis."*

A secret bulletin prepared by the institute and distributed among its members reported frankly on international developments even when they reflected badly on the Soviet Union, according to my informant. For example, the bulletin once concluded that American aid to India had been genuinely helpful and effective, and that the Soviet Union should match it or face up to the possible consequences.

---

* The Arabs did attack, and were badly beaten.

Official intellectuals have influenced major decisions , according to this source. He cited an article published in the institute's public journal in the early 1960s which analyzed the importance of military elites in underdeveloped countries. Soon afterward the Central Committee decided it should be Soviet government policy to court those elites.

The story of a man I will call Igor is not typical of the Russian intelligentsia, because Igor is an untypical fellow, but his life demonstrates what is possible in the contemporary Soviet Union.

Igor is a scientist, a professor of one of Moscow's leading research institutes, though he is still in his forties. He is a strong, self-confident person, certain of what he wants in life and equally certain that he can get it. This alone sets him apart from most other Russian intellectuals.

Igor came to Leningrad as a high-spirited young man determined to make his way in life. He soon decided that there were two possible avenues to success: he could join the KGB, or pursue a scientific career. He took entrance examinations for Leningrad University and for an institute which would have led to membership in the KGB, was admitted to both and chose a scientific faculty at the university. He was lucky to choose as his specialty a branch of chemistry which was of little importance then, but has grown significantly since. He did brilliantly, was taken on at the Moscow institute where he now works, and has progressed steadily ever since.

Igor arranged his private life with comparable determination, through not quite as successfully. He married a fellow student, who bore him a daughter, but the marriage soured. He had several prolonged affairs, but has moved back in with his wife and child, to whom he is devoted. Igor has stayed away from politics, avoiding membership in the Party, and has thrown himself into several hobbies, particularly stamp-collecting and the accumulation of pre-revolutionary Russian paintings. He now has valuable collections of both, and can happily spend long hours with his treasures.

Several years ago Igor was invited to Western Europe with a group of Soviet scientists. He enjoyed the trip enormously. He also made a good impression on a number of the western chemists he met, several of whom invited him back. But Igor calculated that he might impress his own superiors by refusing the first invitations, to show he was not too much enamored of foreign climes. He did so, pleading preoccupation with his own research, and the ploy succeeded. A year later he was permitted to travel *by himself* to Europe, a privilege reserved for very few. On this second trip Igor accepted the gifts—mostly cash—offered by his hosts, and bought large quantities of clothes, records and other trinkets. He also purchased the items requested by a new friend he had made in Moscow—a customs official at the airport who would allow him to bring his own purchases into the country duty-free.

Much of what he bought was distributed as gifts to key colleagues in his institute. "I am consolidating my position," Igor likes to say, "covering my flanks and neutralizing my enemies." He even found a friend who could check his file at the KGB to make sure his record was clean. It was.

A number of Igor's friends have emigrated in recent years. He says he understands why, but wouldn't think of leaving himself—his life is too comfortable. Moreover, he is needed in Moscow: he is one of the best specialists in a small but important field. He quietly acknowledges that his country is being badly run—it's a totalitarian country, he says, there isn't much that can be done with it. But he maintains high personal standards, and imposes them in his laboratory.

Igor has discovered how to play the angles in Soviet life. Intellectuals can find satisfaction in the Soviet Union—as anywhere—by beating the system. I met a young cellist who was about to graduate from the conservatory. He was trying to get a job in the orchestra of the Bolshoi Theater. The work there would be rather dull, playing the same opera and ballet scores night after night, but the Bolshoi's is the only orchestra whose members are exempt from military service. The theater would list them as ballet dancers, who are apparently regarded as a national asset too fragile to be risked on the fields of battle or in basic training.

A family I knew discovered that the Party had blackballed their son at every scientific institute in Moscow because his father had been an active "signer" of protests against persecution of writers. So they quietly sent him to Irkutsk in Siberia, where he was able to enroll in a college, apparently without the knowledge of Party officials in Moscow.

Russians who cannot escape corruption or compromise may still look for ways to redeem their self-esteem. An elderly man who spent his long career studying the languages, culture and history of India attended a meeting of Indianists which was addressed by an official from the Party's Central Committee. The official made a pompous speech about the Soviet Union's efforts to strengthen its ties with India. The old scholar rose and said those were fine words, but in fact the USSR had behaved foolishly, restricting the contacts of Russian scholars and diplomats with ordinary Indians. Rhetoric should conform to reality, he observed. It was a small bit of defiance, but enough to electrify his colleagues, who did not expect an official from the Central Committee to be publicly contradicted.

A scholar who lived in Moscow was once invited to give a series of lectures at a provincial university. The scholar felt he had to tell the dean of the university that he had been in some trouble with the Moscow Party authorities for speaking his mind too openly—to give the dean a chance to reconsider the invitation. "Officially," the dean replied, "that is of no consequence. Unofficially, what you tell me only increases my desire that you speak at our university." This little display of courage gave the scholar an emotional lift which lasted for several weeks.

Small assertions of independence are not rare among Russian intellectuals. I decided they were one manifestation of a desire, shared by many, to try to redeem individual dignity by struggling—at least a little—before succumbing. Many Russians make a game effort to extract the best from a bad situation.

During my first year in Moscow I was invited to a special exhibition of paintings by a man who had been well known in the '20s, but then got into trouble and was little heard from afterward. He is still alive and has gone on painting, though he has not been able to show his works or sell them officially through the Union of Artists. The exhibit I saw was not open to the public, but it was officially sanctioned—apparently a limited concession to the artist or his friends, who probably wanted a full-fledged exhibition but settled for this arrangement. Only people with printed invitations were admitted to the hall. My wife and I got tickets through a friend of friends, also a painter.

When we arrived nearly 200 people were already there. It was a cold winter night and the heat wasn't working, so most people kept their overcoats on. Nevertheless, it was easy to see that this was an unusual Russian crowd. In almost every Russian gathering I was struck by a certain crudeness—which really meant a few people of a kind you don't often see outside Russia, dirty, surly and rude, with no pretense of civilizing varnishes. This group had none of that. Virtually every face looked intelligent and interesting. The crowd had a Bohemian flavor of a kind I associate with Paris between the World Wars—turtleneck sweaters and goatees, and women with long, straight hair. A majority were middle-aged or older, apparently the artist's contemporaries. They talked with each other in calm, assured tones, suggesting a degree of self-confidence not typical of Russians.

The walls of the room, perhaps 20 feet by 60, were hung with pictures painted by this old artist. They were not the paintings of an old man, though they all had been done in the previous four or five years. They were very good: portraits of girls with a feeling reminiscent of the young Picasso; weird landscapes with small human figures; and some wonderful female torsos.

The people had come to see the pictures and pay homage to the artist. After a while a woman called the meeting to order. She was plump, about fifty-five, her hair drawn back in a long, girlish pony-tail that was ill-suited to her age and figure and to her thick black hair streaked with gray. She reminded me of the kind of woman who runs her own jewelry shop in Greenwich Village, though her front teeth capped with steel were unmistakable badges of her true nationality. She sat in the front of the room with the artist, a balding man who wore horn-rimmed glasses. She invited the group to begin a discussion of the painter's work.

A young man stood up and walked to the front of the room. He had studied with the painter, and knew in detail the history of his career. It began in the 1920s, when he worked with many of the famous modernists of that period, a rich one in Russian artistic history (after the Revolution, but before Stalin). The painter's first one-man show took place in 1933. The authorities closed it after a day or two. Later he was criticized in the press. The young man described the difficulties of the '30s, when artists had to "stick to nature" and the official pressures were intense. He did not mention Stalin by name, but the message was clear, particularly to the people in this room, most of whom had lived through the period. The artist's next show was held in 1956, the young man continued, during the thaw that followed Stalin's death. Apparently, this exhibition in 1971 was only the third occasion his pictures had been hung in a public place.

The young man made several recommendations for improving conditions in the Soviet art world. Everyone in the room was familiar with the famous French painters of the early 20th century, he observed, but perhaps it was time to make Russian audiences familiar with contemporary French art. Since relations with France were improving, he hoped that might be possible. He also thought there should be more exhibitions like this one to allow Soviet artists to see what their colleagues were working on. As it was, he said, artists lived in isolation from one another.

A number of the older people also spoke. Another artist, a man with ears that stuck straight out from his head, reminisced about old days and bad times, not explicitly, but in general terms, in a tone which suggested a common understanding in the room of how bad it all was—a shared wisdom, not worth elaborating. Two women praised the artist's "psychological approach," which was indeed unmistakable in his portraits. Each little speech was made with eloquence and poise, the result, I suspect, of Russian schooling, which involves a lot of standing recitations in class.

Good humor abounded in the room. One man got up and said he loved some of the painter's work, but other pictures upset him. "So please," he said, "stop doing the ones I don't like and concentrate on the others." The lady who was officiating rejected this idea sternly: if artists took the advice of the public, she said, there would soon be no more art. The fellow who made the original remark replied, "I like your comments better than what I said," a bit of self-mockery which the crowd appreciated.

The artist responded to many of the comments, always with bright eyes and a smile. (He was, another speaker had said, a man who "always carried a little of his childhood in his pocket.") He said he felt foolish discussing his technique—which was unusual—because it didn't matter. "If you feel, you will feel," he said. "If you can't feel, you won't feel." The artist's feelings and his ability to convey them, the painter thought, were what mattered.

Several people tried to get him to discuss the bad old days, but the author protested repeatedly that "it's not worth it." Some in the crowd audibly disagreed. He did read some of the criticism made against him when his show was closed in 1933. One critic had maligned a painting of a girl reading a newspaper under a streetlight: this was not a proper way to show the wonderful powers of electrification, the critic wrote, a subject that was important to the industrialization of the country. Moreover, the figures in the painting were too small, not heroic like good revolutionaries. The painter read this, then said he hoped he would always qualify for that kind of criticism. It seemed to me that those cruel words, written by some faceless hack nearly 40 years earlier, still stung.

So they cope, these Russian intellectuals; they make do or make the best of it. Is that happiness? Not by my standards, I decided. But then, happiness by my standards has never been the Russians' lot. Suffering has. Suffering and the Russian intellectual tradition are inextricably tied up with each other, and I knew many people who doubted they could ever be separated. "We love our suffering," one confided. "We need it."

Suffering has distorted the values of numerous Russian intellectuals. Those who compromise, who succumb to corruption, are often excused by their friends—just as the man who made that film about Jews in the USSR wanted his old acquaintance to excuse him. Even people who behaved outrageously—by reporting on their friends to the KGB, for example—could ask and receive forgiveness. Too many have made their own compromises to condemn those of others.

This is another of the countless consequences of Stalin's reign which still reverberate through Soviet society. In the 1930s and 1940s everyone compromised or lost his freedom, and perhaps his life. The ranks of Soviet intellectuals were decimated; many disappeared for ridiculous or perverse reasons. Informers were everywhere—many lived in constant fear. I met the members of one family who stayed up every night for five years playing bridge until they dropped off to sleep from exhaustion—it was the only way they could overcome the fear of a knock on the door in the night. Others have blocked out the entire period. "What did we do all those years? I don't remember."

It is difficult to be happy when one is constantly threatened by fickle and uncontrollable forces. Even those who cooperate with the regime are subject to whimsical restrictions. Like the children of parents who are inconsistent disciplinarians, they are left angry and confused—which may just be the intention. Late one night one of the Soviet Union's best writers, very drunk, said, "I would like to know what would have happened to Faulkner if they had banned every other book *he* wrote. I'd just like to know." It was a relevant question, I later learned, because every second book written by this writer has indeed been banned or drastically altered by the Soviet censors.

A Hungarian artist, a young woman, spent a recent summer in the USSR at a resort maintained by the Union of Artists. An attractive and infectiously likable woman, she quickly befriended the Russians living and working there. At the end of the summer many gave her gifts, largely modernist or abstract paintings, the things Russian artists do for themselves and their friends, but not for sale or public show.

The Hungarian woman took the gifts to Moscow and asked her hosts at the Union of Artists to pack her own canvases and the presents for shipment to Budapest. She returned on the day of her departure to pick up the crate the union had made for her. Russian friends took her to the train. On the platform she told them what she had done with their gifts; one of the Russians suggested they open the crate. They did; the gifts were gone. The Union of Artists had seized them all.

Arbitrary pressure is seldom far from a Soviet intellectual's concerns. "I don't want to worry about politics," one of the country's best film directors told me. "Personally, I am bored by politics, I want to make films. But it is impossible! Some boob will be forced upon me in a starring role because of his good political connections; some other boob will suddenly become an important official of the studio, just because he has a friend in the Central Committee. I can't escape politics even though I try to!"

It is the arbitrary, unexpected intrusions that wear down the spirit of even the most determined optimists. Those who knew their books would never be published often seemed to me more content and serene than others who were never sure. Even those who do the best work that official standards allow can become bitterly alienated. One of them, a writer who is rich and famous, astounded me by recounting, at our first and only meeting, the story of his recent trip to Britain. "I got back five weeks ago," he said, "but I just can't get used to life here, I can't readjust to it. I was a free man for three weeks!"

When the despair reaches this level, there is usually an amateur philosopher nearby to reduce the tension. "Yes," I heard one of them say, "but you must remember, you can only understand the best in Russia through the worst." And there are always jokes, like the one about the difference between an optimist and a pessimist:

A pessimist is sure that things will get worse. An optimist is convinced that things *can't* get worse.

The Russian intellectual's last and most effective line of defense is the barrier he can build around his own private world. Privacy is the logical defense for intellectuals who live in a society which regards intellectuals suspiciously. And that is certainly the case in the Soviet Union. The Russian intelligentsia has always been tinged with a certain foreignness. The class was born of relations with Europe, and not so long ago. (Russia didn't get its own university until 1755, 119 years after Harvard College was established in America.) Russian intellectuals have always brought foreign influences into the country, and foreign influences have always made ordinary Russians nervous. Now, when the prejudices of the Russian masses are clearly reflected in national policy, countless intellectuals try to sneak out of official society and find refuge in a private world.

A private world may be a house in the country, like the cottage owned by a violinist I met, who lives with his elderly mother. His life consists of books, music, a few friends and relations, and the BBC, which he tries to listen to every day on an oversized shortwave radio he bought years ago.* He plays in one of Moscow's large symphony orchestras, collects records and tape recordings from Moscow's shops and other collectors, and allows himself a few foreign friends, who bring him records and books he could not otherwise obtain. The orchestra's Party Secretary once indicated that he knew all about the violinist's foreign acquaintances, but no one ever told him to drop them. In the summer the violinist grows flowers and tomatoes in his garden. He travels to Moscow on

---

* Judging by my conversations with Russians all over the country, listening to foreign radio broadcasts is an almost universal custom among educated people. Factory officials, officers of the Young Communist League, Moscow writers all listen to the Russian-language broadcasts of the BBC, Voice of America, German Radio and others. Even Khrushchev, according to his memoirs, listened.

the electric train only when he has to. His mother makes his midday dinner with great care and looks after his clothes.

I glimpsed another private world shared by four artists in Moscow, all of whom paint pictures that fail to meet the standards of realism imposed by the Union of Artists. The four think of themselves as a group or school, not because their work is so similar, but because they share common attitudes toward the struggle for identity and integrity. They are a talented group, producing paintings that might well make most of them rich and famous in the West, but which are little known in Russia outside their immediate circle of friends. I have no idea how many such artists exist in the Soviet Union. There could be many great talents who are known only to their wives or husbands.

The artist's life assumes a special character when he is denied any real audience, any formal criticism, any galleries or dealers. The ego rewards that creative people require must be supplied by a few friends. Each member of this group remembers what the others are working on. When they meet they know what questions to ask, what encouragement to offer.

Life for these four is full of hard work and private pleasures. They have their own studios, improvised in basements or under the eaves of old apartment houses, where they work and entertain friends. Two make their livings as graphic artists designing books; another sculpts official busts of Lenin; and the fourth is supported by his wife. Much of their conversation is dominated by philosophical subjects—the nature of Russia, the meaning of art and of life itself. "We are all working with basic metaphysical issues," one of them told me.

They entertain each other with hot tea, dried fish or tinned sprats, a cake bought in a bake shop or coleslaw made at home, and sit around tiny tables until the early hours of morning. Politics touches their lives only peripherally—for example, when a friend emigrates to Israel (many have) or an artist they know gets in trouble with the union.

Politics is a distraction. An artist who paints abstract canvases of far higher quality than the average "underground" painter in Moscow refused to take part in the outdoor exhibit of unofficial art which the authorities permitted in 1974. Later she explained why:

"There are two possible paths in life—the path outside, in the open, in society, and the path inside. I don't mean simply inside oneself, a closed circuit within oneself, but rather the path to metaphysics, to a deeper understanding of the world. This deeper, ontological understanding of existence demands a certain aloofness from the world of daily events which shape social and political passions. Therefore, my decision not to participate in this exhibit—in an activity that was conducted on the most superficial level of existence—was motivated by a desire to preserve my inner peace, and to preserve the ability to contemplate more deeply."

This could have been a rationalization for avoiding a risky situation. Many of those who took part in the exhibit were later punished. But I know this woman, and suspect she really believed what she said. Her words evoke a romantic-philosophic strain in the Russian character which I saw again and again in Moscow's intellectuals. They are drawn to private philosophizing, to mysticism and religion.

One evening in Moscow I listened to a long conversation about a spiritual medium from Vienna who had somehow made her way to the Soviet Union, and whom my acquaintances had met. They told me about the evening they had spent with her. "She didn't make contact with any spirits of the dead that night," one explained, "but the stories she told were amazing—really persuasive!" They seemed completely convinced of her ability to talk with spirits. These were intelligent, well-read, thoughtful people.

I expressed predictable, liberal, Anglo-Saxon doubts about the plausibility of the medium's claims, which led to a discussion on belief and faith. No, I said when asked, I do not believe in God. "Ah," said one of the Russians, "then you need to live in Russia for a few more years!"

Later, on my way home to the compound for foreigners, I thought about that remark. It seemed wise. My world discourages philosophic rumination or belief in supernatural forces; I can lead my life without them, I don't need them. Could any Russian intellectual say the same?

Russian intellectuals live in Russia—the country, now part of the Soviet Union; the historical tradition; and the culture. They are fiercely patriotic and Russo-centric. That is, Russia occupies the center of their world, and often fills it entirely.

I cannot count the times a Russian mentioned a name to

me—of a writer, an artist or a political figure—expecting me to be familiar with it, only to raise his eyebrows in amazement when he discovered I was not. One of my acquaintances in Moscow met a famous American journalist several years ago and began talking with him about Alexander Tvardovski, a celebrated 20th-century poet who became a hero to Russian intellectuals as editor of the magazine *Novy Mir*, a post he held after World War II and again from 1958 to 1970. It is no exaggeration to say that most of the literature and criticism worthy of note published in the USSR during those years appeared in *Novy Mir*. But the American journalist had never heard of Tvardovski, a fact which shocked and appalled my Russian acquaintance. He talked about it for weeks afterward. "This makes us realize," he said, "that others don't share our interest in Russian problems." To him, that was a revelation!

Lev Navrozov, a recent émigré from the Soviet Union, has written about the Russian attitude toward the two great European cultures:

> ... While appreciating "austere German genius" and "lucid Gallic wit," the traditional Russian intellectual conceived of Germans and French as vaudeville types, and a nobleman's knowledge of French and German did not prevent even Tolstoi from representing them as such, thus showing the reader once again that only the Russian has a *soul*. Even after the cultural elite migrated to France and Germany after [the Bolshevik Revolution in] 1917, many Russian intellectuals never rid themselves of these vaudeville images. Besides, they believed that Western (meaning French and German culture was turning apocalyptically into what Spengler called "civilization," something "scientifically" soulless, cynical, lifeless. ...

The Russian inclination to cultural chauvinism is reinforced by the government's restrictions on travel abroad. Prejudices cannot be tested against reality. Most Russian intellectuals have never had the experience of seeing life, world events, even the stars in the sky from a vantage point radically different from the one they were born to.

The combination of Russo-centrism and isolation has had the curious effect of helping Russian intellectuals accept their lives in the Soviet Union. Most Russian intellectuals are certain in their hearts that it is better to struggle and suffer in Russia than to abandon their homeland. In recent years, for the first time since the 1920s, emigration has become possible for a few Russians, mostly Jews, and quite a large number have taken advantage of the opportunity. But only a tiny fraction of the intelligentsia has left, and only a tiny fraction would leave even if emigration were free to all. Live in some alien land where they don't even know the poems of Pushkin? Impossible. Well, nearly impossible.

Some Russian intellectuals are so immersed in their own country and its traditions that they find it hard to believe that other countries are really different. A distinguished Soviet scientist who was waiting for permission to emigrate to Israel told me about a friend of his, a lawyer, who survived Stalin's prison camps and twice escaped death sentences by good fortune. According to my acquaintance, the lawyer was a thoughtful and intelligent man who himself had decided to try to emigrate to Israel, but he could not imagine that other societies were qualitatively different from his own. My acquaintance argued with him about the existence of a truly free press in the United States. Ridiculous, the lawyer said— the *Washington Post* is just their version of *Pravda,* it speaks for their leaders. What about Watergate? my acquaintance asked him (late in 1973). If Nixon would just get tough, the lawyer replied, it would all blow away.

Russian intellectuals tend to have an exaggerated opinion of their understanding of the outside world. I was often lectured in Russia on the decline of the West, the true meaning of pornography in Times Square, the American electoral process and many other subjects about which those speaking were misinformed.

I don't mean to sound condescending—I also heard wise opinions from Russians on many non-Russian subjects. By no means every Russian intellectual thinks the rest of the world is just like the Soviet Union, or overestimates his own understanding of other countries. But I saw both these phenomena often. Combined with patriotic feelings, they help many Russian intellectuals cope with life in the Soviet Union.

In Moscow the intellectual community seemed almost incestuously intimate. Because they are bound together by the giant unions, the members of one branch of the creative intelligentsia—writers or actors, for instance—may know hundreds of their colleagues. I was most familiar with the writers, who all seemed to know one another. The best place to observe them is the Aeroportski region of Moscow, where the Union of Writers has built many cooperative apartment houses.* The writers tended to know one another even before they became neighbors. Now, living in the same building, they seemed to know one another's mistresses, ex-wives and children, and the fate of everyone's most recent story or book.

Intimacy becomes a form of protection against outside pressures. "We hold each other's hands," one woman who lives in the Aeroportski region told me proudly when we met in the apartment of another writer whose niece had just been interrogated by the KGB, alarming family and friends. I saw this hand-holding repeatedly, in good times and bad. The duties of a friend in this circle can be rigorous. One man told me why a friend of his—a mercurial writer—would be lost if he emigrated to Israel or the United States:

"Here he can really impose on his friends. He can call me up at three in the morning and say, 'I'm coming over,' and I won't complain. I should, but I won't. He'll come over and we'll sit up all night smoking cigarettes. He'll tell me all about the latest girl or some new catastrophe in his life. Now, who will he find in Israel or New York who could take my place?" It seemed to me a good question. In the Anglo-Saxon world we generally abandon that kind of intense friendship soon after adolescence.

Intimacy among the writers has professional implications. It is difficult for a young person without connections in the Leningrad or Moscow literary worlds to get anything published, the domination of these groups is so complete. Many of today's prominent writers went to school together. There is a widespread self-consciousness among literary people which may grow from the realization that they are the heirs to Pushkin, Tolstoi, Dostoevski and the rest—be they worthy heirs or not. Well-known writers, including many without

---

* The Soviet government builds apartments to rent to citizens at subsidized rates, but also authorizes the construction of cooperatives, whose buyers must pay several thousand rubles as a down payment and larger monthly amounts than ordinary renters. This is a means of drawing citizens savings back into the economy and helping to compensate for the cost of subsidized housing.

great talent, become celebrities; friends save every note and letter they write.

Intimacy on a wide scale allows the intellectuals to feel some group solidarity in an uncongenial society. We few understand, they often seem to be saying—we must stick together. "I live in a state called Moscow," an actor said to me late one night, trying to explain his ignorance about his countrymen. "What do I know about Russia?"

Many in this group have adopted a carefree, Bohemian approach to life. Seize the day, the flower, the bottle of vodka, the girl—seize what is seizable, for who knows what tomorrow may bring? In the West, intellectuals grow out of—or into—the middle class, a class which tries to impose a sense of propriety on its members. Not in Russia—at least not in Moscow and Leningrad. Heavy drinking, promiscuous sexual lives, an almost total disregard for possessions, clothes, neatness or even cleanliness are all extremely common and widely accepted. It is a rare member of the intelligentsia who hasn't been married more than once, and marriage is a formality which many couples ignore. Couples were breaking up and coming together at a fantastic rate even among the people I knew in Moscow. I met one woman of thirty-five who had been married three times, had lived with a dozen different men, had had more than 10 abortions (she had lost count) and who thought of herself as entirely normal in every way.

I used to visit a two-room apartment which would make the ideal setting for a play about this class of Muscovites. Its wooden floors had never been varnished or waxed, and in five years had become a hideous dark gray. The beds were never made, and the disarray was always just about total—clothes, toys, books, cassettes for a tape recorder strewn about; a window broken; the walls streaked with crayon, the wallpaper peeling. The only respectable piece of furniture in the apartment was a bookcase. Life was conducted mostly in the kitchen, a small room perhaps eight feet square. Laundry hung from strings across it; the undersized sink was invariably piled precariously high with dirty dishes; on the stove a pot half full of yesterday's *kasha* (a hot cereal made from grain) and the teakettle, usually boiling. More people than a fire marshal would allow were usually crowded around the small table, drinking tea out of a variety of unmatching containers and cutting slices of bread from a stale white loaf.

The woman of the house had come into a pair of Levis, and wore them constantly, day after day for months at a time. It was a wonderful place to spend an afternoon or evening.

The best part of any private world is the pleasure one can find within it, and these Russians know how to arrange their pleasures. They are masters of the gay evening, fueled by vodka and Armenian cognac, entertained by a new record on a scratchy old record-player, filled with laughter, dancing, whatever. A holiday, a birthday, a whim is occasion enough to make a party. The young, especially, make them constantly.

But the greatest pleasure comes from conversation. A Russian intellectual is most comfortable with himself, I decided, when he is sitting at a crowded table in someone's kitchen, talking across a litter of cheese and salami, pieces of bread and cucumber, glasses, vodka bottles and teacups. Visitors may come and go, hosts brew more and more pots of tea, the salami steadily shrinks and the talking goes on and on. This is the setting for what the Russians call "a real Russian conversation." I first heard the phrase from an old man, and asked how he defined it. "A Russian conversation," he said, "is one that touches on every subject there is." He winked. In the 19th century Vissarion Belinski, a famous critic, protested when his wife called a group of friends to the dinner table. What, he said, you want to eat before we have decided whether or not God exists?

I sat through many Russian conversations, and began to realize that this was the aspect of Russian life that I would cherish the longest. Yet they all seemed impossible to remember; so many subjects were covered in the course of one evening, so many jokes and anecdotes. I decided I had to try to set down a Russian conversation immediately after it occurred, in the hope of capturing the anarchic quality, the richness, the fun of a long evening of Moscow talk. So late one night, after several hours spent with a Moscow writer and his daughter-in-law, a fledgling writer herself, I recorded the following:

We began with a discussion of book reviews in Soviet literary journals. The daughter-in-law (I will call her Tanya) had just published a review in a small magazine. It was a review of a book of poetry, she said—bad poetry, but the author's ideas were "normal," a wonderful Russian use of the word which meant she agreed with them. Therefore she was willing to fulfill the magazine's request for a "positive" review of the book. She wrote one, very carefully. She had received a copy of the magazine just that morning. The magazine had given her piece a new title—an enthusiastic slogan—and added a final paragraph saying how splendid the book was in every way. Between those two inventions was, essentially, Tanya's review. "They pay well," Tanya said. "Sixty-five rubles for three and a half pages."

Her father-in-law (Alexei) then recounted how the literary journal *Moskva* (Moscow) had asked him for a positive review of a first novel by a young writer. They sent him the book, he tried to read it, but couldn't—"it was simply awful." So he called the editor back and apologized, but said he couldn't do the review.

From this we went to a new movie that had just opened, a sensational hit by Moscow's standards, then playing in more than 50 movie theaters in the capital. (The theaters exploit a hit in this way, they explained to me, to fulfill their Plans. One popular movie can fulfill a theater manager's Plan for a period of months, enriching the state in the process.) I had found it a fascinating movie, and startling for its departures from the usual run of Soviet films. It concerned a criminal— a departure in itself, since Soviet heroes are meant to be uplifting models of good behavior—who tried to escape his past by building a new life in the far northern countryside. Just as he seemed to be succeeding, his former colleagues in a gang of thieves tracked him down and killed him, for no apparent reason. This defied all the rules of Soviet cinematography—a violent ending, sad and unexpected, with no uplifting moral. Moreover, the film contained unmistakable religious allusions, and left the strong impression that its author, a popular but controversial writer named Vasily Shukshin, was condemning the spiritual emptiness of Soviet life.

We discussed how such a movie could ever be cleared by the censor. Shukskin apparently had a special status with the cultural bureaucrats—and perhaps with the country's senior leaders—because he was not a typical intellectual, but a farm boy who had made good as writer, film director and actor (he played the leading role in this movie). "On top they think he is one of them, not one of us," Alexei said. According to one rumor, a member of the Politburo, perhaps Brezhnev himself, had seen the movie and liked it, recommending it enthusiastically to the State Committee on Cinematography—which had been sitting on the film for several months, not knowing what to do with it. With a high-level endorsement, the committee felt free to distribute the film.

Alexei—like others in Moscow at the time—disliked Shukshin's romantic views of rural life and implicit, unfavorable comparison with the city. Alexei thought he was criticizing values which he, Alexei, respected. Tanya disagreed sharply. She defended Shukshin's view of rural life.

"That's his idea of a way out," Tanya said. "He's entitled to his own theory." Intellectuals of the 1960s, she argued, particularly those associated with the journal *Novy Mir* when Tvardovsky was its editor, had tried to find subtle ways to criticize the status quo, but offered no way out of it. Shukshin had an idea for a way out, albeit a half-baked idea. She thought this was significant. (Shukshin died unexpectedly at age forty-five in 1974.)

Alexei then teased me about a story in a recent issue of *Literary Gazette* which had quoted me as writing in the *Washington Post* that there was no inflation in the Soviet Union. *Literary Gazette* had invented the quotation, but I had to answer for it to Russians for weeks afterward. "You'll make a fine Soviet journalist someday," Alexei told me.

He observed that you could still hear people on the streets say that "things were good under Stalin—he lowered prices." Yes, he lowered prices—this was how: The price of a roll which used to cost ten kopeks in the bakeries was reduced, with much fanfare, to nine kopeks. A few other products might be similarly reduced in price at the same time. Then the papers would be full of detailed analyses explaining how much richer people would be in 10 years, thanks to the money they'd save because of these new, lower prices. Much jubilation would ensue. Then after a few weeks that type of roll (or salami, or cheese, or whatever) would disappear from the stores, replaced by something almost the same which cost thirteen kopeks.

This introduced the subject of Stalin, one that recurs often in such conversations. Alexei recalled the day Stalin's death was announced. At the time he was working as a journalist, and had been assigned to write an article about one of the biggest factories in Moscow. He was interviewing scientists in the research laboratory. When news of the Great Leader's demise was broadcast on loudspeakers, Alexei wandered out onto the factory floor, where people were weeping "in real fear." Many thought, *Well, that's it for us, that's it for the country—we're helpless now.*

Back in the research lab, Alexei found that despair was not exactly universal. There was one man working in the laboratory who—for the rest of the day—repeatedly broke out in song. Each time others shouted at him to be quiet, to stop insulting the memory of Stalin. He apologized and stopped, but a short while later the singing started up again. "Evidently," Alexei said, "he wasn't one of the saddest people that day."

Tanya then told a long story she had heard about the behavior of *kulaks* (wealthy peasants) deported to Siberia during the collectivization of agriculture. The story lasted 45 minutes, and I won't try to repeat it here, but its point was interesting: that, once transplanted, the *kulaks* became utterly dependent on the local authorities in their new Siberian homes, and would do their bidding loyally, even if that meant displacing local populations in the same cruel way the *kulaks* themselves were originally displaced from European Russia.

Somehow the talk got back to literature. Alexei complained that, apart from a brief period in the early years of this century, there has never been "culture for culture's sake" in Russia. Instead literature has always been part of specific social or political conditions. Tanya said she had recently realized that the literary revival of the early 19th century, led by Pushkin, was in a sense a Russian substitute for the Renaissance—which Russia missed out on altogether. This prompted Alexei to undertake a discursive analysis of Pushkin's *The Bronze Horseman*, whose true message, he thought, was that there is no hope of fundamentally improving the human condition.

That led to a discussion about emigration to Israel, which some intellectuals do think of as a way of improving their condition. Many prominent members of the Moscow intelligentsia have emigrated in recent years—the most famous, of course, Solzhenitsyn, whose departure was involuntary. This subject was passionately discussed. Alexei read from a letter he had received from an old friend now living in Jerusalem; its subject was "whether or not to take your umbrella"—a euphemism for trying to emigrate.

Two years earlier, Tanya said, she had desperately wanted to leave the country. That was before she met her current husband and began to get some work as a writer. Now, she said, she wanted to stay. Of course that would mean making compromises. But she was ready for that, up to a point. She could write book reviews like the one just published. She would make the small compromises and cultivate her inner freedom. That is most important—inner freedom—and it is possible, even in Russia.

People born to freedom can never appreciate what it means to achieve that inner freedom in our kind of system, Tanya said. What we have achieved here is something unusual, even precious, but for you (me) it wouldn't mean anything at all. Russians need their suffering, they *want* to suffer. What is love to a Russian? First of all, it is pity. Sex? That's in tenth place. First, they want to pity someone, then to comfort him.

Tanya said she wasn't ready for real individualism, for complete responsibility for herself, yet she knew that's what she would have in the outside world. Russia is really a collective society, not just because of communism, but historically. Look at the Orthodox Church—there the individual has no personal relationship with God, he is simply part of the group worshiping together. Life in the villages, traditional family life—it's all collective. It's in our blood. . . .

My notes end there.

11 · A Rebellious Few

I will sing of Liberty
And scourge the evil that sits on thrones. . . .
—*Alexander Pushkin, 19th-century poet*

Where can people turn in this land?
—*Andrei Sakharov, 20th-century physicist and dissident*

PUSHKIN AND SAKHAROV both belong to an old and distinguished tradition of Russian intellectuals who have yearned for justice and freedom. The yearning is as old as the intelligentsia, yet it has never been satisfied. Pushkin, Dostoevski, Hertzen, Mandelstam, Pasternak, Solzhenitsyn—a long line of great Russian writers has conveyed this yearning to their countrymen and to the world outside, but an equally long line of czars and commissars has persistently frustrated the dream. This is surely one of the great struggles of history, one that will fascinate men for as long as Russian culture survives.

Since the early 19th century the struggle has continued erratically, in bursts followed by long lulls. When circumstances allowed, the protagonists rose up to advance their claim to freedom. But this has never been easy, and each time it has occurred, the strain of the effort has exhausted those who made it. The forces of orthodoxy have always reassumed full control.

In the last few years we have witnessed the most significant uprising of the progressive, liberal intelligentsia in half a century. It has been high drama: on one side, Sakharov, Alexander Solzhenitsyn, the most celebrated writer of Russian prose in several generations, a band of courageous young people, Jewish activists and others; on the other, the KGB and the Communist Party; and—for the first time in Russian history—a huge international audience looking on. This audience, brought into the drama by the mass media of our age, is an entirely new factor in the struggle. Because of it Solzhenitsyn is probably better known in the world than Leonid Brezhnev; he has certainly made a deeper impression on the intellectuals of Russia and the West during these years than has any of the leaders of his own country.

For his efforts Solzhenitsyn is now an involuntary exile; Sakharov, though a Nobel laureate, is isolated and often dejected, hundreds more are in prisons, labor camps, mental hospitals or exile in Siberia. Human tragedy has always accompanied the Russian intelligentsia's periods of assertiveness; the dank and bitter odor of tragedy now surrounds the remnants of this latest episode.

The "dissidents," as they came to be known, first appeared in strength in the mid-1960s. They startled the world then, because the world and Russia itself were used to the silence of the Stalin years. But that silence was dearly bought, and Stalin's successors refused to pay the price to maintain it. They abandoned massive terror, so the level of fear in Soviet society receded. That made the reappearance of some vocal intellectual critics inevitable. Inevitable, because the commissars, like the czars before them, have failed to impose intellectual orthodoxy, but have failed also to make room for intellectual diversity. They cannot convince everyone to think alike (except, perhaps, with terror), nor can they bring themselves to allow anyone to think differently in public. The word for "dissident" in Russian means, literally, "one who thinks differently," a good indication of the conventional mentality.

Eventually, a few of those who privately dispute the official orthodoxy will say so out loud. The impulse to speak out is an ancient human instinct; it is the force which moved the boy in Hans Christian Andersen's fable to shout that the emperor had no clothes. When that happens in the Soviet Union it is dissidence.

The fact that only a few speak out is important. The dissidents represent a small fraction of the educated population, a tiny fraction of the Soviet citizenry. Throughout Russian history they have failed to attract a mass following, and it is hard to imagine that they ever will win over their countrymen. On the basis of their numerical weakness, Soviet officials try to write the dissidents off as an insignificant fringe group. But the harsh official repression of this small band reveals the authorities' true sentiments; they know that, despite their number, the dissidents are important.

The authorities have recently tried to explain dissidence as a consequence of foreign influences. Purely internal dissent is impossible, because "People and Party Are One," according to the sloganeers. At a trial of political dissidents in 1973 the prosecution based its case on the proposition that foreign ideas inspired Soviet dissidence; foreign cameras and typewriters—used by duped Soviet citizens—reproduced those ideas; then foreign news media reported that a "democratic movement" was active in the Soviet Union. In other words, a foreign plot from conception to consecration.

In fact many of the dissidents worked for years as loyal collaborators of the regime. Some, such as Sakharov, admit that their opinions have changed and new ideas have drawn them away from the Party and the government. But others feel strongly that they have not changed in temperament or thinking—the regime has. While they have maintained a consistent outlook, in other words, the official standards have shifted, leaving them exposed; instead of cooperating, they now find themselves isolated.

Perhaps the best example of such figures is Alexander Tvardovsky, whom I have already mentioned. Tvardovsky was a popular poet. He became a national hero at the end of the war when he published an epic poem about a fictional common soldier, Vasily Tyorkin, which captured the national imagination. Stalin himself, according to Khrushchev, hung a "portrait" of Tyorkin on a prominent wall in the Kremlin.

During most of his life Tvardovsky apparently tried to push Soviet literature in a more liberal direction. His first term as editor of *Novy Mir*, the literary journal, ended in 1954 because he had published critical stories and articles which offended the authorities. He got the job back in 1958, as the post-Stalin thaw was beginning, and under his leadership *Novy Mir* became the voice of the progressive intelligentsia. With the permission of the Party's Central Committee, he published Solzhenitsyn's *Ivan Denisovich* in 1963, the most dramatic literary event of the post-Stalin period. In the same year, on Khrushchev's personal order, *Izvestia* published a new Tvardovsky poem about Vasily Tyorkin, but this one had nothing to do with wartime heroics. It was called *Tyorkin in Another World* (that is, in heaven), an hilarious but bitter denunciation of bureaucracy, narrow-mindedness and official censorship. These, too, were the heritage of Stalinism, Tvardovsky seemed to say. Among intellectuals this poem caused almost as much stir as did *Ivan Denisovich*.

Tvardovsky tried to continue publishing Solzhenitsyn; the novel *Cancer Ward* was even set in type before higher authorities banned it for political reasons. From 1964 onward Tvardovsky could only watch helplessly as his greatest literary discovery slipped deeper and deeper into official disgrace. In 1970 it was Tvardovsky's own turn; he was removed as editor of *Novy Mir*.

Tvardovsky was a victim of the same historical process which produced the modern dissidents—which is why I tell his story here. In 1958, when he reassumed the editorship of *Novy Mir*, a large part of the Soviet intelligentsia, particularly the literary intelligentsia, was optimistic and excited. This was the period of the thaw, as Ilya Ehrenburg had called it. Stalin was dead and Khrushchev had denounced him in the famous "secret speech" at the 20th Party Congress in 1956. (It was no secret to the intellectuals in Moscow.) A few books, stories and articles had appeared which flew in the face of Stalin's old standards, and everywhere the old restrictions seemed to loosen. It was easy to believe that a new liberalism was on the way.

This optimism grew steadily through 1963, when *Tyorkin in Another World* and *Ivan Denisovich* were published. Then in 1964 Khrushchev was removed and the first disquieting signs of change began to appear. The turning point was the trial of Sinyavsky and Daniel in February 1966, which I mentioned in the last chapter. Sinyavsky and Daniel were the first intellectuals in the history of the Soviet state to be put on trial for, in effect, disseminating dissenting views—by writing fiction published abroad under pseudonyms. The trial shocked many members of the intelligentsia; hundreds, perhaps thousands of people signed letters and petitions protesting the persecution of writers. Instead of heeding these protests, however, the authorities effectively closed the trial to the public, convicted both defendants (who insisted on their innocence) and sentenced Sinyavsky to seven years, Daniel to five, in labor camps. The convictions of Sinyavsky and Daniel created the energy which produced the dissidents. In the next big political trial the defendants were people who had made and distributed a transcript of the first trial; it, too, attracted letters and petitions. Like-minded people began distributing these documents among themselves, giving birth to *samizdat*, a Russian word meaning "self-published" which came to describe the widespread circulation of protests, declarations and even full-length works of fiction and prose in typescript from hand to hand.* (*Cancer Ward* could not be read in *Novy Mir*, but thousands read it in *samizdat*.) The authorities had embarked on a campaign to stamp out the liberalism that Khrushchev had permitted, but the intellectuals—or a substantial, though small, minority of them—would not give in without a fight. Repression bred protest which bred more repression.

By 1971 the authorities were clearly in control of the situation, and in that year Alexander Tvardovsky died. His death became a political event. The literary bureaucrats—who had never approved of the thaw, and were delighted when something like the old orthodoxy was reimposed—saw to it that Tvardovsky was memorialized only as a poet. His editorship of *Novy Mir* was ignored in the many appreciations that were written when he died and in the speeches made at a memorial service in the House of Writers, a signal that the authorities now saw nothing to praise in Tvardovsky's work as an editor. Zhores Medvedev sneaked into that memorial service (non-members of the Union of Writers were supposed to be excluded, and Medvedev, a biologist, was not a member), and has written this account in *Ten Years After Ivan Denisovich:*

---

* Banned manuscripts have circulated among Russian intellectuals at least since the last century, and there were "dissidents" before the 1960s, but the phenomenon I am writing about here began at that time.

The meeting ... was opened by S. S. Narovchatov, a secretary of the Moscow branch of the Writers' Union. Of all the speakers at the brief gathering, none had been a really close friend of Tvardovsky's. All the speeches had been prepared in advance and had passed through the filter of censorship, so that there should be no mention of the last 10 years of the poet's life, of his journal [*Novy Mir*], his polemical writing, his civic courage, and of *Tyorkin in Another World*. The orators acknowledged only Tvardovsky the poet and even then only as the author of a restricted list of works. When Narovchatov declared the funeral assembly over and requested everyone except the dead man's family and close friends to leave the hall, a young woman in the middle of the hall rose to her feet.

"Why are you closing the meeting so soon?" she cried, so that everyone could hear her. "Is it possible that no one is going to say that we are burying our civic conscience here? That Tvardovsky was forcibly removed from his work, that he was compelled to leave *Novy Mir*, that his last poem [*By Right of Memory*, said to be a moving account of horrors under Stalin] was not published? That they shut his mouth before he shut it of his own accord?" This short speech was followed by the noisy shouting of vigilantes [who were stationed throughout the hall] to try to drown whatever the woman might say next. But she was already pushing her way toward the exit, a scarf thrown over her head. Soon she was lost in the crowd filing out of the hall. Nobody stopped her. Evidently she got away from the House of Writers without being detained—and none of Tvardovsky's friends ever managed to discover her name.

A brazen act of dissidence, right in the main hall of the House of Writers! But what did it consist of? Just an anguished cry of indignation, an attempt to set the record straight. The young woman was presumably a member of the Union of Writers herself—part of the official intelligentsia, in other words.

As I write this book in the second half of 1975, it appears that the KGB and the Party have virtually completed the crackdown against active dissidents which began 10 years ago with the arrests of Sinyavsky and Daniel. At that time hundreds of people in Moscow would sign a protest petition; a decade later it would be a triumph to get two dozen signatures on a similar protest. Hundreds of arrests, hundreds of voluntary and involuntary decisions to emigrate and thousands of private decisions that protest is no longer worth the candle have all but silenced the active dissenters.

But the activists are not the only dissidents. They are unusual for what they do, but not for what they think. Among the intelligentsia there are literally thousands of people—I suspect hundreds of thousands—who share, in a general way, the views of one or another faction of dissidents. But it is a private, silent sharing. The active dissidents speak out, take risks, usually forgo any hope of maintaining an official career, end up in trouble or in jail. Naturally, most people aren't attracted to that sort of life, so most people, even among the group naturally sympathetic to them, don't join the dissidents.

The fact that a large number of intellectuals privately sympathizes with people like Tvardovsky, Solzhenitsyn and Sakharov should not be surprising. Intellectuals, after all, live with ideas. They are by nature thoughtful, often idealistic and hopeful. They are likely to have a personal sense of right and wrong, and a personal understanding of intellectual honesty. In the modern era the Soviet regime has proven incapable of appealing to any of these qualities. The regime demands loyalty for practical reasons, but cannot satisfy the intellectuals' desire for a sense of meaning, a purpose in life. Join us or suffer the consequences of opposing us, the regime demands—but don't ask questions. Don't ask for justifications.

There is no room for questions in the Soviet political process, at least not in public. No one is entitled to ask the most basic questions: Why can't we practice Marx's humanism? Why are we spending so much on armaments? Why are Russians so unpopular among the other Soviet nationalities? Why can't we publish a journal like Tvardovsky's *Novy Mir*, a little more liberal than the straight Party line? Why can't we write the true history of our own country? Why can't we live as well as the Hungarians, let along the French? Those questions—and all others—are ruled out of order by the siege mentality that still prevails in the ruling circles of the country. We are under siege, they seem to be saying, therefore we have no time for diversions—such as these questions. First let us build communism, then we'll worry about what it is like.

Why should this appeal to an intellectual? Obviously it wouldn't. The loyalty of intellectuals comes from patriotism, from fear, from the material rewards for loyalty, and perhaps in a few cases from faith in Marxism-Leninism and the notion that the end, perfect communism, justifies the means, rigidly enforced orthodoxy. (Of the intellectuals I knew, most agreed that a few people still believe passionately in the ideology, but only a few. Some of my acquaintances were certain that no one still believes. Belief, of course, is a difficult word to define.) The combination of patriotism, privileges and fear limits the number of dissidents but cannot eliminate dissidence, if only because stubborn idealism is a trait that recurs in a constant—though small—percentage of humankind, wherever it is found.

The dissidents are a diverse lot, easy to think of as a homogeneous group from afar, but unmistakably varied up close. They mirror the entire intelligentsia. There are religious dissidents whose only concern is the Church and religious literature. More religious writing is distributed in *samizdat* than secular literature or political material. There are extreme Russian nationalists whose program—if it can be called a program—is tinged with monarchism and anti-Semitism. For a while a group of Russian nationalists "published" (that is, typed and distributed) a journal called *Veche,* but eventually gave it up with a declaration that the operation had been thoroughly infiltrated by KGB stooges. There are well-meaning, utterly naïve people who make their protests individually, suffer for them individually and are never known to other people. Zhores Medvedev found a typical example of this sort of dissident in the mental hospital where he was confined. He was "a young man of about twenty-four" who, soon after he got out of the Army, "had begun to write memoranda to different official bodies sharply criticizing the Komsomol [Young Communist League] for having degenerated into a bureaucratic organization. He had proposed the creation of a new, more democratic youth association."

In the past there have been manifestations of dissent from a group which one Moscow engineer described to me as "honest communists," and it is fair to assume that such dissidents still exist. I met one of the "honest communists" who took over the Party Committee at Moscow State University in the mid-1950s. Many of them were later arrested and imprisoned. They believed that Marx and Lenin would be taken seriously and literally. Let us build real communism, they said, eliminate class differences, put the workers in real control of the economy. "We thought we were responding to Khrushchev and his attacks on Stalin," the man I met explained. "In fact we must have scared the pants off him."

Many of the dissidents reflect the strong strain of social-democratic opinion that exists within the intelligentsia. These are people who have lost enthusiasm for Marxism-Leninism. I don't mean they have become opponents of communism as a doctrine, but they have stopped thinking it is important. Most of them seem to prefer socialism to capitalism, but they want to concentrate on basic human rights; freedom of speech and press and absolute legal rights head their list. In my experience, some of the strongest advocates of this position are reformed hard-liners, old Stalinists who once helped enforce rigid orthodoxy. A man who fits this description told me, "The biggest lesson we have learned is the importance of tolerance."

Sakharov, the Moscow Committee for Human Rights which he helped to form, the *Chronicle of Current Events,* a *samizdat* journal which tried to keep up with official repression of dissidents, and many of the most active authors and signers of petitions and protests all fall into this social-democratic catagory. That doesn't mean they have always agreed with one another, but they share a common approach.

There is a division within this group that deserves elaboration. One faction—typified by the Medvedev brothers—has maintained a persistently optimistic point of view, insisting that limited reforms in the system are not only desirable but also possible. Roy Medvedev's book *On Socialist Democracy,* published in English in 1975, amounts to a summation of the optimistic analysis, though it is not very convincing. Medvedev describes the strength of conservative and reactionary elements in the Party and the weakness of progressives like himself, but then insists that the Party will democratize Soviet society because without freedom the country will stagnate.

A second and larger faction speaks out for democratization without regard for the real chances of liberalizing Soviet society. Whether its members are motivated by legalism or by ethical considerations, they share the conviction that the justice and correctness of their position are reason enough to advocate it. This is the essence of Andrei Sakharov's attitude. He insists on speaking out against injustice whenever he finds it because he is sure that is the right thing to do—whether or not there is serious hope of success.

Another group is essentially pessimistic about the Soviet system, and would be glad to see it destroyed or radically changed. Some have concluded that the western democracies have found better solutions to the problems of human society and should be copied. Others—Solzhenitsyn is the best example—doubt that western institutions can be transplanted to Russia, and would prefer not to have them. Solzhenitsyn favors something that sounds like a religious, benevolent autocracy ruled by technocrats. He explicitly rejects freedom in the western sense for Russia. Both Solzhenitsyn and the "westernizers" are contemptuous of the Soviet present.

In 1973-4 disputes broke out among the Medvedevs, Sakharov and Solzhenitsyn. Their argument grew from the distinction between optimists and pessimists. The optimists are tacticians, willing to sacrifice moral principles to gain marginal advantages. For example, the optimists thought it was a mistake for the United States to try to force the Soviet leaders to allow freer emigration of Jews by withholding trade benefits. That may have been the principled stand, the Medvedevs said, but it wouldn't work: the Soviet leaders would rebel against such pressure. They should be encouraged to do the right thing, but not forced. The pessimists put little faith in the Soviet leaders, and generally subscribe to the proposition that they only understand strength. Sakharov and Solzhenitsyn have both welcomed attempts by foreigners to compel the Soviet leaders to do what is morally right. (In the case of Jewish emigration, the Medvedevs' warning proved accurate.)

To identify every dissident with a specific, coherent point of view would be misleading. Many—I suspect a majority—react emotionally to Soviet life, without trying to construct personal ideologies. These are the people who signed so many letters on behalf of Sinyavsky and Daniel. They simply believed that it was wrong to prosecute a writer for a book he had written. They don't want to humiliate their country or overthrow the Party. They only want to find a place within the status quo for fairness, justice and truth. I was startled one evening when an acquaintance of mine, a woman deeply committed to the dissident cause, said: "If we didn't have this system, we'd probably have anarchy, which would be much worse." She really didn't think there was any fundamental alternative to Soviet power. She only hoped that the power could be used more justly.

Resurgent nationalism in the non-Russian Soviet republics probably worries the authorities in Moscow more than any other form of dissidence, because it is not restricted to a narrow intellectual elite. Ukrainians of all kinds, from the humblest peasant to the most educated professor, share a sense of Ukrainian nationality which, if aggravated, can manifest itself in dissident behavior. The submersion of local culture appears to unify the local intelligentsia in virtually every non-Russian republic, creating an "us and them" situation detrimental to the interests of the central authorities. Like the residents of the Soviet dependencies in Eastern Europe, the people of the non-Russian republics don't—with a few exceptions—dream of escaping from Russian domination, but they do hope for more autonomy and less arbitrary controls on local culture.

A final catagory of dissidents may actually include the largest number of individuals who reject the regime's values, but the form of their rejection makes them an impotent force. I have in mind the dropouts—people of all ages and backgrounds who refuse to deal with Soviet life, and turn instead to vodka, or sex, or rural life, or any of 100 other escapes. In Leningrad a group of young writers, painters, photographers and others refers to its members as "the new decadence"; they have as little to do with the Soviet Union as possible. Members of this band refer to Leningrad as St. Petersburg, its original name. They seem to have a weakness for dirty beards, leather trousers and long nights of drinking wine.

One group of dissidents deserves more attention here, both because of their intrinsic interest and because of the stir they have made inside the Soviet Union and in the West: the Jews.

Jews have lived on the territory of what is now the Soviet Union for at least 1000 years, sometimes in bad conditions, sometimes worse. Occasionally the authorities of the day have left them alone. Rarely the Jews have even had a chance to break out of their ghettos and villages and lead full lives. But for most of those 1000 years the Jews have been isolated and persecuted, sometimes mildly, sometimes cruelly.

For centuries they accepted this fate stoically. But in the 19th century three new options emerged, each of which appealed to a different segment of the Jewish population. One was emigration to America. The second was Zionism, the struggle to reestablish a Jewish homeland in Palestine. Most of the founding fathers of Israel were Russian Jews. The third was socialism, a new and powerful political idea which seemed to echo many of the tenets of traditional Jewish law and custom. A disproportionately large number of the earliest Russian revolutionaries was Jewish. So were many of Lenin's colleagues in the first Soviet government.

There may have been greater opportunities for Jews in Russia during the early years after the Bolshevik Revolution than at any other time in history. Lenin personally struggled against anti-Semitism, and the new government eradicated the artificial barriers against Jews imposed by a succession of czars. (It harassed Judaism equally with other religions, however.) But Stalin did not share Lenin's openmindedness. He turned on Lenin's Jewish colleagues (first Trotsky) with a vengeance, eventually transforming them into enemies of the state. Personally prone to anti-Semitism, Stalin reimposed the old prejudices, and eventually—after World War II—conducted a vicious program against Jewish intellectuals. Stalin's successors backed away from this final campaign against the Jews, but they never revived Lenin's original, liberal policies. After Stalin died, Jews found themselves in an uncertain position. They had greater opportunities than before, but were still conscious of prejudice, and were still excluded from certain fields. Stalin's daughter, Svetlana, described the Jews' ambiguous status in the 1960s:

> Not a single Jew worked within the apparatus of the Central Committee ... but when information was required ... then such work was done for that same Central Committee by specialists—Jews. They merely supplied the information: they were never called in to discuss and decide. Often they signed their articles in magazines with Russian pseudonyms.... Compared to 1952 ... even this represented an advance. But that was the full measure of progress in the USSR up to this day.

And when a talented young man with a special diplomatic education had been singled out for work in the Soviet Embassy in the U.S., [Foreign] Minister Gromyko turned him down for one reason only: a Jew. This happened in the year 1966, not in 1952!

The Six Day War in 1967 was an explosive event even inside the Soviet Union. It had two main consequences: First, the war gave Soviet Jews (like Jews all over the world) an enormous emotional lift. Pride in Israel's triumph became pride in their own Jewishness, something most Soviet Jews had never felt before. Second, the Soviet government's bitterly anti-Israel policy became an unspoken mandate for renewed anti-Semitism in the USSR. The state unleashed an "anti-Zionist" propaganda campaign which much of the public seemed to interpret as an anti-Jewish campaign. The distinction was often too fine to draw.

At its worst, the revived anti-Semitism of the post-1967 period has been cruel. I met a man in Israel who had arrived two weeks earlier from one of the largest cities in the Ukraine, an area where anti-Semitism is traditionally strong. He told hair-raising tales of his last months there, yet his calm tone of voice and memory for detail made the story entirely credible. Life began to get measurably worse soon after 1967, he recalled. A new epithet came into common use in those years: "Go to Israel!" Even non-Jews used it with one another. *"Zhid,"* the Russian equivalent of "kike," came into normal conversation vocabulary, whereas before it had been used discreetly.

"I remember once I was riding on the electric train in a car with about 100 other people," this man recalled. "Suddenly a wild-looking Russian began waving a knife and shouting. 'Any kikes on this train? I'll slice up every one of them.' I sat there with my head in my hands, thinking that if he did discover me and start slicing me up, no one in the train would help me. What have we come to?"

Several years ago his son, then four years old, came home from kindergarten and asked to have his curly hair cut off. His mother asked why. "The teacher said I look like a kike with this hair, and I'm not a kike, I'm a Russian."

"Listen," his mother said, "you are Jewish—your father and I are Jewish, and so are you."

"Oh, no!" the boy replied. "You can be what you want to be, but I'm a Russian!"

When this family applied for visas to emigrate, they received threatening telephone calls for three days. Someone threw a brick through the window of their apartment. They quickly moved into a rented room in a remote corner of the city and hid for weeks until they got their visas.

In Moscow anit-Semitism appears in other ways. Alexander Lerner, a mathematician and computer expert and one of the highest-ranking Soviet scientists to apply for a visa to Israel (which, at this writing, he has not received), once offered to write a book on modern management techniques. His boss, a member of the Academy of Sciences, rejected the idea. "We can't have Jews writing books telling Russians how to run things," he said. Soon afterward Lerner applied to emigrate.

The head of a laboratory—a non-Jew—in a scientific-research institute recently had two vacancies on his staff. He proposed to fill them with young scientists who both happened to be Jewish. The director of the institute rejected both candidates: "We have enough Jews in our institute already," he said.

I could tell several dozen more anecdotes of this kind. Many educational institutions have Jewish quotas. Jews find it harder than Russians to get jobs in many fields, from movie acting to nuclear physics. There are only a few token Jews in the upper reaches of the Communist Party. The authorities permit blatant anti-Semitism to appear in the public print. For example, in a book review in the magazine *Our Contemporary* published in March 1974, a critic named G. Manukyan wrote: "Wild as it may seem, the Zionists [also referred to as the world Zionist movement] have serious pretensions—like the Hitlerites before them—to world domination."

And yet the status of Jews is much more complicated than these stories suggest. The wife of that man from the Ukraine, for example, told me that in her apartment house their family was often held up as a model by the 120 other—non-Jewish—housewives. "My husband was the ideal father," she said. "All the Russians and Ukrainians would ask their husbands, 'Why don't you stay sober like he does?' That's the way it is with Jewish families—they're stronger than the others."

There are Jewish intellectuals in Moscow and Leningrad

who have had brilliant careers in science and the arts. Without Jews, Soviet music would have barely a shadow of its present international stature. A large percentage of the progressive intellectuals in Moscow and Leningrad are Jews or partly Jewish. Of the three million ethnic Jews in the USSR,* a large majority consider themselves assimilated and at home. Like Jews in almost any country, they are undoubtedly aware of anti-Semitism, but for this large majority, life in the Soviet Union is not intolerable—or it is more tolerable than any conceivable alternative, particularly emigration to Israel, a prospect that scares many Soviet Jews.

One Jewish woman who has established herself in a good career told me she thought Soviet life could be tolerable because compromise came naturally to Russian Jews—it was part of their heritage. "I already think that if I have some prospects of my own, if I'm not waiting up nights for a knock on my door, if my children are happy and have some prospects—then I can live."

There are tensions within the Jewish community between those who want to emigrate and those who try to make the best of life in the Soviet Union; they can be seen in Moscow's old synagogue on Arkhipova Street. Many of the old men who regularly worship there want no part of the new activism.** They long ago made their peace with Soviet power, and now willingly join in the prayer for the Soviet state which has been added to every service, on the order of State Council on Religious Affairs. These old men devote their energies to prayer, not politics; they rock and chant in the ancient manner of their forebears, threadbare prayer shawls over their shoulders, yarmulkes or work caps on their heads. The younger, more militant Jews regard both these old men and the officers of the congregation, who cooperate with the authorities, as little better than retainers of the state. For

---

* Under Soviet law, Jewishness is a "nationality" that has nothing to do with religion. The children of Jewish parents are automatically designated Jewish in their internal passports. It is common for Jews to bribe the police officials who issue passports to change their nationality to Ukrainian or Russian, which is thought to make life easier in many ways.

** I can't speak for the women, who were segregated from the men—and thus from me—in an upstairs balcony of the handsome old synagogue.

their part, the elders dislike the young troublemakers, and fear that they will have to pay for the activists' excesses. "They'll go to Israel, but we'll be left behind to hear about what traitors they are"—it's a familiar complaint from Jews who have no intention of emigrating, young and old.

The story of Jewish life in the Soviet Union could fill a volume as big as this one. The important point here is that the combination of reinvigorated anti-Semitism and new Jewish "nationalism" which followed the Six Day War of 1967—a year after the trial of Sinyavsky and Daniel—produced the Jewish activism of recent years. After 1967 a minority of Soviet Jews, eventually a substantial minority of well over 100,000 people, made the unprecedented decision to try to leave the USSR.

Once they had made this decision, these Jews did something no other group of unhappy Soviet citizens had ever done: they fought the authorities until they won. In 1968 the Ministry of Interior notified a few JewishJewish families that if they still wanted to go to Israel, they could. Some of them had applied years earlier, never dreaming they would actually receive permission to emigrate. After 1968 the flow of emigrants increased steadily. By 1973, the high point of the new emigration, 2500 Jews were leaving the Soviet Union every month.

The Soviet authorities' decision to open their borders to a group of malcontents was a shock and a surprise to all involved. There was no precedent for this magnanimity. Arguably, pressure from abroad forced the Russians' hand: the Jews' cause had become an international issue, and pressure was brought from virtually every western country, particularly the United States. But I cannot imagine that the Soviet leaders would make such a decision purely because of foreign pressure. It must have suited their internal purposes as well.

In my view, the Jews succeeded because they made so much noise. They conducted protest demonstrations and even a sit-in at the Party Central Committee. They unabashedly established contact with foreigners, accepted moral and material support from them, and sent their own protests abroad for distribution (and rebroadcast to the Soviet Union on foreign radio stations). They declared hunger strikes. One small group even plotted to hijack an airplane to take it out of the country.

All of this must have profoundly alarmed the KGB and its associates. They had no experience of such brazen disloyalty and aggressive self-assertion from a substantial minority of the population. Most upsetting, no doubt, was the example the Jews were setting for other potential troublemakers; if their behavior became a model for others, the consequences could be serious.

The authorities first tried to silence the Jews with brute force. Two of the defendants in the Leningrad hijack trial in 1970 were sentenced to death—not for hijacking, but for attempting to leave the country, which is treasonous under Article 64-A of the Criminal Code. It was an unmistakable warning. But at this point foreign opinion did prove influential. The death sentences provoked an outcry around the world which alarmed the Soviet authorities;* they reduced the sentences and soon afterward began allowing more Jews to emigrate, including the most troublesome activists. The KGB began to solve the problem by getting rid of it.

The authorities must have decided that they could allow the Jews to go because their departure would not create a significant precedent. After all, the Jews were almost "foreigners" anyway, a distinct nationality with its own homeland in Israel. No other malcontents in the Soviet population could make a similar claim (except for about 50,000 Germans, but they were relatively docile, and remain so).

The activist Jews were not an adequate model for other dissident groups because their goals were so limited. All they wanted was permission to leave. An intellectual dissident such as Sakharov hoped for wholesale changes in the Soviet regime, new standards of legality and official behavior. Nevertheless, the Jewish protests had important consequences for the other dissidents, who found numerous unexpected allies among the Jews—soul brothers of a kind who shared the loneliness of protest. The dissidents were heartened by the Jews' success. And the opening of the border for the first time in modern Soviet history provided a new option for the political dissidents as well—particularly for those who were Jewish, or partly Jewish, or married to Jewish spouses, categories which covered quite a few. A few gentile dissidents ac-

---

* These events took place just as the Soviet Union was preparing for the diplomatic offensive which produced what we now call *détente*. Thus there may have been unusual sensitivity to foreign opinion inside the Politburo at the time.

tually married Jews to get out of the country in the early 1970s.

That, to paraphrase the old Jewish joke, is the good news. The bad news is that the Jews' victory was apparently short-lived. The rate of emigration began to decline in 1974, and in late 1975 it is less than half what it was in 1973. There was a brief period when Soviet Jews, Israelis and their American supporters dared to believe that Senator Henry M. Jackson had forced the Soviet Union to allow 50,000 or more Jews to emigrate each year. Those were the terms Senator Jackson laid down if the Russians were to satisfy his "Jackson Amendment," which required freer emigration in return for trade benefits and credits. But after an ambiguous period of uncertainty, the Russians announced they weren't interested. They gave up the credits and tariff preferences and retained strict control over the rate of Jewish emigration.

If the Soviet leaders had accepted Senator Jackson's ulti-matum, it would have been a truly revolutionary develop-ment. Foreigners can best understand this in their own terms. How would Americans react to a foreign power which de-manded they put an end to racism? Or Britons if another na-tion insisted they solve the Ulster problem? And Russians are more xenophobic than Americans or Britons. To me, it was extraordinary that negotiations over Senator Jackson's amendment went as far as they did. Only Henry Kissinger and the Russians know the entire story, and the rest of us may never learn it, but apparently Mr. Brezhnev was prepared to live with the Jackson Amendment. He later changed his mind, perhaps under pressure from colleagues in the Party's leadership. Or perhaps Mr. Kissinger misreported Brezhnev's intentions from the beginning.

This diplomatic maneuvering coincided with other factors which tended to discourage Soviet Jews from trying to emi-grate, and in 1975 the number of applications apparently de-clined quite sharply. (Exact figures are not known.) The Yom Kippur War of October 1973 raised the possibility that Israel might not be a safe place to live, which scared many Soviet Jews. That war disrupted Israel's programs for absorb-ing immigrants, so in 1974 new arrivals had to spend longer periods in temporary housing, and professional people had more trouble finding jobs. News of these developments, which reached the Soviet Union in letters from émigrés, discour-aged many of those Jews who had thought of emigrating to

Israel because they wanted to live better than they could in Russia,* and not out of a desire to live in a Jewish state.

The most effective deterrent to Jewish emigration, though, has been the KGB. If the Jews won a victory by persuading the authorities to let so many of them leave, it was never a victory that the political police recognized. From the beginning the KGB has tried to counteract the Jewish activists. It created a new Jewish Department to conduct the campaign. I heard a rumor in Moscow—"My cousin told me, her sister-in-law works there"—that the entire 1973 graduating class of the KGB Academy was assigned to the quickly growing Jewish Department.

The central element of the KGB's strategy against the Jews, and against the other dissidents, has been patience. Deprived of the power to administer instant justice—the power which made Stalin's secret police so frightening—the KGB has chosen to wear its opponents down. In the case of the Jews, its tactics have been elaborate.

Since the late 1960s the authorities' principal concern has been to dissuade the most productive and useful Jews from emigrating. A high percentage of those permitted to go were elderly people, already on pension, and young children. Of the young adults and heads of families allowed to leave, most were ordinary workers, not trained professionals. Scientists have had the most trouble getting exit visas. Andrei Sakharov once suggested a reason for this: Jews comprise a small percentage of the scientific establishment, he said, but they tend to occupy critical posts—"they are the glue which holds it all together."

The KGB has made it particularly painful for scientists and intellectuals to emigrate—not for every one of them, but for enough to give pause to any others who might contemplate leaving. First they are subject to the normal penalty for making application to leave: immediate expulsion from their jobs and denunciation at a public meeting of the Party organization where they work. In special cases there may be more than one such meeting; I met a man in Israel who had been through 11. At each, former colleagues got up to

---

* The Israelis have discovered that this desire motivates more of the Soviet Jews than they might have liked. Those who came to Israel essentially to improve their standard of living are, as a rule, the most difficult immigrants. Many demand special privileges and complain loudly when they feel aggrieved.

denounce the traitorous Zionist. The most prominent scientists who have asked to leave the country have had to wait for long periods, from months to several years. The highest-ranking, Dr. Benjamin Levich, a chemist and a corresponding member of the Academy of Sciences, is still—in late 1975—waiting for his visa, as are a dozen or more others who applied in the early 1970s. Levich's son was suddenly drafted into the Army and, despite serious physical ailments, was sent to a spartan camp, virtually a prison, inside the Arctic Circle. (In 1975 this son and his brother both got exit visas.) Virtually every prominent Jewish scientist or intellectual who has applied to emigrate has mysteriously lost the service of his telephone, though the post office, which is in charge of telephones, pretends it cannot explain why. These people have lived largely on gifts of money from abroad;* in 1975 the government announced it would reserve the right to impose a new tax on such gifts, apparently a confiscatory tax which could be applied at the government's discretion.

All these measures have taken their toll. The Jews who have applied to leave say that hundreds more would like to do the same—"they're just waiting to see what happens to us." The KGB insures that what they see is sufficiently unappealing to give many potential emigrants pause. There probably are thousands more Jews, particularly intellectuals, who would be tempted to emigrate if they thought the pain involved would not be too severe. But it seems too risky now.

The KGB has had the sense to realize that it should not stop too many of those who apply from emigrating, so most eventually do get out. Once they've asked to go, these people are no longer useful to the Soviet Union, which quickly denounces them. As outcasts they have the courage to fight for their exit visas, and they tend to cause trouble. So they get out. The most determined Jews—which often means those with the strongest Zionist feelings—have probably emigrated already. They presumably made application as soon as it was

---

* The fact that Jews waiting to emigrate—virtual outcasts in their own society—receive money from abroad means they get certificates which allow them to shop in special hard-currency stores. A special office exchanges these certificates for foreign bank drafts, after the state takes 30 percent as a "service charge." With certificates the Jews can buy the Scotch whisky and western fashions which are the envy of the bureaucratic bourgeoisie—the very group responsible for inflicting this punishment on the Jews. A nice Soviet anomaly.

possible to do so, and wouldn't take no for an answer. After waiting a decent interval, the KGB didn't want to give no for an answer. Thus the Jewish community—particularly in Moscow and Leningrad, and no doubt elsewhere too—has lost many of its most active members, those who inspired others to take the risk and seek an exit visa.

Entirely different rules apply in the provinces and non-Russian republics, because what the KGB does in those places is seldom reported to the outside world. In Moscow the Jewish activists have extensive contact with western correspondents, who report official actions against Jews, a factor which has obviously deterred the KGB in many instances. But in Donetsk, Kharkov or Novosibirsk there is no restraining influence. In Israel I heard horrific stories about the fate of Jews in all three of those cities. Many provincial Jews have been put in jail as criminals after they applied for visas. Foreign donations can't reach the provinces, so Jews who lose their jobs face the danger of starvation. No doubt because of harsh official policies, there are many cities with large Jewish populations from which only a few families—or no one at all—have managed to emigrate.

So the Jews won a victory of sorts, but the victory has lost its shine. Anyway it was a strange victory. They forced the ruling elite to relax the traditional controls on emigration and allow them to leave—forever.

Even if emigration never again reaches the level of 1973, though, I think the Jews' victory is likely to have permanent consequences. The authorities are unlikely to close the gates tight again. I expect Soviet Jews will continue to leave the country—in a trickle, not a flood—for years to come. It will be easier to let them go than to try to keep them in.

I have written a long section about Jews, but virtually nothing about Judaism. I suppose that is another subject. Judaism in the Soviet Union is dying; except in a symbolic sense, it will probably be dead in one generation, perhaps two. Important centers of Jewish life such as Lvov and Kharkov no longer even have a synagogue. In Odessa, where Jews have lived for centuries, the few old men who still worship do so in a converted factory. The rabbis are dying off, and the government has allowed only a handful of young men to study at a seminary in Budapest where they can become rabbis. The young don't learn Hebrew or their prayers, don't know the rituals or even the meaning of the holidays.

Official persecution of religion for nearly 60 years has been more effective against Judaism than against the Russian Orthodox Church—not by coincidence, no doubt. The prohibition against religious education is an enormous barrier to the passing of Jewish ritual and tradition from generation to generation; Russian Orthodox ritual is much less complicated. Officially indulged anti-Semitism has encouraged tens of thousands of Jews to deny or disguise their religious heritage. For Judaism to survive in the land of Sholem Aleichem truly would require a miracle of miracles.

Next I want to describe Andrei Sakharov, one of the most interesting personalities in the Soviet Union, and perhaps the best individual symbol of the dissidents. Solzhenitsyn is better known and has made a greater personal impression, but in terms of beliefs and activities Sakharov is a more representative figure.

Andrei Dmitrivich Sakharov isn't exactly a regular fellow. He invented a hydrogen bomb—at least, Nikita Khrushchev gives him credit for inventing a hydrogen bomb. Sakharov himself says he was one of several scientists who made the important discoveries. Sakharov was once a leading citizen of the Soviet Union, decorated, pampered and looked after like a national treasure—but unknown to the general public. (Like the men who made the country's rockets, Soviet weapons scientists have never been permitted any personal fame.) Secretly, Sakharov received the Stalin Prize, the Lenin Prize and was named Hero of Socialist Labor *three times*. Only two other people are known to have received that high honor so often, and both are also associated with the armaments industry. At thirty-two, Sakharov became a full member of the Academy of Sciences, which made him its youngest member. Normally, even distinguished scientists don't become full members until their late forties or afterward.

Sakharov made a crucial contribution to the development of the Soviet hydrogen bomb, yet he has never been anything but a gentle, kind and reflective person. "When, twenty-five years ago, I began working on those horrible weapons," he once recalled, "I subjectively thought that this was work for peace—that it was leading to a balance of power, and thus was useful to my people and—to some extent—to all mankind.

This was how I felt then, and I think this view was shared by many others—the more so since we didn't have any choice at the time."

Because of his enormous intellect, Sakharov was swept into the upper reaches of Soviet society long before he had taken any time away from his physics to reflect on the world and his place in it. Later, when he began to think of such things, a new Sakharov emerged, a man of high principle who made his views known without regard for traditional Soviet protocol. His first cause was to ban nuclear testing.

In his memoirs Khrushchev described Sakharov's efforts to curtail experimental explosions, particularly a petition Sakharov submitted in 1961. "He was obviously guided by moral and humanistic considerations," Khrushchev recalled. "I knew him and was profoundly impressed by him. Everyone was. He was, as they say, a crystal of morality among our scientists. I'm sure he had none but the best of motives." Yet Khrushchev rejected his petition.*

Sakharov feels that in 1962 he may have influenced the limited-nuclear-test-ban treaty subsequently negotiated by the Soviet Union and the United States. Sakharov suggested to the relevant Soviet officials that the best way to overcome the problem of detecting underground explosions was to ignore them and draft a treaty banning tests in "the three environments"—in the atmosphere, in space and in the oceans. That formula was eventually adopted.

In 1964 Sakharov made a speech in the Academy of Sciences attacking the fraudelent genetic theory of Trofim Lysenko, who had persuaded both Stalin and Khrushchev that environment was more powerful than heredity, contrary to the proven laws of genetics. Lysenko dominated Soviet biology for a generation, destroying the careers of many honest men and the science of biology in the USSR. His star began to fade in the mid-1960s, thanks in part to Sakharov.

---

* The episode provides a unique opportunity to test Khrushchev's often self-serving memory against someone else's. Sakharov has recounted the same episode, noting that the proposed H-bomb tests coincided with a Berlin crisis. Khrushchev said in his presence, Sakharov has written, that the tests were necessary as a show of force: "We can't say aloud that we are carrying out our policy from a position of strength, but that's the way it must be." Khrushchev did not recall the Berlin connection when he dictated his memoirs later, and said he had explained to Sakharov that testing was necessary to keep up with the imperialists, and thus protect the Motherland.

In 1966 Sakharov joined the active dissidents for the first time. He wrote a letter to Brezhnev protesting the arrest of four people who had themselves protested against the trial of Sinyavsky and Daniel. He also signed a letter to the Party warning against a revival of Stalinism. In 1968 he wrote and distributed among his friends an essay called "Progress, Coexistence and Intellectual Freedom." The essay is a strong statement of liberal, humanistic principles. In it Sakharov concludes that mankind can be assured of a safe future only if communism and capitalism converge, and if this process is accompanied by universal democratization and demilitarization. This eloquent document reached the West and was published in many languages. It made Sakharov famous.

In August 1968—the month of the Warsaw Pact's invasion of Czechoslovakia—Sakharov was removed from all secret work. Later he was transferred to an academic institute in Moscow, with which he is still (in late 1975) affiliated. At that time he donated his life savings of 139,000 rubles, a gargantuan sum by Soviet standards,* to the Red Cross to help build a new cancer hospital, a gesture he later had cause to regret. "I had no personal contacts with people in need of help" then, Sakharov has said.

It wasn't long before he began meeting people who could have used that money—active dissidents who could find no job of any kind. They were Sakharov's new companions as he became more involved in the dissident cause. In late 1970 he and two others formed the Moscow Committee for Human Rights, a symbolic organization which periodically issues statements about individual cases or broad problems, such as the confinement of political dissidents in psychiatric hospitals. "The very existence of the Committee as a free group of associates independent of the authorities has a unique and very great moral significance for our country," Sakharov has written.

By the time I got to Moscow in August 1971, Sakharov was an established member of the activist dissident community. He was then fifty years old. He had a special status within the group because the authorities continued to indulge him. He kept his job and his membership in the Academy, and was able to lead a relatively normal life. His friends as-

---

* Sakharov's high salary and the cash value of his many state prizes enabled him to accumulate so much.

sumed that the authorities still recognized his great contribution to the state.

Sakharov receives guests in the front room of the two-room flat he has occupied in recent years with Elena Bonner, his second wife. It is in a sturdy gray apartment house on the Garden Ring, a 10-lane circular boulevard which surrounds inner Moscow. The room is dominated by a large double bed, from which the bedclothes are removed during the day, and glass-fronted bookcases along the right-hand wall. Between the books and the glass of the bookcases the Sakharovs keep snapshots of friends. Once when he caught me looking at the pictures, he reached up and brought one down; it showed a smiling man with a dog. "That's Shikhanovich, my friend," Sakharov said. "He is being forcibly treated in a mental hospital. Does he look crazy to you?" He didn't.

I eventually spent many hours in this room, and in the kitchen down the hall. Tea is served in both places. Sakharov is a fanatic for tea—tea with jam, tea with chunks of apple, plain tea. He likes to brew it piping hot, pour a little from his cup into a saucer, then sip it out of the saucer, almost like a cat.

Sakharov reminded me of a gentle old cat. He moves with a deliberate sense of purpose and control, and sits perfectly still for long periods, legs crossed, hands crossed on top of them. He has no discernible nervous habits, but is reserved with new acquaintances, sometimes to the point of allowing long lapses in the conversation while he studies the newcomer with a tilted head. He seemed intrigued by foreigners' mis-pronunciation of Russian.

If Sakharov has any weaknesses, they are tea and sweet cakes. More than once when I arrived at the apartment Mrs. Sakharov was waiting for him to return from the bakery with a new cake.

That this gentle man invented a hydrogen bomb, argued with Nikita Khrushchev or took on the KGB struck me, every time I saw him, as wholly implausible. Everything about him suggests a kindly professor, from his peaked bald head and the perpetually cracked lens in his reading glasses to his omnipresent bedroom slippers. His quiet tone of voice and slight lisp reinforce the professorial impression.

Yet he is a man of remarkable inner strength, borne along by the unswerving courage of his convictions. His words come out of his mouth with a flat, even assurance; he rarely hesitates or loses his train of thought. He has always concentrated on straightforward issues, and refuses to get tangled in esoteric discussion—a rare trait for a Russian intellectual.

From my first visit to the apartment it was obvious that his wife, Elena—"Lucya" to Sakharov—was the single most important thing in his life. She is his second wife; the first bore him three children and died in middle age. Elena Bonner is a fiery woman, part Armenian and part Jewish. Sakharov met her at the trial of a political dissident, and soon fell in love with her—madly in love, with an almost adolescent passion. According to old friends, it was something entirely new for Sakharov. With visitors in the apartment, they often held hands unselfconsciously. I repeatedly caught Sakharov staring at her.

She has a strong influence on Sakharov. An outspoken critic of the Soviet regime, she once boldly announced that she was responsible for sending the poignant prison diaries of Eduard Kuznetsov to the West. (Kuznetsov, convicted as one of the Leningrad hijackers, is serving a 15-year prison sentence.) She encourages her husband to speak out whenever he can against injustice, something he has done so often that friends fear his protests no longer carry any weight, either at home or overseas. Often she speaks for him, even interrupting him in midsentence to strengthen his words.

Issuing appeals and public statements, sending letters and telegrams—this is the substance of Sakharov's dissident activity. He has, in effect, donated his name as a banner to attract attention to various dissident causes. For a time Sakharov was admitted to dissidents' trials when others were excluded, and he sat through several of them in a silent gesture of solidarity. He'll fire off a telegram to Brezhnev or some other official on behalf of anyone who he thinks has been unjustly treated. I was in the apartment one afternoon when a nervous young man from Riga appeared at the door. He was a Jew whose wife and daughter had emigrated to Israel while he was serving a prison sentence for his participation in a Jewish protest. He had prepared a typed appeal to the Soviet leaders, reviewing his case and demanding an exit visa so he could rejoin his wife and child. Sakharov invited him into the front room, put on the reading glasses with the cracked lens and read through the document. He took a pen and scribbled on the bottom of the page, "I endorse this appeal. A. Sakharov."

Then he handed it to me, saying: "Here's some news for you."

Until he received the Nobel Peace Prize, Sakharov received the most public attention for his essay on peaceful co-existence and for a series of interviews he gave in August and September 1973. The first of these, an interview with Olle Stenholm, the Moscow correspondent of Swedish radio and television, provoked a crisis in Sakharov's life.*

Sakharov answered Stenholm's questions about Soviet society bluntly. He attacked the system of privileges and the false pretensions of the welfare state, and outlined his personal credo. After that interview Sakharov was summoned to the office of the Deputy Prosecutor General of the USSR, who warned him against further meetings with foreign journalists.

Sakharov responded by calling a press conference in his apartment. Ten western correspondents attended. We sat in a tight ring on chairs and stools in the front room, and on the bed. Sakharov told us about the warning he had received and his rejection of it. Then he answered questions. In reply to one he advised the western powers against a diplomatic rapprochement with the Soviet Union which did not require the Russians to begin opening up their society. "Such a rapprochement would be dangerous in the sense that it would not really solve any of the world's problems and would mean simply capitulating in the face of real or exaggerated Soviet power," Sakharov said.

After this interview was published, the authorities decided they should respond. They unleashed an unprecedented campaign of vilification against Sakharov, beginning it with a letter signed by fellow members of the Soviet Academy of Sciences reproaching him for opposing *détente*. This was the theme of the campaign, which continued for weeks.

The campaign coincided with a long interview that Solzhenitsyn gave to the Assocated Press and *Le Monde*, and with the show trial of Pyotr Yakir and Viktor Krasin, two dissidents who chose to cooperate with the KGB when they were arrested. The result of this coincidence was an unusual concentration of news about the opinions—and persecution—of Soviet dissidents during the fall of 1973. All this publicity upset the Soviet leaders; Brezhnev denounced it bit-

---

* It caused a crisis for Stenholm, too; he was expelled from the Soviet Union soon afterward.

terly in a major speech. As a practical matter, in 1973 the dissident "movement" had been virtually decimated, yet at that low ebb of its fortunes the outside world suddenly became vividly aware of its plight.

The Soviet authorities responded clumsily to this situation. They gave the dissidents an unprecedented amount of publicity in their own official news media. The publicity was all negative, naturally, but the public responded to it avidly. I saw this at the time at a political lecture in Moscow. The lecturer apparently received dozens of questions about Sakharov and Solzhenitsyn; reading silently through the pile of written queries he'd been handed, the lecturer said, "A lot of people seem to be interested in Comrade Sakharov. They should read what our newspapers have written." He would say no more.

Other lecturers were not so restrained. One told an audience that the real Sakharov had died from overexposure to atomic materials, and that this one was an impostor. Another said the radiation had affected Sakharov's mind. Instructions went out to Soviet journalists, and perhaps other officials, to spread the word that Sakharov was slightly unbalanced—"not quite right in the head," as one journalist told me. Rumor-spreading of this kind is common in the Soviet Union. I found it particularly ugly.

Altogether the authorities managed to display a surprising degree of fear and hate for Sakharov. Yet they had to invent a pretext for their campaign. It was based entirely on the misleading claim that Sakharov opposed *détente* and had invited foreign countries to interfere in the internal affairs of the Soviet Union.

True *détente* could have no stronger adherent than Andrei Sakharov. His opinions are about as objectionable as the Ten Commandments. He is for justice and against arbitrary punishment of people who think or express unfashionable ideas; he is against war and for disarmament; he wants countries to become more like each other by adopting each other's best— that is, fairest, most just—characteristics.

Sakharov's true sin is not that he holds such opinions, but that he expresses them. If Party and People are One, why does this most distinguished Soviet scientist insist on contradicting the Party line? It is an effrontery the authorities will not excuse. They reserve unto themselves the right to articulate ideas; no one else may compete with them. Ideas are the threat, not a tiny band of dissidents.

I was struck by the fact that Sakharov never suggested that his Committee for Human Rights or any dissident activity could be very effective in a political sense. Olle Stenholm asked him if anything could be done to change the Soviet system. He answered:

"It seems to me that almost nothing can be done, because the system has a very strong internal stability. The less free a system is, the greater, ordinarily, its ability to maintain itself."

So why did he bother to continue protesting?

"Well, there is a need to create ideals even when you can't see any route by which to achieve them, because if there are no ideals, then there can be no hope and then one would be completely in the dark, in a hopeless blind alley."

The story doesn't end there. As a matter of fact, I don't know where it ends. As in the case of the Jewish activists, the KGB has chosen to deal with Sakharov patiently, by nibbling away at him. The nibbles have been numerous; added together, they amount to large, painful bites. His wife's children by a previous marriage were among the first to suffer; her daughter was expelled from Moscow State University in her final year. She, her husband and younger brother have all been invited to study in America, but the Ministry of Internal Affairs won't even consider their application for exit visas.

Mrs. Sakharov was next. She was summoned to the KGB for a series of interrogations based on her relations with other dissidents, including Eduard Kuznetsov. Finally, she and her husband announced publicly that she would refuse to respond to any more summonses. I was in Moscow then, and it was obvious that both feared she might be arrested. She wasn't. But an injury sustained in the war began acting up, an eye injury that had left her partially blind. It deteriorated steadily during late 1974 and 1975, and Mrs. Sakharov began to fear for her remaining sight.

Together the Sakharovs have been subjected to a series of harassments. The most dramatic and terrifying was a visit by two Arabs who claimed to be members of the Black September terrorist group. They stayed for nearly 90 minutes, threatening "something worse than killing you." They added, "We never warn people twice," and told Sakharov to stop making public statements about Israel—the reason they gave for their anger. Sakharov was originally convinced that they were genuine Septembrists, but this is highly unlikely. Arab terrorists have never before or since shown their faces in the Soviet Union. And it is hard to believe that two Arabs could locate Sakharov's apartment without official assistance.* For weeks afterward Sakharov continued to get threatening mail from Lebanon and other Arab countries. This was strong, if oblique, confirmation of official Soviet connivance, since Sakharov's mail from abroad is carefully screened and ordinary letters seldom reach him.

By the end of 1974 the telephone exchange no longer allowed Sakharov to talk to persons overseas, cutting off his direct ties to former dissidents now living in Israel or the West. (He had been receiving numerous encouraging calls from foreign scientists and other sympathizers.) Shortly afterward the Sakharovs received an ominous note signed by "the Central Committee of the Russian Christian Party." It warned them to cease their dissident activities or risk danger for Mrs. Sakharov's infant grandson. Sakharov said he assumed the note was a KGB provocation, but it frightened them nevertheless.

Sakharov has retained his composure most of the time. At the height of the campaign against him in late 1973 he told me a joke on himself. "It's a story about two scientists," he said. "One tells the other, 'I can't go along with what Sakharov said in his interview with Swedish radio [the Stenholm interview].'

" 'Why not?' the other asks. 'Do you think we have good medical care?' [Sakharov criticized Soviet medical care and education during the interview.]

" 'Oh, no.'

" 'You think we have good education?'

" 'Oh, no. He could have spoken even more critically about that.'

" 'Then what's the problem?'

" 'I can't go along with a man who throws himself in front of a steamroller.' "

Sakharov told the story with a little grin on his lips.

But he has been scared. He was extremely grateful for a

---

* For the first time in years a four-volume Moscow telephone book appeared in 1973. However, Sakharov and most other dissidents were not listed.

telegram from the president of the American National Academy of Sciences to the Soviet Academy during the campaign of vilification; the American said that if anything happened to Sakharov, future scientific cooperation could be jeopardized. Sakharov thought that might have saved him from arrest or expulsion from the Academy.

Later Sakharov told us that he would like to accept an invitation to Princeton University—in other words, to leave the country. This news horrified many of Sakharov's friends, people who think of him as a symbolic insurance policy for other dissidents. Reacting to their complaints, Sakharov later said he didn't really intend to leave.*

In August 1975 the authorities permitted Mrs. Sakharov to travel to Rome, where she underwent several eye operations. When she left for Italy friends feared that the KGB might never let her return to Moscow.

Official pressure and increasing isolation began to eat away at the "crystal of morality among our scientists," as Khrushchev called him. Sakharov aged noticeably and put on weight. His wrinkles were deeper, his smile less frequent. During the summer of 1975 many who wished him well began to fear for his future, not least because his voice had lost some if its old authority, he had used it so often.

But in October 1975 a committee appointed by the Norwegian parliament threw a thunderbolt into Sakharov's life; it awarded him the Nobel Prize for Peace. Two years earlier some of Sakharov's friends had tried to get him nominated for the Nobel Prize, hoping that if he won it the authorities would be restrained from repressing him. But instead the Nobel Prize went to Henry Kissinger and Le Duc Tho, then to Eisaku Sato and Sean McBride, and Sakharov's friends forgot all about it. Then in 1975 lightening struck.

"For him," the Nobel committee said in its citation to Sakharov, "it is a fundamental principle that world peace can have no lasting value unless it is founded on respect for the individual human being in society."

The second remarkable dissident I want to describe is also a Noble laureate, Alexander Solzhenitsyn. He bears only

---

* Many of Sakharov's friends believe that the KGB will never let him leave the country because of what he knows about Soviet weaponry. Sakharov says his knowledge is outdated, and that he would never discuss it anyway.

slight resemblance to Sakharov; in fact, they have little in common except their status as outcasts, their courage to fight back and their Nobel Prizes.

Solzhenitsyn is bold, vain, dominating, utterly charming when he likes, and self-disciplined to an almost inhuman degree. "He isn't made of the same stuff as the rest of us," an old friend said.

I got to know Solzhenitsyn too, though not as well as I knew Sakharov, because Solzhenitsyn had little time to waste on American journalists. He had work to do. But Hedrick Smith of the *New York Times* and I were chosen—by Solzhenitsyn himself, on the advice of a friend of his who had put us through a series of experiments to test our reliability*—to receive the first interview he had ever given to western journalists.

The interview took place on March 30, 1972. We had known for months it was coming. That winter Smith and I went ice-skating together in Moscow so that out of range of the KGB's listening devices we could discuss the questions we would ask. Solzhenitsyn, we understood, expected a renewed campaign against him to begin in the Soviet press. Friends with official connections had warned him of this. He wanted to respond publicly when it came, which would be the principal object of his meeting with us.

Several days after the interview I wrote out a full account of what happened and sent it to a friend in America for safekeeping. At the time the whole episode was surrounded with excitement and not a little foreboding; we had no idea what the consequences might be for us (expulsion seemed a distinct possibility) or for Solzhenitsyn. What follows is that original account, slightly edited three years later:

We had been told to bring tape recorders and cameras to record the interview, and Solzhenitsyn's family, for posterity. We were also asked to look as inconspicuous as possible. So I wrapped my tape recorder and camera in old copies of *Pravda* and put them in a string bag of the type all Russians carry in their pockets or purses.

I put on dungarees and an old ski parka, an outfit that would pass unnoticed among students at Moscow State Uni-

---

* The friend was Zhores Medvedev, who, is now—like Solzhenitsyn—an involuntary exile living in the West.

versity, and set off from my apartment in the compound for foreigners at 10 A.M.

First I went to the American embassy to tell the consul what we were doing, a precaution we had agreed to in advance. If he hadn't heard from us by 7 P.M., I said (in a note handed across his desk), he should make inquiries. [We had both been in Moscow for only seven months, and still felt self-consciously uncertain about our status there. We took these precautions knowing we would never forgive ourselves if something went wrong because we *hadn't* taken them. Whether they were necessary or even helpful is an open question.] From the embassy I went across the street to Moscow's largest bread store, where I bought a late breakfast of two big sweetrolls. Then, as requested, I started riding buses, trying to confirm that no one was following me. There was no sign of anyone suspicious.

I met Rick around the corner from Solzhenitsyn's flat, which was just off Gorki Street, the principal thoroughfare in downtown Moscow, and walked to his entrance. It was in a courtyard with big gates at each end, a narrow space about 60 yards long. As we walked in, we saw a uniformed policeman standing in front of the door that led to Solzhenitsyn's apartment at the far end of the court. His familiar gray uniform was both alarming and somehow reassuring; it seemed right that the police were there, though it might mean that we would have no interview. We decided to walk back out of the courtyard, around the block and in through the entrance at the opposite end, just next to Solzhenitsyn's entry. When we came back into the courtyard, no more than five minutes later, the policeman was gone. We walked right in and up one flight of stairs to the first-floor landing. Solzhenitsyn's door was right in front of us, but so was a woman ostensibly waiting for the elevator. We stood there awkwardly until she did indeed go into the lift, and then I rang the bell.

A bolt turned and the door opened. It was equipped with a chain lock that allowed it to open only about five inches. It opened that much and there he was, the shaggy beard instantly recognizable. He looked us over. I don't think either of us said anything, but he seemed satisfied, and took off the chain. We stepped in and shook hands. I think he was as nervous as we were in the beginning, because we had to say three times which of us was which.

He introduced us to his wife, a handsome woman of

thirty-two [at the time of the interview—March 1972] whose short-cropped hair was graying. She had a wonderful full mouth and sharp brown eyes. Son Hermolai also appeared, blond, with enormous blue eyes, wearing a striped shirt and coveralls. He strutted about with the uncertain but determined step of a fifteen-month-old, talking excitedly in an indecipherable tongue. Papa exuded pride in this creature, his first child.

Solzhenitsyn was friendly but crisply business-like. He has a superb grin which makes long wrinkles around his eyes and reveals steel molars in the depths of his small mouth. The eyes are stunning: a very brilliant, very dark blue that I don't think I've ever seen before. They could talk for him.

We were ushered into what seemed to be a library. All the curtains were drawn. They both pointed fingers to the high ceiling to inform us that the police were present, if only electronically. The apartment belonged to her family, so it didn't reveal much about him. The walls were lined with bookcases. Many of the books were in sets—collected works of various writers, mostly. A small Sony tape recorder sat on a table at which we were invited to sit—not the tiny kind reporters use, but a small table model that used a reel of tape, not a cassette. It was a strange sight there. Such machines aren't sold in Soviet shops.

We sat on one side of the table, he sat opposite. He shuffled some papers he had apparently been working on, then handed a pile to us. They turned out to be "transcripts" of something he had headed "Interview with the *New York Times* and the *Washington Post*."

We had planned to submit written questions to him a week before our meeting. At the last minute the interview had been advanced five days, and there had been no chance to submit the questions. Now, sitting opposite him, we realized that he had never been interested in our questions. He had always intended to conduct an interview with himself. This put Rick in a nervous state. He had long been afraid that we might be trapped into doing something that served Solzhenitsyn's interests but not ours. I was less alarmed, but certainly wanted to read the document before making any judgment. Solzhenitsyn said he had planned to answer our questions, but since he hadn't received them, he had made up his own. Then he said that he wanted our assurance: that every single word would be published.

We both said immediately that was impossible. The document was too long. We were reporters and could not make editors' decisions. This upset him. We said we would like to read through it, and then we could tell him more realistically what the prospects were. We also gave him a list of 10 questions that we had prepared in Russian—the questions we would have submitted in advance, had there been a chance to do so.

I'm not sure I understood all his reactions during the four hours we were there, but I'm quite certain he was most upset when he realized that he wasn't going to be able to control this encounter the way he wanted to. Taking his wife, he retreated from the room, leaving us to start reading through the document. For the next two hours or so Solzhenitsyn was in and out of the library. His wife spent most of that time with us, helping us with Russian words we didn't know by defining them in simple language. Thanks to our mediocre Russian and his baroque style, we needed a good deal of help. But it was immediately obvious that he had given us an important and fascinating document. It was a detailed reply to what Solzhenitsyn called the authorities' plan "to suffocate me," a defiant response to years of accusations made against him in lecture halls and closed Party meetings. The only serious shortcoming of the document was the form he had put it in. He had phrased his questions so awkwardly that it was obvious real reporters hadn't asked them.

As we read we bantered with Mrs. Solzhenitsyn, a bright person and obviously an important advisor to her husband. We explained to her why some sections would not be of interest in America, how we could not expect to run more than a full page of text ("Nixon doesn't get that much space") and so on. She seemed to catch on. Several times she went out; we thought she was trying to explain the situation to him. She was also reporting our insistence that we get more than this document—we still wanted to ask our original questions. At one point he came in with our list of queries and said that if he answered all of them, the answers would fill another document twice the length of the one he'd given us. It was a fair remark.

Some time later he returned with a proposition. Would we mind if he also gave the "interview" to a Swedish correspondent who would publish every word? We discussed the suggestion. Neither of us liked the idea of pretending that a Swede had been there with us when it wasn't true.

"Don't worry about that," Solzhenitsyn said. He left the room and returned in a moment with a boyish blond whom Rick had never seen before, but whom I vaguely recalled. This was the period when Solzhenitsyn was trying to arrange to receive his Nobel Prize for Literature in Moscow, and this Swedish journalist had some role in that affair. He was a regular visitor to the Solzhenitsyn apartment, and had appeared while we were in the library. When Solzhenitsyn had realized that we were not going to publish every word he had prepared, he must have asked the Swede if *he* would publish it. The Swede had agreed.* After some discussion we hit on a formula that pleased everyone: Rick and I would publish the interview on April 3, the Swede on April 4, and none of us would call it an interview with anyone. It would be published simply as a statement from Solzhenitsyn. As we discussed this, Solzhenitsyn insisted several times that no report of his words appear on April 1, lest someone take it for a joke. Russians are superstitious about April Fools' Day.

With this arrangement agreed on, the Swede withdrew and Solzhenitsyn seemed much relieved. We then persuaded him to answer orally some of the questions from our list. He read through them and discussed each with his wife. They ruled out questions with obvious political overtones. "In general," Solzhenitsyn explained, "a writer decides what he will talk about." One of our questions was whether the persecution of writers was a permanent Russian condition, not tied to communism. He said he couldn't answer this one, it was much too complicated, he would have to do a lot of research to respond. Rick said fine, that's a good answer, just say that. He agreed, so we finally had a live answer to a live question. Rick and I turned on our tape recorders, he turned on his, and he repeated what he had just said. We duplicated this process with several more questions. He discussed every answer with Natalia before giving it; she offered extensive advice, some of which he accepted. The sport of it seemed to please him, though he was obviously nervous about a situa-

---

* To this day I don't know what the Swede had in mind when he gave this pledge. We learned later that he represented the Scandinavian news agencies, not any newspaper, so his promise to publish the entire interview was meaningless. In the end he did not even send the whole thing out on his wire.

tion which he could not fully control. [We learned later that when he played back his tape, he was disappointed that his language wasn't more polished.]

When we had finished taping we moved into another room to take pictures. The curtains remained drawn, so we had to get as much artificial light as possible. Every lamp in the apartment was brought in. First we did family portraits: Solzhenitsyn, Natalia and Hermolai. Papa was terribly concerned that we spell the boy's name correctly. It was unusual for Russian which has no H, but it was an H, he said—he was named for Hermes. [Copy editors at both our newspapers knew better; they renamed the boy Yermolai, which is as close as Russian comes to an H. He has been Yermolai ever since in every article I have read about Solzhenitsyn.] Then Solzhenitsyn posed alone, with a grim scowl on his face. We asked for a smile. "It's time to be serious," he said.

He revealed a little of himself during the afternoon. Once he wanted to mark the paper for emphasis, and he looked all around the room for a red pencil to do this. I offered him a blue pen, but no, he wanted a red pencil. He never found one. His handwriting is tiny but perfectly legible. He smokes a lot, a relatively expensive local brand called Golden Fleece. The index finger of his right hand has a small dot of a nicotine stain. He holds his cigarette between the thumb and third, fourth and fifth fingers, flicking the ash off with the fingernail of his index finger. His voice has a smoker's rasp, and isn't strong. He seemed in good health, and his belly made a bulge of the gray V-neck sweater he wore over a blue shirt. Both looked foreign-made. His hands are the only obvious sign of the years he spent in labor camps. They are stubby and strong. The right thumb looks as though it was once split open badly. It is now scarred and misshapen.

All the time I was with him I felt the presence of one of those dominating human personalities that fill rooms. I think this was because of the face, which is so expressive. I could feel his concentration. He is visibly nervous, his smile is radiant and the amazing eyes seem to do most of the talking. His skin seems rich and thick. He is very sensual; women must find him extremely attractive.

We had been in the apartment nearly four hours when Solzhenitsyn told us it was time to leave. I wrapped up my camera and tape recorder in the old *Pravdas*. We said goodbye. Rick's wife had left a car for us not far away, and we walked to it. He started driving me home, and had stopped to make a U-turn (the legal alternative to left turns in Moscow) when suddenly a taxi smashed into us from behind. We both immediately assumed that the KGB had crashed into the car. In a stern voice Rick said, "Take the stuff and go, go, go!" I had the same idea and was gathering up our equipment and the one precious copy of the prepared interview. Before the taxi driver could pull over, I was out of the car and across the street, climbing onto a trolley bus. I got home by bus half an hour later. The accident turned out to be legitimate—the taxi driver had to pay the *New York Times* for repairs to the car.

That all took place just seven months after I arrived in the Soviet Union. Later I met many of Solzhenitsyn's friends and acquaintances, and saw him again, but I would do nothing to change that original portrait. However, I can add to it.

Later I learned more about Solzhenitsyn's iron self-discipline. He apparently works all day, every day, regardless of what is going on around him. For several years he lived in a cottage on the property of Mstislav Rostropovich, the cellist, on that country lane lined with *dachas* which I described earlier. The KGB stationed a car about 10 yards from the cottage where Solzhenitsyn worked; it was there nearly as often as he was, yet he never let it bother him. He worked even during the final furor that preceded his expulsion from the country in February 1974. He could also put worries about his own plight aside. He asked one old friend during those days what should be done to help the friend. "Don't worry about me, it's you who are in danger," the friend replied. "Oh, let's not worry about that," Solzhenitsyn said, calm as could be.

Because of an error in judgment of the kind journalists have nightmares about, I was skiing in France when Solzhenitsyn was arrested in Moscow and expelled from the country. But thanks to this mistake I saw a side of Solzhenitsyn I would have missed otherwise.

I sped from the French Alps to Heinrich Böll's house in the Eifel Hills of West Germany, where Solzhenitsyn spent his first hours as an exile. The cobbled courtyard of Böll's farmhouse was filled with scores of reporters, television crews and curious neighbors.

Soon after I arrived Solzhenitsyn stepped out of the farmhouse. People jumped up and pressed around him. He looked out into the crowd and recognized me. "Robert!" he shouted, waving at me to come up to him. We had a few minutes of conversation. Completely serene, he told me how he had called my apartment in Moscow three days earlier to read me a statement. The maid had answered, he explained, and said I was in France. "So, I'm sorry, Robert, I had to call the *New York Times.*"

I still don't understand how a man who had been arrested 42 hours earlier, interrogated at length by the KGB, then put on an airplane to a destination he didn't even know until he landed in Frankfurt, could muster the presence of mind to recognize me, one face in a sea of clamoring humanity, and to remember that story. But that was the least of his accomplishments during his first day in West Germany. He also spent several hours discussing fine points of the language in *The Gulag Archipelago* with its Swedish and Norwegian translators. He talked with a lawyer about financial questions and possible residence in Switzerland.

Solzhenitsyn's single-mindedness grows naturally out of his sense of his own role. He considers himself no ordinary man. The propaganda campaign directed against him, he said shortly before his expulsion, was actually directed "against our society . . . and against the conscience of our people." Solzhenitsyn came to view himself as that conscience, and—like Tolstoi before him, whom he had always admired—he assumed a special obligation to help his country.

Whatever Solzhenitsyn thought he was doing, many of his old friends found him increasingly difficult to get along with. He had the habit of writing nasty notes to people who angered him. He wrote one to Rick Smith, whose account of our interview displeased him. His oldest and closest friends, central figures in his literary career and people who had known him since prison-camp days, were not spared. One by one they quarreled with him, many breaking off relations completely. Solzhenitsyn seemed determined to prove that he no longer needed anyone outside himself. Once he was expelled from the country, sadly, many of his oldest friends were actually relieved. "Well, at least we don't have to defend him unreservedly any longer," one said. "Now we can talk honestly about him."

Another old friend said to me before he was exiled: "I've always said it's too bad we don't have a better one—one with better manners, or more patience, or something else. But this is the only one we've got—the only one! So we have to take him the way he is."

The only what? "Our only living classic," as the poet Yevgeni Yevtushenko once said. It was, despite Solzhenitsyn's occasional pomposity and rudeness, an almost universal judgment among the Russians I knew. Solzhenitsyn's name and work would live with the classics, for he was the classic of this age. This was true largely because he alone had written boldly, unreservedly about the horrors of Stalin's reign, horrors known at first hand by millions of Soviet citizens, yet officially denied or ignored before *One Day in the Life of Ivan Denisovich* appeared.

With the publication of that long story, Solzhenitsyn became an instant celebrity. He was elected to the Union of Writers without even applying, and the official reception of *Ivan Denisovich* was rhapsodic. The work was nominated for the Lenin Prize in 1964, and almost won. Solzhenitsyn's fortunes changed as the Party line changed. Khrushchev backed away from de-Stalinization during 1964, and his successors, who took over in October of that year, backed away even further. Each step back had unfortunate consequences for Solzhenitsyn. In 1969 the Writers' Union, which had welcomed him so enthusiastically five years before, expelled him. His novels *Cancer Ward*, *The First Circle* and *August 1914* were published and acclaimed abroad, which brought him more trouble and public denunciation. In 1973 Solzhenitsyn decided to publish a book he had written years before about the history of Soviet prisons and labor camps, a documentary account based on the stories of real victims. This was *The Gulag Archipelago*, a damning indictment, an international sensation and the last straw for the Soviet authorities, who threw him out of the country.

The more he was attacked, the more bitter Solzhenitsyn became. At first he was prepared to cooperate with the cultural authorities—if that meant Tvardovsky at *Novy Mir* and others whom he could respect, and who respected him. He withheld *The Gulag Archipelago* for years because he knew that publishing it would mean inevitable official retribution. He was even afraid that word of its existence would get out. But as the Soviet regime turned against him, Solzhenitsyn responded in kind. In the process he developed new political sensibilities whose full dimensions have become clear only since he went into exile.

Solzhenitsyn—who is so important to the dissident cause, such a powerful symbol of defiance against Soviet orthodoxy—has decided that he is not personally committed to freedom. Truth, justice and Christianity are all more important, according to the political essays he has published in exile. He thinks Russia needs an authoritarian regime, and doesn't seem to mind even if it uses physical coercion on its subjects, provided it also makes them behave justly, speak only the truth and believe in God.* Democracy doesn't satisfy him; it is nothing but "a clash of interests, and no more than interests, a clash regulated [in America] only by the constitution without any all-embracing ethical edifice."

Solzhenitsyn's later political views are barely relevant to his importance in the events of the decade between his first fame and his expulsion. No one understood his significance better than the KGB, which nibbled away at Solzhenitsyn even more effectively than it did at Sakharov—judging, at least, by the results achieved by 1975. The KGB got rid of Solzhenitsyn.

The official campaign against him has been well documented, particularly in Zhores Medvedev's book *Ten Years After Ivan Denisovich*. Solzhenitsyn's fate as a writer is part of the fate of the brief thaw which made him possible in the first place. His personal fate at the hands of the KGB is less well known, to me as well. It appears that dozens of agents were assigned to Solzhenitsyn for years. His mail was intercepted, and people who visited him were often trailed when they left. After leaving the country he even discovered that people in Europe had received letters allegedly from him, over signatures that looked identical to his, but which he had never written. In the interview with Smith and me he cited many of the lies told about him in closed lectures around the country—that he had been a war criminal, that he was really Jewish, that he had worked for the Gestapo, and more.

He often fought back, not only in interviews with American journalists. In early 1972, for example, Solzhenitsyn took

---

* Solzhenitsyn's political ideas appear most vividly in *From Under the Rubble*, a collection of essays by him and other dissidents published in England in 1975.

on the people who were interfering with his mail. In two different letters—one to the lawyer he had retained in Switzerland, another to someone in Sweden—he enclosed an extra message addressed to the KGB. You may read this letter, he wrote, copy it, subject it to chemical analysis and whatever else you wish, but it is your duty to see that it is delivered to the addressee. If it is not, I will publish a public protest against you that will not bring honor to the post office. Both letters reached their proper destinations, minus the extra sheets of paper, and afterward Solzhenitsyn began to receive more of the letters addressed to him. This pleased him enormously, a friend told me at the time.

Eventually the KGB became nasty. Solzhenitsyn and his family received numerous threats, all of which they attributed to the political police. Some came through the carefully censored mail, demanding huge payments of money or threatening bodily injury to the writer and his family. Harassing telephone calls to his wife's flat were also common. For months Solzhenitsyn's divorce from his first wife was delayed in the courts, so his union with Natalia was not legal until after two of their three sons had been born. Once married, Solzhenitsyn was automatically entitled to registration in Moscow (as the spouse of a registered resident of the capital), but a special exception was made in his case; permission was denied.

Solzhenitsyn's greatest moral victory was to survive all of this and go on working. He simply refused to be disrupted. He ignored the police and lived openly in Moscow; he ignored the threats and nothing happened. He finally lost his temper, but just once: when an elderly woman in Leningrad who had typed a version of *The Gulag Archipelago* for him hanged herself after revealing to the KGB where a copy of that manuscript was hidden. This, Solzhenitsyn has said, finally provoked him to publish *Gulag*, as he had long planned to do. He knew how the Soviet authorities would react to it.

The appearance of *The Gulag Archipelago* and the stir it caused in the West convinced the Politburo that something had to be done about Solzhenitsyn. According to a reliable informant, several members of the Politburo thought he should be arrested and tossed in jail, but a calmer view prevailed. In the end Solzhenitsyn won a victory on the scale of the Jewish activists' victories: he was allowed to live, even to remain free, but only in another country.

Solzhenitsyn's career as a writer will thus continue, but he will never again be the political force and symbol he was for the 10 years that followed *Ivan Denisovich*. The best epitaph for that decade that I know appeared in Zhores Medvedev's book about Solzhenitsyn. Medvedev quotes an elderly intellectual, a veteran of the Revolution and the civil war who was an associate of Tvardovsky's on *Novy Mir*:

> Many people think that we had a democracy under Khrushchev [a reference to the widespread nostalgia for the good old days when *Ivan Denisovich* was published.] That is nonsense. There was no democracy. There was *occasional* liberalism, but in the conditions in which we live, that does not mean very much. It's a humane form of arbitrariness. And in any case, as we see, it's a temporary phenomenon. There can only be stable justice when there is genuine, stable democracy.

Sakharov and Solzhenitsyn were never the only active dissidents, but the others—with literally just a handful of exceptions—have met similar or harsher fates. The KGB is a huge agency, a tough and resourceful agency, with every conceivable advantage on its side. Its agents have plodded after the dissident activists for a decade, and though they may have brought discredit to their country abroad, they have fulfilled the task the Party set for them. The courageous band of dissidents who first appeared in the mid-1960s are now gone—to jail, to Siberia, to mental hospitals all over the country, to quiet lives of their own, to Israel or New York in the new wave of emigration.

The KGB's strategy has always been to surround and isolate the dissidents, picking off the activists one by one, counting on each act of repression to deter others from speaking out. The strategy was consistent for 10 years, though that is obvious only now with hindsight. Both Soviet intellectuals and outsiders who followed these events noticed only the high points of repressive activity, especially during 1973 and 1974, when the authorities seemed to crack down at home while they relaxed their policy abroad. In fact what happened in the early 1970s was an inevitable consequence of the fundamental decision, taken in the mid-1960s, to reverse the post-Stalin thaw and reimpose stricter orthodoxy. That decision produced the dissidents—who originally rebelled against it—

and it also insured their eventual elimination, because it meant that no active dissidence would be allowed.

Though the dissidents struggled valiantly, they were never a match for the KGB. The police had too many tools at their disposal. The decision to "treat" dissidents in mental hospitals, for example, was a particularly brilliant improvisation. In effect, mental hospitals became a substitute for Stalin's arbitrary terror. Once the KGB began putting dissidents into hospitals for forcible treatment—sometimes with mind-altering drugs—those who contemplated dissident activity had to take into account the possibility of this punishment. There were people who could endure the idea of being put on trial and jailed, but could not bear the thought of an indefinite term behind the walls of a psychiatric hospital. The authorities have always denied that they used mental hospitals to punish dissidents, but many Russians I knew interpreted the denials as confirmation. Eventually all the dissidents heard of personal acquaintances who had received this treatment, so they knew it really happened. The attempted incarceration of Zhores Medvedev became widely known, and provided final confirmation of the misuse of mental hospitals.

Arrests and trials have also been effective. The KGB's success in converting Pyotr Yakir, a famous dissident, into a police informer in 1973 was particularly demoralizing for the other dissidents. Yakir was an alcoholic, everyone knew, a wild and unpredictable man. So it should not have been surprising that he became an informer, pleaded guilty in his trial and gave a press conference—with Viktor Krasin, his co-defendant—admitting that he had been duped by foreign agents. Yet the spectacle was appalling, and made a deep impression on others.

This was one occasion when I felt an outsider was in a position to feel what the Russians themselves felt. I was summoned, with the entire Moscow press corps, to the press conference at which Yakir and Krasin appeared, but without forewarning of the purpose of the session. The auditorium at the House of Journalists was packed when suddenly the two of them walked onto the stage and took seats behind a long table. At once we all realized what was about to happen. (They had already pleaded guilty in their trial, and it had been known for months that both were cooperating with the KGB.) Not a show trial like those that Stalin staged, but a show press conference. The KGB probably didn't trust its new helpers to act properly through an entire public trial, so the press conference was a substitute. My stomach went to jelly as soon as I saw them.*

As each year passed, fewer and fewer people would sign protests or petitions. Gradually even the most determined optimists had to recognize that the "movement" wasn't going anywhere. This realization was the most demoralizing of all. "The great tragedy of our situation," an old intellectual who sympathized with the dissidents said to me, "is that we have no way out of it. No exit."

In late 1973, after the official propaganda campaign against Sakharov and then Solzhenitsyn, the remaining dissidents began quarreling. "It's impossible to have a balanced philosophical discussion now," one acquaintance complained at the time. "All we dissidents have become dogmatic and angry with one another." Ostensibly the arguments were serious, based on principle and honest disagreement, but I had the impression that they were really based on despair. It reminded me of the ragged survivors of a defeated regiment arguing about what they should have done to win.

The human tragedy the dissidents have experienced is immeasurable. I will never forget the face of Gabriel Superfin, a young man now in a labor camp, whom I met several weeks before he was arrested for spreading "anti-Soviet" material. He was then afraid to live at home; he knew his number was up, that it was only a matter of time. He is a small man, perhaps five feet four, with a gentle face which looked very scared when I saw him. How he can survive five years in a strict-regime labor camp—which is where he now is—I cannot imagine.

Superfin's friends made him a black canvas bag for his personal belongings after he was sentenced. It has to last five years, so they made it strong. They also got him a fur hat. Camp rules require that all hats be covered in black cloth. Someone said a girl named Natalia at a particular tailor shop knew how to do this job. A woman I knew took the hat to Natalia, who was indeed an old hand at adapting fur hats to prison standards. She did a good job and asked for five

---

* The KGB got its money's worth from that press conference. While the journalists listened to Yakir's and Krasin's recantations, a KGB agent with a Sony videotape recorder passed among the crowd, filming the face of every western correspondent in the room.

rubles. My acquaintance wanted to give her more, but Natalia refused. "I cannot profit from an unhappiness," she said.

One of the most famous—and in Moscow most beloved—dissidents was Pavel Litvinov, grandson of Maxim Litvinov, Stalin's Foreign Minister in the 1930s who was later disgraced, though spared. The younger Litvinov, a physics teacher, was one of seven people who staged a brief demonstration in Red Square to protest the invasion of Czechoslovakia in 1968. For that he was sentenced to five years' exile in a Siberian village.

He returned to Moscow in 1973 and soon realized that the situation there was hopeless. The movement was dead, but there was still ample opportunity to get into more trouble. Litvinov feared that this would happen to him, and next time his sentence would be prison or camp, not just internal exile. So he and his wife, Maya, decided to leave. Both have Jewish parents, and the authorities were delighted to be rid of them. They received an exit visa in short order.

I went to a farewell party for them in a Moscow flat whose walls were lined with books and photographs. It was primarily a family gathering. A round table in the front room was loaded with bottles of wine and vodka and plates of open sandwiches. It was a big spread for a big party, but when I arrived it was no party. People sat or stood in small groups, talking quietly, self-consciously. This was not a celebration. Pavel, Maya and their two children were leaving in three days—forever. My wife and I were the only people in the room who expected to see them again. The others knew they would not. So should they laugh? Or cry? Or pretend? In Russia, for the most part, one pretends. The guests made small talk about what time the plane would leave, and how Pavel and Maya would go from Vienna to Rome.

Later Maya's eighty-two-year-old grandfather gave a toast. He said his granddaughter had married a wonderful man, Pavel, who would always take good care of her. The old man said he was very pleased that they would have the chance to start a new life. He came close to tears; the emotion silenced him. Pavel, a huge man who was standing right next to him, leaned down over this diminutive old figure and kissed his bald head. The old man went on with his toast for a few phrases, then he could say no more. His wife, a sturdy woman of seventy-five though she had spent many years in Stalin's prison camps, led him from the room. No one said anything; the silence was a strain. I was crying, so were one or two others. Finally someone got the conversation going again, to the relief of everyone in the room. They seemed anxious to cut that silence, push it aside. They didn't want to cry. They wanted to change the subject.

Is there no hope of making Russia more free? The best answer, I think, is that hope exists, but it may not be justified.

Russian history argues against freedom. Russia is a land of conformity, strong authority, rigid orthodoxy. These are ancient characteristics. The medieval Church was as nervous about non-Orthodox Christian dogma as today's communists are about liberal ideas. Russia missed out on the Renaissance and the Enlightenment, the great intellectual upheavals which established our definitions of freedom, authority and the state. Russia's definitions of those concepts are ancient and absolute. Tyranny is not the Russians' enemy; anarchy is. The Russian antidote to anarchy has always been absolutist rule by a powerful autocracy. Marx certainly did not favor autocratic rule; Lenin probably didn't either, at least not on the traditional model. But on this point (as on so many) Russian history has proven stronger than Marxism-Leninism.

Russian autocrats have traditionally ruled with great condescension. We *know best*, they seem to say; *however, we can't trust everyone to realize that we know best, so we must impose that realization.* And that has meant imposed ideas, imposed orthodoxy, challenged only at the peril of the challenger. The origin of this is the unspoken insecurity of the autocrats, who know in their hearts that they rule first of all to protect the autocracy, and secondarily for the benefit of the citizenry. But they pretend otherwise, and fear that their pretense will be exposed. That is why the last czars were intolerant of dissent, and why the communists have stamped it out. (The communists have proven even less tolerant than the czars—a good indication, I think, that they are even more insecure.)

Outsiders, and particularly liberals from the West, have lionized the few famous dissidents who have come to our attention. This seems natural: the dissidents share our values, and they defend them with a degree of courage that most of us suspect we could not muster ourselves. But a Soviet official is more likely to see the dissidents as a psychological threat—where most people bend and compromise, they fight back, a discomfiting spectacle. Moreover, they fight back at the expense of national unity, putting their own narrow interests ahead of the country's reputation. I suspect the Nixon administration's reaction to Daniel Ellsberg is comparable to the Soviet attitude toward the dissidents of the past decade.

The prospects for more freedom depend on the kind of people who will lead the USSR in the future and the values they respect. Future leaders may be less insecure than those we have known. Unlike today's leaders, who grew up in the years of Stalin's terror and who lack both education and sophistication, future generations will reflect the calmer atmosphere of their youth, and the knowledge and self-confidence gained from broader exposure to the outside world. But there is no reason to expect them to admire liberal values, or to see merit in permitting the country—and particularly its intellectuals—more freedom. Future leaders will still be autocrats, and liberalization inevitably invites trouble for an unelected autocracy.

In the West we put great faith in the civilizing value of education. Our confidence that education enhances respect for liberal ideals is shared by some of our experts on Russia, who have predicted that the Soviet Union will become more liberal as its educated population grows. The nature of Soviet education suggests that this assumption is overly optimistic. The educational system produces the formal intelligentsia (the real intelligentsia, as I said earlier, is largely self-educated), and it trains the country's future leaders. The way it is organized, however, would seem to discourage the spread of liberal values.

Like so many aspects of Soviet life, education is highly formalized and narrowly practical. Its goal is *not* to produce men and women of great intellectual breadth, originality and creativity. On the contrary, none of these is sought. Soviet education is supposed to supply the country with specialists who can make it work, specialists with limited competence in narrow fields.

Today's Soviet intelligentsia still reflects the old German educational tradition, which dominated Russian education until the time of Stalin. Many people are still alive who studied at the old *gymnasia*, rigorous secondary schools which gave their students a broad, classical education. Today's intelligentsia is influenced by men and women who graduated from

Russian universities when they were still centers of serious learning in the old-fashioned European sense. But modern Soviet schools and universities are not training people who will be able to carry on the old traditions.

The distinguishing characteristic of Soviet education is its lack of autonomy. The Soviet university is no ivory tower. Quite the reverse, it is a politicized institution fully integrated into the Party's and state's systems of control. The rectors of all the important universities are members of the Supreme Soviet, the national legislature, a good indication of their status in society.

As an integral part of the system, the country's schools and institutions of higher learning share many of the system's problems. For example, education is dominated by a Plan. A medical student explained the consequences of this. In his institute, he said, the first two years of the six-year course are rigorous, and a high percentage of the students drops out. "From the third year on," he continued, "it's enough just to attend classes. No matter if you never study, from then on virtually nobody flunks out. . . . They have a Plan—according to the Plan, they're supposed to graduate a set number of doctors. . . . That's why they admit twice as many as they need to graduate. Even so, they often fail to fulfill the Plan. So when they've got fewer students left in school than they are supposed to graduate to fulfill the Plan, they want to keep them all."

That student saw professors coach their students during oral examinations to insure their success. "Don't you remember how it was explained in the lecture?" one professor asked the student he was examining.

"Yes, yes, I remember," the student replied. For that he received a three, the passing grade.

This story seemed improbable to me. Then I met a professor of medicine who had been called in to the Party Committee and chastised for being too rough on students. "They demanded that my marks be higher, that my average mark be a four [the equivalent of a B]." Later a schoolteacher told me that she was evaluated according to the "successfulness" of her students; the better the grades she gave, the better teacher she was thought to be. The school director interpreted students' failures as a sign of bad teaching.

Education is subject to political manipulation. Since the late 1960s institutes and universities throughout the country have given special preference to applicants from rural and working-class backgrounds, a policy designed to draw people from "reliable" strata of society into the intelligentsia. Special "workers' faculties" have been established to prepare these students for university-level work. In some cases this program has probably given new educational opportunities to people who might otherwise have had none. But I met many students and educators who told harrowing tales of the crude political overtones of this policy in many institutions.

"There is a pretext of examining their knowledge," one former teacher, now living in Israel, said of these specially chosen students. "A friend of mine is a math teacher, and she sat in on one of the 'meetings' they hold with these kids to find out how much they know. They were asking the simplest questions—things people ought to learn in the seventh grade. But one of them couldn't even answer that stuff, and my friend pointed out how little he knew. They bawled her out for not following the general line. That guy got admitted."

Worst of all, this man thought, is that the young people who benefit from this system realize why they are admitted. "They know they can't possibly be kicked out of school. A teacher can't give them a failing grade. If he did, he'd be called in to the Party Committee and chewed out. So you see seventeen-year-old kids who already realize that in this country, in this system, you don't need to know anything—to have any real knowledge—in order to get ahead."

Numerous educators told me that the quality of higher education in the Soviet Union is declining. Some said it is falling drastically. This, too, is caused by the educational system's lack of autonomy. Promotions based on non-academic criteria tend to dilute the quality of senior academics, and such promotions are common. Many educational administrators are essentially Party bureaucrats pressed into this line of work. Party activity helps many get ahead—for example, the rector of Moscow's Medical Institute Number Two, Yuri Lopukhin, who began his career as secretary of the institute's Young Communist League chapter. The younger generation is widely thought to be less well educated than its elders. "You can see it now in Leningrad," one scholar of medieval history told me. "All the great old men are dying off and retiring, and young careerists with second-rate minds are taking their places."

The non-scientific fields, which are dominated by politics, are the weakest. The brightest young people seem drawn to careers in the natural sciences, which effectively take them out of the class from which the country's leaders are chosen.

Leaders rise up through the Party bureaucracy, from careers in industry, and from special institutions organized to train them. The best known of these is the Moscow State Institute for International Relations, a special college affiliated with the Ministry of Foreign Affairs, whose graduates become diplomats, KGB officers, journalists, trade officials and Party functionaries. A graduate of the institute described it for me in detail. His account deserves a place here because it tells so much about young people who may inherit positions of leadership in Soviet society, and about the society itself.

My informant entered the institute in the mid-1960s. "When you apply [for admission]," he said, "you have to give them a *kharakteristika* [a ubiquitous Soviet document which amounts to a character reference] from the regional committee of the Young Communist League where you live. . . . And there are a lot of extra meetings when you are trying to get in. First a meeting at your regional committee, then at the institute. Then you take the exams, and have still another meeting afterward. They use that last one as a way to weed out people they don't want even though they passed the exams."

The student body was an interesting combination of the sons and daughters of high officials and of famous national figures (for instance, the son of the Minister of Internal Affairs) and young people from more ordinary backgrounds. Preference seemed to go to the children of influential citizens and to provincial young people recruited by the institute and local branches of the Young Communist League. The privileged group set the tone of institute life, according to this former student.

"The school was dominated by the one goal, the one dream that was held up before all of us—the possibility of a trip abroad for practice work. A lot of the students were ready to do whatever was necessary to make that trip abroad—to study well, to do all the right things in the Young Communist League and so on.

"The chance to go abroad comes in the first half of the fifth [and final] year in school. . . . That's the big issue from the first year on. You *may* be able to go abroad—the chance exists. But less than half the students end up going. . . .

"When I went to the institute, I didn't believe in anything to do with communism. For me it was a question of staying out of the Army. I'm personally convinced that none of the others believed in anything at all. As a rule, these are very limited people—they don't read very much, they're not much interested in culture. They're all great consumers, they love to consume. They're great collectors of western records, watches, clothes. They know something about politics, and they know a foreign language not too badly. . . . They're careerists—that's a good word for them. The way the system works, they come out of the institute right into careers that are waiting for them. They know what it will be like—they've heard already from their parents. The parents have given them a taste for the nicer things. . . . It's a privileged class, and they want to stay in it. And, of course, that has nothing in common with communism. . . .

"[Yet] a lot of them are true believers, not in communism, but in the correctness of the Party line, the policies of the day, because those policies suit them completely. They are riding on top of the wave and they know it. . . .

"After a while these people start to think the way they talk. For a long time they say things they don't believe, but after a while it becomes a habit, and they start believing it themselves. . . . They don't worry about the KGB. They know the limits and respect them. . . . So they eat well and sleep well. Their hearts beat evenly. For them, the KGB is an institution that is preserving the laws of the country. . . .

"In every class there was a Komsomol [Young Communist League] bureau. . . . They dealt with questions like the *subotniks* [designated Saturdays when citizens, including students, are supposed to donate labor to the state]. The Komsomol bueau discussed how the students were doing, and who was doing badly, and why. They discussed trips abroad, the writing of character references and a lot of administrative work. A student's life depends a lot on the Komsomol organization. It can punish him—for being drunk, or for amoral behavior. . . . I have to admit I was pretty active in the Komsomol. Why? Well, first of all, you could try to do something good, from within. In our bureau we never kicked anybody out, we gave everybody a good reference. And it was an elected position . . . and, like everybody else, I thought when they elected me, Well, why not go on the Komsomol committee? That was already a good thing, everybody understood that. . . .

"I went to the institute because I didn't want a technical education, I wanted a general education in the humanities. But you know what kind of stuff they teach there—one year of math, which you soon forget, some accounting, then the history of the Party, Marxism-Leninism and so on. A lot of it wasn't really political, it was more ideological, and completely useless. The only good thing was foreign languages. They did that well. There was a good language lab, equipped with Norwegian tape recorders. . . . You have to realize that there is no intrinsic need to graduate from an institute like this one—it's done just to get the necessary piece of paper, not for any kind of education. . . ."

I can't say whether that young man gave a fair description of tomorrow's Soviet elite. The many future leaders who will come up from the ranks of Party and government work, not from special schools like the Institute for International Relations, may have different values and opinions. But I could never find a trace of evidence that suggested the existence of a new spirit among young people, or a new respect for liberal values.

The officials of the Young Communist League who have traveled to America on recent exchanges seem a tough and ambitious lot. They never stray from the Party line in conversation. I did hear one heartening story from an American who hosted one of these groups, however. He put copies of books by Alexander Solzhenitsyn, in Russian, at various spots in his apartment, and told his Russian guests to help themselves to any books they found interesting. At the end of the evening all the Solzhenitsyn books were gone. Was that just curiosity, or something more?

I knew a shrewd and thoughtful scientist in Moscow who theorized that the mid-1970s would mark the beginning of a new period of "totalitarian stability" in Soviet life. Stalin's death and the end of Stalinist terror, he thought, led to a transition period. For 10 years—through 1963—the transition seemed to lead toward liberalization; then for 10 subsequent years it led back toward orthodoxy and stability. Now the transition is ending at a new point of equilibrium. The society is much less rigid than it was, but the ruling autocracy has re-imposed intellectual orthodoxy.

Stalin maintained totalitarian stability by means of fear and ignorance. People were afraid to challenge the status quo, and ignorant of what was really happening at home or abroad. Now the fear is gone, and so is much of the ignorance. Most intellectuals, particularly in Moscow and Leningrad, realize what is going on in the country. They even know something about events abroad. They can complain if they want to, not just at home, but to a stranger on the bus, without fear of a knock on the door in the night.

Louder complaining—by signing a petition, or defending a Solzhenitsyn or a Sakharov—is discouraged by two factors. First are the privileges now enjoyed by the official intelligentsia, which would be lost by protest, and which these people hope to pass on to their children. Second, most intellectuals are now convinced that brave acts of protest are doomed to failure. They see no elasticity in the system, no way to jolt it. Better to stay inside the system and try to change it slowly from within.

Some seriously would like to change it, to replace ideological mumbo-jumbo with practical policies, perhaps even to allow more personal freedom. Others don't think of such things; they devote all their energies to obtaining a new car, a country *dacha*, foreign clothes. But both groups, the scientist concluded, now accept the status quo voluntarily, and that is totalitarian stability.

It is a plausible analysis. But it is based on one assumption that may prove false—that the future evolution of Soviet society is predictable, or at least controllable.

Soviet society is actually changing very quickly, and it may be on the threshold of even greater changes. The younger generation has grown up in a country very different from the one its parents first knew. The old rigidity is crumbling even while the Party and the KGB succeed in stamping out the rebellious dissidents.

Two Muscovites, both members of the official establishment, told me in amazement how their eleven-year-old son had come home from school with a new joke ridiculing Leonid Brezhnev's eyebrows. They were flabbergasted. "You know, both of us grew up, right through the university, believing everything we were told. That was in the 1950s. Do you think anyone is so credulous now?"

Thousands of Soviet citizens have traveled to foreign countries, mostly to Eastern Europe, but some to the West. Foreign radio stations broadcasting in Russian can be easily heard, and millions listen to them regularly. Private apartments are now within the reach of most city dwellers, and private cars are on the way—radical developments in a society whose language has no word for privacy. Countless young Russians know more about the Beatles and Jethro Tull than they do about Rachmaninov and Tchaikovsky.

I left the Soviet Union convinced that the country faces serious new social and political problems. The drastic decline of the birthrate in European Russia is a good example: the authorities helplessly watch it occur, but before long it will have serious consequences. Increased exposure to the outside world will inevitably result in more pressure to match the western standard of living. More prosperity will probably be accompanied by the social dislocations western societies have experienced since the end of World War II. Vagrant youth, increased crime, alienation—they all seem to appear at the level of economic development and standard of living which the Russians are just beginning to reach.

At the same time, the Soviet Union has entered into a new relationship with the outside world. The country is more open to foreigners than at any earlier stage of Russian history. The current leaders have apparently abandoned Stalin's dream of economic autarky, or self-sufficiency. At least they have decided to rely on foreign suppliers for crucial new sectors of their economy, including the motor-vehicle industry, iron-and-steel-fabricating and numerous others. The Soviet leaders have accepted, by treaty, their total vulnerability to an American missile attack, and have joined in an unprecedented variety of international negotiations, many of which will tie them more firmly into an international system they cannot control.

The foreign connection will inevitably influence the evolution of Soviet society, though only a rash prophet would predict how. The men who rule the country have already made unprecedented compromises to assuage foreign opinion. Andrei Sakharov is free, Alexander Solzhenitsyn is in the West and not in prison, 100,000 Soviet Jews now live in Israel or America because of these compromises. As I have tried to show, compromises of this kind have done little to liberalize Soviet society itself—quite the contrary. But a precedent has been established for foreigners to note; it shows

that the Soviet leaders will bargain with outsiders over domestic conditions in their own country.

Which is not to say that foreign pressure can democratize
the Soviet Union. It cannot. Russian society is authoritarian;
it has been cruel to its members for hundreds of years, and
has never tolerated non-conformists for long. Outsiders may
shame the Russians into hiding or even curtailing their harshest impulses, but this is far easier than shaming them into
virtue.

Perhaps that scientist was right. Perhaps all the changes I
see coming in Soviet society will be of no consequence in a
new era of totalitarian stability. Those changes may not touch
the fundamental nature of the society. A joke about
Brezhnev's eyebrows may not shake the system.

Inertia opposes change, even if a new generation should
want to liberalize the country. The autocracy may be trapped
by history. Mistrust of the people is now automatic. The
communist autocrats have fed them invented history and invented information for nearly half a century. Dictatorship is
the expected norm throughout a huge and diverse country.
Can there be any hope for real change?

There is hope, but it may not be justified.

12 · The Russians and the World

> The fundamental and most stable feature of Russian history is the slow tempo of her development, with the economic backwardness, primitiveness of social forms and low level of culture resulting from it.
>
> —The first lines of Leon Trotski's
> *History of the Russian Revolution*

THE SOVIET UNION is rich, varied and complex, but in the end not incomprehensible. It is a huge country and suffers the pains of bigness; it is unwieldly, its population is heterogeneous, its government too big and too powerful. If the object of human society is to organize man's labor and leisure for his maximum benefit and fulfillment, then the Soviet Union is a most unsuccessful society. It is inefficient, stupidly managed, unproductive despite great wealth, stubbornly conservative and therefore disinclined to reform.

The country is ruled arbitrarily, sometimes cruelly, by an autocracy whose rule has never been fully legitimized. The autocrats are insecure in their power, perhaps more insecure than they ought to be, given the apparent stability of their realm. This insecurity explains much in their behavior that would otherwise be inexplicable, particularly their fear of foreigners and foreign ideas, their almost paranoiac concern about domestic "opposition" and their total disregard for objective truth. The autocracy's insecurity dictates the nature of the governmental system and apparently guarantees the survival of many of the country's most irrational features—for example, its inefficient economy and hopeless agricultural system.

The autocrats compensate for their insecurity by invoking the ideology of Marxism-Leninism, which justifies their status as leaders. On its face the ideology is a prescription for a revolutionary, Marxist society, but the Soviet Union is neither of those. Revolutionary zeal is discouraged, except in pursuit of the regime's goals, such as higher coal production. A Russian who dares to ask aloud what has happened to democracy—may find himself in prison or a mental hospital. The humanism of Karl Marx and the high ideals of his utopian vision of socialism have no place in contemporary Soviet society. Nor do the vibrance and excitement of new ideas that one associates with revolution. The Soviet Union has not produced one original idea for the organization of human society or the production of goods and services which any significant foreign society except perhaps China has voluntarily adopted.

Life in this country goes on in recognizable human patterns. The struggle against man's fate fills the lives of the citizenry. The state provides a high degree of economic security and generally eliminates the need for individual initiative or risk-taking, which seems to please most of the people. The population includes a richly talented intelligentsia and a loyal mass of workers, but the system cannot take full advantage of either.

Though known as a super-power, the Soviet Union lacks many of the attributes of Europe's smaller countries—a basic network of good roads, for example. Technologically and economically it cannot compete with the advanced western nations. The national currency is virtually worthless outside the country's borders. The Soviet Union's influence in the world economy is negligible—though it can upset other countries' calculations with unexpected purchases, as it did in 1972 by buying huge quantities of American grain.

And this is the country which has frightened us for nearly 60 years, which convinced us to invest billions in an arms race without end, which established itself as the second super-power and a threat to peace in the minds of several generations of western statesmen. That this has been possible, given their egregious weaknesses, is a great tribute to the men who have ruled the Soviet Union. But it is also a tribute to our foolishness.

The Russians earned the respect and fear of their adversaries by overcoming their weaknesses to produce a powerful military force, one clearly superior to any in the world except America's. This was accomplished by exploiting perhaps the greatest advantage in the Soviet system, the ability to concentrate vast resources on narrow objectives in secret. Yet the West has persistently overestimated the threat posed by Soviet military strength, and has generally ignored the implications of the country's weaknesses in non-military fields. In other words, we have given the Russians more than their due credit for military prowess, and ignored their failings in economic and technological development, social organization and the rest. We have defined strength and power in purely military terms—the terms most favorable to the Soviet Union—and then exaggerated Soviet power.

The misinterpretation of Soviet strength began immediately after World War II. Faulty American intelligence convinced President Truman and his associates that the Red Army remained large and powerful after the war, while the British and American forces were quickly demobilized. In fact the Russians demobilized too, and were seriously weakened by the abrupt cancellation of Lend Lease aid at the end of the war. They did not pose the military threat that western statesmen feared until well into the 1950s.

In the '50s faulty intelligence—encouraged by Soviet bluff—persuaded the Americans that a "bomber gap" existed. The Soviet Union, they feared, had surpassed the United States in the capacity to deliver atomic weapons over long distances. This prodded the Americans into a new program of bomber construction, resulting in overwhelming superiority for the United States. Later the Americans realized there had never been a gap.

In 1957 the Russians jolted the United States with Sputnik. That artificial earth satellite confirmed that the Russians had made intercontinental ballistic missiles which worked, and it terrified Americans. They could stand outside at night and see the tiny sphere speed across the North American sky, yet were helpless to control it or match it. Sputnik—a simple radio beeper in a ball of metal—changed the western world's perceptions of Soviet and American capabilities. For years afterward it was widely believed in the West that the USSR had surpassed America in rocketry, space technology and related fields. This belief, shared by the American Congress, caused a radical change in American priorities involving tens of billions of dollars.

At the time, Professor George Kistiakowsky of Harvard, a remarkable man who was born in Kiev and fought against the Bolsheviks in the Russian civil war, was a member of President Eisenhower's "missile panel," a group of scientists who gave advice on the American rocket program. Kistiakowski understood the state of Russian society, and realized that one Sputnik could not mean that the Soviet Union had surpassed the United States. "I was appalled at the public reaction—that the Russians were ten feet tall—because I knew that in many other areas of science and technology they were far behind," Kistiakowski recalled years later. "I told the President, 'Look, that country was three-fourths destroyed by the Germans. It was very poor in the first place. It is just humanly impossible that they could have passed us.'" Eisenhower, Kistiakowski recalled, said he wanted to believe that. But politically it was impossible to minimize the Soviet accomplishment.

Eisenhower's other advisors were pressing a pessimistic interpretation of Soviet strength. Most dramatic was the "Gaither Report," name for H. Rowan Gaither of the Ford Foundation, who led a committee appointed by Eisenhower to study civil defense in a nuclear attack. Gaither and his colleagues heard official intelligence estimates of Soviet capabilities which terrified them. They gave Eisenhower an extraordinarily gloomy report. The report was secret, but Chalmers Roberts of the *Washington Post* revealed its contents two months later in one of the great journalistic coups of the 1950s. Roberts' story could hardly have been more alarming:

The still top-secret Gaither Report portrays a United States in the gravest danger in its history.

It pictures the nation moving in frightening course to the status of a second-class power.

It shows an America exposed to an almost immediate threat from the missile-bristling Soviet Union.

It finds America's long-term prospect one of cataclysmic peril in the face of rocketing Soviet military might and of a powerful, growing Soviet economy and technology which will bring new political, propaganda and psychological assaults on freedom all around the globe. . . .

This was the origin of the "missile gap" which Senator John F. Kennedy used so effectively in his 1960 campaign for the Presidency. Kennedy—and numerous other critics of the Eisenhower administration—contended that the Soviet Union had surpassed America in the deployment of intercontinental ballistic missiles (ICBMs). In fact photographs of the Soviet Union taken at the time by U-2 spy planes did not reveal a single operational ICBM launching site, according to Professor Kistiakowski, who by then had become Eisenhower's science advisor. Later Kennedy admitted that the U-2* had been right: there had never been a missile gap. But by that time his administration had deployed large numbers of new ICBMs, giving the United States an enormous lead over the Russians.

In 1961 Yuri Gagarin became the first man to fly in space, another jolt which produced another American over-reaction, the race to land men on the moon. For several years the Americans were not sure they could win that race, though in fact it was no contest. If the Russians ever joined it, they dropped out early on.

---

* The most famous U-2, that flown by Francis Gary Powers over the Soviet Union in May 1960, may have given the West another opportunity to overestimate Soviet capabilities. It has long been assumed that Powers' U-2 was shot down by surface-to-air missiles operating at extraordinarily high altitudes. (This was the official Soviet explanation.) But a Norwegian fisherman named Selmer Nilsen, a confessed Soviet spy who served two years in a Norwegian prison for espionage, has said the U-2 was brought down by a bomb planted on the plane before it took off from Pakistan. A KGB officer in Moscow told him this, Nilsen said in a television documentary broadcast in Scandinavia. His story carries some weight since he was assigned to keep track of the U-2s that landed in Norway, and reported on them regularly to the Russians. If true, this would explain how Powers survived. The Americans doubted it was possible to survive the explosion of an anti-aircraft missile in the fragile U-2, which was one reason why the U.S. originally lied about Powers' flight, confident that the lie could not be challenged. Then the Russians produced Powers, alive, to disprove it.

In the mid-1960s, when American superiority in missiles, bombers and atomic submarines was overwhelming, the Pentagon devised a new formula for making itself nervous, the "Greater-Than-Expected Threat." The United States could meet any threat that the military planners could reasonably expect to arise, but what if the planners had underestimated the enemy? In 1966 Robert McNamara, then Secretary of Defense, justified the further development of two new weapons systems, the Poseidon missile-firing submarine and Multiple Independently Targetable Re-Entry Vehicles (MIRVs),* as potential responses to the Greater-Than-Expected Threat. Deployment of these weapons, McNamara said then, "would depend upon how this threat actually evolved." Eventually both weapons were deployed *without* any further evidence that a Greater-Than-Expected Threat might materialize.

Numerous American decisions to build or deploy new weapons—in other words, to escalate the arms race—have been made on the basis of wrong assumptions. Pressure to build an anti-missile missile (ABM) came from an apparent misinterpretation of the purpose of a Soviet anti-aircraft system. American analysts feared that this rocket, code-named Tallinn because it was deployed near the capital of Soviet Estonia, could be "upgraded" from an anti-aircraft weapon to an anti-missile weapon (that is, one that could intercept American missiles before they struck the Soviet Union). In 1966 an American National Intelligence Estimate concluded that Tallinn was purely an anti-aircraft weapon, but still some officials disagreed. This and the "Galosh" anti-missile missile system which the Russians installed around Moscow created strong political pressures on the Johnson administration, particularly in Congress, to deploy an American ABM. Johnson finally succumbed, but obliquely. He agreed to deploy a "thin" ABM system (that is, composed of relatively few anti-missile missiles) which could protect against a rocket

---

* MIRVs are elaborate warheads. A cluster of nuclear bombs in an apparatus called a "bus" is attached to an ICBM. The rocket carries the whole cluster toward the target, but high above the earth the bus—a sophisticated mechanism containing its own computer—begins dispensing the bombs one by one, hurtling them out on computer-designated flight paths at individual targets. Thus a single rocket carrying eight bombs in a bus can wipe out eight different targets hundreds of miles apart.

attack from China (which at that time had no operational rocket capable of reaching the United States).

Johnson was unenthusiastic about ABM, and about the arms race in general, for reasons he explained in 1967 to a group of educators in Nashville, Tennessee. "I wouldn't want to be quoted on this," Johnson began—a useless disclaimer, since there were journalists in the room—"but we've spent thirty-five or forty billion dollars on the space program. And if nothing else had come out of it except the knowledge we've gained from space photography, it would be worth 10 times what the whole program has cost. Because tonight we know how many missiles the enemy has. And, it turns out, our guesses were way off. We were doing things we didn't need to do. We were building things we didn't need to build. We were harboring fears we didn't need to harbor."* So much for the Greater-Than-Expected Threat.

When Richard Nixon became President he decided to continue deploying the ABM, but for a new reason. He wanted to protect America's ICBM launchers near Grand Forks, North Dakota, against *Soviet* attack.** Galosh and Tallinn remained the major reasons why the United States wanted an ABM. Later the Americans concluded that Galosh was a primitive weapon which could not have intercepted American missiles, and was perhaps intended by the Russians as protection against the Chinese.

The Nixon administration decided to deploy MIRVs. MIRV was appealing on many grounds: it was a splendid new weapon that would frustrate an ABM system (by showering it with independently targeted warheads) and give the Americans the option of taking out thousands of different Soviet targets. (In mid-1975, thanks to MIRV, the United States has 8500 individual nuclear warheads capable of delivery against Soviet targets, and the number is still growing.) MIRV was also a brilliant demonstration of American technological superiority, and, as such, an intimidating new factor in the Soviet-American contest.

Unfortunately, MIRV added nothing to the national security of the United States. The weapon it was meant to counteract—the ABM—was banned by the first SALT treaty.

---

* Quoted in *The Nuclear Years* by Chalmers M. Roberts.
** One drawback to the American ABM was its uncertain reliability. Like the comparable Soviet ABM, its efficacy was never certain.

(Each country is now permitted just one battery of ABMs.)
The Russians must have seen MIRV as a symbol of America's technological mastery, and also as a weapon which gave
the United States the option of attacking many more targets
than the Soviet Union could attack. So the Russians decided
they had to have MIRV, too. After years of work (more
years than American experts predicted) the Soviet Union began to make its own MIRVs in the mid-1970s, and will presumably go on deploying them for years to come. The American decision to deploy MIRV reinvigorated the arms race at
a time when both contestants had enough reliable weapons to
destroy each other many times over.

From the beginning of the nuclear-arms race the United
States has tried to maintain a reliable and substantial superiority over the Soviet Union. Since the early 1970s the Americans have said they will accept equality, not superiority, and
the Strategic Arms Limitations Talks (SALT) are pointed in
that direction. Hopefully, both countries can agree on broad
quantitative limits which will give them roughly equal—
though ridiculously large—strategic forces. But still in 1975
the Americans maintain a three-to-one advantage in the number of nuclear weapons they can deliver to the enemy's territory, and they still enjoy the tactical and psychological advantages afforded by a network of bases surrounding Soviet
territory.

The United States has not been uniquely responsible for
the arms race, and the reasons advanced for each successive
escalation have not been invariably insincere. The American
officials who made these decisions may have suffered from an
excess of zeal—I think history will judge them harshly for
that—but they could always justify their behavior as prudent.
An American politician with power over the country's defenses naturally fears that he will be caught out doing too little,
not too much. Too much can be excused, but too little could
be fatal.

The Russians made these American decisions easier by
bluffing about their own accomplishments, by doing everything they could to hide their true capabilities, and by periodically threatening to use their bombs and rockets, especially
in the Khrushchev years. Without reliable evidence about Soviet weapons, Americans logically made conservative, cautious estimates. These often led to American programs which
in fact aggravated Soviet weaknesses, so of course the Rus-

sians struggled to catch up. When the Russians struggled, the Americans often perceived another reason to begin another round.

The nuclear-arms race has been encouraged, in the words of George F. Kennan, the former American ambassador in Moscow, "not by any reason to believe that the other side *would*, but by an hypnotic fascination with the fact that it *could*. . . . There is a Kafkaesque quality to this encounter. We stand like two men who find themselves confronting each other with guns in their hands, neither with any real reason to believe that the other has murderous intentions toward him, but both hypnotized by the uncertainty and the unreasoning fear of the fact that the other is armed."

Kennan described elegantly what the Pentagon calls "worst-case" assumptions—conservative assumptions that the worst one can imagine about the Russians may prove to be true. These assumptions have guided American strategic policy for years. The most basic worst-case assumption is that there may be circumstances in which a Soviet leader would begin a nuclear war. In other words, a madman in the Kremlin might be tempted by some marginal advantage to solve the problem of American "imperialism" once and for all, accepting the consequences of large-scale destruction of the USSR.

This is of course a possibility. Madmen sometimes do come to power. Unfortunately, there is no defense against a madman. The whole system of mutual deterrence which has prevented nuclear war thus far is based on the rationality of both competitors. Each sees that nuclear attack could result in its own destruction, so each refrains from attack. If rationality disappears on either side, no amount of clever contingency planning will make the slightest difference.

To understand the Soviet Union's behavior during the past 30 years, I think we have to abandon the image of the USSR as a bristling, powerful and aggressive nation. Which is not to say, I repeat, that we dreamed up that image. Stalin and Khrushchev both went out of their way to convince the West of their fearsome power and bold intentions. From afar, we saw threats, harangues and occasional intimidating successes such as Sputnik. It was a deceptive combination; it hid the fact that Soviet policy was made by nervous men who were conscious of their own gaping weaknesses and their adversaries' great strength.

A siege mentality has infected the leaders of Soviet society since its birth in 1917. This attitude has ideological origins; Lenin and his colleagues thought of themselves as the vanguard of the international working class, destined to invoke the wrath of the bourgeoisie of every industrial country. Unfortunately, the industrial West reinforced this fear by sending troops to support counter-revolutionary forces in the Russian civil war. This bit of adventurism may have been one of the great diplomatic catastrophes of our time. The capitalists invaded us once, Soviet leaders can now proclaim, so they may do it again. The United States compounded the madness of invading Russia in 1918 by withholding recognition of the Soviet regime until 1933—further proof, in Russian eyes, of capitalist enmity.

Stalin's insecurities were all too evident in his insane behavior of the 1930s, when he virtually wiped out the original Communist Party and the senior ranks of the Red Army and established a personalized totalitarian dictatorship. Insecurity drove him into Hitler's arms, but the Nazi-Soviet pact of 1939 could not save him from war. Once invaded, the Soviet Union had to ally itself with the western democracies, but had to expect the capitalists—the "class enemy," in the Soviet dialect—to be hostile to his country again when the war was finished.*

Stalin seized the buffer zone he craved in Eastern Europe even before the war had ended. In the manner of a ruthless dictator, he was buying insurance against any repetition of the devastation his country had just suffered.

The West tended to discount the consequences for Russia of 20 million dead, industry largely destroyed, cities in ruins. But Stalin could not discount such factors. Nor could he miss the fact that his principal adversary, the United States, had come out of the war strengthened rather than

---

* "Revisionist" historians of the cold war who have argued or implied that Stalin would have been interested in a full and sincere resolution of outstanding disputes in 1945 have failed to advance a single plausible reason for believing this. The capitalist bogeyman was vital to Stalin—as important to his regime as the political police. Only in a state of siege could his kind of rule be justified. He had to maintain the siege at all costs. So tensions with the West were inevitable.

weakened, with unprecedented industrial capacity and an atomic bomb.

Stalin's post-war policies caused alarm in the West. His unsavory appetite for colonies justified renewed suspicions of Soviet intentions. His ill-considered blockade of Berlin in 1948 seemed proof that Stalin was bent on conquest, and hardened western determination. Soon afterward the NATO treaty was signed and the Federal Republic of Germany established.

Yet the Berlin blockade was not a 'forward' action. (Then, as now, Berlin was well inside the Soviet zone of occupation.) The blockade was probably the clearest single signal of Soviet fears, a last desperate effort to dissuade Britain, France and America from establishing a West German state that could rearm and eventually threaten Russia again. Stalin felt helpless when the Americans challenged the blockade, and helpless again when they permitted the formation of a West German government.

My purpose here is not to excuse Stalin's brazen post-war behavior, which was provocative and imprudent. His encouragement of the Korean War was proof enough that he was capable of dangerous miscalculation. Yet even that decision—like all the important Soviet decisions during the early years of the cold war—could be justified as a means of protecting the Motherland and the Revolution. The far east was the border area where Stalin must have felt most vulnerable (assuming, as he undoubtedly did, that Mao could not be trusted). He already controlled half of Korea, and the other half looked weak and tempting. A Soviet victory there might help the communists in Japan, who, Stalin probably hoped, might frustrate remilitarization of Japan under American guidance. Moreover, if the Americans had not come to the defense of Chiang Kai-shek in China, why should Stalin expect them to defend Syngman Rhee's corrupt regime in South Korea?

What Korea demonstrated was Stalin's opportunism, a characteristic that his more cautious successors have inherited. He saw an opportunity and he took it, not counting on President Truman's violent response. Once he realized the Americans were prepared to fight a major war in Korea, Stalin maneuvered the Chinese communists into the front line of defense, and cautiously stepped back from the fray, revealing again the Soviet preoccupation with self-protection.

Neither Stalin nor his successors have been reluctant to strike an aggressive pose when it suited their purposes, but they have always backed away from direct confrontation with the western powers.

They could hardly have done anything else, given the balance of power for at least 25 years after World War II. Despite bomber gaps and Gaither Reports and the reaction to Sputnik and Yuri Gagarin, that balance offered little comfort to a Soviet leader until the 1970s.

In the first years after the war the Americans had the strongest economy in the world's history (while Russia was devastated) and a monopoly on the atomic bomb. Later the Soviet Union developed atomic and hydrogen weapons and built a huge conventional army that was equal or superior to NATO forces in Europe, but this was not enough to close the gap. The NATO powers circled the USSR with bases and bombers that could blanket the country with nuclear weapons, while for years the Russians had no reliable means to deliver a significant number of bombs to targets in America. Until the mid-1960s American nuclear strategy was based on America's capacity to deliver a devastating blow before the Soviets could take any military action, with confidence that this first strike would be so effective that the Soviets could not retaliate. This was no secret from the Russians: successive American Secretaries of Defense advertised it regularly—always with the disclaimer that America had no intention of using this superior force, naturally. But what Soviet leader could allow himself to rely on that assurance? Why did the Americans build those weapons if they had no intention of using them?

Until the Soviet Union mastered the technology of submarine-based missiles in the mid-1960s, an American first strike was a credible threat. (Missiles on submarines at sea provide the capacity to strike back even if one's entire land mass has been destroyed. As long as the submarines remain invulnerable, only a madman would begin a nuclear exchange, for whoever began it would be assured of ultimate destruction. That is the heart of the present balance of terror.) For years the United States had a devastating psychological advantage, one that must have frustrated and infuriated the men who then ruled the Soviet Union. The Americans used the most challenging rhetoric in conjunction with their military superiority. Eisenhower was elected President on a platform which spoke seriously of rolling back communism in Eastern Europe. American Presidents annually celebrated "Captive Nations Week," a holiday the Russians could only interpret as a challenge to their empire. For years the Americans continued to press for reunification of Germany, knowing that nothing scared the Russians more than the prospect of a revived, remilitarized German state. The American position, in sum, appeared to be a position of strength, overwhelming strength which the Soviet leaders always felt was directed against them. Arguably, the Russians were foolish not to see that the NATO countries lacked the unity and determination ever to undertake offensive operations against them. But—being Russians—they took the cautious view, and probably accepted American rhetoric at face value.

Moreover, the Americans kept raising the ante, introducing sophisticated new weapons that the Russians were in no position to match. Despite Sputnik, the Soviet Union could not deploy land-based missiles comparable to the Americans' until the late 1960s. The technology of the Polaris and Poseidon submarines, which could launch intercontinental missiles from underwater, remained out of reach for nearly a decade after the Americans developed them. So did MIRV. The United States exploited its gerat technological advantages, its production skills and its national wealth so effectively that Soviet arms designers and manufacturers must have been panting in exhausted frustration for the last 30 years.

Khrushchev was in power during much of the period when the USSR appeared strong but was in fact weak vis-à-vis the United States. His reaction to Soviet inferiority did little to calm the international atmosphere. He tried to compensate for his weaknesses with brazen threat and bluff, and eventually with the reckless decision to install Soviet missiles in Cuba. His was the behavior of an insecure leader, a man who thought he and his country deserved equal status with the Americans, but who could achieve that status only by bluff and deception. His diplomacy reflected the personality he revealed in his recollections: proud yet fearful, boastful but timid, desperate for respect and admiration.

Khrushchev showed an interest in international adventures which his successors have not entirely eschewed, and which rightly alarms the western world. Soviet support for radical regimes, rebel movements and the competitors in tense confrontations (in the Middle East, for example, or on the In-

dian subcontinent) has contributed to a succession of crises,
some of which could conceivably have grown into serious,
East-West confrontations. One, the Cuban missile crisis,
brought the world to the edge of nuclear war.

But it is important to separate Soviet threats and rocket-
rattling from Soviet behavior under stress. That behavior has
remained consistent since World War II. While advancing
their interests as forcefully as they could, taking advantage of
every opportunity and never relaxing their guard, the Soviet
leaders of these 30 years have persistently avoided the use of
force in international disputes outside their own sphere of influence. They have consistently backed down when they perceived a real danger of strong American action that might
lead to war. Thus Stalin permitted the American airlift
to neutralize the blockade of Berlin, Khrushchev abandoned
his various Berlin "ultimata," Khrushchev withdrew from
Cuba during the missile crisis, and Khrushchev's successors
twice backed away from threatened confrontations in the
Middle East.

The Soviet Union did not land its marines in Lebanon or
put a half-million-man army in Southeast Asia. The Russians
have not permitted any foreign country to draw them into
commitments which necessitated military action. (Hungary
and Czechoslovakia are exceptions, but also special cases,
since they are dependencies of the USSR.) Only in Cuba did
the Soviet Union use military force rashly. In that case
Khrushchev was trying to compensate for Soviet weaknesses,
both strategic and political. He must have hoped that the sudden appearance of his missiles in Cuba, aimed at American
targets, would drastically alter the international climate, allowing for a settlement of outstanding disputes on terms favorable
to him. It was a bold stroke, a departure from traditional (and
subsequent) Soviet diplomacy, and no doubt a factor which
contributed to Khrushchev's removal by disenchanted colleagues two years later.

I don't think the words "aggressive" and "expansionist" adequately describe Soviet behavior in international affairs since
World War II. Future historians, I think, will have to conclude that during this period it was the United States, not the
Soviet Union, which was most prone to misjudge its true interests and take questionable risks by using military force in
international disputes. The Russians have behaved like people

who want to be taken more seriously on the world stage, who crave recognition as the second and co-equal super-power. Their eagerness for status and influence is troublesome, sometimes dangerous, but less worrisome than an actively aggressive, expansionist Soviet policy would be. Like the rest of us, they are principally interested in protecting themselves, and they have often been wiser than the rest of us in perceiving how best to achieve that protection.

In the late 1960s American intelligence-analysts made something of a discovery. They calculated—according to John Newhouse, who has written an excellent book on SALT with the help of many official sources—that the Soviet Union "traditionally spent much more money on defense than on offense. The ratio was about three to one, compared to America's one to one." That figure can be disputed, because it is often impossible to distinguish between offensive and defensive weapons, but the general conclusion is now accepted even in the Pentagon: the United States has spent more than the Soviet Union to acquire an offensive war-fighting capacity.

It would be comforting to be able to report that past western exaggerations of Soviet military power are still valid, and that Soviet armed forces are still inferior to the West's. But that is not the case. At last, from the Russians' point of view, the situation has changed in their favor. Their large conventional forces have finally been matched by strategic weapons which are, roughly, a match for America's. Their atomic missiles are still less sophisticated and probably less reliable than the Americans', but they are no longer vulnerable. In 1962 American power humiliated Khrushchev, an event which may have caused the subsequent build-up of Soviet strategic forces. Whatever its cause, that build-up has succeeded. America can no longer intimidate the Soviet Union.

The cost of catching up has been staggering, and the Russians are not finished yet. They obviously want to continue their build-up of forces until they can honestly claim real parity with the United States in every field, from ICBMs to conventional arms. They will be tempted to seek advantages in each category. That is simply Russian nature, I think; historic insecurity can be assuaged only by achieving indisputable equality, if not superiority.

Soviet military strength is no longer a secret, or the subject merely of guesses. Thanks primarily to the cameras in spy satellites, the United States can now confidently evaluate Soviet forces. According to the best American estimates, this was the USSR's military position vis-à-vis the West in late 1975:

It has more and heavier land-based ICBMs than America, but they are probably less accurate. In 1975 the first of them were fitted with MIRVs, whereas hundreds of America's Minutemen already have MIRV warheads. Its submarine-based missiles are technologically inferior to America's, as are the submarines themselves, but not inferior enough to give the United States any great comfort. America will have more submarine-based missiles than the Russians until the late 1970s, when they will pull even. America has MIRV warheads on submarine missiles, but as of 1975 the Soviets have not yet tested a MIRV—let alone deployed it—on a submarine-based missile.

America has a large advantage in long-range bombers which the Russians show no sign of trying to close. The United States also has a significant geographical advantage which the Soviet Union is helpless to counteract. Americans can launch nuclear weapons against the USSR from all directions, thanks to their network of bases around the periphery of the country.

Conventional forces are the Russians' strongest suit. They have 3.5 million men under arms, compared to 2.1 million for the United States. Moreover, their entire society is militarized in a way no western country is. Schoolchildren and university-level students all receive military training. The universal draft is still in force, though young men with higher degrees usually avoid active duty. The Voluntary Society for Assisting the Army, Air Force and Navy is a huge organization with millions of members who act as activists on the home front.

The Soviet Union and its Warsaw Pact allies have 26,500 tanks in Central Europe, compared to 11,500 for the NATO countries. Other forms of armament are more equally balanced, but western military experts generally agree that the Warsaw Pact has the superior military force in Europe. It also enjoys a geographic advantage, since Central Europe is so far removed from NATO's strongest member, the United States.

The Warsaw Pact force has certain significant weaknesses. Its logistics are poor, and western analysts doubt its capacity to fight a prolonged war. The political reliability of forces from Czechoslovakia, Hungary, Poland and East Germany is open to question. Soviet soldiers are less well trained and less technically competent than their western counterparts.

Nevertheless, this force gives the Russians a comforting sense of security in Europe. Their army is designed so that it can cross West Germany in a modern blitzkrieg, a posture obviously intended to give the NATO powers pause. The Soviet Union might someday try that blitzkrieg to topple the equilibrium in Europe. For many reasons, that seems unlikely—most obviously because of the danger of an instantaneous atomic reply—but the possibility has to be considered seriously.

The Soviet Air Force is large but defensive in its orientation. The United States has a vastly superior capacity to carry an air war deep into an enemy's air space, and to deliver bombs or take action to support troops fighting hundreds of miles from base. The Warsaw Pact has a substantial numerical advantage over NATO in terms of aircraft bases in Central Europe, but America's overall numerical superiority could be quickly exploited in an emergency by flying in more planes. Western planes are more versatile, and their pilots are betted trained and more experienced than Warsaw Pact pilots.

The Soviet Navy has grown dramatically in the past decade, shifting the balance of naval power. Until recently the United States and its allies maintained an effective monopoly on the world's oceans. The Americans got used to the idea that they ruled the seas—a comforting notion, and one that gave the United States numerous options for the use or threat of force around the world. Now the Soviet Union has put an end to the monopoly.

Not surprisingly, this has alarmed the American Navy and many of its supporters. Admiral Elmo R. Zumwalt, Jr., who retired as the American Chief of Naval Operations in 1974, left office with the alarming observation that the United States had lost control of the sea lanes to the Soviet Union.

What Zumwalt meant was that the United States once controlled the sea lanes uncontested, but now the Russians can challenge American control. He did not mean the Soviet

Union has taken over control—its Navy is in no position to do that. Primarily by dint of its vast force of submarines, the USSR has become a formidable sea power, but overall its fleet hardly compares with the NATO navies.

The western powers have 16 aircraft carriers in service; the Soviet Union has none. It is building two small ones which can be used only by vertical-take-off airplanes, and therefore pose only a modest military threat. Though the Soviet Navy has grown impressively, western navies outweigh it in tonnage of surface combatants by three to one. The American Navy can keep 30 percent of its fleet at sea in distant waters at all times; the Soviet Navy has difficulty keeping 10 percent of its fleet on the high seas. NATO ships are fully manned and capable of fighting prolonged battles at sea. Most Soviet ships carry skeleton crews, apparently on the theory that prolonged naval fighting is unlikely. The American Navy, operating from a network of bases around the world, carries enormous firepower and large contingents of men to distant trouble spots; the Soviet Navy has no formal bases in foreign countries and cannot deliver substantial firepower or manpower to distant targets quickly.

Soviet behavior has been determined by more than the simple balance of military forces. The Russians may be imperfect Marxists, but they have a very Marxist sense of power. In the Soviet view, international power comes from a combination of sources: military strength, naturally, but also political strength as measured by the alignments of other nations and the durability of alliances; economic capacity; technology and scientific skills. Soviet political and military literature is filled with appreciation for the importance of non-military factors.

Western statesmen have tended to minimize these factors in their calculations of power, particularly the power of the Soviet Union. The West has concentrated almost exclusively on Soviet military capabilities, which is the best—in fact, the only—way to make the Russians look nearly as formidable as the United States. We have judged them on the basis of their strongest assets, and have misunderstood their weaknesses. The Soviets themselves could not have hoped for the flattering evaluation we have so long accorded them.

Evidence of Soviet weaknesses is not difficult to find. In the crucial areas of economics, technology and science, the Soviet

Union openly advertises not just inferiority, but *dependence* on its principal adversaries. It has turned to the West for a large and still growing number of its basic economic and technological needs, and has demanded long-term credit to pay for them. The USSR has behaved in this area like the developing country it is, not like the second super-power which, in many respects, it is not. The Russians may claim, to others and to themselves, that the large-scale purchase of foreign technology and industrial capacity will be needed only temporarily, but where is the proof of that? The structure of the Soviet economy does not support the hypothesis that after buying foreign technology for a transition period, it will suddenly blossom with new technological capacity of its own. On the contrary, foreign purchases allow the Russians to avoid confronting the structural reasons for their technological inferiority, and thus insure that the inferiority will last.

I am oversimplifying a complicated issue, but fairly. A country that will spend one billion dollars in cash for a new iron-and-steel works—as the Soviets are spending on a plant to be built by West Germany—its demonstrating an indisputable dependence on outsiders. That factory at Kursk will be enormous, and will provide a significant percentage of the country's needs. The Russians argue that they could build it themselves, but prefer to buy it. Perhaps they could—but only at the expense of other projects. Soviet capacity is finite; resources devoted to one project cannot also be used for another. The Russians could not possibly build all the factories they are buying from foreigners, nor even a large portion of them. Which is why they are buying them.

The Soviet Union could survive without these foreign projects, and could maintain its military forces without them. (Trade with the West represents less than 2 percent of Soviet economic activity, though much of it affects vital sectors of the economy.) I am not trying to suggest a desperate dependence or one that would allow the western powers to humiliate or intimidate the USSR. The Soviets obviously calculate that they can purchase western technology without being confronted with unreasonable demands or intimidation. That calculation has proven correct. If they felt they had to, the Russians could get along without the things they have been buying abroad in recent years.

But it is perhaps more significant that they have chosen *not* to go without those factories and machines. They want them, even at the expense of exposing Soviet weaknesses.

The reason they want them, I think, reveals a great deal about the practical, short-term desires of this generation of Soviet leaders. These leaders, who abandoned Stalinist terror, have decided to try to maintain stability in their country by creating a contented public. This may be less dramatic than it sounds, because the leadership wants to buy contentment cheaply. It shows no readiness to radically change the distribution of resources in the Soviet economy, so improvements in the standard of living will continue to be gradual and, by western standards, modest. But outsiders should realize that the Soviet citizen's expectations are low. The effort now being made to satisfy them could be successful.

It is important, I think, that the present leaders no longer ask (or demand) that their people accept great sacrifices and material shortages for the sake of an imprecise revolutionary future. Instead they promise a better life for all, and quickly. And they have begun to provide it, if slowly. The satisfaction of consumer desires has obviously prompted many of the Soviet Union's foreign purchases. One of the first big factories the Russians bought in the 1960s—at a cost of $430 million in hard currency—was the Fiat plant now producing small passenger cars at Togliattigrad.

The Soviet Union's steadily expanding trade with the West exposes another sort of weakness: the world economy which the Russians find increasingly attractive is controlled by their adversaries. We take it for granted that our dollars or pounds are an acceptable currency in the world market, but the Russian ruble is worth nothing in international trade. The Soviet Union must maintain a foreign-currency account outside its normal economy. It has no voice in the World Bank, the International Monetary Fund or the informal councils in which world monetary policy is determined. The Russians borrow from foreign banks to finance their trade. They must sell their diamonds in the West through affiliates of De Beers, the South African firm which dominates the world diamond market.

The Soviet Union cannot compete economically with the western powers in the Third World. The poorer countries need the capital and technical assistance which, with few exceptions, only the western nations and Japan can provide. The Soviet Union cannot have missed the fact that the Arab world's new wealth—earned at the expense of the capitalist powers—is actually tying the Arab states more closely into the capitalist system, a trend that could eventually move the Arabs further away from the Soviet Union.

During the years in which the Soviet Union has managed to achieve military parity with the United States, its political position has deteriorated. This is another point we have tended either to ignore or to minimize, but for the Russians its importance is enormous.

When Stalin died in 1953 there really was a single communist movement—not as monolithic as John Foster Dulles supposed, perhaps, but impressively unified under Soviet direction. Communism, though discredited in many circles, still had a wide following in the West—not just in Italy and France, but even in Britain. The Soviet claim to lead the world's "progressive" forces was still widely recognized, and those forces appeared on the eve of great victories, particularly as the pace of decolonization quickened.

All that has changed. The communist countries are now divided and contentious. Some of them disregard Moscow's desires entirely; the Chinese actually work against them. Even the satellites, whose freedom to maneuver is limited, no longer respond to every Soviet wish. The invasions of Hungary and Czechoslovakia and Khrushchev's revelations of Stalin's crimes wiped out much of the most respectable support for communism in the West. Decolonization has not proven a boon to communism; on the contrary, it has created many contenders for leadership of the "progressive" forces. The Arabs, whom the Russians courted most ardently, have never shown much gratitude, and in the case of Egypt have proven hostile and ungrateful for aid which cost the USSR billions of dollars.

The western powers have become stronger, more prosperous and more unified. The economic miracles in Japan and West Germany strengthened capitalism appreciably. Even Finland, the Russians' supposedly compliant neighbor, has established formal relations with the European Economic Community.

The evolution of China from loyal ally to hostile enemy has been, for the Russians, the single most important development of the last 20 years. Having to share a long border and mutual enmity with the world's most populous nation has disrupted the Soviet Union's political and military calculations. There is no question that Chinese hostility helped push the Brezhnev leadership toward *détente* with the West—as a means of reducing tensions on at least one main front, and perhaps to beat the Chinese to improved relations with the United States. The dispute with China had forced the Russians to station 45 divisions along the Chinese border, including two in Mongolia. This huge army is far removed from supply centers in European Russia. China must now be the Soviet Union's principal foreign preoccupation.

Eastern Europe has also caused the Russians far more trouble and anxiety than is generally recognized. When Stalin ruled the empire, the vassals knew their place. He exploited the satellites ruthlessly and they felt helpless to protest. Stalin's death gave them heart. In June 1953 rioting East German workers inaugurated a series of bold protests by Eastern Europeans which have harassed the Russians at periodic intervals ever since, and which forced Stalin's heirs to abandon the policy of blatant exploitation.

The new policy was one of pacification through limited prosperity. It failed to satisfy the Hungarians in 1956, the Czechoslovaks in 1968, the Poles in 1970, but after each of those crises the Russians returned to essentially the same tactic. Events that followed the invasion of Czechoslovakia were instructive. At first the invasion seemed to portend a general crackdown in the Soviet empire, a return to stricter orthodoxy. In fact, outside of Czechoslovakia it produced the opposite result. Within a few years old-line orthodox leaders in Poland and East Germany were replaced by more progressive and pragmatic men. Economic reform in Hungary gathered momentum. The Russians permitted—and in some cases encouraged—the Hungarian, Polish, East German and Czechoslovak regimes to steadily raise the standard of living in their countries. As a result, the residents of all those countries now live appreciably better than the Soviet population.

The Russians have failed to change the western orientation in any of these countries. I traveled through Eastern Europe for six weeks in 1972 and was deeply impressed by the contrasts between the satellites and the Soviet Union. The atmosphere was utterly different: relaxed, unselfconscious, surprisingly candid. The Eastern Europeans, including some officials of the local Communist Parties, don't try to hide their desire to loosen the ties that bind the Soviet empire. "What we want to achieve," a senior Polish economist told me, "is a new relationship inside the socialist camp—maybe something like the British Commonwealth."

Something like the British Commonwealth would amount to a revolutionary change in the present arrangement, which is based on ultimate control by Moscow. Yet it is an understandable aspiration for proud people with distinguished national traditions. The Eastern Europeans seem to be pushing independently in that direction, though they may never get there. They have steadily expanded independent ties with the capitalist West. Trade has grown steadily and is now substantial. More than 20 percent of all foreign commerce in Hungary and East Germany is conducted with the West; in Poland, more than 30 percent.

The Russians know in their hearts that they are not loved in Eastern Europe. Only the Bulgarians and some of the Yugoslavs feel a historical attachment to Russia. All the others regard themselves as part of Europe and western civilization. For historic reasons the Poles and East Germans despise Russia. The Hungarians and Czechoslovaks have more recent cause for similar emotions. The Soviet Union is still an occupying power in these countries; it must substitute military force for admiration.

So the Soviets are on the defensive with Eastern Europe as with the rest of the world. First they must fear rebellions and an unraveling of their control. This fear has convinced them to indulge policies in Eastern Europe which would never be permitted in the USSR—freer cultural policies, minimal restrictions on travel to the West in several countries, more pragmatic economic policies. Yet by permitting these aberrations the Russians invite another kind of problem. Ideas travel comparatively freely inside the "fraternal socialist camp." Soviet citizens can sometimes find out what is going on in Hungary, East Germany or Czechoslovakia, and they may begin to ask why the Soviet Union remains so different. During the Dubcek era in Czechoslovakia, a magazine printed in Ukrainian for the country's small Ukrainian population was banned from the Soviet Union because it contained such liberal ideas.

I don't think Soviet domination of Eastern Europe is in jeopardy. The Eastern Europeans are still timid, and they see no way to overcome their dependency on the USSR for raw materials and energy. But Soviet domination will never be easy to maintain. Eastern Europe will remain a distracting source of difficulties for the Russians.

My purpose here is not to declare the Soviet Union a pitiful, helpless giant. The Soviet leaders have made the most of the considerable resources available to them, and have not fared badly in international politics during the past 30 years. My point is that the Russians are less formidable than we have imagined, more vulnerable and more nervous. Their ambitions, I think, are less grand than even their own words suggest.

What do these Russians really want? First it is important to understand who "these Russians" really are.

They are something different from the simple embodiment of a nation's or a revolutionary movement's interests. The Soviet leaders who determine their country's foreign policies are the autocrats who have appeared throughout this book—isolated from their public, chosen to rule only by their autocratic peers, insecure about the legitimacy of their power.

They revealed their true colors in the invasion of Czechoslovakia in 1968. They invaded not to further the cause of communism—which was seriously damaged by the spectacle of Soviet aggressiveness—nor to redeem their nation's interest, but to protect their own autocracy.

Alexander Dubcek posed no threat to the USSR; his country is tiny and powerless, and it wanted to maintain the friendliest of relations with the Soviet Union. Nor did he threaten Marxism-Leninism. On the contrary, the new Czechoslovakia attracted admirers in many other countries. But he threatened the Marxism-Leninism practiced in Moscow—the system based on arbitrary rule by the Communist Party, absolute control over the press and mass media, and the pre-eminence of an unelected elite. Dubcek proposed to give up the Communist Party's monopoly of power, to end censorship and implicity to subject the ruling elite to the popular will. The Soviet autocrats calculated that such reforms in the USSR would put them out of business. Dubcek's "socialism with a human face" terrified them.

So they invaded, contrary to most predictions by the western world's Soviet experts, and clearly contrary to the apparent interests of their country and their cause. They invaded because their first priority is neither country nor cause, but self-preservation. They decided that the Czechoslovak reforms were too dangerous, potentially too infectious to permit.

The interests of the ruling autocracy will come first as long as the Soviet system retains its present character. This is only logical: self-preservation is the principal motivation of politicians everywhere. But in the Soviet Union self-preservation has a special meaning, because the politicians are autocrats, not elected or popularly controlled. An analysis of Soviet ambitions and intentions, then, should concentrate on the autocracy's ambitions and intentions.

That said, I want to examine the hypothesis that the Soviet Union is an aggressive, expansionist power which actively seeks to undermine the western world. I can think of three factors that support this hypothesis:

First, the Soviet leaders are vulnerable to traditional Napoleonic instincts, reinforced by geographical imperatives. The Russian empire has historically tended to expand, but it still lacks geographical advantages that must be tempting, most obviously a reliable outlet to the Mediterranean. Aggrandizement for tactical advantage could also tempt the Russians, though they now enjoy a good deal of protection on every frontier save that with China.

The second factor bears more on agressiveness than on territorial ambition—the effect of traditional Russian insecurity. The biggest bully is often trying to hide the biggest fears. There is an aggressive streak in the contemporary Soviet character which I encountered more than once, and which Russians familiar with the Soviet Army told me is common in its ranks, particularly among middle-ranking officers. "There are captains, majors and colonels who think that World War III will bring great victories to the Soviet Motherland," according to a young Russian who had visited numberous Army units as part of his work. I personally heard soldiers boast about the efficiency of the Warsaw Pact's invasion of Czechoslovakia. Western military attachés posted in Moscow repeatedly encounter manifestations of aggressive hostility among their Soviet counterparts.

Aggressiveness born of insecurity could lead to an active Soviet policy of subversion in the West. Subversion which weakens potential adversaries and distracts their attention may tempt the Soviet leaders as a sensible tactic which could serve their interest.

Third, Soviet ideology may require both aggressiveness and expansion. Marxism-Leninism is a dynamic ideology; it holds that communism is the inevitable wave of the future—that "the objective realities of social development have put the revolutionary transition to socialism on the agenda of this century," to quote a Soviet schoolbook.

The ideology justifies the entire system. Marxism-Leninism is the Soviet Union's raison d'être. Therefore, arguably, the Soviet leaders must see to it that the ideology's predictions come true, which may mean stepping in on the side of "the objective realities of social development" to give them a helping hand. Only if communism appears to be a vital, growing force in the world, the leaders may feel, can they claim the legitimacy for their cause which the ideology promises.

Moreover, the ideology implies a constant crisis in Russia's relations with the capitalist West. Tension between the USSR and its class enemy, the international bourgeoisie, justifies the state of permanent siege inside the country—the restrictions on freedom, the arbitrary rule by a tightly knit Party elite. So the Soviet autocracy may want to maintain the tension, and on occasion even to aggravate it, for internal purposes.

In other words, a stable and permanent peace with the West would undermine both the autocracy's legitimacy and its system of internal control, and is therefore out of the question.

None of these arguments is new, and all of them are essentially correct. The Soviet leaders are ambitious, they often seem aggressive in temperament and their ideology does seem to require international tension. Therefore, western statesmen have assumed that the USSR is indeed aggressive and expansionist by nature. I question this assumption, though, because it ignores a whole set of other facts about the Soviet Union which point to a more subtle and very different conclusion.

The most important of these other facts is the lesson of Czechoslovakia—that the Soviet autocracy puts its own interests above all else. From the vantage point of a Soviet leader, communist governments in sovereign nations beyond the USSR's control are a potential *danger*. The best proof of this is the People's Republic of China. Stalin had little to fear from Chiang Kai-shek and he knew it, but Mao Tse-tung has turned out to be a rival for leadership of the communist movement, a rival for prestige and influence in the Third World and a potential enemy in a hot war. What would happen if the Communist Party came to power in France and Italy? Might they not become dynamic forces on the world scene, new models of socialism and a new source of competition for the Soviet leaders? Of course they would. An Italian communist government could easily prove much more provocative and dangerous than Dubcek's Czechoslovakia ever was. But the Russians would not have the option of invading Italy to restore orthodoxy, at least not without enormous risk.

Is it really possible that the Russians don't want communist regimes in the advanced western countries? I realize this is a bold suggestion, given our long-standing prejudices, but I suspect it is the case. Our prejudices come from a misreading of the men who run the USSR. Were they as bold and imaginative as Lenin, or as tough and ruthless as Stalin, my hypothesis would be improbable. But they are completely cut off from Lenin, and much weaker than Stalin. These rulers don't show an appetite for great conquests, or for unpredictable upheavals. They find it hard enough to keep the Soviet Union going, to handle the tactical skirmishes that arise at home and abroad from day to day and month to month.

Their tactics may reveal their true colors. When their central interests are at stake, those tactics are invariably prudent, even when prudence contradicts the aspirations implicit in Marxist-Leninist ideology,

Soviet diplomacy in France is a case in point. Its goal is to maintain favorable relations with the French government and to encourage French independence of America and NATO, but not to help the French Communist Party achieve full or partial power in France. The Russians presumably don't see how the French communists could gain power, and they disapprove of sharing it with the anti-communist or, at least, anti-Soviet French Socialists. So the Russians have thrown their weight with the Gaullists. In 1974 the Soviet ambassador in Paris signaled his support for the Gaullists' candidate. Valéry Giscard d'Estaing, on the eve of his run-off with François Mitterand, the Socialist candidate supported by the French Communist Party. The ambassador made an ostentatious and unnecessary call on Giscard just before the run-off, apparently to bestow Soviet blessing for his victory. In the event he barely won.

In the Arab world the Soviets have befriended fiercely anti-communist regimes for tactical reasons, and have shown little interest in spreading Marxism-Leninism. In 1972

President Sadat of Egypt unceremoniously dismissed more than 10,000 Soviet military advisors, an insult which apparently signaled the failure of a sixteen-year-old Soviet policy in the Middle East, a policy which cost the USSR billions of rubles and dollars. Yet the Soviets accepted Sadat's hostility with remarkable equanimity.

In India the Russians have ordered the local Communist Party to cooperate unreservedly with Indira Gandhi and the Congress Party, a tactic to help a friend and strengthen the anti-Chinese forces in Asia, but one which does not advance the revolutionary cause in India.

No doubt the Soviet leaders excuse these compromises as necessary tactical maneuvers—the steps backward which, Lenin counseled, should be followed by more steps forward. I doubt these leaders think of themselves as compromisers who are indifferent to the future of communism. In their own minds they probably remain ambitious, even aggressive proponents of world revolution. But what these men privately think of themselves is much less important than the way they actually behave toward the rest of us. The significant point is that the Soviet leaders can effectively abandon the ideological goals of communism *without ever admitting that they are doing so*—by saying one thing and doing another. They can behave like the man in the familiar cartoon who, feet up on a chaotic desk, announces, "Tomorrow I've got to get organized."

This is just what they have been doing for many years. The victory of international communism, like the arrival of utopian "pure communism" at home, is quietly set aside for a distant future. Since the men who rule the country are old (on average between sixty-five and seventy), that future is someone else's worry. Once this formula is established, the leaders can go about the pursuit of their self-interest with a clear ideological conscience.

So, for example, they can enter into long-term economic agreements with the capitalistic countries and slip deeper and deeper into the capitalist-dominated world economy on the grounds that this will build a stronger Soviet Union in the future. Similarly, they can allow and even encourage the Eastern Europeans to let their economies become increasingly intertwined with the West. Yet because of these developments the Soviet Union now has a real and growing interest in economic stability in the West. A serious depression in the capitalist world could have traumatic consequences in Eastern Europe and increasingly serious repercussions for the Soviet economy. So the Soviet Union has probably already become an ally—perhaps as yet an unconscious ally—of at least moderate prosperity in the western world.*

The West has long been alarmed by the slogans of Soviet communism and by Soviet-supported efforts to advance the communist cause in other countries. The ruthless, conspiratorial nature of Marxism-Leninism is intimidating. The Russians have long understood this fear, and probably welcomed it. But as a practical matter the Soviet leaders have demonstrated that they are not consumed and driven by their ideological objectives. On the contrary, ideological objectives are selectively altered and ignored to suit more pressing needs.

Before this begins to sound too rosy I must advance an important qualification. There will not be an early end to East-West tensions, or formal changes in Soviet ideology which would allow for the permanent survival of capitalism in peaceful harmony with the Soviet camp. The Soviet leaders welcome and will probably encourage tensions, because tensions help justify the rule of an arbitrary autocracy. Competition for influence around the world can continue and, in the Soviet view, is probably appropriate, since competition for prestige and influence comes naturally to Russians. Nothing need stop the Soviet Union from helping indigenous communist movements as it has in Vietnam, Portugal and elsewhere in the developing world. The Soviet Union will welcome new allies, especially those which are self-supporting or not too expensive. They will welcome harassment of the western powers and a steady deterioration of the West's strength, provided this is not precipitous. If the Communist Party seizes power in Italy, the Russians are not likely to join any effort to overthrow it; instead they will try to make an accommodation.

The Soviet Union can abandon tense, competitive relations with the West only if its leaders can find other props to hold up the autocracy. The "ideological struggle" which they insist on continuing in this era of *détente* is primarily a form of self-protection, only secondarily a kind of political aggression.

---

* There is an ideological justification for supporting western prosperity. According to Soviet theoreticians, it is in times of depression that capitalist countries become the most dangerous. Hitler is advanced as an example of what can happen when economic conditions deteriorate drastically.

If their statements on the ideological struggle are closely examined, it is clear that the Russians are talking about the right to keep foreign ideology (that is, ideas and information) out of the USSR while practicing *détente* in interstate relations.

Prosperity may someday dilute the "ideological struggle," which is largely a tool to protect the Soviet public from knowledge of better living conditions in the outside world. But that won't happen soon.

Soviet foreign policy reflects the interests of the ruling autocracy above all others. That may not be a bad thing for the rest of us. I find it hard to imagine a situation in which the autocrats' self-interest would be served by aggression outside their own empire. Even aggrandizement without aggression is laden with risk. The status quo, viewed from the autocrats' perspective, is surprisingly satisfactory.

The status quo does not have a guaranteed future, however, and to the outside world the most important question about the Soviet Union probably is: What next?

Confident prediction is impossible. The ruling autocracy is not a completely homogeneous group, and one cannot foresee the next generation's reactions to domestic or international issues. The strong Russian nationalist tendencies inside the ruling elite are a potentially powerful influence, but an influence for what? Arguably, if Russian nationalism can replace Leninist internationalism, the aggressive implications of Soviet ideology could diminish. On the other hand, if the country's rulers adopt Russian nationalism as a guiding creed, they will face great strains at home, since Russians are a minority of the Soviet population. Domestic unrest might produce foreign adventures, as it has in so many countries in the past.

Future leaders may be much less insecure than past ones, and with reason. They will be citizens of a militarily invulnerable Soviet Union, and they will have grown up ignorant of Stalinism and the terrible fears it bred. Less insecurity might mean more rational dealings with the outside world; it might also give future leaders the confidence to undertake more dangerous foreign adventures.

I suspect, though, that Russian insecurity is too deeply imbedded to disappear in one or two generations. And the "objective conditions," to borrow a Soviet phrase, which shaped Soviet policy in the last quarter-century could easily last another 25 years. It is reassuring that each group of Soviet leaders since Stalin has decided, sooner or later, that negotiations with the West are preferable to uncontrolled competition. Malenkov and his colleagues jumped to this conclusion after Stalin died, which probably hastened the armistice in Korea. (Stalin died in March 1953; the armistice was signed in July.) Khrushchev found it difficult to choose between negotiations and competitive boasting, and his indecision produced the worst of both worlds; his diplomacy failed, and his boasting encouraged America to compete more earnestly, which put the Soviet Union in a relatively weaker position. The Brezhnev group waited four years before indicating an interest in negotiations (at first on controlling strategic weapons), but by 1971 they had decided on the bold "peace program" which has given us *détente*.

Soviet leaders opt for negotiations because they cannot profit from all-out competition. That realization explains why the USSR has decided to pursue *détente*. Isolated, economically far inferior to the capitalist West, tied to a vulnerable empire and wary of a hostile China, the Russians would be rash indeed to willingly engage the best energies of their adversaries. *Détente*—which the Russians call "the relaxation of international tensions"—reduces the danger of confrontation and provides better opportunities for the Soviet Union to pursue its interests.

Détente is not just a fleeting tactic adopted in Moscow. I think it represents a fundamental decision about the best way the Soviet Union can achieve its international objectives, the first of which is security from hostile forces. The Soviet leaders have said repeatedly that the relaxation of international tensions is a policy intended to last for decades. Soviet officials behave as though they believe this is so.

East-West negotiations of the kind we have seen in recent years serve Soviet purposes on several fronts. Now that the Russians can claim a roughly comparable military establishment, they can bargain with the Americans for contractual equality, a good way to assure their security and, perhaps, eventually to spend less on arms. (For years the American idea of negotiations was to impose contractual inferiority on the Soviet Union.) Negotiations legitimize the Soviet empire and assure the Russians that the West has no plan or hope for rolling back the Iron Curtain. Negotiations calm the western powers and dull their appetitite for all-out competition. Probably most important of all, negotiations of the kind that began with President Nixon's first visit to Moscow in 1972 appear to ratify the Soviet Union's status as the second super-power, almost America's equal.

True equality with America on all counts must be the broad aim of all Soviet policies. Equality (if not superiority) is all that could satisfy Russian insecurity, Russian pride and Russian ambition. Soviet officials speak constantly of surpassing the capitalist world. Soviet statisticians compile tables to show Soviet production as a percentage of American production. This proud, isolated nation, so long the victim of forces beyond its control, yearns for a combination of invulnerability, influence and prestige that would establish it at the head of the international community.

If we understand that *détente* is a Soviet strategy designed to help the USSR achieve genuine super-power equality, we are unlikely to be surprised by Soviet behavior in the years to come. This does not mean a Soviet campaign of world conquest, nor even a dangerous new threat to western interests. The Russians have craved equality for a long time, and the craving is unlikely to be satisfied in the foreseeable future. But they will be pressing and we will have to learn to make room for the Russians in areas where they once had no significance.

The Middle East provides a good example of the tactics the Russians are likely to pursue. First they sent aid and advisors to their new Arab friends. Later they established a naval presence in the Mediterranean Sea, a declaration of intensified interest in the area. Eventually they became the patrons and protectors of the militant Arab faction, adopting its position in international forums and supporting its ambitions with vast assistance. Finally, when events in the region came to a head in the mid-1970s, they insisted on an important place in the negotiations and a role in the future life of the region.

That pattern of behavior suggests an intense desire for recognition and influence. Yet the recent history of the Middle East also demonstrates the large and still insoluble problems the Soviet Union faces if it wants to attain the status of a real super-power. Soviet aid did not buy reliable friends, and in Egypt may have bought new adversaries in the long run. The Soviet naval presence has neutralized the American Mediterranean fleet as a weapon of all-out war (one Soviet cruiser can neutralize a huge American aircraft carrier), but has not given the Russians any great new power or influence. When the time came to try to resolve the Middle East situation with serious negotiations, only the United States had the standing, power and influence to act as honest broker. Henry Kissinger's shuttle diplomacy humiliated the Russians. I was in Moscow when it began; several Soviet journalists and officials urged *me* "not to cut us out of the Middle East." The Soviet press barely reported on Kissinger's early diplomatic triumphs, a clear sign that they infuriated the leadership. Soviet diplomats spent 1974 and much of 1975 maneuvering for a significant role in the Middle East negotiations, preferably in the Geneva conference of which the USSR was co-chairman, but by mid-1975 had given up the idea as hopeless.

This doesn't mean the Russians have been pushed out of the Middle East. On the contrary, the Americans see the value of keeping them in, at least symbolically. What is instructive is the Russians' inability to match the Americans' resources in this situation. An important new factor, after the sharp increase in oil prices, was the Arabs' wealth. The Americans could help them use and invest that money, the Russians could not (unless the Arabs wanted to buy Soviet arms). American flexibility was significant; the Russians didn't even have relations with Israel (cut off to please the Arabs in 1967), and seemed unwilling to reestablish them for fear of alienating their so-called clients. Most important was American trustworthiness. Both sides trusted Kissinger, whereas no statesman in the region would have risked putting faith in any Soviet diplomat or official. The Russians have earned the suspicions of most of the world, including their closest friends and allies.

The growth of the Soviet Navy and its appearance in all the world's major oceans confirms that temporary failure—or imperfect success—won't deter the Soviet Union. The Navy is a good tool for building up one's image. It might also be used to increase one's power, but the Soviets haven't chosen that course yet. Their Navy is a symbolic instrument, undermanned for fighting at sea, unprotected in most waters by Soviet air power and lacking aircraft carriers. Yet simply by sailing into an ocean it deprives the United States of the monopoly it once enjoyed.

Soviet determination is no assurance of success, however. As I hope I have shown, the rigidities of the Soviet system, the weaknesses of the economy, the lack of imagination in the leadership and the isolation of the country all suggest that the Russians are unlikely to achieve real equality with the West. (I am assuming, perhaps rashly, that the West will not collapse of its own foolishness. If it does, nothing I say here will matter.)

The Russians suffer one enormous disadvantage in this competition: their opponents control the rules by which it is played. The super-power game is America's game. The Russians mimic American ways, copy American weapons and equipment, measure their accomplishments against American accomplishments. For some years they have been struggling to catch up with the West's post-war boom, but by the time they do catch up, the West will have moved up into a new era. Success in that era will depend on solutions to the new generation of human problems—overpopulation, poverty, hunger, pollution and interdependence. The Russians are in no position now to contribute significantly to any of them.

A Russian acquaintance of mine, a scientist, read Alvin Toffler's *Future Shock* while I was in Moscow, and was overwhelmed by it. The book is about the pace of man's progress and his inability to control it. "I read that book in amazement," the Russian scientist said. "No one in this country is thinking about such things. The future here doesn't go beyond the next Five Year Plan." He is probably right.

My conclusions here contradict the views of many scholars and diplomats whose credentials as Soviet experts are better than my own. There is no shortage of specialists who hold ominous views of Soviet power and its potential effectiveness. Many believe that the Soviet leaders are supremely confident that history is moving in their direction.

These experts would dispute my impression of Soviet diplomacy as essentially tactical, motivated primarily by insecurity. Instead they perceive a grand design in Soviet policy, a design intended to put the entire world under communist domination.

In recent years some of these experts have fostered the theory of "Finlandization." This is a process by which the Western European states are supposed to relinquish their sovereignty to the USSR gradually, as a consequence of overbearing Soviet power, the way Finland has in the past. Through Finlandization, some have argued, the Russians will first erode the NATO alliance and eventually dominate the western countries entirely.

An alarming prospect, but not yet a serious one, I think. Finland deserves closer attention. Though dependent on the Soviet Union for energy supplies, completely vulnerable geographically and tied closely to the Soviet economy by extensive trade, the Finns maintain a high degree of independence. They have preserved a free, open society, and during the past decade they have moved closer to their Scandinavian neighbors and Western Europe. Recent Finnish history is hardly an advertisement for the effectiveness of Russian pressure.

Which isn't to say that under some circumstances the Soviet Union might not try to intimidate its neighbors. Someday it might. Some future generation of Soviet leaders could decide—and may have good reason to decide—that history really is on the side of Marxism-Leninism, and that communism will conquer the world. If we in the western world continue to mismanage our affairs, we will encourage the Russians to reach that conclusion.

But for now Soviet diplomacy reflects the true "correlation of forces" in the world, to borrow a common phrase from Soviet political analysis. Their Marxism helps the Soviet leaders to understand that the correlation of forces still favors their adversaries, and will probably do so for years to come. They realize that power consists of more than rockets and tanks, and that their economic, political and geographic weaknesses deny them the status and influence they crave.

The most ominous interpretation of Soviet power and intentions, I believe, can be taken seriously only if one ignores the kind of society the Soviet Union is and the way it really works.

I do not mean to suggest that the western world's problems are over. The Soviet Union is responsible for very few of those problems, though it happily exploits many of them. In countries such as Portugal the Russians will be glad to take advantage of opportunities created by years of right-wing dictatorship and western indifference. Spain may be next. The West's political vulnerability—which seems serious—is hardly a consequence of Soviet policy. In Italy, for example, the Communist Party is likely to exploit whatever chances come its way even if a small group of Soviet autocrats would prefer that it not win power. In many countries, accelerated economic development, equitable distribution of income and wealth, equal rights and equal justice are powerful ideas. If the western powers align themselves with the opponents of those popular ideas, future troubles are assured.

Although the Soviet Union may be less formidable an adversary than we have generally thought, it is still a formidable adversary, and it is anxious to do us ill. There is no generosity of spirit in the Soviet Union's attitude toward the West, no high-minded desire to see all men prosper in whatever circumstances they choose. The meanness and competitiveness of the USSR, amply displayed in all its international dealings, cannot be ignored or discounted.

But we have the resources necessary to cope with the Russians. We can cope more effectively if we now recognize the errors of our past evaluations of them. The Soviet enemy we have imagined during the last 30 years bore too little resemblance to reality. It seems to me that we often imagined the sort of enemy we wanted—and, subconsciously, perhaps needed—without due attention to the real character of Soviet society.

The Russians themselves have wanted us to overestimate their strength and their greatness. They are strong and they are great, but those are hardly the only words that should be used to describe the country in which things that just don't happen happen.

Acknowledgments

I SPENT FIVE years preparing for and then writing this book. During that time a great many kind people and generous institutions helped me—too many to list them all here. But I do want to mention a few.

The *Washington Post* deserves my greatest appreciation. Benjamin C. Bradlee, Howard Simons, Philip Foisie and other editors at the *Post* made possible my tour in the Soviet Union, and even prepared me for it. The *Post*, with help from the Ford Foundation, sent me and my wife to Columbia University for a year to study Russian before we went to the USSR. And the *Post* excused me for a year when we returned from Russia so I could write this book.

It was written at Duke University, with the support of the Markle Foundation, and I want to thank both of them. Joel Fleishman, Director of Duke's Institute of Policy Sciences and Public Affairs, made my year there possible.

Simon Michael Bessie was the editor of this book, and he was also its spiritual godfather. He urged me to write it even before I left for Russia, and repeatedly thereafter. Once the writing began he was an invaluable counselor and a constant source of enthusiasm.

Gali Hagel was my research assistant, editor, typist and general helper, and a great boon to the book.

Many people took the time to read various sections of the manuscript and comment on them. I would like to mention especially my mother, Hannah G. Kaiser, Bruce Payne, William Odom, Vladimir Treml, Jerry Hough, Lawrence Goodwyn, John Newhouse, John Ahearne, Chalmers Roberts, Murrey Marder, Marilyn Berger, Dan Morgan, Thomas Powers, Carl Bernstein and Peter Osnos.

Hundreds of Soviet citizens and recent émigrés from the USSR took many hours to try to teach me about their country. Without them there would be no book. Those who can be named are mentioned in the text. The others, I hope, know how much they helped and how grateful I am.

Hannah Jopling Kaiser had more influence on this book than anyone but myself—as a participant in many of the events described, as the best critic I have ever had, and as uncredited co-author of several sections.

A Note on Sources

THE MOST important source for this book was my own experience in the Soviet Union: travels, meetings with officials, conversations with friends, and strangers met by chance.

I have also drawn heavily on published Soviet sources—newspapers, journals and books which I collected during the three years I spent in Moscow. I have not tried to give academic citations for each quotation from published sources, except in the case of books, and ask the professional reader's indulgence for this omission. I would be glad to provide more details on particular references on request.

When I left Moscow I travelled to Rome and then to Israel, where I recorded interviews with dozens of recent émigrés from the USSR. I transcribed more than 50,000 words from these interviews, and excerpts from them appear throughout the book. I recognize the dangers of relying on those who voluntarily left a country for descriptions of it, and I chose to ignore much of what these émigrés told me. I take responsibility for the material from these interviews which I used, all of which I judged to be creditable.

I also take responsibility for altering the details of many anecdotes to protect the anonymity of those who told them to me. These alterations involve names, places and dates, and do not change the essential character of any incident or story.

I have drawn on published works by Russians about their country, all of which are listed below.

Some of the material in this book appeared in different form in the *Washington Post*. I acknowledge with gratitude the *Post*'s permission to use that material.

Works Cited

These books are listed in the order of their first citation in the text.

Gogol, Nikolai Vasilievich. *Dead Souls*. Translated by David Magarshack. London: Penguin Books, 1969.

Hakluyt, Richard. *Voyages and Discoveries*. Edited by Jack Beeching. London: Penguin Books, 1972.

Khrushchev, Nikita S. *Khrushchev Remembers: The Last Testament*. Edited and translated by Strobe Talbott. Boston: Little, Brown and Co., 1974.

Amalrik, Andrei. *Involuntary Journey to Siberia*. Translated by Manya Harari and Max Hayward. New York: Harcourt Brace Jovanovich, 1970.

Newhouse, John. *Cold Dawn*. New York: Holt, Rinehart & Winston, 1973.

Kohler, Phyllis Penn. *Journey for Our Time*. New York: Pellegrini & Cudahy, 1951.

Medvedev, Zhores. *The Medvedev Papers*. Translated by Vera Rich. London: Macmillan & Co., 1971.

Medvedev, Roy. *On Socialist Democracy*. Translated by Ellen deKapp. New York: Alfred A. Knopf, 1975.

Alliluyeva, Svetlana. *Only One Year.* Translated by Paul Chavchavadze. New York: Harper & Row, Publishers, 1969.

Eisenhower, Dwight D. *Crusade in Europe.* New York: Doubleday & Co., 1952.

Pares, Sir Bernard. Russia: *Between Reform & Revolution.* Edited by Francis B. Randall. New York: Shocken Books, 1962.

Hollander, Paul. *Soviet and American Society, a Comparison.* New York: Oxford University Press, 1973.

Lyons, Eugene. *Assignment in Utopia.* New York: Harcourt, Brace & Co., 1937.

Amalrik, Andrei. *Will the Soviet Union Survive Until 1984?* New York: Harper & Row, Publisher, 1970.

Vladimirov, Leonid. *The Russian Space Bluff.* New York: The Dial Press, 1973.

Medvedev, Zhores. *Ten Years After Ivan Denisovich.* Translated by Hilary Sternberg. New York: Alfred A. Knopf, 1973.

Roberts, Chalmers M. *The Nuclear Years.* New York: Praeger Publishers, 1971.

Index

ROBERT G. KAISER was born in Washington, D.C., in 1943. He graduated from Yale and took a masters degree at the London School of Economics. He has worked for the *Washington Post* in various capacities since 1963, first as a part-time reporter while still in college, later as an irregular correspondent from London, a city reporter, Saigon correspondent and, from 1971 to 1974, chief of the Moscow bureau. His first book, *Cold Winter, Cold War*, a history of the origins of the Truman Doctrine, appeared in 1974. Mr. Kaiser's journalism has been published in *Esquire, New York* magazine, *The Observer* of London and many other journals. He now writes on the *Washington Post*'s national staff and lives with his family in Washington. Mr. Kaiser's dispatches from Moscow were awarded the Overseas Press Club's prize for the best foreign correspondence of 1974.